FINANCE ETHICS

The *Robert W. Kolb Series in Finance* series provides a comprehensive view of the field of finance in all of its variety and complexity. The series is projected to include approximately 65 volumes covering all major topics and specializations in finance, ranging from investments, to corporate finance, to financial institutions. Each volume in the *Kolb Series in Finance* consists of new articles especially written for the volume.

Each *Kolb Series* volume is edited by a specialist in a particular area of finance, who develops the volume outline and commissions articles by the world's experts in that particular field of finance. Each volume includes an editor's introduction and approximately thirty articles to fully describe the current state of financial research and practice in a particular area of finance.

The essays in each volume are intended for practicing finance professionals, graduate students, and advanced undergraduate students. The goal of each volume is to encapsulate the current state of knowledge in a particular area of finance so that the reader can quickly achieve a mastery of that special area of finance.

FINANCE ETHICS

Critical Issues in Theory and Practice

John R. Boatright

The Robert W. Kolb Series in Finance

WILEY

John Wiley & Sons, Inc.

Library of Congress Cataloging-in-Publication Data:

Boatright, John Raymond, 1941–
   Finance ethics : critical issues in theory and practice / John R. Boatright.
      p.   cm. – (The Robert W. Kolb series in finance)
   Includes bibliographical references and index.
   ISBN 978-0-470-49916-0 (hardback); ISBN 978-0-470-76809-9 (ebk);
ISBN 978-0-470-76810-5 (ebk); ISBN 978-0-470-76811-2 (ebk)
  1. Business ethics.   2. Finance–Moral and ethical aspects. I. Title.
   HF5387.B64 2010
   174′.4–dc22   2010010867

10 9 8 7 6 5 4 3 2

Contents

PART I

Overview

CHAPTER 1

Ethics in Finance*

JOHN R. BOATRIGHT
The Raymond C. Baumhart, S.J., Professor of Business Ethics,
Graduate School of Business, Loyola University Chicago

INTRODUCTION

Although finance raises many ethical issues, the academic study of finance ethics has received surprisingly little attention from scholars in either finance or business ethics. The neglect by finance scholars is understandable given the research paradigm in the field, which not only excludes normative questions from study but also demands the use of particular analytical tools and methodologies. For most finance scholars, the task of addressing ethical issues is simply not what they are trained to do. Business ethicists, who have the training, often ignore finance ethics due to unfamiliarity with financial theory and practice. This book is intended to advance the understanding and appreciation of the critical ethical issues in financial theory and practice and to encourage academic research and instruction by scholars in both finance and business ethics. To this end, it draws together the contributions of distinguished scholars from a wide range of disciplines, including finance, economics, philosophy, management, and law, and from many parts of North America and Europe. Because this book offers authoritative surveys of problem areas as well as original scholarly works, it constitutes a valuable resource for students and general readers interested in finance ethics. The task of this introductory chapter is to provide an overview of the field of finance ethics that organizes the ethical issues in finance and introduces the various chapters that follow.

Finance may be defined broadly as the generation, allocation, exchange, and management of monetary resources. The main topic areas in finance so defined are (1) *personal finance* by which individuals save, invest, and borrow money in order to conduct their private lives; (2) *corporate finance* by which business organizations raise capital through the issuance of securities and allocate it to its most productive uses; and (3) *public finance* by which government raises revenue through taxation and borrowing and spends it to provide services to its citizens. These activities are facilitated or mediated by a variety of financial *markets* and financial *institutions*, such as securities and commodities exchanges, commercial and investment banks, insurance companies, mutual and pension funds, and the like. In addition, finance includes the academic subject called finance that is

---

*This chapter is drawn in part from Boatright (1999, 2008a, and 2008b).

studied in business schools and constitutes the training that people in finance—both scholars and practitioners—receive. Accordingly, the subject of finance ethics can be conveniently divided into four parts: finance theory, financial markets, financial services, and financial management. This framework is employed in this book as the major organizing principle.

Finance ethics as an academic field is concerned with the moral issues that arise in each of these four areas and with the moral norms that apply to the activities that take place in them. Although the academic study of finance ethics is relatively new, the examination of these issues and norms is of long standing since they form the basis of much of the regulation of financial markets and institutions, including industry and firm self-regulation, and underlie much of the popular concern with financial activity that is reflected, among other places, in the business press. From the very beginning of rudimentary financial activity, people have raised questions about what is fair in markets and what are the rights and duties of participants in these markets. And as financial institutions have grown in size and importance, ethical concerns about fairness, rights, and duties have arisen about their operation. Despite the popular cynical view that there is no ethics in finance, a moment's reflection reveals that finance could not exist without it. Without an assurance of fairness and the observance of basic rights and duties, no one would make exchanges in a market or place their assets with financial institutions. So even if finance ethics as an academic field of study is relatively new, consideration of the ethical issues in finance has a long and rich history.

Given this history of concern, it is the lack of recognition of ethics in finance, and not the present attention it is receiving, that requires explanation. One reason for this oversight is the ubiquity of law and regulation in finance, which has had two effects. One effect is to obscure the role that ethics has played in the development of law and regulation, which has been guided by moral considerations to the extent that in advanced economies much of what is unethical is also illegal. Ethical issues in finance are often perceived as *merely* legal or regulatory matters, thus disguising the role of ethics in law and regulation. The other effect is to leave the role of prescribing conduct and developing rules to law and regulation or to public policy. People who work in the financial world often believe that the task of creating and enforcing ethical rules and standards is the job of legislators and regulators, not themselves. Within finance theory, ethical issues are typically conceptualized as side constraints, externalities, or market failures, which they often are; but the effect of this conceptualization is to dismiss these issue as problems to be addressed by law and regulation or by public policy and not considered within the field of finance. Conversely, people in finance often contribute to the discussion of ethical issues and even lobby, sometimes aggressively, on proposed laws, regulations, and public policies without realizing that they are addressing ethical matters. Thus, ethics is actually a pervasive subject of concern in finance without being recognized as such.

FINANCE THEORY

Finance as an academic field is an area of applied economics that is scarcely more than half a century old. Prior to 1950, the main concerns of modern finance theory—namely, the functioning of credit markets and the pricing of assets—were largely ignored or dismissed by economists as unsuitable topics for economic analysis. Financial markets were viewed by economists such as John Maynard Keynes as mere "casinos" or "beauty contests," in which assets were not priced in any rational way that could be described by economic laws. Before the development of finance theory, practicing traders operated by gut feelings or rules of thumb derived from experience, which they thought enabled them to take advantage of underlying trends that could be detected and charted but whose sources remained mysterious.

The field of finance is generally dated from the development of modern portfolio theory (MPT) in the 1950s, which demonstrates the possibility of constructing an optimal portfolio that offers the highest return for any given level of risk. This possibility frees portfolio selection from any need to consider specific risk and allows (diversified) investors to consider only systemic risk. The next step for finance theory was to develop a means for assessing the risk-to-return characteristics, and hence the specific risk, of any given security or asset. This was done with the development of the capital asset pricing model (CAPM) in the 1960s, which allows the calculation of the expected return on an asset that compensates an investor for the additional risk of that asset above the return on a risk-free asset. The problem of pricing options, which had been vexing, was eventually solved in the 1970s with the Black-Scholes option pricing model.

Other building blocks of modern finance include the Miller-Modigliani hypothesis or theorem (M-M) and the efficient market hypothesis (EMH). According to M-M, the capital structure of a firm is irrelevant to its valuation insofar as investors can adjust their personal portfolios to achieve the desired risk/reward ratio. In consequence, the market will not reward firms for their management of specific risk. Finally, EMH holds that markets are generally efficient in that the prices of assets reflect all available information. If this is true, then investors cannot "beat the market" without having any new information that has yet to be registered in the market. With all these elements, which were in place by the 1980s, modern finance theory as it is conceived and practiced today was largely complete.

As Robert W. Kolb observes in Chapter 2, "Ethical Implications of Finance," finance theory is regarded, at least by its adherents, as ethically neutral or without normative import. However, the main assumptions of the theory, such as those about rational or self-interested behavior, and the outlook induced by adopting the theory, including CAPM and EMH, lead to conclusions about how people (morally) ought to behave, as well as to how firms (morally) ought to be organized and operated. For example, the propositions that firms ought to be controlled by shareholders and that they ought to be managed so as to maximize shareholder wealth are thoroughly normative. One writer observes that a critical transition occurs when ideas that may be initially ethically neutral are advocated as a basis for decision making (Horrigan 1987, 97). Thus, if everyone in a world thinks in the terms of modern finance, there are consequences that need to be morally evaluated, and, in the view of this writer, the world of modern finance "is not a nice place ethically" (Horrigan 1987, 107). Niall Ferguson (2008) has coined the term "Planet Finance" to describe a world in which financial thinking has resulted in the creation of the vast edifice of exotic collateralized and derivative securities that collapsed in the recent financial crisis. Clearly, whether Planet Finance is a good place to live is a fit subject for moral inquiry.

Kolb begins this inquiry with an examination of the ethical implications of the basic assumption of economics that rationality is the maximal satisfaction of individual preferences or utility and of the key concepts of finance theory, such as the time value of money and the reward for risk taking. These assumptions and concepts, as well as the basic tools of finance, such as the capital asset pricing model and option pricing theory, raise normative concerns, in Kolb's account, mainly when they are used in practice to guide individual portfolio management or the management of business corporations. Although the elements of modern finance were in place by the mid-1980s, Kolb discerns two more recent developments that also involve ethical issues, namely the nascent fields of enterprise or integrated risk management and behavioral finance. As a result of MPT, CAPM, and M-M, which consider mainly systemic risk, finance theory has tended to minimize the need to manage specific risk and along with it the impact of corporate decisions on employees and other stakeholder groups, who are affected by specific risk. However, finance today has a greater appreciation of the importance of managing total risk—both systemic and specific—in increasing the value of a firm, which also leads to a greater concern for all stakeholders and not merely shareholders. Finally, the field of behavioral finance is the result of advances in psychology that yield a more realistic understanding of people's actual financial decision making. The result has been to replace the simple view of *homo economicus* as a perfect utility maximizer with a more complex conception that must be considered by managers in their efforts to increase firm value.

The remaining chapters in Part II on finance theory provide more thorough treatment of the subjects introduced in Kolb's chapter. In Chapter 3, "Behavioral Assumptions of Finance," author John Dobson examines the basic assumption of economics and finance that economic agents are purely self-interested utility max-imizers. Ranging far and wide from the Scottish enlightenment thinkers Adam Smith and David Hume, who fathered economics, to modern game theorists, so-cial psychologists, evolutionary biologists, and neuroscientists, Dobson compiles an extensive body of evidence to counter the simplistic view of *homo economicus* that underlies economics and finance. The conclusions of this chapter not only bear on finance theory but also have practical implications for corporations—for example, in the design of incentives that were critical in, among other cases, the collapse of Enron—and for business education with its narrow focus on managerial effectiveness. In Dobson's view, a more realistic understanding of human rational-ity might perhaps return business education to a traditional, broader focus that includes moral development.

Nien-hê Hsieh's Chapter 4, "Efficiency and Rationality," offers a more de-tailed and technical account of rationality than that found in the preceding chapter by Dobson, and it introduces in the book a related key concept of economics and finance, namely efficiency. The aim of the chapter is to explain how these two concepts are defined and employed in economics and finance and to dis-cuss the normative issues surrounding them. Whereas rationality is normative mainly as a prescription about how decisions ought to be made—by maximiz-ing preferences—efficiency is normative as a criterion for evaluating outcomes: In general, more efficient outcomes ought to be preferred. Hsieh notes that the two concepts of efficiency—the efficient market hypothesis and Pareto efficiency—are normative and raise ethical issues in their use, especially in cases of imperfect conditions where the assumptions of a perfect market fail to obtain.

A fundamental tenet of finance is that a return is due investors for the time an investment is made and for the risk taken. Whereas the time value of money is discussed in Chapter 2, Chapter 5, "Returns, Risk, and Financial Due Diligence," by Christopher L. Culp and J. B. Heaton, explains the concepts of risk and return and the relationship between them. According to modern portfolio theory, investors seek the highest return for any level of risk. Generally, the return that investors receive along this *efficient frontier* is morally justified, and the main task is the technical one of determining the portfolio that produces the optimal risk/return ratio. This task requires some means for pricing assets according to risk so as to find the *alpha*, the amount of return in excess of this risk-adjusted return. Culp and Heaton explain and evaluate several forms of risk/return analysis, including CAPM and its variants. Aside from their use in portfolio selection, these models for asset pricing are useful for identifying the kind of too-good-to-be-true returns that occur in Ponzi schemes, such as the notorious Madoff funds. Culp and Heaton show how these models might have been used to exercise financial due diligence in discovering Bernard Madoff's massive fraud.

Risk is usually understood as merely financial risk—and systematic rather than specific risk at that—but the recent development of enterprise or integrated risk management has focused attention on other kinds of risk. One of these is risk to a company's reputation that can impose a cost greater than a failed strategy or external shocks. Chapter 6 by Ingo Walter, entitled "Reputational Risk," explains what it is, why it arises, and how it can be valued. Although reputation can be easily understood as an object of risk, the difficulty of assessing how these risks might arise, what might be done to reduce them, and how to compare the costs and benefits of risk reduction pose difficult operational challenges. These challenges are especially great for financial services firms due to their special role as intermediaries, which depends so much on trust. The value of this chapter lies not only in identifying reputation as an object of risk but in showing how this risk can be measured and what can be done to reduce it through a combination of market discipline, effective government regulation, and company investment in self-regulation.

Finance theory has been enriched by theoretical developments unrelated to its core concerns of credit markets and asset prices. Among these are related developments in the study of the agent-principal relationship, which is ubiquitous in finance, and the structure of the firm. Both of these developments—agency theory and the theory of the firm—are the fruits of interdisciplinary work in economics, sociology, political theory, and law. Agency theory is useful for analyzing the economic, managerial, and legal structure of the relationships between agents and principals, which are designed to overcome the problems that result from such factors as opportunism, information asymmetry, uncertainty, and transaction costs. Agency theory also incorporates the related concepts (originally from insurance) of moral hazard and adverse selection, which figure prominently in finance theory. Thus, this theory is commonly applied in finance to the relationships of employer-employee, stockbroker-client, bank-customer, and the like. Agency theory was introduced into finance most prominently by Michael C. Jensen and

William H. Meckling (1976) to analyze the relationship between managers and stockholders, which leads directly into the theory of the firm as a nexus of contracts between the firm and its input providers. Corporate governance, which is the contract between a firm and its investors, is structured to ensure that managers act as faithful agents for the shareholder-principals.

Chapter 7, "Agency Theory," by Joseph Heath, is concerned mainly with defending agency theory, as it is used in finance and other fields of study, against criticism from some business ethicists. These critics oppose agency theory for its alleged role in supporting several positions that they find morally objectionable, including its assumption of rational, self-interested agents; the doctrine of shareholder primacy, by which shareholders exercise exclusive control rights over corporations; and the possible use of the agent-principal relationship to avoid responsibility by engaging agents to perform acts that are forbidden to the principals. Heath follows Kolb, Dobson, and Hsieh in questioning the assumption of rational self-interest as an accurate description of human behavior, but holds that "sophisticated practitioners" of agency theory are aware of the limitations of this methodological assumption and make allowances for them. With regard to agency theory and shareholder primacy, he argues that there is no necessary connection between them—shareholder primacy neither implies nor is implied by agency theory—but holds that agency theory may still be a valuable analytical tool in understanding the shareholders' role. Finally, the objection that agency relationships wrongly permit agents to do what is denied to principals is simply a conceptual error on the part of business ethicists. Agency theory is vindicated in Heath's analysis as a valuable tool in finance theory.

The doctrine of shareholder primacy, which Heath holds is not logically tied to agency theory, is nevertheless a central part of finance theory with links to other elements, most notably efficiency. The theory of the firm as it has developed in recent decades starts with the assumption that the firm has evolved in a market through a search for the most efficient forms of economic organization. Finance theory conceives the firm as a nexus of contracts. That is, for analytical purposes, the firm is understood in finance as the totality of all the contracts that are formed with various groups in the process of production. These groups include employees, suppliers, customers, and, of course, investors. On the assumption that each group as well as the managers of firms are operating in a market with a view to maximizing their own gain, the organization that results—that is, the result of this totality of contracts—represents a search for the most efficient ways of organizing the productive process. If any given form of organization is not fully efficient, then, in theory, another firm that is more efficient will drive it out of business.

Shareholder primacy—the doctrine that shareholders have the right of control and a right for their interests to be the objective of the firm—is considered in finance to be, in most instances, the most efficient form of governance. A question that must be left to ethics, though, is whether such an arrangement is not merely efficient but also ethically ideal. That is, is shareholder primacy morally justified? In Chapter 8, "The Financial Theory of the Firm," Wayne Norman examines both the financial argument that the standard investor-owned firm is efficient and the ethical argument that it is also morally justified. Although some ethicists, especially those who espouse stakeholder theory as an alternative to the stockholder- or shareholder-centered firm, criticize shareholder primacy as giving undue prominence to shareholders in corporate governance, the ethical argument shows that shareholder control actually serves the interests of all groups and, moreover, is justified, in part because it is based on voluntary contracting in a market.

FINANCIAL MARKETS

Much of the activity of finance takes place in markets, in which currencies, commodities, and financial instruments, such as stock, bonds, futures, options, swaps, and derivatives, are traded. Commonly, these markets are organized exchanges, such as stock and bond markets or currency or commodities or futures exchanges, which operate according to established laws, rules, and procedures. However, transactions can also take place privately, through dealers or middlemen in over-the-counter markets, or face-to-face between a buyer and a seller, as when an individual or company secures a loan from a bank or an insurance policy from an insurer. These are all market transactions.

The fundamental ethical requirement of financial markets is that they be *fair*. Fairness in financial markets can be analyzed by identifying instances of unfairness. These may be due to unfair *trading practices*, such as manipulation and fraud; unfair *conditions*, which are commonly described as an unlevel playing field; or unfair *contracts*, in which one party has taken morally impermissible advantage of another. Unfair conditions or an unlevel playing field typically result from asymmetries in information, bargaining power, or other resources. Whether an asymmetry is a cause of unfairness and ought to be corrected by regulation or other means is a difficult question that generally hinges on other rights and duties. Thus, a prospectus may be required for the issuance of a security, thereby correcting an information asymmetry, because investors are judged to have a *right* to make an informed decision. Similarly, insider trading is considered to be wrong because it involves a breach of a fiduciary *duty*. Fairness may be defined either *substantively*, as when a security is accurately priced, or *procedurally*, as when a security is sold with full disclosure so that the buyer can assess its value. Thus, *blue-sky laws*, which require expert evaluation of securities offered for sale, aim at substantive fairness, whereas regulations that merely require disclosure of relevant information aim at procedural fairness.

Fairness is a notoriously complex moral concept that has a wide range of application and standards. In some instances it denotes impartiality or a lack of bias, in others an equitable outcome or a distribution based on merit or desert. Fairness may be applied to discrete market transactions, market rules, or market outcomes and also to practices and institutions, such as insider trading or a tax system. Fairness is often regarded as being the same as *justice*, while some distinguish the two concepts. Chapter 9, "Fairness in Financial Markets," by Eugene Heath, explores the elusive complexity of the concept of fairness. Taking a philosopher's perspective, Heath describes not only the many aspects of fairness but also the ways in which moral philosophers have attempted to formulate the essential thread that runs through all these disparate uses. Following this, he shows how the concept of fairness can be applied to diverse financial matters, including lending and securities transactions.

The most commonly adopted means for ensuring fairness in markets is government regulation, although a significant degree of industry- and firm-level self-regulation is also employed in finance. A great deal of deregulation has occurred in the past several decades, especially in the United States and Britain, but financial markets around the world still remain highly regulated. In addition to the amount of regulation, the parties to this debate also disagree on the most effective forms of regulation. The recent financial crisis has renewed and sharpened the debate over regulation, with opponents of deregulation placing blame for the crisis on the reduction in regulation and calling for a rollback of recent deregulation and an overall increase. Chapter 10, "Regulation," by Edward Soule, contributes to this debate, first by rejecting the claim that deregulation or too little regulation was at fault in the recent financial crisis. He argues that regulators had sufficient authority under the law to effectively prevent financial institutions from taking excessive risks; the fault lies rather with the use regulators made, or failed to make, of their authority. The solution, however, is not merely more diligent enforcement but also a change in the focus of regulation to the detection of weaknesses in the risk management culture of financial firms. This proposal is similar to the practice in auditing of not merely verifying the financial records of a firm but also assessing the effectiveness of its internal controls.

One particular kind of unfair market practice is insider trading, in which corporate insiders trade on information that they alone possess. As Peter-Jan Engelen and Luc Van Liedekerke observe in Chapter 11, "Insider Trading," this practice is part of a larger question of how much and what kinds of asymmetric information market participants may fairly use. Although insider trading is generally held to be unethical and is almost universally outlawed, the ethical justification for this ethical and legal prohibition is difficult to articulate. And some critics have held that the practice is, on the whole, beneficial and ought to be permitted for the reason that insider trading registers information about prices quickly at low cost. Engelen and Van Liedekerke survey the main arguments against insider trading, including those based on consideration of its alleged harmful consequences, market fairness in the possession of and access to information, property rights in information, and a market morality perspective. Their discussion leads to an understanding of both the ubiquitous condemnation of the practice and the difficulties in providing a cogent rationale for legal prohibitions.

Concerns about fairness and other ethical aspects of financial markets are not confined solely to market transactions but extend to the financial instruments that are created and subsequently sold and traded in these markets. The past decade has seen the remarkable development of exotic new products that offer great benefits in managing standard risks, even as they create new risks of their own. Chief among these new products are derivative contracts, which Warren Buffett has famously described as "financial weapons of mass destruction." James A. Overdahl, the chief economist of the Securities and Exchange Commission, examines these financial instruments in Chapter 12, "Derivative Contracts: Futures, Options, and Swaps," first by defining them and then by describing the five types of such contracts: forward contracts, futures, options, swaps, and structured products. After giving data on the size of the derivatives contract market, he discusses how they can be properly used—and possibly abused. Overall, he concludes that, despite Buffett's knock on them, derivative contracts are valuable financial products.

The participants in financial markets are most commonly individuals and institutional investors, such as banks, insurance companies, mutual funds, and pension funds, which are still acting as custodians for the assets of individuals and other organizations. Investment banks engage in some proprietary trading for their own account, and although such activity occasionally gives rise to ethical issues, these have been, until recently, little different from the unfair trading practices that can also arise for individuals, such as market manipulation and fraud. However, many of the ethical issues in the recent financial crisis were the result of investment banks' activities in originating and securitizing loans and selling these collateralized debt obligations (CDOs) to others, as well as in buying and selling credit default swaps (CDSs). There are two other types of institutions of recent origin, though, that have become major market participants and whose activities raise ethical concerns. These are hedge funds and sovereign wealth funds.

Hedge funds are lightly regulated pools of capital, usually from wealthy individuals and large institutional investors—including pension funds and university endowments—which seek above-market rates of return (or *alpha*) by exploiting diverse markets with innovative (and usually proprietary) investing strategies. Because of their size and heavy use of leverage, hedge funds pose some risk to capital markets, as witness the collapse of Long Term Capital Management and Amaranth Advisors. In addition to the question of whether these funds should be more closely regulated to prevent this risk, they also raise ethical issues about their fee structures—the usual "2 and 20," a 2 percent management fee and 20 percent of the returns—and about the tax treatment of returns. (The returns are classified as *carried interest* and thus are taxed at capital gains rates rather than the higher personal income rate.)

As Thomas Donaldson notes in Chapter 13, "Hedge Funds," the main ethical issue is the opaqueness or lack of transparency, which is defended as essential to protect the proprietary nature of a fund's strategy. Donaldson argues that attempts by government to regulate hedge funds, given their opaqueness, run into two limits, which he calls *regulatory recalcitrance*, namely the cost of collecting and interpreting the data in a timely manner, and the impact that regulation would have on the use of innovative investment strategies. He does not conclude that no regulation should be imposed but recommends that it take the form of industry self-regulation in order to circumvent the problems of regulatory recalcitrance. Industry self-regulation involves, in Donaldson's view, the development of norms—which he calls *microsocial* norms—that solve collective action problems for hedge funds and serve to protect the impact on third-party stakeholders.

Sovereign wealth funds (SWFs), which are investment funds owned and controlled by nation states, usually funded by trade surpluses, raise many fears about their impact on financial markets, in part because of their size but mainly due to their control by a foreign government. The basic concern is that decisions by SWFs may be influenced less by standard financial or market considerations and more by national interests. Colleen Baker, in Chapter 14, "Sovereign Wealth Funds," argues that the ethical objections to such funds can be grouped under the single label of *corruption*: "corruption of national security, corruption of market processes, corruption of information integrity, corruption of the rule of law, and corruption of domestic industry competitiveness." Although these matters are serious, the potential problems are not insurmountable. Like hedge funds, SWFs do not appear to have played a disruptive role in the current financial crisis, and, indeed, they may have played a constructive role by providing American banks with much-needed capital infusions. Moreover, the influence of SWFs may have peaked. Baker notes that several codes or guidelines have been developed, including the International Working Group of Sovereign Wealth Funds' *Sovereign Wealth Funds Generally Accepted Principles and Practices* (the Santiago Principles) and the Organisation for Economic Co-operation and Development's *Guidance on Sovereign Wealth* (OECD Guidance). She believes that these documents provide a workable blueprint for responsible conduct on the part of SWFs.

FINANCIAL SERVICES

Financial services firms—which include banks, insurance companies, brokerage firms, mutual and pension funds, and financial planners—provide a vast array of financial services to individuals, businesses, and governments, as well as to each other. In so doing, these firms act primarily as financial *intermediaries*, by enabling their clients to consummate transactions through third parties rather than by themselves. This intermediary role utilizes the specialized knowledge and skill of finance professionals, as well as the unique capabilities of large financial institutions. For example, an individual might be able to manage a personal portfolio without expert advice and service, but only a bank can turn the savings of individual depositors into home mortgages, and only an insurance company can pool the risks of fire to home owners.

In acting as intermediaries, financial services firms typically become *agents* or *fiduciaries*. These roles have morally and legally defined obligations or duties, which are different from the ethics of market participants in arm's-length economic transactions. Much of the activity of financial services firms, as well as of markets generally, consists in the formation of *contracts*, which also create morally and legally binding obligations or duties, such as the duty to make loan payments, to settle insurance claims, or to honor derivative contracts. Indeed, agency and fiduciary relationships can be understood as the result of specialized kinds of contracts. In addition to the obligations or duties created by financial contracts of all kinds, financial services providers are also bound by the ethics of the marketplace to avoid fraud, violations of rights, and various kinds of unfair advantage taking.

Financial services firms operate as businesses, and like any business, they have the ethical obligation, as well as a legal duty, to observe accepted standards of business conduct. Thus, in their sales practices, firms should avoid deception, provide adequate information, ensure that products are suitable for customers and clients, and avoid abusive sales practices. Financial firms also have many of the other obligations for businesses generally—for example, to respect privacy rights, to avoid discrimination, to manage conflicts of interest, and not to participate in bribery and corruption. Banks have a particular role to play in preventing money laundering and tax evasion. Banks and other financial institutions also have social impacts that need to be managed according to best practices of social responsibility, and some institutions go further by facilitating socially responsible investing and providing credit to the very poor in less developed countries in a process known as *microlending* or *microfinance*.

Part IV on financial services begins with Chapter 15, "Marketing of Financial Services," by George G. Brenkert, who has written widely on marketing ethics. After developing an ethical framework for marketing ethics generally—which includes identifying the relevant values and determining how they apply in practice—Brenkert focuses on three areas of marketing financial products to individuals that are subject to the greatest controversy. These are home mortgages, credit cards, and so-called payday loans. The first is controversial recently for the role that subprime mortgages played in the housing bubble, the wave of mortgage defaults and home foreclosures, and the subsequent collapse of the mortgage-backed securities market and the resulting credit squeeze; the second, for alleged abusive practices involving excessive fees and high interest rates; and the third, for the possibly usurious interest rates on such loans and the cycle of indebtedness that sometimes results when these short-term loans are rolled over. Although many of the ethical issues surrounding credit cards have been addressed in the United States by the Credit Card Accountability, Responsibility, and Disclosure Act of 2009, Brenkert observes that the other two sources of controversy are currently subjects of much proposed regulation.

The regulation of the marketing and delivery of financial services is achieved both by externally imposed government regulation and by a significant amount of internal self-regulation by professions, industries, and individual firms. The motivation for this self-regulation is not only to avoid more onerous government regulation but also to meet public expectations and to instill public confidence. In particular, finance practitioners in many areas seek to attain the status of professionals, which requires a certain amount of self-regulation and also a commitment to service in the public interest. All of these aims are achieved by the promulgation of a code of ethics. Chapter 16, "Financial Codes of Ethics," by Julie A. Ragatz and Ronald F. Duska, examines the major codes of ethics that have been adopted by various professional organizations of financial services practitioners, including bankers, accountants, financial analysts, and financial planners and advisers. They find in the codes seven basic principles, namely integrity, objectivity, competence, fairness, confidentiality, professionalism, and diligence. Although these principles are easily recognized, the effectiveness of the codes depends on the interpretation of these principles and the manner in which they become embedded in practice. It is easy to be skeptical about the effectiveness of these codes and to suspect that they are mere "window dressing." Accordingly, Ragatz and Duska conclude with an assessment of code effectiveness.

Banking is the financial service that touches the life of the most people, whether through checking and savings accounts, credit cards, consumer loans, home mortgages, or trust administration. In addition to providing essential services to customers, commercial banks serve the important economic function of aggregating people's savings and making the funds available to individuals and businesses that need them. The economic health of any community depends on the soundness and the competence of its banks, especially in their money management and lending practices. In addition, investment banks provide some of these services as well as advisory, underwriting, and financing services for corporations that seek new capital or are engaging in a merger or acquisition. Investment banks can also engage in proprietary trading for their own account. All of these activities require not only strong technical skills but also an ability to address myriad ethical issues. These issues arise because of the important interests at stake in managing such large amounts of money and the conflicts that occur among different interests in typical bank dealings.

Chapter 17, "Banking," by Christopher J. Cowton, describes the activities and functions, mainly of commercial banks, and identifies the main ethical issues banks face. The ethical challenges to banks are grouped in the chapter under the twin heads of *integrity*, which is essential for generating the trust that banking requires, and *responsibility* in carrying out the activities and functions of banking effectively. In addition, Cowton explores a third area of *affinity*, which is a possibility that banks have only lightly exploited to bring together groups with similar interests in social causes. Affinity in banking shares similarities with socially responsible investing and microfinance, which are covered in other chapters of this volume.

Chapter 18, "Mutual Funds," by D. Bruce Johnsen, examines the ethical issues in two forms of mutual funds brokerage commission rebates: soft dollars and directed brokerage. Both practices are common in the mutual fund industry despite persistent criticism from academics and practitioners, who consider them to be ethically suspect. Soft dollars are credits that a brokerage firm provides to a mutual fund to pay for research and other fund expenses, and directed brokerage is a commitment by a brokerage firm to market a fund's shares. Both are means that brokerage firms use to compensate mutual funds for selecting them to execute their trades. Although they may appear to be a kind of kickback or bribe, Johnsen argues that, contrary to appearances, both practices may be efficient arrangements that benefit investors. The argument is that these arrangements effectively solve, at relatively low cost, a major problem for mutual fund managers, namely how to monitor the performance of a broker when the quality of the execution is difficult to assess. Although a fund manager may want high-quality execution, the manager will be unwilling to pay for it unless he or she can be assured of getting the (hard to detect) high quality. Soft dollars and directed brokerage may thus be a way for a broker to provide a bond to guarantee the quality of the execution. Although these two forms of commission rebates may be efficient, it does not follow that they are ethical. Johnsen completes the argument by using integrative social contracts theory, developed by Thomas Donaldson and Thomas Dunfee (1999), to show that such efficient arrangements are also ethical in virtue of being in accord with legitimate microsocial norms, as postulated in that theory.

For most individuals, their pension is the single most valuable asset they possess. However, much of the control over this asset is in the hands of pension managers, who have a fiduciary duty to manage a fund in the interest of the beneficiaries. Because of this third-party control, pension holders are at considerable risk from the mismanagement of their funds. In addition, the design of pension plans, and especially the choice between defined benefit and defined contribution plans, involves questions of how risk is to be shared by employees and employers. In Chapter 19, "Pension Funds," David Hess sets out the ethical issues for both private and public pension plans. In view of the risk involved, he writes, "What fiduciary duties require of individuals is at the heart of many of the ethical issues for pensions." Although the fiduciary duty of pension fund managers is imposed by law, the law itself does not resolve all questions about the meaning and application of this duty. In addition to exploring some of the gray areas of fiduciary duty in pension fund management, Hess also discusses the ethics of shareholder activism and social investing, especially by public pension plans.

Although insurance raises many ethical issues, especially about sales practices and product quality, Chapter 20, "Insurance," by Julie A. Ragatz and Ronald F.

Duska, focuses mainly on the social role of insurance and the challenges the industry faces in meeting the expectations of society. Insurance serves an essential role by pooling risks and sharing the burden of misfortune, but fulfilling this role requires an immense amount of trust that the resources will be available when misfortune strikes. After noting that some ethical problems, such as moral hazard and adverse selection, are present in all kinds of insurance, the authors explore the issues specific to three major types of insurance, namely life insurance, property and casualty insurance, and health insurance. Some of these issues, such as those involved in attempting to insure against major catastrophes like Hurricane Katrina and to provide health insurance for everyone, are among the most difficult faced by society today. They rightly conclude that the resolution of these ethical issues is, at bottom, "a question of economic justice."

When people think about ethics in finance, the socially responsible investing movement (SRI) often comes to mind. SRI is certainly an area of financial activity in which ethical concerns are most consciously considered. Céline Louche and Steven Lydenberg, who are, respectively, an academic and an industry professional, bring their separate perspectives to a study of the movement. In Chapter 21, "Responsible Investing," they observe that SRI is both an investment *product* bought by individual investors and a *practice* on the part of fund managers to engage with companies to improve their socially responsible activities. After presenting the history of SRI, which stretches back to the eighteenth century, Louche and Lydenberg describe how SRI is carried out in practice, how the industry itself is organized, and what challenges confront the industry. They note that the financial crisis of 2008–2009 poses both a challenge and an opportunity. SRI stands in opposition to modern portfolio theory, which has led, to some extent, to the financial crisis; and although the crisis creates an opportunity for a different approach to investing, it can be seized only if SRI advocates can successfully develop an alternative theoretical framework for this investment approach.

Another area of finance that visibly involves ethics is microfinance, which is widely praised as an effective means for alleviating poverty and empowering women in less developed countries. This practice gained global recognition in 2006 when Muhammad Yunus and the Grameen Bank, which he founded, were awarded the Nobel Peace Prize. Chapter 22, "Microfinance," by Antonio Argandoña, examines the ethical issues involving this practice. Despite its noble aims and achievements, microfinance is open to criticism for such features as the high interest rates charged and the social pressures used to enforce loan collections. Argandoña observes that much of the criticism both inside and outside the movement results from an unresolved tension between the social mission of microfinance and the need for financial viability. This tension has become more acute as commercial banks have entered this market with a greater profit orientation than the Grameen Bank.

FINANCIAL MANAGEMENT

Financial management is a function within a corporation, usually assigned to a chief financial officer (CFO), that is concerned with raising and deploying capital. In a sense, a CFO is making investment decisions and managing a portfolio, but these decisions are not about which securities to hold but about what business opportunities to pursue and especially how they are financed. Every corporation must have a financial structure in which capital is divided between equity, debt, and other types of obligations. All of these decisions are guided by the objective of maximizing shareholder wealth. In the United States, the Sarbanes-Oxley Act assigns the CFO a responsibility to personally attest to the accuracy of financial statements, and the act also requires that corporations have a code of ethics for their top financial managers.

The ethical issues in financial management fall into two broad categories: the ethical obligations or duties of financial managers of a corporation, and the ethical justification for organizing a corporation with shareholder control and the objective of shareholder wealth maximization. The former category bears on the decisions made by financial managers in fulfilling the finance function of a corporation, and involves the fiduciary duties of financial managers to a corporation and its shareholders. The latter is a matter largely for government in establishing the laws of corporate governance; it concerns more theoretical matters about property rights and social welfare.

The first chapter in Part V on financial management covers this latter category of the meaning and justification of shareholder wealth maximization (SWM) as the objective of the corporation, which finance theory posits as the touchstone of all corporate financial decisions. In Chapter 23, "Shareholder Wealth Maximization," the author, Duane Windsor, focuses primarily on the standard interpretation and justification of this objective in the finance literature, and on the criticism of this purely financial view from the perspectives of corporate law and business ethics, the latter of which encompasses the literatures of corporate social responsibility and stakeholder theory. These critiques are relevant to the assessment of SMW because, as Windsor writes, "the public corporation is simultaneously private property, a web or nexus of contracts, a governmentally licensed and traded securities registrant, a social benefits entity, and a locus of stakeholder relationships." He concludes that the financial view, which is based largely on property rights, may be inadequate both as a justification of the corporate objective in law and as a practical managerial guide.

Although a company's financial records are maintained by internal accountants and certified by external auditors, the CFO of a corporation has ultimate oversight over financial reporting and is responsible for the presentation of financial records to investors and the government. In carrying out this responsibility, CFOs may be tempted to present the records in the most favorable light in ways that may be described as *earnings management*. In Chapter 24, "Earnings Management," Leonard J. Brooks, an expert in accounting ethics, explores the large gray area between the permissible and impermissible in reporting a company's earnings and offers practical guidance to CFOs and investors about the acceptable limits of this widespread practice. Of particular usefulness is his discussion of the red flags that can alert users of financial statements to questionable or impermissible earnings management.

In addition to required financial reports, which may be subject to earnings management, most large corporations maintain an office, staffed by finance professionals, to communicate regularly with investors about all manner of financial information. This investor relations office is typically headed by an investment relations officer (IRO). Like earnings management, investor relations raises a host of ethical questions about what information to disclose and how to disclose it.

These questions are addressed by Cynthia Clark Williams and Lori Verstegen Ryan in Chapter 25, "Investor Relations." The answers to these questions, they argue, are determined, in part, by considerations of what rights investors have to certain information. In the United States, these questions have been given additional urgency by SEC Regulation FD on fair disclosure, which requires that information be disclosed to all investors and not merely a select few. In addition, many investor relations offices collect information about the corporations' own shareholders, thus raising additional issues about ethical information collection practices.

Risk is commonly applied in finance to the probability of the expected return on an investment, as explained in Chapter 26, "Risk Management," by Peter Young. In traditional discussions of risk and ethics, the main focus has been on the concept of moral hazard. However, the concept of risk can also refer to all of the factors that bear on the profitability and, indeed, the survival of a firm. These factors, which move beyond mere moral hazard, must be considered in some manner by the top managers of a corporation, including the CFO, and be reflected in the decisions they make. Although the management of specific risks has long been done on a piecemeal basis, a significant change in recent years has been the integration of these previously disconnected efforts into a coordinated function called enterprise risk management (ERM). Some firms have even created the position of chief risk officer to discharge this function. In this chapter, Young seeks to elucidate how this modern-day ERM is related to ethics. He finds the main link between ERM and ethics in the way in which risk management is necessarily connected to an organization's core values. Indeed, risk management is itself a value that must be deeply embedded in a corporation's culture for it to be practiced successfully. And when practiced well, he writes, "risk-based thinking serves to articulate an organization's values with respect to risk, uncertainty, complexity, and ambiguity, and to inform the decisions and actions that are taken."

Bankruptcy raises an immense number of ethical issues not only for financial managers dealing with a financial crisis but also for legislators and judges who must craft and administer the Bankruptcy Code. For a corporation facing insolvency, the decision whether to file for bankruptcy protection and for which kind of protection deeply affects its financial operation and structure. Whether the choice is to liquidate or reorganize, the firm will have to work with its creditors to satisfy their claims. If the firm attempts to reorganize, it typically seeks debtor-in-possession financing to raise new capital. Even before a decision about bankruptcy, a corporation may make many financial decisions in an effort to avoid bankruptcy, some of which may benefit shareholders at the expense of bondholders and other creditors. And a solvent business may take advantage of the Bankruptcy Code to pursue strategic aims, such as reducing legal judgments or breaking contracts. In drafting a bankruptcy code, legislators must first overcome the traditional view that bankruptcy is a moral failing that should not be rewarded, and then draft a code that strikes the right balance between the rights and interests of debtors and creditors and between economic efficiency and social well-being. Chapter 27, "Bankruptcy," by Ben S. Branch and Jennifer S. Taub, explores these myriad ethical issues in both the historical and contemporary forms and also offers some illuminating cross-national comparisons.

Like bankruptcy, a merger, acquisition, or takeover is a corporate event that deeply affects a wide range of constituencies or stakeholder groups and thus raises ethical concerns. Although the hostile takeovers of the 1980s, which were strongly criticized for their adverse effects on workers and communities, are now less frequent occurrences, the pace of friendly mergers and acquisitions has increased as companies struggle to remain competitive. A challenge for management in these sometimes wrenching transformations is to maintain the support of employees, customers, suppliers, and other groups that are critical to a company's competitiveness. As Anthony F. Buono and Roy A. Wiggins III observe in Chapter 28, "Acquisitions, Mergers, and Takeovers," making a merger or acquisition work often involves attention to such ethical considerations as fair treatment of all parties and the minimization of adverse impacts. They recommend that, in addition to the financial, strategic, and legal analyses that are typically undertaken, companies should also develop a plan for managing the conflicts that inevitably occur in acquisitions and mergers.

Perhaps no issue involving finance raises greater ethical concern than that of executive compensation. Outrage is the most common response, according to John J. McCall in Chapter 29 on this topic, "Executive Compensation." The fervency of this outrage is not matched, however, by a clear understanding of exactly what might be wrong. Is the ethical problem with the form of executive pay, which is largely in stock options? Is it with the absolute level of pay or with the way in which pay is set? Why are people outraged with the high compensation to some executives but not others? Emotion is no substitute for rigorous ethical analysis. Although McCall sides with the critics of executive compensation, he supports his view with a careful examination of the arguments in the academic literature that criticize and support the current system and attempt to answer the more specific questions.

Boards of directors are ultimately responsible not only for executive compensation but for all financial matters of a corporation from decisions about financial structure to capital expenditures. Boards are also critical in controlling a firm so as to avoid financial irregularities. Indeed, many provisions of the Sarbanes-Oxley Act, passed in 2002 in response to the collapse of Enron, address the composition and operation of boards, including the requirement that there be a majority of independent directors. This focus on boards reflects the judgment of Congress that the financial scandals of that period were due, in large measure, to a lack of director independence. The need for the independence of directors is dictated not only by long experience but also by theory, specifically agency theory, which is discussed in Chapter 7 as an important component of finance theory. According to this theory, director independence is essential to overcome the agent-principal problem inherent in the separation of ownership and control. If managers also serve as directors, then they are, in effect, monitoring themselves. This problem is especially acute when the CEO of a corporation also serves as the chairman of the board, so-called *duality*. However, CEO duality, which is prevalent in U.S. corporations, is dictated by organization theory generally and, in particular, by the idea of the *unity of command*. The result is identified by Dan R. Dalton and Catherine M. Dalton as "a collision of theories and a collapsing of application." In Chapter 30, "Boards of Directors," these management scholars examine the issues of director independence and CEO duality and the conflict between theories with a view to contributing to both theory and practice in corporate governance.

CONCLUSION

Although finance ethics may lack recognition as a distinct field of study, the chapters in this volume show that the individual topics involved have long been examined from an ethical point of view and are rich in ethical content. No single volume could contain all the possibly relevant topics, and some readers may find a subject of interest omitted. This volume is an attempt, however, to bring together not only the major topics but also the key scholars in the nascent field of finance ethics to provide a foundation for further work. The rest is left to the readers of this volume with the hope that the field of finance ethics flourishes.

REFERENCES

Boatright, John R. 1999. Finance ethics. In *A companion to business ethics*, ed. Robert E. Frederick. Malden, MA: Blackwell Publishers.

Boatright, John R. 2008a. *Ethics in finance*. 2nd ed. Malden, MA: Blackwell Publishers.

Boatright, John R. 2008b. Finance, ethics of. In *Encyclopedia of business ethics and society*, ed. Robert W. Kolb. Thousand Oaks, CA: Sage Publications.

Dunfee, Thomas W., and Thomas Donaldson. 1999. *Ties that bind: A social contracts approach to business ethics*. Boston: Harvard Business School Press.

Ferguson, Niall. 2008. *The ascent of money*. New York: Penguin.

Horrigan, James O. 1987. The ethics of the new finance. *Journal of Business Ethics* 6:97–110.

Jensen, Michael C., and William H. Meckling. 1976. Theory of the firm: Managerial behavior, agency costs, and ownership structure. *Journal of Financial Economics* 3:305–360.

ABOUT THE AUTHOR

John R. Boatright is the Raymond C. Baumhart, S.J., Professor of Business Ethics in the Graduate School of Business at Loyola University Chicago. He has served as the executive director for the Society for Business Ethics and is a past president of the Society. He is the author of two books, *Ethics and the Conduct of Business*, in six editions, and *Ethics in Finance*, in its second edition. He has contributed chapters to many books, and has published widely in major journals, including *Academy of Management Review, Journal of Banking and Finance, Business Ethics Quarterly, Journal of Business Ethics, Business and Society Review, American Business Law Journal,* and *Business and Professional Ethics Journal*. He serves on the editorial boards of *Business Ethics Quarterly, Journal of Business Ethics,* and *Business and Society Review*.

PART II

Finance Theory

CHAPTER 2

Ethical Implications of Finance

ROBERT W. KOLB
Professor of Finance and the Consider Chair of Applied Ethics,
Loyola University Chicago

INTRODUCTION

Finance is essentially a daughter discipline of economics, and ways of thinking in finance owe much to the general field of economics. Yet during the last half of the twentieth century, finance scholars have developed the general economic conceptual framework toward a distinctive finance view of the world. This chapter proceeds by considering the most salient features of the finance view of the world and examining these key finance perspectives from a normative point of view.

The finance discipline often attempts to present itself as an objective science and to insist that it offers no normative prescriptions. But the finance discipline is, in fact, essentially prescriptive and normative. For example, the first finance class that is required of all business students is a course in financial management. In this course, students are instructed in the proper manner of managing the financial affairs of a corporation. In virtually all such instruction the course turns on the familiar models of finance, such as share price maximization and the theory of efficient markets, which are described later in this chapter.

While finance may posture as a purely scientific discipline and may develop models in which simplified views of society, firms, and individuals play a crucial role, the discipline faces the recurring problem of reifying its admittedly simplistic assumptions. In other words, it is a short intellectual leap from "assume that individuals are selfish and concerned only with cash flows" to "a rational actor is selfish and concerned only with cash flows" to "one *ought* to act so as to maximize the present value of future cash flows." Thus, there is a tendency for characterizations of human psychology that are consciously adopted as methodological fictions to harden into descriptions of the ways that people actually think and behave, and eventually to become even a prescription for how people ought to think and behave.

This chapter considers a number of key concepts in finance. Each section proceeds by briefly describing some key ideas and then indicating some of their ethical implications.

KEY ASSUMPTIONS IN FINANCE

At the outset, it is important to emphasize that the characterization of the finance view of the world in this chapter is a simplification and, to some extent, a carica-ture. Further, for many in finance the finance view of the world is a methodological fiction. In particular, for some the truncated view of human psychology that is part of the finance view of the world is a conscious abstraction designed only to further the study of financial markets and financial behavior, but it is not intended to be an accurate characterization of people in general. The two most important views of human psychology that infuse the classical finance view of the world are a specif-ically narrow view of rationality and strong assumptions about the wellsprings of human motivation. The finance worldview also makes strong assumptions about the nature of the firm. As we will see later in this chapter, some of the verities of this finance view of the world are under attack from within the discipline, most notably the rather limited psychology that characterized the discipline of finance until the past 20 years.

Rationality and Self-Interest

Perhaps one of the most important ideas taken over almost *in toto* from the broader field of economics is a narrow view of rationality. In the narrowest finance view, a rational person is one who takes effective means to secure a given end. The choice of ends is, of course, conceptually distinct from, but closely related to, the idea of rationality. We all tend to view someone else from our own point of view and to judge as irrational people who pursue ends that we regard as self-destructive. As Herbert Simon makes the point: "Economics sometimes uses the term 'irrationality' rather broadly and the term 'rationality' correspondingly narrowly, so as to exclude from the domain of the rational many phenomena that psychology would include in it."[1]

Kenneth Arrow (1986, S388) traces this kind of narrow view of rationality to the founders of the economic discipline in the eighteenth and nineteenth cen-turies: "Among the classical economists, such as Smith and Ricardo, rationality had the limited meaning of preferring more to less: capitalists choose to invest in the industry yielding the highest rate of return; landlords rent their property to the highest bidder, while no one pays for land more than it is worth in product." At base, Arrow identifies the economic conception of rationality, especially in the early development of economics, as being concerned with the maximiza-tion of utility under a budget constraint. For their part, Dobson and Riener (1996, 21), critics of the ethical implications of finance, find that rationality in economics and finance is often "defined strictly in terms of the individual pursuit of pecuniary wealth,"[2] although even here it might be more accurate to say that rationality in finance is the pursuit of wealth and the avoidance of risk.

Dobson and Riener's definition of rationality moves from the realm of meth-ods to that of ends. Rather than economics including the pursuit of money in its conception of rationality, it is more accurate to view the assumption about ends as an additional assumption of the discipline. Thus, rationality is about means, while economics makes additional assumptions about ends. Formally, the typical end that individuals are presumed to seek in the economics discipline is *utility*, a term that is defined as pleasure by some, but more broadly as a kind of satisfaction by others. This way of specifying the ends that individuals seek stems from the utilitarians of the nineteenth century, most notably John Stuart Mill, who provided the classic statement of utilitarianism, and who was also a great early economist.

Saying that individuals maximize utility is highly consonant with the finance view of the world, because finance tends to regard individuals as supremely self-interested. However, the notion of utility is so vague that economics reduces it further and specifies it more precisely in terms of monetary wealth. Money is the most fungible of goods, and the finance discipline often assumes that the self-interested ends of human life can be expressed in terms of money alone, as they certainly could be if all aspects of the goods of human life really could be expressed in monetary terms. More particularly, finance generally assumes that individuals maximize utility by capturing high monetary returns while avoiding financial risk. Based on this key intuition or assumption, finance uses various mathematical descriptions of investors in which monetary gain contributes to, and risk detracts from, an individual's utility.

When these assumptions about human psychology are challenged, virtually all finance theorists readily acknowledge that they are not realistic. Yet the discipline as a whole seeks to justify these assumptions using this view of human rationality and ends on two basic grounds. First, the narrow view of rationality, the assumption of self-interest, and the collapse of human values to monetary terms are defended as being methodological simplifications of reality that make it possible to proceed with financial investigations. There is a tendency (or wish) to liken the making of these assumptions to the unrealistic assumptions that have proven so useful in physics—for example, to assume a feather falls in a vacuum. The study of bodies falling in a vacuum has proven to be of great value in understanding bodies that fall in our atmosphere, and the methodological hope is that simplifying assumptions about human nature will be fruitful and elucidating in a similar way for the field of finance.

Second, these restrictive assumptions about human nature are defended along the lines that are common in the philosophy of science. Financial economists often make the argument that the effort upon which they are embarked is not necessarily to describe the world as it really is in its full complexity, but rather to create a useful heuristic. In terms of the philosophy of science, the defense is that finance does not hold a position of scientific realism, but rather that finance takes an instrumental approach to its discipline in which the value of the discipline can be judged not by how well its theories correspond to the full complexity of reality, but by how well finance theories allow us to predict economic behavior and to explain observed market prices.

Instead of attempting to limn reality, according to this line of reasoning, finance theory is a mere instrument, and simplifying the world as it does keeps the discipline tractable, yet allows it to make useful predictions.[3] And it is the correspondence of these predictions with subsequent realities that provides the test of finance and justifies the reasonableness of its simplifying assumptions about human psychology. Milton Friedman provided the classic statement of this view: "Positive economics is in principle independent of any particular ethical position or normative judgments. As Keynes says, it deals with 'what is,' not with 'what ought to be.' Its task is to provide a system of generalizations that can be used to make correct predictions about the consequences of any change in circumstances. Its performance is to be judged by the precision, scope, and conformity with experience of the predictions it yields. In short, positive economics is, or can be, an 'objective' science, in precisely the same sense as any of the physical sciences."[4]

The Financial Theory of the Firm

Turning from individuals to firms, finance also embraces several strong propositions. In particular, in the finance view of the world, the corporation is the property of the shareholders, and the properly managed firm is operated for the sole benefit of the shareholders. In the modern corporation, the managers of the firm are employees. So in accordance with this outlook, the managers are agents of the shareholders, who are the principals.

It is often thought that this view of the corporation implies a disregard of other stakeholders, such as customers, suppliers, and employees. Further, it is often argued that the corporation, in seeking to maximize benefits for shareholders, will impose externalities on society. For example, it is often argued that corporations will pollute rather than internalize the waste products of their own industrial processes. While these are topics addressed more fully elsewhere in this volume, the feared consequences need not prevail.

First, the interaction of other stakeholders with the firm is achieved through contracts, which might be implicit or explicit. In fact, the corporation is often viewed as a *nexus of contracts*. According to this view, the firm essentially is a contracting mechanism. Taking employees as an example, the firm acquires labor services by contracting with individuals. Presumably, the employees agree to work for the firm of their own volition and judge themselves better off from so doing. On this view, employees (and stakeholders, *mutatis mutandis*) receive adequate compensation to induce them to willingly provide their services to the firm. Second, with respect to externalities, virtually all actors face incentives to impose costs on others rather than to internalize them, and this is certainly true of corporations. But law, custom, and social pressure restrain firms from fully imposing externalities on others.

In the finance view of the world, we might say that the firm faces a constrained optimization problem: Maximize the value of shareholder wealth, subject to a variety of constraints. Those constraints include factors such as fair dealing with stakeholders, along with laws, regulations, and social pressures that effectively require the firm to internalize many of the costs it would prefer to externalize. The remainder of this chapter considers a number of key concepts in finance. Each section proceeds by briefly describing the key idea, and then indicating some of its ethical implications.

THE TIME VALUE OF MONEY

The simple idea that money has a time value is the foundational concept of all finance: A dollar received today is worth more than a dollar received tomorrow. The proof of the idea is that a dollar in hand today, a present value, can be converted into a larger number of dollars in the future, a future value, by investment. The relationship between present value, PV, and future value, FV, is mediated by the rate of interest per period, r, and the number of periods between the present value and future value dates, T, and can be expressed formally as:

$$PV = \frac{FV}{(1+r)^T}$$

In freely functioning financial markets, except in the most bizarre and extraordinary instance, the interest rate is above zero, and the future value will exceed the present value. The value of r depends primarily on three factors: the real rate of return on physical capital at the margin,[5] the expected inflation rate over the horizon from the present to the future value date, and the riskiness of the borrower to whom money is lent or the risk of the investment that is undertaken.

The time value of money relates directly to the concept of usury, the unethical demanding of interest on a loan. Usury comes in two forms. First, some claim that charging any interest for a loan is unethical, and so demanding any interest is also unethical. This view is most often associated with religious traditions such as the Islamic concept of *riba* and the Orthodox Jewish and traditional Roman Catholic proscription against charging any interest. A weaker concept of usury stipulates that it is unethical to charge an inappropriately high or excessive rate of interest. Even in contemporary times, this weaker concept of usury is enshrined in the laws of many countries.[6]

In the strict finance view of the world, usury is meaningless. Instead, interest rates are devoid of moral significance, and any interest rate that emerges from the interplay of supply and demand in markets free of deception and coercion is entirely unproblematic. Because the time value of money is *the* essential concept of finance, those who believe that either kind of usury is unethical must find also that finance is fundamentally unethical. However, many finance academics and practitioners would concede that some practices of charging interest can be excessive and abusive, especially when the borrower is poor or naïve.

RISK, RISK AVERSION, AND EXPECTED RETURN

Consider a situation in which investment in a U.S. Treasury obligation can earn 6 percent over the next year. This investment is riskless in the sense that there is no risk that the debtor will fail to pay as promised. (In finance, such an investment is said to have zero credit risk.) Now consider a class of investments that are similarly structured, except that these investments have a 20 percent chance that the borrower will default on the loan and will repay nothing at all, so that the lender loses both the promised interest as well as the principal that was lent. To expect to capture the same return of 6 percent, lending to this riskier class of borrowers would have to be at a rate of 32.5 percent, because there is only an 80 percent chance that the borrower will make the promised payment. (For example, assume the loan amount is $1,000. Then there is an 80 percent chance the borrower will pay the principal plus interest of $1,325, and a 20 percent chance the borrower will pay zero. The expected payoff is then: $0.8(\$1,325) + 0.2(0) = \$1,060$, for a 6 percent expected return.) Thus, given the finance view of the world in which the goal is to maximize monetary gain, risky investments must have a higher promised return than riskless investments, and so those who are thought to have a higher risk of defaulting on their financial obligations must be charged a higher promised rate of interest.

The actual situation is much harsher than this simple example would suggest. In that example, the arithmetic of lending shows that a promised return of 32.5 percent must be required to yield an expected return of 6 percent if there is a 20 percent chance of the borrower defaulting. But lending at 32.5 percent to the risky borrower only offers an *expected* return of 6 percent. Yet lending to the U.S. Treasury in this example yields a *certain* return of 6 percent. Why would anyone invest to get a risky return of 6 percent when a certain return of the same amount is available? From the finance point of view, the answer is that no one would make the risky loan without demanding an interest rate even higher than 32.5 percent.

The discipline of finance assumes that people are *risk averse*—that is, that they prefer to avoid risk. This assumption reflects a view of human nature that is well-confirmed for most people in most situations. If a lender is risk averse, the lender must be compensated with the promise of higher expected returns to be induced to lend to a risky borrower. In our continuing example, charging a rate of 32.5 percent only gives a risky expected return of 6 percent, which merely equals the certain return from investing in U.S. Treasuries. If lenders are risk averse, they must be promised an extra return over 32.5 percent to yield a risky expected return that exceeds the certain 6 percent return on offer from the U.S. Treasury. This additional expected return is necessary in order to overcome the lender's risk aversion.

If people are risk averse, then they will prefer to avoid risk. Yet there is unavoidable risk in the world. If risky, yet beneficial, investments are to be undertaken, such as starting businesses, building new plants, engaging in pharmaceutical research, and so on, then someone must bear the risk of those investments. The finance discipline looks at the bearing of risk as a service to society, and the bearing of risk is a service that must be, and deserves to be, compensated with a higher expected return. From the finance point of view, the rational promised yield on the loan of the example must exceed 32.5 percent to compensate for the expected defaults and for the service of risk bearing. Note that we have not said how much more than 32.5 percent the promised interest rate must be—that depends on the degree of risk aversion of those in the market.

The line of reasoning illustrated by the previous example helps to explain some frequently observed business practices that are often held to be immoral. For example, it is a commonplace that businesses which operate in poor neighborhoods charge higher prices than those that operate in wealthier neighborhoods. Further, it seems to be the case that borrowers who are generally more financially naïve, poorer, of color, and less able to bear the hardship of higher interest rates are exactly those people who are charged the highest interest rates. In the finance view of the world, all of those factors are irrelevant. The goal of running a business or making loans is to maximize financial gain while avoiding risk, not to aid the borrower or to alleviate the hardships of the less well-off. Instead, it is a simple fact that to keep oneself financially whole, loans to riskier borrowers must bear a higher promised rate of interest. Similarly, if the location of a business makes it more subject to greater pilferage, greater hazard of vandalism, greater chance of customers' failing to pay, and so on, that business must charge higher prices to earn the same risk-adjusted return that is available elsewhere.

Firms are often criticized for those business practices that the risk-adjusted approach to investing counsels. If firms charge more in ghettos, they are seen as exploitative, for example. But for the firm committed to shareholder wealth maximization the alternative would be to abandon such markets altogether, leaving potential customers in those markets even worse off.

THE PRICE OF RISK-BEARING SERVICES

The previous section explained why the service of bearing risk is valuable to society and why those who bear risk demand compensation for that service, at least according to the finance view of the world. However, the previous section made no attempt to specify the price that investors require for bearing risk. Pricing the service of risk bearing has been one of the greatest problems faced by finance, and giving reasonable answers to this question has been one of the greatest achievements of the discipline. Statistical methods for the measurement of risk are typically used in finance and become mathematically complex. However, this section discusses the measurement and pricing of risk in more conceptual terms.

Consider again the example of lending to a borrower with a 20 percent chance of complete default. If a bank makes one loan of $100 to a single customer, the outcome will be either the repayment of the $100 plus interest in excess of 32.5 percent or zero. Obviously, the difference between these outcomes is extreme, and for a single loan the default experience will be either zero or 100 percent, neither of which is even remotely close to the 20 percent chance of default stipulated in the example. However, if the bank makes thousands of such loans to many such borrowers, it can expect the overall performance of the loan portfolio to match the terms of our example much more closely. That is, with a large sample of loans, and assuming that the probability of default of any one borrower is 20 percent, the default experience for the total portfolio of loans should be close to 20 percent.

Whether this turns out to be the actual result depends in large part on the accuracy of the prediction of a 20 percent chance of default for a single borrower, but it also depends on how likely the defaults are to be correlated across borrowers. For example, if an economic recession affects many borrowers, then there are likely to be more defaults than the 20 percent predicted. This example shows that diversifying across risky investment projects—the loans to individual borrowers in our example—can reduce the risk of the overall investment project, and that the effectiveness of the diversification will depend on the degree of correlation among the different individual investment projects.

In terms of our example, for any one loan made at 32.5 percent with a 20 percent chance of default, the expected return on the loan would be 6 percent, but making one such loan is extremely risky. By diversifying across many borrowers, each with a 20 percent chance of default that is uncorrelated with other borrowers, the expected return on the portfolio of loans would still be 6 percent, but the riskiness of that entire portfolio would be much lower than the risk of a single loan. Thus, one of the great contributions of finance in the twentieth century was to provide a

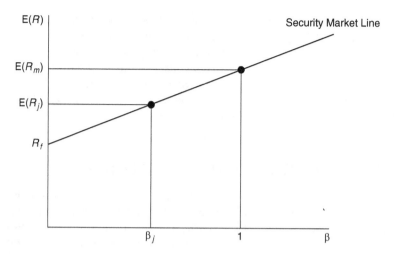

Exhibit 2.1   The Capital Asset Pricing Model with the Security Market Line

mathematical measure of investment risk, to show how diversification reduces that risk, and to develop a technique to calculate the total risk of a diversified portfolio based on the risk of the individual investments in the portfolio and the degree of correlation in investment returns among the individual assets that comprise the investment.

According to the capital asset pricing model (CAPM), the expected rate of return on an asset j, $E(R_j)$, equals the risk-free rate of interest, R_f, plus a measure of the undiversifiable risk associated with that asset, β_j, the asset's beta, times the expected return on the market minus the risk-free rate, $E(R_m) - R_f$:

$$E(R_j) = R_f + \beta_j[E(R_m) - R_f]$$

Exhibit 2.1 presents the security market line (SML), which shows the equilibrium expected rate of return as a function of undiversifiable, or systematic, risk. The SML indicates that the minimum expected return for an asset is the risk-free rate which compensates an investor merely for the use of funds over time, but not for bearing risk. By definition, the entire market, the market portfolio, has a beta of 1.0, and earns a premium over the risk-free rate that is determined by the willingness to bear risk of the collection of individuals that comprise the entire economy. Assets with less undiversifiable risk (a lower beta) than that of the market have a lower expected return, such as asset j in the graph.

Thus, if the market is in equilibrium, an investor receives the risk-free rate for sacrificing the use of money plus a risk premium for bearing undiversifiable risk. So, in the finance view of the world, we might even say that an investor is *entitled* to the risk-free rate for sacrificing the current use of money, and *deserves* compensation for bearing undiversifiable risk, which is a service to society. While the CAPM is presented as a purely descriptive analysis of how the market functions, the model also clearly has a normative subtext.

One of the most striking implications is the focus on only systematic risk, as this is the only risk that the market prices according to the CAPM. The development of the CAPM assumes that transaction costs are zero, so investors can trade to fully diversify their portfolio. In contrast with a fully diversified portfolio a single security embodies a total amount of risk, which can be partitioned into two kinds of risk: systematic risk or nondiversifiable risk, and nonsystematic or diversifiable risk. By holding a fully diversified portfolio, all of the diversifiable risk of all of the securities is eliminated, and the remaining risk of the portfolio is simply systematic or nondiversifiable risk.

If a firm holds constant its systematic risk, but increases its nonsystematic risk, there should be no effect on prices, it might seem. This implies that firms should not worry about bankruptcy risk and its effect on employees and other stakeholders of the firm. Further, it also implies that firms should not attempt to manage bankruptcy risk, as it is a waste of resources from the shareholders' point of view, because investors can diversify away the nonsystematic risk of each particular firm. As we will see in the discussion of risk management later in this chapter, this line of argument, although once widely regarded as persuasive, requires significant modification.

NET PRESENT VALUE AND CORPORATE FINANCIAL MANAGEMENT

The normative dimension of the CAPM becomes apparent in the teaching of the practice of the financial management of corporations. In virtually all business schools, the first finance course required of all business majors focuses on the financial management of corporations, and, more specifically, it concentrates on how the firm *should* be operated. In particular, in the finance view of the world the key task of the financial manager is capital budgeting—the allocation of the firm's capital to investment projects in order to increase the value of the firm and create wealth.

The key principle of capital budgeting is that the firm *should* undertake projects that have a positive net present value (NPV) because these projects increase the value of the firm. A project has a positive NPV if all incremental cash flows associated with the project, including both cash outflows for investment outlays and cash inflows from revenues, have a positive value when they are discounted to the present—the time when the investment decision is made.

Key to this analysis is selecting the appropriate interest rate at which to discount the future cash flows associated with the project. This discount rate is given by the SML, because a project with a given systematic risk should be discounted at the market's equilibrium rate of return commensurate with that level of systematic risk. Exhibit 2.2 shows the security market line with two new projects, Project x and Project y. In terms of the graph, the financial manager should invest in projects that lie above the security market line (e.g., Project x) and refuse to invest in projects that lie below the SML (e.g., Project y). (The financial manager should be indifferent to projects that lie on the SML: They merely earn the required rate of return (RRR)

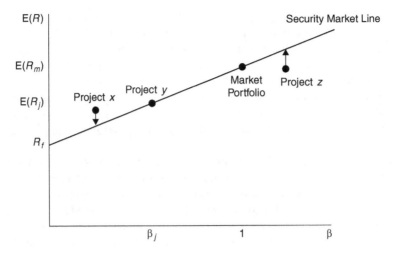

Exhibit 2.2 The Capital Asset Pricing Model with Projects in Disequilibrium

and neither augment nor diminish the value of the firm.) In Exhibit 2.2, note that Project x has a lower expected return than Project y, but Project x is nonetheless desirable, because it has an expected return above its RRR, which is a function of the project's systematic risk. Accepting or rejecting Project y is a matter of indifference, as its expected return is just commensurate with its systemic risk, and Project z should be rejected as its expected return lies below its RRR.

FINANCE, CORPORATE GOVERNANCE, AND THE GOAL OF THE FIRM

Implicit in the standard analysis of capital budgeting and the CAPM is a very clear view of the nature of the firm and the principles that should govern the practice of finance in firms. The goal of capital budgeting is to find and invest in projects that increase the value of the firm in general and, more specifically, increase shareholder wealth, or equivalently, the price of the firm's shares. Whether such a project benefits society as a whole or contributes to the public weal in some way is completely irrelevant in financial management. However, it should be emphasized that firms that undertake profitable investment projects contribute to the wealth of society and that this is a major contribution of business to societal well-being.

Consider a project that earns exactly its RRR, but throws off benefits to the community as a whole. Such a project does not benefit the firm's shareholders but would benefit others. In the finance view of the world, the firm should be indifferent to this project. It might be argued that such a project would indirectly benefit the firm's shareholders by enhancing the reputation of the firm and inducing higher sales for the firm. But in a proper capital budgeting analysis, those reputational benefits and the higher sales associated with them should be included in the capital budgeting analysis, which would make the project have a positive NPV, thereby contributing to the total wealth and well-being of society.

So the acid test of capital budgeting is simply whether a project is expected to benefit the firm's shareholders after all incremental effects of the project on shareholder wealth are considered. A project that is expected to earn even the slightest amount below its RRR, yet yield huge benefits to others, should be rejected. In the finance view of the world, the firm is not an eleemosynary institution!

Thus, the finance view of the world embodies a particular view of the nature and goal of the firm. Specifically, the shareholders own the firm, and the financial manager is an agent of the shareholders whose job is to identify and undertake projects that contribute to the wealth of the firm's owners. This agency theoretic view of the firm contrasts with the stakeholder theory, which maintains that the firm should aim to benefit a wide variety of the firm's constituents, or stakeholders, which would include shareholders, employees, customers, suppliers, and the wider community at large. While the firm operated along agency theoretic lines does not aim at benefiting these other stakeholders, it certainly does so through its relationship with them. For example, the firm contracts with employees, customers, and suppliers in voluntary relationships that bring benefits to all parties. Further, firms benefit the broader society by the wealth they create and the taxes they pay, along with aiding all of the parties who enter into voluntary relationships with the firm.

Agency theory and stakeholder theory are discussed at length elsewhere in this volume. But the important contrast here turns on the goal of financial management. A firm operated in strict accordance with the finance view of the world may, in fact, treat its employees and other stakeholders just as well as a stakeholder-operated firm. In the finance view of the world, the right way to treat employees, for example, is determined by the policy that will benefit the firm's shareholders. Subject to constraints of law and societal demands, the firm should treat employees in a way that maximizes the firm's share price, and this goal might justify the most generous treatment of employees, but it might just as well warrant the most niggardly terms of employment. The same comment would apply to other stakeholders, such as customers, suppliers, and so on.

The Efficient Markets Hypothesis

A market can be efficient in either an operational or an informational sense. An operationally efficient market functions smoothly, rapidly, and accurately by conveying orders to the market, executing them quickly at the best price available, and reporting the results of the transaction in a timely manner. A market is informationally efficient if prices in a market fully reflect a particular body of information. The efficient market hypothesis (EMH) is a theory that pertains to informational efficiency in financial markets, such as the stock market or the market for U.S. Treasury securities. The EMH does not pertain to nonsecurity markets such as the market for labor, homes, and other services or real assets. Stated more formally: A market is efficient with respect to a given information set if prices in that market at all times fully reflect that information.

Thus, different versions of the EMH can be elaborated by specifying alternative information sets. Based on Eugene Fama's classic article (1970), it is customary to distinguish three versions of the EMH: the weak, semi-strong, and strong. According to the weak form of the EMH, security prices fully reflect all historical price data. The information set for the semi-strong hypothesis is all publicly available information, including earnings announcements, news articles, government statistics, and so on. Finally, the strong form EMH asserts that markets fully reflect all information, whether public or private. Private information includes unannounced company information such as sales data, pending earnings announcements, pending merger announcements, contemplated Federal Reserve actions, and new discoveries not yet made public. The truth of a given version of the EMH implies that it is impossible to use the specified information set to direct a profitable trading strategy.

For a long period, ongoing research strongly confirmed the weak form EMH, essentially supported the semi-strong EMH, and continually provided evidence against the strong form EMH. In recent years, the weight of evidence has been swinging against the semi-strong EMH, and today few believe that the semi-strong version is true. Nonetheless, most finance theorists still agree that the semi-strong version provides a useful heuristic or starting point for the examination of security markets and that the approximate semi-strong efficiency of well-developed financial markets justifies a very critical examination of claims of inefficiency.

The EMH can be related to the security market line of Exhibit 2.1. If the EMH is true, and if the market is in equilibrium, then all securities lie on the SML. Note that the EMH pertains only to security markets, not to real investment opportunities, such as developing new cars or discovering new pharmaceuticals. Thus, even if the EMH is literally and exactly true, real investment can still earn economic rents.

Research continues to support the weak form EMH, and the strong form has long been shown to be false. Further, nonpublic information is essentially inside information, and using most forms of nonpublic information to guide a trading strategy is illegal. If the weak form were shown to be false, and the strong form shown to be true, but the information pertaining to the strong form is generally illegal to exploit and only available to insiders anyway, the semi-strong EMH is the most important, focusing as it does on information available to all with a reasonable prospect of being useful to the investor. Thus, this section focuses on the semi-strong form of the EMH, which for a long period garnered the allegiance of many in finance and still provides a key starting point for understanding security markets.

If the semi-strong version of the EMH is true, many normal activities that one might pursue as an investor make no sense. For the investor there is no point in studying financial statements issued by firms, and economic data are useless. If the semi-strong EMH is true, all of that information is already reflected in security prices and none of that information can be used to derive profits from investing. In such a situation, an investor might just passively hold a fully diversified portfolio to avoid unsystematic risk, such as a stock market index fund or exchange-traded fund (ETF).[7]

While presented as an empirical hypothesis, the truth of the EMH would entail a strong prescriptive element and should change investors' behavior. The semi-strong EMH effectively counsels: "Don't waste your time studying markets or economic data; all such information is already reflected in security prices." But this counsel masks an inherent paradox. If information is already reflected in prices, it must be because market participants have already absorbed that information and acted on it in their own trading. It is actual buying and selling that moves prices and makes the current price reflect the new information. So the truth of the EMH effectively depends on the immediate absorption of the information that the EMH holds to be irrelevant to guiding a trading strategy. If the semi-strong EMH is true, investors have the opportunity to be free riders, not paying attention to the flow of financial and economic news, but knowing that others have already considered this and ensured that the value of that news is reflected in security prices. Of course, this practice has the general ethical difficulty of all free rider problems. Some have even seen this paradox as leading to investor nihilism about the value of studying markets (Horrigan, 1997).

If the semi-strong version of the EMH is true, then the current market price is always right in the sense of being the best attainable estimate of the true value of a security. The truth of this hypothesis short-circuits much ordinary discourse that appears to be reasonable. To argue that a security is overpriced, for example, would be foolish, because the market would already have aggregated all useful information. Similarly, saying that tech stock prices were inflated in 2000 or that U.S. home prices were excessively high in 2006 could hardly be plausible or meaningful, given the truth of the semi-strong EMH hypothesis. In short, the semi-strong hypothesis renders otiose much of our normal talk about the value of securities and other financial assets.

OPTION PRICING THEORY

One of the simplest kinds of options is a plain vanilla option to buy a stock, which is a *call*, or to sell a stock, which is a *put*. These options trade on organized exchanges, such as the Chicago Board Options Exchange. There is no preexisting supply of options. Instead, options are contracts that traders create when they trade. For a transaction to occur, there must be a buyer and seller for every option. This means that, ignoring transactions costs, option trading is a zero-sum game, with the buyer's gains being the seller's losses, and vice versa.[8] While this may make it appear that option trading has no social value and is merely a form of gambling, this is definitely not the case. As explained elsewhere in this volume, option trading plays a crucial role in managing risk and in providing price information to market participants.

In buying a call option, the purchaser pays the option price (premium), and owning the option confers the right to purchase the underlying stock at a given price (the strike price or the exercise price) with that right persisting until a specified time (the option's expiration). The seller of a call receives payment of the option premium and promises to deliver the underlying stock in exchange for the strike price if the option purchaser so demands. Put options work similarly, but give the owner the right to sell the option at a specified price, while the put seller promises to buy the underlying stock at the strike price if the purchaser of the put option so demands.

One of the great triumphs of modern finance is the option pricing model, which was first definitively developed by Myron Scholes and Fischer Black and almost immediately extended by Robert Merton.[9] (Scholes and Merton received the Nobel Prize in economics for their work on options; Black died before the award was made.) For a standard stock option, option pricing theory expresses the value of an option as a function of five factors: the stock price, the exercise price, the time until expiration, the risk-free rate of interest, and the riskiness of the stock. Most interestingly, the riskiness of the underlying stock is extremely crucial to the pricing level, and the value of an option increases with the riskiness of the stock.

Option pricing theory was soon extended to the analysis of many types of financial instruments besides options themselves, and it soon developed that many other kinds of nonfinancial contracts and investment opportunities can be understood by using the insights of option pricing theory. For example, consider a corporation with two securities, stock and debt. We may view the stockholders as holding a call option on the value of the firm, with the exercise price being the promised payments to the bondholders. That is, if the firm pays off the bondholders, the stockholders own the firm free and clear. But because owning a stock is effectively owning a call option on the firm, management can increase the value of the stock by increasing the overall risk of the firm. Surprising the bondholders with a big increase in risk makes the firm's bonds riskier and worth less, but this policy makes the shares more valuable and effectively transfers wealth from the bondholders to the stockholders.

If the firm is operated solely for the benefit of the shareholders in accordance with the precepts of the agency theoretic view of the firm, then the managers have a strong incentive to posture as a low-risk firm, issue bonds, and then suddenly increase the risk of the firm. Obviously, such a practice involves considerable deceit to fool the bondholders. If the bondholders are not tricked into believing that the firm will maintain the low-risk policies, they will demand a higher rate of interest to cover the firm's greater risk. (Potential bondholders are well aware of this possibility of deceit, and complicated bonding and signaling arrangements help to mitigate these adverse incentives. Discussion of these more technical topics is beyond the scope of this chapter.)

Many financial contracts have option features as well, and some of these have become extremely important in the financial crisis of 2007–2009. For a home buyer with a mortgage, the mortgage gives the buyer at least two important options. First, the mortgage contains the option for the buyer to prepay the mortgage. When market interest rates drop below the loan rate on the mortgage, home owners routinely exercise their mortgage by prepaying the original loan and refinancing at the new lower rates. The second option is more interesting from a normative point of view. When one buys a home with mortgage financing, the buyer promises to make a specified sequence of payments, and this promise is not conditional on the future value of the home. Nonetheless, in some states, the home owner has the option by law to default on the mortgage, and the lender cannot attempt to seize the defaulter's other assets.[10] This option only has value to the home owner if the mortgage balance exceeds the value of the house—that is, if the house is *underwater*. In defaulting, the mortgagor loses the down payment (which is the purchase price of the option from the point of view of option theory) and delivers the house to the lender. In option terms, the profit to the home owner from defaulting (exercising the option) is the difference between the higher mortgage balance the home owner escapes paying and the lower value of the home the defaulter sacrifices. In this situation, the mortgagor effectively exercises a put option to compel the lender to pay the outstanding mortgage balance for a house worth less than this amount.

It may be argued plausibly that option pricing theory is a purely intellectual endeavor, but it may also be the case that coming to see the world in terms of options may stimulate unethical behavior. For example, in the case of the firm with bondholders, the analysis clarifies the firm's incentives to posture as a low-risk form to deceive and exploit the bondholders. Similarly, viewing the financing of a house as, in part, the acquisition of a put option may lead home owners to default on their promised payments. During the crisis of 2007–2009, there were many televised discussions of this kind of strategy with some pundits explicitly advising this kind of default. At the same time, others publicly denounced such a practice and insisted that the promised payments were a valid obligation, even if the mortgage balance exceeded the value of the home.

The ethics of exercising this default option are quite interesting. Should we view the mortgage contract as containing an option that is understood by both parties and reflected in the interest rate embedded in the mortgage? Perhaps the lender reasons: "This state requires that I give the home owner the option to default on the mortgage loan without my having any remedy. Therefore, I must charge a higher interest rate to cover the chance of this eventuality." Viewed in such a context, the defaulter might be justified in taking advantage of just one among many terms in the mortgage. After all, viewed in this way, the home owner has been effectively paying the lender for granting the option by paying the higher interest rate that the lender demanded to cover the granting of the option to default. Alternatively, the default might be viewed as the simple breaking of the mortgage promise, with the borrower having no real right to exercise the option. A more likely understanding is that the financial institution is well aware of this mortgage feature at inception and the home buyer is unaware of the option. When the property becomes distressed, the buyer then might turn to default as a desperate expedient.

When options are traded in security markets, the rights and privileges associated with purchasing and exercising options are clear. Problems arise in more complicated situations such as the shareholder/bondholder and mortgagee/mortgagor examples. The shareholder/bondholder situation involves at least an implicit representation that the firm will be operated in one manner, but making the option more valuable by raising the risk level of the firm requires deceiving the bondholders. For the mortgagor, viewing the home financing in option terms may encourage debtors to ignore their promise of repayment with its moral obligation and to follow a path of greater financial expediency.

RISK MANAGEMENT

Finance is an infant intellectual discipline, tracing its origins only to the 1950s.[11] To this point, this chapter has described a kind of classical view of the field as it was developed up until about 1980–1985. So it is perhaps not surprising that early models in the field are excessively abstract and fail to capture the full complexity of human thought and behavior. But there are at least two developing subfields within finance that call into question the initial verities that seemed so secure at one time, such as the CAPM, the efficient markets hypothesis, and the view that a psychology of purely self-interested behavior was sufficient to understand financial markets. These two new developments are a greater appreciation of risk management and the emergence of behavioral finance. This section discusses briefly some recent thinking regarding risk management, while the next section considers behavioral finance.

In the classical view of finance, securities are priced according to the CAPM and investors need only consider the systematic risk of securities, so the nonsystematic risk that results from corporate decision making need not be considered. One of the implications of this outlook is that a firm has no need to avoid the risks of bankruptcy and the possible dissolution of the firm because well-diversified investors can insulate themselves very effectively from the demise of a single firm. Viewed in the harshest light, a firm operated in such a manner would give no weight to the interest of employees in maintaining their employment and incomes, for example. Nonetheless, virtually all firms invest heavily in risk management aimed at preventing bankruptcy. This almost universal risk management behavior presents a challenge to the classical view of finance.

One of the explicit assumptions that buttresses the CAPM is the assumption that there are no transaction costs. But this is clearly false in actual markets and for actual firms. Financial distress and bankruptcy, to take a particularly salient example, involve real costs. For example, if a firm is in financial distress, it is unable to undertake profitable investment opportunities. Similarly, when firms enter bankruptcy, real assets (e.g., plant and equipment) are left idle and fail to earn a return that would otherwise be garnered. Thus, one simple justification of risk management is that it can reduce the future expected real costs of financial distress and bankruptcy, thereby increasing the current value of the firm. Finance theorists are not only now working to develop new techniques of risk management but are also striving to justify the risk management behavior that businesses continue to pursue.[12]

From this simple example it is possible to derive a basic lesson about the future of finance and its implication for the ethical management of firms. The disregard of employees and other stakeholders counseled by standard finance theory has long been decried as an unethical implication of finance and its focus on shareholder wealth maximization. With the presently emerging understanding of how managing total risk contributes to maximizing the value of the firm, there is also a greater understanding of firm policies that protect employees and other stakeholders by justifying more concern with firm survival. In short, a richer understanding of finance helps to ameliorate the apparent conflict between the counsels of finance theory and the treatment of nonshareholder stakeholders. This is even more apparent in the field of behavioral finance.

BEHAVIORAL FINANCE

Much business and investor behavior is irrational—at least if we limit our conception of rationality to that of the rational economic man, an actor who merely seeks to maximize utility defined in terms of securing monetary gain while avoiding risk. Behavioral finance documents departures from this kind of rationality and attempts to extend the boundaries of the finance discipline to understand the broad range of human behavior that fails to conform to this truncated conception of rationality.[13] This section focuses on just two important aspect of behavioral finance: the attack on the EMH and the importance of fairness.

In standard finance theory, the current stock price equals the present value of all future dividends from the stock. Changes in the price of the stock reflect changing assessment of the value of that future dividend stream, and buying and selling the stock over time may give capital gains and losses to some investors, but the value of the share, like any asset, is the present value of the stream of cash flows that come from that asset. As such, the current stock price is an estimator of those future cash flows. If that is the case, the EMH implies that the current stock price, the estimator, should be less volatile than that which is estimated, namely the present value of the future stream of dividends. Yet this is not the case. Stock prices seem to exhibit excessive volatility, indicating that the market cannot be efficient (Shiller 1989, 2003). In other words, stock prices fail to conform to the so-called rational model of classical finance. Early evidence against the EMH was greeted with a strong defense of the EMH, but now behavioral finance seems to have prevailed, and most scholars agree that the claims of the EMH now require significant modification.[14]

This kind of realization opens the door to a better understanding of asset bubbles, such as the historical tulip craze in Holland, the dot-com frenzy of the turn of the twenty-first century, and the U.S. housing bubble of 2003–2006. The realization that problems with the EMH suggest that humans are not purely rational and unemotional financial discounting machines opens the door to a richer understanding of human rationality that has strong ethical implications. As a second strand of behavioral finance indicates, a richer finance theory has to take into account our ideas of fairness as well.

Consider a simple experiment, the ultimatum bargaining game, which requires only two players. One person is given $100 and told that she can divide the cash into two portions in any way she sees fit. She keeps one portion and offers the second portion to the other person. If the second person accepts the offered portion, both parties keep their respective portions. But if the second person refuses the offer, then both parties receive zero. If people behave in accordance with the classical finance definition of rationality, she who allocates the portions will retain $99.99 and grant only $0.01 to the second person. Likewise, the second person realizes that a penny is better than nothing and that his utility will increase if he accepts the meager grant.

But of course, people do not behave this way, as mere reflection quickly confirms and as formal experiments have validated. If the second person receives too little, he will punish the divider by withholding acceptance and forgoing the meager grant, even though inflicting the punishment requires sacrificing some money. An extremely unequal (or perhaps any unequal) division offends against our sense of fairness, and we tend to punish those who treat us unfairly. As one of the founding articles in behavioral economics has noted: "Even profit-maximizing firms will have an incentive to act in a manner that is perceived as fair if the individuals with whom they deal are willing to resist unfair transactions and punish unfair firms at some cost to themselves" (Kahneman, Knetsch, and Thaler, 1986, S285).

Thus, the firm that seeks to maximize shareholder wealth by treating other stakeholders according to the precepts of rational economic man will fail to secure the intended goal. All successful firms know that they must treat their employees and customers with a modicum of dignity, respect, and fairness. They cannot treat these constituencies with blatant unfairness and escape reprisal. Thus, an adequate finance theory must expand its conception of rationality to correspond more accurately to human nature and must adjust its prescriptions for financial management to a model more true to human behavior.

CONCLUSION

The basic argument of this chapter has focused on the truncated concept of human psychology that originated in economics and has been embraced by finance in which humans are presumed to maximize their personal utility by seeking only monetary wealth while avoiding financial risk. While this conception of human rationality may have been postulated initially as a pure methodological fiction, it soon hardened into a description of how people actually behave, and even became a presumption about how one ought to manage firms and investments. During the period of classical finance, say from 1950 to 1985, this model of human nature and its financial implications were applied to the particular problems of finance, such as the time value of money, capital asset pricing, diversification, portfolio management, and option pricing theory.

Of course, the real world of business has never operated with the impoverished understanding of humans which the classical period of finance presupposed, although many particular firms and individuals may have erred in that direction. The ethical problems of finance generally stem from acting too strongly in accordance with this diminished view of humans as rational economic men. Yet this conception of human nature, limited as it obviously is, allowed finance to offer a powerful, if incomplete, view of human behavior in financial markets. The field of finance is now in a process of maturation, and this chapter has argued that much of that maturation turns on an enlarged understanding of the wellsprings of human actions, which will enrich the field of finance in the predictive power of its positive aspect and should improve the normative guidance that the field offers to financial managers.

NOTES

1. Simon (1986).
2. Dobson and Riener (1996).
3. This is the contrast between scientific realism and instrumentalism. According to scientific realism, science describes the world as it really is, so the entities that science acknowledges create an entire ontology. By contrast, instrumentalism holds that science is concerned with making useful and testable predictions, and its postulation of various entities is undertaken for the purpose of facilitating scientific discourse and making predictions, not to build an ontology. For the contrast between these views, with a decided preference for scientific realism, see Sellars (1965).

4. Friedman (1966, 3–16). This is a clear statement of Friedman's preference for instrumentalism over scientific realism.

5. A simple example of return on physical capital is agricultural investment, such as planting wheat and reaping a harvest, or acquiring a machine and using it to make a product. In a running economy, the most beneficial real investments have already been undertaken, yet some opportunities remain, even if they earn a lower return. The marginal real rate of capital in a given economy is the rate of return on the most productive investment opportunity that remains available.

6. For a discussion of the historical meaning of *usury* and a discussion of the ethics of usury, see Lewison (1999); and Mews and Ibrahim (2007). For two articles that give strong emphasis to the history of ideas, see Taeusch (1942); and Persky (2007).

7. For a recent appraisal of criticisms of the EMH, and for a spirited defense of the EMH, see Malkiel (2003).

8. For a discussion of option pricing and other issues related to financial derivatives, see Kolb and Overdahl (2010); and Robert W. Kolb and James A. Overdahl (2007).

9. For the original articles, see Black and Scholes (1973); and Merton (1973).

10. These are states with *nonrecourse* mortgage lending laws. Other state allow recourse, while some states offer nonrecourse terms to certain kinds of borrowers (e.g., the elderly), but deny this protection to others.

11. Many would identify modern finance as beginning with the development of portfolio theory in 1952: Markowitz (1952).

12. For a defense of risk management in the face of the received view of classical finance, see Smithson and Simkins (2005).

13. For surveys of behavioral finance see Barberis and Thaler (2003); Elster (1998); Rabin (1998); Shefrin (2007); and Shiller (2003).

14. Not surprisingly, leading proponents of the EMH initially respond by defending the theory or conceding at most that the theory needed a bit of a "touch-up." See, for example, Fama (1998); and Miller (1986). But now, even the strongest proponents of the EMH seem to recognize that the theory has serious deficiencies and limitations. See, for example, Fama and French (2008).

REFERENCES

Arrow, Kenneth J. 1986. Rationality of self and others in an economic system. *Journal of Business* 59:S385–S399.

Barberis, Nicholas, and Richard Thaler. 2003. A survey of behavioral finance. In *Handbook of the Economics of Finance, Volume 1B*, George Contantinedes, Milton Harris, and René M. Stulz. Amsterdam: Elsevier, B. V.

Black, Fischer, and Myron Scholes. 1973. The pricing of options and corporate liabilities. *Journal of Political Economy* 81:637–654.

Dobson, John, and Ken Riener. 1996. The rationality of honesty in debt markets. *Managerial Finance* 22:20–37.

Elster, John. 1998. Emotions and economic theory. *Journal of Economic Literature* 36:47–74.

Fama, Eugene F. 1970. Efficient capital markets: A review of theory and empirical work. *Journal of Finance* 25:383–417.

Fama, Eugene F. 1998. Market efficiency, long-term returns, and behavioral finance. *Journal of Financial Economics* 49:283–306.

Fama, Eugene F., and Kenneth R. French. 2008. Dissecting anomalies. *Journal of Finance* 63:1653–1678.

Friedman, Milton. 1966. The methodology of positive economics. *Essays in Positive Economics* Chicago: University of Chicago Press.

Horrigan, James O. 1997. Ethics of the new finance. *Journal of Business Ethics* 6:97–110.

Kahneman, Daniel, Jack L. Knetsch, and Richard H. Thaler. 1986. Fairness and the assumptions of economics. *Journal of Business* 59:S285–S300.

Kolb, Robert W., and James A. Overdahl. 2010. *Financial derivatives*. Hoboken, NJ: John Wiley & Sons.

Kolb, Robert W., and James A. Overdahl. 2007. *Futures, options, and swaps*. 5th ed. Oxford: Blackwell Publishers.

Lewison, Martin. 1999. Conflicts of interest: The ethics of usury? *Journal of Business Ethics* 22:327–339.

Lintner, John. 1965. The valuation of risk assets and the selection of risky investments in stock portfolios and capital budgets. *Review of Economics and Statistics* 47: 13–37.

Malkiel, Burton G. 2003. The efficient market hypothesis and its critics. *Journal of Economic Perspectives* 17:59–82.

Markowitz, Harry. 1952. Portfolio selection. *Journal of Finance* 7:77–91.

Merton, Robert C. 1973. Theory of rational option pricing. *Bell Journal of Economics and Management Science* 4:141–183.

Mews, Constant J., and Abraham Ibrahim. 2007. Usury and just compensation: Religious and financial ethics in historical herspective. *Journal of Business Ethics* 72:1–15.

Mossin, Jan. 1966. Equilibrium in a capital asset market. *Econometrica* 34:768–783.

Persky, Joseph. 2007. From usury to interest. *Journal of Economic Perspectives* 21:227–236.

Rabin, Matthew. 1998. Psychology and economics. *Journal of Economic Literature* 36:11–46.

Sharpe, William F. 1964. Capital asset prices: A theory of market equilibrium under conditions of risk. *Journal of Finance* 19:425–442.

Sellars, Wilfred. 1965. Scientific realism or irenic instrumentalism: A critique of Nagel and Feyerabend on theoretical explanation. *Boston Studies in the Philosophy of Science II*, ed. Robert Cohen and Marx Wartofsky. New York: Humanities Press.

Shefrin, Hersh. 2007. *Beyond greed and fear: Understanding behavioral finance and the psychology of investing*. New York: Oxford University Press.

Shiller, Robert J. 2003. From efficient markets theory to behavioral finance. *Journal of Economic Perspectives* 17:83–104.

Shiller, Robert J. 1989. *Market volatility*. Cambridge, Mass.: MIT Press.

Simon, H. A. 1986. Rationality in psychology and economics. *Journal of Business* 69:S209–S224.

Smithson, Charles, and Betty J. Simkins. 2005. Does risk management add value? A survey of the evidence. *Journal of Applied Corporate Finance* 17:8–17.

Taeusch, Carl F. 1942. The concept of 'usury': The history of an idea. *Journal of the History of Ideas* 3:291–318.

ABOUT THE AUTHOR

Robert W. Kolb holds two PhDs (philosophy, finance) from the University of North Carolina at Chapel Hill and has been a finance professor at the University of Florida, Emory University, the University of Miami, the University of Colorado, and currently at Loyola University Chicago, where he holds the Considine Chair of Applied Ethics. Kolb's recent writings include *Futures, Options, and Swaps* with James A. Overdahl (Oxford: Blackwell, 2007). Edited works include the *Encyclopedia of Business Ethics and Society*, a five-volume, 1.5-million-word work. Current projects include *Employee Stock Options: Financial, Social, and Ethical Issues* and *The Financial Crisis of Our Time*, forthcoming from John Wiley & Sons, Inc., and Oxford University Press, respectively.

CHAPTER 3

Behavioral Assumptions of Finance

JOHN DOBSON
Professor of Finance, California Polytechnic State University

I carved a massive cake of beeswax into bits and rolled them in my hands until they softened.... Going forward I carried wax along the line, and laid it thick on their ears. They tied me up, then, plumb amidships, back to the mast, lashed to the mast, and took themselves again to rowing. Soon, as we came smartly within hailing distance, the two Seirênês, noting our fast ship off their point, made ready, and they sang.... The lovely voices in ardor appealing over the water made me crave to listen, and I tried to say 'Untie me!' to the crew, jerking my brows; but they bent steady to the oars.

—Homer, *The Odyssey*

INTRODUCTION

In his classic paper "The Determinants of Corporate Borrowing," Myers (1977) employs the above excerpt from Homer's *The Odyssey* (c. 900 B.C.) to illustrate the behavioral assumptions of finance. In Myers's model, lenders (e.g., banks, financial institutions, etc.) have to decide on the appropriate interest rate to charge borrowers. Given that this model is developed within the conventional behavioral assumptions of financial economics, lenders assume that borrowers are opportunists. Thus, lenders assume that borrowers will take only those actions that are directly and explicitly in their own interests. So, for example, if borrowers are faced with the choice of whether to undertake a project that, albeit profitable, does not generate sufficient profits to cover the interest cost of the money borrowed to undertake the project, then borrowers will simply not bother to undertake the project. Specifically, even though this is a profitable project, and even though these profits will go some way to paying the interest cost owed to lenders, borrowers will not undertake it. Borrowers will not "rationally" undertake it because the project will not materially benefit them personally. Also, given equity-type investments—where the downside to the borrower is limited but the upside is potentially unlimited—borrowers will rationally risk-shift toward the riskier but higher potential payoff investments. Simply put, borrowers are assumed not to give a fig about the welfare of lenders, or anyone else for that matter; all borrowers care about is themselves. Indeed, the atomistic nature of the rationality assumption precludes any individual borrower from caring—except strategically—about any other borrower. Each rational opportunist is an island unto himself or herself.

Cognizant of the opportunistic nature of borrowers' rationality, lenders charge a higher interest rate in the expectation that borrowers will act opportunistically and underinvest or risk-shift, or both (i.e., will reject certain low-payoff profitable projects and will choose high-risk projects). These phenomena are termed the *underinvestment problem* and the *risk-shifting problem*, respectively, in the agency theory literature of financial economics. Thus, the actions of lenders in setting higher interest rates ensure that agents—in this case borrowers—pay the price for opportunism even before they act; they are lashed to the mast of opportunism. The possibility that at least some agents may be honest or trustworthy—in the sense that they may feel some obligation to temper their opportunism and honor as far as possible their agreement with lenders—is never considered, and indeed can never be considered given the prevailing rationality rubric. Indeed, the very nature of the resulting equilibrium, in which lenders charge a higher interest rate *a priori*, really discourages the cultivation of any sense of obligation. Trust is never offered, and agents are universally assumed to fall victim to the Seirênês' song of opportunism. So why should agents feel any compunction to act differently? The agent will lie, cheat, steal, and so on, so long as this behavior is construed as wealth maximizing. Noreen, for example, defines this opportunistic notion of rationality as one in which individuals always pursue personal material gain with "if necessary guile and deceit" (1988, 359). Opportunism, in essence, is built into financial economics in a most fundamental way.

The current global financial crisis is often attributed, at least in part, to this guileful opportunism on the part of financial agents. The implicit assumption underlying much of the rhetoric, in both academe and the business press, is that financial agents—whether managers, traders, analysts, or whoever—are irremediably opportunistic. Indeed, just how narrow this behavioral assumption has become is reflected in the recent remarks of Alan Greenspan. In comments regarding his former role as chairman of the U.S. Federal Reserve in precipitating the current crisis, Greenspan bemoaned the fact that his assumption regarding the behavior of bankers had been too naïve: "All of the sophisticated mathematics and computer wizardry essentially rested on one central premise: that enlightened self-interest of owners and managers of financial institutions would lead them to maintain a sufficient buffer against insolvency by actively monitoring and managing their firms' capital and risk positions" (2009, 1). The fact that managers of financial institutions did not adhere to these tenets of "enlightened self-interest" left Greenspan "deeply dismayed." But note that his naïveté did not arise from a failure to recognize that bankers would act in their self-interest; rather, according to Greenspan, it was a failure to recognize that bankers would act *so* narrowly and opportunistically—to, as we now know, a self-destructive extent. For these financial agents, the Seirênês' song was all too seductive. Thus, recent events in actual financial markets appear to have reinforced these narrow behavioral assumptions of finance theory.

But, historically, such a presumption of opportunism or narrow self-interest has not always been the case. Economic agents have not always been invoked in such conceptually narrow terms. An investigation into the early origins of economic philosophy in the writings of, for example, Adam Smith and David Hume reveals "the incredible finesse with which Smith and his contemporaries analyzed the human psyche ... [versus] the pitiful impoverishment that befell us, sometime in the nineteenth century, when Marxism and liberal economics conspired to assert the supremacy of interest and thus to extinguish an older and subtler tradition of moral psychology" (Holmes 1990, 268).

As the following quotes illustrate, these classic economic philosophers envisaged a far richer paradigm of human interaction in the economic sphere. In the case of David Hume: "The epithets sociable, good-natured, humane, merciful, grateful, friendly, generous, beneficent, or their equivalents, are known in all languages, and universally express the highest merit, which human nature is capable of attaining."[1] And in the case of Adam Smith (1937b):

> All members of human society stand in need of each other's assistance, and are likewise exposed to mutual injuries. Where the necessary assistance is reciprocally afforded from love, from gratitude, from friendship, and esteem, the society flourishes and is happy. All the different members of it are bound together by the agreeable bonds of love and affection, and are, as it were, drawn to one common centre of mutual good offices.[2]

So it appears that, in evolving from the self-interest invoked by Smith and Hume (1955) to the self-interest of finance theory, something has been lost. We have in essence regressed in the past 200 years from a morally inclusive concept of self-interest to one in which the notion of what Adam Smith (1937a) called "moral sentiment" has absolutely no *rational* place. In the late nineteenth century, for example, the economist F. Y. Edgeworth declared that "the first principle of Economics is that every agent is actuated *only* by self-interest" (1881, 16, emphasis added).

THE AXIOMS OF RATIONALITY

This modernist notion of self is reflected in the mathematical modeling of human behavior in finance. The first comprehensive derivation of the rationality premise of contemporary financial economics is generally attributed to the five axioms of cardinal utility, as enumerated by von Neumann and Morgenstern (1947). These five axioms define rationality in terms of an individual's ability to make consistent preference orderings over a broad spectrum of choices: "We wish to find the mathematically complete principles which define 'rational behavior' for the participants in a social economy, and derive from them the general characteristics of that behavior" (von Neumann and Morgenstern 1947, 31). Furthermore, "people are assumed to be able to make these rational choices among thousands of alternatives" (Copeland and Weston 1988, 80).

The Axioms of Rationality

1. Comparability: The individual can make comparisons between preferences.
2. Consistency: These comparisons are consistent over an array of alternatives.
3. Independence: Original preference orderings are independent of new preference alternatives.
4. Measurability: Preferences are measurable.
5. Ranking: Preferences can be consistently and ordinally ranked.

The axioms are thus based on a very mathematical and instrumental notion of what it means to be rational. They primarily encompass notions of consistency and transitivity in preference orderings. For example, if you are an investor choosing stocks in which to invest, and you prefer IBM to Microsoft, and you prefer Microsoft to Netscape, then to be rational you must prefer IBM to Netscape. Also, your degree of preference for one investment over another must stay constant no matter how many more stocks are added to your opportunity set. Note that this type of axiom makes no normative statement concerning whether the agent has any specific goal, or what the goal of the agent should be; the axioms simply require that the agent act in a consistent manner in ordering preferences.

Contemporary financial-economic theory, however, adds a sixth axiom. This axiom has just such normative thrust. As Copeland and Weston (1988, 80) put it, in their seminal textbook on corporate finance: "Having established the five axioms we add to them the assumption that individuals *always* prefer more wealth to less" (emphasis added). In relating the five axioms of von Neumann and Morgenstern to this sixth axiom, a useful distinction can be made between *instrumental rationality* and *substantive rationality*. Instrumental rationality concerns how the agent goes about achieving the desired objective, whereas substantive rationality concerns identifying the desired objective itself. For example, Moore (1991) distinguishes between the two concepts as follows:

> *The primary feature of instrumental rationality is that it does not choose ends, but accepts them as given and looks for the best means to achieve them. In instrumental rationality, reason is subordinated to and placed at the service of ends outside itself. In . . . [substantive rationality], in contrast, reason is free ranging. It is not the servant of any end. Rather, it subjects every end to its own standards of evaluation and criticism.*[3]

Von Neumann and Morgenstern's five axioms clearly pertain to instrumental rationality. They do not stipulate an ultimate objective but merely require that agents pursue some given objective in a consistent and logical manner. The substantive rationality premise of financial economics is provided by the sixth axiom: the opportunistic and atomistic pursuit of material gain *ad infinitum*.

Substantive Rationality in Finance

In reference to finance's sixth axiom, Bowie notes that "there is considerable confusion as to whether the profit maximization claim is a universal empirical claim, an approximate empirical claim, a heuristic assumption, or an ethical obligation" (1991, 14). Bowie's intimation that finance's concept of substantive rationality is synonymous with profit maximization is somewhat of an oversimplification, but only somewhat. The broad acceptance of this sixth axiom of profit maximization is reflected in the behavioral assumptions made by financial economists in some of the classic models of finance theory. Leland and Pyle, for example, in their capital structure signaling model, state that "the entrepreneur is presumed to maximize his expected utility of wealth" (1977, 373). John and Nachman directly transfer the traditional objective of the firm to managers when, in their investment model, they assume that management's "overall objective is to . . . invest in nonnegative NPV [net present value] projects" (1985, 867). Diamond, in his model of reputation acquisition in debt markets, defines management's objective as an endeavor to "maximize discounted expected consumption over T periods" (1989, 833). Some models assume management is risk averse or effort averse, or both, and therefore maximizes some measure of utility of wealth. But this utility is always strictly a positive function of wealth ad infinitum. Thus the sixth axiom holds throughout.

Despite its potential ambiguity, then, the term *wealth maximization* captures succinctly the primary characteristic common to all finance-objective functions, namely that they are purely acquisitive in nature, entailing solely the accumulation or consumption, or both, of pecuniary goods. These six axioms also subsume any competing notions of rationality. This is made clear by Thaler:

> *The same basic assumptions about behavior are used in all applications of economic analysis, be it the theory of the firm, financial markets, or consumer choice. The two key assumptions are rationality [the five axioms] and self-interest [the sixth axiom]. People are assumed to want to get as much for themselves as possible, and are assumed to be quite clever in figuring out how best to accomplish this aim.*[4]

Viewing the finance rationality paradigm in terms of the aforementioned dichotomy between instrumental and substantive rationality reveals that this paradigm's rationality premise has only a partial foundation in logic. The logic of the instrumental part of what the finance paradigm regards as rational behavior finds a sound foundation in the five axioms enumerated previously by von Neumann and Morgenstern. The same cannot be said, however, for finance's substantive rationality premise. This premise is applied merely by arbitrarily assuming—for reasons of mathematical convenience—that agents are atomistic and opportunistic wealth maximizers.

These agents are atomistic in that they never adopt any communal notion of self-interest. To be sure, the agents may at times cooperate, but only when they perceive such cooperation to be in their own personal self-interest. Their decisions are not affected by the impact that these decisions might have on other agents, except to the extent that this impact might, in turn, impact their own personal wealth. In other words, there is no such thing as empathy or a sense of community. The agents are opportunists in that they are assumed to take whichever action maximizes their wealth, regardless of prior commitments or agreements. So contracts may be honored, but only if the agent believes the penalty for reneging is too great. In the case of explicit contracts, this penalty might be a fine or other legal sanction; in the case of implicit contracts, it might be the cost of potential litigation and/or reputation damage leading to a loss of future business.

IMPLICATIONS OF THE SIX AXIOMS

Descriptively, do the six axioms of financial rationality simply reflect how people actually behave in financial environments? Are they simply reflecting laws of nature?

The recent financial meltdown, as discussed earlier, might imply this. But there are many possible reasons for this meltdown. And even to the extent that narrow wealth-maximizing self-interest is to blame, the question still remains whether such behavior is indeed a law of nature or whether it is engendered by the environment in which financial agents currently operate. In other words, are agents irremediably self-interested to this self-destructively narrow extent, or are they acculturated into such behavior? Is it nature or nurture?

The nascent discipline of behavioral finance is challenging these traditional assumptions. Behavioral finance can loosely trace its origins to the pioneering work of Kahneman and Tversky (1979) on prospect theory: Individuals' utility functions are not fixed but rather are framed in terms of potential gains and losses around a given reference point; the function resembles an S-shape implying loss aversion where utility losses are more pronounced than utility gains around this reference point. In essence, Kahneman and Tversky showed that behavior is far more complex than the traditional six axioms imply. Following their early work, an increasing body of research is questioning these traditional assumptions on two broad fronts. First, from a descriptive perspective, the validity of finance's simple personal-wealth-maximization assumption is being challenged by a growing body of empirical and experimental evidence. Second, arguments have been made to the effect that the descriptive accuracy of economic rationality is inseparable from its prescriptive desirability. Agents change their behavior when confronted with role models or assumptions about how other agents behave. In other words, *is* inevitably implies *ought*. The next two sections of this chapter summarize these two broad challenges to the six axioms of traditional finance. Are the behavioral assumptions of finance—as encapsulated in the six axioms—descriptively accurate? Are they prescriptively desirable, either economically or ethically? And to what extent, if any, are these two questions separable?

THE DESCRIPTIVE ACCURACY OF THE BEHAVIORAL ASSUMPTIONS OF FINANCE

There is increasing evidence that the six axioms of financial rationality do not reflect the complexity and multifaceted nature of behavior in many financial contexts. For example, Schmidtz notes that "like *Homo economicus* [e.g., the six axioms] we have preferences, but unlike *Homo economicus*, we have preferences directly relating to the welfare of others" (1994, 250). Similarly, while commenting on the notion of economic rationality as premised on wealth maximization, Sen notes that while this view of economics is quite widely held (i.e., the view of rationality as atomistic and opportunistic wealth maximization), there is nevertheless something quite extraordinary in the fact that economics has evolved in this way, characterizing human motivation in such spectacularly narrow terms. One reason why this is extraordinary is that economics is supposed to be concerned with real people. It is hard to believe that real people could be completely unaffected by the reach of the self-examination induced by the Socratic question, "How should one live?" (Sen 1987, 1–2).

Similarly, C. R. Plott notes that "the weakest forms of the classical preference hypothesis [i.e., wealth maximization] are systematically at odds with the facts" (1986, 302). H. A. Simon suggests that "we stop debating whether a theory of substantive rationality and the assumptions of utility maximization provide a sufficient base for explaining and predicting economic behavior. The evidence is overwhelming that they do not" (1986, 223). Specifically, several consistent divergences from financial-economic rationality have been observed in financial markets (Nofsinger 2008). They include the following:

Behavioral Biases in Finance

- Investors tend to sell their profitable investments too quickly while holding on to their unprofitable investments too long.
- Investors tend to be overconfident concerning their ability to time peaks and troughs in the stock market (men more than women) and so tend to trade more frequently than is optimal.
- When deciding whether to continue or abandon a capital project, managers are unwilling to admit defeat and so tend to continue with projects long after the point at which they should be abandoned.
- Market participants tend to frame their decisions on the basis of recent and familiar experience rather than taking the broader perspective that economic rationality requires.
- Conceptions of fairness often eclipse wealth maximization criteria in determining behavior.
- Managerial hubris leads to the apparently excessive premiums paid for target firms in takeover battles.

Thus, even in strictly financial environments, human psychology renders behavior far more complex, multifaceted, and unpredictable than that modeled by the six axioms.

THE ULTIMATUM GAME

One simple laboratory way to test the empirical validity of narrow self-interest is the ultimatum game. The basic ultimatum game involves two players and a single iteration. Player 1, known as the *proposer*, is allocated a sizable amount of money. She is then instructed to offer some portion of the amount to player 2, known as the *responder*. Both proposer and responder know the amount of the original allocation. The responder is instructed to either accept the offer or refuse it. Refusal leads to the loss of all the original allocation of money to both players. If the proposer's offer is accepted by the respondent, both players can keep their respective shares.

The behavioral assumptions of finance—as encapsulated in the six axioms previously outlined—dictate a single simple strategy for this game: The proposer should offer to share a very small percentage of the original allocation, say 5 percent. The rational expectation is that it will be accepted by the respondent because it is better than nothing.

But when individuals play this game, few act in accordance with this rationality paradigm (Lawrence 2004): The typical allocation is 20 to 50 percent. Respondents who are offered less than 20 percent generally refuse the offer: they seemingly irrationally take nothing rather than accept an offer that seems to them unfair. In other words, the principle of fairness has intrinsic value to them, and they are prepared to uphold that principle even in the face of a guaranteed material loss.

There is some evidence that exposure to the behavioral assumptions of finance can change this behavior. For example, experiments involving economics students indicate that they tend to place less intrinsic value on fairness

(Frank, Gilovich, and Regan 1993). A reason for this might be the acculturation to narrow self-interest in business education via the widespread use of game theory. In the introduction to *Games and Information*, Rasmusen notes that "game theory has become dramatically more important to mainstream economics" (1989, 13); the rationality assumption in this methodology is typically narrow and focused on the individual attaining some atomistic payoff through competitive interaction with one or more other individuals. For example, in their extensive review of economic game theory, Hausman and McPherson noted that game theory "does not rule out altruism or sympathy . . . but it does rule out a collective perspective, a perspective that considers what we should do and what the consequences will be for us" (1993, 718). Indeed, regardless of its descriptive accuracy, game theory's distorted view of human interaction is attracting concern among ethicists. Grant (2004) recently summed up these concerns as follows:

> *Employment of game theory . . . involves much more than the adoption of the neutral strategy that this approach itself professes to be. This method of analysis comes with built-in visions of ourselves, of the nature of business, and of the nature of reality as such. It assumes and promotes an individualistic as opposed to a social view of human life, a preference for calculative over reflective reason, and a vision of reality that undermines appreciation of finer human virtues and the spiritual aspirations that sustain these.[5]*

ANIMAL BEHAVIOR

But if the behavior espoused in financial-economic theory and rewarded in game theory is not natural human behavior, what is? Recent research on nonhuman primates provides some intriguing answers. The results of the ultimatum game indicate that many humans place some intrinsic value on fairness or fair distribution. This trait is not unique to humans; studies of primate behavior have found a similar tendency. De Waal (1997), for example, played a variant of the ultimatum game with two chimpanzees kept in adjoining chambers. One subject was given food and was given no incentive to share it. The chimpanzee originally given the food did, however, voluntarily share the food with its neighbor. As with humans, chimpanzees appear to place an intrinsic value on fair distribution (Flack and de Waal 2004).

Nonhuman primate communities also exhibit a rudimentary sense of justice. Senior group members have been observed to intervene in disputes to arbitrate between the antagonists. Exhaustive observation of primate groups by many researchers over many years indicates that these social animals exhibit many behavioral traits that could be considered ethical, in the sense of being consistent with the type of behavior prescribed in a typical human code of ethics: "Sympathy-related traits such as attachment, succorance, emotional contagion and learned adjustment in combination with a system of reciprocity and punishment, the ability to internalize social rules and the capacity to work out conflicts and repair relationships damaged by aggression, are found to some degree in many primate species, and are fundamental to the development of moral systems" (Flack and de Waal 2004, 31).

Another particularly revealing finding from these studies concerns the acculturation of newcomers. The behavior adopted by new arrivals to any group depends heavily on how they think the group expects them to behave. If a newcomer believes that the group expects him to be aggressive, he will be aggressive. If the newcomer believes that the group expects him to be peaceable and cooperative, he will be peaceable and cooperative: the moral tenor of the group determines the moral tenor of the individual. This primate adaptability to social norms was found through observation of olive baboons: "... [M]ales new to the group somehow picked up on how they were expected to behave by watching what was going on.... Cultural transmission of, for want of a better word, manners, has never before been observed outside *homo sapiens*" (Sapolsky and Share 2004, 77).

NEUROSCIENCE

As discussed earlier, the fact that individuals may deviate from strictly rational decision making in financial markets is now well documented in behavioral finance. Indeed, this burgeoning field has identified a broad array of behavioral biases. These are often categorized into biases associated with motivation, cognition, and emotion (Nofsinger 2008). However, they all share a common neurological origin: Brain evolution has conditioned certain unconscious responses that override our conscious attempts to make rational decisions.

Our understanding of the underlying mechanisms behind these unconscious biases has increased markedly in recent years. Salvador and Folger (2009) note that the number of published studies in neuroscience has increased from around 100 in 1991, to over 1,000 by 2006. For example, as noted earlier, humans have many innate tendencies toward what is traditionally regarded as ethical behavior: We naturally feel empathy and compassion, and we naturally have genuine concern for the welfare of others. Indeed, humans use moral criteria in preference to other criteria in making judgments. For example, Messick (2004) undertook a series of experiments to determine the most natural way in which people evaluate stimuli. He tested various *scales of evaluation* (the semantic differential) people might use in making judgments and found the following: Concepts could be rated on a series of bipolar scales, like "strong–weak," "good–bad," "beautiful–ugly," and "active–passive." The ratings on a large series of such scales were then statistically analyzed to see which clusters of scales were intercorrelated in order to identify the underlying dimensions of judgment. The results of many studies in all parts of the globe indicated that the most basic dimension was an evaluative dimension, a "good–bad" dimension of judgment (Messick 2004, 131).

Evaluative judgments are so natural that we are often not consciously aware of them. Take, for example, an experiment used by child psychologists called the "Charlie Task." Cosmides and Tooby summarized the experiment and its implications as follows:

> *A child is shown a schematic face ("Charlie") surrounded by four different types of candy. Charlie's eyes are pointed toward the Milky Way bar (for example). The child is then asked, "Which candy does Charlie want?" Like you and I, a normal four-year-old will say that Charlie wants the Milky Way—the candy Charlie is looking at. In contrast, children with autism fail the Charlie Task, producing random responses. However—and this is important—when asked which candy Charlie is looking at, children with autism answer correctly. That is, children with this developmental disorder can compute eye direction correctly, but they cannot use that information to infer what someone wants.*[6]

This inference concerning the desires of another, which the autistic child is unable to make, is, in a fundamental way, natural. To survive as a social animal, evolution has hard-wired us with an innate awareness of the wants and desires of others. Recent developments in brain scanning and imaging techniques have enabled researchers to monitor brain activity during moral deliberation. Certain behavior stimulates certain parts of the brain: "There is a little inference circuit—a reasoning instinct—that produces this inference" (Cosmides and Tooby 2004, 99).

In summarizing the work of several behavioral psychologists, Messick explicitly makes the connection between the type of natural inference identified in the Charlie Task and ethical behavior: "There is good reason to think that empathy, vicarious emotionality, is hardwired in some way ..." (Messick 2004, 130). In broader motivational terms, Lawrence and Nohria (2002) suggest that the human brain directs activity in accordance with a desire to satisfy four basic drives:

1. To acquire.
2. To defend.
3. To learn.
4. To bond.

They summarized the actual brain function involved in satisfying these drives as follows:

Neural signals from our sense organs are fed through the limbic modules and there pick up markers that code them as opportunities or threats to the fulfillment of these drives. These coded signals move on to the pre-frontal cortex, the seat of consciousness, where they are manifested as emotion-laden representations. At this point the relevant skill sets and memories are activated and drawn into the working memory to aid in formulating a variety of action scenarios. These possible lines of response are weighted for their promise in fulfilling the drives (all four if possible) in the current situation. ... The chosen action plan is moved back through the limbic area to be energized and then sent to the motor centers for activation.[7]

Although this mental process appears lengthy when it is spelled out, the entire process takes only a fraction of a second; as with the Charlie Task response, it is largely subconscious. And, as the studies cited here indicate, these subconscious responses can easily swamp any rational decision-making process. Indeed, from an empirical perspective on financial markets, Thaler has amassed a disquieting array of behavioral "anomalies" and concludes that "assumptions aside, the theory [of opportunism] is vulnerable just on the quality of the predictions" (Thaler 1992, 4). He notes: "We can start to see the development of a new, improved version of economic theory. The new theory will retain the idea that agents try to do the best they can, but these individuals will also have the human strengths of kindness and cooperation, together with the limited human abilities to store and process information" (Thaler 1992, 5).

In concluding his book *On Ethics and Economics*, Sen makes a plea for this "new theory": "The wide use of the extremely narrow assumption of self-interested behavior has, I have tried to argue, seriously limited the scope of predictive economics, and made it difficult to pursue a number of important economic relationships that operate through behavioral versatility" (1987, 79).

In short, reasonable or rational behavior is more complex and multifaceted than simple opportunism. Although by no means exhaustive, the preceding examples illustrate the weight of evidence suggesting some broader notion of behavior than that currently embraced by conventional finance theory.

PRESCRIPTIVE IMPLICATIONS

The behavioral assumptions of finance have implications beyond their descriptive role in finance theory. Descriptive assumptions have a tendency to become prescriptive admonitions. "People change their behavior when confronted with assumptions about how other people behave," observes Bowie (1991, 9). He notes that business school students "believe that they will have to be unethical to keep their jobs. They believe that everyone else will put their [own] interests first. . . . But the evidence here is not merely anecdotal. . . . Economics graduate students are more inclined to behave in a self-interested fashion" (1991, 9). Bowie's assertion is supported by an extensive study by Frank, Gilovich, and Regan (1993). In a laboratory study, they involved business students and nonbusiness students in over 200 prisoners' dilemma-type scenarios. Frank and colleagues found that the business students defected (i.e., failed to cooperate by choosing the economically rational opportunistic move) 60 percent of the time, while nonbusiness students defected only 30 percent of the time. Also, when compared to students in different disciplines, business students were found to be less honest in hypothetical situations, and less likely to donate to charity. Also in a laboratory setting, Thaler finds that individuals tend not to adhere very closely to the dictates of economic rationality. Furthermore, those who do adhere tend to be financially compromised as a result:

> *The conclusion that subjects' utility functions have arguments other than money is reconfirmed. . . . We have seen that game theory is unsatisfactory as a positive model of behavior. It is also lacking as a prescriptive tool. While none of the subjects in . . . [the laboratory] experiments came very close to using the game-theoretic strategies, those who most closely approximated this strategy did not make the most money.*[8]

Thus Thaler's findings imply that economic rationality is not descriptively accurate; nor is it prescriptively desirable even from an economic perspective. In his article "Challenging the Egoistic Paradigm," Bowie concludes that "[l]ooking out for oneself is a natural, powerful motive that needs little, if any, social reinforcement. . . . Altruistic motives, even if they too are natural, are not as powerful: they need to be socially reinforced and nurtured" (1991, 19). Such nurturing is clearly not to be found in the rationality assumptions of behavioral finance. In a similar vein, Dees argues that the value systems of business theory influence those of business practice. He observes that "how concepts are introduced in an academic setting can have a significant influence on their use later on" (1992, 38). While commenting on the value system underlying business theory, Duska notes that "as it gets accepted as a legitimating reason for certain behavior in our form of life, it becomes subtly self-fulfilling" (1992, 149).

> *In a broader context, the susceptibility and suggestibility of human behavior was made very clear in the famous laboratory experiments conducted by Stanley Milgram (1974): Ordinary people, simply doing their jobs, and without any particular hostility on their part, can become agents in a terrible destructive process . . . even when the destructive effects of their work become patently clear, and they are asked to carry out actions incompatible with fundamental standards of morality, relatively few people have the resources needed to resist authority.*[9]

Thus, human behavior is malleable and suggestible. And in financial markets nothing provides a greater behavioral suggestion than money. There is ample evidence that explicit money-based incentives work. At windshield-replacement firm Safelite AutoGlass, for example, the replacement of a standard hourly wage with an incentive system tied directly to number of windshield installations resulted in a productivity gain of 44 percent within a year (Roberts 2004).

But windshield replacements are readily observable, and quality is easily verified. This is generally not the case for corporate executives. Explicit rewards in this context can often lead to distortions that actually destroy firm value. At the H. J. Heinz Company, for example, division managers received bonuses based on the year-on-year increase in corporate earnings. The result was that these managers manipulated the timing of shipments and payment systems in a way that, while maximizing their bonuses, actually destroyed firm value. Similarly, Sears' Auto Center division instigated an incentive system whereby bonuses were paid for the number of replacement brake, steering, and suspension systems installed. The result was unsuspecting customers receiving new parts unnecessarily (Roberts 2004).

The ongoing executive-stock-option backdating scandal, which now involves several hundred firms, is yet another example of incentive system distortion. The widespread adoption of executive stock options in the 1990s was the direct result of the work of agency theorists in the previous two decades advocating better alignment of the interests of managers with those of stockholders (Jensen and Meckling 1976; Jensen and Murphy 1990). The extent to which executive stock options have achieved this alignment is still under debate, but there is increasing evidence that in many cases, far from aligning the interests of shareholders and managers, stock options have furthered the interests of those who design and allocate them, namely managers, at the expense of the very group they were supposed to benefit, namely outside stockholders (Dobson 2002).

The classic example of incentive distortion and the accompanying socialization is undoubtedly Enron Corporation. Consistent with the recommendations of agency theorists, the bulk of managerial compensation at Enron was linked directly to various profitability measures and to Enron's relative stock price performance. The acculturation at Enron was achieved through the infamous Performance Review Committee (PRC). The PRC promulgated ruthlessly the pursuit of stock price appreciation. Those who contributed to this goal were rewarded handsomely, mostly in stock options, which further motivated the manager to focus on stock price appreciation. Whether managers were identifying and undertaking projects that were genuinely contributing to overall corporate value, or were just super-ficially profitable, mattered little to the PRC. Managers who were either unable or unwilling to create or fabricate profitable deals did not last long. CEO Jeffrey Skilling's division alone replaced about 15 percent of its workforce every year (Dobson 2002). As Driggers concludes, Enron "thrived on spending big. Everything had to be better and flashier, and no gesture seemed too lavish" (2002, 374).

Clearly, the tragedy at Enron was *not* that the incentive system failed to motivate managers. As Baker, Jensen, and Murphy observe, the problem with Enron-type incentive systems is "not that they are ineffective but rather that they are *too* effective: strong pay-for-performance motivates people to do exactly what they are told to do" (1988, 597). Managers who are sufficiently incentivized and socialized to meet some explicit target—whether it be stock price, earnings, or sales volume—will move heaven and earth to meet that target, often with little regard for ethics, law, or overall corporate value. In short, if incentive structures are based on the assumption of narrow self-interest (i.e., the conventional behavioral assumptions of finance), these structures will tend to induce just such behavior.

In addition to—and preceding—the behavioral assumptions of finance, the pedigree of modern corporate incentive structures can be traced back, through agency theory, to neoclassical economic utility theory. Recognition is growing, however, that this classic theory's mathematically amenable notion of human motivation in terms of maximum wealth for minimum effort may be dangerously simplistic. Kreps, for example, suggests that "[w]orkers may take sufficient pride in their work so that effort up to some level increases utility" and acknowledges that this calls into question conventional notions of motivation: "Answers involve looking into the utility functions of individuals, *terra incognita* for standard microeconomics" (1997, 361). Sen, who does venture into this terra incognita, warns of the dangers "imposed by taking an overly narrow view of human motivation" (1997, 750f).

One particularly vexing problem is the increasing evidence that under certain conditions individual utility may actually be increasing in effort and decreasing in wealth, the exact inverse to that conventionally assumed. So increasing the level of performance pay compensation may have no effect on effort, or may actually induce the manager to exert *less* effort *even in the task being explicitly rewarded*: "Economic theory seems to have drawn the wrong distinction between work creating disutility and leisure providing utility. Rather, people want to be adequately challenged" (Frey and Stutzer 2002, 107). Furthermore, the provision of explicit monetary incentives may actually crowd out these subtler—yet potentially no less powerful—intrinsic motivations for a job well done: "[I]f intrinsic happiness and motivation are expected (or even desired) to have an effect on behavior, external intervention, for example, in the form of performance pay may have counterproductive effects" (Frey and Stutzer 2002, 182).

The original evidence for these phenomena came from a study by Titmuss (1970) on blood donations. He found that when monetary incentives were offered to blood donors, the amount of blood donated actually declined. Since Titmuss's work, similar phenomena have been observed in a variety of contexts. When monetary fines are imposed on parents for picking their children up late from day-care centers, *more* parents are tardy (Gneezy and Rustichini 2000). In various laboratory settings, students who receive *zero* monetary reward tend to work harder and longer than those who are so rewarded (Deci and Ryan 1985). Residents who are offered monetary compensation if they agree to a nuclear-waste storage facility being built in their area are *less* likely to agree than residents who are offered no explicit monetary compensation (Frey and Oberholzer-Gee 1997).

Various psychological explanations can be given for these observations. Their relevance in the current context is to illustrate the breadth of factors, intrinsic as well as extrinsic, that can motivate individuals: There are many "warm glows." The behavioral assumptions of finance have traditionally focused entirely on the warm glow of monetary rewards, and as such have tended to extinguish these other subtler—but potentially no less powerful—motivations.

EDUCATIONAL IMPLICATIONS

The behavioral assumptions of finance, and the acceptance and promulgation of these values in business schools, did not arise in a vacuum. Throughout the nineteenth and early twentieth century, education in the United States was viewed as inseparable from morality. *Moral* education was part and parcel of *any* educational program. As noted by Bok in *Universities and the Future of America*, professors and university administrators were committed to creating an "educated class committed to a principled life in the service of society" (1990, 66).

By the end of World War II, however, the Christianity-based moral certainties of earlier generations began to unravel. As Menzel observes: "[E]ducation on America's campuses had largely given way to the competing claims of Darwinism, Marxism, and science [with] . . . the eventual domination of 'big' science and its stepchild, technology" (1997, 518).

It was into this environment, in the 1950s and early 1960s, that the modern American business school was born. From the outset, business education was viewed as value-neutral in a moral sense. The business school graduate was purely a technician, trained to apply management science. But, as several twentieth-century philosophers have observed, the claim to moral neutrality of technology and science and their application is a chimera. For example, as MacIntyre notes in *After Virtue*, "there are strong grounds for rejecting the claim that effectiveness is a morally neutral value" (1984, 74).

As this chapter has demonstrated, the notion of managerial *effectiveness*, as it has evolved in American business schools, is premised on a single narrow concept of rationality. Within this rubric, a rational agent is simply one who pursues personal material advantage ad infinitum. In essence, to be rational in business management is to be individualistic, materialistic, and competitive. Business is a game played by individuals; as with all games the object is to win, and winning is measured solely in terms of material wealth. Within the business school, this rationality concept is rarely questioned.

In addition, the behavioral assumptions of finance have been presented as prescriptively (i.e., morally) neutral, thus failing to recognize that this narrow and rigid invocation of self-interest has moral implications. Not only do these assumptions have an implicit moral agenda, but they also tend to promote this agenda through the modern business school. We can only hope that real-world events in the form of the ongoing financial crisis—combined with recent academic developments in behavioral finance and financial ethics—will lead to a descriptive and prescriptive broadening, which will render the behavioral assumptions of finance both more descriptively accurate and more prescriptively desirable.

NOTES

1. Taken from an essay, An Enquiry Concerning the Principles of Morals, originally published in 1751. In *Writings in Economics*, ed. Eugene Rotwein (Madison, WI: University of Wisconsin Press, 1955).
2. Adam Smith, *Wealth of Nations* (New York: Modern Library, 1937; originally published in 1776.
3. Jennifer Moore, Autonomy and the Legitimacy of the Liberal Arts, In *Business Ethics: The State of The Art*, ed. R. Edward Freeman (New York: Oxford University Press, 1991).
4. Richard H. Thaler, *The Winner's Curse: Paradoxes and Anomalies of Economic Life* (New York: The Free Press, 1992).
5. Colin Grant, The Altruists' Dilemma, *Business Ethics Quarterly* 14 (2004):315–328.
6. Leda Cosmides and John Tooby, Knowing Thyself: The Evolutionary Psychology of Moral Reasoning and Moral Sentiments, *Business Ethics Quarterly*, Ruffin Series no. 4 (2004):93–128.
7. Paul Lawrence and N. Nohria, *Driven: How Human Nature Shapes Our Choices* (San Francisco, CA: Jossey-Bass, 2002).
8. Richard Thaler, Anomalies: The Ultimatum Game, *Journal of Economic Perspectives* 2 (1988):195–206.
9. Stanley Milgram, *Obedience to authority: An experimental view* (New York: Harper & Row, 1974), 6.

REFERENCES

Baker, George P., Michael C. Jensen, and Kevin J. Murphy. 1988. Compensation and incentives: Practice vs. theory. *Journal of Finance* 43:593–616.

Bok, Derek. 1990. *Universities and the future of America*. Durham, NC: Duke University Press.

Bowie, Norman E. 1991. Challenging the egoistic paradigm. *Business Ethics Quarterly* 1:1–21.

Copeland, Thomas, and Fred Weston. 1988. *Financial theory and corporate policy*. 3rd ed. Reading, MA: Addison-Wesley.

Cosmides, Leda, and John Tooby. 2004. Knowing thyself: The evolutionary psychology of moral reasoning and moral sentiments. *Business Ethics Quarterly*, Ruffin Series 4: 93–128.

Deci, E. L., and R. M. Ryan. 1985. *Intrinsic motivation and self-determination in human behavior*. New York: Plenum Press.

Dees, Gregory J. 1992. Principals, agents, and ethics. In *Ethics and agency theory*, ed. Norman E. Bowie and R. Edward Freeman. New York: Oxford University Press.

de Waal, F. B. M. 1997. The chimpanzee's service economy: Food for grooming. *Evolution and Human Behavior* 18:375–386.

Diamond, Douglas W. 1989. Reputation acquisition in debt markets. *Journal of Political Economy* 97:828–861.

Dobson, John. 2002. Enron's corporate culture and ethics. In *Enron and beyond*, ed. Julia K. Brazelton and Janice L. Ammons. Chicago: CCH Incorporated.

Driggers, Stephen G. 2002. Executive compensation and employee retirement plans at Enron. In *Enron and beyond*, ed. Julia K. Brazelton and Janice L. Ammons. Chicago: CCH Incorporated.

Duska, Ronald. 1992. Why be a loyal agent? A systematic ethical analysis. In *Ethics and agency theory*, ed. Norman E. Bowie and R. Edward Freeman. New York: Oxford University Press.

———. 1993. To whom it may concern. Unpublished letter to the editor of the *Harvard Business Review*, July 12.

Edgeworth, Francis. 1881. *Mathematical psychics*. London: Kegan Paul.

Flack, Jessica C., and F. B. M. de Waal. 2004. Monkey business and business ethics. *Business Ethics Quarterly*, Ruffin Series 4:7–42.

Frank, R., T. Gilovich, and D. Regan. 1993. Does studying economics inhibit co-operation? *Journal of Economic Perspectives* 7:159–171.

Frey, Bruno S., and Felix Oberholzer-Gee. 1997. The cost of price incentives: An empirical analysis of motivation crowding-out. *American Economic Review* 87:746–755.

Frey, Bruno S., and Alois Stutzer. 2002. *Happiness and economics*. Princeton, NJ: Princeton University Press.

Gneezy, U., and A. Rustichini. 2000. A fine is a price. *Journal of Legal Studies* 29:1–18.

Grant, Colin. 2004. The altruists' dilemma. *Business Ethics Quarterly* 14:315–328.

Greenspan, Alan. 2009. Mea culpa. *Financial Times* (January 7):1.

Hausman, Daniel M., and Michael S. McPherson. 1993. Taking ethics seriously: Economics and contemporary moral philosophy. *Journal of Economic Literature* 31:671–731.

Holmes, Stephen. 1990. The secret history of self-interest. In *Beyond self-interest*, ed. Jane J. Mansbridge. Chicago: University of Chicago Press.

Homer. 1961. *The odyssey*. Trans. R. Fitzgerald. Garden City, NJ: Anchor Press/Doubleday.

Hume, D. 1955. *Writings in economics*, ed. Eugene Rotwein. Madison, WI: University of Wisconsin Press.

Jensen, Michael C., and William M. Meckling. 1976. Theory of the firm: Managerial behavior, agency costs and ownership structure. *Journal of Financial Economics* 3:305–360.

Jensen, Michael C., and Kevin J. Murphy. 1990. Performance pay and top-management incentives. *Journal of Political Economy* 98:225–264.

John, Kose, and D. Nachman. 1985. Risky debt, investment incentives and reputation in a sequential equilibrium. *Journal of Finance* 40:863–877.

Kahneman, Daniel, and Amos Tversky. 1979. Prospect theory: An analysis of decisions under risk. *Econometrica* 47:263–291.

Kreps, David. 1997. Intrinsic motivation and extrinsic incentives. *American Economic Review* 87:359–364.

Lawrence, Paul. 2004. A biological base for ethics. *Business Ethics Quarterly*, Ruffin Series 4:59–80.

Lawrence, Paul, and N. Nohria. 2002. *Driven: How human nature shapes our choices*. San Francisco, CA: Jossey-Bass.

Leland, Hayne E., and David H. Pyle. 1977. Informational asymmetries, financial structure, and financial intermediation. *Journal of Finance* 32:371–387.

MacIntyre, Alasdair. 1984. *After virtue*. 2nd ed. Notre Dame, IN: University of Notre Dame Press.

Menzel, Donald C. 1997. Teaching ethics and values. *Political Science and Politics* 30:518–524.

Messick, David M. 2004. Human nature and business ethics. *Business Ethics Quarterly*, Ruffin Series 4:129–134.

Milgram, Stanley. 1974. *Obedience to authority: An experimental view*. New York: Harper & Row.

Moore, Jennifer. 1991. Autonomy and the legitimacy of the liberal arts. In *Business ethics: The state of the art*, ed. R. Edward Freeman. New York: Oxford University Press.

Myers, S. C. 1977. Determinants of corporate borrowing. *Journal of Financial Economics* 5:147–175.

Nofsinger, John R. 2008. *The psychology of investing*. 3rd ed. Upper Saddle River, NJ: Prentice, Hall.

Noreen, Eric. 1988. The economics of ethics: A new perspective on agency theory. *Accounting Organizations and Society* 13:359–369.

Plott, C. R. 1986. Rational choice in experimental markets. *Journal of Business* 59:S309–S327.

Rasmusen, Eric. 1989. *Games and information: An introduction to game theory.* Oxford: Basil Blackwell.

Roberts, John. 2004. *The modern firm: Organizational design for performance and growth.* New York: Oxford University Press.

Salvador, Rommel, and Robert G. Folger. 2009. "Business ethics and the brain." *Business Ethics Quarterly* 19:1–32.

Sapolsky, Robert, and Lisa Share. 2004. The peacemakers. *Economist* (April 17):77.

Schmidtz, David. 1994. Choosing ends. *Ethics* 104:226–251.

Sen, Amartya. 1987. *On ethics and economics.* Malden, MA: Basil Blackwell.

———. 1997. Maximization and the act of choice. *Econometrica* 65:745–779.

Simon, H. A. 1986. Rationality in psychology and economics. *Journal of Business* 59:S209–S224.

Smith, Adam. 1937a. *The theory of moral sentiments.* New York: Modern Library (originally published in 1759).

———. 1937b. *Wealth of nations.* New York: Modern Library (originally published in 1776).

Thaler, Richard H. 1988. Anomalies: The ultimatum game. *Journal of Economic Perspectives* 2:195–206.

———. 1992. *The winner's curse: Paradoxes and anomalies of economic life.* New York: Free Press.

Titmuss, Richard M. 1970. *The gift relationship.* London: Allen and Unwin.

von Neumann, J., and O. Morgenstern. 1947. *Theory of games and economic behavior.* 2nd ed. Princeton, NJ: Princeton University, Press.

ABOUT THE AUTHOR

John Dobson's primary research area is business ethics—in particular, how the theory of ethics relates to the financial side of business activity. He has published articles on ethics and finance in various academic journals, and has published two books, both of which investigate the synthesis of business and ethics. His current research focuses on the extent to which business activity can be viewed less as a technical enterprise, and more as an artistic (i.e., aesthetic) pursuit.

CHAPTER 4

Efficiency and Rationality

NIEN-HÊ HSIEH
Associate Professor of Legal Studies and Business Ethics, Wharton School,
University of Pennsylvania

INTRODUCTION

The concepts of rationality and efficiency are central to contemporary economics and finance. Contemporary scholars of economics and finance take individuals' choices as a starting point in their analyses. Rationality is the standard by which choices are evaluated, and for purposes of theory building and empirical analysis, choices are often assumed to be rational. Efficiency is the main, if not sole, standard used to evaluate the outcomes that result from the choices and interactions of individuals.

This chapter has two broad aims. The first is to provide nonspecialists with background on the way in which the concepts of rationality and efficiency are commonly defined and deployed in contemporary economics and finance. The thought is that in order to analyze ethical issues in finance, it will help to be familiar with foundational concepts in the fields of economics and finance. The second aim is to put these conceptions of rationality and efficiency into critical perspective by discussing some descriptive and normative issues surrounding their use.[1]

RATIONAL CHOICE

This section outlines the main features of the concept of rationality as commonly deployed in contemporary economics and finance. Because the rationality of an agent's choice is characterized in terms of the rationality of her preferences, the section begins by defining the concept of a *preference*.

Preference Satisfaction

A preference is a relative ranking between two alternatives. Although alternatives are often conceived as bundles of goods, a more general approach is to conceive of each alternative as an outcome or a complete description of a state of affairs. If A and B are two alternatives, the agent *strictly prefers A to B* (*A is strictly preferred* to *B*) if it is a better state of affairs from the perspective of the agent that A is realized rather than B. In contrast, the agent *prefers A to B* (*A is preferred* to *B*) if it is at least as good a state of affairs from the perspective of the agent that A is realized rather than B. An agent is *indifferent* between A and B if A is preferred to B and B is preferred to A.

Three points are worth noting. First, the rankings are understood to be subjective. Rationality does not require that different agents have the same rankings over the same alternatives. Second, an agent may have preferences regarding alternatives even if she is not faced with choosing between them. Third, what underlies an agent's preferences is open-ended. Although phrases such as "a better state of affairs" suggest that judgments of goodness underlie preferences, this need not be the case. On most accounts, the concept of a preference is thought to be sufficiently general to be able to reflect nonconsequentialist judgments about different alternatives. For example, if the choice is between lying and not lying, and the agent believes it would be wrong to lie, the agent could be said to prefer not lying. More generally, preferences need not reflect evaluative judgments; they may be taken to reflect brute desires or wants.

An agent's preferences are considered *rational* if two conditions are met.[2] First, her preferences must be *complete*. That is, for any two alternatives, A and B, it is the case that she prefers A to B or that she prefers B to A or both. Second, the agent's preferences must be *transitive*. That is, if A is preferred to B, and B is preferred to C, then A is preferred to C. In turn, an agent's choice of an alternative is *rational* if her preferences are rational and there is no other available alternative that she strictly prefers to what she has chosen.

Utility Maximization

If an agent's preferences are rational, then her preferences can be represented by an *ordinal function*.[3] An ordinal function assigns every alternative a real number in a way that preserves the underlying preference ranking over the alternatives. For example, if A is strictly preferred to B, then the number assigned to A is greater than the number assigned to B. If the agent is indifferent between A and B, then A and B are assigned the same number. The function is ordinal in the sense that the absolute magnitude of the numbers is not relevant. What matters is their order.

The ordinal function that represents an agent's preferences is referred to as a *utility function* and the real number assigned to an alternative is referred to as the *utility* of an alternative. The agent's choice of an alternative is considered rational if that alternative has the highest utility among the available alternatives. If there are two or more alternatives that qualify, then the choice of any of those alternatives is considered rational. In this manner, choosing rationally is defined as utility maximization.

As used here, *utility* does not mean anything like *goodness*, *benefit*, or *pleasure*—terms normally associated with the concept of utility as used in ethical theory (Broome 1991a). The utility function is a representation of the agent's preferences, and as previously noted, what underlies her preferences is left open-ended. In choosing rationally, the agent is not assumed to be aiming to maximize her own benefit or the greater good. Nor is it assumed that by choosing rationally she ends up maximizing her own benefit or the greater good. If there is a connection between utilitarianism and rationality as utility maximization, it seems closest in the idea that choices are evaluated in terms of their outcomes, rather than as acts. Even then, however, it has been argued that preference rankings can encompass the act of choice by making preferences over final outcomes contingent on how they come about (Sen 1997) or by including the act of choice in a description of the outcome itself (Sandbu 2007). It is only with further restrictions on an agent's preferences that anything substantive can be assumed about the rationality of agents and the resulting outcomes of rational choices.

Expected Utility

Thus far the discussion has assumed that if an alternative is chosen, the outcome of choosing that alternative is known with certainty. Many choices, however, involve uncertainty regarding the outcome realized by the choice of an alternative.[4] In such cases, rationality is conceptualized by specifying restrictions on preferences over *lotteries*.

A lottery is a way to represent an alternative that can randomly result in one of a number of outcomes if chosen. It specifies the probability with which each outcome will be realized, with the probabilities summing to one.[5] Imagine, for example, that an agent faces a choice between two alternatives: an asset A that pays a return (A_1) with certainty and an asset B that could pay one of two returns (B_1, B_2) with probability p for the first return, B_1. The second alternative (B) can be represented by a lottery, L, such that

$$L = p \times B_1 + (1 - p) \times B_2$$

If the agent's preferences over lotteries meet the requirements discussed shortly, then a utility can be assigned to B that takes the following form:

$$u(B) = p \times u(B_1) + (1 - p) \times u(B_2)$$

Here $u(B_1)$ is the utility assigned to the return B_1 if the agent were to receive it with certainty and $u(B_2)$ is the utility assigned to the return B_2 if the agent were to receive it with certainty. In other words, the agent's utility for B is the expected value of the utilities of each of the possible outcomes that can result from choosing alternative B. The agent's utility for alternative B is represented by an *expected utility function*, also commonly referred to as a *von Neumann-Morgenstern utility function*.[6] The agent's choice is rational if she chooses the alternative with the highest expected utility.

For an agent's preferences to be represented by an expected utility function, her preferences over lotteries must be *complete*, *transitive*, *continuous*, and *independent*. The first three requirements are analogous to the requirements on preferences over alternatives whose outcomes are realized with certainty, as discussed in the previous subsection.[7] The fourth requirement holds that if two lotteries differ only in one outcome, then the agent's preference between the lotteries tracks her preference between the outcomes. Building on the previous example, suppose there is a lottery, L' that differs from L only in terms of the second outcome. Rather than B_2, the second outcome is B_3. Suppose the agent prefers B_2 to B_3. The requirement of independence holds that she prefers L to L'. The requirement is sometimes referred to as the "sure-thing principle" (Hausman and McPherson 2006, 51), because if the agent prefers B_2 to B_3, in a choice between L and L' she is no worse off with respect to B_1 and she is better off given the choice of B_2 over B_3.

On this account, the agent's preference between A and B reflects her attitude toward risk. To continue with the current example, suppose $B_1 < A_1 < B_2$ and the expected monetary value of asset B is equal to return A_1. The agent is *risk averse* if she strictly prefers A to B. She would be willing to accept less than A_1 with certainty rather than a higher expected return that involves uncertainty. The less she is willing to accept with certainty, the more risk averse she is. The agent is *risk neutral* if she is indifferent between A and B. What matters to her is the expected monetary value independent of considerations of uncertainty. The agent is *risk seeking* if she strictly prefers B to A. For the agent to give up a risky alternative for a certain alternative, the certain alternative would have to pay more than the expected value of the risky alternative. The more she needs to be paid with certainty, the more risk seeking she is.

Rationality does not specify what the agent's attitude toward risk should be. Given the form of the expected utility function, the agent's attitude toward risk is determined by her underlying preferences over the monetary values of A_1, B_1, and B_2. The agent is risk averse if her preferences display *diminishing marginal utility of money*—each additional unit of money increases her utility less than the previous unit of money. The less money the agent has, the greater the utility she receives from a given unit of money. The intuitive relation to risk aversion is that even though B_2 is greater than A_1, the agent prefers having A_1 with certainty than risk the possibility of receiving B_1, which is less than A_1. The agent is risk seeking if her preferences display *increasing marginal utility of money*—each additional unit of money increases her utility even more than the previous unit of money. For a risk-seeking agent, the utility of B_2 is that much greater than the utility of A_1 such that she prefers risking the possibility of ending up with B_1 for the possibility of receiving B_2. For the risk-neutral agent, each additional unit of money increases her utility the same amount as the previous unit of money. An agent's attitude toward risk may vary over levels of wealth. For example, one can imagine an agent who is highly risk averse at low levels of wealth, decreasingly risk averse at higher levels of wealth, and then risk seeking over a certain threshold of wealth at which her needs are met.

Rational Expectations

In the discussion thus far, what rationality requires of an agent's beliefs arises in a limited way—specifically, with respect to the assignment of probabilities to uncertain outcomes. Consider, for example, a horse race. The race cannot be run multiple times to ascertain the frequency of each horse winning the race. Instead, the probabilities assigned to different horses winning the race are better understood as expressions of the agent's subjective degree of belief in the likelihood of each outcome. For the agent's preferences to be represented by an expected utility function, her probability assignments must obey basic axioms of probability theory (e.g., the probabilities sum to one).[8]

The restrictions imposed by probability theory involve the internal consistency of beliefs. The requirement of *rational expectations* goes further. In addition to being internally consistent, this requirement holds that the agent's assignment of probabilities must reflect the best guess of future outcomes using all available information. This requirement is defined in at least three different ways (Cowen 2004, 219–220). On one interpretation, the agent understands the "true model" of the economy such that she is able to predict market equilibrium results in the manner of a macroecononomist. On a second, less stringent interpretation, the agent's estimates of economic variables are correct on average. This may hold at the individual level, in which case the errors made by any one agent average to zero over time, or at the group level, in which case the individual estimates at any point in time are scattered around the correct mean of the variable. On a third interpretation, the agent's errors in an estimate of an economic variable have no predictive power with respect to her future estimates of the variable. Under all three interpretations, there are no systematic deviations in agents' estimates of economic variables.

Rationality in Strategic Interaction

The rationality of an agent's beliefs is also relevant to contexts involving *strategic interaction*—a situation in which the payoffs that agents receive depend on the choices made by other agents. In *game theory*—the field devoted to the study of such strategic interaction—there is debate as to what constitutes an appropriate conception of rationality in such contexts. The aim of this subsection is to provide some insight into this debate by discussing two examples of strategic interaction with widespread applicability to economic contexts that also are discussed in normative ethics.

The first example is the *prisoner's dilemma*, Exhibit 4.1. In the standard telling of this example, two suspects are arrested by the police. The police have enough evidence for convictions that will put each suspect in jail for one year. The police separately offer the suspects the following deal. If one testifies against the other and the other remains silent, then the one who testifies will go free while the one who remains silent will face a ten-year prison sentence. If both testify, they each face five years in prison. The suspects are not able to communicate with one another before making their decision. The situation can be illustrated as in Exhibit 4.1; in each box, the number on the left (right) is the outcome for Agent 1 (Agent 2). The assumption usually made is that the suspects are self-interested in the sense that each seeks only to minimize his own time in prison.

		Agent 2	
		Don't testify	Testify
Agent 1	Don't testify	1 year, 1 year	10 years, 0 years
	Testify	0 years, 10 years	5 years, 5 years

Exhibit 4.1 Prisoner's Dilemma

		Agent 2	
		Fix bridge 2	Do nothing
Agent 1	Fix bridge 1	3, 3	−1, 0
	Do nothing	0, −1	0, 0

Exhibit 4.2   Assurance Game

In the case of the prisoner's dilemma, it does not matter what beliefs each agent holds about the other's preferences or expected behavior. Testifying, under the assumption of self-interest, is a *dominant strategy*—that is, no matter what the other agent prefers or does, it is rational for the agent to testify.

Most situations, however, do not allow for dominant strategies. Consider the example of the *assurance game* (Sen 1967), Exhibit 4.2. In this telling of the example, there is a road that can be used only if both bridges are in working order, and right now both happen to be broken.[9] Agent 1 is in a position to fix the first bridge and Agent 2 is in a position to fix the second bridge. Both know this, and the bridges are too far apart for the agents to communicate. Fixing a bridge is costly to an agent, but if both bridges are in working order, then the net benefit to the agent is positive. Not fixing a bridge costs the agent nothing. The situation can be illustrated as in Exhibit 4.2; in each box, the number on the left (right) is the net benefit to Agent 1 (Agent 2).

In this situation, what each agent believes about the likelihood of the other agent's actions affects what she ought to do from the perspective of rationality. For example, if Agent 1 could be assured that Agent 2 will fix bridge 2, then it is rational for Agent 1 to fix bridge 1. Similarly, if Agent 1 believed with certainty that Agent 2 will not fix the bridge, then it is rational for Agent 1 not to fix the bridge. Rationality, as defined thus far, however, provides little guidance as to what Agent 1 ought to believe. Further restrictions on beliefs are required, and much of game theory concerns itself with developing a plausible conception of rationality as regards beliefs.

EFFICIENCY

This section discusses two commonly used conceptions of efficiency in contemporary economics and finance. The first is found in the efficient market hypothesis. The second is Pareto efficiency. As part of this discussion, this section highlights the role of rationality in each conception of efficiency and the relation between the two conceptions of efficiency.

The Efficient Market Hypothesis

As discussed in finance, the efficient market hypothesis (EMH) is an empirical claim about the operation of financial markets, and is central to contemporary finance (Cowen 2004, 221). The general idea is that stock prices reflect information relevant to the value of publicly traded companies in a manner such that an investor will not be able to earn more than the market rate of return by picking individual stocks based upon further analysis of information. An investor may earn more than the market rate of return by random luck. The point is that the investor cannot systematically earn more than the market rate of return.

There are three basic versions of the hypothesis, each involving different assumptions about the rationality of market participants and the information reflected in stock prices.[10] The *weak form* assumes little about the rationality of market participants. Market participants may be irrational or systematically biased in their predictions. What matters is that these irrationalities and biases are unpredictable to rational investors. In turn, rational investors will not be able to do better than the market rate of return by engaging in *technical analysis*—the analysis of securities market information, such as stock price movements and trading demand. Investors, however, may be able to earn more than the market rate of return through *fundamental analysis*—the analysis of information about a company, including earnings and balance sheet variables, as well as macroeconomic information that may affect the company's success.

According to the *semi-strong form*, investors are not able to do better than the market rate of return by engaging in either technical analysis or fundamental analysis. As in the weak version, the semi-strong version allows for irrational or systematically biased market participants. In contrast to the weak version, the semi-strong version assumes there is at least one rational investor with an accurate understanding of the fundamental values of companies and that capital markets are perfect or nearly perfect. If capital markets are perfect or nearly perfect, that investor is able to borrow unlimited funds (against the value of the purchased stocks) to purchase stocks that are not priced in line with companies' fundamental values. As a result, deviations in a stock's price from the price at which it should trade based on a company's fundamental values will be short-lived. Accordingly, fundamental analysis does not allow investors to earn more than the market rate of return.

The weak and semi-strong versions of the EMH allow for the possibility that investors can earn more than the market return if they have *insider information*—that is, information about a company not publicly available to market participants. The *strong form* of the EMH rules out this possibility. According to the strong version, the stock price reflects not only all publicly available information, but also all relevant privately held information.

Pareto Efficiency

The concept of Pareto efficiency is used to characterize the allocation of goods, services, or resources, usually within the context of a market.[11] An allocation X is a *Pareto improvement* over allocation Y if no one prefers Y to X and at least one person strongly prefers X to Y. An allocation is *strongly Pareto efficient* if there are no other feasible allocations that represent Pareto improvements over it. An allocation is *weakly Pareto efficient* if there are no other feasible allocations that everyone strictly prefers to that allocation. As connoted by the use of the terms *strong* and *weak*, allocations that are strongly Pareto efficient are also weakly Pareto efficient, but not vice versa.

According to what is commonly called the *first fundamental welfare theorem*, if agents are free to trade in an economy characterized by *perfect competition*, the resulting *equilibrium* will be strongly Pareto efficient. The economy is said to be in equilibrium when markets clear—that is, the price for a good or service is such that the amount demanded at that price is equal to the amount supplied at that price. For an economy to be characterized by perfect competition, there must be markets for all possible goods and services, no barriers to entry or exit from markets, and enough agents such that no one agent can influence prices. Also, it is assumed that agents are rational and in possession of perfect information, and that their utilities are not interdependent. That is, an agent's utility is assumed to depend only on the bundle of goods and services that she herself consumes (Hausman and McPherson 2006, 65–66). Usually not made explicit is one other assumption—namely, that there is a private property regime such that once an agent comes into possession of a good or service, she is guaranteed its possession and use until she voluntarily relinquishes it in an exchange. Under these conditions, markets lead to an allocation of goods and services such that no agent prefers another outcome and at least one agent strongly prefers that allocation. Furthermore, the economy is characterized by *productive efficiency*—meaning that no good or service can be produced in greater amount without a reduction in the production of some other good or service.

The prisoner's dilemma is often used to illustrate the contrasting situation in which individually rational behavior leads to a Pareto inefficient outcome.[12] In the preceding example, the Pareto improvement is an outcome in which both suspects do not testify and each receives only one year in prison. Many human interactions, such as the provision of public goods, are characterized as prisoner's dilemmas. Goods are *public* if individuals cannot be excluded from enjoying them and their enjoyment does not interfere with the enjoyment by others. From a purely self-interested individual's perspective, if others contribute, she does best by not contributing and enjoying the good. If others do not contribute so there is no good available, she does best by not contributing. The social science literature contains much discussion on possible solutions to the problem of the provision of public goods and whether it is correct to characterize public goods provision as a prisoner's dilemma.[13]

Consider now two possible allocations: allocation X, which gives \$1,000 to agent A and \$2,000 to agent B, and allocation Y, which gives \$2,000 to agent A and \$1,900 to agent B. Assuming that each agent prefers more money to less, from the perspective of Pareto efficiency, neither allocation is superior. Nevertheless, it has been argued that something can be said in favor of allocation Y on grounds of efficiency. The argument relies on the idea of a *potential Pareto improvement* (Hicks 1939; Kaldor 1939).[14]

An allocation R is a *potential Pareto improvement* over allocation Q if there is some allocation R' that is an actual Pareto improvement over allocation Q and the total sum of allocated resources in R' does not exceed the total sum of allocated resources in R. The idea of a potential Pareto improvement is often expressed in terms of the possibility of *compensation*. That is, those who prefer moving to R from Q gain enough resources such that they would still prefer the move even if part of their resources were transferred to the "losers" to leave them with at least as many resources as they have under *R*. To be clear, actual compensation need not occur. In the preceding example, *Y* is a potential Pareto improvement over *X*. Under *Y*, $100 could be transferred from agent *A* to agent *B* to leave *B* in the same position as she was under *X*.

The conceptions of efficiency in the first fundamental welfare theorem and the EMH are not formally related. However, there is reason to hold that the efficiency of markets in the manner specified by the EMH is a requirement for an economy to be Pareto efficient. The thought is that if prices did not reflect all available information, then a Pareto efficient outcome would not be guaranteed by market exchange; there would be information that could be used to allow for a Pareto improvement (Ross 2008).

DEBATES ABOUT DESCRIPTIVE CLAIMS

As discussed previously, the concepts of rationality and efficiency are central to many descriptive claims in contemporary economics and finance. Questions have been raised, however, about the plausibility of describing the choices of agents as rational and economic outcomes as efficient. This section discusses some of these debates.

Satisficing

In economic and financial decisions, two sorts of complexity can arise. The first is informational—the information required to assign probabilities to certain outcomes may not be easily available, and some possible outcomes may not even be anticipated. The second is computational—there may be limits to people's ability to calculate expected utilities.

In such situations, individuals may engage in *satisficing*. Satisficing, as first proposed by Herbert Simon (1955), is an approach to decision making that involves two simplifications: (1) the categorization of outcomes as "satisfactory" or "unsatisfactory," and (2) choosing an alternative that guarantees a satisfactory outcome. One example of satisficing is the use of a *stopping rule*. To borrow an example from Michael Byron, suppose an individual seeks a bottle of wine that pairs well with dinner. Rather than seek the bottle of wine that best fits, an individual engaged in satisficing would stop once she found one that is satisfactory (Byron 2004, 4). Because an alternative need not maximize utility in order to qualify as satisfactory, satisficing has the appearance of being irrational.

There is debate as to whether satisficing should be described as irrational (Byron 2004). Suppose the individual in our example prefers to avoid spending time and effort in choosing a bottle of wine. She may find it difficult to determine which wine is most appropriate or she may prefer to appear decisive and knowledgeable to her dinner companions. Suppose also she has reason to believe that no bottle of wine in the available set surpasses a certain level of fittingness. In this situation, there is a level of fittingness such that once she comes across a bottle of that level, she would be worse off to continue her search, even knowing that she may find a bottle that fits even better with dinner. The bottle of wine she chooses need not be the one that would best satisfy her preferences had it been given to her with dinner, and yet she best satisfies her preferences by following the stopping rule.

The considerations underlying a preference to avoid time and effort in finding an appropriate bottle of wine are often described as *search costs*. Making explicit such costs and incorporating them into an agent's preferences provides a way for her choice to be described as consistent with maximizing the satisfaction of her preferences.

Transitivity

Questions also have been raised as to whether people choose in a manner that is consistent with having preferences that are transitive. Experiments have been conducted, for example, in which subjects are shown to be willing to pay more for a bet that they judged to be worse than another bet (Lichtenstein and Slovic 1971, 1973; Hausman 1992). One way to interpret this result is as an instance of intransitive preferences.[15]

On the whole, results such as these do not trouble economists (Mas-Collel, Whinston, and Green 1995). One reason is that individuals with intransitive preferences can be turned into "money pumps." Suppose an individual prefers A to B, B to C, and C to A. If she prefers C to A, she is willing to pay some amount of money to exchange A for C. Similarly, she is willing to pay some amount of money to exchange C for B and to exchange B for A. Now she is back where she started with A, but also poorer. If such money pumping is transparent or its effects are apparent, the thought is that individuals will change their preferences to avoid being made poorer in this way. It also has been argued that economic agents with such preferences are unlikely to survive long in a market context, and as such, agents are unlikely to hold such preferences (Hausman 1992).

Independence

This subsection discusses an early question raised about expected utility theory as a description of choice that has helped to frame much of the subsequent analysis. The question concerns the plausibility of describing people's preferences over lotteries as being consistent with the independence requirement.

Maurice Allais posed the question by way of what has come to be known as the *Allais paradox* (Allais 1979). The Allais paradox involves two pairs of lotteries. All four lotteries involve an urn that contains 1 red ball, 89 white balls, and 10 blue balls, from which one ball is drawn. The payoffs are summarized in Exhibit 4.3.

The "paradox" arises because many individuals express a preference over the first pair of lotteries and a preference over the second pair of lotteries that violate the independence requirement. For the second pair, one preference often expressed is for lottery 2B over 2A—a preference for a 10 percent chance of winning $5 million over an 11 percent chance of winning $1 million. For the first pair, the same individuals often express a preference for lottery 1A—a 100 percent chance of winning $1 million. Note that the first pair of lotteries is simply the second pair of lotteries with the addition to each lottery of an 89 percent chance of winning $1 million. According to the independence requirement, this addition of the same gamble to each lottery should not change the individual's preferences over the lotteries, and yet in expressing a preference for 2B over 2A and then a preference for 1A over 1B, the individual reverses her preference over the lotteries.

		Red (1%)	White (89%)	Blue (10%)
First Pair	Lottery 1A	$1 million	$1 million	$1 million
	Lottery 1B	$0	$1 million	$5 million
Second Pair	Lottery 2A	$1 million	$0	$1 million
	Lottery 2B	$0	$0	$5 million

Exhibit 4.3 Allais Paradox—Lottery Payoffs

One explanation for the apparent preference reversal makes reference to the experience of regret. With the addition of an 89 percent chance of winning $1 million, lottery 1A now gives the agent the opportunity to win $1 million with certainty. With lottery 1B, the agent may win nothing and, as a result, experience regret for not having chosen $1 million with certainty. Put another way, she may view her choice of 1B as giving up $1 million with certainty, something she is likely to regret. Note that this explanation does not involve risk aversion, as previously defined. Risk aversion refers to how much the agent is willing to forgo a potentially larger but uncertain payout in return for a lower but certain payout because of the diminishing marginal utility of money. That is distinct from the idea of regret, which refers to the experience of having wished that one had done otherwise once an uncertain outcome is realized. That is to say, it is not the certainty of winning $1 million that makes lottery 1A preferable (which could be related to risk aversion), but rather the avoidance of regret from not having chosen it if one wins nothing.

Prospect Theory and Behavioral Finance

The case of intransitive preferences and the Allais paradox are two examples in which the choices made by individuals appear to violate the requirements of rationality. Prompted in part by such examples, a number of scholars—largely in psychology, economics, and decision theory—have studied ways in which people's behavior departs from the requirements of rationality and have sought to develop alternate accounts that better conform to this observed behavior. Among the best known of these alternative accounts is *prospect theory*, as developed by Daniel Kahneman and Amos Tversky. This section highlights three main themes in the research on prospect theory and ways in which these themes relate to developments in *behavioral finance*—an approach that aims to explain economic and financial phenomena by characterizing the behavior of individuals in ways that depart from the standard of rationality as described earlier.[16]

The first theme concerns the weights attached to variations in the probability of an outcome. As a description of choice, expected utility theory holds that individuals weight variations in the probability of an outcome in a linear fashion—hence the paradox in the Allais paradox. In contrast, prospect theory accommodates weights that do not vary in a linear fashion, thereby accommodating preferences such as those expressed in the Allais paradox.

The second theme involves *reference-dependence* and *loss aversion*. Under expected utility theory, outcomes are characterized as the resulting states of affairs. In the case of monetary gambles, for example, each outcome specifies the individual's total amount of wealth after the gamble. *Reference-dependence* is the idea that outcomes of choices under uncertainty are understood as gains and losses relative to the starting point of the agent. *Loss aversion* refers to the idea that people weight more heavily the possibility of a loss than the possibility of a gain (Tversky and Kahneman 1991).

The third theme involves *framing effects* and *mental accounting*. *Framing effects* refer to instances in which two decision problems that are identical from the perspective of rationality result in different choices, ostensibly because of the way in which the problems are described. *Mental accounting* refers to the cognitive processes by which agents categorize and evaluate advantages and disadvantages in economic choices, mainly in the realm of financial decisions. As an illustration of these two concepts and their relation, consider the following experiment (Kahneman and Tversky 1984).

In the experiment, one group of subjects was asked to imagine purchasing a jacket for $125 and a calculator for $15, and then was told that the calculator was on sale for $10 at the other branch of the store. A second group was given the same scenario with the initial prices of the jacket and calculator reversed, and then was told that the calculator was on sale for $120 at the other branch. In the first scenario, 68 percent of respondents were willing to drive to the other store. In the second scenario, only 29 percent of respondents were willing to do so. Underlying this framing effect, according to Kahneman and Tversky (1984), is a tendency in mental accounting to categorize problems spontaneously as *topical* rather than *comprehensive*. A *topical* account evaluates the alternatives relative to a reference level set by the nature of the problem. A *comprehensive* account includes all of the features of the problem as well as considerations outside of the problem, such as the impact on monthly household savings. Although there is no difference between the two scenarios under a comprehensive account, there is a difference under a topical account in which the topic is the purchase of a calculator and the purchase price sets the reference level.

Prospect theory has been invoked to explain financial market phenomena that cannot be easily explained under an expected utility framework. One such phenomenon is the *equity premium puzzle*. Given that stocks are riskier than bonds, it is expected that stocks will offer a higher return to attract investors, and that the more risk averse investors are, the greater the difference in returns. The puzzle arises because the difference in returns suggests that investors are much more risk averse than suggested by estimates from other contexts. Shlomo Benartzi and Richard Thaler (1985) argue that if investors are loss averse and follow a mental accounting process of evaluating their portfolios annually, the premium on equities is consistent with previously estimated parameters of prospect theory. The intuition is that because loss-averse investors are more sensitive to decreases in financial returns than to increases, they are less willing to hold risky assets. Along similar lines, loss aversion has been used to explain the observation that investors are more likely to sell winners than losers when reducing their portfolio of stocks (Odean 1998).[17]

These examples point to predictable and potentially exploitable features of financial markets. If capital markets were perfect and some investors were rational, then these features should not persist according to the EMH. For these reasons, a number of scholars have called the EMH into question. For example, Robert Shiller (2005) argues that investors tend to overreact to small pieces of information, which gives rise to price movements that are disproportionate to the significance of the information. Along these lines, it has been argued that having the suffix ".com" in a firm's title alone added value during the Internet stock market boom and subtracted value during the subsequent stock market bust (Cowen 2004, 222).

The Role of Preferences

The preceding debates concern observations about people's choices and the functioning of financial markets, and the extent to which these observations are consistent with different accounts of choice, including expected utility theory and prospect theory. Much research has been devoted to trying to support or refute expected utility theory as a description of choice as well as to develop plausible alternatives to it. This is a highly active line of research.

At the same time, it may help to put this line of research into perspective. The conceptions of rationality discussed in this chapter take preferences as given. This suggests that much of the description and explanation of people's choices depends on describing and explaining their preferences, something that falls outside the realm of debates about rationality as defined in this chapter. In turn, there is reason to doubt that settling questions about rationality as a descriptive claim can settle questions about the description and explanation of people's choices.

For example, it is often claimed that a rational agent will testify in the prisoner's dilemma. If an agent is concerned with more than minimizing the amount of time that she spends in prison, however, this claim need not be correct. Suppose an agent also cares (though to a lesser degree) about the time that the other agent spends in prison. If each agent attaches a weight of one-half to the amount of time that the other spends in prison, the agents face an assurance game, as shown in Exhibit 4.4.

Testifying is no longer the dominant strategy, even if there is no change in the sense that agents are considered to be rational.

		Agent 2	
		Don't testify	Testify
Agent 1	Don't testify	1.5 years, 1.5 years	10 years, 5 years
	Testify	5 years, 10 years	7.5 years, 7.5 years

Exhibit 4.4 Prisoner's Dilemma Modified to Assurance Game

At first, it might be thought that in the case of financial markets, individuals seek to maximize their financial wealth and so a fuller description of people's preferences is not required. It turns out, however, there is research to suggest that individuals act on considerations, such as status, that are independent of financial wealth and may even go against their financial interests (Frank 1985, 1988, 2000). There also is a growing sociological literature emphasizing the role that networks of social relationships play in influencing the dynamics of financial markets (Granovetter 1985; Poldony 2001; Preda 2008; White 1981). For example, it has been argued that pricing practices are influenced by considerations of prestige and status in these networks that are independent of considerations of wealth maximization (Poldony 2005).

None of this is to deny the importance of trying to determine whether people choose rationally if the concept of rationality is invoked in trying to explain and predict individual choices and market phenomena. Rather, the point is that because rationality concerns only the relations among preferences, descriptive claims about individual choices and market phenomena cannot be settled without considering the actual preferences that individuals have.

NORMATIVE ISSUES

This chapter closes by discussing some normative issues that arise from the way in which rationality and efficiency are defined and used in contemporary economics and finance.

Normative Commitments and Descriptive Claims

The money pump and the Allais paradox are offered as examples of behavior that, if observed, would challenge the descriptive claim that people behave rationally. There is a question, however, whether the examples can be understood to serve this function without further normative commitments about the nature of rationality.

Consider the following agent. In the case of the money pump, the agent claims that A when given the choice of A and B is not the same as A when given the choice of C and A. If we designate the first A as *A1* and the second A as *A2*, the agent has rational preferences; she prefers *A1* to B, B to C, and C to *A2*. In the case of the Allais paradox, the agent claims that the outcome of choosing lottery 1B when a red ball is drawn is not $0, but rather $0 plus regret. With such an interpretation of the alternatives, choosing lottery 1A and lottery 2B would not violate the requirement of independence.

The researcher confronted with such an agent could conclude that the agent's choices do not violate the requirements of rationality. However, given that the money pump and the Allais paradox are offered as examples of behavior that do not conform to the requirements of rationality, there is reason to believe that most researchers hold further normative commitments about what rationality requires for the evaluation of alternatives.[18]

Rationality and Comparison

Rationality concerns what one has reason to do. By taking preferences as given and focusing largely on the consistency among preferences, the conception of rationality in this chapter places few restrictions on what is required to conform with reason. Accordingly, if this conception of rationality is to guide what one ought to do, it must be accompanied by standard sorts of ethical inquiry and more general inquiry regarding what one has reason to do.

Although the conception of rationality at hand is consistent with a wide range of ethical views, there is reason to doubt it accommodates all plausible ethical views. One issue, alluded to earlier, concerns the extent to which preferences accommodate considerations about the act of choice. Another issue concerns the comparative nature of rationality.

Some scholars argue that for certain pairs of alternatives, it is not true that one alternative is at least as good as the other or that each is at least as good as the other. Alternatives for which this is the case are often referred to as *incomparable*.[19] One argument grounds the incomparability of alternatives in *value incommensurability*—the idea that some values lack a common measure against which to rank alternatives that are each favored by different values. Another argument holds that incomparability is constitutive of certain goods and values. Suppose one is offered a significant amount of money to leave one's spouse for a month. The indignation that is typically experienced, according to Joseph Raz, is grounded in part in the symbolic significance of actions (Raz 1986, 349). In this case, "what has symbolic significance is the very judgment that companionship is incommensurable with money" (Raz 1986, 350).[20]

In requiring preferences to be complete, the conception of rationality at hand does not readily accommodate views in which there is good reason to judge alternatives to be incomparable. Indeed, this feature of rationality has been used to defend the view that the responsibility of managers is to maximize the long-run market value of the firm (Jensen 2002). Jensen's defense involves rejecting *stakeholder theory*—the view that managers ought to take into account the interests of all stakeholders—on grounds that it lacks a single measure against which to evaluate trade-offs among competing interests and to evaluate whether an alternative is at least as good as all others. Jensen argues that in contrast, the long-run market value of the firm provides just such a measure.

One response is to reject the requirement that rational choice involves the choice of an alternative that is at least as good as all other alternatives.[21] Amartya Sen (1997, 2000), for example, argues that rationality only requires the choice of an alternative that is not worse than all other alternatives. Because incomparable alternatives qualify as not worse than one another, this alternate conception of rationality is able to accommodate the incomparability of alternatives. In turn it has been argued that those who understand rationality to require the choice of an alternative that is at least as good as all other alternatives have no reason to reject this alternate account of rationality (Hsieh 2007a).

Efficiency and Well-Being

The first fundamental welfare theorem is often invoked in favor of the use of markets to allocate goods, services, and resources. For example, a Pareto efficient state of affairs is often described as a situation in which no one can be made better off without making someone worse off. In principle, this is the sort of claim that could count in favor of the use of markets. However, there is no necessary connection between preference satisfaction and what is better for a person. This subsection takes up making this connection along with the normative significance of Pareto efficiency more generally.

There are two ways in which the connection is made between the satisfaction of an agent's preferences and her well-being. The first involves the *desire-satisfaction* account of well-being. According to this account, a person is made better off simply in virtue of the satisfaction of her preferences. The second involves the assumption that is frequently made in descriptive economics. The assumption is that agents are self-interested and well-informed about what alternatives best serve their interests and well-being. If this assumption is adopted, then an agent's preferences reflect what is better for her, and a Pareto efficient allocation is one in which no one can be made better off without someone being made worse off (Hausman and McPherson 2006, 64).

In turn, three features of a Pareto efficient allocation seem to make it morally desirable. First, to shift away from a Pareto efficient allocation entails making someone worse off. The Pareto criterion captures the intuition that if there is no good reason to do so, it is morally objectionable to make someone worse off. Second, if an allocation is not Pareto efficient, someone is denied the possibility of being made better off without anyone else being made worse off. This state of affairs strikes many as wasteful. Third, the criterion of Pareto efficiency does not require ranking a change in one agent's well-being against a change in another agent's well-being. Such a comparison would require a common measure of well-being, something considered controversial by many scholars, especially if well-being is understood in terms of preference satisfaction.[22] The criterion of Pareto efficiency requires only examining whether each individual is better off or worse off relative to how she fares under other allocations.

This case for Pareto efficiency as an evaluative criterion raises a number of issues. First, it calls into question the appeal of potential Pareto improvements. An allocation may qualify as a potential Pareto improvement even if someone is made worse off, but this contradicts one basis for the appeal of Pareto efficiency as an evaluative criterion. The question is what distinguishes Kaldor-Hicks efficiency from a principle of maximizing aggregate resources.

The second issue concerns the plausibility of connecting preference-satisfaction to well-being. A number of scholars reject the desire-satisfaction view of well-being,[23] and as previously discussed, there is reason to question the extent to which individual preferences are self-interested and well-informed. More generally, there seems to be a tension between an account of rationality that professes to be open-ended with regard to the content of preferences and an account of efficiency that relies upon the assumption that preferences are self-interested.

The third issue concerns the robustness of Pareto efficiency as an evaluative criterion. Consider a situation in which one individual is starving and the only way to feed her is to redistribute resources from a wealthy individual. The redistribution of resources is not a Pareto improvement, and yet it may be morally justified on grounds of justice or beneficence. Also, there are situations in which it seems wrong to distribute resources unequally, even if this means that some resources are not used to make individuals better off. Such a situation arises, for example, when considerations of fairness or solidarity are paramount.[24] These brief examples are taken to represent instances in which considerations such as justice, beneficence, or solidarity are prior to efficiency in evaluating an allocation of resources. The question is the extent to which the Pareto efficient nature of an allocation provides sufficient reason on its own to count in favor of one allocation over another.

None of this is to deny that there are advantages associated with the use of markets as a means of allocation. For example, markets have been defended on grounds that they enhance choice[25] or that they enable coordination of information that only individual economic agents possess.[26] The point is that the efficiency of markets—understood in terms of the satisfaction of preferences and well-being—may not be among the stronger reasons to favor the use of markets.

CONCLUSION

This chapter highlights a number of questions that have been raised about the ways in which efficiency and rationality are conceptualized and deployed in contemporary economics and finance. In the case of efficiency, these questions suggest the need for additional criteria to evaluate economic and financial outcomes and institutions, especially if well-being is conceived in terms of preference satisfaction. In the case of rationality, the chapter points to questions about its use in describing economic behavior in the light of apparently irrational behavior; the accommodation of such behavior by alternate accounts of choice, such as prospect theory; and the role of preferences in explaining choices. The chapter also raises questions about whether the account of rationality at hand is able to accommodate nonconsequentialist moral views and views that regard certain alternatives as incomparable. None of this requires rejecting the use of efficiency and rationality as commonly conceptualized in economics and finance. However, it does suggest that if considerations of efficiency and rationality are invoked, then care must be taken to clarify what can and what *cannot* plausibly be claimed about human behavior and the desirability of certain economic policies and institutions.

NOTES

1. There is an extensive literature on rationality and efficiency. Within the context of economics, two useful guides to this literature are Cowen (2004) and Hausman and McPherson (2006). For a guide to the philosophical literature on rationality see Mele and Rawling (2004).

2. Sometimes, the requirements of rationality are characterized using three conditions: complete, transitive, and reflexive. Reflexivity holds that A is at least as good as A. Reflexivity is implied by completeness. Hence it is dropped as an explicit requirement of rationality.

3. Strictly speaking, this is not correct. The agent's preferences also must be *continuous*. Intuitively, this requirement holds that as alternatives vary slightly, there are no sudden "jumps" or "breaks" in the agent's ranking of the alternatives. A lexicographic preference ranking is one kind of noncontinuous preference ranking. Suppose there are two goods, X and Y, and alternatives consist of different combinations of X and Y—for example, one alternative might be (5 units of X, 3 units of Y). With lexicographic preferences, between any two alternatives, the agent prefers the alternative with the greater amount of one good, say X, no matter how much of Y the other alternative might have. For example, she prefers (5 units of X, 3 units of Y) to (4 units of X, 1,000 units of Y). It is only in the case of a tie between the amounts of X that she prefers the alternative with more units of Y. For example, she prefers (5 units of X, 3 units of Y) to

(5 units of X, 2 units of Y). With such preferences, holding X constant, the agent prefers alternatives that increase in the amount of Y. However, as soon as there is an alternative with an infinitely small increase in X, she prefers that alternative to all of the previous alternatives. This is the sense in which the agent's preferences are not continuous. To use the terminology of mathematics, preferences are continuous if the set of alternatives is a topological space; then the set of alternatives strictly preferred to an alternative A and the set of alternatives to which alternative A is strictly preferred are both open. Because continuity is something of a technical requirement, it is left aside for purposes of this chapter.

4. In this chapter, the terms *risk* and *uncertainty* will be used interchangeably with the assumption that for the most part, the possible outcomes and probabilities are known. In doing so, it overlooks the distinction made by Frank Knight (1921). Knight uses the term *risk* for circumstances in which the outcomes and probabilities are known and the term *uncertainty* for circumstances in which some of the probabilities and potentially the outcomes are not known.

5. To keep things simple, assume that each of the outcomes is itself an alternative over which the agent has a preference ranking when the alternatives are realized with certainty. This is a *simple* lottery. The assumption leaves aside the possibility that the lottery is a *compound* lottery—namely, one in which at least one of the outcomes is another lottery. Because complex lotteries can be converted to simple lotteries under the requirements for rationality presented here, the discussion of rationality uses simple lotteries in this chapter.

6. See von Neumann and Morgenstern (1947).

7. Her preferences over lotteries are complete if for any two lotteries, L and L', L is preferred to L', L' is preferred to L, or both. If L is preferred to L' and L' is preferred to L'', and if L is preferred to L'', then her preferences over lotteries are transitive. Her preferences over lotteries are continuous if there is a probability, p, such that if L is preferred to L' and L' is preferred to L'', then the agent is indifferent between $p \times L + (1 - p) \times L''$ and L'.

8. If the agent's preferences are intended to track some objective standard, then there is a further requirement on beliefs. For example, suppose the agent is motivated exclusively by considerations of her own well-being. Her preferences would be rational only if the preferred alternatives did, in fact, maximize her well-being. In this case, her beliefs about the impact of the alternatives on her well-being would have to be correct for her preferences and choices to be rational. Notice, however, that this requirement about the agent's beliefs is limited to circumstances in which the agent's preferences are meant to track some underlying set of considerations, but this is not a requirement of rationality. On the conception of rationality under discussion, the agent's preferences may be simply brute preferences or desires without any underlying considerations. In that case, the issue of the rationality of her beliefs as discussed here need not arise.

9. This is adapted from Hausman and McPherson (2006), 241–242.

10. This discussion draws on Lo (2008) and Ross (2008).

11. The concept is named after the Italian economist Vilfredo Pareto (1848–1923).

12. Individually rational behavior also need not lead to a Pareto efficient outcome under conditions of uncertainty. See, for example, Hammond (1983) and Levi (1990).

13. For discussion of the prisoner's dilemma, see Axelrod (1984). On the question of whether public goods are best understood as prisoner's dilemmas, see for example Hardin (1982) and Hampton (1987).

14. The idea is often referred to as Kaldor-Hicks efficiency.

15. Let X be a bet that the subject judges to be worse than another bet, Y, and yet the subject is willing to pay more for X (say \$11) than she is for Y (say \$10). The agent expresses the following preferences: (1) She is indifferent between \$11 and X; (2) she is indifferent between \$10 and Y; and (3) Y is at least as good as X. If she is indifferent between \$11 and X, then X is at least as good as \$11, and if she is indifferent between \$10 and Y, then Y is at least as good as \$10. This means that \$10 is at least as good as Y, Y is at least as good as X, and X is at least as good as \$11. Assuming she prefers \$11 to \$10, her preferences are intransitive.

16. This draws from Kahneman (2000). A *prospect* is a simple lottery as defined earlier. For a guide to the behavioral finance literature, see Bloomfield (2008).

17. Thaler (1999) discusses a range of financial behavior that mental accounting is thought to help explain.

18. For some discussion, see Broome (1991b), Chapter 5.

19. For more on the topic of incommensurable values, see Hsieh (2008), on which the current discussion draws.

20. To be clear, Raz does not say that companionship is more valuable than money. If such a view were correct, then those who forgo companionship for money would be acting against reason (1986, 352). For another discussion on value incommensurability and rationality, see Anderson (1993).

21. Another response to Jensen's argument is that there are ways in which to incorporate long-run market value and other considerations, such as the interests of nonshareholders, into a single measure that allows for comparisons of alternatives (Hsieh 2007b).

22. For one discussion, see Elster and Roemer (1991).

23. See, for example, Parfit (1984).

24. Consider the following example: "You are a kindergarten teacher (Teacher) with a tradition of giving every member of your class a 'kindergarten cub' sticker on graduation day, a symbol of class solidarity. Although those stickers cost next to nothing and peel off within days, in past years students preserved them as cherished mementos. This year, you find that you have miscounted; you have one fewer sticker than students. You should not, we suppose, distribute the stickers you possess to the children, leaving one without a sticker at the graduation ceremony. Instead you should keep the stickers until you have enough for all, perhaps never distributing them if you never get enough, certainly seeking an alternative expressive device if the stickers remain scarce" (Hsieh, Strudler, and Wasserman 2006, footnote 13).

25. Friedman (1962). For two responses to this view, see Peter (2004) and Waldfogel (2007).

26. For a classic statement of this view, see Hayek (1945).

REFERENCES

Allais, Maurice. 1979. The foundations of a positive theory of choice involving risk and a criticism of the postulates and axioms of the American school. In *Expected utility hypothesis and the Allais paradox*, ed. Maurice Allais and Otto Hagen. Dordrecht, The Netherlands: Reidel.

Anderson, Elizabeth. 1993. *Value in ethics and economics*. Cambridge, MA: Harvard University Press.

Axelrod, Robert. 1984. *The evolution of cooperation*. New York: Basic Books.

Benartzi, Shlomo, and Richard Thaler. 1985. Myopic loss aversion and the equity premium puzzle. *Quarterly Journal of Economics* 110:73–92.

Bloomfield, Robert. 2008. Behavioral finance. In *The new Palgrave dictionary of economics online*, ed. Steven N. Durlauf and Lawrence E. Blume. New York: Palgrave Macmillan.

Broome, John. 1991a. Utility. *Economics and Philosophy* 7:1–12.

———. 1991b. *Weighing goods*. Oxford: Blackwell.

Byron, Michael. 2004. Introduction. In *Satisficing and maximizing*, ed. Michael Bryon. Cambridge: Cambridge University Press.

Cowen, Tyler. 2004. How do economists think about rationality? In *Satisficing and maximizing*, ed. Michael Byron. Cambridge: Cambridge University Press.

Elster, Jon, and John Roemer, eds. 1991. *Interpersonal comparisons of well-being*. Cambridge: Cambridge University Press.

Frank, Robert. 1985. *Choosing the right pond: Human behavior and the quest for status*. New York: Oxford University Press.

———. 1988. *Passions within reason: The strategic role of the emotions*. New York: W.W. Norton.

———. 2000. *Luxury fever: Money and happiness in an era of excess*. Princeton: Princeton University Press.

Friedman, Milton. 1962. *Capitalism and freedom*. Chicago: University of Chicago Press.

Granovetter, Mark. 1985. Economic action, social structure and embeddedness. *American Journal of Sociology* 91:481–510.

Hammond, Peter. 1983. Ex-post optimality as a dynamically consistent objective for collective choice under uncertainty. In *Social choice and welfare*, ed. Prasanta Pattanaik and Maurice Salles. Amsterdam: North-Holland.

Hampton, Jean. 1987. Free-rider problems in the production of collective goods. *Economics and Philosophy* 3:245–273.

Hardin, Russell. 1982. *Collective action*. Baltimore: Johns Hopkins University Press.

Hausman, Daniel. 1992. *The inexact and separate science of economics*. Cambridge: Cambridge University Press.

Hausman, Daniel, and Michael McPherson. 2006. *Economic analysis, moral philosophy, and public policy*. 2nd ed. Cambridge: Cambridge University Press.

Hayek, Friedrich von. 1945. The use of knowledge in society. *American Economic Review* 35:519–530.

Hicks, John. 1939. The foundations of welfare economics. *Economic Journal* 49:696–712.

Hsieh, Nien-hê. 2007a. Is incomparability a problem for anyone? *Economics and Philosophy* 23:65–80.

———. 2007b. Maximization, incomparability, and managerial choice. *Business Ethics Quarterly* 17:497–513.

———. 2008. Incommensurable values. In *The Stanford encyclopedia of philosophy (Fall 2008 ed)*, ed. Edward N. Zalta. http://plato.stanford.edu/archives/fall2008/entries/value-incommensurable/.

Hsieh, Nien-hê, Alan Strudler, and David Wasserman. 2006. The numbers problem. *Philosophy and Public Affairs* 34:352–372.

Jensen, Michael. 2002. Value maximization, stakeholder theory, and the corporate objective function. *Business Ethics Quarterly* 12:235–256.

Kahneman, Daniel. 2000. Preface. In *Choices, values, and frames*, ed. Daniel Kahneman and Amos Tversky. Cambridge: Cambridge University Press.

Kahneman, Daniel, and Amos Tversky. 1984. Choices, values, and frames. *American Psychologist* 39:341–350.

Kaldor, Nicholas. 1939. Welfare propositions of economics and interpersonal comparisons of Utility. *Economic Journal* 49:549–552.

Knight, Frank. 1921. *Risk, uncertainty and profit*. Chicago: University of Chicago Press.

Levi, Isaac. 1990. Pareto unanimity and consensus. *Journal of Philosophy* 89:481–492.

Lichtenstein, Sarah, and Peter Slovic. 1971. Reversal of preference between bids and choices in gambling decisions. *Journal of Experimental Psychology* 89:46–55.

———. 1973. Response-induced reversals of preference in gambling: An extended replication in Las Vegas. *Journal of Experimental Psychology* 101:16–20.

Lo, Andrew. 2008. Efficient Markets Hypothesis. In *The new Palgrave dictionary of economics online*, ed. Steven N. Durlauf and Lawrence E. Blume. New York: Palgrave Macmillan.

Mas-Colell, Andreu, Michael Whinston, and Jerry Green. 1995. *Microeconomic theory*. Oxford: Oxford University Press.

Mele, Alfred, and Piers Rawling. 2004. *The Oxford handbook of rationality*. Oxford: Oxford University Press.

Odean, Terrance. 1998. Are investors reluctant to realize their losses? *Journal of Finance* 53:1775–1798.

Parfit, Derek. 1984. *Reasons and persons*. Oxford: Oxford University Press.

Peter, Fabiene. 2004. Choice, consent, and the legitimacy of market transactions. *Economics and Philosophy* 20:1–18.

Poldony, Joel. 2001. Networks as the pipes and prisms of the market. *American Journal of Sociology* 107:33–60.

———. 2005. *Status signals: A sociological study of market competition*. Princeton, NJ: Princeton University Press.

Preda, Alex. 2008. The sociological approach to financial markets. In *Issues in heterodox economics*, ed. Donald George. Oxford: Blackwell Publishing.

Raz, Joseph. 1986. *The morality of freedom*. Oxford: Clarendon Press.

Ross, Stephen. 2008. Finance. In *The new Palgrave dictionary of economics online*, ed. Steven N. Durlauf and Lawrence E. Blume. New York: Palgrave Macmillan.

Sandbu, Martin. 2007. Valuing processes. *Economics and Philosophy* 23:205–235.

Sen, Amartya. 1967. Isolation, assurance, and the social rate of discount. *Quarterly Journal of Economics* 81:112–124.

———. 1997. Maximization and the act of choice. *Econometrica* 65:745–779.

———. 2000. Consequential evaluation and practical reason. *Journal of Philosophy* 98: 477–502.

Shiller, Robert. 2005. *Irrational exuberance*. 2nd ed. New York: Broadway Books.

Simon, Herbert. 1955. A behavioral model of rational choice. *Quarterly Journal of Economics* 69:99–118.

Thaler, Richard. 1999. Mental accounting matters. *Journal of Behavioral Decision Making* 12:183–206.

Tversky, Amos, and Daniel Kahneman. 1991. Loss aversion in riskless choice: A reference dependent model. *Quarterly Journal of Economics* 106:1039–1061.

von Neumann, John, and Oskar Morgenstern. 1947. *Theory of games and economic behavior*. 2nd ed. Princeton: Princeton University Press.

Waldfogel, Joel. 2007. *The tyranny of the market*. Cambridge: Harvard University Press.

White, Harrison. 1981. Where do markets come from? *American Journal of Sociology* 87:517–547.

ABOUT THE AUTHOR

Nien-hê Hsieh is an associate professor in the Legal Studies and Business Ethics Department at the Wharton School, University of Pennsylvania, with a secondary appointment in the Department of Philosophy. He also serves as co-director of the Wharton Ethics Program. He writes about ethical issues in economic activity and ways to structure economic institutions to meet the demands of justice. He was a postdoctoral fellow at Harvard Business School, and has held visiting fellowships at Harvard University, Oxford University, and the Research School for Social Sciences at the Australian National University.

CHAPTER 5

Returns, Risk, and Financial Due Diligence*

CHRISTOPHER L. CULP
Senior Advisor at Compass Lexecon and Adjunct Professor of Finance, Booth School
of Business, The University of Chicago

J. B. HEATON
Partner, Bartlit Beck Herman Palenchar & Scott LLP, and Lecturer, The University of
Chicago Law School

Returns are the prospective financial rewards from investment. Risk is the potential for fluctuations in returns to engender losses. If investors are risk averse—as most appear to be—then they should demand higher expected returns from riskier investments.

In the wake of the credit crisis and the Bernard Madoff scandal, investors and regulators are clamoring for more rigorous *financial due diligence* by fund managers, institutional investors, and other market participants. Financial due diligence is the process by which investors try to ascertain, among other things, the potential risks and returns of a contemplated investment.

Both qualitative and quantitative methods are used to determine whether a given investment offers a fair risk/return trade-off (and what that trade-off is). Due diligence analysts use qualitative methods to examine hard-to-quantify variables—for example, portfolio manager reputation, internal control quality, reporting adequacy, and regulatory compliance. Investors employ quantitative methods to examine matters that more naturally lend themselves to empirical analyses—especially the risk and return characteristics of contemplated investments.[1]

Some potential investments can appear undesirable until the due diligence analyst properly measures their risks and returns, at which point the investment may seem more attractive. Alternatively, other potential investments can look

*We are grateful to John Cochrane and Dan Fischel for their comments on earlier drafts. The usual disclaimer applies, however; the opinions expressed herein are the authors' alone and do not necessarily reflect those of any organization with which the authors are affiliated or their customers and clients.

appealing until the due diligence analyst appropriately analyzes risks and returns and determines that the investment is unpalatable.

Part of the process of identifying investments with fair risk/return trade-offs includes spotting investments that seem too good to be true. As Judge Richard Posner observed in a Ponzi scheme case, "Only a very foolish, very naive, very greedy, or very Machiavellian investor would jump at a chance to obtain a return on his passive investment of 10 to 20 percent a month (the Machiavellian being the one who plans to get out early, pocketing his winnings, before the Ponzi scheme collapses). It should be obvious that such returns are not available to passive investors in any known market, save from the operation of luck."[2] Financial due diligence helps investors avoid becoming one of those "very foolish, very naive, very greedy, or very Machiavellian investor[s]" that Judge Posner and other actors in the courts look for in such situations.

In this chapter, we first explain basic concepts of risk and return in financial economics with an eye toward the task of financial due diligence. We then illustrate the applications of these concepts in financial due diligence using the example of Bernard Madoff Investment Securities.

BASIC CONCEPTS OF RISK AND RETURN IN FINANCIAL ECONOMICS

The *return* on an asset over some period of time (returns are always relative to some time period, whether an instant, day, month, year, etc.) is its payoff over that time period relative to its initial value (i.e., the value of the asset at the beginning of the period). We summarize some of the most popular ways of measuring returns in Appendix A. Most generally, the net return on a financial asset from time t to $t + 1$ is

$$r_{t+1} = \frac{x_{t+1} - p_t}{p_t} = \frac{d_{t+1} + p_{t+1} - p_t}{p_t} \qquad (5.1)$$

where p_t is the price of the asset at time t
x_{t+1} is the payoff to investors at time $t + 1$
d_{t+1} reflects distributions to investors (e.g., dividends or interest) at time
$t + 1$
p_{t+1} is the price of the asset or portfolio at the end of the holding period

The *risk* of an asset is the potential for returns to fluctuate unexpectedly. Returns vary for a number of reasons, including, but not limited to, changes in prices and interest rates (market risk), the nonperformance of counterparties or obligors (credit risk), cash flow shortfalls (funding risk), and forced liquidations of losing positions at unreasonable prices or spreads (liquidity risk).

A key premise of modern financial economics is that return and risk are related—in particular, investors expect a higher return for bearing higher risk. When an asset pays off a known amount with certainty, that asset is called *risk-free*. Competition in the market for risk-free assets will force the rate payable on riskless assets to the risk-free rate.[3]

Excess Returns and Alpha

Risk-averse investors will demand a return in excess of the risk-free rate to compensate them for bearing risks they prefer to avoid. Risks to which investors are averse are risks that lead to losses—so-called *downside* risks. Some investors are content with low returns as long as they face limited downside risk. Others are willing to bear more downside risk in the pursuit of higher returns.

In theory, only downside risks that investors cannot eliminate by diversification should earn higher expected returns. Such risks are called *systematic* risks. Because no investor can eliminate systematic risk simply by adding other assets with systematic risk to a diversified portfolio, the asset must offer a return commensurate with its systematic risk to persuade the investor to hold the asset.

Risks that the investor can eliminate by holding the asset in a diversified portfolio, by contrast, are called *idiosyncratic* risks. In equilibrium, investors should not earn a return for bearing idiosyncratic risk, which *is* diversifiable by most investors.[4] Otherwise, all investors would have an incentive to add any asset offering a return for idiosyncratic risk to their already diversified portfolio. The idiosyncratic risk would disappear in the portfolio, leaving only the return. Such free lunches cannot survive in competitive capital markets.

Much research in financial economics aims at understanding the risks for which investors demand compensation in capital markets. That is, financial economists seek to understand the sources of systematic risk and the returns that investors demand for bearing those risks. If we could measure systematic risk perfectly, we then could estimate the expected return actually being offered by the asset, $E(r)$, and compare it to the expected return $E(r*)$ that compensates for the asset's systematic risk. The difference, if any, between the two is known as alpha:

$$\alpha = E(r) - E(r^*)$$

A zero or negative alpha indicates that the investment is just compensating or undercompensating investors for the risks that affect the underlying payout on the security or portfolio. But if alpha is positive, the investment is overperforming relative to its measured risks. That is the reason many investors claim to "seek alpha"—investments with positive alpha are offering expected returns that more than compensate for their risk.

How much return an asset should pay to compensate for its systematic risk depends on the sources of systematic risk, the exposure of the asset to those sources, and the premiums that investors demand for bearing that risk. Answering those questions requires a model of market equilibrium for capital assets, often referred to as *asset pricing models*. Different asset pricing models will, in general, assume the existence of different sources of systematic risk and thus typically give rise to different estimates of $E(r^*)$.[5]

The Capital Asset Pricing Model

The capital asset pricing model (CAPM) is the simplest and best-known theoretical asset pricing model. In the CAPM, the only source of systematic risk is the extent to which an asset's return moves together (covaries) with the return of the weighted average of all other assets, where the weights are the market values of all of the other assets in the world.

The idea is fairly simple. Suppose that you could buy a little bit of every asset in the world and that your own personal portfolio had the same rate of return as the weighted average of all assets in the world—that is, your own portfolio of risky assets is just a tiny version of the whole portfolio of world wealth. Suppose further that you prefer more money to less but that, at your current wealth, the pain of losing a dollar hurts more than the pleasure of gaining a dollar feels good.

Now consider any one asset in the world. If the asset performs well (earns good returns) when all of your other assets are doing well, that is doubtless a good thing. But the problem is that you are earning money from that asset when you are already earning money on everything else. And it works the other way. If that asset is moving with the rest of your wealth then it is going to perform poorly when the rest of your assets also are doing poorly. That's not good. So the more an asset's return covaries with the rest of the wealth in the world, the more you are going to want to get paid to hold that asset—that is, the higher the expected return you will demand.

In the CAPM, the systematic risk is the strength of the covariance between the returns on a given asset and the returns to the rest of the wealth in the world. That is, the CAPM return that investors can expect on some asset or portfolio j, $E(r_j^*)$, is related to its systematic risk as follows:

$$E(r_j^*) - r_f = \beta_j [E(r_m) - r_f] \tag{5.2}$$

where r_j is the return on asset or portfolio j
         r_m is the return on the market portfolio of world-invested wealth
         r_f is the risk-free rate
         β_j is a measure of the extent to which the returns r_j and r_m move together—namely, the coefficient in a regression of asset j's excess returns on the market's excess returns

or

$$\beta_j = \frac{Cov(r_j, r_m)}{Var(r_m)}$$

The only source of systematic risk in the CAPM—and the only thing driving differences in expected returns given r_m and r_f—is the asset's β.

To determine whether there is any alpha, we take a sample of N historical returns on a portfolio j and run the following regression:

$$r_{j,t} - r_f = \alpha + \beta_j [r_{m,t} - r_f] + \varepsilon_{j,t} \tag{5.3}$$

$$for \ t = 1, \ldots, N$$

If the asset earned returns that compensated for its CAPM risk and the CAPM correctly models asset returns (this is an important assumption), then the estimated intercept α in regression (3) should be zero. A positive estimated alpha is evidence that the asset earned more on average than the CAPM predicted.

Interpretations of positive estimated alphas can be challenging. If the CAPM is true, the estimated alpha is good evidence of positive abnormal returns—in other words, an investment that beat the market. But it is much more difficult to interpret the positive alpha if the CAPM is not a good description of asset pricing. In that case, the positive alpha may be due entirely to the omission of some other risks for which the investors holding the asset were compensated but which is not reflected in the CAPM. The asset will have earned higher average returns than the CAPM predicted not because of any mispricing that reflected the opportunity for returns above those necessary to compensate for risk, but instead because those returns compensated for sources of risk omitted from the CAPM.

Other Asset Pricing Models

Much empirical evidence suggests that the CAPM does not adequately capture all sources of systematic risk in asset returns. The co-movement of returns with other variables helps explain these deviations from the CAPM. Asset pricing models that include these variables often characterize expected excess returns as

$$E(r_j^*) - r_f = \beta_{1,j}\delta_1 + \beta_{2,j}\delta_2 + \cdots + \beta_{k,j}\delta_k \qquad (5.4)$$

where β_{kj} is the kth regression coefficient of asset j's excess return on the kth risk factor

δ_k is the risk premium of the kth risk factor

The risk factors are proxies for economic variables with which investors are concerned in defining good and bad times. In the CAPM, the only such risk factor was co-movement with the market.

A currently popular version of the general model shown in equation (5.4) is the Fama and French (1993) three-factor model, which describes expected excess returns on an asset or portfolio j in terms of three systematic risk factors:

$$E(r_j^*) - r_f = \beta_m\delta_m + \beta_{SMB}\delta_{SMB} + \beta_{HML}\delta_{HML} \qquad (5.5)$$

where δ_m is the excess return on the market (the same factor used in the CAPM)

δ_{SMB} is a variable formed from the difference in returns to big versus small market capitalization stocks (designed to capture the observed factor of firm size in explaining differences in average returns across stocks)

δ_{HML} is a variable formed from the difference in returns on stock with high versus low book-to-market ratios (designed to capture the observed explanatory factor of such measures in explaining differences in average returns across stocks)

The various β's are the respective regression coefficients. A four-factor version of the model also includes a variable designed to capture the tendency of recent good and bad performance to continue, known as the *momentum effect*.

Like the CAPM, running a regression of the form in equation (5.5) generates an estimated intercept that should be zero if the Fama-French model is a true representation of the relation between expected excess returns and systematic risk. A positive estimated intercept indicates that the average return of the asset or portfolio exceeds the risk-free rate by more than the systematic risk premium. Also like the CAPM, the positive intercept may reflect abnormal performance unexplained by risk or, alternatively, misspecification of the asset pricing model that has omitted proxies for the true sources of systematic risk.

Measures of Total Risk

To augment or obviate the search for an appropriate asset pricing model to estimate alpha, many analysts also employ measures of returns relative to some measure of total risk that does not attempt to decompose return fluctuations into systematic and idiosyncratic components. One such measure is the Sharpe ratio:[6]

$$SR_j = \frac{\bar{r}_j - r_f}{\sigma_j}$$

where SR_j is the Sharpe ratio on asset or portfolio j
   $\bar{r}_j$ is the average return on asset or portfolio j
   σ_j is the volatility of returns on that asset or portfolio

Volatility is often estimated as the standard deviation of returns over an historical period, perhaps using rolling moving averages or more structured models of the evolution of volatility over time.[7]

A problem with using the Sharpe ratio for financial due diligence, however, is its measurement of risk using only the volatility of excess returns. Volatility is a symmetric measure of risk that reflects deviations both above and below average returns. But if the true return distribution is negatively skewed or fat-tailed, volatility is an incomplete description of return dispersion. And, as noted earlier, it is the downside risk with which most investors are more concerned.

Consider, for example, a portfolio that consists of short positions in out-of-the-money equity put options. The portfolio earns a premium as long as stock prices do not decline significantly. But if stock prices collapse, the options move into-the-money and the value of the portfolio crashes. Yet the volatility of the payoff on the short option portfolio is lower than the volatility of a similar portfolio invested in the stocks underlying the puts. In both portfolios, investors lose when share prices decline. But in the stock portfolio, investors make money when prices rise, unlike the option portfolio in which the maximum payoff is the premium collected. The distribution of payoffs on the option portfolio thus is truncated, which reduces the estimated volatility of returns. That lower volatility, however, results from chopping off the potential *upside* of the strategy. Volatility thus has been reduced at the expense of negative skewness and fat tails in the payoff distribution. As such, it is by no means clear that the option portfolio is less risky than the stock portfolio even though the returns on the former are less volatile than on the latter.

To measure the risk/return ratio for an asset or portfolio with skewed and/or fat-tailed returns, an analyst may instead evaluate average excess return relative to an estimate of downside risk (DSR). Unlike volatility, DSR measures the risk of only those returns below the average or some target. The analogue of the Sharpe ratio for measuring average excess returns per unit of DSR is the Sortino ratio:

$$Sortino\ Ratio = \frac{\bar{r} - r_f}{DSR}$$

Quite a few different ways of measuring DSR can be used to calculate the Sortino ratio. One such measure, the downside semi-standard deviation (DSSD), is defined as

$$DSSD = \sqrt{\frac{1}{M} \sum_{\substack{1 \\ \{s,t,r_t < \bar{r}\}}}^{M} (\bar{r} - r_t)^2}$$

where M is the number of returns in the sample below the average return. DSSD thus measures the so-called bad part of the standard deviation. If the underlying return distribution has a fat left-hand tail, the DSSD provides a better measure of risk than volatility.

Another popular measure of DSR is value at risk (VaR). For an estimated distribution of potential returns, VaR measures the return threshold that the investor expects to exceed $(1 - X)$ percent of the time, where X is usually set at 1 percent or 5 percent. A 99 percent monthly VaR of –15 percent, for example, means that the portfolio is expected to generate monthly returns below –15 percent only 1 percent of the time. The underlying return distribution used to compute VaR can be generated parametrically, nonparametrically, by simulation analysis, or with some mixture of those methods.[8]

A significant drawback of VaR is that it does not tell us the magnitude of potential losses below the critical level. A 99 percent monthly VaR of –15 percent suggests that returns should not be below –15 percent more than 1 percent of the time, but it does *not* tell us whether the 1 percent of violations consist of, say, –16 percent returns or –1,600 percent returns. To address this, market participants sometimes define VaR in terms of conditional expected loss, otherwise known as *tail VaR* or *t-VaR*.

Analysts typically compare a calculated risk/return ratio with the risk/return profile of similar assets. For example, Exhibit 5.1 shows historical return, risk, and return/risk ratios for the CRSP Value-Weighted Portfolio of NYSE, NASDAQ, and AMEX stocks from 1947 to 2008. All of the measures of return relative to risk are below 0.50. The definition of risk, moreover, changes the results noticeably. The Sortino ratio using 95th percentile VaR as a measure of DSR, for example, is appreciably lower than the Sharpe ratio.

Exhibit 5.1 Risk and Return Statistics on the CRSP Value-Weighted Portfolio of
NYSE, NASDAQ, and AMEX Stocks, 1947 to 2008

	Monthly	Annual
Returns:		
Average Market[a] Return	0.924%	11.981%
Average 30-day T-Bill Return	0.377%	4.659%
Average Excess Return[b]	0.546%	7.323%
Risk:		
Volatility of Excess Returns	4.251%	18.149%
DSSD of Excess Returns	4.723%	20.897%
95th Percentile VaR of Excess Returns [c]	6.513%	22.293%
Return/Risk Ratios:		
Sharpe Ratio	0.1286	0.4035
Sortino Ratio (DSSD)	0.1157	0.3504
Sortino Ratio (VaR)	0.0839	0.3285

[a] CRSP Value-Weighted Portfolio (including distributions).
[b] Average market return minus average 30-day T-bill return.
[c] Absolute value of fifth percentile excess return.
Source: Center for Research in Security Prices.

PUTTING THEORY INTO PRACTICE—THE MADOFF EXAMPLE

We now illustrate the application of risk/return analysis to financial due diligence by examining the detection of a Ponzi scheme. In a Ponzi scheme, the promoter solicits funds from customers for investment in some portfolio or strategy, but little or no investing actually occurs. Redemption requests and distributions are financed by cash received from new participants in the scheme—robbing Peter to pay Paul, as it were—and the remaining cash is distributed to the participants in the fraud.

Because almost all investment managers who appear to have abnormally high average returns will attribute their results to skill, the self-reported performance explanations of investment managers are likely to hold little weight in the due diligence analysis. Investment managers do not, after all, self-proclaim their fraudulent investments.

The problem is especially difficult when Ponzi schemes do not promise super-high returns. When long-run average returns are just high enough to be enticing but not so high as to be obviously unrealistic, then the tools we have discussed thus far can be valuable components of the due diligence process. We illustrate using the case of Bernard L. Madoff Investment Securities ("Madoff" in the pages that follow).

Madoff's Ponzi Scheme

In the largest investor fraud by an individual in history, Madoff primarily marketed a single investment strategy—known as a *split strike conversion*—in which he claimed to be purchasing blue-chip stocks in the S&P100 Index and simultaneously selling out-of-the-money calls and buying out-of-the-money puts on the S&P 100

Index. Normal enough in its own right, a split strike conversion strategy is essentially just a stock index arbitrage program and, as such, should have relatively low risk and generate modest returns.

Yet Madoff boasted average returns of nearly 10.5 percent per annum for the 17 years during which the Ponzi scheme went undetected. Even when the market fell nearly 40 percent through November 2008, Madoff was still reporting a positive 5.6 percent year-to-date return (Applebaum et al. 2008).

Ponzi schemes generally fall apart when larger-than-expected redemptions occur. But that never happened with Madoff. If not for the collapse of equities during the credit crisis, Madoff's fraud might have remained undiscovered for many more years. Madoff's scheme apparently went undetected for so long part because it was an *affinity fraud* aimed at the wealthy Jewish community in New York and Palm Beach. Within that community, Madoff was a well-known figure with impeccable references; his investors trusted him. Indeed, some within Madoff's target affinity group report having tried to invest with him but having been turned away—no doubt adding to his appeal.[9] In addition, Madoff's returns were generally not so high as to be completely ridiculous on their face.

A Risk/Return Analysis of a Madoff Feeder Fund

Most of Madoff's money came from feeder funds that secured investments from customers and then used Madoff as either the investment manager or broker. To analyze the risk and return of Madoff's scam, we obtained returns from July 1989 through December 2000 on one of Madoff's largest feeder funds.[10] Although some of Madoff's feeder funds had other investments, we understand that the fund we examined was invested almost exclusively with Madoff.

Alpha
Exhibit 5.2 shows Madoff's estimated alpha from the CAPM and the Fama-French model regressions—equations (2) and (5), respectively. If we run a CAPM regression of the feeder fund's excess returns on the market portfolio's excess returns, we get a statistically significant estimated α of 0.7251 percent per month. In the naïve CAPM world, it looks like Madoff was earning about 75 basis points per month above the return commensurate with the systematic risk of the market. The Fama-French regression yields a similar estimate of 0.7209 percent per month; adding the two additional proxies for systematic risk only reduces average returns by about half a basis point per month.

Using both the CAPM and Fama-French models, it appears as though Madoff's feeder fund was adding significant value in excess of the systematic risk of the fund. As noted earlier, these positive alpha estimates could be the result of model misspecification. But part of the due diligence process is identifying red flags like this one and following up with additional qualitative and quantitative analysis.

Returns Relative to Total Risk Measures
Exhibit 5.3 shows monthly returns from July 1989 through December 2000 on the CRSP Value-Weighted Portfolio compared to Madoff's monthly returns. The average monthly return on Madoff was 1.18 percent, as compared to an average monthly return on the market of 1.24 percent over this period. As Exhibit 5.3 also

Exhibit 5.2   Alpha Regressions of Madoff Feeder Fund Returns

	CAPM	Fama-French
α	0.007251**	0.007209**
β_m	0.053397**	0.053783**
β_{SMB}	n/a	−0.04799*
β_{HML}	n/a	−0.01809
N	138	138
R^2	0.0727	0.1147

$^*p < 5\%$.
$^{**}p < 1\%$.

shows, however, Madoff's returns exhibited very low volatility—0.83 percent per month as compared to 4.08 percent per month for the market.

Despite average returns slightly below the market, the Sharpe and Sortino ratios for Madoff are well above the market, as shown in Exhibit 5.4. The Sharpe ratio over this period was 0.9516 for Madoff, as compared to 0.2028 for the market. And Madoff's Sortino ratios (measured with DSSD and VaR, respectively) were 1.0730 and 2.9515, compared to the market Sortino ratios of 0.1741 and 0.1465.

Moving down the rows in Exhibit 5.4, average returns are divided by increasingly conservative measures of risk. As expected, the risk/return ratios for the market decline as the measure of risk in the denominator increases. But the

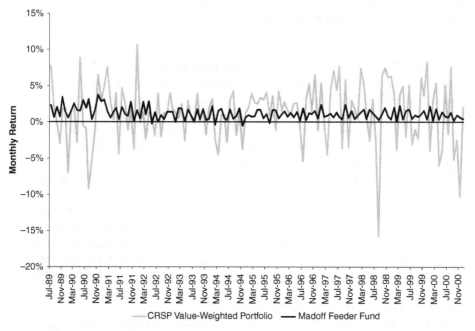

Exhibit 5.3 Monthly Returns on the Market versus Madoff Feeder Funds, July 1989 through December 2000
Source: Center for Research in Security Prices.

Exhibit 5.4 Sharpe and Sortino Rations, Madoff versus CRSP Value-Weighted Portfolio, July 1989 through December 2000

	Madoff	Market
Sharpe Ratio	0.9516	0.2028
Sortino Ratio (DSSD)	1.0730	0.1741
Sortino Ratio (VaR)	2.9515	0.1465

Madoff portfolio shows the opposite pattern—*increasing* risk/return ratios for progressively more conservative measures of risk. That indicates extremely thin tails in Madoff's return distribution vis-à-vis the market. In other words, not only do Madoff's returns exhibit little variation around the average, they also include few bad months.

Both the levels of the risk/return ratios and the thin-tailed distributions they indicate represent additional red flags. Although fraud is not the only possible explanation for the patterns in Exhibit 5.4, the data indicate that further due diligence is likely warranted.

Persistence and Serial Correlation

Another indicator of potentially too-good-to-be-true investments is excessive persistence in returns. Efficient capital markets are generally thought to follow close to random walks, especially over holding periods of a month or longer. As such, significant persistence in returns is a red flag to ask additional questions about why the performance of an asset or portfolio is seemingly so stable over time.

Return persistence is measured statistically by looking at serial correlation (aka autocorrelation). Specifically, we can run the following regression:

$$r_{t+1} = \rho_0 + \sum_{k=1}^{q} \rho_k r_{t-k} + \varepsilon_{t+1}$$

where q is the number of lagged returns that we want to examine. The regression coefficient ρ_k is the partial autocorrelation of returns at the kth lag. If returns fluctuate randomly, ρ_k should be zero at all lags. Positive estimated autocorrelations indicate persistence in returns—that is, an unusual high return in one period is likely to be followed by an unusually higher return in the next period.

The number of autocorrelation lags that an investor should examine depends on the frequency of available mark-to-market returns and the quality of that data. In annual returns, statistically significant positive autocorrelations at the one-year lag should be enough to raise an eyebrow. With monthly returns, looking at two or three lags is probably adequate.

Positive autocorrelation also reduces estimated volatility. Returns that exhibit persistence thus will tend to be less volatile and to have higher Sharpe ratios than returns following a random walk. The greater the persistence of returns, the lower is the estimated volatility of returns and the higher the Sharpe ratio. So even if positive autocorrelations show up for good reasons, further due diligence still may well be indicated.[11]

The first three partial autocorrelation coefficients on market portfolio returns are all statistically indistinguishable from zero, just as we would expect. But for Madoff, the partial autocorrelations are –0.19, 0.24, and 0.19 for the first three lags, all of which are statistically significant.

The positive autocorrelation on the second and third lags show persistence in returns that might be expected from a Ponzi scheme. Although returns persistence can be generated by infrequent marking to market of the underlying securities, Madoff's supposed focus on highly liquid S&P 100 stocks and options suggests that those autocorrelations cannot be explained by nonsynchronous trading or illiquidity alone.

The estimated autocorrelation at the first lag, however, is negative. That is more traditionally associated with phenomena such as market overreactions or prices that bounce between bids and offers. The same thing would also be consistent with a fictional pricing scheme that took average prices and then marked them up one month and down the next. But the explanation is not immediately obvious from the data.

So once again, we have a potential red flag—but only a potential one. Although the autocorrelations in the Madoff fund are consistent with a fictional-price Ponzi scheme, there are other explanations for these estimates. The autocorrelations thus are not conclusive on their own but should be the catalyst for asking additional questions.

CONCLUSION

In theory, identifying opportunities that are seemingly too good to be true can be accomplished by looking for abnormally high alphas. The problem, of course, is that the appearance of uncharacteristically high average excess returns may arise for different reasons: (1) the investment manager or trader is engaged in willful deception or fraud; (2) the investment manager or trader is pursuing authorized and legitimate investments but the measurement does not provide a true picture of risk and return due to errors in data or methodology; (3) the investment manager has been lucky; or (4) the investment manager has genuine skill. But in practice, the seemingly insurmountable empirical difficulties in testing asset pricing models makes it virtually impossible to distinguish between alphas that are *actually* positive and positive alpha *estimates* that are positive because of a misspecified asset pricing model.

In the Madoff example, warning signs were present in the data as of late 2000. But even with the benefit of hindsight, those warning signs were not unambiguously indicative of fraud in and of themselves. Nevertheless, the warning signs were sufficient to indicate that additional analysis—both quantitative and qualitative—may well have been warranted.

APPENDIX A: COMMON DEFINITIONS OF RETURN

A return is the payoff on a financial asset or portfolio relative to the initial value of that investment. Returns generally can be measured in one of three ways: discrete holding period returns, continuously compounded returns, or investment accounting returns.

Discrete Holding Period Returns

A holding period return is the return on an investment over some period of time during which the investor is presumed to hold the asset. The two most basic measures of holding period returns are gross and net per-period returns:

$$R_{t,t+1} = \frac{d_{t+1} + p_{t+1}}{p_t}$$

$$r_{t,t+1} = \frac{d_{t+1} + p_{t+1} - p_t}{p_t} = R_{t,t+1} - 1$$

where p_t is the time t price of the asset and d_{t+1} reflects any distributions to the investor such as dividends or interest payments.[12]

We also often want to know the effective N-period return on an asset, assuming the payoff on the asset is reinvested at the end of each holding period successively for N periods. An investment of \$1 at time t that is rolled over for N periods yields a time $t + N$ value of

$$V_{t+N} = \prod_{j=1}^{N} (1 + r_{t+j-1,t+j})$$

The effective return over N periods is then calculated as

$$r_{t,t+N} = V_{t+N}^{\frac{1}{N}} - 1$$

$$r_{t,t+N} = [(1 + r_{t,t+1})(1 + r_{t,t+1}) \cdots (1 + r_{t+N-1,t+N})]^{\frac{1}{N}} - 1$$

$$r_{t,t+N} = [R_{t,t+1} R_{t+1,t+2} \cdots (R_{t+N-1,t+N}]^{\frac{1}{N}} - 1$$

Careful attention must be paid to the presumed compounding frequency in multiperiod return calculations. In general, an asset whose return is compounded q times per year over N years has an N-year effective holding period return of

$$r_{t,t+N} = q \left[\left(\frac{V_{t+N}}{V_t} \right)^{\frac{1}{qN}} - 1 \right]$$

where

$$V_{t+N} = V_t \prod_{j=1}^{qN} \left(1 + \frac{r_{t+j-1,t+j}}{q} \right)$$

Continuously Compounded Returns

A continuously compounded return is the *instantaneous* return on an investment, assuming that all distributions are continuously reinvested. In general, the continuously compounded return (aka geometric return) can be calculated from the corresponding holding period return r as follows:

$$r^{cc} = ln(1+r)$$

In practice, continuously compounded returns are often computed as the log difference in prices between two periods. An N-period geometric return, for example is

$$r^{cc} = ln\left(\frac{p_{t+N}}{p_t}\right)$$

Investment Accounting Returns

Investment managers must calculate returns to conform to regulations or guidelines promulgated by supervisors and accounting organizations. Such investment accounting measures of return are often more difficult to calculate than holding period returns because they must take into account any contributions or withdrawals.

The ideal investment accounting measure is a true time-weighted return—essentially a holding period return in which individual holding periods are defined as trading days. At the end of any day t the value of the portfolio is defined as

$$V_t^e = p_t + d_t$$

where p_t is the mark-to-market value of the portfolio at the end of day t and d_t reflects any income or distributions on day t. The value of the portfolio at the beginning of day t is

$$V_t^b = V_{t-1}^e + C_{t-1}$$

where C_t reflects any cash withdrawals or contributions at the end of prior holding period $t - 1$. The time-weighted gross return over day t then is just

$$R_t^{TWR} = \frac{V_t^e}{V_t^b}$$

and the N-period net holding period return is

$$r_{t,t+N}^{TWR} = \left(\prod_{j=0}^{N} R_{t+j}^{TWR}\right) - 1$$

The principal reason that a true time-weighted return requires daily holding periods is that cash contributions and withdrawals may occur at any time. A manager thus needs to know values and returns on each day in order to account for cash distributions properly.

Many portfolio managers, however, do not have access to daily mark-to-market prices or are concerned about the quality of daily prices on illiquid positions. As an alternative, investors often compute approximate time-weighted returns (often misleadingly referred to as dollar-weighted returns) using the Modified Dietz method in which the N-period return is approximated as

$$r_{t,t+N}^{MDietz} = \frac{V_{t+N} - V_t - \sum_{j=0}^{N} C_{t+j}}{V_t + \sum_{j=0}^{N} C_{t+j} \tau_{t+j}}$$

where C_j is any cash withdrawal or contribution on date j, and

$$\tau_{t+j} = \frac{\tau_{t,t+N} - \tau_{t,t+j}}{\tau_{t,t+N}} \tag{5.6}$$

where $\tau_{t,t+j}$ is the total number of days in the holding period from t to $t+j$.

Finally, some investment managers compute a naïve dollar-weighted return on a portfolio as follows:

$$r_{t,t+N}^{DWR} = \frac{V_{t+N} - V_t}{V_t}$$

where

$$V_{t+N} = \sum_{k=1}^{K} C_k (1 + vk)^{\tau_k}$$

where K is the total number of days on which a contribution or withdrawal occurred in the holding period from t to $t+N$
   k is an index variable indicating each of those withdrawal dates
   τ_k is as defined in equation (5.6)
   v_k is the internal rate of return on the portfolio at k

NOTES

1. Not all market participants and due diligence analysts are created equal. Most of our comments here are intended to apply to relatively sophisticated institutional investors.

2. *Scholes v. Lehman*, 56 F.3d 750, 760 (7th Cir. 1995).

3. The risk-free rate will differ depending on the timing of the certain payoff, of course. The risk-free rate for an investment that pays off in a year will in general be different from the risk-free rate for an investment that pays off in two years, and so on.

4. There are some exceptions, most of which owe to capital market frictions. For a discussion, see Cochrane and Culp (2003).

5. For a review of the main asset pricing models, see Cochrane (2005).

6. See Sharpe (1966 and 1994).

7. Because we are really interested in knowing what the risk of an asset or portfolio *will be* and not what it *was*, measures of risk in the Sharpe ratio can be even more useful

when based on estimates of expected future volatility reflected in market prices. Option-implied volatility, for example, is a forward-looking estimate of volatility.

8. One popular method of measuring VaR, known as the *parametric normal* method, uses volatility to compute VaR. As a scaled measure of standard deviation, this does not add much to risk estimates that rely on volatility directly. But this is just one possible way to measure VaR. In general, VaR can also be measured in ways that do not rely exclusively on volatility and that allow for skewed and fat-tailed return distributions. See, for example, Culp (2001).

9. See Biggs (2009).

10. Subsequent references to Madoff's performance refer to this single feeder fund. We are grateful to Andy Lo for providing us with the feeder fund return data.

11. Various methods are available to adjust Sharpe ratios and other performance measures for autocorrelation that arises when hedge funds and private equity funds engage in *return smoothing* (for either legitimate or questionable purposes). For a good discussion, see Getmansky, Lo, and Makarov (2004) and Lo (2001 and 2008).

12. If distributions are paid before the end of the holding period, they can easily be restated to time $t + 1$ values.

REFERENCES

Applebaum, B., D. S. Hilzenrath, and A. R. Paley. 2008. All just one big lie. *Washington Post* (December 13).

Biggs, B. 2009. The affinity Ponzi scheme. *Newsweek* (January 12).

Cochrane, J. H. 2005. *Asset pricing*. Rev. ed. Princeton, NJ: Princeton University Press.

Cochrane, J. H., and C. L. Culp. 2003. Equilibrium asset pricing and discount factors: Overview and implications for derivatives valuation and risk management. In *Modern risk management: A history*, ed. Peter Field. London: Risk Books.

Culp, C. L. 2001. *The risk management process*. New York: John Wiley & Sons.

Fama, E. F., and K. R. French. 1993. Common risk factors in the returns on stocks and bonds. *Journal of Financial Economics* 33:3–56.

Getmansky, M., A. W. Lo, and I. Makarov. 2004. An econometric model of serial correlation and illiquidity in hedge fund returns. *Journal of Financial Economics* 74:529–609.

Lo, A. W. 2001. Risk management for hedge funds: Introduction and overview. *Financial Analysts Journal* 57:16–33.

———. 2008. *Hedge funds: An analytic perspective*. Princeton, NJ: Princeton University Press.

Sharpe, W. 1966. Mutual fund performance. *Journal of Business* 39:119–138.

———. 1994. The Sharpe ratio. *Journal of Portfolio Management* 21:49–58.

ABOUT THE AUTHORS

Christopher L. Culp is a senior advisor with Compass Lexecon; adjunct professor of finance at The University of Chicago's Booth School of Business; Honorarprofessor at Universität Bern in the Institut für Finanzmanagement; managing director of Risk Management Consulting Services, Inc.; and an adjunct fellow at the Competitive Enterprise Institute. He teaches graduate courses on structured finance, insurance, and derivatives, and provides consulting services and testimonial expertise in those areas. He is the author of four books, the co-editor of two books, and has published numerous articles. He holds a PhD from The University of Chicago's Booth School of Business.

J. B. Heaton is a litigation partner with Bartlit Beck Herman Palenchar & Scott LLP. He received his MBA, JD, and PhD (financial economics) from the University of Chicago in 1999. He regularly lectures and publishes on topics in law and finance. Dr. Heaton's law practice focuses on litigation for hedge funds and private equity funds. Dr. Heaton teaches as a lecturer at the University of Chicago Law School and previously has taught as an adjunct professor at Northwestern University Law School and as an adjunct professor of finance at Duke University.

CHAPTER 6

Reputational Risk*

INGO WALTER
Seymour Milstein Professor of Finance, Corporate Governance and Ethics,
Stern School of Business, New York University

INTRODUCTION

The global financial crisis of 2007–2009 was associated with an unprecedented degree of financial and economic damage. For investors and financial intermediaries, the estimates seem to have risen to over $4 trillion or so worldwide by the time things began to stabilize, according to the International Monetary Fund (2009). Along with the financial damage has come substantial reputational damage for the financial services industry, for financial intermediaries and asset managers, and for individuals.

At the industry level, for example, Josef Ackermann, CEO of Deutsche Bank and chairman of the International Institute of Finance, noted in April 2008 that the industry was guilty of poor risk management with serious overreliance on flawed models, inadequate stress-testing of portfolios, recurring conflicts of interest, and lack of common sense, as well as irrational compensation practices not linked to long-term profitability—with a growing perception by the public of "clever crooks and greedy fools." He concluded that the industry has a great deal of work to do to regain its reputation.[1] Crisis-driven reputational damage at the firm level can be inferred from remarks by Peter Kurer, former supervisory board chairman of UBS AG, who noted at the bank's annual general meeting in April 2008 that "We shouldn't fool ourselves. We can't pretend that there has been no reputational damage. Experience says it goes away after two or three years."[2]

Perhaps it does, perhaps not, but the hemorrhage of private client withdrawals at the height of the crisis suggests severe reputational damage to the world's largest private bank—to the point that it was surpassed in assets under management by Bank of America (after its acquisition of Merrill Lynch) in 2009. The number of financial firms—ranging from Santander in Spain to Citigroup in the United States and Union Bancaire Privée in Switzerland—that have reimbursed client losses from the sale of bankrupt Lehman bonds, collapsed auction-rate securities, and investments in Bernard Madoff's fraudulent scheme suggests the importance of reputational capital and the lengths to which financial firms must go to maintain

---

*The author is grateful for helpful comments by John Boatright and Ed Hartman on earlier drafts of this article.

it. And at the individual level the world is full of disgraced bankers whose hard work, career ambitions, and future prospects lie in tatters.

Whether at the industry, firm, or individual level, the reputational costs of the financial crisis have been enormous. The first section of this chapter considers the special nature of financial services and traces the roots of the reputational risk that firms in the industry invariably encounter. The second section defines what reputational risk is and outlines the sources of reputational risk facing financial services firms. The third section considers the key sources of reputational risk in the presence of transactions costs and imperfect information.[3] The fourth section surveys available empirical research on the impact of reputational losses imposed on financial intermediaries, including the separation of reputational losses from accounting losses. The chapter concludes with some governance and managerial implications.

THE SPECIAL CHARACTER
OF FINANCIAL SERVICES

Financial services comprise an array of *special* businesses. They are special because they deal mainly with other people's money, and because problems that arise in financial intermediation can trigger serious external costs. In recent years, the roles of various types of financial intermediaries have evolved dramatically. Capital markets and institutional asset managers have taken a greater portion of the intermediation function from banks. Insurance activities conducted in the capital markets—such as credit default swaps and weather derivatives—compete with classic reinsurance functions. Fiduciary activities for institutional and retail clients are conducted by banks, broker-dealers, life insurers, and independent fund management companies. Intermediaries in each cohort compete as vigorously with their traditional rivals as with players in other cohorts, and the competition has been intensified by deregulation and rapid innovation in financial products and processes. Market developments have periodically overtaken regulatory capabilities intended to promote stability and fairness as well as efficiency and innovation. The regulatory arbitrage that can result has a great deal to do with the dynamics of the financial crisis of 2007–2009, and is being addressed in many of the regulatory efforts that have been proposed and implemented.

It is unsurprising that these conditions would give rise to significant reputational risk exposure for financial firms. For their part, investors in banks and other financial intermediaries are sensitive to the going-concern value of the firms they own, and hence to the governance processes that are supposed to work in their interests. Regulators, in turn, are sensitive to the safety, soundness, and integrity of the financial system and will, from time to time, recalibrate the rules of the game. Market discipline, operating through the governance process, interacts with the regulatory process in ways that involve both costs and benefits to market participants and are reflected in the value of their business franchises.

WHAT IS REPUTATIONAL RISK?

There are substantial difficulties in defining the value of a financial firm's reputation, the extent of damage to that reputation, the origins of that damage, and, therefore, the sources of reputational risk. Reputation itself may be defined as the opinion (more technically, a social evaluation) of the public toward a person, a group of people, or an organization. It is an important factor in many fields, such as education, business, online communities, and social status. In a business context, reputation helps drive the excess value of a business firm and such metrics as the market-to-book ratio. However, both a precise definition and data are found to be lacking. Arguably many deficiencies in both definition and data can be attributed to the fact that theory development related to corporate reputation has itself been deficient. Such problems notwithstanding, common sense suggests some sources of gain/loss in reputational capital:

- The cumulative reputation of the firm, including its self-promoted ethical image.
- Economic performance—market share, profitability, and growth.
- Stakeholder interface—shareholders, employees, clients, and suppliers.
- Legal interface—civil and criminal litigation and enforcement actions.

Consequently, proximate symptoms of sources of loss in reputational capital include:

- Client flight and loss of market share.
- Investor flight and increase in the cost of capital.
- Talent flight.
- Increases in contracting costs.

For practical purposes, reputational risk in the financial services sector is therefore associated with the possibility of loss in the going-concern value of the financial intermediary, which is to say the risk-adjusted value of expected future earnings. Reputational losses may be reflected in reduced operating revenues as clients and trading counterparties shift to competitors; increased compliance and other costs required to deal with the reputational problem, including opportunity costs; and an increased firm-specific risk perceived by the market. Reputational risk is often linked to operational risk, although there are important distinctions between the two. According to Basel II, operational risks are associated with people (internal fraud, clients, products, business practices, employment practices, and workplace safety), internal processes and systems, and external events (external fraud, damage or loss of assets, and force majeure). Operational risk is specifically *not* considered to include strategic and business risk, credit risk, market risk or systemic risk, or reputational risk.[4]

If reputational risk is bracketed out of operational risk from a regulatory perspective, then what is it? A possible working definition is as follows: Reputational risk comprises the risk of loss in the value of a firm's business franchise that extends beyond event-related accounting losses and is reflected in a decline in its share performance metrics. Reputation-related losses reflect reduced expected revenues and/or higher financing and contracting costs. Reputational risk, in turn, is related to the strategic positioning and execution of the firm, conflicts of interest exploitation, individual professional conduct, compliance and incentive systems, leadership, and the prevailing corporate culture. Reputational risk can frequently be rooted in conflicts of interest—between the firm and its clients, between clients, or within the financial firm itself.[5] Reputational risk is usually the consequence of management *processes* rather than discrete *events*, and, therefore, requires risk control approaches that differ materially from operational risk.

According to this definition, a reputation-sensitive event might trigger an identifiable monetary decline in the market value of the firm. After subtracting from this market capitalization loss the present value of direct and allocated costs, such as fines and penalties and settlements under civil litigation, the balance can be ascribed to the impact on the firm's reputation. Firms that promote themselves as reputational standard-setters will, accordingly, tend to suffer larger reputational losses than firms that have taken a lower profile—that is, reputational losses associated with identical events according to this definition may be highly idiosyncratic to the individual firm.

In terms of the overall hierarchy of risks faced by financial intermediaries, reputational risk is perhaps the most intractable. In terms of Exhibit 6.1, market risk is usually considered the most tractable, with adequate time-series and cross-sectional data availability, appropriate metrics to assess volatility and correlations, and the ability to apply techniques such as value at risk (VaR) and risk-adjusted return on capital (RAROC). Credit risk is arguably less tractable, given that many credits are on the books of financial intermediaries at historical values. The analysis of credit events in a portfolio context is less tractable than market risk in terms of the available metrics, although many types of credits have over the years become *marketized* through securitization structures such as asset-backed securities (ABSs) and collateralized loan obligations (CLOs), as well as derivatives such as credit default swaps (CDSs). These financial instruments are priced in both primary and secondary markets, and transfer some of the granularity and tractability found in market risk to the credit domain. Liquidity risk, by contrast, has both pluses and minuses in terms of tractability. In continuous markets, liquidity risk can be calibrated in terms of bid-offer spreads, although in times of severe market stress and flights to quality, liquidity can disappear.

If the top three risk domains in Exhibit 6.1 show a relatively high degree of manageability, the bottom three are frequently less manageable. Operational risk is a composite of highly manageable risks with a robust basis for suitable risk metrics

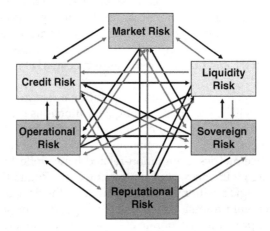

Exhibit 6.1 A Hierarchy of Risks Confronting Financial Intermediaries

together with risks that represent catastrophes and extreme values—tail events that are difficult to model and, in some cases, have never actually been observed. Here management is forced to rely on either simulations or external data to try to assess the probabilities and potential losses. Meanwhile, sovereign risk assessment basically involves applied political economy and relies on imprecise techniques, such as stylized facts analysis, so that the track record of even the most sophisticated analytical approaches is not particularly strong—especially under conditions of macro-stress and contagion. As in the case of credit risk, sovereign risk can be calibrated when sovereign foreign-currency bonds and sovereign default swaps (stripped of nonsovereign attributes like external guarantees and collateral) are traded in the market. This leaves reputational risk as perhaps the least tractable of all—with poor data, limited usable metrics, and strong fat-tail characteristics.

The other point brought out in Exhibit 6.1 relates to the linkages between the various risk domains. Even the most straightforward of these—such as the linkage between market risk and credit risk—are not easy to model or to value, particularly in a bidirectional form. There are 36 such linkages, exhibiting a broad range of tractability. It can be argued that the linkages that relate to reputational risk are among the most difficult to assess and to manage.

SOURCES OF REPUTATIONAL RISK

Where does reputational risk in financial intermediation originate? It may emanate in large part from the intersection between the financial firm and the competitive environment, on the one hand, and from the direct and indirect network of controls and behavioral expectations within which the firm operates, on the other hand, as depicted generically in Exhibit 6.2.[6] The franchise value of a financial institution as a going concern is calibrated against these two sets of benchmarks. One of them, market performance, tends to be relatively transparent and easy to reward

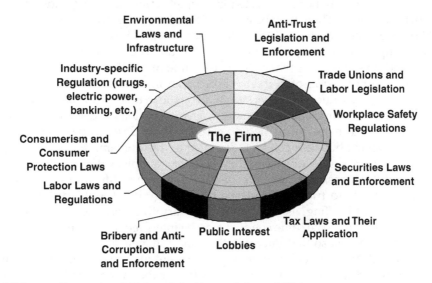

Exhibit 6.2 Reputational Risk and the External Control Web

or punish. The other, performance against corporate conduct benchmarks, is far more opaque but potentially more critical as a source of risk to shareholders.

Management must work to optimize with respect to both sets of benchmarks. If it strays too far in the direction of meeting the demands of social and regulatory controls, it runs the risks of poor performance in the market, punishment by shareholders, and possibly a change in corporate control. If it strays toward unrestrained market performance and sails too close to the wind in terms of questionable market conduct, its behavior may have disastrous results for the firm, its managers, and its shareholders. Such are the rules of the game, and financial intermediaries have to live with them.

But the rules are not immutable. There is constant tension between firms and regulators about appropriate constraints on corporate conduct. Sometimes financial intermediaries win battles (and even wars) leading to periods of deregulation. Sometimes it is possible to convince the public that self-regulation and market discipline are powerful enough to obviate the need for external control. Sometimes the regulators can be convinced, one way or another, to go easy. Then along comes another major transgression, and the constraint system reacts and creates a spate of new regulations. A wide array of interests get into this constant battle to define the rules under which financial business gets done—managers, politicians, the media, activists, investors, lawyers, and accountants—and eventually a new equilibrium gets established which will define the rules of engagement for the period ahead.

There are some more fundamental factors at work as well. Laws and regulations governing the market conduct of firms are not created in a vacuum. They are rooted in social expectations as to what is appropriate and inappropriate, which in turn are driven by values imbedded in society. These values are rather basic. They deal with lying, cheating, and stealing, with trust and honor, with what is right and wrong. These are the *ultimate* benchmarks against which conduct is measured and which may be the origins of key reputational losses. But fundamental values in society may or may not be reflected in people's *expectations* as to how a firm's conduct is assessed. There may be a good deal of slippage between social values and how these are reflected in the public expectations of business conduct.

Build-up of adverse opinion in the media, the formation of special-interest lobbies and pressure groups, and the general tide of public opinion with respect to one or another aspect of market conduct, can be reputationally debilitating. Moreover, neither values nor expectations are static in time. Both change. But values seem to change much more gradually than expectations. Indeed, fundamental values such as those previously noted are probably as close as one comes to constants in assessing business conduct. But even in this domain, things do change. As society becomes more diverse and mobile, for example, values tend to evolve. They also differ across cultures. And they are sometimes difficult to interpret. Is lying to clients or to trading counterparties wrong? What is the difference between lying and bluffing? Is the *context* necessary to determine how particular behavior is assessed? The same conduct may be interpreted differently under different circumstances, so that interpretations may change significantly over time and differ widely across cultures, giving rise to unique contours of reputational risk. There is additional slippage between society's expectations and the formation of public policy on the one hand, and the activities of public interest groups on the other.

Things may go on as usual for a while despite occasional media commentary about inappropriate behavior of a firm or an industry in the marketplace. Then, at some point, some sort of social tolerance limit is reached. A firm goes too far. A consensus emerges among various groups concerned with the issue. The system reacts through the political process, and a new set of constraints on firm behavior develops, possibly anchored in legislation, regulation, and bureaucracy. Or the firm is subject to class action litigation.[7] Or its reputation is so seriously compromised that its share price drops sharply. As managers review the reputational experiences of their competitors, they cannot escape an important message. Most financial firms can endure a credit loss or the cost of an unsuccessful trade or a broken deal, however large, and still survive. These are business risks that firms have learned to detect and limit their exposure to before the damage becomes serious. Reputational losses may be imposed by external reactions that may appear to professionals as unfocused or ambiguous, even unfair. They may also be new—a new reading of the rules, a new finding of culpability, something different from the way things were done before.

Although regulators and litigants, analysts, and the media are accepted by financial professionals as facts of life, such outsiders can be influenced by public uproar and political pressure, during which times it is difficult to defend an offending financial firm.[8] In the United States, for example, tighter regulation and closer surveillance, aggressive prosecution and plaintiff litigation, unsympathetic media and juries, and stricter guidelines for penalties and sentencing make it easier to get into trouble and harder to avoid serious penalties. Global brokerage and trading operations, for example, involve hundreds of different, complex, and constantly changing products that are difficult to monitor carefully under the best of circumstances. Doing this in a highly competitive market, where profit margins are under constant challenge and there is considerable temptation to break the rules, is even more challenging. Performance-driven managers, through compensation and promotion practices, have sometimes unwittingly encouraged behavior that has inflicted major reputational damage on their firms and destroyed some of them.

The reality is that the value of financial intermediaries suffers from such uncertain reputation-sensitive conditions. Since maximizing the value of the firm is supposed to be the ultimate role of management, its job is to learn how to run the firm so that it optimizes the long-term trade-offs between profits and external control. It does no good to plead unfair treatment—the task is for management to learn to live with it, and to make the most of the variables it can control.

The overall process can be depicted in the diagram in Exhibit 6.3, which represents the firm and its internal governance processes in the center and various layers of external controls affecting both the firm's conduct and the reputational consequences of misconduct—ranging from hard compliance components near the center to soft but potentially vital issues of appropriate conduct on the periphery. Clearly, serious reputational losses can impact a financial firm even if it is fully in compliance with regulatory constraints and its actions are entirely legal. The risk of reputational damage incurred in these outer fringes of the web of social control are among the most difficult to assess and manage. Nor is the constraint system necessarily consistent. There are important differences in regulatory regimes (as well as expectations regarding responsible conduct) across markets in which a firm is active, so that conduct which is considered acceptable in one environment may give rise to significant reputational risk in another.

Exhibit 6.3   Performance Gaps, Competition, and Conflict

VALUING REPUTATIONAL RISK

Recent research has attempted to quantify the impact of reputational risk on share prices during the 1980s and 1990s.[9] Given the nature of the problem, most of the evidence has been anecdotal, although a number of event studies have been undertaken in cases where the reputation-sensitive event was clean in terms of the release of the relevant information to the market.

Exhibit 6.4 summarizes shareholder value losses in a reputation-sensitive situation involving the aforementioned sources of loss: (1) client defections and revenue erosion; (2) increases in monetary costs comprising accounting write-offs associated with the event, increased compliance costs, regulatory fines, and legal settlements, as well as indirect costs related to loss of reputation, such as higher financing costs, contracting costs, and opportunity costs; and (3) increases in firm-specific (unsystematic) risk assigned by the market as a result of the reputational

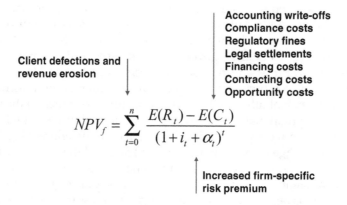

$$NPV_f = \sum_{t=0}^{n} \frac{E(R_t) - E(C_t)}{(1 + i_t + \alpha_t)^t}$$

Exhibit 6.4   Reputation-Sensitive Events in a Simple Going-Concern Valuation Framework

event in question. In order to value the pure reputational losses, it is necessary to estimate the overall market value loss of the firm to a reputation-sensitive event, and then deduct the monetary losses identified in Exhibit 6.4. Consider the following example.[10] On December 28, 1993, the Bank of Spain took control of the country's fourth largest bank, Banco Español de Crédito (Banesto). Subsequently, shares of J.P. Morgan, a U.S. bank holding company closely involved with Banesto, declined dramatically. Such a reaction appeared inconsistent with market rationality, given that the impact of the event on Morgan's bottom line was trivial inasmuch as the accounting loss to Morgan was unlikely to exceed $10 million after taxes. Perhaps something more than the underlying book value of J.P. Morgan was moving the price of the stock. In particular, the central bank takeover of Banesto may have affected the value of Morgan's corporate franchise in some of the firm's core business areas, notably securities underwriting, funds management, client advisory work, and its ability to manage conflicts of interest that can accompany such activities in nontransparent environments. J.P. Morgan was involved in Banesto in four ways, in addition to normal interbank transactions relationships:[11]

1. In May 1992, it began raising funds for the Corsair Partnership, LP, aimed at making noncontrolling investments in financial institutions. By February 1993, Morgan had raised over $1 billion from 46 investors, including pension funds and private individuals. Morgan served as general partner and fund manager, with an investment of $100 million. The Corsair Partnership's objective was to identify troubled financial institutions and, by improving their performance, earn a significant return to shareholders in the fund. The Corsair Partnership's first investment, undertaken in February 1993, was a share purchase of $162 million in Banesto, thereby giving Morgan a $16.2 million equity stake in the Spanish bank.
2. A vice-chairman of JP Morgan served on the Spanish bank's board of directors.
3. Morgan was directly advising Banesto on its financial and business affairs.
4. As part of an effort to recapitalize Banesto, Morgan was lead underwriter during 1993 of two stock offerings that totaled $710 million. The Corsair Partnership was intended to search for troubled financial institutions in the United States and abroad. The objective was to restructure such institutions by applying Morgan's extensive expertise and contacts. Morgan indicated that Corsair investors could expect a 30 percent annual return over 10 years. Although Morgan had a separate investment banking subsidiary (J.P. Morgan Securities, Inc.), Corsair was believed to be the first equity fund organized and managed by Morgan since the Glass-Steagall Act separated banking and securities activities in 1933, a separation which ended in 1999. The business concept of searching for troubled financial institutions emerged from a time of turmoil in the United States and foreign banking sectors. When the U.S. banking industry started to improve as a result of a favorable interest rate environment, Corsair ventured abroad. Corsair's first stake in Banesto was taken in February 1993. By August 1993, it had invested $162 million (23 percent of the funds raised) in the Spanish bank. The overall J. P. Morgan–Banesto relationship is depicted in Exhibit 6.5.

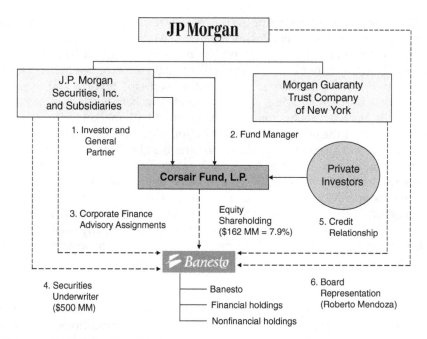

Exhibit 6.5   Reputational Risk Exposure: J.P. Morgan and Banco Español de Crédito, 1993

Banesto's problems stemmed from rapid growth and a convoluted structure of industrial holdings, followed by a serious downturn in the Spanish economy. The bank's lending book decreased from 4 trillion pesetas in 1988 to Pta. 2.3 trillion in 1991, a period when its competitors were growing at a quarter of that rate. Banesto bid aggressively for deposits, increasing interest rates by 51 percent while competitors increased theirs by 40 percent.

When the Spanish economy weakened, the bank was stuck with an array of bad loans and losses on its industrial holdings. In October 1992, after a partial audit, the Bank of Spain was forced to lend the troubled institution a substantial amount. A full audit released at the end of December 1993 revealed that Banesto assets of Pta. 5.5 trillion ($385 billion) were overvalued in excess of Pta. 50 billion ($3.5 billion). In April 1994, Banesto was bought for $2.05 billion by Banco Santander, leaving costs of $3.7 billion to be borne by the Spanish banks and by taxpayers.

Morgan had been advising Banesto on various deals since 1987. In July 1992, Morgan's involvement became more extensive when it began advising Banesto on how to raise capital. By August 1993, Morgan had assisted Banesto in two rights issues to raise $710 million. During the period of these rights issues, Corsair invested $162 million in Banesto. In a letter dated December 27, 1993, Morgan wrote to the Bank of Spain's governor, outlining how Banesto could continue to raise capital, including a bond issue that Morgan was planning to launch in the first quarter of 1993.

Instead, the Bank of Spain took control of Banesto on the following day, December 28, 1993. Citing mismanagement and reckless lending, the governor justified the action as being necessary to avoid a run on the deposits of the bank, whose share prices were falling sharply on the Madrid Exchange.

Given Morgan's multifaceted involvement in Banesto and potential conflicts imbedded in that relationship, the announcement of the takeover could have had a large effect on the value of Morgan's reputation and business franchise and hence its stock price. In order to test the impact of the Banesto case on the J.P. Morgan share price, the authors of a study of this case use conventional event study methodology.[12]

They create a sample prediction of returns on Morgan stock and compare the predicted returns with actual returns on Morgan shares after the Banesto event announcement.[13] The difference is considered the excess return attributable to the event, which is to say the difference between what shareholders would have received had they sold their shares in the market 50 days prior to the announcement and what they would have received if they had sold them on subsequent days. If the reputation effect hypothesis is correct, the market response to the Bank of Spain's announcement on December 28, 1993, should have significantly exceeded the firm's book exposure to Banesto.[14]

Prior to the announcement, Morgan stock behaved as predicted based on its behavior during the 250 days before the event period. A few days before announcement, the stock price began to decline. Thereafter, an essentially steady decline occurred. A cumulative loss of 10 percent of shareholder equity value is apparent 50 days after the announcement translates into a loss in J.P. Morgan market capitalization of approximately $1.5 billion versus a maximum direct loss of only $10 million from the Banesto failure.

This analysis suggests that the loss of an institution's franchise value can far outweigh an accounting loss when its reputation is called into question, a finding similar to that of Smith (1992) in the case of Salomon Brothers, Inc. Reasons for the adverse market reaction can only be conjectured. The takeover of Banesto could have been seen as compromising Morgan's reputation in precisely those areas key to its future. Inability to turn Banesto around may have called into question Morgan's ability to successfully advise clients. Banesto, as the dominant participant in the Corsair portfolio, may have suggested flaws in Morgan's ability to organize and manage certain equity funds. Difficulties with underwriting stock issues and placing shares with important investor-clients raises questions about its ability to judge risks in underwriting securities. Service on Banesto's board suggests problems with monitoring, and the configuration of Morgan's various involvements with Banesto suggests the potential for conflicts of interest or lack of objectivity. Whatever the linkages, here was a case of a financial services firm of exceedingly high standing, which in no way violated legal or regulatory constraints but whose shares nevertheless appeared to have been adversely affected by the market reaction to the way a high-profile piece of business was handled. In recent years, event studies such as this have yielded a growing body of evidence about share price sensitivity to reputational risk.

For example, Cummins, Lewis, and Wei (2006) undertook a large sample study of operational and reputational events contained in the Fitch OpVar database. Exhibit 6.6 shows the results in terms of the magnitude of the losses using three-factor estimation models in terms of cumulative abnormal returns (CARs) and number of trading days before and after the announcement. The authors, however, do not distinguish between operational losses and reputational losses, as defined earlier.

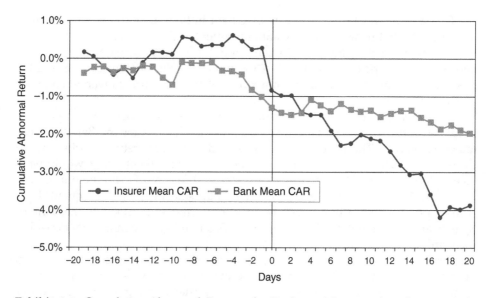

Exhibit 6.6 Cumulative Abnormal Returns for Banks and Insurers in a Large-sample Study of Operational and Reputational Events (Three-factor Models)
Source: J. David Cummins, Christopher M. Lewis and Ran Wei, "The Market Impact of Operational Risk Events for U.S. Banks and Insurers," *Journal of Banking and Finance* 30, no. 10 (October 2006): 2605–2634.

De Fontnouvelle et al. (2006) use loss data from the Fitch OpVar and SAS OpRisk databases to model operational risk for banks that are internationally active. In a series of robust statistical estimates, they find a high degree of regularity in operational losses that can be quantified. This would justify maintaining significant capital reserves against operational risk—see Exhibits 6.7 (page 115) and 6.8 (page 116). The paper also segments the losses by event type and by activity line, as well as whether the operational losses occurred in the United States. The largest losses involved retail and commercial and retail/private banking activities in terms of type of event. As in the case of other studies, the authors do not distinguish the associated accounting losses due to legal settlements, fines, penalties, and other explicit operational risk–related costs from reputational losses. As such, these estimates are relevant from a regulatory perspective but probably materially understate the losses to shareholders.

In a pilot study of 49 reputation-sensitive events, using the aforementioned definition and excluding operational events, we find negative mean CARs of up to 7 percent and $3.5 billion, depending on the event windows used.[15] Exhibit 6.9 (page 117) shows the results graphically, and the tables in Exhibits 6.10 (page 117) and 6.11 (page 118) show the numerical results. The results do not, however, distinguish between the associated monetary losses and the pure reputational losses.[16]

The only study to date that attempts to identify pure reputational losses is Karpoff, Lee, and Martin (2006). The authors attempt to distinguish book losses from reputational losses in the context of U.S. Securities and Exchange Commission enforcement actions related to earnings restatements or "cooking the books." The authors review 2,532 regulatory events in connection with all relevant SEC enforcement actions from 1978 to 2002 and the monetary costs of these actions in the ensuing period through 2005. These monetary costs are then compared with the

Exhibit 6.7 Operational Losses by Event Type

Event Type	SAS OpRisk % of All Losses	Percentiles ($M) 50%	75%	95%	Fitch OpVar % of All Losses	Percentiles ($M) 50%	75%	95%	Wilcoxon Test
All Event Types	100.0%	6	17	88	100.0%	6	17	93	90.2%
Internal Fraud	23.0%	4	10	42	27.0%	6	16	110	1.2%
External Fraud	16.5%	5	17	93	16.6%	4	12	70	33.2%
EPWS	3.0%	4	14	–	3.3%	5	11	–	95.0%
CPBP	55.5%	7	20	95	48.1%	7	20	99	96.3%
Damage to Physical Assets	0.4%	18	–	–	0.3%	20	–	–	92.9%
BDSF	0.2%	36	–	–	0.4%	10	–	–	38.0%
EDPM	1.3%	9	27	–	4.2%	4	11	–	14.6%
Kruskal-Wallis Test	6.4E-06				9.1E-05				

Panel B, Losses that occurred outside the U.S.

All Event Types	100.0%	10	36	221	100.0%	13	46	288	16.7%
Internal Fraud	48.5%	9	35	259	42.9%	15	62	381	1.5%
External Fraud	15.3%	7	27	–	21.6%	10	28	136	27.3%
EPWS	0.8%	7	–	–	1.6%	2	7	–	75.3%
CPBP	32.6%	14	51	374	28.6%	13	51	359	99.6%
Damage to Physical Assets	0.0%	–	–	–	0.3%	163	–	–	–
BDSF	0.8%	7	–	–	0.5%	3	–	–	42.3%
EDPM	1.9%	29	–	–	4.6%	5	19	–	8.1%
Kruskal-Wallis Test	11.8%				5.5E-05				

Source: Patrick de Fontnouvelle, Virginia DeJesus-Rueff, John S. Jordan, and Eric S. Rosengren, "Capital and Risk: New Evidence on Implications of Large Operational Losses," Federal Reserve Bank of Boston Working Paper, September 2006.

cumulative abnormal returns estimated from event studies to separate them from the reputational costs. The results are depicted in Exhibit 6.12 (page 118). Note that the reputational losses (66 percent) are far larger than the cost of fines (3 percent), class action settlements (6 percent), and accounting write-offs (25 percent) resulting from the events in question.

It is likely that the broader the range of a financial intermediary's activities, (1) the greater the likelihood that the firm will encounter exploitable conflicts of interest and reputational risk exposure; (2) the higher will be the potential agency costs facing its clients; and (3) the more difficult and costly will be the safeguards necessary to protect the value of the franchise. If this proposition is correct, costs associated with reputational risk mitigation can easily offset the realization of economies of scope in financial services firms—scope economies

Exhibit 6.8   Operational Losses by Business Line

Business Line	SAS OpRisk % of All Losses	Percentiles ($M) 50%	75%	95%	Fitch OpVar % of All Losses	Percentiles ($M) 50%	75%	95%	Wilcoxon Test
All Business Lines	100%	6	17	88	100%	6	17	93	90.2%
Corporate Finance	6%	6	23	–	4%	8	23	–	55.8%
Trading and Sales	9%	10	44	334	9%	10	27	265	89.2%
Retail Banking	38%	5	11	52	39%	5	12	60	73.1%
Commercial Banking	21%	7	24	104	16%	8	28	123	13.3%
Payment and Settlement	1%	4	11	–	1%	4	11	–	65.8%
Agency Services	2%	22	110	–	3%	9	28	–	10.3%
Asset Management	5%	8	20	–	6%	3	22	165	80.8%
Retail Brokerage	17%	4	12	57	22%	4	13	67	98.0%
Kruskal-Wallis Test					1.0E–12				

Panel B. Losses that occurred outside the U.S.

Business Line	SAS OpRisk % of All Losses	50%	75%	95%	Fitch OpVar % of All Losses	50%	75%	95%	Wilcoxon Test
All Business Lines	100%	10	36	221	100%	13	46	288	16.7%
Corporate Finance	2%	13	–	–	3%	12	27		69.3%
Trading and Sales	9%	30	125	–	12%	25	66	–	35.3%
Retail Banking	41%	6	27	101	44%	9	29	272	10.4%
Commercial Banking	30%	15	42	437	21%	35	91	323	2.4%
Payment and Settlement	1%	5	–	–	1%	13	–	–	17.7%
Agency Services	2%	45	–	–	3%	20	77	–	49.6%
Asset Management	3%	5	47	–	5%	7	23	–	90.1%
Retail Brokerage	12%	10	42	–	11%	8	34	–	42.6%
Kruskal-Wallis Test	6.6E–04				1.1E–05				

Source: Patrick de Fontnouvelle, Virginia DeJesus-Rueff, John S. Jordan, and Eric S. Rosengren, "Capital and Risk: New Evidence on Implications of Large Operational Losses," Federal Reserve Bank of Boston Working Paper, September 2006.

that are supposed to generate benefits on the demand side through cross-selling (revenue synergies) and on the supply side through more efficient use of the firm's business infrastructure (cost synergies). As a result of conflict exploitation, the firm may win and clients may lose in the first instance, but subsequent adverse reputational and regulatory consequences (along with efficiency factors such as the managerial and operational cost of complexity) can be considered diseconomies of scope.

Breadth of engagement with clients may create conflicts of interest that can be multidimensional and involve a number of different stakeholders at the same time. Several examples came to light during the corporate scandals in the early 2000s. Following the $103 billion bankruptcy of WorldCom in 2002, for example, it appeared that Citigroup, a multifunctional, global financial conglomerate, was serving as equity analyst, supplying assessments of WorldCom to institutional and (through the firm's brokers) retail clients, while simultaneously advising WorldCom management on strategic and financial matters. Citigroup's equity

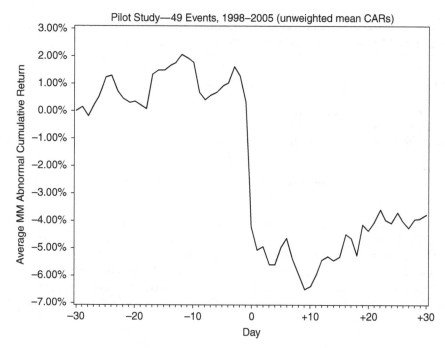

Exhibit 6.9 Reputational Impact and Share Prices
Source: Gayle De Long, Anthony Saunders, and Ingo Walter, "Pricing Reputation-Sensitive Events in Banking and Financial Services," New York University, Department of Finance Working Paper (in draft).

analyst at times participated in WorldCom's board meetings. As a major telecommunications-sector commercial and investment banking client, Citigroup maintained an active lending relationship with WorldCom and successfully competed for its securities underwriting business. At the same time, Citigroup served as the exclusive pension fund adviser to WorldCom and executed significant stock option trades for WorldCom executives, while at the same time conducting proprietary trading in WorldCom stock and holding a significant position in the

Exhibit 6.10 Relative CARs—Reputational Loss Pilot Study

Cumulative Abnormal Returns—Statistical Summary

Event window	(−5,3)	(−5,10)	(−1,3)	(−1,10)
Mean	−6.24%	−7.02%	−6.79%	−7.57%
Patell Z-score	−10.02	−7.63	−14.37	−9.41
Median	−4.59%	−4.92%	−4.55%	−4.96%
Bottom 95% loss	−38.17%	−44.97%	−35.88%	−44.37%
Bottom 99% loss	−62.57%	−47.52%	−63.78%	−48.73%
90% skew	−1.0907	0.1740	−1.2563	0.0538
90% kurtosis	0.0696	−4.6151	0.9144	−4.7431

Source: Gayle De Long, Anthony Saunders, and Ingo Walter, "Pricing Reputation-Sensitive Events in Banking and Financial Services," New York University, Department of Finance Working Paper (in draft).

Exhibit 6.11   Absolute CARs—Reputational Loss Pilot Study

Reputational Losses in Market Capitalization—Statistical Summary

Event window	(−5,3)	(−5,10)	(−1,3)	(−1,10)
Mean	−$3,300,009	−$3,485,131	−$1,765,038	−$1,950,161
p-value	0.0000	0.0013	0.0007	0.0049
Median	−$984,421	−$555,256	−$700,940	−$616,721
Bottom 95% loss	−$14,875,021	−$24,140,182	−$10,704,029	−$13,227,960
Bottom 99% loss	−$18,375,026	−$28,360,334	−$13,971,351	−$20,261,036
90% skew	−1.5269	0.2562	−0.5088	−1.3309
90% kurtosis	2.4720	−0.4915	0.1960	1.6990

company's stock through its asset management unit. Additionally, Citigroup advised the WorldCom CEO, financed his margin purchases of company stock, and provided loans for one of his private businesses.

On the one hand, Citigroup was very successfully engaged in the pursuit of revenue economies of scope (cross-selling), simultaneously targeting both the asset and liability sides of its client's balance sheet, generating advisory fee income,

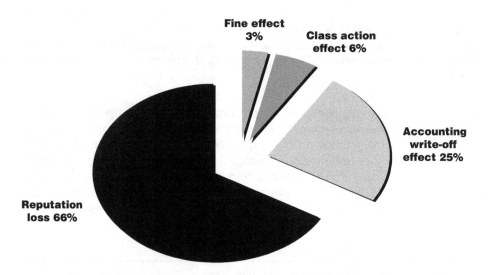

Data: All SEC enforcement actions 1978–2002 (2,532 regulatory events).
Actions and penalties tracked through November 15, 2005.
Mean CAR −38.06% = mean market value loss $397 million (24% higher for surviving firms).

Partitioned for sample:
Fines imposed on firms	$5.01 million
Class action payments	$8.59 million
Accounting write-off	$37.4 billion
Reputation loss	$101.5 billion

Exhibit 6.12   Decomposing CARs Related to Earnings Restatement
Source: Jonathan M. Karpoff, D. Scott Lee, and Gerald S. Martin, "The Cost to Firms of Cooking the Books," Social Science Research Network, March 8, 2006. Available at http://ssrn.com/abstract=652121.

managing assets, and meeting the private banking needs of WorldCom's CEO. However, that same success caught the firm in simultaneous conflicts of interest relating to retail investors, institutional fund managers, WorldCom executives, and shareholders, as well as Citigroup's own positions in WorldCom credit exposure and stock trades. WorldCom's bankruptcy triggered a large market capitalization loss for Citigroup's own shareholders, only about a third of which can be explained by a $2.65 billion civil settlement the firm reached with investors in May 2004.[17]

It seems plausible that the broader the range of services that a financial firm provides to a given client in the market, and the greater the cross-selling pressure, the greater the potential likelihood that conflicts of interest and reputational risk exposure will be compounded in any given case, and, when these conflicts of interest are exploited, the more likely they are to damage the market value of the financial firm's business franchise once they come to light. Similarly, the more active a financial intermediary becomes in principal transactions such as affiliated private equity businesses and hedge funds, the more exposed it is likely to be to reputational risk related to conflicts of interest.

CONCLUSION

This chapter attempts to define reputational risk and to outline the sources of such risk facing financial services firms. It then considers the key drivers of reputational risk in the presence of transactions costs and imperfect information, and surveys available empirical research on the impact of reputational losses imposed on financial intermediaries. We conclude that market discipline, through the reputation effects on the franchise value of financial intermediaries, can be a powerful complement to regulation and civil litigation. Nevertheless, market discipline–based controls remain controversial. Financial firms continue to encounter serious instances of reputation loss due to misconduct despite its effects on the value of their franchises. This suggests material lapses in the governance and management process.[18]

Dealing with reputational risk can be an expensive business, with compliance systems that are costly to maintain and various types of walls between business units and functions that impose significant opportunity costs due to inefficient use of information within the organization. Moreover, management of certain kinds of reputational exposure in multifunctional financial firms may be sufficiently difficult to require structural remediation. However, reputation losses can cause serious damage, as demonstrated by reputation-sensitive, apparent accidents that seem to occur repeatedly in the financial services industry. Indeed, it can be argued that such issues contribute to market valuations among financial conglomerates that fall below valuations of more specialized financial services businesses (Laeven and Levine 2005; Schmid and Walter 2006).[19] The massive shrinkage of market values of financial firms in 2007–2009 depicted in Exhibit 6.13 certainly embodies reputational damage that will make it even more difficult to recover after the crisis ebbs.

Managements and boards of financial intermediaries must be convinced that a good defense is as important as a good offense in determining sustainable competitive performance. This is something that is extraordinarily difficult to put into practice in a highly competitive environment for both financial services firms and

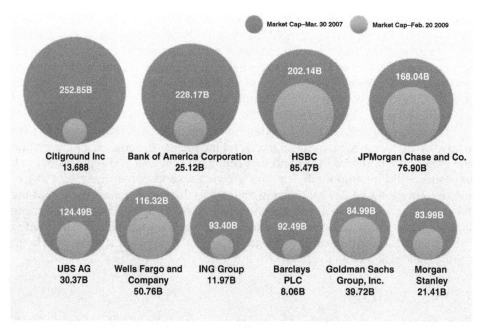

Exhibit 6.13   Declines in Market Capitalization of Major Banks, 2007–2009
Source: MyBankTracker.com.

for the highly skilled professionals that comprise the industry. A good defense requires an unusual degree of senior management leadership and commitment (Smith and Walter 1997). Internally, there have to be mechanisms that reinforce the loyalty and professional conduct of employees. Externally, there has to be careful and sustained attention to reputation and competition as disciplinary mechanisms. In the end, it is probably leadership more than anything else that separates winners from losers over the long term—the notion that appropriate professional behavior reinforced by a sense of belonging to a quality franchise constitutes a decisive competitive advantage.

NOTES

1. For the ensuing report, see http://www.iasplus.com/crunch/0804iifbestpractices.pdf.
2. See http://careers.hereisthecity.com/front_office/corporate_and_investment_banking/press_releases/124.cntns.
3. Earlier studies focusing on reputation include Chemmanur and Fulghieri (1994), Smith (1992), Walter and De Long (1995), and Smith and Walter (1997).
4. Basel II at http://www.bis.org/publ/bcbs107.htm.
5. See for example Attorney General (2003), Demsky (2003), Herman (1975), Krozner and Strahan (1999), Saunders (1985), Schotland (1980), and Walter (2004).
6. For an early discussion of external conduct benchmarks, see Galbraith (1973).
7. For a discussion, see Capiello (2006).
8. For a full examination of these issues, see Smith and Walter (1997).

9. For one of the early studies, see Smith (1992).

10. Walter and DeLong (1995).

11. For a journalistic account, see various 1994 issues of the *Wall Street Journal* and *Euromoney*. These matters were discussed there in great detail.

12. De Long and Walter (1994). For event study methodology, see Brown and Warner (1985).

13. In order to create this prediction, we regressed the daily return of Morgan stock on the daily return on the market index as well as on an industry-group index. The industry-group index included 20 financial institutions with characteristics showing some degree of overlap with those of J.P. Morgan. This was the unweighted average of share prices for Banc One, BankAmerica, Bank of Boston, Bank of New York, Bankers Trust NY, Barnett Bank, Bear Stearns, Chase Manhattan, Chemical Bank, Citicorp, Continental Bank, First Chicago, First Fidelity Bancorp, First Virginia, Merrill Lynch, Morgan Stanley Group, NationsBank, Paine Webber Group, Salomon Inc., and Wells Fargo. We used data from 300 days to 50 days prior to the announcement date (December 28, 1993). The resulting coefficients were then multiplied by the returns on the market and industry indexes from 50 days prior to 50 days after the announcement, in order to obtain an estimation of the daily stock return during this period. Then the excess return was calculated at the predicted return minus the actual Morgan stock returns for the period, and the cumulative excess return was plotted. In order to translate these results into the monetary effect on J.P. Morgan stock, the cumulated excess return was multiplied by the total market value of equity (shares outstanding times price per share) 50 days before the announcement.

14. We regressed Morgan's stock returns against the value-weighted NYSE index and the industry group composed of 20 banking and securities firms. While autocorrelation can be a problem in using daily stock returns, J.P. Morgan stock was heavily traded, so that daily carryover is unlikely to be significant. Indeed, when we controlled the industry for this potential problem by including the lagged market index as a regression, the resulting coefficient was negative and statistically insignificant. We obtained the following model, estimated over days −300 to −50 prior to the announcement date:

$$R_{JPMt} = -0.00014 + 0.5766 \times R_{Mt} + 0.2714 \times R_{Gt} + u_t$$

where R_{JPMt} = return on J.P. Morgan stock
R_{Mt} = return on NYSE composite (value-weighted) index
R_{Gt} = return on group of companies in the same industry.

The excess return attributable to the event is the calculated residual (u_t) from 50 days prior to 50 days after the announcement.

15. Based on an ongoing empirical study of reputational risk being conducted at the Stern School of Business, New York University.

16. Based on ongoing empirical work on reputation-sensitive financial services events with Gayle De Long and Anthony Saunders.

17. Similar issues surfaced in the case of the 2001 Enron bankruptcy. See Batson (2003) and Healy and Palepu (2003).

18. These issues are explored in Daniel Hoechle, Markus Schmid, Ingo Walter, and David Yermack, "Corporate Governance and the Diversification Discount," available at http://papers.ssrn.com/sol3/papers.cfm?abstract_id=1341006.

19. See also Kanatas and Qi (2003) and Saunders and Walter (1997).

REFERENCES

Attorney General of the State of New York. 2003. *Global settlement: Findings of fact*. Albany, NY: Office of the State Attorney General.

Batson, Neal. 2003. *Final report*, Chapter 11, Case no. 01-16034 (AJG), United States Bankruptcy Court, Southern District of New York, July 28.

Brown, Stephen J., and Jerold B. Warner. 1985. Using daily stock returns: The case of event studies. *Journal of Financial Economics* 14:3–31.

Capiello, S. 2006. Public enforcement and class actions against conflicts of interest in universal banking: The U.S. experience vis-à-vis recent Italian initiatives. Working Paper, Bank of Italy, Law and Economics Research Department.

Chemmanur, Thomas J., and Paolo Fulghieri. 1994. Investment bank reputation, information production, and financial intermediation. *Journal of Finance* 49:57–86.

Cummins, J. David, Christopher M. Lewis, and Ran Wei. 2006. The market impact of operational risk events for U.S. banks and insurers. *Journal of Banking and Finance* 30:2605–2634.

De Fontnouvelle, Patrick, Virginia DeJesus-Rueff, John S. Jordan, and Eric S. Rosengren. 2006. Capital and risk: New evidence on implications of large operational losses. Working Paper, Federal Reserve Bank of Boston (September).

De Long, Gayle, and Ingo Walter. 1994. J.P. Morgan and Banesto: An event study. Working Paper, New York University Salomon Center (April).

Demsky, Joel S. 2003. Corporate conflicts of interest. *Journal of Economic Perspectives* 17:51–72.

Galbraith, John Kenneth. 1973. *Economics and the public purpose*. New York: Macmillan.

Herman, Edward S. 1975. *Conflicts of interest: Commercial banks and trust companies*. New York: Twentieth Century Fund.

Healey, Paul M., and Krishna G. Palepu. 2003. The fall of Enron. *Journal of Economic Perspectives* 17:3–26.

International Monetary, Fund. 2009. *Global financial stability report*. Washington, DC: IMF (April).

Kanatas, George, and Jianping Qi. 2003. Integration of lending and underwriting: Implications of scope economies. *Journal of Finance* 58:1167–1191.

Krozner, Randall S., and Philip E. Strahan. 1999. Bankers on boards, conflicts of interest, and lender liability. Working Paper no. W7319, National Bureau of Economic Research (August).

Laeven, Luc, and Ross, Levine. 2007. Is there a diversification discount in financial conglomerates? *Journal of Financial Economics* 85:331–367.

Saunders, Anthony. 1985. Conflicts of interest: An economic view. In *Deregulating Wall Street*, ed. Ingo Walter. New York: John Wiley & Sons.

Saunders, Anthony, and Ingo Walter. 1997. *Universal banking in the United States: What could we gain? What could we lose?* New York: Oxford University Press.

Schmid, Markus M., and Ingo Walter. 2009. Do financial conglomerates create or destroy economic value? *Journal of Financial Intermediation* 14:78–94.

Schotland, R.A. 1980. *Abuse on Wall Street: Conflicts of interest in the securities markets*. Westport, CT: Quantum Books.

Smith, Clifford W. 1992. Economics and ethics: The case of Salomon Brothers. *Journal of Applied Corporate Finance* 5:23–28.

Smith, Roy C., and Ingo Walter. 1997. *Street smarts: Linking professional conduct and shareholder value in the securities industry*. Boston: Harvard Business School Press.

Walter, Ingo. 2004. Conflicts of interest and market discipline in financial services firms. In *Market Discipline Across Countries and Industries*, ed. Claudio Borio, William Curt Hunter, George G. Kaufman, and Kostas Tsatsaronis. Cambridge: MIT Press.

Walter, Ingo, and Gayle DeLong. 1995. The reputation effect of international merchant bank-
    ing accidents: Evidence from stock market data. Working Paper, New York University
    Salomon Center.

ABOUT THE AUTHOR

Ingo Walter is the Seymour Milstein Professor of Finance, Corporate Governance
and Ethics at the Stern School of Business, New York University, and dean of
faculty. He has taught at New York University since 1970, and served a number of
terms as associate dean for academic affairs, chair of International Business, chair
of Finance, and, from 1990 to 2003, as director of the New York University Salomon
Center for the Study of Financial Institutions. Since 1985 he has also been affiliated
with INSEAD in Fontainebleau, France, and serves as a consultant to various
corporations, banks, government agencies, and international institutions, and has
authored or co-authored numerous books and articles in the fields of international
trade policy, international banking, environmental economics, and economics of
multinational corporate operations. Among his recent publications are *Governing
the Modern Corporation* (Oxford University Press, 2006) and "Can Microfinance
Reduce Portfolio Volatility?" *Economic Development and Cultural Change*, 58 (2009).

CHAPTER 7

Agency Theory

JOSEPH HEATH
Professor, Department of Philosophy and School of Public Policy and Governance,
University of Toronto

INTRODUCTION

Agency theory, or principal-agent theory, is a methodological approach that involves the application of game theory to the analysis of a particular class of social interactions, namely "situations in which one individual (the agent) acts on behalf of another (the principal) and is supposed to advance the principal's goals" (Milgrom and Roberts 1992, 170). The term *agent* is used differently here than in certain other contexts, such as commercial law, where the *law of agency* assigns a much narrower meaning to the term (see Clark 1985, 56). In the legal sense, an agent is one who is entitled to negotiate on behalf of a principal or bring the principal into a contractual relation with some third party. The game-theoretic sense is much broader, dealing (at least in principle) with any sort of interaction between two individuals where one is trying to influence the actions of the other. In part because of this potential for confusion, some agency theorists have taken to redescribing their work as simply "the theory of incentives" (Laffont and Martimort 2002; Campbell 1995).

Agency theory is highly relevant to the field of finance, because the dominant approach to understanding the structure of the corporation involves analyzing it as a set of agency relations (Jensen 2000, 5–6). Traditional microeconomic models of the market economy are built using the assumption that firms maximize profits. Yet this in no way follows from the standard microeconomic behavioral assumption that individuals maximize utility. Even if one assumes that increased wealth and increased utility correspond fairly neatly, the fact that individuals maximize their own utility does not imply that, when they get together as a group, they will naturally or spontaneously act in such a way as to maximize some joint utility function. They may just as easily fall into collective action problems. Thus, many theorists consider it the role of a theory of the firm to explain "how the conflicting objectives of the individual participants are brought into equilibrium so as to yield this result"—that is, profit maximization (Jensen 2000, 84). In this respect, an agency-theoretic approach to the theory of the firm is a natural extension of economic theory from an analysis of markets to an analysis of the internal structure of corporations, in order to bridge the gap between the utility-maximization hypothesis and the profit-maximization assumption.

CONFLICT WITH BUSINESS ETHICS

This approach has been met with fairly hostile response by business ethicists (e.g., Bowie and Freeman 1992), primarily because game theory comes freighted with a number of substantive theoretical assumptions, including most prominently a commitment to an instrumental (or economic) model of rational action. This approach is famous for classifying certain forms of moral action as irrational, or else rationalizing morality through the discovery and ascription of some underlying nonmoral incentive. Thus, ethicists often complain that agency theorists, by adopting an economic model of action, thereby assume that rational individuals are self-interested, or that they act only from egoistic and not altruistic motives (Dobson 1997, 3–7). This is, from their point of view, equivalent to endorsing moral skepticism and is, therefore, unhelpful as a point of departure for the development of a system of applied ethics. Others have gone further, arguing that it is positively pernicious. Sumantra Ghoshal argued that "by propagating ideologically inspired amoral theories, business schools have actively freed their students from any sense of moral responsibility," which in turn has encouraged "many of the worst excesses of recent management practice" (Ghoshal 2005, 76; see also Khurana, Nohria, and Penrice 2005; and Kulik 2005).

The standard response from agency theorists to this criticism is to say that the economic model of rationality does not privilege self-interest or egoism. Utility is defined with respect to the preferences of individuals, and preferences reflect whatever desires individuals happen to have, whether egoistic or altruistic (Jensen 2000, 5). Thus, what creates the need for incentives in principal-agent relations, strictly speaking, is not the fact that the principal and the agent have egoistic preferences, but merely the fact that they have *different* preferences. Principal-agent theory is about how individuals manage situations involving "goal incongruity" between two or more persons (Dees 1992, 37–38). It does not matter whether they are selfish or not; what matters is that each acts in pursuit of his or her *own* goals, and that the goals of the other show up only insofar as they affect that agent's goals, or ability to satisfy these goals.

Yet while agency theorists may be justified in thinking that much of the criticism coming from ethicists is predicated upon an incomplete or faulty understanding of the underlying model, this does not mean that agency theory is entirely innocent from the moral point of view or that it has not served as a source of mischief in many organizations. In order to clarify the issues, it is important first to get clear on the sort of theoretical commitments that are essential to agency theory, in order to distinguish between agency theory itself and certain incorrect interpretations that have become widely promulgated. It is also important to be more specific about the different ways that agency theory can be used to analyze relations within the firm, in order to determine whether it is the use or the abuse of agency theory that has become a source of mischief. Finally, it is important to be more specific about the circumstances in which moral obligations can arise out of agency relations. Only then is it possible to develop a more balanced appreciation of the contribution that agency theory can make to the study of finance ethics.

AGENCY THEORY AND SELF-INTEREST

The idea that game theorists are committed to the claim that individuals care only about money is clearly mistaken. Indeed, as Ken Binmore once pointed out, "it was game theorists who were largely responsible for constructing modern utility theory because it was so obvious to them that it is inadequate to model people as maximizers of money" (1999, 33). Such assurances, combined with the fact that satisfaction of altruistic preferences can serve as a source of utility, has led some business ethicists to conclude that agency theory is perfectly neutral, from the moral point of view. Allen Buchanan takes this position when he writes:

> *If, in applying principal/agent theory, it were necessary to assume that motivation is exclusively or primarily self-interested, this would greatly reduce if not vitiate the enterprise. However, we need not do so. Instead, we can proceed on the assumption that the conflicts of interest that give rise to agency-risks may result from a variety of motivations, on the part of agents and principals. All that is necessary is that there be conflicts of interest (Buchanan 1996, 421).*

Of course, in fairness to those business ethicists who have complained about the self-interest assumption, it should be noted that one can search the economic "theory of the firm" literature for a very long time before finding an actual example of an agency analysis that ascribes altruistic motives to any of the parties involved. Even if the theoretical framework does not force them to do so, agency theorists often do make unflattering empirical assumptions about individual preferences, by stipulating in their models that, for example, work effort has negative utility, money rewards have positive utility, and individuals have no other relevant motives (Dees 1992, 29). Strictly speaking, however, such assumptions are not essential to the economic model of rationality, and so theorists like Binmore and Buchanan are quite correct to point out that agency theory per se entails no commitment to such claims. It would be premature, however, to conclude on this basis that the economic conception of rationality is neutral from the standpoint of ethics. There are a number of other substantive theoretical commitments associated with the instrumental model that are hostile from the perspective of the ethicist and that cannot be purged from the model so easily.

The first of the two outstanding problems stems directly from the tendency among game theorists to *black-box* all questions of motivation. While this theoretical strategy does allow them to sidestep disputes over altruism and egoism, it also leaves them without a developed theory of preference formation, and thus without any ability to model the way that preference changes arise out of social interactions (Knight 1992, 18). Preferences are taken as given, and are also taken to be independent of strategies. Thus, players in a standard game-theoretic model cannot change each other's preferences through their actions. This is closely related to the fact that in standard game-theoretic models players are explicitly precluded from communicating with one another (Nash 1951). Furthermore, insofar as they *are* able to communicate with one another, standard game-theoretic solution concepts, such as Nash equilibrium, do not apply (Heath 2001, 73–78). This nontrivial restriction on game-theoretical models is often conveniently forgotten by those who are eager to apply them to the analysis of empirical interactions.

Because there is no generally accepted theory of endogenous preference change in games, agency theorists have devoted almost all of their time and attention to studying the way that external incentives can be used to bring about greater alignment of goals in cases of incongruity. This often turns into a classic case of economists searching where the light is best. For instance, in their widely used management textbook on organizational theory, game theorists Paul Milgrom and John Roberts (1992) dedicate an entire chapter to the subject of moral hazard and agency relations within the firm. They canvass an exhaustive range of strategies for controlling employee shirking, including monitoring, incentive contracts, performance pay, ownership stakes, employee bonding, and promotional systems. At the same time, they fail to mention such absolutely elementary factors as whether employees enjoy their jobs, and whether they love or hate the firm that they work for (1992, 179–192). Similarly, in their chapter on human resources policy, Milgrom and Roberts have a lengthy discussion of employee retention strategies, which does not once mention the fact that employees sometimes feel a sense of loyalty toward the firm (and that managers have it within their power to cultivate such loyalties).

Once again, though, this emphasis on external incentives is not a necessary consequence of the commitment to the economic conception of rational action. There is nothing intrinsic to agency theory that prevents people from taking an interest in the way that *internal* incentives such as preference change can be used to overcome agency problems; it is just that game theorists have no idea how to model such processes, and so have largely chosen to ignore them. Thus, the emphasis on external incentives is simply a case of methodologically induced bias, which could be corrected through the development of more sophisticated modeling techniques—or even just a frank acknowledgment of the need for qualitative analysis in this domain. So again, there is no reason in principle for the ethicist to object to the use of agency theory.

The second outstanding problem, however, has no quick fix. It involves the commitment on the part of the agency theorist to the view that individuals will behave *opportunistically* whenever given the chance to do so. There are two components of opportunism in the standard (i.e., dictionary) sense of the term: first, that of taking advantage of circumstances as they arise, and second, that of acting without regard for principle. Entering into a cooperative agreement, then reneging once the other party has performed, is the paradigm example. Agency theorists routinely assume that regardless of what people *say* they are going to do, they will always update their plans as the situation unfolds, and renege on any prior commitments whenever it is in their interest to do so. Thus, a farmer may hire workers who promise to harvest his crop, but find himself facing a strike threat at a critical time during the season when it is too late to bring in replacement workers (Milgrom and Roberts 1992, 128). An insurance company may agree to indemnify any policy holder who suffers a particular sort of loss, but then drag its feet when the time comes to pay the claim (e.g., by proposing unusual legal interpretations of certain exclusion clauses). Employees may agree to give some particular job their full attention, but then shirk in various ways in situations where their effort level is unobservable, and so on.

Along with this characterization of opportunistic behavior comes the assumption that individuals are unable to credibly commit themselves to refraining from opportunism, unless they are able to create some external incentive structure that changes their own future incentives (such as posting a bond to guarantee perfor-mance). Promises to perform are basically cheap talk, and the rational principal will disregard them when it comes to managing agency relations.

Ethicists are unlikely to regard this as a satisfactory framework for analysis, since it suggests that rationality encourages individuals to exhibit a variety of vices, including fickleness (in Machiavelli's sense of the term), dissimulation, treachery, and guile. It also follows very closely upon this that rational agents will treat each other with distrust and suspicion. Thus, agency theory seems to take some of the worst assumptions about human nature and build them into its central definition of rationality. Furthermore, in this case the standard evasive response is not available to the agency theorist. Unlike the egoism postulate, which is in fact peripheral to the instrumental conception of rationality, the assumption of opportunistic behavior is absolutely central to the model. The fact that agents are unable to make commitments is one of the defining postulates of noncooperative game theory (Nash 1951).

What we typically refer to as *opportunistic* behavior is a direct consequence of agents acting in accordance with the general game-theoretic principle known as *sequential rationality*. This is simply the view that, in a multistage game, a rational strategy must not only be utility-maximizing at the point at which it is chosen, but each of its component actions must also be utility-maximizing at the point at which it is to be performed. The sequential rationality postulate is what licenses, among other things, the use of backward induction as a method for solving multistage or repeated games (Fudenberg and Tirole 1991, 72–74), as well as the *subgame perfection* solution concept, which is the most uncontroversial refinement of Nash equilibrium (Selten 1975). It is so deeply entrenched that, in most cases, game theorists don't even bother to mention it. Eric Rasmusen, for example, in his widely used textbook on game theory, discusses the principle only once, in order to explain why he will not be mentioning it again:

> The term sequential rationality *is used to denote the idea that a player should maximize his payoffs at each point in the game, re-optimizing his decisions at each point and taking into account the fact that he will re-optimize in the future. This is a blend of the economic idea of ignoring sunk costs and rational expectations. Sequential rationality is so standard a crite-rion for equilibrium now that often I will speak of "equilibrium" without the qualifier when I wish to refer to an equilibrium that satisfies sequential rationality (Rasmusen 1989, 95).*

Opportunism, from this perspective, is just a somewhat moralizing way of de-scribing the phenomenon of reoptimization, and as such, it is not easy to get rid of as a game-theoretic assumption. On the contrary, it comes very close to capturing the essence of the *strategic* conception of rationality. Central to this conception is the consequentialism postulate, which states simply that the value of an action is a function of its anticipated consequences, and nothing else (the commitment to reoptimization follows almost immediately from this consequentialism). Yet consequentialism precludes the possibility that a rational agent might incorporate *deontic constraints*—principles associated directly with actions, independent of their consequences—into his deliberations (or what Robert Nozick [1974, 28–32] refers to as "side constraints"). Since genuine loyalty, commitment, conformity to social norms, and respect for moral rules are all forms of deontic constraint, this is a very significant restriction.

Thus, when a critic like Eric Noreen claims that "at the heart of agency theory, as expounded in accounting, finance and economics, is the assumption that people act unreservedly in their own narrowly defined self-interest with, if necessary, guile and deceit" (1988, 359), he is only partially mistaken. While it is incorrect to say that self-interest, narrowly defined, is at the heart of agency theory, it is correct to associate agency theory with the view that people act unreservedly, using guile and deceit—not only when necessary, but whenever it is advantageous for them to do so. Thus, the image of employees loafing around whenever the boss isn't looking, faking disabilities, calling in sick during hunting or fishing season, exaggerating the difficulty of their assignments in order to make their performance appear more impressive, and so on (Milgrom and Roberts 1992, 170), is a nonaccidental consequence of the agency perspective. Because of this, business ethicists do have some legitimate concerns about the agency theory framework, insofar as it incorporates a controversial conception of rationality, one that presupposes the correctness of a certain form of moral skepticism.

AGENCY THEORY AND SHAREHOLDER PRIMACY

There is a second issue with agency theory that has been a source of concern among ethicists. In many people's minds there is a very close connection between agency theory and the doctrine of shareholder primacy. Margaret Blair, for instance, in her influential work on team production theory, starts out by defining the "principal-agent" model of the firm as the view that "public corporations are little more than bundles of assets collectively owned by shareholders (principals) who hire directors and officers (agents) to manage those assets on their behalf" (Blair and Stout 1999, 248). Similarly, Milgrom and Roberts, after defining the principal-agent relationship, go on to assert that "senior executives of corporations are charged with advancing the interests of the stockholders, who are the owners of the corporation," and that these executives are therefore "agents of the stockholders" (1992, 181). Michael Jensen and William Meckling, after offering a brief introduction to agency theory, argue that "the relationship between the stockholders and the managers of a corporation fits the definition of a pure agency relationship" (1976, 309), and proceed to analyze the firm on that basis.

Jensen and Meckling present this as though it were purely an empirical observation—a *positive* claim about the structure of the firm, not a *normative* claim about how the firm should be organized. Yet it is not clear that describing a particular relationship as a "principal-agent" relationship can ever be normatively neutral. This is because, in any sort of social interaction, both parties influence one another to varying degrees. Thus, any purely positive definition of the agency relationship is bound to create ambiguity concerning who is the agent and who is the principal. Donald Campbell, for instance, in his textbook on incentive theory, states that "the principal is the individual whose welfare is to be served and this welfare is affected by an agent who makes decisions on behalf of the principal" (1995, 8). He then illustrates this with the standard example of a person taking a taxi from the airport, with the passenger as principal and the driver as agent. Yet in this interaction, as in many others, both individuals make decisions that affect the welfare of the other. The only way to infer the "correct" agency relationship is to understand the phrases "whose welfare is *to be served*" and "makes decisions *on behalf of*" in normative terms. The principal is the one whose welfare *ought* to be served; and the agent is the one who is under an obligation to serve the principal faithfully (and, typically, is in a position to abuse an information asymmetry).

With Milgrom and Roberts's definition, this normative structure is much more apparent. As we saw earlier, they define the agent as the one who is *supposed* to advance the principal's goals. One can see, however, that with this sort of definition, it is not uncontroversial to say that the relationship between managers and shareholders is that of agent to principal (Newton 1992, 100–101; Blair and Stout 1999, 252). Indeed, proponents of normative stakeholder theory would regard it as straightforwardly question-begging to say that the manager is *supposed* to advance the interests of shareholders, to the exclusion of other constituency groups. Similarly, it is not obvious that employees are agents of their superiors. Workers also depend upon managers to make decisions that will protect their jobs and preserve the value of the firm-specific human capital that they have accumulated (Blair 2000, 67; Dees 1992, 37). Or, to take a less controversial example, with respect to the management of defined-benefit pension schemes it is natural to describe employees as the principals, with managers of the firm serving as their agents.

Jensen and Meckling define an agency relationship as "a contract under which one or more persons—the principal(s)—engage another person—the agent—to perform some service on their behalf that involves delegating some decision-making authority to the agent" (1976, 308). Yet, as stakeholder theorists are fond of pointing out, managers have no explicit contract with shareholders, nor do they stand in a fiduciary relationship to them. They have contracts with the *firm*, and are fiduciaries for the *firm* (Blair and Stout 1999, 292). The relationship between the firm and its shareholders is, in turn, very complicated, making it difficult to say that shareholders have "hired" managers or engaged them "to perform some service on their behalf." The standard response is to say that there is an *implicit* contract in this case (Easterbrook and Fischel 1991, 99–93), but again, that will be disputed by anyone who does not accept the general thrust of the shareholder primacy doctrine. Typically, the sort of implicit contracts that are posited are simply implied by the theory of the firm that the person who is doing the ascribing happens to endorse.

But despite these controversies, none of them add up to a criticism of agency theory per se. Anyone who tries to map the principal-agent framework onto the relationship between shareholders and management is clearly *presupposing* the doctrine of shareholder primacy (i.e., the managers *ought* to serve the interest of shareholders). Thus, it would be question-begging to argue that managers should serve the interests of shareholders *because* they are agents of the shareholders. But a theorist could quite easily employ agency theory as a framework for understanding various relationships within the firm without presupposing the doctrine of shareholder primacy. Indeed, it is worth recalling that R. Edward Freeman makes liberal use of agency vocabulary in his work on stakeholder theory. He even introduces an "agency principle" in his Doctrine of Fair Contracts, specifying that "any agent must serve the interests of all stakeholders" (1994, 417; 1998, 134). In his view, the best way to think of stakeholder management is in terms of a set of agency relationships between members of the board of directors and the various constituency groups that have a *stake* in the success of the firm. Thus, the connection between agency theory and the doctrine of shareholder primacy is not a necessary one.

There are, of course, many powerful arguments for the doctrine of shareholder primacy that rely upon agency-theoretic premises and analysis. For instance, there is the observation that those who are residual claimants with respect to the revenues of the firm are likely to suffer the most serious agency risks in their dealings with management, and therefore have the greatest interest in exercising the sort of formal control associated with ownership (Hansmann 1996, 35–38). Thus one way of understanding shareholder control is to see it as a way of minimizing agency costs in the firm. Thanks to arguments such as this, many agency *theorists* are committed to the doctrine of shareholder primacy. Nevertheless, agency *theory* is not.

AGENCY THEORY AND MISPLACED LOYALTY

Another prominent line of objection to agency theory is centered upon the claim that agency relationships, even fiduciary relationships, cannot serve as a genuine *source* of moral obligation; rather, they serve only to *transmit* moral obligations from one person to another. More often, however, agency relationships are used as an excuse for unethical conduct, as agents seek to avoid responsibility by claiming that they are merely "following orders" or "serving the client." From this perspective, agency theory is nothing but a giant distraction, a way of passing the buck when it comes to confronting the problem of unethical behavior in business. Either the agent's action is ethical, in which case the agency relationship has nothing to do with it and the source must be traced back to some obligation imposed upon the principal; or it is unethical, and the agency relationship serves only to obscure that fact, by suggesting that it was done out of loyalty or obligation to the principal. In both cases, the agency relationship has nothing to do with the moral obligations that individuals are subject to, and so business ethicists gain nothing by focusing upon it.

Kenneth Goodpaster has tried to provide a principled basis for this critique, by introducing what he calls the *nemo dat* principle. The reference is to the Latin proverb (and legal rule), *nemo dat quod non habet*, or "Nobody gives what he doesn't have." Goodpaster uses this to draw attention to the fact that agency relationships are unable to create moral permissions where previously none existed. Principals cannot (ethically) hire someone to do on their behalf what they could not (ethically) do themselves (Goodpaster 1991, 68). In a similar vein, Richard DeGeorge takes pains to emphasize that "acting for another does not give one ethical license," and that "all persons are ethically responsible for their actions, whether performed under command or performed on behalf of another" (1992, 6). Yet, since the agency relationship cannot be a source of moral permissions, it is then claimed that whether managers act as agents of shareholders, or of anyone else for that matter, is an issue that is simply lacking in moral significance.

This view does have some prima facie plausibility. It is a well-known feature of conventional morality that promising to help a friend commit a crime, for example, does not generate a moral obligation on one's part to commit that crime. To allow this would be to permit the unlimited laundering of unethical acts into ethical ones. Yet many people seem to believe that professional roles do permit laundering of this sort. Thus, for example, what might ordinarily be regarded as lying is sometimes presented not just as permissible but as morally obligatory when done by a lawyer who is seeking to advance the interests of a client. Arthur Applbaum draws out the absurd consequences of such a view of role obligations by developing a profile of Sanson, the "executioner of Paris," who carried out his duties with consummate professionalism throughout the final years of the *Ancien Régime*, the French Revolution, the Reign of Terror, and the Thermidorian Reaction (Applbaum

1999, 16–27). Sanson remained above the fray throughout, insisting that he was merely a loyal agent, carrying out legal executions, and was thus not to be held responsible for any of the excesses committed by one or another of the various principals he had served.

Many business ethicists take this sort of example as a *reductio ad absurdum* of the idea that agency relationships might serve as a source of moral obligation. So rather than denying that managers are agents of shareholders (as stakeholder theorists are inclined to do), they simply deny that such relationships have any significance, from the moral point of view (e.g., Michalos 1995, 45; Newton 1992, 100). There is, however, some danger of equivocation in the way that the *reductio* argument is formulated. With respect to agents, it is important to distinguish the deontic modality of *permission* from that of *obligation*. Critics of the agency perspective are perfectly correct in noting that agency relations cannot create permissions. This is in fact why theorists who are heavily influenced by the agency perspective, such as Buchanan, are at pains to specify that the moral obligation of managers is to advance the *legitimate* interests of shareholders (not just any old interests) (Buchanan 1996, 422–423). Even Milton Friedman qualified his defense of profit-maximization with the stipulation that shareholders will "generally" want "to make as much money as possible while conforming to the basic rules of the society, both those embodied in law and those embodied in ethical custom" (1970). Thus, no one is committing the elementary error of believing that agency relations can turn impermissible conduct into permissible conduct (or wrong into right).

What critics of the agency perspective generally fail to note is that professional roles can serve as a genuine source of moral obligation in one important sense: They can transform actions that are merely *permissible* for the principal into ones that are *obligatory* for the agent. This is in fact Applbaum's final observation in his book *Ethics for Adversaries*. In response to the (rhetorical) question, "Why take professional roles seriously, from the moral point of view?" he replies, "Though roles ordinarily cannot permit what is forbidden, they can require what is permitted" (Applbaum 1999, 259). Thus, from the standpoint of business ethics, if it can be shown that shareholders are merely *permitted* to claim the residual earnings of the firm, and that managers are their agents, it then follows that managers are *obliged* to serve them loyally in this regard. This is morally salient, because the relationship creates that moral obligation by transforming a permission into an obligation. The *nemo dat* principle is misleading in this regard; when it comes to obligations, principals do in fact give that which they do not have.

The idea that managers might be morally obliged to maximize the profits of shareholders (or to act as "agents for the greedy" [Newton 1992]) does strike many people as intuitively implausible. Indeed, part of the success of Friedman's famous article is no doubt due to its title ("The Social Responsibility of Business Is to Increase Its Profits"), precisely because it *sounds* paradoxical. But upon closer examination, it turns out to be perfectly defensible (at least *pro tanto*). One need only show that it is permissible for individuals to seek a return on equity investments, and that managers owe some sort of loyalty to investors in the firm.

WHAT'S THE PROBLEM?

The preceding discussion has surveyed three potential problems with agency theory from the perspective of the business ethicist: (1) that it treats all motivation as self-interested; (2) that it presupposes shareholder primacy; and (3) that it encourages violation of the *nemo dat* principle. We have seen, however, that the identification of rational choice theory with self-interest is something of an oversimplification (agency theory leads us to expect *opportunism* on the part of individuals, but not necessarily self-interest); that agency theory is not committed to the doctrine of shareholder primacy; and finally, that the *nemo dat* principle, correctly understood, does not diminish the moral significance of agency relationships.

Thus, the only really significant issue outstanding is the first one, having to do with opportunism. How important is it that agency theory downplays the significance of social norms, moral principles, and intrinsic motives in explaining human conduct? The standard defense of the agency theorist will be to say that this is all just positive theory; no one is recommending universal opportunism. As an empirical tool for understanding the way organizations function and for explaining various aspects of organizational structure, agency theory has proven its value. Why should that be of concern?

The first step in formulating an answer to this question lies in noting that, because it is based upon a flawed conception of human rationality, agency theory generates predictions that are at variance with what one can actually observe in the behavior of individuals and the structure of organizations. Of course, many of the *potential* problems identified by agency theory are genuine—this is why the theory resonates with so many people. There is, for example, a notable *tendency* toward moral hazard. Similarly, individuals have a *tendency* to act noncooperatively in collective action problems. Usually, however, these show up only as tendencies, even when game-theoretic analysis predicts universal defection. In particular, while moral hazard in the firm can be a serious problem, empirically it is much less of a problem than any straightforward application of game-theoretic analysis to principal-agent relations would lead one to predict. In particular, while employees do sometimes shirk, most of the time they shirk a lot less than they could in fact get away with.

The empirical limitations of game-theoretic models have been exhaustively studied and documented by experimental game theorists. It is well-known, for instance, that large numbers of individuals cooperate in one-shot prisoner's dilemmas, knowing full well that there is no possibility of reciprocation (Dawes and Thaler 1988; Schneider and Pommerehne 1981; Kim and Walker 1984; Isaac, McCue, and Plott 1985), or make fair offers in an ultimatum game (see Henrich et al. 2001). Given these experimental findings, it would not be surprising to find that agency theory consistently overstates the agency costs that may arise within organizations, simply because real human beings often behave cooperatively, exhibit loyalty, and refrain from acting opportunistically, even in the absence of external incentives. This fact is well understood by sophisticated management theorists, even those quite friendly to the agency perspective (Eisenhardt 1989, 71–72).

Indeed, the general upshot of a lot of agency analysis of the firm is that many organizations, especially those that exhibit what Oliver Williamson calls "information impactedness," simply would not function if the *only* tools that managers had at their disposal were external punishments and rewards (1973, 318). Bengt Holström (1982) showed very early on how imperfect observability could make it impossible to devise efficient incentive schemes for individuals working in teams. George Baker (1992) and others drew attention to the fact that, when effort or output was not fully observable, a system of sharp incentives focused upon one aspect of the task could produce results that were much worse than a system of dull incentives applied to the task as a whole. Much of the agency literature wound up sounding a very skeptical note on the subject of performance pay, and provided unexpected support for the old-fashioned practice of paying employees a flat salary (Gibbons 1998). Results such as these suggested that, insofar as real-world corporations do actually succeed in extracting reasonable levels of cooperative effort from their employees, there must be more than just external incentives and instrumental rationality at work.

Given these results, one might wonder where the harm could be in business schools teaching agency theory, or in managers using it as an analytic tool. And perhaps there would be no problem, except for the fact that the limitations of the theory are often overlooked or understated. This can lead to mischief in several different ways, as outlined next.

Improper Understanding of Incentives

People who are overly impressed by economic methodology often subscribe to the instrumental conception of rationality in a form that makes the model essentially unfalsifiable. As a result, when particular agency problems do not show up where agency theory predicts that they should, rather than concluding that there must be some relevant sort of internal constraint at work, these theorists assume that the external incentives must be there, but that they simply have not been discovered yet. Economists have in fact invested extraordinary ingenuity and effort in the task of devising baroque external incentive schemes as a way of explaining phenomena that in fact admit of far more straightforward internal explanations.

To take just one example, there are two prominent interpretations of the so-called *efficiency wage* phenomenon. Henry Ford set the relevant precedent, by voluntarily increasing the pay of his workers to $5 a day at a time when average wages in the automobile industry were less than half that. He was rewarded with a significant increase in worker productivity. The commonsense explanation would be to suppose that Ford tapped into an underlying norm of reciprocity (see Fehr et al. 1996; Akerloff 1982). According to this perspective, the notion of a "fair day's work for a fair day's pay" plays a powerful role in determining employee effort levels (Hausman and McPherson 1996, 55–56). So when the boss agrees to pay you a rate that is, by common admission, far in excess of what he is obliged to pay, he has in essence done you a favor. And since one good turn deserves another, you then owe it to him to put more effort into your work (or, at the very least, to refrain from shirking). One might also expect this obligation to be enforced informally in the relations between workers on the shop floor, thus removing an important barrier to observability and leading to a dramatic reduction in moral hazard problems.

It should also be noted that, apart from its common sense appeal, there is significant empirical evidence to support this "norm of reciprocity" explanation of efficiency wages (Gneezy 2003). Nevertheless, many economists have felt the need to resist this explanation. The more popular suggestion has been that, by paying workers an above-market wage rate, Ford essentially created an economic rent associated with employment at his firm. This made workers more averse to losing their jobs, by making it unlikely that they would find work at comparable wages elsewhere. This, combined with the queues of workers that began to assemble outside Ford's factory looking for work, created enough fear of dismissal to motivate the existing workers to shirk less (Fraser and Waschik 2002, 291). According to this view, the efficiency effects of the wage increase can be explained entirely through reference to traditional monetary incentives, and without appeal to any obscure internal motivational factors, such as a sense of fairness or a commitment to reciprocity. (Of course, few people would doubt that the external explanation represents a *part* of the story, perhaps even an important part. The question is whether it represents the *entire* story.)

John Boatright has argued that this methodologically induced bias toward explanations in terms of external incentives can have a psychological "framing effect" that, when translated into practical managerial decision making, "might result in mistaken solutions to problems or even incorrect assessments of the problems to be solved" (1999, 48; see also Dees 1992, 35). For example, the agency perspective "is apt to lead to a distrust of agents and a reliance on mechanisms of control. Such an approach is warranted in certain situations, but when applied in a business setting it may result in an overinvestment in monitoring and other contractual solutions and a corresponding underinvestment in building trust in an organization, and in fostering traits like loyalty and professionalism" (Boatright 1999, 49; see also Frey and Osterloh 2002).

The other potential source of mischief is caused by the assumption that, whenever a particular sort of agency cost *fails* to arise, there must always be an explanation in terms of external incentives. This can encourage individuals in such agent positions to act in a purely instrumental fashion, by leading them to assume that there must already be a system of checks and balances in place to mitigate the negative impact of any opportunistic actions that they take, even if they cannot see it. If they believed, however, that the situation called for moral restraint on their part as the only way of avoiding an agency cost or a collective action problem, then they might be less willing to act opportunistically or noncooperatively. They would certainly be deprived of one powerful rationalization for unethical conduct.

Crowding Out of Moral Incentives

As we have seen, the methodological biases of agency theory generate an overemphasis on external incentives as a way of addressing agency risks, along with a comparative neglect of internal incentives. Thus an enormous amount of time and energy has been spent designing increasingly clever incentive schemes, to the neglect of more obvious strategies for securing employee loyalty and dedication. Yet while this may be a waste of time, one might be inclined to think that it also can do no *harm*. Even if an organization depends heavily upon voluntary moral constraint on the part of its employees in order to avoid certain potential agency problems, surely it can't hurt to layer on some additional external incentives, in order to create a greater alignment of interests?

Of course, the agency literature itself is full of cautionary examples of how incentive schemes can distort incentives, and thus of how poorly designed incentive schemes can exacerbate agency problems. Yet there is a more general problem that has until recently been entirely ignored, namely that even a well-designed system of external incentives has the potential to undermine moral motivation, and thus to create agency costs where previously none existed (Fehr and Gächter 2002; Tenbrunsel and Messick 1999). Bruno Frey and Felix Oberholzer-Gee (1997) refer to this phenomenon as the "crowding out" of moral incentives (see also Frey and Osterloh 2005, 102–5). Their research highlights some of the ways in which pecuniary incentives can have the effect of undermining moral incentives. People may be acting cooperatively merely because they consider it the right thing to do. When they are subsequently offered an external incentive, it may have the effect of changing their perspective, so that they no longer consider the question from the moral point of view, but rather examine it from the standpoint of their self-interest (Tenbrunsel and Messick 1999). If the rewards being offered fail to outweigh the free-rider benefits, then the incentive scheme may easily have the effect of undermining cooperation, thereby creating real collective action problems where previously there were only potential ones.

This is something that was well known to previous generations of organizational theorists (e.g., McGregor 1960), but it has become so thoroughly sidelined by the rise of agency theory that serious experimental research has been required to reestablish the importance of the basic phenomenon. One particularly nice example is a study conducted by James Heyman and Dan Ariely (2004). Students were asked to perform a somewhat boring task (dragging around circles on a computer screen). One group was paid a flat fee of $5 to participate in the experiment, another was paid a "piece rate" of 10 or 50 cents per circle dragged, and the final group was simply asked to do it as a "favor." Those who were paid 50 cents per circle dragged more than those paid only 10 cents, as an economist would be inclined to predict. However, those who were paid the flat rate of $5 dragged far more circles than those who were paid a piece rate, while those who were simply asked to do it as a favor dragged the most circles of all (Ariely 2008, 68–69). "Money," Ariely concludes, "is very often the most expensive way to motivate people" (2008, 84). More important, what the experiment suggests is that internal and external incentives are not necessarily complementary or cumulative, even when in theory they are correctly aligned to promote the same outcome. In practice, they may be mutually antagonistic (e.g., if one were to take the students who were dragging the circles as a favor and start offering them money, one might likely see a decline in performance).

Furthermore, there is good reason to think that the type of incentive schemes often promoted by agency theorists for use within corporations have considerable potential to undermine moral motivation. Far from intensifying work effort, the incentive scheme may simply communicate the message that management does not trust workers. One need only recall the way that workers have historically responded to sharp incentives such as piece rates, along with the monitoring systems that are required in order to implement them, to see the consequences this sort of thinking can have.

Cryptonormativism

No matter how strenuously agency theorists may insist that theirs is only a positive theory of the firm, and thus entails no value judgments, the fact is that the basic approach has as its foundation a *normative* theory of practical rationality, one that categorizes certain forms of action as *rational* and certain other forms as *irrational*. The fact that moral rules (or cooperation) get consistently categorized within such models as irrational, and opportunism (or defection) as rational, might easily lead more impressionable minds to the conclusion that they should learn to ignore moral constraints (Miller 1999).

This can have two pernicious consequences. First, in the interests of acting more "rationally," individuals may begin to plan their own behavior in accordance with the dictates of the instrumental model, and thus begin to act more opportunistically. Second, even if they do not change their own deliberative processes, they may begin to expect higher levels of opportunistic behavior from others, and therefore feel justified in engaging in preemptive defection in order to protect themselves from the anticipated defection of others. Thus, Ronald Duska observes that the instrumental conception of rationality has the potential to become a self-fulfilling prophecy: "If I think humans are always going to be selfish, and cannot help but be so, it becomes the height of foolishness to sacrifice myself, or to predict their behavior on any other than selfish grounds" (Duska 1992, 149; see also Argyris 1973, 264–266). Yet the type of "I did it to him to prevent him from doing it to me" reasoning that this generates provides another one of the classic techniques of neutralization used to excuse antisocial behavior (see Sykes and Matza 1957, 668).

There is some evidence to support this concern about instrumental rationality becoming a self-fulfilling prophecy (Ferraro, Pfeffer, and Sutton 2005). It was widely reported, for instance, that one of the only significant anomalies discovered in experimental trials of the "public good" game in North America occurred when the game was played among economics graduate students. There the rate of cooperation fell to only 20 percent, whereas it remained over 40 percent when played by students in other disciplines (Marwell and Ames 1981; also Frank, Gilovich, and Regan 1993). In a series of follow-up questions, students were asked whether a concern over "fairness" played a role in their decisions. Whereas virtually all noneconomists answered yes, "more than one-third of the economists either refused to answer the question regarding what is fair, or gave very complex, uncodable responses.... Those who did respond were much more likely to say that little or no contribution was 'fair.' In addition, the economics graduate students were about half as likely as other subjects to indicate that they were 'concerned with fairness' in making their decisions" (Marwell and Ames 1981, 309).

This is important because, contrary to the widespread conviction that the willingness to act morally is primarily dependent upon ethical *character*, which in turn is instilled through childhood socialization, empirical studies have generated strong support for the contention that the willingness to act morally is in fact highly situational, and that individuals rely to an exceptional degree upon social cues in their immediate environment in order to determine what to do (Doris 2002). Thus, it would be no surprise to discover that a social environment in which the dominant assumption is that "it's every man for himself" is one that would not only encourage unethical behavior, but could become positively criminogenic.

CONCLUSION

The use of agency theory brings to the fore two sets of ideas that ethicists have traditionally been very uncomfortable with: (1) the economic model of rational action, and (2) the doctrine of shareholder primacy, with its commitment to profit maximization. With regard to the first, I have suggested that business ethicists have been at least partially justified in their reservations. The economic model is based upon an inadequate conception of rational action, precisely because it classifies an important category of moral action as irrational. Indeed, it classifies all genuine rule-following as irrational and is, therefore, unsuitable for use as a general theory of rational action. Sophisticated practitioners of agency theory are familiar with these limitations, but a large number of enthusiasts are not. Because of this, agency theory can serve as a source of considerable inadvertent mischief when treated as an accurate representation of reality.

With regard to the doctrine of shareholder primacy and the extent to which agency theory encourages this perspective, I have tried to emphasize that there is no simple connection between the two sets of ideas. Of course, agency theory can be used to argue that the owners of a firm are in a vulnerable position with respect to management, and that a fiduciary relation may be justifiable for that reason (Marcoux 2003). So while the commitment to agency analysis neither presupposes nor entails a commitment to the doctrine of shareholder primacy, the gain in conceptual clarity afforded by the agency perspective may provide a powerful source of arguments in favor of that doctrine. This does not mean that one cannot use the agency framework to make the opposite claim, and it is certainly the case that many stakeholder theorists have sought to articulate and clarify their moral ideas using this framework.

It is perhaps this gain in conceptual clarity that constitutes the most important contribution of agency theory to the field of finance ethics. It has certainly not escaped the attention of many observers that the Wall Street scandals of the past decade—from the Enron-era bankruptcies to the subprime mortgage fiasco—occurred at precisely the points within both organizations and markets that agency-theoretic analysis identifies as major fault lines. Concepts like *moral hazard*, developed and refined by agency theorists over the years, have moved out of the textbooks and into the realm of popular commentary, becoming part of the basic tool kit for understanding the problems that can arise in these domains. This suggests that agency theory, whatever its limitations, can play an important heuristic role in the reflections of business ethicists, helping them to identify the points at which, absent some form of moral constraint, serious collective action problems are likely to arise.

REFERENCES

Akerloff, G. 1982. Labor contracts and partial gift exchange. *Quarterly Journal of Economics* 84:488–500.

Applbaum, A. I. 1999. *Ethics for adversaries*. Princeton, NJ: Princeton University Press.

Argyris, C. 1973. Some limits of rational man organizational theory. *Public Administration Review* 31:253–67.

Ariely, D. 2008. *Predictably irrational*. New York: HarperCollins.

Baker, G. P. 1992. Incentive contracts and performance incentives. *Journal of Political Economy* 100:598–614.

Binmore, K. 1999. Game theory and business ethics. *Business Ethics Quarterly* 9:31–36.

Blair, M. M. 2000. Firm-specific human capital and theories of the firm. In *Employees and corporate governance*, ed. M. M. Blair and M. J. Roe. Washington, DC: Brookings.

Blair, M. M., and L. A. Stout. 1999. A team production theory of corporate law. *Virginia Law Review* 85:248–328.

Boatright, J. 1999. *Ethics in finance*. Oxford: Blackwell.

Bowie, N. E., and R. E. Freeman, eds. 1992. *Ethics and agency theory*. Oxford: Oxford University Press.

Buchanan, A. 1996. Toward a theory of the ethics of bureaucratic organizations. *Business Ethics Quarterly* 6:419–440.

Campbell, D. E. 1995. *Incentives*. Cambridge: Cambridge University Press.

Clark, R. C. 1985. Agency costs versus fiduciary cuties. In *Principals and agents*, ed. John W. Pratt and Richard J. Zeckhauser. Boston: Harvard Business School Press.

Dawes, R. M., and R. H. Thaler. 1988. Anomalies: Cooperation. *Journal of Economic Perspectives* 2:187–197.

Dees, J. G. 1992. Principals, agents and ethics. In *Ethics and agency theory*, ed. N. E. Bowie and R. E. Freeman. Oxford: Oxford University Press.

DeGeorge, R. T. 1992. Agency theory and the ethics of agency. In *Ethics and agency theory*, ed. N. E. Bowie and R. E. Freeman. Oxford: Oxford University Press.

Dobson, J. 1997. *Finance ethics: The rationality of virtue*. Lanham, MD: Rowman & Littlefield.

Doris, J. 2002. *Lack of character*. Cambridge: Cambridge University Press.

Duska, R. 1992. Why be a loyal agent? A systemic ethical analysis. In *Ethics and agency theory*, ed. N. E. Bowie and R. E. Freeman. Oxford: Oxford University Press.

Easterbrook, F. H., and D. R. Fischel. 1991. *The economic structure of corporate law*. Cambridge, MA: Harvard University Press.

Eisenhardt, K. H. 1989. Agency theory: An assessment and review. *Academy of Management Review* 14:57–74.

Fehr, E., and S. Gächter. 2002. Do incentive contracts crowd out voluntary cooperation? Working Paper 34, University of Zurich. http://www.iew.unizh.ch/wp/iewwp034.pdf.

Fehr, E., S. Gächter, and G. Kirchsteiger. 1996. Reciprocal fairness and noncompensating wage differentials. *Journal of Institutional and Theoretical Economics* 152:608–640.

Ferraro, F., J. Pffefer, and R. I. Sutton. 2005. Economics language and assumptions: How theories can become self-fulfilling. *Academy of Management Review* 30:8–24.

Frank, R. H., T. Gilovich, and D. T. Regan. 1993. Does studying economics inhibit cooperation? *Journal of Economic Perspectives* 7:159–171.

Fraser, T. C. G., and R. G. Waschik. 2002. *Managerial economics: A game-theoretic perspective*. London: Routledge.

Freeman, R. E. 1994. The politics of stakeholder theory: Some future directions. *Business Ethics Quarterly* 4:409–421.

———. 1998. A stakeholder theory of the modern corporation. In *The corporation and its stakeholders*, ed. M. Clarkson. Toronto: University of Toronto Press.

Frey, B. S., and F. Oberholzer-Gee. 1997. The cost of price incentives: An empirical analysis of motivation crowding-out. *American Economic Review* 87:746–755.

Frey, B. S., and M. Osterloh, eds. 2002. *Successful management by motivation: Balancing intrinsic and extrinsic incentives*. Berlin: Springer Verlag.

Frey, B. S., and M. Osterloh. 2005. Yes, managers should be paid like bureaucrats. *Journal of Management Inquiry* 14:96–111.

Friedman, M. 1970. The social responsibility of business is to increase its profits. *New York Times Magazine*, September 12.

Fudenberg, D., and J. Tirole. 1991. *Game theory*. Cambridge, MA: MIT Press.

Ghoshal, S. 2005. Bad management theories are destroying good management practices. *Academy of Management Learning and Education* 4:75–91.

Gibbons, R. 1998. Incentives in organizations. *Journal of Economic Perspectives* 12:115–132.

Gneezy, U. 2003. *Do high wages lead to high profits? An experimental study of reciprocity using real effort*. Chicago: University of Chicago Graduate School of Business.

Goodpaster, K. E. 1991. Business ethics and stakeholder analysis. *Business Ethics Quarterly* 1:53–73.

Hansmann, H. 1996. *The ownership of enterprise*. Cambridge, MA: Harvard University Press.

Hausman, D. M., and M. S. McPherson. 1996. *Economic analysis and moral philosophy*. Cambridge: Cambridge University Press.

Heath, J. 2001. *Communicative action and rational choice*. Cambridge, MA: MIT Press.

Henrich, J., R. Boyd, S. Bowles, C. Camerer, E. Fehr, H. Gintis, and R. McElreath. 2001. Cooperation, reciprocity and punishment in fifteen small-scale societies. *American Economic Review* 91:73–78.

Heyman, J., and D. Ariely. 2004. Effort for payment. *Psychological Science* 15:787–793.

Holström, B. 1982. Moral hazard in teams. *Bell Journal of Economics* 13:324–340.

Isaac, M., K. F. McCue, and C. R. Plott. 1985. Public goods provision in an experimental environment. *Journal of Public Economics* 26:51–74.

Jensen, M. C. 2000. *A theory of the firm*. Cambridge, MA: Harvard University Press.

Jensen, M. C., and W. J. Meckling. 1976. Theory of the firm: Managerial behavior, agency costs and ownership structure. *Journal of Financial Economics* 3:305–360.

Khurana, R., N. Nohria, and D. Penrice. 2005. Management as a profession. In *Restoring trust in American business*, ed. J. W. Lorsch, L. Berlowizt, and A. Zelleke. Cambridge, MA: MIT Press.

Kim, O., and M. Walker. 1984. The free rider problem: Experimental evidence. *Public Choice* 43:3–24.

Knight, J. 1992. *Institutions and social conflict*. Cambridge: Cambridge University Press.

Kulik, B. W. 2005. Agency theory, reasoning and culture at Enron: In search of a solution. *Journal of Business Ethics* 59:347–336.

Laffont, J. J., and D. Martimort. 2002. *The theory of incentives: The principal-agent model*. Princeton, NJ: Princeton University Press.

Marcoux, A. 2003. A fiduciary argument against stakeholder theory. *Business Ethics Quarterly* 13:1–24.

Marwell, G., and R. E. Ames. 1981. Economists free ride, does anyone else? *Journal of Public Economics* 15:295–310.

McGregor, D. 1960. *The human side of enterprise*. New York: McGraw-Hill.

Michalos, A. C. 1995. *A pragmatic approach to business ethics*. Thousand Oaks, CA: Sage.

Milgrom, P., and J. Roberts. 1992. *Economics, organization and management*. Upper Saddle River, NJ: Prentice Hall.

Miller, D. T. 1999. The norm of self-interest. *American Psychologist* 54:1053–1060.

Nash, J. 1951. Non-cooperative games. *Annals of Mathematics* 54:289–295.

Newton, L. 1992. Agents for the truly greedy. In *Ethics and agency theory*, ed. N. E. Bowie and R. E. Freeman. Oxford: Oxford University Press.

Noreen, E. 1988. The economics of ethics: A new perspective on agency theory. *Accounting, Organizations and Society* 13:359–369.

Nozick, R. 1974. *Anarchy, state and utopia*. New York: Basic Books.

Rasmusen, E. 1989. *Games and information*. 3rd ed. Oxford: Blackwell.

Schneider, F., and W. W. Pommerehne. 1981. Free-riding and collective action: An experiment in public microeconomics. *Quarterly Journal of Economics* 96:689–704.

Selten, R. 1975. Reexamination of the perfectness concept for equilibrium points in extensive games. *International Journal of Game Theory* 4:25–55.

Sykes, G. M., and D. Matza. 1957. Techniques of neutralization: A theory of delinquency. *American Sociological Review* 22:664–670.

Tenbrunsel, A. E., and D. M. Messick. 1999. Sanctioning systems, decision frames, and cooperation. *Administrative Science Quarterly* 44:684–707.

Williamson, O. E. 1973. Markets and hierarchies: Some elementary considerations. *American Economic Review* 63:316–325.

ABOUT THE AUTHOR

Joseph Heath is a professor in the Department of Philosophy and the School of Public Policy and Governance at the University of Toronto. He is the author of numerous books and articles, including *Communicative Action and Rational Choice* (MIT Press, 2001) and *Following the Rules* (Oxford University Press, 2008). He has written extensively on the subject of practical rationality, rational choice theory, and business ethics.

CHAPTER 8

The Financial Theory
of the Firm*

WAYNE NORMAN
Mike and Ruth Mackowski Professor of Ethics, Department of Philosophy and Kenan
Institute for Ethics, Duke University

INTRODUCTION

Finance ethics is largely about who owes what to whom, and why. What duties do various agents, groups, and entities have, and whose rights must they
respect? Almost all of the chapters in this book consider either (1) what firms
owe to other firms or individuals, including their own employees and investors,
the society at large, and even in some cases members of other societies; or (2)
what individuals owe to the firms they work for, manage, or direct. But what is
this thing we call a *firm* or *corporation*?[1] It turns out that the answers to many
of the normative questions central to these chapters either presuppose or serve
to support some answer to this rather abstract question. Different theories of the
firm go hand-in-hand with differing views about, for example, the objective of
shareholder wealth maximization, fair executive compensation, or corporate social responsibility. This chapter inquires about how we might reasonably choose
among various theories of the firm that have been developed over the past century
or so. It pays particular attention to how the most prominent theory of the firm in
modern finance—the so-called *nexus-of-contracts* or *contractual* theory[2]—addresses
some of the more basic questions about who owes what to whom, and why, in the
corporate world.

WHAT KIND OF THEORY IS THE
"THEORY OF THE FIRM"?

So what *kind* of theory is a theory of the firm, and what specifically is it a theory *of*?
In fact, these are misleading questions because any given theory of the firm is really
a rather eclectic *bundle* of theories, principles, and concepts that are drawn from a

---

*I am indebted to an unusual degree in this chapter to Emily White for her research assistance
and for her persistence during a series of stimulating discussions throughout the winter and
spring of 2009.

variety of disciplines—from economics and law to sociology, ethics, and political economy. Our theory of the firm will consist of answers to several empirical, legal, normative, and even metaphysical questions (e.g., questions about what sorts of things *exist* or what kind of existence they enjoy).[3] Firms or corporations are obviously social constructions and human institutions. Or as Adolf Berle put it in 1967, they "are essentially political constructs" (Berle and Means 1991, xxxviii). And they are creatures of the law: You cannot *be a corporation* merely by selling goods or services, any more than you can *be married* merely by cohabiting with someone—in both cases you need to obtain a legal status. Along with that status come a large number of governance constraints within corporate law, but also a range of options for how a corporation might structure its own relations among various *constituencies* or *stakeholder groups*.

From the perspective of one particular theory of the firm (albeit the dominant one in recent scholarship), and speaking of only one particular *type* of firm (albeit the dominant one in all Western economies now), Michael Jensen picks out most of the context and basic elements for a theory of the firm:

> The public corporation is the nexus for a complex set of voluntary contracts among cus-
> tomers, workers, managers, and the suppliers of materials, capital, and risk bearing. This
> means the parties contract, not between themselves bilaterally, but unilaterally with the
> legal fiction called the "corporation," thus greatly simplifying the contracting process.
> The rights of the interacting parties are determined by law, the corporation's charter, and
> the implicit and explicit contracts with each individual.[4]

The *theory* of the firm is itself, if you will, a nexus of a complex and interdisciplinary set of investigations into the relations between a firm, these core constituency groups, and the laws that structure their interactions. It is concerned *empirically* with the implications of various actual or possible laws and contracts, and *normatively* with the interpretation or reform of law, on the one hand, and with the justification of the rights and duties assigned to different agents or groups involved with the firm, on the other. I would follow Hansmann and Kraakman (2004, 6) in leaving open for now the question of whether "the relationship between the firm and its participants can be described exhaustively in contractual terms." I would also suggest that we do not begin by *assuming*, as Jensen seems to here, that the rights (and duties) of interacting parties are *entirely* determined by law, the corporation's charter, and implicit and explicit contracts. There is no need to rule out *by definition* the possibility of beyond-compliance corporate obligations or responsibilities. We, of course, return to this important question about the normative implications of a theory of the firm (and of the nexus-of-contracts theory in particular) later in the chapter.

COMING TO TERMS WITH
THE PUBLIC CORPORATION

As noted, not all firms are corporations, and not all corporations are public corporations. But it is safe to say that the overwhelming majority of the scholarship on the theory of the firm has focused on the large modern public corporation with widely dispersed share ownership. Indeed, it is not uncommon for other forms of firm governance to be described mainly to shed light on the distinctive arrangements that characterize the public corporation.

We might also say that this is how modern scholarly debates into what we now call the theory of the firm began with the groundbreaking 1932 book, *The Modern Corporation and Private Property* (1932/1991), by Columbia law professor Adolf A. Berle and Harvard economist Gardiner C. Means. Berle and Means drew attention to what they saw as dramatic recent changes in American capitalism. These developments challenged the conventional wisdom (reflected in court rulings up to that time) that corporations were the private property of their owners and managed for their benefit. By emphasizing the separation of *ownership* (widely dispersed among uninformed, and largely indifferent, shareholders) and *control* (in the hands of a professional management clique able to amass corporate power to consolidate its own interests), they helped to transform our concepts of ownership and property in a corporate setting, and they focused attention on what would come to be seen as the agency problem at the heart of corporate governance.[5] With the separation of ownership and control of the firm, how do we ensure that professional managers act in the interest of the firm's owners, and even of the society as a whole, rather than in their own interest? It is no exaggeration to say that a large part of scholarly work on the theory of the firm ever since has tried to understand how best to deal with problems raised by the separation of ownership and control in the public corporation (see, e.g., Fama and Jensen 1983; Butler 1988; Bainbridge 2008, 6–8).

The young Ronald Coase's audacious paper "The Nature of the Firm" (1937) appeared five years after the publication of *The Modern Corporation and Private Property*, and it, too, helped to set the course of scholarly debates on the theory of the firm to this day. Eschewing the rich analysis of history, law, and political economy that characterized Berle and Means's approach, Coase asked a question that could be answered within the abstract models of economics, namely: Why should there be *some* firms rather than *none*? Why, if free markets are so efficient, do organizations built around hierarchical nonmarket command structures survive against competitors relying entirely on market transactions? His answer, famously, is that firms can avoid some of the *transaction costs* of purely contractual relations in the market. Ever since, the search has been on to identify other exotic costs and benefits within the operations of increasingly complex firms and management systems that help to explain not only why firms do better than markets alone, but also why firms with certain types of governance will do better than other kinds of firms.[6]

In effect, Coase asked a very stark version of a more general question that continues to frame scholarly debates: Why should we expect firms with some particular governance structure to outperform and perhaps come to dominate or supplant firms with some other governance structure? And also, why would freely contracting parties come to prefer cooperating within some type of governance arrangement rather than others? This is why he is widely viewed as the father of the contractual theory of the firm (see, e.g., Alchian and Demsetz 1972; Boatright 1996, 217). The governance structures in question may be dictated in part by the corporate law in a firm's jurisdiction (which is a state responsibility in the United States); in part by other regulatory law, such as federal SEC rules or legislation like the Sarbanes-Oxley Act in the United States; in part by nongovernmental regulators, such as stock exchanges; in part by the firm's charter; and in part by board or management initiatives. The question of what it means to *outperform* is contested (since this depends on, among other things, what we think the purpose or objective of a firm is), though not often by economists, who tend to presume this is a matter of efficiency. It goes without saying that since the public corporation is the type of firm that has *in fact* come to dominate most sectors in developed market economies (particularly now that an old rival, the state-owned enterprise, has disappeared from many of the sectors it once literally monopolized in many Western states),[7] most debates over the theory of the firm concentrate on explaining, justifying, or reforming the special features of the corporate form.

Drawing on a transnational survey by Hansmann and Kraakman (2004, 5–15; page numbers without a name or date in the following list refer to this book), we can identify at least five essential features of the modern corporation in all major market economies. These features have become nearly universal despite the fact that the traditions of corporate law around the world differ significantly on other points.

1. *Legal personality.* The reason it makes sense to think of a firm as a "nexus of contracts" is that it is "the single contracting party that coordinates the activities of suppliers of inputs and consumers of products and services" (6). The often-overlooked core element of corporate legal personality is "the ability of the firm to own assets that are distinct from the property of other persons, such as the firm's investors" (7). That is, in a very real sense, the corporation owns itself. The creditors of its shareholders and managers, for example, have no right to any of its assets.

2. *Limited liability.* By the same token, the creditors of the firm can go after the assets of the firm alone; they have no right to those of the shareholders or managers. Since an individual's creditors and a corporation's creditors both have a comparative advantage at monitoring their respective debts, the combination of legal personality and limited liability should lower the cost of capital for both the firm and its investors (9). In addition, "by shifting downside business risk from shareholders to creditors, limited liability enlists creditors as monitors of the firm's managers, a task which they may be in a better position to perform" (10). This in turn reduces agency costs associated with the next feature of the corporation.

3. *Delegated management with a board of directors.* Corporate law in the United States and elsewhere treats the board as formally distinct from both management and shareholders, though major shareholders and senior managers are typically elected to boards. It also quite clearly invests the board with authority and control. As the Delaware code puts it, the corporation's "business and affairs . . . shall be managed by or under the direction of the board of directors" (Del. Code Ann., tit. 8, s. 141(a), quoted in Bainbridge 2008, 34). According to Stephen Bainbridge, who argues for the controversial "director primacy" model of the corporation, "under U.S. corporate law the board of directors is not a mere agent of the shareholders, but rather a *sui generis* body whose powers are 'original and undelegated.' . . . In all states, the corporation code provides for a system of nearly absolute delegation of power to the board of directors, which in turn is authorized to further delegate power to subordinate firm agents [i.e., managers]."[8] Of course, while

the directors may have *formal* power, we know all too well that in practice their ability to monitor or control managers can be very limited.

4. *Transferable shares.* Unlike partnerships, owners of corporate shares can freely transfer their shares. This allows "the firm to conduct business uninterruptedly as the identity of its owners changes" (10). Having shares with this amount of liquidity also enables investors to diversify their holdings and minimize their risk, and in so doing it, too, reduces the cost of capital for the firm.

5. *Investor ownership.* Ownership is a normative concept, largely defined in terms of specific rights, and often quite explicitly excluding other rights or adding duties. As Berle and Means observed, the nature of corporate ownership, and the de facto ownership rights of shareholders, evolve over time. And so have the legal rights of owners, as defined by corporate law statues and judicial interpretations (Easterbrook and Fischel 1991; Boatright 2008, 177–182). The two rights that typically define corporate ownership are "the right to control the firm, and the right to receive the firm's net earnings" (13). As we shall see, these rights are, in practice, severely curtailed for most shareholders. The "right to control" in the influential Delaware code (where most major U.S. firms are registered) amounts to little more than a right to vote for or against a proposed slate of directors, and also for or against charter or bylaw amendments, mergers, sell-offs of the company's assets, and voluntary dissolution (Bainbridge 2008, 51–52). And the "right to receive a share of net earnings" is at the discretion of the board. For example, Google, an extremely profitable corporation, announces in its investor relations FAQ that "we have never declared or paid a cash dividend nor do we expect to pay any dividends in the foreseeable future." Nevertheless, the so-called "market for corporate control," which allows an investor or group of investors to gain majority ownership of an underperforming firm and to replace its directors or management, remains a powerful tool for reducing the agency costs arising from the separation of ownership and control.

It is noteworthy that every one of these core elements of the corporation is defined by the assignment of rights and duties to the members of different key constituencies or stakeholder groups in the nexus of contracts. And these are simply the *core* elements of the firm, stated in very general terms. Corporate law, along with all of the other sources of corporate governance noted earlier, fills out the meaning and implications of these very general rights with countless more specific provisions. For example, in reference to the so-called market for corporate control, just mentioned, there are many specific rights in both corporate law and permissible corporate charters that make it difficult for raiders to gain control of a corporation against the wishes of the incumbent management or board. Chiefly, there is the question of whether the firm can have so-called "poison pills" and "shark repellant" to make a hostile takeover prohibitively expensive for the raider. Some corporate law jurisdictions allow for the use of these provisions, and some do not; and some corporations within the permissive jurisdictions allow for the use of these provisions, and some do not.

It is an open question whether management or boards should have spe-cial rights to resist hostile or coercive takeovers.[9] On the one hand, the threat of a hostile takeover provides an incentive for managers to serve the interests of the corporation (and of society) by making more productive use of the firm's assets and resources; so enabling managers to shield themselves from this potential discipline may allow lazy, incompetent, and corrupt man-agers to maintain their power even if this is not in the interest of other stake-holders (including shareholders). On the other hand, management and the board may have good reason to believe that a particular takeover would *not* be in the firm's or the shareholders' interest, and since it is their duty to serve these interests, they also need some rights to enable them to perform this duty.

Now, my aim here is not to get bogged down in this particular issue about the optimal set of legal and contractual rights and duties for structuring the market for corporate control. Rather, the point is to emphasize (1) how *normatively infused* all of the contractual and quasi-contractual relations are between the constituencies interacting with the firm; and (2) how many deeper ethical and political issues seem to arise as we try to describe the rationale or justification for either the handful of core elements that structure the firm or the myriad specific rights and duties that ultimately determine how these rights work in practice. What is the ultimate purpose or justification of corporate law, and what kinds of considerations are appropriate for judging whether any particular right or duty assigned by corporate law is justified? What is the purpose or objective of the corporation? Whose interests should it serve? What is the role of management and to whom do senior managers owe fiduciary duties? Why should one group (shareholders) enjoy such a privileged position, with rights to control and to residual earnings, while being protected from having to shoulder the liabilities of the corporation? (Or alternatively, why is one group—shareholders—so vulnerable, with few real means to protect their interests either by contract or by real control over management and the board?) Who, if anybody, *owns* the firm? And what should ownership entitle them to, or what duties should it impose on others? What duties do firms (or their managers or directors) have to those adversely affected by their activities who are *not* among the parties to the nexus of contracts (e.g., people living downstream from polluting factories, run over by delivery vans, or injured when customers use or misuse the firm's products)?

All of these are genuinely open ethical questions. They cannot be answered merely by explaining how things work in the real world, or how they might work if we changed some rules. Or, put another way, if the current provisions in corporate law (and in other forms of legislation, contractual arrangements, and so on) that structure the modern firm *are justified*, there must be ethically sound answers available to questions like the ones just posed. Either way, providing defensible answers to these background normative questions is part of the task for a theory of the firm.

The fact that these fundamental normative issues require justification has not escaped either defenders or critics of the contractual theory of the firm or the theories of corporate governance and corporate law that it shapes. The rest of this chapter briefly surveys some of these debates.

TAKING RIGHTS AND DUTIES IN (AND OUT OF) THE NEXUS OF CONTRACTS SERIOUSLY

Justice is the first virtue of social institutions, as truth is of systems of thought. A theory however elegant and economical must be rejected or revised if it is untrue; likewise laws and institutions no matter how efficient and well-arranged must be reformed or abolished if they are unjust. Each person possesses an inviolability founded on justice that even the welfare of society as a whole cannot override. For this reason justice denies that the loss of freedom for some is made right by a greater good shared by others. It does not allow that the sacrifices imposed on a few are outweighed by the larger sum of advantages enjoyed by many.[10]

These are the first lines of the first section of the most influential treatise on justice in political philosophy of the past half-century. By the time one has read the 500-plus pages that follow this declaration it becomes clear that there is no *direct* or deductive way of applying this vision of justice to particular policies or institutions. John Rawls (1971) defends two particular principles of justice, which in turn help us think about what a just constitution might look like; and from there we can think about what lawmakers and judges in a just society might take into account.

But Rawls, like most of his colleagues in political philosophy, said virtually nothing about that major social institution we call the corporation. It is true that many political philosophers have evaluated the justice of markets,[11] but like neoclassical economists, they have usually treated the firm as a *black box* designed to maximize profits.[12] But to see the firm in this way is to define away the agency problems arising from the separation of ownership and control, which are the gateway to most of the serious thinking about the rights and duties of corporate governance. Of course, it should be clear by now that the legal scholars, judges, and economists who take the theory of the firm and corporate governance seriously do *not* treat the firm as a black box, and it is also not difficult to grasp the principles they use to justify governance rights.

What are these principles? Typically they consist of a commitment to two interrelated families of values: respect for autonomy and freedom of choice on the one hand, and promoting human well-being or preference-satisfaction (or *value*) on the other. We see the first set of values at play when we encounter arguments for a governance arrangement based on the fact that it is what all parties would voluntarily agree to. And the second set comes to the fore when a governance arrangement is preferred because it would be more efficient or create more value or wealth (say, by reducing transaction costs or the cost of capital). Corporate governance theorists do not generally defend these higher-level principles or basic values themselves; but since they are time-honored principles in most liberal-democratic societies, there are certainly both defenses and criticisms readily available in the history of ethics and political philosophy. Indeed, both sets of values have a prominent place within the architecture of Rawls's theory of justice, where his first principle of justice proclaims that "each person is to have an equal right to the most extensive scheme of equal basic liberties compatible with a similar scheme of liberties for others" (Rawls 1971, 60), and where various components of or conditions for well-being (including income and personal property) are listed among his set of so-called primary goods (Rawls 1971, 92).

With this background in mind, let us finish now with a brief survey of some of the fundamental normative debates in the theory of the firm, which were raised at the end of the previous section. Many of these fundamental normative questions we have been asking are interrelated, and indeed we can see something of a sequence where answers to fairly concrete specific questions are based on answers to more general or abstract questions.

The flashpoint for many political and scholarly debates, for example, is often the allegedly privileged position of shareholders in the modern corporation. Why do *shareholders* have a right to all of the profits, and a right to control the corporation and to demand that managers maximize their (i.e., the shareholders') return?

In order to answer this question adequately we are led to the more general questions, like: What is the ultimate purpose or objective of the corporation? Whose interest ought it to serve? What roles and responsibilities do directors and managers have to ensure that it serves these interests and fulfills these objectives and purposes?

Our answers to those questions are likely to depend on our answers to questions like these: What is the purpose or objective of corporate law? What is the purpose of markets, and what principles do we use to evaluate their success?

And of course, our answers here will be based on some of the most general, abstract, and fundamental theories of justice and political economy of the sort Rawls was alluding to at the beginning of this section. This is obviously not the appropriate place to try to make progress on parsing debates at this most abstract level. But it is useful to approach the other three types of normative questions by descending from the most abstract to the most concrete.

What Is the Purpose or Objective of Corporate Law?

As noted already, whether they address this question explicitly or not, theorists of the firm and of governance (coming primarily from economics and law) almost always appeal to two families of values when justifying particular reforms to corporate law or the *raison d'être* of corporate law itself: roughly, protecting autonomy and promoting well-being. It must also be said that a strong libertarian current in law-and-economics circles (especially in the so-called Chicago school) is also inclined to believe that protecting freedom and autonomy within free markets is the best way to promote well-being. (In many traditions, these families of values are seen to be interrelated, so we will often see them both playing a role in justifications for institutions or laws.) Here is a classic Chicago-school statement of the "protecting autonomy" justification for corporate law, from what is probably the most widely cited work in corporate law of the past generation, Frank Easterbrook and Daniel Fischel's *The Economic Structure of Corporate Law* (1991):

> We treat corporate law as a standard-form contract, supplying terms most venturers would have chosen but yielding to explicit terms in all but a few instances. The normative thesis of the book is that corporate law should contain the terms people would have negotiated, were the costs of negotiating at arm's length for every contingency sufficiently low. . . . It is enabling rather than directive. The standby terms grant great discretion to managers and facilitate actual contracts. They leave correction to the interplay of self-interested actors rather than to regulators. (Easterbrook and Fischel 1991, 15)

Why not abolish corporate law and let people negotiate whatever contracts they please? The short but not entirely satisfactory answer is that corporate law is a set of terms available off-the-rack so that participants in corporate ventures can save the cost of contracting. Corporate law fills in the blanks and oversights with the terms that people would have bargained for had they anticipated the problems and been able to transact costlessly in advance (Easterbrook and Fischel 1991, 34). Most liberals across the political spectrum (i.e., from social democrats to economic conservatives) accept that contracts or agreements between free individuals that don't harm anyone else are, *at the very least*, prima facie justified. This argument justifies corporate law by claiming that it is the contract that parties would agree to if they had the time and knowledge; and, moreover, that where their specific knowledge suggests they should contract in some other way, corporate law typically allows them to do so. It should be noted that the voluntary agreements being referred to here are presumed to involve any of the standard stakeholders in the nexus of contracts, not just, say, investors and managers.

Critics, who may be broadly in favor of the sanctity of free agreements, have tended to focus on two background assumptions in this argument. The first assumption is that all of the contracting between firms and members of various stakeholder groups is really free and voluntary, and that nobody will voluntarily enter into a contract that does not make them better off. But why should we not rather presume, the critics argue, that the "resulting contract defining the terms of corporate governance . . . mirrors the pre-existing market power of the various parties" (Greenfield 2006, 18)? Workers in remote areas or lacking special or basic skills may have few employers to choose from; or they may have extensive firm-specific skills that will be of little value if they leave their current employer. "To say that a contract optimizes the interests of the parties may be true in that it allows the parties to improve on what would be their lot without such a contract. But it is emphatically not the case that all contracts are fair, just, supportive of human dignity, or consistent with the interests of society as a whole" (Greenfield 2006, 18).

A second common critique of contemporary corporate law in general, and the rationale articulated by Easterbrook and Fischel in particular, is that even if it does facilitate voluntary contracts, it is *not* the case that these contractual relations have no negative implications for third parties. As Greenfield observes:

> By centralizing power in management, limiting the involvement of other stakeholders in corporate decision making, and imposing a requirement that the firm's management care about making money first and foremost, the law has created an entity that is guaranteed to throw off as many costs and risks onto others as it can. If a corporation can make money by polluting a river, it will likely do so. If a corporation can make money by paying its workers low wages or making them work in unsafe conditions, it will likely do so. If a corporation can make money disregarding the harms of a product . . . it will likely do so (Greenfield 2005, 16).[13]

There is, of course, a massive literature in economics, public policy, and law on how best to deal with this problem of externalities. One of the standard responses in the context of this particular debate is to remind the critics that corporate law is only *one* of the tools that citizens, organizations, and the state can use to regulate corporate behavior, and there are reasons to think it is not the best way to deal with many problems such as externalities. Greenfield, one of the more sophisticated critics, scoffs at this response. "Other [nonshareholding] stakeholders are left to depend on mechanisms outside corporate law, primarily in the form of express contracts or government regulation, both seriously imperfect, to protect their interests" (Greenfield 2005, 16).

All theorists of the firm rely routinely on autonomy-based arguments to make the case for why some particular structures of firms, or rules in corporate law, would be better than others. If a change would be welcome by all affected by it, then it is presumed to be worthwhile. But it is also possible to make people better off even if everybody would not agree to a particular rule, and this has always been one of the justifications of coercive law and regulations. This "well-being-based" or utilitarian justification for corporate law is endorsed explicitly by Hansmann and Kraakman (who nevertheless are in broad agreement with the kind of corporate law provisions advocated by Easterbrook and Fischel):

> *As a normative matter, the overall objective of corporate law—as of any branch of law—is presumably to serve the interests of society as a whole. More particularly, the appropriate goal of corporate law is to advance the aggregate welfare of a firm's shareholders, employees, suppliers, and customers without undue sacrifice—and, if possible, with benefit—to third parties such as local communities and beneficiaries of the natural environment. This is what economists would characterize as the pursuit of overall social efficiency. (Hansmann and Kraakman 2004, 18)*

They note, as any good utilitarian should, that whether, in fact, "the pursuit of shareholder value is generally an effective means of advancing social welfare is an empirical question on which reasonable minds may differ." They are also quick to add that endorsing this goal for corporate law is not to say that *actual* corporate law always serves that goal. "[C]orporate law everywhere continues to bear the imprint of the historical path through which it has evolved, and reflects as well various non-efficiency-oriented intellectual and ideological currents that have sometimes influenced its formation" (Hansmann and Kraakman 2004, 19).

This broadly utilitarian approach to corporate law has not attracted the same level of criticism even though, again, it can be used to justify the very same models of corporate law that critics assail. Interestingly, many contemporary critics of capitalism rely, perhaps unwittingly, on utilitarian arguments. They certainly draw attention to what they believe are devastating negative externalities (not offset by gains for shareholders or executives), from climate change and ecological disaster to the direct or indirect oppression of workers at home and abroad. If political philosophers in the Rawlsian and other traditions turned their attention to this conception and justification of corporate law, they might be concerned for all the standard reasons they are suspicious of utilitarianism as a moral and political theory.

Near the top of these concerns is the one expressed by Rawls himself in the passage quoted at the head of this section. The law or policy that maximizes aggregate welfare or overall social efficiency might also violate rights, trample on basic liberties, distribute wealth unfairly, or be otherwise unjust. And this type of criticism is explicitly or implicitly behind many of the more urbane criticisms of contemporary capitalism and corporate governance. These include worries about inequalities generated by exorbitant compensation packages for CEOs (especially in the United States); about the way corporate governance encourages risky behavior in the financial services industry that leads to big Wall Street bonuses when risks pay off, and taxpayer bailouts when they do not; about exporting of jobs offshore, which benefits executives and shareholders, but harms their fellow working-class citizens; or even worries that the amassing of wealth in the hands of big business will inevitably corrupt the democratic political system.

Hansmann and Kraakman (2004) do not defend their utilitarian approach beyond the passages quoted. But a defense is possible, and it need not be a defense of utilitarianism. In the passage quoted they claimed that the goal of any branch of law is "to serve the interests of society." This is most plausible if we do not assume that "serving the interests of society" is simply a matter of maximizing aggregate welfare. The criminal law, for example, seeks to punish the guilty and not punish the innocent in part as a way to discourage crime and keep dangerous people off the street, to be sure; but also as a matter of justice. And while it is possible to concoct sophisticated utilitarian theories to justify the criminal law, tort law, or redistributive justice, the impulse behind these bodies of law and policy is most easily understood in terms of fairness and egalitarian justice.

But it is in principle possible to accept, on the one hand, the utilitarian-like goal for the design and regulation of markets and corporate governance in order to create more wealth and maximize the size of the economic pie, so to speak; and to use other branches of regulatory law, tax law, and public programs in health care, public health, education, and so forth, to ensure that the pie is divided up more equitably. One of Rawls's principles—the so-called *difference principle*, which is but a small part of his overall theory of justice—called for a distribution of primary goods that would maximize the share for those who are worst off (Rawls 1971, 303). It is empirically possible that the best way to achieve this decidedly nonutilitarian distribution involves, among other government laws and policies, a system of corporate governance that aims, in Hansmann and Kraakman's words, to advance the aggregate welfare of the firm's shareholders, employees, suppliers, and customers (without undue externalities). In a footnote they articulate this vision "more precisely in the language of welfare economics as pursuing Kaldor-Hicks efficiency *within acceptable patterns of distribution*" (Hansmann and Kraakman 2004, 18n). The burden of proof for critics is to show why a reform of corporate law would do more to serve the interests of the less well off, and would do so more efficiently, than would, say, investing in better schools or public health clinics in poor neighborhoods.

One final feature of the aims and justification of corporate law is worth highlighting, though it is rarely discussed explicitly in the theory-of-the-firm literature. The legal and ethical rules that guide the behavior of firms and their constituents must be rules that are *designed for the competitive, adversarial nature of the markets in which these firms operate*. In many realms we structure *essentially adversarial systems* in the hope that competition will lead to innovation, diligent effort, and efficiency—which in turn creates positive externalities for those both inside and outside the adversarial arena.[14] For example, in an adversarial legal system we ask lawyers to fight hard (within carefully delimited boundaries) to defend their clients. This, in turn, forces law enforcement and prosecution agencies to do a more thorough and ethical job in arresting and building a case against a suspect. Something similar happens with the system of competitive elections, where we hope that a tough competitive battle between candidates or parties (again, within certain rules) leads to more innovative and transparent policies, and allows voters to better understand what they are voting for.

Similarly with firms in the market: We want them, within the rules of the game, to be focused on how they can maximize their returns, how they can add the most value to their inputs, and even how they can gain an advantage over competing firms. We want them to respect the rules, and even (as I discuss further in the next section) to go beyond what is strictly required by the rules in some cases. But we should be careful not to undermine the positive externalities produced by the whole game by asking the firms who are players in the game to distribute benefits themselves as they see fit. In sum: We should not be expecting that the kinds of rules appropriate for the governance of firms in the heat of battle, so to speak, will be similar to those used by other kinds of organizations not operating in an essentially competitive context.

With this general understanding of debates about the goal and justification of corporate law in mind, we can turn rather briefly to the two more concrete challenges that are typically made to the nexus-of-contracts theory of the firm and the type of corporate law that sustains it. For as we shall see, the standard defenses and criticisms of the theory follow closely from the ones discussed in this section.

What Is the Ultimate Purpose or Objective of the Corporation? Whose Interests Ought It Serve?

Given the adversarial context of the markets in which the corporation operates, there are several reasonable ways we might answer these questions. In highly competitive markets, the objective of the corporation is often just to survive. And it does this by producing outputs that are worth more in the marketplace than its inputs. That added value will show up as profits or residual earnings, so we can say that the objective of a firm is to maximize its profits, or at least produce a "satisfactory" level of profit (Anthony 1960; Boatright 2008, 192). We could also say that its purpose, as a nexus of voluntary contractual relationships, is to manage these relationships so that the best parties (e.g., the most innovative and diligent employees, the highest-quality suppliers, the financiers willing to offer the best terms) want to continue combining their resources in the firm's team production. And this implies, as Hansmann and Kraakman (2004) emphasize, that it should advance the aggregate welfare of its primary stakeholder groups.

But we can get even more specific than that: Any given firm is entitled to set almost *any* (legal) objective for itself, including objectives that require forgoing profit. The *New York Times* is often cited in this context. It is a closely held public corporation with a charter that shields it from takeover. And its primary stated aim is to stay profitable enough to be able to deliver a quality news service for the good of society. Interestingly enough, the kinds of theorists most closely associated with the shareholder-wealth-maximization objective for business—people like Milton Friedman (1970)—have no problem with firms giving themselves explicitly non-profit-maximizing objectives, as long as they announce this up front when seeking investment. As Easterbrook and Fischel (1991) put it:

> An approach that emphasizes the contractual nature of a corporation removes from the field of interesting questions one that has plagued many writers: what is the goal of the corporation? Is it profit, and for whom? Social welfare more broadly defined? Is there anything wrong with corporate charity? Should corporations try to maximize profit over the long run or the short run? Our response to such questions is: who cares?

One suspects that when many people ask what the *ultimate* aim of the corporation is, what they are really asking is what is the ultimate aim of the market, or of the capitalist system. But this is a much broader question for political economy and theories of justice, not a theory of the firm (although clearly those theories will inform the theory of the firm in ways we have already seen). Whatever the best way to characterize the ultimate aim of the game in an adversarial context, the aim of the players in the game is to win (within the letter and the spirit of the rules of the game), or at least to survive to fight another day. For the sake of the many stakeholders who literally have a stake in the firm's thriving, good corporate law and corporate governance should be designed to give a firm at least a puncher's chance.

Why Do Shareholders Have a Right to All of the Profits, and a Right to Control the Corporation and to Demand That Managers Maximize the Shareholders' Return?

This leads finally to the most concrete normative question or challenge about the theory of the firm that seems to be entrenched in the corporate law and capitalist systems in most developed economies today. To quote the subtitle of a paper by John Boatright (1994), "What's so special about shareholders?" We have now covered most of the elements of an answer to this question. The short answer, from the point of view of a contractual theory of the firm is, in a sense, "Nothing." As should be clear by now, the "folk theory of the firm,"[15] whereby shareholders are special because they *own* the firm as a piece of private property, is dead. At the very least, it is anathema in the nexus-of-contracts approach. This view persisted in judicial rulings up through the 1920s, but has since given way to an implicit theory of the firm along the lines of the contractual theory. Shareholders, or equity investors, are, as radical stakeholder theorists long ago insisted, *just another* stakeholder group.

The mistake of some stakeholder theories was assuming that this implied that all other stakeholder groups should get a piece of what the shareholders get: namely, control and a share of profits. In fact, given a realistic choice, rarely would any other stakeholder group want to be in the place of shareholders. Workers, for example, might like the idea of controlling the board and distributing the profits to themselves; but rarely would they choose to have this kind of contractual relation with the corporation *instead of* a contractually guaranteed wage. Of course, if they do want that kind of control, they are free to form a worker-owned cooperative. The fact that so few do so, and/or the fact that firms with that model of governance have difficulty competing against firms with access to equity capital, tells us something about the real efficiency gains available in the shareholder-controlled firm. In certain sectors, such as law and other professional services, worker-owned co-ops have thrived. Other kinds of co-ops have also thrived in other sectors. For example, in the apartment buildings market, tenant-owned co-ops (i.e., condos) have competed well against corporations that own buildings and rent to tenants. A significant amount of the cheese and butter in the United States is produced by supplier-owned co-ops. These examples tell us as much about the importance or lack of importance of shareholders as the success of public corporations does in most other sectors.

We owe this insight to the Yale legal scholar Henry Hansmann, who stands out as a highlight at our end of the long contractualist tradition of the theory of the firm that began with Coase. His book *The Ownership of Enterprise* (1996) may well be the most influential work on the theory of the firm or corporate governance among business ethics scholars today. Like Coase, Hansmann wants to explain why firms with some kinds of governance structure come to dominate; and he does this by taking seriously why different constituencies or stakeholder groups (he calls these groups different "patrons" of the firm) would voluntarily bargain to accept their particular place in the nexus of contracts. His brilliant realization is that the public corporation is really just an investor-owned co-op. So any question about why shareholders should be given rights of control and rights to residual earnings can be rephrased this way: Under what conditions do stakeholder groups freely contract to coordinate their joint production in one form of co-op rather than another? And why, in particular, has the investor-owned co-op come to dominate most sectors?

His answer is long, detailed, and fascinating; and it incorporates many of the insights into governance costs (such as transaction and agency costs) that have emerged in the scholarly tradition that began with Coase. A very short answer is that there are great costs and burdens in controlling a firm, especially in properly monitoring the agency relation with senior managers. For various reasons, these costs are almost always lower for investors, not least because they have more of a unity of interests as a group. (If workers ran the board, or worse yet, if several different stakeholder groups were represented on the board, there would be so much conflict and debate that opportunistic managers could exploit the board's weakness to their advantage.) The bottom line for Hansmann (1996, 23) is that it makes sense for the group that has the lowest combined ownership and contractual transaction costs (where such costs are often linked to distortions of market power) to control the firm and have the right to its residual earnings.

Another way of putting this is that other stakeholder groups will generally do better if the group with these lower costs serves that role. And this is another way of arguing that shareholder control is usually in the best interests of—and would be chosen by—other stakeholder groups. This is not to deny that in the real world shareholders and the boards they are stuck with often do a very poor job of monitoring the CEO or making strategic decisions. But when shareholders and the board fail in these ways, they provide an opportunity for another firm that is governed or managed more effectively.

CONCLUSION

I have tried in this chapter to sketch the general nature of firms and of theories of firms, and to survey some argument for and against. Once again, assumptions and theories at this level of abstraction are very close to the surface in a great many other ethical issues and theoretical concepts that are discussed elsewhere in this volume.

NOTES

1. I use the terms *firm* and *corporation* interchangeably. Technically speaking, all corporations are firms, but some firms are not corporations. They may be cooperatives, partnerships, or not-for-profit businesses, for example. This distinction usually will not matter, because I am primarily concerned in this chapter with the ethical implications of a theory of the firm appropriate for understanding the world of finance; and here the public corporation is the primary player.

2. The language—or image—of the nexus of contracts comes from Jensen and Meckling (1976). The theory itself has been developed by Jensen and various co-authors ever since, and is now broadly accepted as the mainstream view by economists and corporate lawyers. I use the terms *nexus-of-contracts theory of the firm* and *contractual theory of the firm* interchangeably.

3. Even lawyers have to tackle these quasi-metaphysical questions about what kind of entity, if any, a firm is. See, for example, Horwitz (1985) and Bainbridge (2008, 24–30).

4. Jensen (2000, 1).

5. See Boatright (2008, 179), and for a critique of Berle and Means's reading of American legal history, see Werner (1981).

6. See, for example, Alchian and Demsetz (1972) on the difficulties in metering outputs of team production and shirking; Cheung (1983) on the information cost of knowing a product; or Hansmann (1996) on the unattractiveness for most constituencies of various ownership costs.

7. For an argument explaining why state-owned enterprises generally foundered because of their inability to solve agency problems arising from their forms of governance, see Heath and Norman (2004).

8. Bainbridge (2008, 34–35). The internal quote is from *Manson v. Curtis*, 119 N.E. 559, 562 (NY 1918).

9. See Easterbrook and Fischel (1991, Chapter 8) for the canonical "Chicago-school" analysis of these debates.

10. Rawls (1971, 3–4).

11. A list of citations here could be a very long one, beginning with a young Hegelian named Karl Marx. For a particularly astute contemporary analysis in the Rawlsian tradition see Allen Buchanan (1985/2001).

12. Boatright (2008, 177). For a pioneering treatment of the firm by a political philosopher, see McMahon (1994).

13. This is a common refrain in contemporary critiques of capitalism. See, for example, Bakan (2004) or the documentary *The Corporation* based on this book—or *any* movie by Michael Moore.

14. The argument in this paragraph has its roots in Adam Smith's famous "invisible hand" metaphor for the positive externalities of market competition. The best contemporary analysis and defense of the logic of adversarial ethics is Heath (2006).

15. I believe this expression was coined by Joseph Heath, though I am not sure if he has used it in print. It comes from the concept of folk psychology, which consists of a large number of essentially false psychological beliefs that ordinary people live by.

REFERENCES

Alchian, Armen A., and Harold Demsetz. 1972. Production, information costs, and economic organization. *American Economic Review* 62:777–795.

Anthony, Robert N. 1960. The trouble with profit maximization. *Harvard Business Review* 38:126–134.

Bainbridge, Stephen M. 2008. *The new corporate governance in theory and in practice*. Oxford: Oxford University Press.

Bakan, Joel. 2004. *The corporation: The pathological pursuit of profit and power*. New York: Free Press.

Berle, Adolf, and Gardiner Means. 1991. *The modern corporation and private property*. New Brunswick, NJ: Transaction Publishers. (Reprint of the 1967 reprint, with a new introduction, of the 1932 book.)

Boatright, John R. 1994. Fiduciary duties and the shareholder-management relation; Or what's so special about shareholders? *Business Ethics Quarterly* 4:393–407.

———. 1996. Business ethics and the theory of the firm. *American Business Law Journal* 34:217–238.

———. 2008. *Ethics in finance*. 2nd ed. Malden, MA: Blackwell Publishing.

Buchanan, Allen. 1985/2001. *Ethics, efficiency, and the market*. Oxford: Oxford University Press.

Butler, Henry N. 1988. The contractual theory of the firm. *George Mason Law Review* 11:99–123.

Cheung, Stephen N. S. 1983. The contractual theory of the firm. *Journal of Law and Economics* 26:1–22.

Coase, Ronald M. 1937. The nature of the firm. *Economica*, 4:386–405.

Easterbrook, Frank H., and Daniel R. Fischel. 1991. *The economic structure of corporate law*. Chicago: University of Chicago Press.

Fama, Eugene F., and Michael Jensen. 1983. Separation of ownership and control. *Journal of Law and Economics* 26:301–325.

Friedman, Milton. 1970. The social responsibility of business is to increase its profits. *New York Times Magazine*, September 13.

Greenfield, Kent. 2006. *The failure of corporate law: Fundamental flaws and progressive possibilities*. Chicago: University of Chicago Press.

Hansmann, Henry. 1996. *The ownership of enterprise*. Cambridge, MA: Harvard University Press.

Hansmann, Henry, and Reiner R. Kraakman. 2004. What is corporate law? In *The anatomy of corporate law: a comparative and functional approach*, ed. Kraakman et al. Oxford: Oxford University Press.

Heath, Joseph. 2006. An adversarial ethic for business: Or when Sun-Tzu met the stakeholder. *Journal of Business Ethics* 72:359–374.

Heath, Joseph, and Wayne Norman. 2004. Stakeholder theory, corporate governance and public management: What can the history of state-run enterprises teach us in the post-Enron era? *Journal of Business Ethics* 53:247–265.

Horwitz, Morton J. 1985. Santa Clara revisited: The development of corporate theory. *West Virginia Law Review* 88:173–224.

Jensen, Michael C. 2000. *A theory of the firm: Governance, residual claims, and organizational forms*. Cambridge MA: Harvard University Press.

Jensen, Michael C., and William H. Meckling. 1976. Theory of the firm: Managerial behavior, agency costs, and ownership structure. *Journal of Financial Economics* 3:301–325.

McMahon, Christopher. 1994. *Authority and democracy: A general theory of government and management*. Princeton, NJ: Princeton University Press.

Rawls, John. 1971. *A theory of justice*. Cambridge, MA: Harvard University Press.

Werner, Walter. 1981. Corporation law in search of its future. *Columbia Law Review* 81:1611–1666.

ABOUT THE AUTHOR

Wayne Norman is the Mike & Ruth Mackowski Professor of Ethics, Department of Philosophy and Kenan Institute for Ethics, Duke University. A political philosopher by training, Wayne Norman has authored or co-edited five books; most recently *Negotiating Nationalism: Nation-building, Federalism, and Secession in the Multinational State* (Oxford University Press, 2006). He was introduced to business ethics while teaching in an MBA program more than ten years ago, and now writes mostly on the normative evaluation of business and markets. His work has appeared in *Ethics, Business Ethics Quarterly* and the *Journal of Business Ethics*, among other places.

PART III

Financial Markets

CHAPTER 9

Fairness in Financial Markets

EUGENE HEATH
Professor of Philosophy, State University of New York, New Paltz

Fairness is an important ethical principle, though not the only one. The actions of individuals, the rules and practices of institutions and organizations, and the regulations of public policies may be assessed in terms of fairness, though they may also be assessed in terms of other moral criteria, such as their contributions to welfare, equality, or liberty. In its broadest sense, fairness is a moral concept concerned with the comparative treatment or assessment of individuals (or groups of individuals): To be treated fairly is to be treated similarly to others with respect to a rule, agreement, or recognized expectation. For example, a person may treat another unfairly by failing to bestow the same benefit on that individual as was given to another person similarly situated. A rule may be unfair if it fails to require the same conduct from one person as is demanded from others who are relevantly similar.

We have an intuitive sense of fairness, for the term is invoked in various and broad contexts. One may refer to a "fair deal," a "fair profit" or a "fair wage." Alternatively, an accountant might ask whether a financial statement "fairly represents" the position of a firm or corporation. Or a loan officer might ask whether a bank's lending policy is "fair to all applicants" or reflects a "fair or level playing field." These samples illustrate a wide and varied usage, but they also indicate that within the practices of commerce there is a place for consideration of fairness.

Of course, some might contend that the primary aim of business transactions is profit. We often evaluate markets and businesses merely by their productivity or efficiency; for example, an appeal to efficiency provides a valuable reminder that the legal and regulatory framework of bank lending should provide the conditions for productivity. However, the value of this sort of analysis does not vitiate the importance of moral considerations such as those of fairness. A normative or moral evaluation of businesses and markets examines commercial practices in terms of their foundational principles or in terms of the operations and interactions that arise once these principles are set in place. The concept of fairness, for example, may be invoked to consider the foundational framework of markets as well as the rules and regulations of ongoing exchanges—the practices of business firms or the conduct of professionals and clients.

Even if it is charged that fairness and business do not mix—because the business person is nothing but a rational maximizer of profit—it must be recalled that the very idea of profit maximization is a postulate of theoretical models. Such a theoretical assumption entails no description of the motives of actual businesspersons, nor does it even purport to be part of any description of the processes of commercial competition. As a matter of fact, the motives and preferences of persons in business may diverge from a simple assumption of profit maximization (Kahneman et al. 1986). Indeed, to seek profit is not the same as seeking *maximum* profit, but even the latter is constrained by norms of market exchange: At its most minimal level, trade is a voluntary activity in which agents must attempt to persuade another person to take "this" for "that." At the very least, the items for trade must be presented honestly and without force or fraud, so that each party agrees voluntarily to the exchange.

A consideration of the application of fairness to the foundations and operations of markets, especially financial markets, illuminates central moral and political questions and suggests that the ethical evaluation of complex social and economic phenomena demands careful analysis. In the first section of this chapter, a general and simplified portrait of the market is offered in which some of the foundational elements of trade and exchange are noted, including the fact of financial markets. In the subsequent section, a general account of fairness, both procedural and substantive, is set forth. The third section broaches specific topics concerning fairness and the foundations of markets—the distribution of income and wealth, public debt, and the administration of a currency. In the fourth section, the focus is on fairness in the operations of financial markets, including the disclosure of information, discriminatory lending, and insider trading. Throughout the chapter, the discussion is presented with an eye to illuminating salient issues and indicating contestable claims and assumptions.

MARKETS AND FINANCIAL MARKETS

One of the virtues of markets is that they generate wealth. This is a remarkable feature, but it is even more so when one considers that the production of wealth occurs without any single directing or guiding hand. Adam Smith was one of the first to recognize how the steady attempt of each person to better his position, in conjunction with a division of labor, could generate unintended prosperity:

> [E]very individual necessarily labours to render the annual revenue of the society as great as he can. He generally, indeed, neither intends to promote the publick interest, nor knows how much he is promoting it. By preferring the support of domestick to that of foreign industry, he intends only his own security; and by directing that industry in such a manner as its produce may be of the greatest value, he intends only his own gain, and he is in this, as in many other cases, led by an invisible hand to promote an end which was no part of his intention (Smith 1976, vol. 1, 456).

Unintended benefits arise as individuals respond to particular circumstances, use their knowledge, and strive, as Smith said, to "better [their] own condition" (Smith 1976, vol. 1, 540).

The foundational framework of a market must permit individuals to labor, produce, create, and trade. In order for production to take place, individuals need a recognized or demarcated sphere—whether defined in terms of property or contractual relations—in which they can be secure in the expectation that they will have an opportunity to reap a reward from their labors, whether physical or mental. One need not labor in isolation, however, for productivity can be vastly improved from cooperation with others. One may sell one's own products or one's labor, skill, or knowledge in exchange for the goods or services of someone else. Each party seeks to trade something that is good for the other party. Except in cases of barter, such exchange involves the medium of money: The apple seller values his apples less than the money received in exchange for them; the apple buyer values the apples more than the money relinquished. Each party to the exchange seeks to gain something of greater value than what is surrendered. In this sense, each party seeks a profit. Thus, markets are composed of for-profit trades (even though the participants need not be profit maximizers). Profits also serve as signals of where to invest one's time and resources, as do prices, for the price of an item reflects the preferences of individuals in relation to the supply of the item. The fluctuating prices of goods indicate changes in preferences and suggest how best to allocate one's own resources in order to gain a profit.

As individuals act within the foundational rules that allow for production and trade, so do they make myriad choices. These activities and choices, as regulated by government or influenced by industry, constitute the operations of markets. Some individuals, known as entrepreneurs, enter a market in order to produce, create, or transport goods to sell. What is saleable for a profit depends, ultimately, upon the choices and values of consumers. The entrepreneur must take into account what is desired and how to produce it. To produce a good requires both capital and labor, as well as the knowledge of how to employ that capital and labor in such a way that the costs of production are less than the revenue received for selling the finished goods. Exchange occurs at all levels of production but also in the securing of capital and labor. The prices of all commodities reflect the valuations of the parties and the supply and demand of the good or service.

The capital required for production will include land, buildings or machines and the money necessary for securing the raw materials and hiring the labor. These items may be purchased with the entrepreneur's own funds, but it is more likely that he requires a loan to finance the business. Perhaps he turns to a financial institution such as a bank or investment company; or the entrepreneur may seek to establish a corporation, in which case he sells stock or shares of ownership in exchange for monetary capital. (The funds loaned to the entrepreneur, or the assets of those who invest in stock, exist because some individuals have forgone consumption and saved.) Once the business is operating at a profit, then those who work for the firm may be able to save some of their own earnings and perhaps even invest some portion of their wages or salaries in stocks or bonds.

In this brief and simple narrative one glimpses how markets presuppose ownership, as well as the freedom to exchange goods and services, and a medium of exchange or money. Money facilitates production and exchange and renders possible certain financial instruments, such as loans. Yet it is inevitable, given human circumstance, fortune, skill, and effort, that the wealth of markets will not accrue equally to all persons. This is not unexpected: The value of one person's knowledge may be vastly greater than that of another; the product of one firm may secure a wider customer base than that of a competitor. Incomes will differ and wealth will accumulate in unequal ways. Before turning to consider how fairness may relate to both the foundations and the operations of markets, let us consider more carefully the very idea of fairness.

FAIRNESS: FORMAL AND SUBSTANTIVE

Fairness is one sort of moral principle or standard of right. In being fair one does not fulfill all of the aims of ethical conduct, so fairness should not be identified with the whole of ethics. As but one element of ethical conduct, fairness concerns, at least minimally, the comparative treatment of persons in relation to some rule, agreement, or recognized expectation. For example, if there is a rule or set of criteria that applies to all loan applicants, then a loan officer treats all applicants fairly if that officer utilizes the criteria in determining the creditworthiness of the applicants. It would be *unfair* to subject one applicant or some subset of applicants to new criteria. In the case of agreements, the violation of a contract has its own wrongness, irrespective of any unfairness. However, to the extent that some group of persons is cooperating or acting within some agreement, tacit or explicit, then the terms of that agreement—its benefits or burdens—should fall upon all who had so agreed. And in a similar case in which various parties have recognized and accepted an expectation regarding some practice or benefit, then a failure to meet that expectation would usually be unfair.

Although fairness and justice are similar, they should not be equated. Aristotle contended that the unjust person is also unfair (1941, 1143a10). Justice may, therefore, presuppose a certain fairness. However, justice and fairness may diverge, for some demands of fairness could require a violation of the constraints of justice. Aristotle also asserted that justice involves giving to equals equally and to unequals unequally (1941, 1131a). Even this formal account, emblematic of consistency itself, suggests something important about fairness: At some minimal level, fairness refers to the wrongness of making exceptions in the application of a rule, or to playing favorites and giving privileges to some but not to others. In addition, it may be possible to understand fairness in relation not only to the treatment of persons but to the retrieval, presentation, and evaluation of information: The fair accountant is one who does not favor one interpretation of events over a plausible alternative but tries to ensure that the financial facts are presented without privileging a desired outcome (e.g., the appearance of financial soundness) over another (e.g., the reality of debt). Or unfairness might occur insofar as one manipulates a rule from its accepted meaning so that it favors some outcomes or persons over others.

The discussion so far takes up fairness in relation to a rule, agreement, or recognized expectation. This sort of fairness, sometimes referred to as "procedural fairness" (Hooker 2005, 329), is important, and its violations may be inequitable, wrong, or hurtful. Rules, agreements, or recognized expectations seem to generate claims on the part of those to whom the rules, agreements, or expectations apply. (This conceptual link between fairness and claims is suggested by Broome 1990.) For example, if a code of conduct specifies that no employee may trade a company's stock on the basis of certain types of proprietary or *inside* information, then with respect to this provision all employees of the corporation have a similar claim.

A claim is a kind of reason. We have various types of moral reasons (keeping a promise, not violating a right, or distributing goods fairly), but one of these is concerned with what we owe others; these reasons are claims (Broome 1990, 92). Some reasons (e.g., that we ought to maximize happiness) have nothing to do with claims, and in many instances a person may not have any claims to be satisfied. However, in the event that a person has a claim, then to treat the person fairly is to ensure that the claim is satisfied in proportion to its strength: Fairness requires "that *claims should be satisfied in proportion to their strength*" (Broome 1990, 95). That we should honor claims in proportion to their strength does not entail that fairness trumps all other obligations. For we may have obligations not to violate rights, and these obligations may function as side constraints (so that whatever we do, we should not violate these constraints).

Procedural fairness concerns the application of a rule, agreement, or expectation to which the individual has some claim. However, a rule, agreement, or recognized expectation might itself be *unfair*. One may apply fairly an unfair rule: For example, a rule, consistently applied, that rewards some but not others (relevantly situated) is unfair. If fairness is a kind of moral reason, then the idea of fairness can be applied to the very *substance* of rules, agreements, or expectations. Following Broome, we can assert that fairness at both a substantive and procedural level involves the proportional satisfaction of claims (about rules, agreements, or expectations) or the proportional satisfaction of claims existing prior to the making of rules, agreements, or expectations. The latter sort of claims may relate to needs, to desert, or to other prior agreements.

It is at this substantive level that fairness becomes a more contestable topic, morally and politically. It is one thing to assert that a rule, agreement, or expectation generates a claim on behalf of those to whom it applies (procedural fairness); it is a more fraught question to consider whether we owe something to individuals, or to identify the claims that individuals may have, simply as human beings. Some might say, for example, that all individuals have a claim on some minimal level of basic goods—housing, health care, food, and education. If individuals do have such claims, then fairness dictates that they ought to be satisfied in proportion to their strength. One might argue, in some instances, that the claims are only alleged: They cannot be *real* claims for they presuppose that there are such basic goods in existence. Such basic goods appear not by a snap of the fingers but by the labors of others whose very efforts may have established prior claims on their products or creations.

Another element of contestability arises from the fact that there are moral reasons distinct from the claims of fairness. The appeal to fairness does not, necessarily, trump all other moral considerations. In some instances it may be better to maximize the general welfare than to treat everyone fairly. After all, it is not evident that all acts of unfairness constitute harms (Hooker 2005, 336). If an unfair act does not constitute a harm, then it may not be the sort of act that must be prohibited; in this sense, the claims of fairness do not function as rights which must be enforced. For example, if two individuals apply for a loan, then procedural fairness would dictate that each individual has a claim on being evaluated with regard to the criteria for issuing loans. If both individuals are relevantly similar in terms of credit history, income, and so on, and if the bank has the funds available, then there would be no reason for granting one person the loan and denying it to the other. To do so would treat unfairly the person denied the loan. What is less clear is whether this denial constitutes a harm. One might contend that a harm is done if the person has a *right* to the loan in the sense that the person has an enforceable claim to receive a loan if the person meets the relevant criteria. Yet in the absence of a clear right, there is neither an enforceable claim nor a harm. Without a right (or some equivalent claim) there is no enforceability. And if the failure to receive the loan does not leave one worse off, then there is no harm.

FOUNDATIONS OF MARKETS

With this account in hand, we may return to the market, specifically to financial markets. The concept of fairness is often invoked in evaluating the foundations of markets and their operations. The sections that follow offer some brief considerations as to how fairness might apply to some of the salient features and institutions of markets, including differences in income and reward, the use of public debt to finance government, and the administration of a currency.

Income and Rewards

The legal and institutional foundations of markets set the parameters of exchange and contract, delineate the kinds of firms that may exist, and establish a monetary system. As individuals interact they receive differential rewards for their labor, goods, or services; as a result, inequalities of income and wealth emerge. These inequalities result from consumer preferences and from how individuals with certain skills, traits, and luck are able to respond to these preferences in a timely fashion. The rewards that individuals receive are not distributed separately from the processes of production and exchange. As Robert Nozick puts it, "There is no *central* distribution. . . . What each person gets, he gets from others who give to him in exchange for something, or as a gift" (1974, 149). Yet the inequalities of income, wealth, and status may seem unfair. How can this unfairness be understood?

John Rawls (1999) contends that in a market system (such as Adam Smith's "system of natural liberty"), inequalities of income and wealth are the "cumulative effect of prior distributions of natural assets—that is, natural talents and abilities—as these have been developed or left unrealized, and their use favored or disfavored over time by social circumstances and . . . chance contingencies" (63). In Rawls's estimate, an unfettered market allows the distribution of income and reward to be influenced by features, such as natural and social assets, that are "arbitrary from a moral perspective" (1999, 64). It is important to note that Rawls does not assert that the distribution of natural or social assets is *unfair*, only that it is arbitrary.

To overcome the inequalities conditioned by such arbitrary elements, Rawls proposes a theory that he calls "justice as fairness" (1999, 3). The principles of justice that undergird and inform the structure of society are precisely those principles that would be selected in a situation of choice that is itself fair (15). The fairness of the choice situation is constituted by the fact that the individuals in the original position of choice are not able to tailor the principles of justice to favor their natural talents or social circumstances, or even their particular conception of good. Thus, the fair situation of choice as described by Rawls is one in which the individuals make their decisions behind a "veil of ignorance" (118) in which the parties do not know facts about themselves, including education, social status, intelligence, or their conception of the good.

Rawls can plausibly describe such a situation as fair because he assumes that a society is "a mutually advantageous cooperative venture" (1999, 96). If society is such a venture of mutual cooperation, then each person has a claim on society to advance that individual's good. Such claims should be satisfied equally since no one may assert that his own claim is more important than anyone else's. If each person has such a claim, then it would be unfair to allow any person to select rules of justice that would structure society in such a way that some goods or traits are favored over those of others. As it turns out, the principles that are chosen are two: that each person has a right to basic liberties; and that social and economic inequalities are permissible only if these inequalities benefit the "least advantaged" and are "attached to offices and positions open to all" (Rawls 1999, 53).

Setting aside the actual principles of justice—compatible with markets as well as with a strong public sector (Rawls 1999, 234–242)—the Rawlsian project raises interesting challenges. For present purposes, it is useful to consider how the very idea of society as a "cooperative venture" may relate to fairness. Rawls explains that society is a "self-sufficient association of persons" (1999, 4). The idea that we have embarked together on a "venture" or formed an "association" suggests that any one person's goods, traits, or situations should not be favored or disfavored in comparison to those of others. However, even if society involves cooperation among and between individuals, society itself may not be a "cooperative venture" to which we have somehow consented. Without the underlying idea of society as an agreed-upon venture, the appeal to fairness must find some other footing.

Robert Nozick (1974) charges that Rawls' account of justice is so designed that the parties will neglect any consideration of a rights-based theory of cooperation and interaction. As an alternative to Rawls, Nozick proposes an entitlement theory of justice according to which a property holding is justified provided that its sequence of transfers and original acquisition were just. Such a theory, Nozick contends, is historical rather than patterned: It takes into account not what people have now—how their income and wealth is distributed currently—but how their holdings arose over time. If one's income and wealth came about through actions that did not violate rights—which function as side constraints on everyone's conduct (Nozick 1974, 28–30)—then one's income or wealth is just. On this account, even if an individual treats another person unfairly, such treatment is permissible (though morally condemnable) so long as it does not violate a side constraint. Even if one thinks it unfair or, at best, unfortunate that some have vastly greater incomes than others, it does not follow that a government (or anyone else) would have a right to interfere so as to alter the patterns of income and wealth unless these patterns resulted from violations of rights.

Nozick's argument rests on his basic assumption of rights as side constraints. Another view of justice and markets is that of F. A. Hayek (1976) who contends that the outcomes of markets—the differential rewards of buying and selling—are neither just nor unjust. Outcomes are just or unjust only if they are the results of intentional or deliberate actions (Hayek 1976, 31). The market is grounded on rules of justice, characterized as prohibitions, generalizable to all persons, that protect domains of freedom. These rules allow for the emergence of an unintended or spontaneous order. The monetary rewards that accrue to individuals acting within the market cannot be analyzed as just or just, or fair or unfair, for these rewards are the unintended outcomes of a vast and complex series of interactions. Hayek writes, "the impersonal process of the market . . . can be neither just nor unjust, because the results are not intended or foreseen, and depend on a multitude of circumstances not known in their totality to anybody" (Hayek 1976, 70).

The Hayekian insight suggests that an understanding of markets should lead one to reassess whether the concept of justice (or fairness) even applies to certain kinds of outcomes and interactions. In point of fact, there may be evidence that what is counted as fair or unfair depends on whether one is evaluating a market or a nonmarket institution (Isaac et al. 1991; Zajac 2002, 383). As an empirical question, a person's tendency to assess rules or outcomes in terms of fairness may provide evidence of distinct understandings of how the market functions and of the differences between for-profit businesses and nonprofit organizations. Nonetheless, at this foundational level of permissions and requirements, the question of fairness remains, and its appropriate application often pivots on significant and contestable issues of political thought.

Fairness and Public Finance

A government provides the legal framework in which exchange takes place. However, the institutions of government require revenue to function: Laws must be enforced and justice met; the programs and services of the state must proceed. How is the government to finance its activities? In the modern era, governments have typically financed their activities through taxation. In democratic governments, voters elect representatives who make decisions about programs, services, infrastructure, and defense; these same representatives also determine how to finance these endeavors. In a representative democracy, it is ultimately the voting citizen who determines what the government will do and how the revenue will be raised. But it turns out that taxation is only one means of generating the funds for government. An alternative mode of financing is issuance of public debt: A government receives revenue through the sale of government bonds; in turn, the government promises the buyer of the bond the return of the face value of the bond plus the payment of interest.

The great philosopher Immanuel Kant warned against the use of public debt to wage war, for it "provides a military fund which may exceed the resources of all the other states put together" (1970, 95). However, one could also argue that the financing of government via public debt, rather than taxation, raises questions of fairness. In the case of taxes, the current taxpayer receives the government services that the taxes provide. In the case of public debt, the current taxpayer receives the government services and the bondholder receives interest payments; however, it is not the current but the *future* taxpayer who must pay the bond! It might be considered a recognized expectation of democracies, if not a tacit agreement, that the current services and programs of the government should be paid for by the current taxpayers. All taxpayers, current and future, have a claim against bearing a financial burden to which they did not consent. But the financing of government by public debt shifts the financial liability to future taxpayers, even as the current generation enjoys the services or programs (Buchanan 1999).

The alleged unfairness rests on two principles: Those who receive benefits should pay the costs, and those who bear the costs should have some say in whether they are imposed. However, public debt financing allows some voters to determine the obligations of future voters. The Nobel laureate James M. Buchanan summarizes the idea thusly: "The essence of public debt, as a financing question, is that it allows the objective cost of currently financed expenditure projects to be postponed in time" (2000, 358).

There are at least two ways of dealing with this problem: A constitutional amendment could proscribe or limit the use of public debt, or the nation could inculcate or revivify a moral constraint against the use of public debt. Apart from these possible resolutions, some might challenge Buchanan's argument by contending that, in fact, there is no unfairness because, as it is often said, "we owe it to ourselves." According to this objection, Buchanan fails to see how the decision to raise revenue via public debt involves transfers to ourselves: Government services are a transfer *to* us and the payment of the bonds is a transfer *from* us. This argument requires, however, that one regard the nation as a single collective whole. However, Buchanan's point is about individuals, and a view of the economy as a collective whole "does not take seriously," as Rawls says about the doctrine of utilitarianism (Rawls 1999, 24), "the distinction between persons."

The Administration of a Currency

Some scholars contend that the increase in the use of public debt is, in part, a consequence of monetary inflation (Hülsmann 2008, 166). Monetary inflation may itself raise questions of fairness. Markets of any complexity require a medium of exchange, money, which itself is a commodity subject to the forces of supply and demand. Whatever the form of money—precious minerals such as gold or silver, a paper currency backed by such minerals, or the legal tender authorized by law—its value should be stable. Not only does the instability of the value of money increase the costs of doing business, but if monetary prices are to provide information, then these prices should signal real changes in supply and demand, not increases or decreases in purchasing power.

The Federal Reserve Act of 1913 created an institution whose mission is "to promote effectively the goals of maximum employment, stable prices, and moderate long-term interest rates" (Federal Reserve Board 2005, 15). The Federal Reserve holds a monopoly on the issuance of currency, and until 1971 it allowed the dollar to be backed by gold. Since that year, dollar notes are not redeemable but are simply "legal tender." There are, no doubt, significant and interesting questions related to whether monetary stability is best achieved through a government monopoly or whether money should be allowed to emerge through the market itself. If a government monopoly on money tends to produce inflation, and if this inflation is unfair, then this is one reason for considering whether inflation would be diminished if there were a market in currencies. (In a free banking system, banks would likely hold gold reserves as a backing for their notes. A currency backed by a precious metal will more likely find acceptance among the public than a paper currency with no backing. Indeed, without the enforced monopoly of the government there seems no reason why any purely paper currency would attain any circulation at all. See Hülsmann [2008, 29–33] and Selgin [1996].)

Inflation can be defined as an increase in the supply of money, which in turn diminishes the purchasing power of money and raises prices. For much of history, inflation would occur through the shaving or clipping of coins or through the substitution of a lesser for a more valued metal. However, governments have the power to increase the supply of money, thereby lowering its purchasing power and distorting "the prices of goods, services, materials, and labor" (Federal Reserve

Board 2005, 15). There are two ways in which the control of the money supply may be used unfairly.

If the Federal Reserve is to administer the money supply so that prices are stable, then it must retain, as its mission stipulates, a genuine independence from both the political process and the economy. Those who administer the currency must not, in other words, seek to affect the value of money in order to alter or affect political decision making, economic rewards, or the production of goods and services. There are strong economic reasons for such independence, including the simple fact that citizens should be able to trust that their currency is stable, but there is also an issue of fairness: Citizens, including those engaged in politics or holding political office, have a claim that their currency should be a *medium* of exchange for goods and services. To affect the value of a currency for political ends (or to favor a narrow economic interest) serves to benefit some citizens at the expense of others and thereby fails to respect the claims of all citizens to a currency whose value is independent of particular projects, industries, or aims.

There remains a more significant and obvious question of fairness. Any inflation of the currency tends to benefit some at the expense of others. An inflated currency devalues monetary assets, and a steady inflation of the currency ensures that the purchasing power of money is steadily reduced. This also affects conduct: Saving money is no longer sufficient, and it loses its traditional function. To retain the purchasing power of one's money, one must not simply save but *invest* (Hülsmann 2008, 183–184). But the real unfairness is that inflation is hard on those who have fixed incomes, those who have interest-bearing savings accounts, and anyone who has lent money. The real value of their assets is diminished. Conversely, inflation helps borrowers and anyone with hard assets.

To alter the value of money is essentially no different than taking something without someone's permission. The unfairness arises because each individual enters an exchange with a claim on money as a store of value; an intentional increase in the supply of money changes that value so that some are advantaged and others disadvantaged. However, all originally had the same claim on the money as possessing a certain value.

THE OPERATIONS OF FINANCE

Acting within the legal foundations that permit production, contract, and exchange, market participants engage in a variety of activities and enterprises. Firms and individuals raise capital or secure loans and mortgages. Investors buy stocks and bonds and utilize other financial instruments. Firms and companies track and assess their own performance using the knowledge and standards of accountancy; corporations offer financial statements to disclose information relevant to investors. Financial rules, practices, and regulations not only guide and inform the behavior of owners, managers, and executives, but they determine the conduct of professionals such as advisers, stockbrokers, and accountants.

It is often assumed that the rules and regulations of finance are and should be judged in terms of either fairness or efficiency (Shefrin and Statman 1992, 8; Boatright 2008, x). It may be true that legislators and regulators attend only to the trade-offs that occur as they "attempt to enhance both *efficiency* and *fairness*" (Shefrin and Statman 1992, 1). However, there exists significant scholarly literature grounded on "the theory that purportedly public-interested regulation is almost always an effort to create a cartel or to serve some private interest at the public expense" (Sunstein 1997, 271; see also Macey 1994). Even if efficiency and fairness provide the primary criteria for assessing a rule, regulation or practice, this does not entail that these criteria are the primary motivations or intentions of legislative bodies or of regulators.

Fairness and Disclosure

There are three significant questions in financial disclosure: How do financial statements *fairly present* the financial position of a firm? Should companies, as a matter of fairness, *disclose* certain information to the public? How should financial professionals *represent* themselves and their products to their clients? The first question concerns accounting ethics, the second public policy, and the third professional obligation.

In the field of accountancy, an internal accountant or an external auditor may be called on either to provide or to verify a firm's financial statement. In drawing up or testifying to the financial condition of a company, the accountant has the duty to present the information *fairly*. The Code of Conduct of the American Institute of Certified Public Accountants (AICPA) requires integrity, objectivity, independence, and due care in the performance of the profession. This suggests that the accountant must report objectively and without bias the information that he receives (Monti-Belkaoui and Riahi-Belkaoui 1996, 3). Whether a fair presentation extends beyond the use of "generally accepted principles of accounting" is a matter of debate (Monti-Belkaoui and Riahi-Belkaoui 1996, 10–12; Duska and Duska 2003, 118–119). Nonetheless, there is solid justification for employing the concept of fairness in the presentation or verification of financial statements. These statements purport to report clearly, fully, and relevantly the "underlying events and transactions" (Monti-Belkaoui and Riahi-Belkaoui 1996, 10) of the firm. All facts germane to these events and transactions have a claim on being presented. In this sense, a fair presentation is one in which all of the elements of the company's financial picture receive their appropriate notice in accordance with the rules or principles of accounting.

Some have argued that fairness in accounting should also involve a more expansive presentation of material and social as well as financial information (Williams 1987). True fairness in accounting should include an objective statement of how the firm is fulfilling its social responsibilities and whether the firm's engagements and activities have costs to third parties not otherwise manifest in their balance sheets (Monti-Belkaoui and Riahi-Belkaoui 1996, 58–59). This approach remains controversial. For example, given the variety and contestability of what counts as a "social responsibility" it is not obvious that such statements would be easily consistent with the AICPA's appeal to objectivity.

Turning from accounting to public disclosure, the Securities Act of 1933 and the Securities Exchange Act of 1934 provide the regulatory background for the disclosure of material deemed relevant for the prudent investor. Prior to the act of 1934, the information disclosed was left up to the corporation unless it was listed on an exchange which required that the balance sheets and income statements be made public (Benston 1982, 170). So even prior to the regulations of 1934 there was disclosure. In fact, there are market incentives for disclosing information. Any corporation that wishes to sell stock has a strong interest in providing the information that a reasonable investor would want to know, thereby demonstrating that the corporation is in sound condition and well run (Benston 1982, 172–173). "There is almost no evidence to support the assertion that the financial statements of publicly traded companies were fraudulently or misleadingly prepared in the years prior to the passage of the securities act" (Benston 1982, 185). Those disclosures were not necessarily made for reasons of fairness, but they do reveal how market incentives can accomplish precisely what the advocate of fairness might demand. This is an important consideration, if only because a regime of mandatory disclosure will have its own costs (Benston 1982, 177, 191; Shefrin and Statman 1992, 38).

Shefrin and Statman delineate three thresholds of disclosure. The first is "buyer beware," in which there is no guarantee of truthfulness; a second is disclosure in which there is no *mis*representation, even if there is not full disclosure of what a prudent and reasonable investor would want; the third stage is mandatory disclosure (Shefrin and Statman 1992, 34). They contend that any shift from a framework of buyer beware to that of no misrepresentation is a move toward fairness because it serves to equalize the information available to investors, though it still allows for the inequalities of "cognitive errors and imperfect self-control" (Shefrin and Statman 1992, 42).

Why is disclosure deemed fair? Setting aside that nondisclosure is distinct from willful misrepresentation, disclosure is often thought to be a step toward a fair playing field in which all investors have access to the same information. This could mean that "the parties to a trade [either] actually *possess* the same information or have equal *access* to information" (Boatright 2008, 33). There is, clearly, no meaningful sense in which parties could possess the same information, but there is a sense in which the access to the information could be more or less equal (Boatright 2008, 33). After all, one must expend effort to secure the information, and the ability to comprehend, process, or analyze information will vary widely. Thus, even if companies disclose to the public all material information, the qualities of individuals—their natural talents or educational levels—may affect how well they can process the information. Perhaps those who have a better education or greater financial aptitude will make better investment decisions than others (or perhaps not!). However, if the prices of stocks reflect all available information, as held by the efficient market hypothesis, then the same information is available to everyone. Moreover, as Boatright acknowledges, "this kind of equal information is possible only if people with superior information are allowed to trade on it" (Boatright 2008, 33; see also Benston 1982, 188).

Turning to the responsibilities of financial professionals, the Securities and Exchange Commission states that brokers and dealers are to "treat investors fairly and honestly, putting investors' interests first" (SEC 2009, 3). One of the functions of a dealer or broker is to serve as a pillar of trust. Trustworthy financial firms help individuals to make sense of the plethora of investing options. A crucial responsibility for a broker or dealer in financial securities is, therefore, not to misrepresent a security.

Taking into account that a misrepresentation is an instance of fraud, not unfairness, an additional question arises: Should the financial profession offer clients investment vehicles that are *suitable* to the client's circumstances, aims, and risk profile? There are two levels of suitability. In the first, the broker recommends a security based on the unverified information that the client discloses to the broker; in the second and higher (or paternalistic) level, the broker must "elicit and verify information" from clients and use this to determine the clients' appropriate financial needs (Shefrin and Statman 1992, 55). The rules about suitability, especially the paternalistic ones, reduce efficiency by deterring a customer from buying the securities he wants and by thwarting those customers who are less risk averse than other investors (Shefrin and Statman 1992, 63–64). However, insofar as brokers or dealers voluntarily opt to recommend suitable investments, they may be responding to what customers want and expect.

From the perspective of the client, the broker who does not take into account even the first level of suitability may appear to be attempting to secure commissions at the client's expense, perhaps taking advantage of a client's lack of experience, knowledge, or prudence. This would be unfair in the sense that the client may have formed an expectation, encouraged by the broker, that the broker is working for the client (suitability of at least the first level). To the extent that the broker encourages this expectation but fails to conform to it, then the broker has engaged in a kind of deception. But is this also unfair? To understand how it may be unfair, one must appeal to a more traditional standard of fairness, the golden rule: Do unto others as you would have them do unto you. The failure to adhere to the first threshold of suitability is unfair in the sense that if the broker were the client, then that broker would want the expectation of first-level suitability fulfilled. The unfairness is captured by the fact that the broker is not demanding his own adherence to the expectation of suitability, though he would do so if he were the client.

Fairness in Lending

To grant a benefit to one person and to refuse it to a person who is relevantly similar and equally situated would seem to be unfair. Such unfairness is part of what is at issue in instances of discrimination, including discriminatory lending. When a bank lends money it must exercise a kind of legitimate discrimination in that it must evaluate the person to whom it is lending in order to determine whether that person will be able to repay the loan with interest. The creditworthiness of the person who seeks a loan is not only relevant but essential. (Many contend that the encouragement of home loans to those who did not meet the traditional criteria is one more factor in the financial crises of 2008. See Sowell 2009.)

In 1992, the Federal Reserve Bank of Boston published a study (Munnell et al. 1992) that suggested that banks were in fact engaging in racial discrimination. The Federal Reserve study has been the subject of numerous and serious criticisms, but it also has its defenders (see Ross and Ringer 2002). The first question to ask is whether such discrimination has, in fact, occurred (Boatright 2008, 115). Following Becker (1957, 5–9), if bankers harbor prejudices or discriminatory tastes, then they will be punished by the market. So if a bank is discriminating in the application of its lending criteria, then other lenders should be attracted to the opportunity to grant loans to those who have been the victims of discrimination. Still, even if there are disincentives to discriminatory lending, any discrimination is unfair because all applicants have claims to be evaluated by the relevant criteria for bank loans. However, if one adopts the Nozickean view that rights are side constraints, then lenders may have rights to discriminate even if there are market incentives for overcoming genuine discrimination.

Fairness and Insider Trading

Of the two major ethical arguments deployed *against* insider trading, one employs a conception of fairness, the other the idea of property rights. The property rights argument presumes that information is a scarce and valuable good; if information originates within a corporation, then that corporation has a right to use that information and may stipulate that no employee is permitted to trade on the information. If a corporation elects to allow such trading, then that is permissible from a property rights perspective. Indeed, from the standpoint of efficiency, some argue that insider trading should be permitted (Shefrin and Statman 1992, 83; Manne 1966).

The fairness argument turns on the question of whether insider trading upsets a level or fair playing field. If one accepts that investors should have equal access to information, then those who are insiders have information that is simply not available to the public. No matter how strenuously one tries, a private investor cannot gain the knowledge that the insider gleans from working for the corporation (Shefrin and Statman 1992, 83). However, there are many alternative circumstances in which there are inequalities of information and knowledge (Moore 1990, 153), and these inequalities, which often reflect a division of labor, do not seem unfair, nor does it seem unfair to profit from these inequalities. Considerations such as these weaken the argument of unfairness.

Typically, insider trading is conceptualized in terms of the buying or selling of a stock. Another kind of unfairness may arise, however, if one considers not the phenomenon of insider trading but the enforcement of its prohibition. Insofar as the price of a stock may appreciate over time, then insider knowledge may also be used as the basis for *holding* a stock, on the assumption that it will appreciate. Once the inside knowledge is made public and raises the price of the stock, then one may sell. The unfairness of such a pattern of enforcement is that the person who buys or sells is arrested but the person who holds and sells later gets rich (Boudreaux 2009, W2)!

CONCLUSION

Fairness proves to be a concept of some breadth and application. To invoke this idea in the context of financial ethics is to discover deep and interesting questions of law, policy, and morals. At the foundational level of markets, the concept of fairness generates interesting but contestable issues regarding income inequality, rights, and liberty. Moreover, the extent to which a government utilizes public debt as a source of revenue may reveal a bias toward current as opposed to future taxpayers. And the inflation of currency may prove unfair to those whose money or savings lose purchasing power.

Within the operational practices of finance and business, fairness has wide application and is often used as a justification of various kinds of financial disclosure. There is a genuine sense in which an accountant must construct a financial statement so that it "presents fairly" a picture of a company. However, there is greater controversy as to whether mandatory disclosure of a corporation's financial status is necessary or whether there is a meaningful sense in which such disclosure is considered fair. For financial professionals, the responsibility of ensuring that a client finds investments suitable for that person's circumstances and risk profile may fulfill fairness. Finally, in the case of bank and mortgage loans, it seems clear that discriminatory lending, if it exists, is unfair; it is less than obvious whether there is any unfairness in insider trading.

REFERENCES

Aristotle. 1941. Nicomachean ethics. In *The basic works of Aristotle*, ed. Richard McKeon. New York: Random House.

Becker, Gary S. 1957. *The economics of discrimination*. Chicago: University of Chicago.

Benston, George J. 1982. Security for investors. In *Instead of regulation: Alternatives to federal regulatory agencies*, ed. Robert W. Poole Jr. Lexington, MA: D. C. Heath and Company.

Boatright, John. 2008. *Ethics in finance*. 2nd ed. Malden, MA: Blackwell.

Boudreaux, Donald J. 2009. Learning to love insider trading. *Wall Street Journal*, October 24–25, W1–2.

Broome, John. 1990. Fairness. *Proceedings of the Aristotelian Society* 91:87–102.

Buchanan, James M. 1999. *Public principles of public debt: A defense and restatement [1958]. Vol. 2, The collected works of James M. Buchanan*. Indianapolis: Liberty Fund.

———. 2000. Confessions of a burden monger [1964]. In *Debt and Taxes, Vol. 14, The collected works of James M. Buchanan*. Indianapolis: Liberty Fund.

Duska, Ronald F., and Brenda Shay Duska. 2003. *Accounting ethics*. Malden, MA: Blackwell.

Federal Reserve Board. 2005. *The Federal Reserve system: Purposes and functions*. 9th ed. Washington, DC: Board of Governors of the Federal Reserve System.

Hayek, F. A. 1976. *Law, legislation, and liberty. Vol. 2, The mirage of social justice*. Chicago: University of Chicago Press.

Hooker, Brad. 2005. Fairness. *Ethical theory and moral practice* 8:329–352.

Hülsmann, Jörg Guido. 2008. *The ethics of money production*. Auburn, AL: Ludwig von Mises Institute.

Isaac, R. M., D. Mathieu, and E. E. Zajac. 1991. Institutional framing and perceptions of fairness. *Constitutional Political Economy* 2:329–370.

Kahneman, Daniel, Jack L. Knetsch, and Richard H. Thaler. 1986. Fairness and the assumptions of economics. *Journal of Business* 59:S285–S300.

Kant, Immanuel. 1970. Perpetual peace: A philosophical sketch [1795]. In *Kant's political writings*, trans. H. B. Nisbet, ed. Hans Reiss. Cambridge, MA: Cambridge University Press.

Macey, Jonathan. 1994. Administrative agency obsolescence and interest group formation: A case study of the SEC at sixty. *Cardozo Law Review* 15:909–949.

Manne, Henry G. 1966. *Insider trading and the stock market*. New York: Free Press.

Monti-Belkaoui, Janice, and Ahmed Riahi-Belkaoui. 1996. *Fairness in accounting*. Westport, CT: Quorum Books.

Moore, Jennifer. 1990. What is really unethical about insider trading? *Journal of Business Ethics* 9:171–182.

Munnell, Alicia H., Lynn E. Browne, James McEneaney, and Geoffrey M. B. Tootell. 1992. Mortgage lending in Boston: Interpreting the HMDA data. Working Paper 92-7, Federal Reserve Bank of Boston.

Nozick, Robert. 1974. *Anarchy, state, and utopia*. New York: Basic Books.

Rawls, John. 1999. *A theory of justice* [1971]. Rev. ed. Cambridge, MA: Harvard University Press.

Ross, Stephen L., and John Ringer. 2002. *The color of credit: Mortgage discrimination, research methodology and fair-lending enforcement.* Cambridge, MA: Massachusetts Institute of Technology.

Securities and Exchange Commission. 2009. The investor's advocate: How the SEC protects investors, maintains market integrity, and facilitates capital formation. www.SEC.gov/about/whatwedo.shtml.

Selgin, George. 1996. *Bank deregulation and monetary order.* London: Routledge.

Shefrin, Hersh, and Meir Statman. 1992. *Ethics, fairness, efficiency, and financial markets.* Charlottesville, VA: The Research Foundation of the Institute of Chartered Financial Analysts.

Smith, Adam. 1976. Wealth of nations [1776]. In *An inquiry into the nature and causes of the wealth of nations,* ed. R. H. Campbell, A. S. Skinner, and W. B. Todd. Oxford: Oxford University Press.

Sowell, Thomas. 2009. *The housing boom and bust.* New York: Basic Books.

Sunstein, Cass R. 1997. *Free markets and social justice.* New York: Oxford University Press.

Williams, Paul F. 1987. The legitimate concern with fairness. *Accounting Organizations and Society* 12:169–192.

Zajac, Edward E. 2002. What fairness-and-denial research could have told the Florida Supreme Court (and can tell the rest of us). *Independent Review* 6:377–397.

ABOUT THE AUTHOR

Eugene Heath is a professor of philosophy, State University of New York at New Paltz. Specializing in eighteenth-century British moral philosophy and business ethics, he has published on Bernard Mandeville, Adam Smith, and Adam Ferguson. He is the co-editor, with Vincenzo Merolle, of a two-volume collection on Ferguson: *Adam Ferguson: History, Progress and Human Nature* and *Adam Ferguson: Philosophy, Politics and Society.* His work in business ethics includes *The Morality of the Market: Ethics and Virtue in the Conduct of Business,* and essays on virtue and business, genetic commerce, and responsibility and pensions.

CHAPTER 10

Regulation

EDWARD SOULE

Associate Professor, McDonough School of Business, Georgetown University

The fact is that bankers are in the business of managing risk. Pure and simple, that is the business of banking.

—J. Pierpont Morgan[1]

INTRODUCTION

A dreadful chapter in U.S. commercial history is being written. When complete, it will chronicle institutional carnage of staggering proportions. The casualty list from a single month in 2008 included AIG, Lehman Brothers, Bear Stearns, Fannie Mae, Freddie Mac, Washington Mutual, Wachovia, and Merrill Lynch. Although debates as to the cause of the wider financial crisis will continue for years, this much is indisputable: A number of major financial institutions became insolvent—abruptly and without warning. That phenomenon, and what should be done about it, are the focus of this chapter.

Two general claims are defended here: (1) Defective risk management practices were to blame for the spate of firm failures; and (2) regulators with ample authority to constrain financial institutions from taking excessive risks did not do so. Aside from increased vigilance, a sensible response to these findings would include innovative regulatory strategies, ones that provide advance warnings of risk management catastrophes. As against these claims, advocates of regulatory reform blame other factors: from the housing bubble to credit default swaps. And rather than the performance of regulatory agencies, they blame the regulatory framework applicable to the financial services industry. Thus, for instance, the Obama administration proposes to reconfigure the regulatory agencies that oversee banks and broker-dealers and increase the scope of their authority (see Appendix A). As such, it takes aim at the wrong target, offers nothing in the way of novel strategies, and, therefore, is likely to disappoint. Or so it will be argued here.

The chapter proceeds as follows. The first section sketches the regulatory framework and dispels the widely shared but misleading belief that the financial services industry was deregulated. The second section argues that the relevant regulatory agencies were sufficiently empowered to discharge their legislative mandates; their failure to avert risk management breakdowns is not an indictment of the laws and regulations in force but the performance of individual agencies.

The third section is a proposal for improved regulation of banks and broker-dealers by focusing supervisory attention on their risk cultures. Fostering a culture that places a high priority on risk management is a critical responsibility of management; ensuring that it has been discharged should be a top priority of regulatory supervisors.[2]

THE REGULATORY FRAMEWORK

Among the universe of regulatory targets, the financial services industry is a particularly difficult one to hit. This section provides a brief sketch of the effort. It is not comprehensive but is designed to serve two purposes: (1) to describe the nature and scale of the regulatory project; and (2) to dispel the misconception that deregulation is to blame for the lax oversight of banks and broker-dealers.

The regulatory framework applicable to financial institutions has been erected over the course of nearly a century. Construction began with foundational legislation: the Federal Reserve Act of 1913 for banking and several Depression-era laws for broker-dealers. These acts established the broad contours of financial regulation and delegated implementation and enforcement authority to government agencies. Subsequent market conditions and business trends produced targeted legislation like the Bank Holding Company Act of 1956. More recently, ever-narrower initiatives have produced legislation with titles that include the words *reform*, *improvement*, or *efficiency*, signifying the remedial nature of laws like the Financial Institutions Reform, Recovery and Enforcement Act of 1989 and the Market Reform Act of 1990.

Three government agencies have primary responsibility for the safety and soundness of nationally chartered banks and thrifts: the Board of Governors of the Federal Reserve System (Fed), the Office of Thrift Supervision (OTS), and the Office of the Comptroller of the Currency (OCC).[3] The Securities and Exchange Commission (SEC) is responsible for the financial integrity of broker-dealers. The authority of these agencies is delineated in their enabling legislation and is bounded by the purposes and limitations specified therein or in subsequent legislation. Courts tend to defer to agency expertise and to uphold an agency's actions that have not exceeded its legislative purpose. There are exceptions: "arbitrary and capricious" actions, abuses of discretion, and so forth. But within the limits of reasonableness, regulators enjoy broad power and are given wide berth in using it.

Agencies have two means of bringing the law to bear on financial institutions: regulation and supervision. The former refers to the issuance of regulations, rules, and sundry guidelines and interpretations. Supervision entails everything else: monitoring, assessing, and enforcing compliance with the rules and regulations. The OCC, OTS, and Federal Reserve subject banks and thrifts to continuous monitoring, targeted examinations, and annual ratings. The SEC and the Financial Industry Regulatory Authority (FINRA), a self-regulatory organization with legislative origins, rely on periodic reports and annual examinations of broker-dealers. In order of importance, the success or failure of the regulatory project turns on supervision. Assiduous supervision can compensate for ambiguous or incomplete regulations, but the most comprehensive and explicit rules cannot make up for superficial oversight or feckless enforcement. This dynamic stems from the formidable powers that Congress vested in financial regulators. Those with a reputation for using it command attention, and supervision proceeds informally and privately between agency officials and firm management.

The informal and nonpublic dimension of agency supervision is well suited for the financial services industry. Rigid rules are inherently imperfect for rapidly changing and inordinately complicated institutions with a propensity to generate lethal risks out of seemingly benign activities. Try as they may, agencies have struggled to craft rules that cannot be interpreted opportunistically or otherwise circumvented. As such, supervision is a rational response to the formidable obstacles to achieving legislative objectives.[4]

From the point of view of most industry participants, there are at least two more layers of oversight: state laws and commissions of banking and securities, and the regulatory schemes of other nations. The cumulative effect is a robust and pervasive framework of laws, regulation, and supervision. Its reach and complexity is evident from the annual reports of major banks and broker-dealers. For instance, describing the regulatory environment applicable to Goldman Sachs required 6,514 words in its 2008 Form 10-K. Wells Fargo & Company required 4,043 words in its filing. Combined, these disclosures exceed the length of this chapter. In contrast, nonfinancial firms make passing references to regulation; Proctor & Gamble did so in 162 words in its 2008 Form 10-K.

Some prominent and authoritative voices would take issue with the foregoing characterization. Robert Kutner (2007) observed that "this old-fashioned panic is a child of deregulation." In particular, he cited legislation that repealed "the 1933 Glass-Steagall Act, which prohibited the same financial company from being both a commercial bank and an investment bank." Joseph Stiglitz (2008) lambasts "the wisdom of leaving markets to themselves" and compares U.S. financial regulation to the Chilean experiment in "free banking" under Augusto Pinochet. A less trenchant version of this criticism was advanced by then-Senator and presidential candidate Barack Obama in a speech entitled "Renewing the American Economy" (Obama 2008):

> ... [W]e have deregulated the financial services sector, and we face another crisis. A regulatory structure set up for banks in the 1930s needed to change because the nature of business has changed. But by the time the Glass-Steagall Act was repealed in 1999, the $300 million lobbying effort that drove deregulation was more about facilitating mergers than creating an efficient regulatory framework.

President Obama reiterated his belief that financial regulation had been "gutted" (Obama 2009). Thus, it is fair to associate him with those who endorse the following line of thought: By repealing the Glass-Steagall Act, the Gramm-Leach-Bliley Financial Services Modernization Act of 1999 (GLB Act) deregulated the financial services sector and, thereby, created the conditions for the financial crisis. If this deregulation narrative is accurate, then reparative legislation is clearly needed. Thus, the veracity of its core tenet warrants scrutiny: Was the Glass-Steagall Act a significant feature of the regulatory landscape before passage of the GLB Act? It will be argued here that it was not.

By way of background, the Glass-Steagall Act (technically, the Banking Act of 1933) introduced safeguards that were intended to restore the integrity of a very battered banking system.[5] Thus it is reasonable to believe that eliminating those safeguards would weaken the regulatory system, perhaps catastrophically. However, the Glass-Steagall Act was dismantled in stages, beginning with the Depository Institutions Deregulation and Monetary Control Act of 1980 and ending with the GLB Act of 1999. That last installment eliminated provisions that were intended to protect depository institutions by inhibiting them from engaging in securities businesses. But as Jackson (1987, 2) notes, *inhibiting* is not the same as *prohibiting*:

> *Although Glass-Steagall seemed to maintain the barriers between "banking" and "commerce" for half a century, depository financial, industrial, and securities firms have increasingly blended the businesses of banking and brokerage, using "loopholes" in the Act and other tactics. . . . Since 1982, as a result, banks and the financial arms of non-depository firms have become competitors to some extent.*

Or as Barth, Brumbaugh, and Wilcox (2000, 1) explain,

> *Since the barriers that separated banking from other financial activities have been crumbling for some time, the GLB Act is better viewed as ratifying, rather than revolutionizing, the practice of banking.*

Thus, to claim that the GLB Act enabled "broad" or "free" banking, or that it "dismantled" or "gutted" financial regulation, ignores prevailing practices at the time of its passage. Indeed, the likes of J.P. Morgan had fully diversified: Based on its 1999 annual report, the firm earned less from traditional banking activities than it did from its underwriting, trading, derivatives, and mergers and acquisitions businesses. A better characterization of the GLB Act is that it streamlined the process whereby depository and other financial institutions could operate within a holding company structure. And as former President Clinton noted in his defense of having signed the GLB Act (Bartiromo 2008), it has provided a vital tool in combating the financial crisis. For instance, unless the Glass-Steagall prohibition had been nullified, the government could not have called on JPMorgan Chase to take over Bear Stearns, and Bank of America would not have been able to rescue Merrill Lynch.

Historical accuracy aside, the deregulation narrative is at odds with recent events: The commingling of commercial and investment banking has not been a significant factor in the financial crisis. Depository institutions have been seriously or fatally damaged; but not because of the activities of a related firm in the securities industry. Rather, the failures of banks and thrifts stemmed primarily from residential and commercial real estate, quintessentially traditional banking businesses. Similarly, investment banks have suffered crippling losses, but not to the detriment of depository institutions. For instance, the losses that jeopardized the viability of Merrill Lynch did not threaten the safety or soundness of Merrill Lynch Bank & Trust Co., FSB. Nor did the investment-related liquidity crisis of AIG threaten the solvency of AIG Federal Savings Bank. Contrary to the deregulation narrative, we have not witnessed a repeat of the toxic mixture of activities that gave rise to the Glass-Steagall Act.

Granted, the GLB Act contains many other provisions, one of which limits the reach of regulatory authority. Another could (arguably) reduce the effectiveness of financial holding company regulation. Those provisions will be examined shortly, and their significance will be discounted. For now, suffice it to say that neither of them created serious gaps or otherwise impaired the regulatory framework applicable to banks and broker-dealers.

In sum, the deregulation narrative is an exercise in exaggeration if not an outright myth. The onslaught of failed financial institutions lends intuitive plausibility to this line of thought, but it does not comport with the facts. When accepted uncritically, the deregulation narrative motivates reform initiatives that seek to fix putative flaws in the regulatory framework, flaws that are cited as reasons for the lax oversight of banks and broker-dealers. A case in point is the Obama administration's proposal. But if agency authority was adequate, then these proposals are taking aim at the wrong target. Such is the claim of the next section.

ADEQUACY OF REGULATORY AUTHORITY

Whether regulation is adequate depends on its intended purpose. Some would argue that it should prevent financial crises, perhaps by targeting market bubbles and other known catalysts of financial dislocations. However, the history of financial crises, well documented by Kindleberger (1996), is a saga of human psychology run amok. There may not be a regulatory solution to market bubbles but there is a realistic strategy for ameliorating their damages: Limit the high-risk activities of major financial institutions. That objective is consistent with the legislative mandate of the agencies with responsibility for the financial integrity of U.S. banks and broker-dealers. Thus it will be assumed to be the appropriate objective for these purposes. Insofar as the agencies have fallen so short of achieving that goal, it is reasonable to ask, "What went wrong?"

The answer on offer here is performance: Regulatory agencies failed to use their authority to constrain the risk-taking activities of some major banks and broker-dealers. By way of pinpointing the failure, consider that there are two lines of defense against the hazards that can imperil financial institutions. The first consists of internal risk management systems and strategies and the second is agency supervision of that effort. The claim being made here is that regulators failed to intervene in deficient risk management practices. That interpretation is based on the beliefs that the risks were identifiable, that the agencies had adequate authority to constrain them, and that there were no impediments to its use. The following examples are intended to substantiate those beliefs and the claim they support.

Perhaps the most blatant risk management failures were related to subprime and other nontraditional residential mortgages. The blunder was not the mortgages per se but the size of the exposure in relation to capital, the financial cushion for absorbing losses. For instance, the Office of Thrift Supervision (2008) reported that as of June 30, 2008, Washington Mutual Bank (WMB) maintained $24 billion of capital in support of $307 billion of assets. Such leverage is not necessarily menacing; but it is downright treacherous when that asset base includes $122 billion of nontraditional mortgage loans.[6] A mere 10 percent decline in the value of those holdings stood to cut the bank's capital in half. Thus, it is not surprising that the OTS declared the company to be "in an unsafe and unsound condition" (OTS 2008, 1) on September 25, 2008. What is surprising is the OTS's longstanding assessment that "WMB met the well-capitalized standards" (OTS 2008, 2), a stance that was altered by receivership.

IndyMac, another OTS-supervised thrift, presented a similar risk profile to that of WaMu, was accorded the same "well capitalized" designation, and failed in a similarly abrupt fashion. As for the quality of its mortgage loan portfolio, FDIC chief operating officer John Bovenzi (2008) commented that "Most of the loans have little or no documentation, including no verification of income." As was the case with WMB, unambiguously imprudent banking practices were to blame for the failure of IndyMac, practices that were not identified by the OTS.

Risk management blunders were not limited to OTS-supervised thrifts. The Federal Reserve is the umbrella regulator of Citigroup, and the OCC and the OTS are the functional regulators of its banks and thrifts, respectively. Thus, any of these agencies could have intervened in the multiyear activities that culminated in the following risk profile on March 31, 2008: $48 billion of exposure to nontraditional mortgages; $48 billion of commercial real estate; $38 billion of loan commitments to highly leveraged borrowers; $17 billion of private equity investments; $7 billion of auction rate notes; and a $34 billion contingent liability to several structured investment vehicles, a now-defunct off-balance-sheet scheme that Citibank had pioneered. All told, $192 billion of hazards bore down on $127 billion of capital.[7] It is no surprise that Citigroup exists by dint of massive government support. But it is baffling that a trio of regulators did not act to halt the self-destruction of such a critically important balance sheet.

These episodes illustrate the nature and magnitude of the risk management failures that destroyed or crippled so many banks and thrifts. As portrayed, the hazards of imprudent balance sheet management and cavalier underwriting were unambiguously hazardous and within clear view. As against that characterization, it has been argued that regulators should be excused for not acting proactively with regard to the risks of nontraditional mortgages. Such is the stance of John Dugan, Comptroller of the Currency, in his defense of his agency's performance:

> *Collateralized debt obligations (CDOs) backed by subprime mortgages were the prime example of the need for better efforts here. Despite the inherent risk of the underlying collateral, the industry and regulators were lulled into a false sense of security by the triple-A ratings given to the super-senior tranches of these securities. Some of the exposure [to subprime mortgages] was masked in off-balance-sheet vehicles in ways that clouded the full extent of exposure. (OCC 2008, 2)*

This comment warrants unpacking. First, "the industry" was not lulled into a false sense of security by flawed credit ratings. In actuality, some banks were and some were not; but precious few institutions had lethal levels of exposure to subprime mortgages. Second, it is not the case that major banks were naïve buyers of nontraditional mortgages; after all, they were sponsors of CDOs and the same firms that have been accused of improperly engineering the triple-A ratings. Third, Dugan ignores the fact that to overconcentrate in an unproven asset class is to violate a basic tenet of prudent risk management—regardless of its credit rating. Finally, complex arrangements should not have impeded the OCC's ability to identify risk. Agencies can specify the format of information; "Enterprise-wide Exposure to Subprime Mortgages" could have been a line item in a mandatory report. Simply put, there is no justification for managers weighing down a balance sheet with nontraditional mortgages; and there is no good excuse for supervisors condoning it.

Dugan concludes his defense of the OCC with the following comment.

Indeed, some senior bank management thought they had avoided subprime risk by deliberately choosing to avoid originating such loans in the bank—only to find out after the fact that their investment banks had purchased subprime loans elsewhere to structure them into CDOs.

This is alarming. A CDO production desk requires specialized personnel, sophisticated systems, and significant capital. It is frightening to consider that such an operation could have been maintained without rigorous oversight. The fact that senior management learned of it after the fact is not indicative of a risk management flaw, it is a classic sign of a risk management system that had utterly failed. Dugan points to this example as evidence of the inscrutability of subprime mortgage risks. It is a better example of how a wholesale risk management breakdown could evade detection by a regulator that dedicates 27 examiners to each of the largest U.S. banks (OCC 2008, 13).

As for SEC supervision of broker-dealers, three episodes warrant attention: Lehman Brothers, Merrill Lynch, and Bear Stearns. As with bank and thrift failures, overconcentration in asset classes was a factor, but the broker-dealers had smaller margins for error. Citigroup supported $1.251 trillion of assets with $99 billion of equity capital at December 31, 2007, for an asset-to-capital ratio of 12.6 to 1. Merrill Lynch supported $1.020 trillion of assets with $31 billion of equity, a ratio of 33 to 1. Such extreme leverage entails extreme vulnerability when a firm does not properly align its assets with its liabilities. Such was the case with these firms, each of which was perilously dependent on overnight funding of illiquid and volatile positions. The risk management practices of these broker-dealers were not beyond the purview of SEC constraint. Indeed, they had been anticipated in the applicable law and regulations.

To explain, the SEC reduced the mandatory capital requirements of broker-dealers in 2004.[8] The increased leverage that ensued would not necessarily have been problematic had the Commission monitored the composition and alignment of firm balance sheets. Doing so required sweeping authority that cut across holding company structures, but such powers had been granted by the Market Reform Act of 1990. And a monitoring plan was developed: the Broker-Dealer Risk Assessment Program, the cornerstone of which was a comprehensive quarterly report of disaggregated nonpublic information. As designed, the SEC was able to assess "the risks ... that may stem from affiliated entities, including holding companies, and keep apprised of significant events that could adversely affect broker-dealers ..." (SEC IG, 2008: iii). In other words, the Commission was well positioned to curtail haphazard risk management practices.

Unfortunately, execution left much to be desired. A comment from a 2002 IG audit is revealing: "... the effectiveness of the broker-dealer Risk Assessment Program has been compromised by the lack of a supervisor ..." (SEC IG, 2002). The report describes an overburdened group of five accountants, two economists, two support staff, and no leader. To have assigned a staff of nine individuals to such a vital program is telling. To put that in perspective, the OCC has a staff of 467 assigned to the 17 largest banks or an average of 27 examiners and support personnel per bank (OCC 2008, 13). But an equally worrisome finding was that firms were filing incomplete information because the SEC had not finalized the applicable regulations.

In the past, underfunding may have explained such a feeble effort. However, that excuse dissolved after the Enron era corporate scandals and the enactment of Sarbanes-Oxley (SOX). As explained by then-Chairman of the SEC Christopher Cox, "[B]etween fiscal 2002 and 2004, the SEC hired more than 1,000 new employees—the largest staffing increase in the agency's history" (SEC 2005, 2). Jickling (2004) notes that the SEC budget increased from $423 million in fiscal year 2003 to $913 million in fiscal year 2005. And yet the Inspector General (IG) conducted another audit in 2008 and discovered that the regulations were still not finalized and the information was still not being filed. Worse yet, the temporary regulations were not being enforced and "nearly one-third of the firms failed to file [the report] ..." (SEC IG 2008, v). Of those that filed partial information, the IG noted that six received in-depth reviews but the other 140 were not reviewed at all. As an indicator of how assiduously the SEC was supervising the risks of broker-dealers, this is damning evidence.[9]

Advocates of regulatory reform could concede that lax supervision was a factor in the demise of financial institutions, but they excuse it or downplay its importance based on factors beyond the control of regulatory agencies. Two often-mentioned items, products of the GLB Act, are the unregulated status of credit default swaps and putative gaps in the supervisory coverage of financial holding companies. These items can be dismissed as excuses for dismal performance by examining the episode that culminated in the government takeover of American International Group, Inc. (AIG). Following is a brief synopsis of what transpired at AIG.

A subsidiary of AIG, AIG Financial Products Corp. (AIGFP), had initiated a large volume of credit default swaps (CDSs), a form of insurance on debt instruments. Although issuers of CDSs do not maintain reserves as would a traditional insurance company, they agree to maintain collateral over the life of the contract. The amount of the collateral is based on a number of factors, all of which went against AIGFP in late 2007. The resulting demands for additional collateral exceeded the liquid resources of AIGFP and its parent, AIG. If not for government intervention, AIGFP would have defaulted; and its counterparties, including several major financial institutions, would have realized losses of a potentially destabilizing magnitude.

As for the status of CDSs, the fact that they are unregulated means that the parties to a CDS can contract as they see fit. But if one (or both) of them is a bank or a registered broker-dealer, then a regulatory agency can specify the accounting treatment of the transaction on the books of the regulated entity, the method for computing the carrying value of the so-called insured security, and, thereby, its impact on regulatory capital. Thus, while CDSs are beyond the purview of regulation, the risk they pose to banks and broker-dealers is not. This is not to say that CDSs should remain unregulated—that is a separate matter. It is to say that there is ample authority to limit their risks to banks and broker-dealers.

As for alleged gaps in the coverage of financial holding companies, AIGFP did not evade regulatory oversight. Since the creation of AIG Federal Savings

Bank in 1999, AIG has been subject to regulation by the OTS. As described in the company's Form 10-K, this authority extends to "enforcement authority over AIG and its subsidiaries," and it "permits the OTS to restrict or prohibit activities that are determined to be a serious risk to the financial safety, soundness or stability of AIG's subsidiary savings association, AIG Federal Savings Bank."

Nonetheless, there remains an entrenched impression that "AIG exploited a huge gap in the regulatory system." That quotation is a response to a question that Senator Tim Johnson had posed to Donald Kohn, vice chairman of the Fed.[10] Asked to elaborate on the gap, Kohn stated that "... no one was responsible for the whole company ... and there was a piece of the company, Financial Products, that wasn't being supervised and regulated by anybody." At the conclusion of his comments, Scott Polakoff, the then-acting director of OTS, set the record straight:

> ... it's time for OTS to raise their hand and say, "We have some accountability and responsibility here." This entity [AIG] was deemed a Savings and Loan Holding Company and we were deemed the acceptable regulator for both U.S. domestic and international operations. The segment, this AIG Financial Products, was an unregulated, as that term is defined, subsidiary of AIG but part of the overall consolidated regulatory responsibilities of OTS.

While there is not enough evidence to explain the dismal performance of U.S. financial regulators, there are some early indicators of what went wrong. A recent Government Accountability Office (GAO) examination of the banking agencies reported a common refrain: Officials admitted that "they did not fully appreciate the risks to the institutions under review" (GAO 2009, 4). If, after further study, that explanation holds, then the performance breakdowns can be chalked up to errors in judgment. While every supervisory protocol is vulnerable to human error, those employed by financial regulators would appear to be particularly worrisome. All of them use similar techniques and none of them acted proactively with regard to momentous risk management failures. This would appear to call for novel supervisory strategies, protocols unlike any in current use. One possibility is introduced in the next section.

REGULATING ROOT CAUSES

Losses from imprudent lending, reckless trading, and ill-conceived investments are unavoidable facts of life in the financial services industry. However, they rarely incapacitate firms in which risk management is embedded in the culture: when risk is a top-of-mind consideration for traders, investment bankers, lending officers, and other employees in risk-prone positions. Conversely, debilitating losses and outright failures are lively possibilities when those employees have little concern for the downside of their conduct. Thus, the effectiveness of risk management is not a function of the sophistication of the systems or the rigor of regulatory oversight alone. Rather, it turns on an intangible factor: the culture in which those systems are situated.

This relationship between formal controls, organizational culture, and performance is well supported by scholarly research; Treviño and Nelson (2004) and Treviño and colleagues (1999) are two good examples. And it has been confirmed empirically: The Ethics Resource Center (2007) has conducted multiple examinations of employee conduct, the upshot of which is that culture tends to trump controls in terms of how people behave. This was borne out by the Enron-era scandals (Soule 2005). That is, deviant conduct was not deterred by an array of internal controls and a number of external gatekeepers; nor did threats of legal sanctions alter the course of events. Post-hoc examinations of Enron, WorldCom, and other scandal-ridden companies revealed what scholarly research and empirical studies would have predicted: The offending conduct was the manifestation of corporate cultures that valued short-term profitability and personal enrichment, regardless of how the earnings were created or the risks they entailed. In short, internal controls and external constraints were no match for the values, beliefs, and attitudes of the people doing the work.

Although the literature and studies are focused primarily on ethical conduct, the findings are germane to risk management. Both are compliance efforts. In the case of ethics, the objective is conduct that meets the ethical expectations of society, as expressed in a code of conduct or otherwise communicated. In the case of risk management, the objective is conduct in conformity with principles of prudential risk management, as expressed in operational directives and compliance documents. Based on this alignment, it would follow that if employees believe that risk management is one of those things that "really matters around here," then it will. Losses would still be incurred, but the chances of catastrophic damage would be minimized. Alternatively, if employees believe that risk management is not taken seriously, or if it is of secondary importance to short-term profits, then potentially lethal losses are lively possibilities. Following is a side-by-side illustration of this phenomenon.

As previously discussed, Citigroup was hobbled by the cumulative effect of a long list of imprudent activities. JPMorgan Chase & Co. (JPM), a similarly configured firm with overlapping businesses, avoided them. The company had a small exposure to subprime mortgages and none to the more exotic varieties. JPM did not sponsor structured investment vehicles and did not participate in esoteric structured finance products. And the JPM balance sheet was conservatively managed: Capital and liquidity levels were above industry averages and funding sources were properly aligned with its assets. The contrast with Citigroup could not be more striking. In terms of damages sustained, JPM has preserved $171 billion of market capitalization while Citigroup owes its very existence to the U.S. Government.[11]

Given the size and sophistication of these two firms, it is safe to assume that their internal control and risk management systems are equally sophisticated. So what might account for their disparate performances? In his 2008 shareholder letter, CEO Jamie Dimon offered the following explanation of JPM's performance:

> *Our culture of strong risk management (proper due diligence, documentation, auditing, among other measures) is consistent with our philosophy of putting clients' interests first and has enabled us to avoid many of the negative developments that surfaced last year. (JPM 2009, 7).*

Tett (2009) confirms the veracity of this comment. It is also borne out by Cisafulli (2009), a study of Dimon that includes a chapter entitled, "Never, Ever Forget the Downside." As for Citigroup, the equivalent letter from CEO Vikram Pandit contains no mention of culture, except in a reference to his determination to build a "culture of meritocracy" (Citigroup 2009, 3). However, there is a reference to "risk culture" buried deep in the body of the 2008 annual report:

> *Significant focus has been placed on fostering a risk culture based on a policy of "Taking Intelligent Risk with Shared Responsibility, without forsaking Individual Accountability." (Citigroup 2008, 51)*

One can only wince at such a pronouncement. Worse yet is the string of legalistic definitions that follows it:

> *'Taking intelligent risk' means that Citi must carefully identify, measure and aggregate risks, and must fully understand downside risks.*

> *'Shared responsibility' means. . . . [And so forth]*

It is jarring to consider that someone in a position of authority in the nation's largest bank thought it was necessary to specify the importance of identifying and measuring risk on an enterprise-wide basis. To have done so in such uninspiring text is evidence that risk management was probably not a deeply entrenched, top-of-mind consideration for Citigroup traders or bankers.

Another example of a culture that promotes conservative risk management is the Royal Bank of Canada (RBC). As the largest of the so-called "Big Five" Canadian banks, RBC has been virtually unscathed by the financial crisis. That performance cannot be attributed to its location, insofar as banks headquartered in London, Paris, Zurich, and elsewhere around the world suffered severe damages. Nor can it be attributed to its size or activities. RBC is engaged in the same businesses as other global banks, and with a market capitalization of $82 billion at the end of 2007, it was larger than many of the banks that suffered severe damages. But the following excerpt from the RBC 2008 Annual Report is illuminating:

> *Our management of risk is supported by sound risk management practices and effective enterprise risk management frameworks including capital management and liquidity management. The cornerstone of these frameworks is a strong risk management culture, supported by a robust enterprise-wide set of policies, procedures and limits which involve our risk management professionals, business segments and other functional teams. (RBC 2009, 83)*

Finally, consider a study of the 11 largest financial institutions by senior regulatory officials of the United States, the United Kingdom, France, Germany, and Switzerland. Through interviews and analysis, the group identified factors that account for successful risk management performance. Primary among them was the following:

> *An overarching difference is apparent in the balance that senior management achieved between expanding the firms' exposures in what turned out to be high-risk activities and fostering an appropriate risk management culture to administer those activities. (Senior Supervisors Group 2008, 7)*

The report containing this finding goes on to explain what "an appropriate risk management culture" entails. With a few modifications for context, it could have been abstracted from a study of ethical culture: hands-on leadership involvement, enterprise-wide communication, elevating the importance of minimizing risk, and so forth.

Granted, anecdotes do not constitute data. But the foregoing illustrations provide compelling reasons to anticipate a corollary to the connection between the ethical performance of an organization and its culture: that an organization's propensity to manage risk is a function of its culture. At a minimum, the role of organizational culture should be a pressing concern to regulatory agencies.

As against this emphasis on the role of culture, there are alternative accounts of what went wrong and what warrants regulatory attention. However, their plausibility is in doubt. The more compelling of them violate a basic principle of social science: A universal condition does not explain aberrant phenomena. Following is an example of this flawed reasoning.

Rebonato (2007) faults the use of statistical risk models (e.g., value at risk or VaR) for risk management failures. Taleb (2007) agrees. But since virtually every large bank employed VaR, the casualties should have been nearly universal. Why did just a subset of banks experience catastrophic breakdowns? RBC management explains that "VaR is a risk measure that is only meaningful in normal market conditions. To address more extreme market events, stress testing is used . . ." (RBC 2009, 183). Likewise, Nocera (2009) reported that Goldman Sachs disregarded its statistical models during periods of market turmoil. Since the inherent flaws of statistical risk models were well known at the time, what inclined the managers of RBC, Goldman, and many other firms to abandon the models while others slavishly followed them? A satisfactory answer to that question must refer to some distinguishing characteristic(s) of the firms that successfully managed risk. Organizational culture is a lively possibility because unlike the use of VaR, it is a firm-specific factor.

Jickling (2009) assembled a list of 26 other explanations of what went wrong. Next to each entry is a synopsis of the argument in support of it; and next to that is a reason why the account is not plausible. Like the preceding illustration, each explanation cites a general market condition or practice that would have applied with more or less equal force to all similarly situated firms (e.g., the glut of inexpensive funds) or practices that were in widespread use (e.g., securitization and credit default swaps). The list was comprehensive when published and remains exhaustive.

Suffice it to say that it would behoove regulatory supervisors to concentrate their efforts on the risk cultures of banks and broker-dealers. Indeed, unlike many performance metrics, insight into the culture of an organization can provide advance warning of calamitous developments. For instance, consider New Century Financial Corp., a critical organization at the bottom of the subprime mortgage feeding chain. The company originated $56 billion in loans in 2005 (2005 Form 10-K). As the economy softened, portfolio losses mounted. Additional losses were incurred when the company was required to repurchase underperforming loans that had been sold to investment banks. To compound matters, New Century was unable to renew its lines of credit. On April 2, 2007, the company petitioned for bankruptcy protection. Although New Century was not subject to banking regulation, it was publicly traded and, therefore, subject to SEC disclosure requirements and the internal control provisions of Sarbanes-Oxley.

New Century's abrupt demise was not foreseeable from any of its publicly disclosed information. But what is not evident from any public disclosure is a complete disregard for prudent lending practices. Such qualitative information would have emerged from an assessment of New Century's culture, a process that would have involved structured interviews with "employees in the know," as Treviño and colleagues (1999) and Treviño and Nelson (2004) dubbed them. By way of example, consider the following excerpt from an interview that Cho (2007) conducted with a New Century appraiser.

> *Maggie Hardiman cringed as she heard the salesmen knocking the sides of desks with a baseball bat as they walked through her office.* Bang! Bang!
> *'You cut my [expletive] deal!' she recalls one man yelling at her. 'You can't do that.' Bang! The bat whacked the top of her desk. As an appraiser for a company called New Century, Hardiman was supposed to weed out bad mortgage applications. Most of the mortgage applications Hardiman reviewed had problems, she said. But 'you didn't want to turn away a loan because all hell would break loose,' she recounted in interviews. When she did, her bosses often overruled her and found another appraiser to sign off on it.*

If that episode was representative of New Century's underwriting practices, then the company's risk culture was utterly corrupt—vital information for gauging the firm's viability. A competent assessment of the culture in several New Century loan production offices would have revealed more about what was in store for New Century stakeholders—and investors in subprime mortgages—than all of its other disclosures combined. Indeed, it would have signaled that those disclosures should not be relied upon. Unfortunately, accurate assessments of organizational culture do not automatically emerge. The degenerate situation at New Century evaded detection by KPMG in the course of its audits, notwithstanding the increased scrutiny of a SOX-mandated audit of internal controls. And it evaded detection by a court-appointed examiner (Missal 2008) whose report notes minimal irregularities in the company's practices. This, and similar such episodes, suggest that unless the culture of an organization is the target of a systematic examination then it will not receive the attention it deserves.

To be clear, New Century was not subject to regulatory supervision. But based on the IndyMac episode, it is not obvious that an OTS examiner would have focused sufficient attention on cultural factors. Not to single out the OTS, culture is simply not a priority from a regulatory point of view. Case in point: Fed examiners are instructed that "the CEO should establish and communicate a corporate culture that promotes safe, sound, and prudent business practices." That quote is from the Federal Reserve Bank Holding Company Supervision Manual (3070.0.1.4), on page 731 of a 1,661-page tome in which "culture" appears only nine more times (ignoring those instances where it is preceded by "agri"). The OCC Examination Handbook includes references to culture but none of them treat it as an attribute worthy of rigorous evaluation. And the OTS Examination Handbook contains no references to culture. The impression that culture is not a priority for any of these agencies is confirmed by the absence of a protocol for assessing it.

The failure to systematically assess the risk culture of financial organizations is a grievous oversight but a promising opportunity. And it is not farfetched; the importance of culture has crept into at least two regulatory regimes. Following is a sketch of each.

The first requires a little background. The U.S. Sentencing Commission issues guidelines for use by Federal courts in determining fines and prison sentences. In the case of businesses, the Federal Sentencing Guidelines for Organizations (FSGO) specifies a basic fine that considers the nature of the misconduct and the damages inflicted. Courts can increase or decrease it, depending on a variety of considerations that are expressed numerically as a culpability score multiplier (CSM). A troubling realization emerged in the wake of the scandals of 2001–2002: Enron and WorldCom—poster children of corporate malevolence—would have earned favorable CSMs by dint of their sophisticated compliance and ethics programs. In response, the Commission amended the Guidelines so that simply installing and maintaining these programs would no longer qualify. In the future, they would have to be effective. The section that defines "effective" reads in pertinent part as follows:

> To have an effective compliance and ethics program . . . an organization shall . . . promote an organizational culture that encourages ethical conduct and a commitment to compliance with the law.[12]

The second example involves the Public Company Accounting Oversight Board (PCAOB), the agency that supervises auditors of publicly traded companies. Its chairman, Mark Olson (2006), explained a key consideration in the inspection of public accounting firms:

> PCAOB inspections begin by looking at the professional environment in which audits are performed and focuses on the influences—both good and bad—on a firm's audit practice. These influences include a firm's culture and the relationships between the firm's audit practice and its other practices, as well as between engagement personnel in field or affiliate offices and a firm's national office.

The U.S. Sentencing Commission does not specify how to determine whether an organization has fostered a culture that encourages ethical conduct, and the PCAOB does not publicize its methodology for assessing the culture of public accounting firms. However, models are available, and one in particular warrants mention. The U.S. Chemical Safety and Hazard Investigation Board (CSB) conducts "root cause investigations" of industrial chemical accidents. Insofar as the root cause of the most serious industrial accidents are defective organizational cultures, the agency's methodology is a case study in how to rigorously assess the operative values, beliefs, and attitudes of employees in risk-prone areas of organizations. Following is a sketch of one such exercise.

The CSB investigated the explosion of a British Petroleum (BP) refinery on March 23, 2005, that claimed 15 lives and injured 180 people. The investigation uncovered equipment malfunctions and operator errors, but focusing on what took place on the morning of March 23 "misses the underlying and significant cultural, human factors, and organizational causes of the disaster that have a greater preventative impact" (CSB 2007, 19). The underlying cause was described as follows:

> *The Texas City disaster was caused by organizational and safety deficiencies at all levels of the BP Corporation. Warning signs of a possible disaster were present for several years, but company officials did not intervene effectively to prevent it. The extent of the serious safety culture deficiencies was further revealed when the refinery experienced two additional serious incidents just a few months after the March 2005 disaster. (CSB 2007, 18)*

That conclusion is based on the results of a systematic assessment of the BP safety culture. As detailed in the Report of the BP U.S. Refineries Independent Safety Review Panel (January 2007), 700 in-depth interviews were conducted with current employees and retirees at all levels of the organization. Additionally, an extensive and thoughtfully designed survey was administered to 10,348 refinery employees and contractors; 7,450 or 72 percent of them responded. Many of these workers were not from the Texas City refinery and served as a control group for questions like the following: "In my work group, process safety concerns are secondary to achieving production goals." In one refinery, 82 percent of the operations personnel disagreed with that statement, but in the Texas City refinery only 7 percent did so. Not surprisingly, the results of this study were not disputed by BP.

Industrial safety would appear to be unrelated to the safety and soundness of financial institutions. But the disasters that occur in each domain are of the same category: They are wide-scale organizational failures or, to put it less abstractly, management failures. As such, it is not surprising to find a common denominator between chemical plant disasters and catastrophic bank failures. Such was the finding of a 1988 study by the OCC Administrator of National Banks. Contrary to the perception that external factors (e.g., economic conditions) cause banks to fail, the Administrator examined 171 bank failures and discovered that they were the result of "poor management and other internal problems" (OCC 1988).

In summary, there are ample reasons to focus supervisory attention on the risk management culture of banks and broker-dealers. For these purposes, to "focus attention" would entail a formal protocol specifying the manner and frequency of assessments. The assessment need not be as extensive as the CSB assessment of the BP disaster, but two aspects of it warrant inclusion. First, it is proactive. Employees are not inclined to use anonymous whistleblower hotlines, but they are responsive to surveys and very responsive to interviews. The CSB approach does not passively await information but harvests it from the only credible source. Second, the CSB engaged outside experts to design and administer the data gathering process. The results speak for themselves: The questions are carefully worded and the results are unambiguous and authoritative.

The CSB is an obscure federal agency with a budget of less than $12 million, a fraction of the cost of operating a financial regulator (e.g., $775 million for the OCC in fiscal year 2009). Ideally, the expertise of that tiny agency would also be resident in its colossal cousins. But unlike the CSB, financial regulators have the ability to act before disasters strike. Periodically assessing risk cultures provides advance warnings, but the process itself stands to alter the course of events. To increase the transparency of an organization's culture is to increase the chances that it will be managed in a manner that comports with regulatory objectives.

CONCLUSION

The finding that culture can trump compliance implies that the safety and soundness of any given bank or broker-dealer could be impervious to conventional supervisory strategies. Simply put, the arsenal of techniques is ill suited for large, complex organizations whose leaders accord so little importance to risk management that traders, loan officers, and investment bankers have little concern for the downside risks of their conduct. That sad reality flies in the face of the conventional approach to the supervision of financial institutions. But it is consistent with the history of the financial services industry: a chronicle of prominent institutions abruptly imploding in a maelstrom of recklessness.

This is not to say that traditional supervisory approaches should be abandoned. They are formidable forces in fostering and maintaining a healthy risk culture. The ideas advanced here would add a supervisory protocol: one that places a feature of organizational culture on the same footing as operational and financial metrics. At present, the latter have monopolized attention while the former is ignored. This proposal would elevate the importance of culture to the point that it would be systematically assessed, just like any other indicator of the performance and condition of federally supervised financial institutions.

In closing, the core idea of this paper was expressed by John Stumpf, CEO of Wells Fargo & Company. The setting was a hearing before the House Financial Services Committee on February 11, 2009. Representative Melvin Watt asked whether there is a need for "an even more aggressive regulatory framework for larger banks or other institutions that have systemic risk potential." Stumpf responded as follows: "I think success and failure is more a condition of culture and leadership and values than it is [a matter of] small or large. In our case, we have a strong culture; we are able to buy a firm, merge with a firm, using our own money."

Unfortunately, the Congressman cut him off at that point. Had he been allowed to continue, Representative Watt would have learned what has gone so tragically wrong with some prominent financial institutions, and the futility of trying to fix it by passing a law.

APPENDIX A
CURRENT LEGISLATIVE ACTIVITY

As this chapter goes to press, several reform proposals are in circulation. Although the ultimate outcome defies prediction, the main contenders share a key feature: a tilt toward consolidated regulation. For instance, the Obama administration would increase the authority of the Fed to include "all firms that could pose a threat to financial stability, even those that do not own banks" (U.S. Department of the Treasury 2009, 3). Additionally, the plan entails a merger of the OCC and the OTS into a new entity, the National Bank Supervisor. The Senate Committee on Banking, Housing, and Urban Affairs and the House Committee on Financial Services have authored similar plans, albeit with different mechanisms. Insofar as some version of consolidated regulation would appear to be a lively possibility, the concept warrants a brief examination.

It is important to stipulate that none of the proposals creates any new supervisory authority; rather, they concentrate existing authority in fewer agencies and expand the universe of entities subject to it. But because the most severe risk management failures transpired within banks and broker-dealers, an expanded universe of regulated entities would not have averted the institutional breakdowns on display lately. Thus, any improvements from the proposals will come from the increased efficiency and efficacy of vesting authority in fewer agencies, two in the case of the Administration's plan. Because this plan has been in circulation the longest and its details are easier to discern, it will be the focus of the discussion that follows.

As for the efficiency of consolidated regulation, size and complexity are the bane of agency performance, and the Federal Reserve stands to be a significantly larger organization with a considerably more complex mission. It would seem to be a more streamlined approach, but the benefits of consolidation could be confounded by the nature of what would be consolidated. Realistically, it is not feasible for a single group of professionals to supervise every type of financial business—the work is too specialized. Rather, a discrete staff with expertise in securities will be needed; another for banking; and another for commodities and futures. The result is likely to resemble a mini-SEC, a mini-OCC, and a mini Commodity Futures Trading Commission (CFTC). Whether a regulatory conglomerate would be more efficient than the current configuration of stand-alone specialized agencies under an umbrella regulator is anyone's guess. Granted, interagency rivalries would be eliminated; but interdepartmental conflicts can be equally counterproductive.

Likewise, the efficacy of consolidation is questionable. Most significantly, the recent performance of the Federal Reserve in supervising bank holding companies does not inspire confidence in its expanded role—a span of authority that would make the Federal Reserve way too big to fail. Nor does the performance of what advocates of consolidation hail as "the world's premiere consolidated agency" (Jackson 2008, 1), the British Financial Services Agency. In 2008, the Agency's tenth year of operation, Northern Rock plc was nationalized. Shortly thereafter, two diversified banking concerns, the Royal Bank of Scotland Group and Lloyds Banking Group, were bailed out. Finally, a £400 billion ($692 billion) bailout plan for a group of large UK banks was announced on October 8, 2008 (BBC 2008). More recently, the program has been enlarged. This scenario should seem eerily familiar to American observers. And it should dampen enthusiasm for consolidation.

This is not to say that consolidation is a bad idea—the Canadian regime is consolidated and its banks were ranked first in soundness by global business leaders (Porter and Schwab 2009). It is to say that consolidated regulation is the wrong idea. It has been billed as the elixir for what ails a flawed framework. This study has urged a different diagnosis: substandard agency performance. If that is an accurate assessment then the reform proposals on offer are apt to disappoint. Not only are they bereft of supervisory innovations, it is improbable (at best) that combining substandard performing agencies will dramatically improve their performance. And to be sure, the safety and soundness of U.S. financial institutions calls for nothing short of dramatically improved agency performance.

NOTES

1. Quotation from Buder (2009, 143).
2. The scope of this investigation is limited to the safety and soundness of depository institutions (i.e., banks, thrifts, and savings associations) and securities broker-dealers (i.e., brokerage firms and investment banks). Thus, references to "financial institutions"

do not include insurance companies nor government-sponsored enterprises (GSEs) such as Fannie Mae and Freddie Mac.

3. The safety and soundness of state-chartered banks and thrifts that are not a part of the Federal Reserve System are supervised by the Federal Deposit Insurance Corporation (FDIC). Insofar as these institutions have not figured prominently in the financial crisis, the agency is not germane to this study.

4. These observations were informed by a decade of personal experience as a senior financial manager in the financial services industry.

5. But as Barth, Brumbaugh, and Wilcox (2006) point out, subsequent studies dispute the assumption upon which Glass-Steagall was enacted. Benston (1989) and Puri (1996) reject the notion that the securities businesses of commercial banks were to blame for the bank failures that ushered in the Great Depression. And Kroszner and Rajan (1997) cite evidence indicating that that commingling the two businesses was beneficial.

6. The balance included $16 billion of subprime and $52.9 billion of payment-option adjustable-rate mortgages plus $53.4 billion of home equity lines of credit.

7. This data was included in Citigroup's first quarter 2009 earnings review dated April 17, 2009. It can be downloaded from http://www.citigroup.com/citi/fin/qer.htm.

8. Alternative Net Capital Requirements for Broker-Dealers That Are Part of Consolidated Supervised Entities (17 CFR Parts 200 and 240), http://www.sec.gov/rules/final/34-49830.pdf.

9. Lest these remarks be interpreted as uncharitable or unnecessarily trenchant, I am on record as having respected and admired the work of the SEC in years past (Soule 2002). It is not clear when or why that aggressive watchdog became so passive.

10. The setting was a hearing before the U.S. Senate Committee on Banking, Housing, and Urban Affairs on March 5, 2009.

11. As reported by the *Wall Street Journal* on March 12, 2010.

12. FSGO, §8B2.1(2).

REFERENCES

Barth, J., R. Brumbaugh, and J. Wilcox. 2000. The repeal of Glass-Steagall and the advent of broad banking. *Journal of Economic Perspectives* 14:191–204.

Bartiromo, M. 2008. Bill Clinton on the banking crisis, McCain, and Hillary. *BusinessWeek*, September 24. http://www.businessweek.com/print/magazine/content/08_40/b4102000409948.htm.

BBC. 2008. Rescue plan for UK banks unveiled. BBC News, October 8, http://news.bbc.co.uk/1/hi/business/7658277.stm#chart.

Benston, G. 1989. *The separation of commercial and investment banking: The Glass-Steagall act revisited and reconsidered.* New York: Oxford University Press.

Bernanke, B. 2009. Speech to the Council of Foreign Relations, Washington, DC, March 10.

Bovenzi, J. 2008. The role of deposit insurance in financial crises: Past and present. Speech in Arlington, VA. October 29. http://www.fdic.gov/news/news/speeches/archives/2008/chairman/spoct2908.html.

Buder, S. 2009. *Capitalizing on change: A social history of American business.* Chapel Hill, NC: University of North Carolina Press.

Cho, David. 2007. Pressure at mortgage firm led to mass approval of bad loans. *Washington Post*, May 7, A01.

Citigroup, Inc. 2009. 2008 Annual Report. New York: Citigroup, Inc. http://www.citibank.com/citi/fin/data/ar08c_en.pdf.

Cisafulli, P. 2009. *The house of Dimon*. Hoboken, NJ: John Wiley & Sons.

Ethics Resource Center. 2007. National business ethics survey. Washington, DC: Ethics Resource Center. http://www.ethics.org/research/NBESOffers.asp.

Government Accountability Office (GAO). 2009. Financial regulation: Review of regulators' oversight of risk management systems at a limited number of large, complex financial institutions. GAO-09-499T. U.S. Governmental Accountability Office: March 18.

Jackson, H. 2008. A pragmatic approach to the phased consolidation of financial regulation in the United States. Working Paper. SSRN. November 12. http://ssrn.com/abstract=1300431.

Jackson, W. 1987. Glass-Steagall act: Commercial vs. investment banking. *Congressional Research Service*, June 29. http://digital.library.unt.edu/ark:/67531/metacrs9065/.

Jickling, M. 2004. Barriers to corporate fraud: How they work, why they fail. *Congressional Research Service*, December 27. http://assets.opencrs.com/rpts/RL32718_20041227.pdf.

———. 2009. Causes of the financial crisis. *Congressional Research Service*, January 29. http://fpc.state.gov/documents/organization/116693.pdf.

JP Morgan Chase & Co (JPM). 2009. 2008 Annual Report. New York: JPM. http://investor.shareholder.com/jpmorganchase/annual.cfm.

Kindleberger, C. 1996. *Manias, panics, and crashes: A history of financial crises*. New York: John Wiley & Sons.

Kroszner, R., and R. Rajan. 1997. Organization structure and credibility: Evidence from commercial bank securities activities before the Glass-Steagall act. *Journal of Monetary Economics* 39:475–516.

Kutner, R. 2007. The bubble economy. *The American Prospect*, September 24. http://www.prospect.org/cs/articles?article=the_bubble_economy.

Missal, M. 2008. Final report of bankruptcy court examiner. In re: New Century TRS Holdings, Inc., a Delaware corporation, et al., Debtors. February 29, 2008.

Nocera, J. 2009. Risk mismanagement. *New York Times Magazine*, January 2, MM24.

Office of Thrift Supervision (OTS). 2008 Fact Sheet on Washington Mutual Bank. Washington, DC: Office of Thrift Supervision. http://files.ots.treas.gov/730021.pdf.

Office of the Comptroller of the Currency (OCC). 1988. Bank failure: An evaluation of the factors contributing to the failure of national banks. Washington, DC: Office of the Comptroller of the Currency. http://www.occ.treas.gov/bankfailure.pdf.

———. 2008. Annual Report. Washington, DC: Office of the Comptroller of the Currency. http://www.occ.treas.gov/annrpt/annual.htm.

Obama, Barack. 2008. Renewing the American economy. Speech in New York, March 17. http://www.barackobama.com/2008/03/27/remarks_of_senator_barack_obam_54.php.

———. 2009. Speech to joint session of Congress, February 24. http://www.whitehouse.gov/the_press_office/remarks-of-president-barack-obama-address-to-joint-session-of-congress/.

Olson, M. 2006. Testimony before the House committee on financial services. September 19. http://pcaobus.org/News/Speech/Pages/09192006_OlsonHouseFinancialServicesCommittee.aspx.

Porter, M., and K. Schwab. 2008. The global competitiveness report: 2008–2009. Geneva: World Economic Forum.

Puri, M. 1996. Commercial banks in investment banking: Conflict of interest or certification role? *Journal of Financial Economics*. 40:373–401.

Rebonato, R. 2007. *Plight of the fortune tellers: Why we need to manage financial risk differently*. Princeton, NJ: Princeton University Press.

Royal Bank of Canada (RBC). 2009. 2008 Annual Report. Toronto: Royal Bank of Canada.

Securities and Exchange Commission (SEC). 2005. *U.S. Securities and Exchange Commission: 2005 performance and accountability report*. Washington, DC: SEC. http://www.sec.gov/about/secpar2005.shtml.

Securities and Exchange Commission, Office of Inspector General (SEC IG). 2002. Broker-dealer risk assessment programs, audit no. 354. August 13. http://www.sec.gov/about/oig/audit/354fin.htm.

———. 2008. SEC's oversight of Bear Stearns and related entities: Broker-dealer assessment program. Report no. 446-B, September 25. http://www.sec-oig.gov/Reports/AuditsInspections/2008/446-b.pdf.

Senior Supervisors Group. 2008. Observations on risk management practices during the recent market turbulence. March 6. http://www.newyorkfed.org/newsevents/news/banking/2008/SSG_Risk_Mgt_doc_final.pdf.

Soule, E. 2002. *Morality and markets: The ethics of government regulation.* Lanham, MD: Rowman & Littlefield.

———. 2005. *Embedding ethics in business and higher education: From leadership to management imperative.* Washington, DC: Business-Higher Education Forum. http://www.eric.ed.gov/ERICDocs/data/ericdocs2sql/content_storage_01/0000019b/80/42/c7/7b.pdf.

Stiglitz, J. E. 2008. Reversal of fortune. *Vanity Fair.* October. http://www.vanityfair.com/politics/features/2008/11/stiglitz200811.

Taleb, N. 2007. *The black swan: The impacts of the highly improbable.* New York: Random House.

Tett, G. 2009. *Fool's gold: How the bold dream of a small tribe at J.P. Morgan was corrupted by Wall Street greed and unleashed a catastrophe.* New York: Free Press.

Treviño, L. and K. Nelson. 2004. *Managing business ethics.* Hoboken, NJ: John Wiley & Sons.

Treviño, L., G. Weaver, D. Gibson, and B. Toffler. 1999. Managing ethics and legal compliance: What works and what hurts. *California Management Review* 41 (Winter): 131–151.

U.S. Chemical Safety and Hazard Investigation Board (CSB). 2007. Investigation report: refinery explosion and fire, BP Texas City, Texas March 23, 2005. Washington, DC: CSB. http://www.csb.gov/assets/document/CSBFinalReportBP.pdf

U.S. Department of the Treasury. 2009. *Financial regulatory reform: A new foundation.* June 17. http://www.financialstability.gov/docs/regs/FinalReport_web.pdf.

ABOUT THE AUTHOR

Edward Soule is an associate professor at the McDonough School of Business, Georgetown University, where he teaches courses in business ethics and corporate social responsibility. His research is focused on the ethical dimensions of commercial life with an emphasis on management and regulation. Teaching and writing is Ed Soule's second career. The first was in business and included his work as a CPA and as the chief financial officer of Edward Jones from 1986 to 1995. Between his business and academic careers he earned a PhD in moral and political philosophy from Washington University in St. Louis, Missouri.

CHAPTER 11

Insider Trading

PETER-JAN ENGELEN
Associate Professor of Finance, Utrecht University, Netherlands

LUC VAN LIEDEKERKE
Professor of Business Ethics, University of Leuven, Centre for Ethics, Leuven, Belgium,
University of Antwerp, Antwerpen, Belgium

INTRODUCTION

In December 2001 the CEO of ImClone Systems sold $5 million shares just before the public announcement of the U.S. Food and Drug Administration's rejection of the company's experimental cancer drug, which led to a share price drop of 16 percent on the announcement date. He also tipped his father and daughter to dump their shares (SEC 2003, 2005). The broker handling the sale order tipped his client Martha Stewart about the transaction, leading her to sell shares as well (SEC 2006). The latter turned into a high-profile media case in the United States (CNN 2004).

The spouse of a board member of the Belgian-based industrial company Bekaert purchased stocks prior to the public announcement of a special interim dividend. The Court of Appeal acquitted both the husband and wife for lack of evidence. An economic analysis of the case revealed the information not to be privileged or material (Engelen 2006).

R. Foster Winans was a financial journalist of the *Wall Street Journal* column "Heard on the Street," in which he gave positive or negative outlooks on the future share price movements of specific stocks. He was involved in a scheme of buying or selling the shares before the publication of the column. Although Winans was convicted for insider trading, it is strange from an economic point of view because the input for his articles was only publicly available information.

DEFINING INSIDER TRADING

The preceding examples illustrate the wide range of activities and actors involved when we talk about insider trading. It is quite difficult to give an exact definition of the phenomenon of insider trading. The point of view from which one looks at insider trading will outline the answer, because an economic, legal, or ethical perspective might answer this question differently (Exhibit 11.1). Not every case of insider trading from an economic point of view will be considered insider trading from a legal or ethical point of view. Or a case might not be considered insider

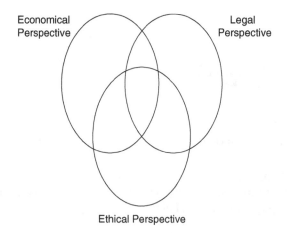

Ethical Perspective

Exhibit 11.1   Different Ways to Look at Insider Trading

trading from a legal point of view, even though it is considered problematic from an economic or ethical point of view.

It is clear that insider trading involves a situation of asymmetric information. This occurs when some market participants utilize information that other market participants do not possess. From an economic point of view, inside *information* refers to every situation in which some market participants are better informed and others are less well informed about the relevant aspects of the valuation of a share of a certain company. A situation in which market participants are subsequently trading on the stock exchange based on the superior knowledge arising from this information asymmetry can be labeled as *trading* on inside information. It is clear that trading on inside information is not automatically reprehensible or punishable (Engelen 2005).

The crucial question will be how much asymmetric information market participants are permitted to use. And the answer to this might differ from a legal or from an ethical point of view. Generally, legal rules determine the threshold of admissible versus inadmissible use of asymmetric information. The legal definition of insider trading must therefore be more restrictive than the economic definition because otherwise no trading could occur on a stock exchange, because informational asymmetry is inevitable in the stock markets. In general, we can define *insider trading* as trading on the basis of nonpublic information of a certain company-specific event that can influence the stock price of a company, but the precise legal interpretation of insider trading obviously depends upon the legal system one analyzes. Moreover, an ethical perspective might consider certain acts as unacceptable, while such acts might be legally acceptable. Before moving to the ethical analysis, we briefly outline the legal rules on insider trading in the United States and in Europe.

LEGAL RULES FOR INSIDER TRADING

Following a European Directive, most European countries enacted insider trading regulations in the early 1990s. Among these countries were Italy and Denmark in 1991, Austria in 1993, and Spain and Germany in 1994.[1] The EU updated its regulation with the introduction of the Market Abuse Directive (MAD) in 2003.[2] The MAD prohibits primary and secondary insiders to engage in three types of behavior: (1) to use their inside information in conducting a transaction, (2) to disclose the inside information to a third party, and (3) to recommend a transaction to a third party (Kristen 2005; Engelen 2007).[3]

The U.S. insider trading rules are governed by the statutory authority from Section 10b of the Securities Exchange Act of 1934. Based on this authority, the SEC enacted Rules 10b-5 and 14e-3, which it applied to impersonal stock exchange transaction beginning in 1961 (Bainbridge 2005). Moreover, milestone U.S. Supreme Court rulings (*Dirks v. SEC, Chiarella v. United States, United States v. O'Hagan*) further determined the scope of application of those rules. In *Chiarella v. United States*, the U.S. Supreme Court rejected the SEC's equal access to information policy. Insiders are only liable if they breach a fiduciary duty to the source of the information. In *Dirks v. SEC* the U.S. Supreme Court extended this view to recipients of insider tips ("tippees"), requiring a breach of the tipper's fiduciary duty before the tippee becomes liable.[4] In *United States v. O'Hagan*, the U.S. Supreme Court accepted the misappropriation theory, which bases insider trading liability on "a breach of a duty owed to the source of the information." A misappropriator is thus liable if he fails to disclose to his principal the use of confidential information for his personal gain while having a duty of loyalty or a duty of confidentiality.[5] The U.S. regulation shows that legal prohibition is an evolving field developed by court decisions (Bainbridge 2005).

The seriousness of trading based on privileged information is well documented. Empirical studies examining the profitability of reported legal insider trading clearly show that insiders earn abnormal returns (e.g., Givoly and Palmon 1985; Seyhun 1986; Lin and Howe 1990; Seyhun 2000; Atkas et al. 2008).[6]

Another line of the empirical literature focuses on examining illegal insider trading using detailed data on the illegal inside trades. Cornell and Sirri (1992) report an abnormal return of 5.4 percent during the month insiders were trading, while Meulbroek (1992) finds an abnormal return realized by insiders of about 3 percent on the day of the insider trade.

Finally, a third strand of literature examines insider trading around major corporate events, such as dividend announcements (John and Lang 1991), earnings announcements (Sivakumar and Waymire 1994; Hillier and Marshall 2002), new issue announcements (Karpoff and Lee 1991), stock repurchases (Lee, Mikkelson, and Partch 1992), corporate sell-offs (Hirschey and Zaima 1989), capital structure changes (Karpoff and Lee 1987), and corporate control transactions (Keown and Pinkerton 1981; Schwert 1996; and Linciano 2003). In broad lines, those three strands of literature demonstrate that corporate insiders earn abnormal returns.

A Classification of Insider Trading Transactions

Since Manne (1966, 1970), the distinction between insider trading and market manipulation is omnipresent in the economic literature on insider trading. Coming back to our definition of insider trading as any form of trading based on nonpublic information that is relevant for the fundamental value of a company (and thus the stock price), it follows that there is a strong link between insider trading

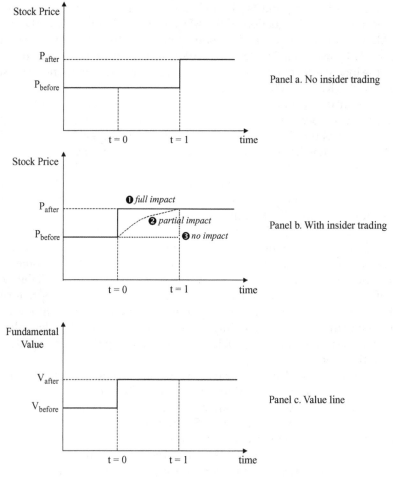

Exhibit 11.2   The Impact of Insider Trading on Security Prices
Source: Engelen and Van Liedekerke (2007).

and market efficiency defined as information efficiency.[7] Since insider trading is based upon private information that is crucial for the evaluation of a stock price, bringing this information into the open will automatically imply that the price of a stock moves closer toward its fundamental value. Insider trading will therefore by definition increase market efficiency. Market manipulation, by contrast, takes place whenever nonpublic information is used to push the price of a stock away from its fundamental value.[8] Again, by definition, market manipulation will decrease market efficiency. To visualize this distinction, consider Exhibit 11.2.

Assume a price-sensitive event occurs at moment $t = 0$, increasing the fundamental value of the stock (panel c in Exhibit 11.2). If there is no insider trading, the stock price will remain at its pre-event level until the news is announced at moment $t = 1$ (panel a of Exhibit 11.2). If insider trading were allowed, the informed trading by the insider at $t = 0$ signals to the market that some value-relevant event has occurred, and the stock price will adjust according to the solid line (1) in panel b of Exhibit 11.2. If insiders, fearing criminal charges because of insider trading regulation, try to disguise their trading, the signal will be less clear and stock prices may adjust according to the dashed line (2) in panel b of Exhibit 11.2. Not surprisingly, Vermaelen (1986) concludes that "reduction of insider trading will reduce, rather than increase market efficiency because it will slow down the speed with which information will be reflected in security prices" (compare panels a and c in Exhibit 11.2).

Suppose, by contrast, that false information is released that pushes the stock price below its fundamental value (V_{before} in panel c before $t = 0$) or above its fundamental value (V_{after} after $t = 0$). By this action the stock price moves away from its fundamental value. At that moment, market manipulation is taking place and results in a decrease of market efficiency (again, by definition).

This conceptual distinction, which is paramount in the economic literature, is relatively absent from the philosophical literature. For although a conceptual distinction is always possible, ethicists argue that it is unclear whether it reflects a reality. And if one cannot distinguish insider trading from market manipulation when trading takes place, the distinction itself becomes problematic when one is looking for a moral judgment on insider trading. Empirical studies, however, indicate that it is possible to distinguish between market manipulation and insider trading. Meulbroek (1992) examines the transactions of 320 individuals charged with insider trading by the SEC during the period 1980–1989. The results show that in 81 percent of all cases, insider trading led to quick price changes that follow the pattern indicated in panel b of Exhibit 11.2. Other empirical studies that corroborate these results are Cornell and Siri (1992) and Chakravarty and McConnell (1997). Examining legal insider trading, Atkas et al. (2008, 1391) find that the "insiders do contribute significantly to faster price discovery on insider trading days." Many cases of insider trading therefore have the information effect that Manne predicted in his initial study and definitely augment information efficiency in markets. We must therefore conclude that empirical studies confirm the possibility to discriminate between forms of inside trading that augment information streams in markets (which economists label insider trading), and other forms that hamper information streams in financial markets (which can be labeled as market manipulation). Whether they like it or not, philosophers have to take the distinction between insider trading and market manipulation seriously and adapt their argumentation accordingly.

The second distinction we want to elucidate is between insider traders and misappropriators. The term *insider trader* has gradually extended its scope from corporate insiders such as officers or directors to persons other than corporate insiders like tippees (people who get information from corporate insiders), temporary insiders (people who are temporarily inside the company), or people who happen to stumble upon crucial information (the innocent passerby who picks up a fax). As Moore puts it: "Increasingly the term *insider* has come to refer to the kind of information a person possesses rather than the status of the person" (Moore 1990, 172). But when Manne (1966) discusses the issue his eye is firmly on the corporate insider, the manager leading the company who is mainly responsible for the creation of information that is valuable to the operation of the firm, and that is still how economists look upon the insider. Misappropriators are essentially all the rest, contributing nothing to the value of the firm. Once you take this

Exhibit 11.3   Classification of Different Types of Alleged
Wrong Transactions

	Insider	Misappropriator
Insider trading	I	II
Market manipulation	III	IV

Source: Engelen and Van Liedekerke (2007).

distinction seriously, it becomes possible for shareholders to use inside information as a compensation scheme, and that is precisely what Manne argued for in his 1966 study.

Manne has essentially two arguments in favor of insider trading. The first is the market efficiency component stressed earlier: Insider trading will release information early into the market and make prices stick closer to their real value. The second argument is Schumpeterian in nature and stresses the fact that by allowing insiders to cash in on their private information, a more creative, productive, risk-taking breed of managers will be attracted to the firm. From the point of view of the shareholders, allowing insider trading has the double advantage that these new managers will create more value for the firm (and its shareholders), while at the same time being less costly because the fixed salary/benefit package can be reduced. All that is needed for this mechanism to work is a clear labor contract stipulating that shareholders hand over the right to deal on inside information to corporate insiders and to nobody else, thereby excluding all misappropriators.

Given both basic distinctions, we now have four different types of insider transactions, as shown in Exhibit 11.3. When Manne discussed insider trading, he thought about type I transactions. The legal and philosophical literature, however, often mixes these different types. For instance, it uses correct arguments to condemn type III or IV transactions in order to condemn type I transactions.[9]

We will hereafter round up most arguments against insider trading and order them in four classes. When we discuss these arguments, it is vital for the reader to keep both distinctions in mind. When we refer to insider trading, we refer to transactions of type I and II, but not III and IV (where market manipulation takes place). Likewise, when we talk about insiders, we talk about the corporate insider and not about anybody else who might be involved in an inside transaction. Basically we will find out that many arguments against allowing inside transactions hold for type II, III, or IV transactions, but it will prove to be very hard to find a sound argument against type I transactions.

In the remainder of this chapter we analyze insider trading from a utilitarian perspective, a fairness perspective, a property rights perspective, and a market morality perspective.

UTILITARIAN PERSPECTIVE

Assessing insider trading from a utilitarian perspective implies balancing pros and cons of insider trading with respect to social utility to decide upon its ethical acceptability. Arguments both for and against insider trading can be found. Since this mainly coincides with an economic analysis of insider trading, our coverage of the utilitarian perspective will be brief.

The previous section already showed that insider trading contributes to market efficiency. Empirical research shows that security prices will better and faster reflect the real fundamental value by incorporating the private information due to the transactions of insiders. This is an important finding since it demonstrates that the allocation efficiency of the security market will definitely improve by allowing insider trading. This allows security prices to become a more reliable criterion for the optimal allocation of scarce financial resources at a *fair* price, which is one of the central functions of the stock market in our economy.

Another aspect of the efficiency argument is the fact that insider trading creates an additional method for communicating information (Carlton and Fischel 1983). This is especially the case with diffuse, complex information that is not readily encapsulated in a public announcement (King and Roell 1988). The case study of CUC International in Healy and Palepu (1995) shows that it is sometimes difficult to disclose value-relevant information effectively through an official public announcement. In such cases, insider trading can act as an efficient replacement for public disclosure.

An argument that is often used to ban insider trading is the fact that it allegedly harms the insider's counterparty on the other side of a trade. Haddock and Macey (1986a) demonstrate that insiders do not harm the counterparty. On the contrary, he is better off than in a situation in which insiders do not use their privileged information. This can be illustrated by means of an example. Suppose an event occurs that has a negative impact on the value of the firm (bad news). In this case insiders can realize a profit based on their inside information by selling the security before the news is announced (see Exhibit 11.4). By this, the security price p_1 will decrease between the price-sensitive event date t_1 and the announcement date t_3 (see the dashed line AC). If no insider trading occurs, the price will move along the solid line ABC and fall to price p_3.

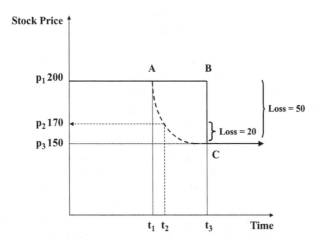

Exhibit 11.4 Alleged Damage to Counterparty in the Case of Negative News
Source: Haddock and Macey (1986a).

Suppose the original price at the moment t_1 amounts to EUR 200. Because of the bad news, insiders sell their securities so that the stock price falls as a result of the extra supply. Suppose an insider sells his security to the outsider buyer for EUR 170. Hereafter, the price falls to EUR 150. By this, the outsider buyer loses EUR 20. But without insider trading this buyer would have bought the security for EUR 200 and he would have suffered a loss of EUR 50. Precisely by the extra supply of the insiders, the buyers are better off than when they buy without the transactions of the insiders.

Analogously, in case of good news it can be demonstrated that "if insider trading increases share prices before the announcement, all current shareholders who were planning to sell before the announcement are better off (while the other ones are not made worse off) than if no such insider trading occurred" (Vermaelen 1986, 439).

Since the insider's counterparty is not damaged, there is no credible investor injury story. Bainbridge (2000) therefore points out that it is difficult to see why insider trading should undermine investor confidence in the integrity of the securities markets. As insider trading improves the efficiency of the security market, the confidence of a rational investor in the security market will not be damaged. It is irrelevant to him whether an insider can earn abnormal profits, because the investor can always buy or sell the security at a fair price, namely its fundamental value. In an efficient market an investor can rely on the accuracy of the market prices because every piece of information is already reflected in security prices, without the necessity to collect and process the information himself. If all information is reflected in security prices, investors can *trust* market prices. This is precisely the difference between insider trading and market manipulation. While insider trading moves stock prices closer to their fundamental value, market manipulation moves stock prices away from their fundamental value, thereby decreasing the allocative efficiency of market prices.

Moreover, no empirical study has ever shown a decrease in the confidence of investors if insider trading were allowed. For instance, Young (1985) points out that the number of small individual investors on the U.S. stock markets sharply increased during the 1980s, despite the many cases of insider trading during the same period. Interestingly, different cultures might have a different perception of the fairness of insider trading (Statman 2009). Statman finds significant differences between U.S., Taiwanese, and Chinese students with respect to their view of the fairness of insider trading. Carlton and Fischel (1983, 860) as well point out that in Japan insider trading was considered proper and that "there has never been a reported case under the limited insider trading prohibition currently in effect." This has not limited the development of the Japanese stock market. Macey and Kanda (1990) point out that the Tokyo Stock Exchange is highly automated, enjoys a high liquidity, is of the same size as the New York Stock Exchange, and has higher price/earnings ratios than the NYSE. This makes Bainbridge (2000) conclude that insider trading does not seriously threaten investors' confidence.

Besides market efficiency, another major goal of securities regulation is liquidity. Investors value a liquid stock market because it allows a quick and cheap disposal of their securities. There exist several theoretical models for making predictions about market liquidity in cases of insider trading, though these predictions differ widely. Different assumptions about the relative importance of insiders, liquidity traders, noise traders, or market makers lead to different outcomes.[10] For instance, Kyle (1985) predicts less liquid stock markets, while Grossman (1986) and Holden and Subrahmanyam (1992) predict just the opposite, that is, an increase of market liquidity. The argument that banning insider trading increases liquidity ignores the liquidity enhancing role of the insiders themselves and of some noise traders (Kabir and Vermaelen 1996). Ultimately, the question of the impact on liquidity is an empirical issue.

The sparse amount of empirical studies on this aspect shows that a ban on insider trading could cause stock markets to become less liquid. Kabir and Vermaelen (1996) examined the effect of the introduction of insider trading restrictions on the liquidity of the Amsterdam Stock Exchange. They clearly show that liquidity decreased after the introduction of these restrictions on insider trading, while the amount of company-specific information did not change. The authors conclude that this is an example of "regulatory overkill" because market liquidity decreased while the main objective was to increase liquidity by eliminating insider trades. Examining a clinical case of insider trading, Cornell and Sirri (1992) report that insider trading did not reduce market liquidity, mainly because of the increase in uninformed trading volume. Chakravarty and McConnell (1997) lastly also indicate that there is no evidence that the insiders' trades decrease market liquidity.

Finally, by allowing corporate insiders to trade based on their inside information, small investors will benefit by the enhanced shareholder value creation because of the equity-linked compensation of management (as outlined later in this chapter). In case of a ban on trading by corporate insiders, market professionals obtain the benefits of the insider trading regulation, while imposing the cost on a large number of small investors. The latter will not seriously challenge the current rules because these costs are distributed at a low per capita rate. Both Haddock and Macey (1987) and Tighe and Michener (1994) clearly show that a ban on insider trading causes the largest gains to be earned by market professionals, instead of transferring trading profits from corporate insiders to small investors, as is generally assumed. In the end, the prohibition of insider trading does not solve the informational asymmetry or the so-called "unfair" situation (as is explained shortly). It merely rearranges the ranking of winners and losers. As such, the so-called fairness argument is in reality a problem of distributing insider trading profits. Insider trading rules thus redistribute resources but not necessarily in a fairer way.

Balancing the pros and cons of insider trading, one has to observe from the preceding analysis that from a utilitarian (welfaristic) point of view it is actually very hard to point out the damage done by insider trading. On the contrary, the balance seems more positive then negative. First, one has to stress the social gains from informationally efficient capital markets. The more accurately prices reflect information, the better prices guide capital investment in the economy. Moreover, it creates an additional signaling device for management to communicate complex news in a credible way. The confidence of investors cannot be expected to decline because empirical studies showed no decrease of market liquidity. And the noninformed counterpart of the insider is not harmed but is, on the contrary, benefited. Another important social benefit from insider trading is the market-based compensation scheme, which makes it also possible to reward the innovative and entrepreneurial inputs of corporate insiders. Therefore, there is little ethical basis on utilitarian grounds for banning insider trading, since such an argument for banning insider trading would require that the harm of insider trading exceed the benefit.

FAIRNESS PERSPECTIVE

It is often argued that insider trading is unethical because it is simply "unfair" (Schotland 1967; Mendelson 1969). Werhane (1991) refers to the lack of a level playing field because "it gives the outsider an unfair comparative disadvantage that skews competition." Analogously to Lawson (1988), we can distinguish two versions of the fairness argument: the absolute equality version and the equal access view.

Absolute Equality Version

The first version focuses on the possession of information and pursues an absolute equality between market participants. Levmore (1982) defends this full disclosure theory on the basis of a general moral obligation to treat others as we would ourselves. Insider trading is thus unfair because one party uses superior information that the other party does not possess. Such a strict notion of fairness would make every transaction in which there is asymmetric information unethical. This is counterintuitive.

To understand why, take the classical example of the antique dealer who buys a genuine antique piece below price at a jumble sale. Moore (1990) points out that one is "not morally obligated to tell those who deal with [him] *everything* that it would be in their interest to know." For instance, it is standard practice in news reporting that a journalist who discovers some important news facts doesn't share this information with his colleagues, but instead scoops the competition. Among journalists this is considered professional behavior and one that might even reward you with a Pulitzer Prize. Notice that in this case, like in the case of insider trading, money is made on nonpublic information. Machan (1996) correctly asks why this should be different with respect to insider trading. Without a substantive moral theory that tells us when it is permissible to allow the interest of some person to take priority over the interests of others, the absolute equality rule gives no guidance to assess insider trading.

Following a similar reasoning, Moore (1990) and Machan (1996) also conclude that the absolute equality version of the fairness argument fails. Moreover, there may be relevant differences between the parties that make the informational advantages fair. For instance, a doctor charging for his services is clearly profiting from an informational advantage but is, according to most people, not acting unethically. Again, one has to observe that informational advantages motivate almost every transaction in a market economy (Macey 1988).

Equal Access View

The second version of the fairness argument was advocated by Brudney (1979) and focuses on the access to inside information rather than the unequal possession of it, because unequal possession is an advantage which "cannot be competed away since it depends upon a lawful privilege to which an outsider cannot acquire access" (Brudney 1979, 346). Again, this ethical argument is far from self-evident because the notion of equal access is unclear (Lawson 1988). Easterbrook (1981) shows that access to information is not an absolute matter, but a function of the cost of obtaining such information. The resulting inequality of information is, therefore, a result of the division of labor, which in itself need not be unfair. Just as one can decide to become a plumber to have equal access to specialized plumber information, people can invest time and human capital to become a corporate insider with superior access to information (Moore 1990). Since the equal access view does not explain why inequality in some means of access to information is morally more significant while other inequalities are not, it offers no solid ethical basis against insider trading. Any such attempt to provide a further explanation would quickly lead to a more general theory of property rights in information (Lawson 1988).

Werhane (1991, 730) rejects insider trading because it ignores two conditions necessary for fair competition: "an efficient market where as much complete information as possible is available to everyone, and the ideal of an equal comparative advantage between competitors." However, she fails to see how these conditions can be reached by the market mechanism itself. In an efficient market, an investor can rely on the fact that every piece of information is already reflected in security prices, without the necessity to collect and process the information himself. In this way, efficiency provides individual investors a low-cost access to the production and dissemination of all relevant information to value securities because in an efficient market, investors only have to observe market prices and rely on the market to incorporate information into securities prices, without the need to spend private resources to acquire and process information that is almost immediately publicly available through the pricing mechanism (Levine 1997). As a result, equality among market participants is reached through the pricing mechanism itself.

Ideally, one would like stock markets to be strong form informationally efficient. Currently, stock markets seem to be semi-strong form informationally efficient. Because security prices only reflect all publicly available information, but not the nonpublic information, the transactions of insiders will reveal the private information component to the market (as outlined earlier). Although market efficiency in itself is certainly not a sufficient ethical basis for allowing insider trading, the equal access view does not provide an ethical justification for prohibiting insider trading.

Closely related to the equal access theory is the argument that insider trading is like a poker or casino game where some players "have marked cards" (Werhane 1991, 730) or with "two sets of rules" (Werhane 1989, 841). As Ma and Sun (1998) point out, these rules are clearly stated before the start of the game. Investors are fully aware ex-ante that some market participants are better informed and that insider trading may be possible. Even if we assume that investors would require an extra return to compensate for this nondiversifiable risk,[11] thereby causing a decline in stock prices, it still "is not an argument about fairness, but about . . . whether the decrease in share prices is outweighed by the incentives to produce valuable information, efficient stock pricing, and efficient managerial compensation that insider trading might provide" (Lawson 1988, 758). Basically, we are again on utilitarian ground.

PROPERTY RIGHTS PERSPECTIVE

If one thing is clear about insider trading it is that information has value. Privileged corporate information can be seen as a valuable, intangible property right. The existence of property rights in intangibles such as patents, copyright, trademarks, trade secrets, and information is well established (Kitch 1980; Easterbrook 1981; Bainbridge 2000). Since material nonpublic information is also some kind of property, it is argued that insider trading is wrong because it involves a violation of property rights and can be seen as a form of theft. Irvine (1987) refers to this as the "theft theory"; others have labeled it the misappropriation theory.

In order to analyze this argument we follow Macey (1988), who offers a two-step procedure for answering the question of whether property rights are violated. First, one has to determine who holds the ownership rights over the material nonpublic information. Second, the relationship between the trader and the owner has to be determined. If the trader is also the rightful owner of the information, then there is no ethical problem.[12] If he is not, then one has to determine whether he has the actual or implied authority of the owner to use the information. Only in the case where he has not will there be a violation of property rights.

So the central issue here is to determine who is the owner of the inside information. Or as Lawson (1988, 766) puts it: "The moral inquiry with respect to insider stock trading thus centers on where the network of contracts between the firm and its shareholders, suppliers, lawyers, accountants, investment bankers, printers, and so on, places the right to trade on the information." From a Lockean point of view the information belongs to the one who created it.[13] Rightful acquisition of unowned property takes place when a person mixes his labor with the property. Therefore, Moore (1990) assigns the property rights to most inside information to the company. In this case, insider trading is wrong only when the company has not permitted the use of the property right. Under the Lockean approach of property rights, insider trading is only unethical when the company withholds permission to trade on the inside information.

Efficiency-Based Property Rights

In the law and economics literature, Easterbrook (1981) sees the right to trade on some piece of information about a company as a part of the larger question of whether and how to allocate property rights in intangible assets. In general, the term *property rights* refers to a bundle of exclusive rights of use. In particular, possession of a right means that a person controls at least a three-element bundle of rights in which each of the rights can be separated from the others (Demsetz 1998). First, the bundle of rights includes the right to use a scarce resource. Second, it includes the right to exclude others from exercising this right of use without permission. Finally, it includes the right to transfer control of the three-element bundle to other potential owners (the right of alienation).

As the regulation of insider trading can be seen as an allocation of property rights within the company, the relevant question in the law and economics literature is how these property rights can be allocated efficiently. Assigning property rights to those who created the information gives them incentives to produce socially valuable information. In this way, social welfare is increased. A rule allowing insider trading assigns the property right to the insider, while a rule prohibiting insider trading assigns this right to the company (Bainbridge 2000). Depending on whether the property right in inside information is more valuable to the managers or to the shareholders, allowing insider trading will be beneficial or not (Carlton and Fischel 1983). The property right to inside information should therefore be allocated to the party that values it most.

No uniform legal rule is a solution to this allocation, because it depends on who is the next-best information processor after the insiders. In such a situation the best legal rule is contractual in nature (Macey 1991)[14] because Coase (1960) has shown that property rights will be allocated to their highest-valuing user (absent of transaction costs). It is thus irrelevant to which party the property rights are allocated initially, because the parties can engage in a value-maximizing exchange by allocating the property right to its highest-valuing user (Haddock and Macey 1986b). As long as parties are free to contract around the initial rule, they can allocate the property rights in a way that increases the total value of the firm.

Of course, this solution depends upon the level of transaction costs. The cost of including provisions specifying the preferred insider trading rule in the corporate charter or in employment contracts is insignificant (Carlton and Fischel 1983). One could argue that the enforcement costs of such contracts are high, but this is a separate issue unless one can show that all companies have attempted to limit insider trading by contract. Otherwise, a uniform legal rule banning inside trading displaces efficient private contracts with inefficient regulatory solutions (Carlton and Fischel 1983). First, the cost-effectiveness of enforcement by a governmental body was never demonstrated. Second, even if it is more efficient to enforce a ban on insider trading by such a supervisory authority, this does not prevent individual companies from customizing their own rules (Haddock and Macey 1986b).

Mediating the Economic and Ethical Approaches

An efficiency-based property rights approach to insider trading is largely absent from the philosophical literature, basically because "the conceptual difference [between the two approaches] . . . is enormous" (Lawson 1988, 770). But if a system of property rights based on natural law is efficient, the practical difference between a Lockean and an efficiency-based property rights approach is minimal. The link between both is offered by Miller (1987), leading Macey (1988) to conclude that there is actually no difference between the two approaches.

Miller (1987) examines the relationship between economic efficiency and the so-called Lockean proviso. Although people can justly acquire unowned property by mixing their labor with the property, Locke adds a limiting condition by stating that "Labour being the unquestionable Property of the Labourer, no Man but he can have a right to what is once joyned to, at least where there is enough, and as good left in common for others." Miller (1987, 410) demonstrates that the Lockean proviso is not violated, "so long as the value of the property that one has taken in excess of one's pro rata share is less than or equal to the benefits to others that flow from the appropriation of his excess land."

Suppose someone takes land out of the commons in excess of his pro rata share. Is this consistent with the Lockean proviso? Miller examines three possible cases depending on the market value of the land taken in excess of the pro rata share. In the first case, where the market value of the land is zero, no problem arises with respect to the Lockean proviso because it is certain that the benefits to others that flow from the extra enclosure will equal or exceed the loss of value of the extra land enclosed.[15] The second case is where the excess land has a positive value, but it is lower than the value that flows to the others. Again, the enclosure is still consistent with the Lockean proviso because the others receive "as good" in exchange for what they give up. In the third case, when the positive value of the excess land exceeds the benefits to others, the Lockean proviso would rule out the enclosure—that is, unless the appropriator is willing to pay compensation to the others for his action. In this scenario the others receive through compensation, again, "as good" as what they lose. So appropriation is permitted if at least one person is made better off and no one is made worse off than he was before. In this sense the Lockean proviso rules out appropriations that are Pareto-inferior. In fact, the Lockean proviso ". . . has a function not unlike the role of certain efficiency criteria in modern economic thought." In this way, Miller (1987, 410) clearly bridges the gap between a Lockean and an efficiency-based property rights approach.

Reinforcing Fiduciary Relationships

Contrary to Moore (1990), we don't see insider trading as a threat to the fiduciary relation between shareholders and managers. In many cases, insider trading can even strengthen this fiduciary relationship. Because of the separation between ownership and control in publicly traded companies, agency problems may occur (Jensen and Meckling 1976). Because of divergence of interests between shareholders and managers, the latter, driven by their personal utility function, will not act automatically in the interest of shareholders when adopting investment and financing policies (Fischel 1982; Coffee 1999). This might lead to actions, for example in terms of investment decisions, that diverge from those that are maximizing shareholder value. However, several corporate governance mechanisms exist to align the interests of shareholders and managers.

One of these mechanisms is the use of remuneration schemes that link compensation to the creation of shareholder value (as measured by the increase in the stock price). This mechanism to align the interest of shareholders and managers is very adequate (Brindisi 1985; Baker, Jensen, and Murphy 1988). Several writers—Larcker (1983); Brickley, Bhagat, and Lease (1985); Murphy (1985); Morck, Shleifer, and Vishny (1988); and Mehran (1995)—confirm the positive relationship between stock price increase and the introduction of equity-linked compensation systems. By substituting a part of the fixed wage with a variable equity-linked part, interests of shareholders and managers are better aligned. Surprisingly, an overview of equity-linked compensation schemes is always limited to bonuses, stock options, shares, and the like. Insider trading by corporate insiders is always excluded a priori. Since nobody would argue seriously that salaries, options, bonuses, and other compensation schemes allow insiders to profit at the expense of shareholders, why should insider trading be treated differently (Carlton and Fischel 1983)?

The problems with respect to insider trading as a compensation scheme are no different in nature than any other form of equity-linked compensation schemes (Macey 1999). Traditional counterarguments against allowing insider trading as a compensation scheme include the following (Easterbrook 1981; Moore 1990; and Scott 1998):

- If insider trading were allowed, managers could also trade on negative inside information.
- Managers would be focused on short-term stock price movements to exploit insider trading opportunities.
- Managers could create false information to induce stock price movements to capture profits based on inside information at the expense of shareholders.
- Managers would choose risky projects to increase the volatility of stock prices in order to increase profits based on inside information.
- The general meeting of shareholders would lose control over the amount of compensation of management.

But take a careful look at these arguments and you will see that exactly the same problems exist with respect to executive stock options (see Engelen 2005). This has not brought us to the point where executive stock options have been eliminated; on the contrary, they are widely used, and we believe that all the problems listed here can be contained under a proper labor contract. Moreover, insider trading as a compensation scheme could have some clear benefits compared to these traditional remuneration devices. By its automatic and market-based compensation for the creation of shareholder value by management, insider trading avoids any slow and costly (re)negotiations between the company and its management about the correct amount of remuneration (Engelen 2005). As long as one cannot show that other remuneration schemes yield the same benefits at a lower cost, insider trading can therefore not be excluded as a valid compensation scheme (Carlton and Fischel 1983).

Choice Left to the Company

It follows from the Coase theorem that companies and managers have a strong incentive to allocate the property right in valuable information to its highest-valuing user (Fischel 1984). As a result, the distribution of the gains from inside information should be a matter of contract (Macey 1999). In this way, regulating the use of inside information is simply an applied executive compensation problem. Regulating the use of inside information by means of contract allows companies to specify which insiders may trade on private information and which may not, because a company might want to prohibit some individuals, but not others, from trading on the same information (Fischel 1984). For instance, a company might want managers to trade, but not lawyers, accountants, or consultants. Or it might choose to exclude members of the board of directors from a right to trade on inside information. Moreover, it allows companies to specify in the contract what type of private information insiders may trade. For instance, a company might want to allow managers to trade on private information, but exclude any information related to an impending merger or acquisition.

Haddock and Macey (1986a) show that the allocation to the highest-valuing user depends on the identity of the next-best information processor. Who the next-best information processor is after the insiders (which might be market professionals, dominant shareholders, or small shareholders) determines whether the property rights are assigned to the corporate insiders or to the shareholders. So, again, the key question is who captures the benefits when insiders cannot. Haddock and Macey (1987), Tighe and Michener (1994), and Engelen (2005) argue that in companies with widely dispersed share ownership, it will mostly be the market professionals who will capture the gains from the new information when insider trading is banned. Neither the insiders nor the small shareholders will benefit from this rule. So a ban on insider trading is not necessarily beneficial to small shareholders. Even the opposite might be true since, turning back to Manne (1966), allowing insider trading can limit the fixed salary package of the managers and, again following Manne, could invoke a more innovative breed of managers who create more shareholder value (Haddock and Macey 1986b). Similar conclusions can be drawn from the model in Zhang (2001), which suggests that insiders can be allowed to trade on private information so long as this trading also brings benefits to shareholders. These benefits result from better shareholder control over corporate decisions because the insider trading is a useful mechanism to convey managerial private information. In order for this mechanism to operate properly, two conditions must be satisfied. First, the insider is required to report his trading activity, and second, he is prohibited from profiting by making short-term reversals of his trading position.

However, Haddock and Macey (1986a) indicate situations in which a corporation is more likely to assign the property rights to the shareholders instead of to the insiders.[16] Such a situation arises when shareholders are the next-best information processors. This is the case of dominant shareholders who closely monitor the company. When the profits from trading on the inside information (when insiders are banned) are likely to exceed the benefits from fixed salary reduction, dominant shareholders will prefer a ban on insider trading by corporate insiders. They show that this will be especially the case if insiders are more risk averse because the inside trading profits are less certain, thereby making them unwilling to give up a fixed salary. So, depending on the next-best information processor, insiders and shareholders will reach an arrangement that would make both sides better off.

MARKET MORALITY PERSPECTIVE

The remaining argument that occurs regularly in the literature is the effect that legalized insider trading would have on general market morality. In several publications, Werhane (1989 and 1991) goes back to Adam Smith in order to clarify the need for a basic market morality, carried by values like fairness in competition, or a form of self-interest that is restrained by reason as necessary conditions for a free market. The problem about insider trading then becomes that the practice is connected to a "Boeskyian greed culture" (Werhane 1989) that undermines market morality and, if it takes the upper hand, destroys the market itself. It is very hard to argue with this type of general argument, and on the whole we are rather sympathetic to it.

However, if you dismiss insider trading along these lines, it seems very difficult to see why one would not want to dismiss other forms of equity-linked executive compensation on the same grounds. The excesses of stock option compensation that occurred the past decade seem to invoke the same greed culture as insider trading. Still, stock options are considered far less problematic while insider trading is deemed to be inacceptable. If shareholders regulate insider trading in a contractual manner, this compensation mechanism comes very close to stock option compensation and should therefore have the same moral effects (Machan 1996). Nevertheless, the ban on insider trading has grown dramatically while stock option compensation is still hailed as a compensation system that allows us to solve the agency problem.

CONCLUSION

Many examples of insider trading are problematic when looked upon from a normative point of view. Valuable inside information can be used in order to manipulate share prices, or a fax containing the information may get stolen on the way to its receiver. Misappropriation of information and manipulation of share prices can be highly problematic. There is, however, another form of insider trading, identified by Manne (1966), that is much harder to reject on normative grounds. It is a form of insider trading executed by somebody who creates real value for the company and who is authorized to use this information, for instance, as part of a compensation scheme. We evaluate specifically this type of insider trading (labeled type I) and find it hard to reject.

From a utilitarian (welfarist) point of view, its main impact is that it increases market efficiency, and this implies a number of positive effects which we believe greatly outweigh the possible negative effects. On top of this, several supposedly negative welfare effects (loss of confidence in the market, evaporating liquity) are not confirmed either in theoretical models or in the empirical literature.

Fairness is an often-used argument against insider trading. But, again, it is very hard to formulate exactly which type of unfairness is involved and to understand why this unfairness is unacceptable while other forms of unfairness based on informational asymmetries are quite common in markets (and in fact drive markets). A highly problematic argument against insider trading is that we need to ban it in order to create a level playing field. But there is no such thing as a level playing field in financial markets, certainly not for the small investor. There are several types of actors active in financial markets, and if we eliminate the informational advantage from insiders, the advantage simply switches to another group, often institutional investors. In fact, one could even look upon the rise of insider trading regulation as a shift in power relations in financial markets in the direction of institutional investors.

From a property rights perspective one can argue that the right to this valuable form of information should go to the party that values it the most. In a situation with referential shareholders, it is often these shareholders who have the most to gain from keeping this information. From the point of view of small shareholders this might differ and bring us to the situation that Manne believed to be the best option: Managers are paid by handing them the right to insider trading, thus reducing the fixed cost of management and (hopefully) creating an innovative type of managers who generate shareholder value. There are, of course, serious risks involved in handing over to managers the right to trade on inside information. We do not dismiss these arguments lightly; on the contrary, this is a permanent risk. But it is a risk connected to any type of equity-linked executive compensation, and that is all too often forgotten. Creating a good, functioning labor contract around executive compensation is a real challenge, as became abundantly clear in recent years. Using insider trading as equity-linked compensation is essentially no different from these other types of compensation, but probably less costly to the small investor.

A final argument against insider trading refers to a basic market morality necessary in order to let a free competitive market flourish. This is a very abstract argument but in a sense the most convincing of all. It is the case that a well-functioning market is very different from a jungle in which anything goes. A "Boeskyian greed culture" could very well turn the market into such a jungle. But so did the compensation schemes at Enron, Worldcom, Citibank, Fortis, and so on. If we believe that saving market morality is the basic argument, why do we need to eliminate insider trading when there are a number of other activities that are just as questionable but continue to be practiced on a massive scale?

NOTES

1. European Directive 89/592/EEC of November 13, 1989, for the Coordination of the Regulations of Insider Trading, *O.J.*, L334/30.

2. European Directive 2003/6/EC of the European Parliament and of the Council of January 28, 2003, on Insider Dealing and Market Manipulation (Market Abuse), *O.J.*, L96/16, 12 April 2003.

3. A primary insider is a person with access to information because of his capacity as a corporate insider (like managers and board members), a large shareholder, and/or a person with access to inside information due to his employment, profession, or duties (like lawyers, consultants). A secondary insider is a person who is not a primary insider, but who possesses inside information while he knows or ought to have known that it is inside information that was disclosed in a breach of a fiduciary duty.

4. In the context of takeover bids, Rule 14e-3 prohibits insiders of the bidder and target to tip inside information to persons likely to buy shares of the target for their own account (Bainbridge 2005).

5. The novelty of O'Hagan is that he was not in a fiduciary relationship with the company whose stock he traded (Pillsbury) but in a fiduciary relationship with the takeover company (Grand Met). The court rules in effect that this makes no difference. A fiduciary to Grand Met is enough to constitute insider trading in Pillsbury stock.

6. Legal insider trading refers to the transactions by corporate insiders that have to be reported to the market authority. Several countries, such as the Netherlands, Germany, the United Kingdom, and the United States, use this system. For instance, in the United States officers, directors, and beneficial owners of more than 10 percent of any class of stock are obliged to disclose their fraction of share ownership and their transactions in shares of their company (Section 16a-3 (a) Securities Exchange Act of 1934). This legal insider trading has to be distinguished from illegal insider trading prohibited by Section 10b of the Securities and Exchange Act of 1934 and SEC Rule 10b-5.

7. A financial market operates efficiently if security prices instantaneously and fully re-flect all relevant available information. In an efficient financial market, market prices are therefore a reliable criterion for the investment value of securities. A more explicit definition can be found in Malkiel (1992): "A capital market is said to be efficient if it fully and correctly reflects all relevant information in determining security prices. Formally, the market is said to be efficient with respect to some information set if security prices would be unaffected by revealing that information to all participants. Moreover, efficiency with respect to an information set implies that it is impossible to

make economic profits by trading on the basis of that information set." One method to measure the efficiency of a financial market is thus to ask what set of information is reflected in securities prices. Traditionally three types of information can be distinguished: information in historical market prices, publicly available information, and all information, irrespective of its public or nonpublic character. Based on these three types of information, three forms of the efficient market hypothesis can be distinguished: the weak form, the semi-strong form, and the strong form of market efficiency (Fama 1970, 1991).

8. A security price is equal to its fundamental value when it accurately reflects investors' expectations about the present value of the expected future cash flows, discounted at the appropriate risk-adjusted discount rate.

9. Examples are Moore (1990) and Shaw (1990). Both excellent articles do not believe in the possibility of a distinction between market manipulation and insider trading. For Moore, allowing type I transactions will result in type III and IV transactions, and because types III and IV are wrong, type I should also be excluded. Shaw argues that insider trading harms investors, but that is hard to accept once you believe in the possibility of an information-enhancing form of insider trading.

10. Noise traders are investors who trade on the basis of what they believe, falsely, is special information. See Black (1986). In this case, they are investors who trade on fundamentals and who fail to recognize the extent of the inside information reflected in security prices and thus incorrectly believe they have superior information.

11. Notice that it does not have to be the case and that it has not been empirically demonstrated.

12. Macey (1988) gives the example of a tender offer or purchasing stock in the target company before disclosing the takeover plans to the target's shareholders.

13. In *The Second Treatise of Government*, Locke argues that "Every Man has a Property in his own Person. This no Body has any Right to but himself. The Labour of his Body, and the Work of his Hands, we may say, are properly his. Whatsoever then he removes out of the State that Nature hath provided, and left in, he hath mixed his Labour with, and joyned to it something that is his own, and thereby makes it his Property. It being by him removed from the common state Nature placed it in, hath by this Labour something annexed to it, that excludes the common right of other Men" (Locke 1967).

14. Historically, companies have made little or no attempt to prohibit insider trading (Carlton and Fischel 1983). Or as Manne (1985, 940) puts it: "Clearly the overwhelming number of companies, when they were perfectly free to contract their way into such a rule, did not do so. This failure of corporations to design internal rules against insider trading could not have been an accident or oversight." The behavior of companies suggests that insider trading may be beneficial (Fischel 1984). However, this does not imply that insider trading will be beneficial in all situations.

15. The benefits come from increased productivity of the enclosed land. Others will gain through lower purchase prices of the produce of the land and through higher salaries for their labor.

16. The model of Hu and Noe (2001) also predicts situations in which shareholders will benefit and situations in which insiders will benefit from insider trading.

REFERENCES

Aktas, N., E. de Bodt, and H. Van Oppens. 2008. Legal insider trading and market efficiency. *Journal of Banking and Finance* 32:1379–1392.

Bainbrige, S. 2000. Insider trading. In *Encyclopedia of law and economics, Volume III: The regulation of contracts*, ed. B. Bouckaert and G. De Geest. Cheltenham: Edward Elgar.

———. 2005. An overview of U.S. insider trading law: Lessons for the EU? *European Company Law* 1:22–26.

Baker, G. P., M. C. Jensen, and K. J. Murphy. 1988. Compensation and incentives: Practice versus theory. *Journal of Finance* 43:593–616.

Black, F. 1986. Noise. *Journal of Finance* 41:529–543.

Brickley, J., S. Bhagat, and R. Lease. 1985. The impact of long range managerial compensation plans on shareholders' wealth. *Journal of Accounting and Economics* 7:115–129.

Brindisi, L. 1985. Creating shareholder value: A new mission for executive compensation. *Midland Corporate Finance Journal* 3:56–66.

Brudney, V. 1979. Insiders, outsiders and the informational advantages under the federal securities laws. *Harvard Law Review* 93:322–376.

Carlton, D. W., and D. R. Fischel. 1983. The regulation of insider trading. *Stanford Law Review* 35:857–895.

Chakravarty, S., and J. McConnell. 1997. An analysis of prices, bid/ask spreads, and bid and ask depths surrounding Ivan Boesky's illegal trading in Carnation stock. *Financial Management* 26:18–34.

CNN. 2004. Stewart convicted on all charges. CNNMoney.com, March 10.

Coase, R. 1960. The problem of social cost. *Journal of Law and Economics* 3:1–44.

Coffee, J. C. 1999. The future as history: The prospects for global convergence in corporate governance and its implications. *Northwestern University Law Review* 93:641–707.

Cornell, B., and E. Sirri. 1992. The reaction of investors and stock prices to insider trading. *Journal of Finance* 47:1031–1059.

Demsetz, H. 1998. Property rights. In *The new Palgrave dictionary of economics and the law*, ed. P. Newman. London: Macmillan.

Easterbrook, F. 1981. Insider trading, secret agents, evidentiary privileges, and the production of information. *The Supreme Court Review* 309–365.

Engelen, P. J. 2005. *Remedies to informational asymmetries in stock markets*. Antwerp/Oxford: Intersentia Publishers.

———. 2006. Difficulties in the criminal prosecution of insider trading—A clinical study of the Bekaert case. *European Journal of Law & Economics* 22:121–141.

———. 2007. Structural problems in the design of market abuse regulations in the EU. *Journal of Interdisciplinary Economics* 19:57–82.

Engelen, P. J., and L. Van Liedekerke. 2007. The ethics of insider trading revisited. *Journal of Business Ethics* 74:497–507.

Fama, E. 1970. Efficient capital markets: A review of theory and empirical work. *Journal of Finance* 25:383–417.

Fischel, D. R. 1982. Use of modern finance theory in securities fraud cases involving actively traded securities. *The Business Lawyer* 38:1–20.

———. 1984. Insider trading and investment analysts: An economic analysis of Dirks v. Securities and Exchange Commission. *Hofstra Law Review* 13:127–146.

Givoly, D., and D. Palmon. 1985. Insider trading and the exploitation of inside information: Some empirical evidence. *Journal of Business* 58:69–87.

Grossman, S. 1986. An analysis of the role of insider trading on futures markets. *Journal of Business* 59:129–146.

Haddock, D., and J. Macey. 1986a. A Coasian model of insider trading. *Northwestern University Law Review* 80:1449–1472.

———. 1986b. Controlling insider trading in Europe and America: The economics of the politics. In *Law and economics and the economics of legal regulation*, ed. J. M. Graf von der Schulenberg and F. Skogh. Dordrecht: Kluwer.

———. 1987. Regulation on demand: A private interest model, with an application to insider trading regulation. *Journal of Law and Economics* 30:311–352.

Healy, P. M., and K. G. Palepu. 1995. The challenges of investor communication: The case of CUC International, Inc. *Journal of Financial Economics* 38:111–140.

Hillier, D., and A. Marshall. 2002. Are trading bans effective? exchange regulation and corporate insider trading transactions around earnings announcements. *Journal of Corporate Finance* 8:393–410.

Hirschey, M., and J. Zaima. 1989. Insider trading, ownership structure, and the market assessment of corporate sell-offs. *Journal of Finance* 44:971–980.

Holden, C., and A. Subrahmanyam. 1992. Long-lived private information and imperfect competition. *Journal of Finance* 47:247–270.

Hu, J., and T. Noe. 2001. Insider trading and managerial incentives. *Journal of Banking and Finance* 25:681–716.

Irvine, W. B. 1987. Insider trading: An ethical appraisal. *Business & Professional Ethics Journal* 6:3–33.

Jensen, M. C., and W. H. Meckling. 1976. Theory of the firm: Managerial behavior, agency costs and ownership structure. *Journal of Financial Economics* 3:305–360.

John, K., and L. Lang. 1991. Insider trading around dividend announcements: Theory and evidence. *Journal of Finance* 46:1361–1389.

Kabir, R., and T. Vermaelen. 1996. Insider trading restrictions and the stock market: Evidence from the Amsterdam Stock Exchange. *European Economic Review* 40:1594–1603.

Karpoff, J., and D. Lee. 1987. Insider trading around announcement of capital structure changes: Evidence on information signaling. Working Paper, University of Washington.

———. 1991. Insider trading before new issue announcements. *Financial Management* 20:18–26.

Keown, A. J., and J. M. Pinkerton. 1981. Merger announcements and insider trading activity: An empirical investigation. *Journal of Finance* 36:855–869.

King, M., and A. Roell. 1988. Insider trading. *Economic Policy* 6:165–187.

Kitch, E. 1980. The law and economics of rights in valuable information. *Journal of Legal Studies* 9:683–723.

Kristen, F. 2005. Integrity on European financial markets: Backgrounds, objectives, reasons, overall contents and implications of the market abuse directive. *European Company Law* 1:13–21.

Kyle, A. 1985. Continuous auctions and insider trading. *Econometrica* 53:1315–1336.

Larcker, D. 1983. The association between performance plan adoption and corporate capital investment. *Journal of Accounting and Economics* 5:3–30.

Lawson, G. 1988. The ethics of insider trading. *Harvard Journal of Law and Public Policy* 11:727–783.

Lee, D., W. Mikkelson and M. Partch. 1992. Managers' trading around stock repurchases. *Journal of Finance* 47:1947–1961.

Levine, R. 1997. Financial development and economic growth: views and agenda. *Journal of Economic Literature* 35:688–726.

Levmore, S. 1982. Securities and secrets: Insider trading and the law of contracts. *Virginia Law Review* 68:117–160.

Lin, J., and J. Howe. 1990. Insider trading in the OTC market. *Journal of Finance* 45:1273–1284.

Linciano, N. 2003. The effectiveness of insider trading regulation in Italy. Evidence from stock-price run-ups around announcements of corporate control transactions. *European Journal of Law and Economics* 16:199–218.

Locke, J. 1967. *Two treatises of government*, ed. P. Laslett. Cambridge: Cambridge University Press.

Ma, Y., and H. L. Sun 1998. "Where should the line be drawn on insider trading ethics." *Journal of Business Ethics* 17:67–75.

Macey, J. R. 1988. Ethics, economics and insider trading: Ayn Rand meets the theory of the firm. *Harvard Journal of Law and Public Policy* 11:785–804.

Macey, J. R. 1991. *Insider trading: Economics, politics, and policy.* Washington, DC: AEI Press.

Macey J. R., and H. Kanda. 1990. The stock exchange as a firm: The emergence of close substitutes for the New York and Tokyo stock exchanges. *Cornell Law Review* 75:1007–1051.

———. 1999. Securities trading: A contractual perspective. *Case Western Reserve Law Review* 50:269–290.

Machan, T. R. 1996. What is morally right with insider trading. *Public Affairs Quarterly* 10:135–142.

Malkiel, B. 1992. Efficient market hypothesis. In *The new Palgrave dictionary of money and finance.* ed. P. Newman, M. Milgate, and J. Eatwell. London: Macmillan.

Manne, H. G. 1966. *Insider trading and the stock market.* New York: Free Press.

———. 1985. Insider trading and property rights in new information. *Cato Journal* 4:933–943.

———. 1970. Insider trading and the law professors. *Vanderbilt Law Review* 23:547.

Mehran, H. 1995. Executive compensation structure, ownership, and firm performance. *Journal of Financial Economics* 38:163–184.

Mendelson, M. 1969. Book review: The economics board of insider trading reconsidered. *University of Pennsylvania Law Review* 117:470–492.

Meulbroek, L. 1992. An empirical analysis of illegal insider trading. *Journal of Finance* 47:1661–1699.

Miller, G. P. 1987. Economic efficiency and the Lockean Proviso. *Harvard Journal of Law and Public Policy* 10:401–410.

Moore, J. 1990. What is really unethical about insider trading? *Journal of Business Ethics* 9:171–182.

Morck, R., A. Shleifer, and R. W. Vishny. 1988. Management ownership and market valuation: An empirical analysis," *Journal of Financial Economics* 20:293–315.

Murphy, K. 1985. Corporate performance and managerial remuneration: An empirical analysis." *Journal of Accounting and Economics* 7:179–203.

Schotland, R. 1967. Unsafe at any price: A reply to Manne, insider trading and the stock market. *Virginia Law Review* 53:1425.

Scott, K. 1998. Insider trading. In *The new Palgrave dictionary of economics and the law,* ed. P. Newman. London: Macmillan.

SEC. 2003. *Litigation Release No. 18408 [Securities and Exchange Commission v. Samuel D. Waksal and Jack Waksal, Defendants, and Patti Waksal, Relief Defendant, 02-CIV-4407 (NRB)(S.D.N.Y.)],* October 10.

———. 2005. *Litigation Release No. 19039 [Securities and Exchange Commission v. Samuel D. Waksal And Jack Waksal, Defendants, and Patti Waksal, Relief Defendant, 02-CIV-4407 (RJH)(S.D.N.Y.)],* January 19.

———. 2006. *Litigation Release No. 19794 [Securities and Exchange Commission v. Martha Stewart and Peter Bacanovic, 03 Civ. 4070 (RJH) (S.D.N.Y.)],* August 7.

Schwert, W. 1996. Markup pricing in mergers and acquisitions. *Journal of Financial Economics* 41:153–192.

Seyhun, H. N. 1986. Insiders' profits, costs of trading, and market efficiency. *Journal of Financial Economics* 16:189–212.

———. 2000. *Investment intelligence from insider trading.* Cambridge, MA: MIT Press.

Shaw, B. 1990. Shareholder authorized insider trading: A legal and moral analysis. *Journal of Business Ethics* 9:913–928.

Sivakumar, K., and G. Waymire. 1994. Insider trading following material news events: Evidence from earnings. *Financial Management* 23:23–32.

Statman, M. 2009. The cultures of insider trading. *Journal of Business Ethics* 89:51–58.

Tighe, C., and R. Michener. 1994. The political economy of insider trading. *Journal of Finance* 47:1661–1699.

Vermaelen, T. 1986. Encouraging information disclosure. *Tijdschrift voor Economie en Management* 31:435–449.

Werhane, P. H. 1989. The ethics of insider trading. *Journal of Business Ethics* 8:841–845.

———. 1991. The indefensibility of insider trading. *Journal of Business Ethics* 10:729–731.

Young, S. D. 1985. Insider trading: Why the concern? *Journal of Accounting, Auditing and Finance* 8:178–183.

Zhang, G. 2001. Regulated managerial insider trading as a mechanism to facilitate shareholder control. *Journal of Business Finance and Accounting* 28:35–62.

ABOUT THE AUTHORS

Peter-Jan Engelen is an associate professor of finance at Utrecht University, the Netherlands. He holds a PhD in economics, an MSc in finance and tax management, and an MSc in economics. He also read law, obtaining an LLB and LLM. Some recent research topics include real options, law and finance, IPOs, insider trading, reputational penalties, securities regulation, and the ethics of financial markets. In 2002 he was awarded with the prestigious European Joseph de la Vega Prize, and in 2006 he was awarded as Best Researcher in Economics at Utrecht University.

Luc Van Liedekerke is professor of business ethics at the universities of Leuven and Antwerpen. He is the director of the Centre for Economics and Ethics, KULeuven, and the outgoing president of EBEN (European Business Ethics Network), the overarching network of business ethics in Europe. He holds an MSc in Economics and a PhD in philosophy. He specializes in financial ethics and neo-Kantian business ethics and published among others *Explorations in Financial Ethics* (Peeters, Leuven, 2000). He holds positions in the board of several national and international organizations.

CHAPTER 12

Derivative Contracts: Futures, Options, and Swaps*

JAMES A. OVERDAHL
Chief Economist, U.S. Securities and Exchange Commission

INTRODUCTION

Derivatives are financial contracts that derive their principal source of value from some underlying asset, reference rate, reference credit, or index. When used prudently, derivatives offer an efficient mechanism for financial institutions, commercial enterprises, governments, and individuals to hedge preexisting risk exposures—that is, to transfer risk from those who do not want it to those who are willing to accept it for a price. In addition to providing an efficient means for hedging preexisting risks, derivatives also serve an important function in the price-discovery role of markets.

Although derivatives offer many benefits to our economy, they also hold the potential for being misused or misunderstood. The main ethical criticism of derivative products stems from their potential for misuse. A look to newspaper headlines over the years reveals several instances in which derivatives were allegedly misused, leading to financial fiascos or scandals. For example, in 2008, American International Group, Inc. (AIG) sought government protection to avoid defaulting on payments owed to counterparties under the terms of AIG's credit default swaps—a popular kind of derivative based on the credit characteristics of a single firm or an index of the credit characteristics of many firms. In 2002, the Allfirst unit of Allied Irish Bank (AIB) lost $750 million due to the unauthorized derivatives trading of a single rogue employee. In 1995, Barings Bank, an institution that had epitomized prudent financial management throughout its 200-year-old history, was brought down by the actions of an unsupervised employee who had placed large bets on Barings' behalf using derivative contracts written on Japanese equities. Because of their potential for misuse, derivatives have become inviting targets for criticism. For example, Berkshire Hathaway chairman Warren Buffett has referred to derivatives as "time bombs" and "financial weapons of mass destruction."[1]

*The Securities and Exchange Commission, as a matter of policy, disclaims responsibility for any private publication or statement by any of its employees. The views expressed herein are those of the author only and do not necessarily reflect the views of the Securities and Exchange Commission or of the author's colleagues on the staff of the Commission.

Buffett's criticism refers to the potential of derivatives, when misused, to create or amplify risk instead of serving as tools for risk mitigation. In addition, the complex structure of certain kinds of derivatives can lead to ethical considerations regarding the duties owed by better-informed market participants to lesser-informed participants. One noteworthy case involved Bankers Trust Securities Corporation (BT) and Gibson Greetings, Inc., where Gibson claimed that BT had breached the fiduciary duty it owed Gibson as its financial adviser. At the center of the dispute was the duty owed by BT to Gibson in valuing derivative contracts between the two parties. A taped conversation between a BT managing director and his supervisor includes the following passage: "From the beginning, [Gibson] just, you know, really put themselves in our hands like 96 percent. . . . And we have known that from day one . . . these guys have done some pretty wild stuff. And you know, they probably did not understand it quite as well as they should. . . . And that's like perfect for us."[2] This case led to greater specificity in the structure of derivative contracts concerning the roles and responsibilities of contract participants.

This chapter begins by defining a derivative contract. The next section discusses five types of derivative contracts: forward contracts, futures, options, swaps, and structured products. In succeeding sections, we describe the size of the market, and how derivatives are used.

DERIVATIVES DEFINED

First and foremost, derivatives are contracts, or agreements, between contract counterparties. Unlike many market transactions where ownership of an underlying asset is immediately transferred from the seller to the buyer, a derivatives transaction involves no actual transfer of ownership of the underlying asset at the time the contract is initiated. Instead, a derivative contract simply represents a promise, or agreement, to transfer ownership of the underlying asset at a place, price, and time specified in the contract. In fact, most derivative contracts are offset prior to contract expiration without transfer of ownership ever occurring. The counterparty that contracts to buy is said to have established a *long* position. A counterparty that contracts to sell is said to have established a *short* position. Because of the bilateral nature of a derivatives contract, the value of the contract depends not only on the value of its underlying asset, but also on the creditworthiness of the counterparties to the contract.

Derivative contracts are characterized by the fact that for every long position, there is a corresponding short position. Prior to the agreement of the long and the short, the contract defining the terms of future exchange for that asset did not exist. This means the aggregate net value of derivative positions held across the economy is zero.

Another characteristic of a derivative contract is that it must be based on at least one *underlying*. An underlying is the asset, reference rate, or index from which a derivative inherits its principal source of value. In practice, derivatives cover a diverse spectrum of underlyings, including stocks, bonds, exchange rates, interest rates, credit characteristics, weather outcomes, political events, and stock market indexes. Practically nothing limits the financial instruments, reference rates, or indexes that can serve as the underlying for a financial derivative contract. Moreover, some derivatives can be based on multiple underlyings. For example, the value of a financial derivative may depend on the difference between a domestic interest rate and a foreign interest rate.

Consistent with the characteristics described thus far, we can define a derivative as a "zero net supply, bilateral contract that derives its principal source of value from some underlying asset, reference rate, or index."[3] The reader should be aware, however, that there are many competing definitions of derivatives. Economists, accountants, lawyers, and government regulators have struggled to develop a precise, universal definition. That the term *derivatives* is difficult to define arises from the fact that derivatives, in a pure economic sense, are not fundamentally different from other financial instruments that can be used to manage risk.

TYPES OF DERIVATIVES CONTRACTS

This section briefly describes the various types of derivative contracts: forward contracts, futures contracts, options (both exchange-traded and over-the-counter versions), swaps, and structured notes. The main features of each type of contract are discussed as well as how these features can be used to meet particular risk management objectives.

Forward Contracts

A forward contract is the most basic form of a derivative. A simple forward contract might specify the exchange of 100 troy ounces of gold one year in the future for a price agreed upon today, say $400/oz. If the spot price of gold—that is, the price for immediate delivery—rises to $450/oz. one year from now, the purchaser of this contract makes a profit equal to $5,000 ($450 minus $400 multiplied by 100 ounces), due entirely to the increase in the price of gold above its initial agreed-upon value. Suppose instead the spot price of gold in a year happened to be $350/oz. Then the purchaser of the forward contract loses $5,000 ($350 minus $400 multiplied by 100 ounces); and he would prefer to have bought the gold at the lower spot price at the maturity date.

For the short, every dollar increase in the spot price of gold above the price at which the contract was negotiated causes a $1 per ounce loss on the contract at maturity. Every dollar decline in the spot price of gold yields a $1 per ounce increase in the contract's value at maturity. If the spot price of gold at maturity is exactly $400/oz., the forward seller is no better or worse off than if he had not entered into the contract.

Implied in this example is the fact that the value of the forward contract will depend not only on the price of gold but also on the creditworthiness of the contract's counterparties. Each counterparty must trust that the other will perform under the terms of the contract. A default by the counterparty owing money means that the other counterparty will not receive what he is owed under the terms of the contract. The possibility of default means that this kind of forward contract can take place only between creditworthy counterparties or between counterparties who are willing to mitigate the credit risk they pose by posting collateral or other credit enhancements.

In the preceding example, the forward contract is physically settled at maturity. Many forward contracts, however, are cash-settled, meaning that at maturity, the long receives a cash payment if the spot price on the underlying prevailing at the contract's maturity date is above the purchase price specified in the contract. If the spot price on the underlying prevailing at the maturity date of the contract is below the purchase price specified in the contract, then the long makes a cash payment.

A key characteristic of a forward contract is that the counterparties to the contract intend to take delivery (if they are long) or make delivery (if they are short). Forward contract specifications require that counterparties satisfy their obligations by completing the delivery terms of the contract. However, the counterparties can at any time negotiate a separate agreement, apart from the forward contract's terms, calling for early termination of the forward contract. This process typically involves a cash payment from the party seeking early termination.

Forward contracts are important not only because they play an important role as financial instruments in their own right but also because many other financial instruments embodying complex features can be decomposed into various combinations of long and short forward positions.

Futures Contracts

A futures contract is essentially a forward contract that is traded on an organized financial exchange such as the Chicago Mercantile Exchange (CME).[4] Organized futures markets as we know them arose in the mid-1800s in Chicago. Futures markets began with grains, such as corn, oats, and wheat, as the underlying asset. Today, in addition to futures contracts written on agricultural commodities, futures based on currencies, debt instruments, individual stocks, stock indexes, and energy trade actively and represent a vast majority of the volume of futures traded on-exchange.

The early 1970s began an evolution in the futures industry with the introduction of futures on financial products. In 1971, President Richard Nixon removed the United States from the gold standard, causing the U.S. dollar to float in relation to other currencies. The CME ventured into financial products first, establishing the International Monetary Market (IMM) in 1972 to trade foreign currency futures.

During that same period in the early 1970s, interest rates were very volatile, and the Chicago markets expanded their financial offerings to address this challenge. The Chicago Board of Trade (CBOT) introduced contracts on government-backed mortgage certificates in 1975, and two years later began trading futures on long-term government debt instruments. The IMM in 1981 launched its Eurodollar contract to shift risk associated with short-term interest rates.

Equity futures, which are another major source of financial futures trading activity in the United States, were initiated in the early 1980s on indexes such as the Value Line Index at the Kansas City Board of Trade, the Standard & Poor's S&P 500 at the CME, and the Dow Jones Industrial Average at the CBOT.

Foreign currency futures are futures contracts calling for the delivery of a specific amount of a foreign currency at a specified future date in return for a given payment of U.S. dollars. Interest rate futures take a debt instrument, such as a Treasury bill or Treasury bond, as their underlying financial instrument. With these kinds of contracts, the trader must deliver a certain kind of debt instrument to fulfill the contract. In addition, some interest rate futures are settled with cash. A popular cash-settled interest rate futures contract is the CME's Eurodollar futures contract, which has a value at expiration based on the difference between 100 and the then-prevailing London Interbank Offer Rate (LIBOR) for three-month Eurodollar certificates of deposit. Eurodollar futures are currently listed with quarterly expiration dates and up to 10 years to maturity. The 10-year deferred contract, for example, has an underlying of the three-month U.S. dollar LIBOR expected to prevail 10 years hence.

Futures on individual stocks and stock indexes are also traded. For futures on individual stocks, called *single stock futures*, contracts are generally settled through physical delivery, at least in the United States. For futures on broad-based stock indexes, such as the S&P 500, rather than attempt to deliver a basket of the 500 stocks in the index, traders settle their accounts by making cash payments that are consistent with movements in the index.

For many years, a substantial share of futures transactions in the United States occurred through the open-outcry trading process, in which traders literally cry out their bids to go long and offers to go short. This process is still used but is becoming less common as trading volume has migrated to electronic trading platforms. Open-outcry trading helps ensure that all traders in the central marketplace (called a *pit* because of the bowl-like tiered arrangement in which traders stand) have access to the same information about the best available prices. Over the past decade, open-outcry trading has been superseded by electronic platforms that attempt to replicate the trading pit. Some of the largest futures exchanges in the world now handle all order entry and trade execution electronically.

Forwards versus Futures

To say that a futures contract is a forward contract traded on an organized exchange implies more than may be apparent at first blush. This is because trading on an organized exchange involves key institutional features aimed at overcoming the biggest problems traders face in using forward contracts: credit risk exposure, the difficulty of searching for trading partners, and the need for an economical means of exiting a position prior to contract termination.

To mitigate credit risk, the exchange-affiliated clearinghouse will require periodic recognition of gains and losses. At least daily, the clearinghouse will mark the value of all futures accounts to current market-determined futures prices. Any gains in value from the previous marking-to-market period can be withdrawn by the winners, and those gains are financed by the losses of the losers over that period.

Marking-to-market creates a difference in the way futures and forward contracts allow traders to lock in prices. With a forward contract, the price of the asset exchanged at delivery is simply the price specified in the contract. With a futures contract the buyer pays, and seller receives, the spot price prevailing at the delivery date. If this is so, then how is the price locked in? The answer is that gains and losses on a futures position are recognized daily so that over the life of the futures contract the accumulated profits or losses—coupled with the spot price at delivery—yield a net price corresponding with the futures price quoted at the time the futures position was established. The marking-to-market procedure requires that customers post a performance bond that, loosely speaking, covers the maximum daily loss on their futures position. Those who fail to meet their margin call have their positions liquidated by the clearinghouse before trading resumes. Marking-to-market coupled with daily price limits serves to reduce exposure to credit risk.

To further mitigate credit risk, futures exchanges use clearinghouses to serve as the central counterparty to all transactions. If two traders consummate a transaction at a particular price, the trade immediately becomes two legally enforceable contracts: a contract obligating the buyer to buy from the clearinghouse at the negotiated price, and a contract obligating the seller to sell to the clearinghouse at the negotiated price. Thus, individual traders never have to engage in credit risk evaluation of other traders. All futures traders face the same credit risk: the risk of a clearinghouse default. To further mitigate credit risk, futures exchanges employ additional means, such as capital requirements, to reduce the probability of clearinghouse default.

A second problem with a forward contract is that the heterogeneity of contract terms makes it difficult to find a trading partner. The terms of forward contracts are customized to suit the individual needs of the counterparties. To agree to a contract, the unique needs of contract counterparties must correspond. Searching for trading partners under these constraints can be costly and time consuming, leaving many potential traders unable to consummate their desired trades. Organized exchanges, by offering standardized contracts and centralized trading, economize on the cost of searching for trading partners.

A third and related problem with a forward contract is the difficulty in exiting a position, short of actually completing delivery. In fact, forward contracts do not contemplate offset as a means for exiting a position. Users of forward contracts, who tend to be commercial users, intend to take or make delivery when they enter the contract. As noted previously, in some instances, one party to the forward contract may decide that it is no longer desirable to complete the contract through the delivery process. Early termination of a forward contract requires new negotiation between the counterparties, a process that can be expensive for the party seeking early termination, who typically must pay cash to induce the counterparty to agree to the new arrangement. An organized exchange makes it easy for traders to complete their obligations without actually making or taking delivery. In fact, fewer than 2 percent of futures contracts (by volume) are settled by delivery.

Because of credit risk exposure, the cost and difficulty of searching for trading partners, and the need for an economical means of exiting a position early, forward markets have always been restricted in size and scope.[5] Futures markets have emerged to standardize contract terms and mitigate the credit risk associated with forward contracts. An organized exchange also provides a simple mechanism that allows traders to exit their positions at any time.

Options

In 1973, the Chicago Board Options Exchange (CBOE) began trading options on individual stocks. Since that time, the options market has experienced rapid growth, with the creation of new exchanges and many different kinds of new option contracts. Contracts include options written on individual stocks and bonds, foreign currencies, stock indexes, exchange-traded funds (ETFs), and futures contracts.

There are two major classes of options: call options and put options. Ownership of a *call* option gives the owner the right to buy a particular asset at a certain price, with that right lasting until a specified date. For example, if IBM is selling at $120 and an investor has the option to buy a share at $100 (the strike price), this option must be worth at least $20, the difference between the price at which you can buy IBM ($100) through the option contract and the price at which you could sell it in the open market ($120). Such an option is said to be *in-the-money*. If the market price of IBM is equal to the strike price, then this option would be *at-the-money*. If the market price of IBM is below the strike price, the option would be *out-of-the-money*.

Ownership of a *put* option gives the owner the right to sell a particular asset at a specified price, with that right lasting until a particular date. For example, if IBM is selling at $120 and an investor has the option to sell a share at $140 (the strike price), this option must be worth at least $20, the difference between the price at which you can buy IBM ($120) in the open market and the price you can sell it ($140) through the option contract. Such an option is said to be *in-the-money*. If the market price of IBM is equal to the strike price, then this option would be *at-the-money*. If the market price of IBM is above the strike price, the option would be *out-of-the-money*.

Like other forms of derivatives, for every option there is both a buyer and a seller. In the case of a call option, the seller receives a payment from the buyer and gives the buyer the option of buying a particular asset from the seller at a certain price, with that right lasting until a specified date. Similarly, the seller of a put option receives a payment from the buyer. The buyer then has the right to sell a particular asset to the seller at a certain price for a specified period of time.

Selling an option does commit the seller to specific obligations. The seller of a call option receives a payment from the buyer, and in exchange for this payment, the seller of the call option (or simply, the *call*) must be ready to sell the given asset to the owner of the call, if the owner of the call wishes. The discretion to engage in further transactions always lies with the owner or buyer of an option. Option sellers have no such discretion. They have obligated themselves to perform in certain ways if the owners of the options so desire.

There are eight options exchanges in the United States trading options on a variety of financial instruments, reference rates, and financial indexes. In many respects, options exchanges and futures exchanges are organized similarly. To buy an option, a trader simply needs to have an account with a brokerage firm holding a membership on the options exchange. The trade can be executed through the broker with the same ease as executing a stock transaction. The buyer of an option will pay for the option in full at the time of the trade. In selling a call option, the seller is agreeing to deliver the stock for a set price if the owner of the call so chooses. This means that the broker will need to ensure that the seller has the necessary financial resources to fulfill all obligations. The broker needs financial guarantees from the seller of the option (called the *writer*) because the full extent of the seller's obligations is not known when the option is sold. In the case of a call, the writer may already own the shares of stock and deposit these with the broker. Writing call options against stock that the writer already owns is called *writing a covered call*. This gives the broker complete protection, because the shares that are obligated for delivery are in the possession of the broker. If the writer of the call does not own the underlying stocks, he has written a *naked* option, in this case a naked call. In such cases, the broker may require substantial deposits of cash or securities to ensure that the trader has the financial resources necessary to fulfill all obligations.

The Options Clearing Corporation (OCC) serves as a guarantor to ensure that the obligations of options contracts are fulfilled for the selling and purchasing brokerage firms. Brokerage firms are either members of the OCC or affiliated with members. The OCC provides credit risk protection by enforcing rigorous membership standards and margin requirements. The OCC also maintains a self-insurance program that includes a guarantee trust fund. As an additional safeguard, the OCC has the right to assess additional funds from member firms to make up any default losses. As in the futures market, the buyer and seller of an option have no direct obligations to a specific individual but are obligated to the OCC. Later, if an option is exercised, the OCC matches buyers and sellers and supervises the completion of the exercise process, including the delivery of funds and securities.

Over-the-Counter Options

Not all options are traded on exchanges. Over-the-counter (OTC) options markets, where financial institutions and corporations trade directly with one another in principal-to-principal (P2P) transactions are becoming increasingly popular. Trading in OTC options is particularly active on interest rates and foreign exchange.

The main advantage of an OTC option is that it can be tailored by a financial institution to meet the precise needs of corporate clients. Nonstandard features can be incorporated into the design of the option. For example, the option might specify that it can be exercised only on specific days during the option's life. OTC options containing nonstandard features are referred to as *exotic* options. At one time, exotic options seemed fanciful and gained attention only as academic curiosities. Although the name is still used, many exotic options are today commonly used by corporate treasury departments and other end users.[6]

OTC Interest Rate Products

Over-the-counter interest rate options masquerade under a variety of names, including caps, caplets, floors, floorlets, and collars. Most people are familiar with caps in the context of interest rates since so many mortgage contracts offer borrowers the opportunity to protect against the rate of interest on a floating-rate loan going above some level over some specified period of time. If the rate of interest on the loan does rise above the cap rate, the seller of the cap (i.e., the lender) is responsible for the difference.

A *cap* is simply a call option on interest rates. A cap on interest rates guarantees that the borrower (the buyer of the cap) will pay the lesser of the cap rate and the prevailing rate. Suppose that the rate on a loan is reset every three months equal to three-month LIBOR and that the borrower has capped the loan at 10 percent. Since the loan is written for more than three months with several reset dates, the cap can be viewed as a portfolio of options. The individual options are referred to by practitioners as *caplets*.

A *floor* guarantees that the lender (the buyer of the floor) will receive the greater of the floor rate and the prevailing rate. Therefore, a floor can be thought of as a put option on interest rates. For example, the loan contract just considered may require a minimum payment of 5 percent. Since the loan is written with several reset dates, the floor, like the cap, can be viewed as a portfolio of options. The individual options are called *floorlets*.

Caps are often used in conjunction with floors to create *collars*. The combination of a purchased cap and a written floor results in a collar for a borrower. For example, the borrower may purchase a cap at 12 percent and sell a floor at 8 percent. Purchasing a collar is sometimes viewed as a way for a borrower to reduce the cost of a cap by accepting the obligation to make payments if rates fall below the floor rate. A lender can also purchase a collar by purchasing a floor and simultaneously selling a cap. For example, a lender may purchase a floor at 8 percent and sell a cap at 12 percent. Like the collared borrower, the collared lender views a collar as a way of reducing the cost of purchasing a floor.

Swaps

A swap is an agreement between two or more parties to exchange sets of cash flows over a fixed period of time in the future. Swaps are privately negotiated derivatives. They trade in an off-exchange, over-the-counter environment. Swap transactions are facilitated by dealers who stand ready to accept either side of a transaction (e.g., pay-fixed or receive-fixed) depending on the customer's demand at the time.

The origins of the swaps market can be traced to the late 1970s, when currency traders developed currency swaps as a technique to evade British controls on the movement of foreign currency. The first interest rate swap occurred in 1981 in an agreement between IBM and the World Bank. Since that time, the market has grown rapidly.

There are five basic kinds of swaps: interest rate swaps, currency swaps, equity swaps, commodity swaps, and credit swaps. Swaps can also be classified as *plain vanilla* or *flavored*. Some types of plain vanilla swaps can be highly standardized, not unlike the standardization of contract terms found on an organized exchange. With flavored swaps, numerous terms of the swap contract can be customized to meet the particular needs of the swap's counterparties.

An interest rate swap obligates the counterparties to exchange interest payments periodically for a specified period of time. In the most common form of interest rate swap, called a *fixed-for-floating* swap, one payment is based on a floating rate of interest that resets periodically (e.g., three-month LIBOR) and the other on a rate fixed at the inception of the contract. The actual amounts exchanged are calculated based on a notional principal amount. Interest rate swaps can also involve multiple underlyings.

Currency swaps are similar to interest rate swaps in that one party makes a series of fixed or floating-rate payments to its counterparty in exchange for a series of fixed or floating receipts. In a currency swap, though, the payments and receipts are in different currencies, and the principal amounts of each currency *are* exchanged at the beginning of the swap and returned at its conclusion. The principal of a currency swap is therefore *not* notional because the principal amounts are actually exchanged.

An equity swap is similar to an interest rate swap in that there is an underlying notional principal, a fixed tenor (i.e., the time until maturity as defined in the contract), and one party paying a fixed rate of return on the underlying individual equity or equity index while the other pays a floating rate. The difference is that the floating rate is determined by the rate of return on a stock index.

In a commodity swap, the counterparties make payments based on the price of a specified amount of a commodity, with one party paying a fixed price for the good over the tenor of the swap, while the second party pays a floating price. In general, the commodity is not actually exchanged, and the parties make only net payments.

A credit swap is a privately negotiated, OTC derivative designed to transfer credit risk from one counterparty to another. The payoff of a credit swap is linked to the credit characteristics of an underlying reference entity, also called a *reference credit*. A reference credit can be an individual firm or an index of individual firms. Credit swap contracts will also specify the types of credit events that will trigger payouts from protection buyers to protection sellers. These events may include bankruptcy of the reference entity or failure to pay on a reference obligation. Credit swaps enable financial institutions and corporations to manage credit risks.

Counterparty credit risk is a significant concern of end-users and dealers in the swaps market. Credit risk arises from the possibility of a default by the swap counterparty when the value of the swap is positive (i.e., in-the-money). Current credit exposure is measured by the swap's current replacement cost—that is, the amount required to replace the swap in the event of a counterparty default today. Only positive swap values are of interest in determining swap credit exposure. This is because with negative- or zero-value swaps (i.e., out-of-the-money or at-the-money swaps), the counterparty owes nothing in the event of a default. In other words, the only time money is at risk is when the default occurs with a counterparty owing money.

Current replacement cost represents current credit exposure. However, current replacement cost alone does not accurately portray the potential credit risk over the life of the swap. A counterparty might default at some future date with swap values significantly different than current swap values. The potential loss is larger because the replacement cost can potentially become larger over the life of the swap.

In assessing potential counterparty credit risk in swaps, risk managers must account for what a bankruptcy court would do in the event of a default. For example, in one legal scenario, a bankruptcy court may determine the replacement cost of each swap in the portfolio and simultaneously close out all positions. In an alternate legal scenario, a bankruptcy court may allow each swap to run until its settlement, maturity, or expiration date, and then close out only those swaps that have positive replacement cost. Selectively closing out only those swaps with positive value is called *cherry picking*. The possibility of cherry picking is a scenario that must be accounted for in measuring potential counterparty credit exposure.

Structured Notes

A *structured note* can be defined as a debt security whose cash flows can be decomposed into the cash flows on a traditional, straight debt security (e.g., a level-coupon or zero-coupon bond) and a derivatives contract.[7] For that reason, structured notes are also sometimes called *derivative securities* or *hybrid debt*. By offering the debt and derivative features in a combined contract, the issuer believes he can reduce the cost of debt over a stand-alone debt offering.

A simple option-based structured note is a commodity-linked note. Consider the Standard Oil Company of Ohio's issue of an oil-indexed zero-coupon note in 1986. At maturity, the holder of the note received $1,000 plus the excess of the crude oil price over $25 per barrel multiplied by 170 barrels. The payout in excess of $25 per barrel was capped at $40 per barrel. The market value of the notes was contingent on the price of oil in the future. Thus, the cash flows on the note were equivalent to the cash flows of a regular note plus a long call option exercisable at $25 per barrel plus a short call exercisable at $40 per barrel.[8]

THE SIZE OF THE MARKET FOR DERIVATIVES

Derivatives activity can be tracked on a regular or semi-regular basis through several sources. Exchange-traded derivatives data is maintained and distributed by the exchanges themselves. For privately negotiated derivatives activity, perhaps the most regular and reliable source of data is contained in surveys conducted twice a year by the Bank for International Settlements (BIS). The Office of the Comptroller of the Currency (OCC) is another reliable source of market information, at least for derivatives activity at U.S. dealer banks. The OCC compiles and reports derivatives information from call reports submitted by banking organizations.

Exchange-Traded Derivatives

For exchange-traded derivatives, including futures and options on futures, Exhibit 12.1 provides the breakdown of 2008 annual global volume by product type. The table shows that exchange-traded derivatives can be characterized as contracts with financial, rather than physical, underlyings.

Exhibit 12.2 shows total exchange-traded derivatives volume by region. North America, which was once virtually unchallenged in the international arena, is now just one of several areas of the world in which derivatives trading flourishes.

Exhibit 12.1 Global Exchange-Listed Derivatives Volume (Futures and Options), 2008

Type of Underlying	Number of Contracts Traded
Equity Index	6,488,620,434
Individual Equity	5,511,194,380
Interest Rates	3,204,838,617
Agricultural Commodities	888,828,194
Energy Products	580,404,789
Foreign Currency	577,156,982
Precious Metals	180,370,074
Other Metals	175,788,341
Other	45,501,810
TOTAL	17,652,703,621

Source: Futures Industry Association.

Exhibit 12.2 Total Exchange-Listed Derivatives by Region

| | Contracts Traded | | Change | |
	2008	**2007**	**Percent**	**Contracts (millions)**
Asia-Pacific	4,974,727,462	4,289,600,329	16.0%	685,127,133
Europe	4,167,116,664	3,592,095,161	16.0%	575,021,503
North America	6,995,493,016	6,137,204,923	14.0%	858,288,093
Latin America	854,405,219	1,048,627,318	−18.5%	−194,222,099
Other	660,961,260	459,104,373	44.0%	201,856,887
Global Total	17,652,703,621	15,526,632,104	13.7%	2,126,071,517

Source: Futures Industry Association.

Exhibit 12.3 shows the top 10 global futures contracts in 2008 by volume, again confirming the popularity of financial products. Exhibit 12.4 presents the 10 most active global exchanges ranked by 2008 volume.

Privately Negotiated Derivatives

Measuring the size and growth of privately negotiated derivatives is difficult. Quantifying privately negotiated derivatives activity is problematic, largely because disclosure and reporting are not required on a widespread basis.

Data that provide information on privately negotiated derivatives activity are routinely reported. Two popular measures are notional principal amounts and replacement cost. Notional principal is simply the total principal amount outstanding on privately negotiated derivatives of a particular variety. However, although some products, such as currency swaps, have principal that actually is exchanged, many products such as interest rate swaps do not—hence, the term *notional*. The notional amount underlying a swap reveals nothing about the capital actually at risk in that transaction. If one party to a swap agrees to pay 5 percent of

Exhibit 12.3 Top 10 Global Listed Derivatives Contracts (by 2008 Volume)

Rank	Product	Exchange	Contracts (millions)
1	Kospi 200 Options	KRX	2,766.5
2	E-mini S&P 500 Futures	CME	633.9
3	Eurodollar Futures	CME	597.0
4	DJ Euro Stoxx 50 Futures	Eurex	432.3
5	DJ Euro Stoxx 50 Options	Eurex	400.9
6	SPDR S&P 500 ETF Options	Multiple	321.5
7	Euro-Bund Futures	Eurex	257.8
8	10-Year T-Note Futures	CME	256.8
9	Euribor Futures	Liffe	228.5
10	Eurodollar Options on Futures	CME	228.2

Source: Futures Industry Association.

Exhibit 12.4 Top 10 Global Derivatives Exchanges (by 2002 Volume)

Rank	Exchange	Contracts (millions)
1	CME Group	3,277.7
2	Eurex	3,172.7
3	Korea Exchange	2,865.5
4	NYSE Euronext	1,675.8
5	Chicago Board Options Exchange	1,194.5
6	BM&F Bovespa	741.9
7	NASDAQ OMX	722.1
8	National Stock Exchange of India	590.2
9	JSE South Africa	513.6
10	Dalian Commodity Exchange	313.2

Source: Futures Industry Association.

a $100 million notional amount while the other party pays LIBOR as a percentage of $100 million, using $100 million as a measure of the swap's value is of little practical relevance. In most cases, the cash flows actually exchanged are many times smaller than the notional principal amount. Because of the problems associated with notional value, replacement cost is often used as an alternative measure for reporting the extent of a firm's derivatives activity.

Exhibit 12.5 shows annual estimates of privately negotiated derivatives activity by product type from 2004 through 2008. The exhibit shows that interest rate and currency derivatives represent the largest segment of privately negotiated derivatives activity, whereas equity, commodity, and other derivatives have a smaller showing. Exhibit 12.5 also shows that the size of the market for credit swaps grew nearly 10 times between 2004 and 2008 to $57 trillion as of June 2008.

HOW ARE DERIVATIVES USED?[9]

Users of exchange-traded and privately negotiated derivatives include commercial and investment banks, thrifts, financial corporations (e.g., insurance and finance companies), nonfinancial corporations (e.g., airlines and manufacturing firms),

Exhibit 12.5 Privately Negotiated Derivatives Notional Amounts Outstanding ($ billions)

Year	Total	Interest Rate	Currency	Equity	Commodity	Credit
2008	$683,726	$458,304	$62,983	$10,177	$13,229	$57,325
2007	$595,341	$393,138	$56,238	$8,469	$8,456	$57,894
2006	$414,845	$291,582	$40,271	$7,488	$7,115	$28,650
2005	$297,666	$211,971	$31,360	$5,793	$5,435	$13,908
2004	$257,894	$190,502	$29,289	$4,385	$1,443	$6,396

Source: Bank for International Settlements.

institutional investors (e.g., pension funds), governments, and specialized trading firms. Some of the ways these institutions use derivatives are described in this section.

Perhaps the most important use of derivatives is to efficiently manage preexisting risk exposures—that is, to hedge. Interest rate swaps, for example, help banks to hedge the asset/liability mismatches inherent in funding long-term assets, such as mortgages, with short-term liabilities that are revalued more frequently, such as certificates of deposit. Currency forwards, options, and swaps help importers, exporters, and multinational corporations better manage the foreign exchange risk inherent in their ordinary business operations.

To see how derivatives can be used to hedge preexisting risk, consider a pension fund that expects to receive $1,000,000 in three months to be invested in stocks. If the fund manager waits until the money is in hand, the fund will have to pay whatever prices prevail for stocks at that time. This exposes the fund to risk because of the uncertain value of the stocks three months from now. To hedge this risk, the fund manger could establish a long position in stock index futures expiring in three months and establish the effective price the fund will pay for the stocks it will purchase in three months. If the stock market rises over the next three months, the fund benefits by being in the futures market. However, if the stock market falls over the next three months the fund is worse off by being in the futures market. By establishing a futures position, the fund locks in the price it will pay for the stocks it wishes to purchase in three months. This decision reduces risk. The decision protects against rising prices, but it sacrifices the chance to profit from falling stock prices.

Using derivatives to hedge does not make sense for everyone. In particular, publicly held corporations must ask whether hedging adds value to shareholders. For corporations, reducing risk comes at the expense of reducing expected return, and hedging may not improve the trade-off between risk and return. Companies are organized using the corporate form specifically to spread risk across many shareholders, who further spread risk through their individual ownership of diversified portfolios of stocks from many corporations. In a sense, a publicly held corporation is hedged naturally through its ownership structure. Shareholders are therefore likely to be at best indifferent to hedges constructed at the corporate level. Yet, in spite of this indifference, many publicly held corporations are observed to hedge. We must assume that since capital market discipline creates powerful incentives for corporations to make value-maximizing decisions, not all observed hedging is done over the objections of shareholders.[10]

In addition to hedging, derivatives are also used by financial institutions in order to lower funding costs. A U.S. corporation, for example, might borrow 75 million euros in German capital markets, then use a currency swap to convert the euro currency exposure to a U.S. dollar exposure. The final result could be a lower cost of funds in U.S. dollars than if the firm had sought direct financing in U.S. capital markets. International differences in taxation, regulation, and controls on capital often make these types of transactions *persistently* advantageous for some firms.

Many institutions engage in derivatives transactions as a profit center, thus making derivatives a part of a firm's primary line of business. For example, a bank may enter into a proprietary derivatives transaction aimed at exploiting a perceived profit opportunity. When a firm has a view on the direction or volatility of asset prices or interest rates, it may use derivatives to exploit that view while still reducing its overall capital at risk.

Finally, derivatives provide a low-cost and effective means for both corporations and institutional investors to respond quickly and cheaply to new information and manage their portfolios of assets and liabilities more efficiently as a result. A fully invested equity fund, for example, can reduce its market exposure expeditiously and at low cost by using futures on stock indexes, instead of selling off that part of its cash equity assets that comprises the index. Corporate borrowers can also effectively manage their liability structure, fixed/floating debt ratio, and currency composition by using interest rate and currency swaps and futures. Derivative instruments can be substantially less costly to trade than the underlying instrument itself. Without access to derivative instruments, altering risk exposure in response to new information, for example, would be much more costly to accomplish.

NOTES

1. See Annual Report to Shareholders, Berkshire Hathaway Corporation, April 2003.

2. Barry Schachter and James Overdahl, "Derivatives Regulation and Financial Management," *Financial Management* (Spring 1995).

3. This definition comes from Christopher L. Culp and James A. Overdahl, "An Overview of Derivatives: Their Mechanics, Participants, Scope of Activity, and Benefits," in *The Financial Services Revolution*, ed. Clifford E. Kirsch (Chicago: Irwin Professional Publishing, 1997).

4. We say "essentially" because in some legal proceedings over-the-counter swap transactions have been alleged to be futures for purposes of invoking the antifraud provisions of the Commodity Exchange Act. See, for example, CFTC docket no. 95-3 concerning disputed swaps transactions between Gibson Greetings, Inc., and BT Securities Corporation.

5. There is a notable exception in the forward market for foreign currency, where the forward market is extremely large and overshadows the futures market.

6. For a more detailed discussion of exotic options, see *Futures, Options, and Swaps*, 5th edition, by Robert W. Kolb and James A. Overdahl (Malden, MA: Blackwell Publishing, 2007); or *Options, Futures, and Other Derivatives*, 7th edition, by John C. Hull (Saddle River, NJ: Prentice Hall, 2008).

7. Structured securities can also involve the combination of equity securities with derivatives. For a survey of some of these, see Jack Clark Francis, William W. Toy, and J. Gregg Whittaker, eds., *The Handbook of Equity Derivatives* (Chicago: Irwin Professional Publishing, 1995).

8. See C. L. Culp, and R. J. Mackay, "Structured Notes: Mechanics, Benefits, and Risks," in *Derivatives Risk and Responsibility*, ed. R. A. Klein and J. Lederman (Chicago, IL: Irwin Professional Publishing, 1996).

9. For an excellent reference on the use of derivatives, see Christopher L. Culp, *Risk Transfer: Derivatives in Theory and Practice* (Hoboken, NJ: John Wiley & Sons, 2004).

10. For more information on the subject of when corporations should hedge (and when they should not), see Smith and Stulz, "The Determinants of Firms' Hedging Decisions," *Journal of Financial and Quantitative Analysis* 20 (1985), 391–405.

REFERENCES

Berkshire Hathaway Corporation. 2003. Annual Report to Shareholders.

Francis, Jack Clark, William W. Toy, and J. Gregg Whittaker, eds. 1995. *The handbook of equity derivatives*. Chicago: Irwin Professional Publishing.

Culp, Christopher L. 2004. *Risk transfer: Derivatives in theory and practice*. Hoboken, NJ: John Wiley & Sons.

Culp, Christopher L., and Robert Mackay. 1996. Structured notes: Mechanics, benefits, and risks. In *Derivatives risk and responsibility*, ed. R. A. Klein and J. Lederman. Chicago, IL: Irwin Professional Publishing.

Culp, Christopher L., and James A. Overdahl. 1997. An overview of derivatives: Their mechanics, participants, scope of activity, and benefits. In *The financial services revolution*, ed. Clifford E. Kirsch. Chicago: Irwin Professional Publishing.

Hull, John C. 2008. *Options, futures, and other derivatives*. 7th ed. Upper Saddle River, NJ: Prentice Hall.

Kolb, Robert W., and James A. Overdahl. 2007. *Futures, options, and swaps*. 5th ed. Malden, MA: Blackwell Publishing.

Schachter, Barry, and James Overdahl. 1995. Derivatives regulation and financial management. *Financial Management* 24:68–78.

Smith, Clifford, and René Stulz 1985. The determinants of firms' hedging decisions. *Journal of Financial and Quantitative Analysis* 20:391–405.

ABOUT THE AUTHOR

James A. Overdahl is chief economist of the U.S. Securities and Exchange Commission. Prior to joining the SEC, he served as chief economist of the Commodity Futures Trading Commission. He received his BA degree from St. Olaf College and his PhD in economics from Iowa State University. He has written extensively on market microstructure, risk management, and investments, and is co-author, with Robert W. Kolb, of three textbooks: *Financial Derivatives* (John Wiley & Sons, 2002), *Understanding Futures Markets* (Wiley-Blackwell, 2006), and *Futures, Options, and Swaps* (Wiley-Blackwell, 2007). He and Robert W. Kolb also edited *Financial Derivatives: Pricing and Risk Management* (2010) as part of Wiley's Kolb Series in Finance.

CHAPTER 13

Hedge Funds*

THOMAS DONALDSON
Mark O. Winkelman Professor of Legal Studies and Business Ethics, Wharton School,
University of Pennsylvania

INTRODUCTION

Hedge funds are targets of ethical criticism, and most criticism has focused on their opacity. Hedge funds are structured to block transparency for strategic reasons—that is, they systematically deny information to their own investors and to governments in order to protect their competitive advantage, typically a proprietary strategy. They resolutely hold their financial details and their strategies close, even though the information they hide holds tremendous significance for the interests of both groups. This particular form of asymmetry in information is not unique to hedge funds, but it is emblematic of them.

In this chapter I detail the major ethical allegations made against hedge funds, and explain why hedge fund opacity creates intractable conflicts, many of which cannot be resolved through government regulation. Sometimes opacity can be regulated away; but hedge funds are subject to what I call *regulatory recalcitrance*. These considerations suggest strongly that, in the end, only tightly designed government measures to enforce limited transparency, combined with industrywide voluntary moral coordination, can succeed. Moreover, any successful ethical and regulatory approach to hedge funds involves distinguishing among four key stakeholder groups of hedge funds: direct investors, indirect investors, the global public, and the national public.

BACKGROUND ON HEDGE FUNDS

Hedge funds are privately owned financial firms that raise money from large investors, including individuals, pension funds, and charities, for the purpose of increasing the value of the investment. They grew dramatically from 1998 to 2008, and according to a report by the Zurich-based Financial Stability Forum commissioned by G8 governments, in 2008 they managed assets of $1.6 trillion (*New York Times* 2007).

---

*Some material in this chapter appeared originally in Thomas Donaldson, "Hedge Fund Ethics." *Business Ethics Quarterly*, 2008, *18*(3): 405–416. I thank John Boatright for his excellent scholarly and editorial help with this chapter.

In contrast to traditional investment firms such as brokerage houses and banks, hedge funds successfully avoided traditional government regulation for years. At least until 2009, U.S. firms did not have to file quarterly reports with the Securities and Exchange Commission (SEC). It has, hence, been extraordinarily difficult over the years to get accurate information about either their strategies or their earnings (Cassidy 2007). This privileged position offered them almost unlimited freedom in designing investment strategies, and indeed the term *hedge fund* is a loose-fitting blanket that covers a bewildering array of financial strategies. Hedge funds can invest in the distressed debt of a foreign country; can buy equities *long* (buy stocks or bonds hoping they will rise in value); can buy *short* (buy stocks or bonds expecting they will fall in value); can invest and trade using a complex computer-driven algorithm (*quant* strategies); can speculate in foreign currencies; can arbitrage commodity futures, and so on. In short, they can do anything sufficiently profitable to justify the fees they charge to investors.

The economic crisis and worldwide recession that began in 2008 promised to impose more regulations on this heretofore elusive industry. In 2009, SEC head Mary Schapiro argued that her agency needed the ability to inspect and examine the books and records of hedge funds as well as some rulemaking authority (Poirier 2009). In addition, legislation seemed virtually certain requiring the registration of hedge funds with the SEC. Even more invasive regulatory measures, detailed later in this chapter, were proposed by the European Community in 2009.

The most salient feature of hedge funds is that they charge huge fees to their investors. The usual cost to an investor is "2 and 20," meaning that the fund receives annually 2 percent of the value of the invested money (i.e., two cents each year for every dollar it manages), plus 20 percent of any profit it happens to make for investors. Sometimes the formula is even "3 and 30." As has been noted, this can be a "heads I win, tails you lose" proposition. If the fund loses badly for investors, it still receives more than twice the normal fees charged to large investors. But if the fund wins for investors, it receives not only twice the normal fee, but 20 percent of the profits. Fees are considered "carried interest" for tax purposes and are taxed at the capital gains rate. Because most hedge fund managers pay only capital gains rates on their remuneration (currently 15 percent in the United States) instead of income tax rates for top bracket earners (currently 35 percent in the United States), it is little wonder that in 2006 three hedge fund managers—James Simons of Renaissance Technologies, Kenneth Griffin of Citadel Investment Group, and Edward Lampert of ESL Investments—received more than a billion dollars each in after-tax remuneration (Cassidy 2007).

But there is no reason to condemn prosperity per se. Making large sums of money is not itself morally objectionable. One must ask, then, whether there are genuine moral issues raised by hedge funds. At least three moral allegations are often made: that they (1) receive unfair tax benefits, (2) dupe investors, and (3) cause social harm. Let us examine these moral allegations in turn, in order to see the extent to which, if at all, each involves the problem of transparency.

ALLEGED UNFAIR TAX BENEFITS

Critics point out that hedge fund managers and also private equity fund managers pay only the capital gains tax on their remuneration, in contrast to the income tax rate that others in the highest tax bracket pay. Even the salaries of executives in investment banks and brokerage firms are taxed as income, not as capital gains. What is more, taxes are even lower for the many firms legally based in tax havens. About 75 percent of the world's hedge funds are said to be based in the Cayman Islands.

As a *Wall Street Journal* article noted, in 2006 Stephen Schwarzman, chairman and co-founder of the Blackstone Group, earned almost double the combined pay of the bosses of Wall Street's five largest investment banks (Schuman 2007). This appears to violate a basic principle of tax fairness: namely, like should be taxed alike. The secretaries of hedge fund managers, indeed, usually pay a higher tax rate than their bosses, who are earning hundreds of millions of dollars. In the United States in 2007, legislation was introduced that would have removed this tax perk. It was supported by prominent senators including the chairman of the Senate Finance Committee, Max Baucus, Democrat from Montana, and Charles Grassley of Iowa, who is the ranking Republican on the committee (Anderson and Sorkin 2007). The legislation was fought vigorously by the industry and as of early 2010, the congressional effort had failed.

Fund managers argue that the lower rate is appropriate because of the risky nature of hedge fund investments. This is, in effect, the same argument often used to justify lower tax rates on investments generally. The critics, however, note that most fund managers have very little of their own money at risk. They raise and manage the money of other investors and in this sense function as investment managers and advisers—just as managers of investor stock portfolios do. If it walks like a duck and quacks like a duck, critics allege, then it *is* a duck and should be taxed accordingly.

ALLEGED INVESTOR DUPING

Hedge funds are said to dupe investors with false or misleading claims. The data are hazy, but there is no solid evidence to support the claim that the average hedge fund performs any better than a traditional investment in the stock market. Since 2000, the average hedge fund does not appear to have done any better, after fees, than the market as a whole. Interestingly, very large funds, many of which are not open to new investments, appear to outperform the market after fees, while smaller ones underperform (Leonhardt 2007).

Given the fact that many hedge funds at the time of this writing (2009) have some exposure to subprime investments, the slow unwinding of leverage over the next few years may be painful for hedge fund investors and depress profits even further. Warren Buffett, in a 2008 letter to Berkshire Hathaway share owners, called the fee arrangements of hedge fund managers "grotesque" and warned shareholders not to expect high returns. Moreover, it is not only the rich who invest in hedge funds anymore: Pension funds are now invested heavily, and many middle-income Americans are indirectly exposed to hedge fund risk through their pension funds.

A physicist is said once to have quipped that "the most powerful force in the universe is compound interest" (Kay 2008). The 2 percent annual fee charged by hedge funds seems modest, but compounded over years its effect is staggering on a given investment. In an intriguing set of calculations set out in the *Financial Times* by

John Kay, one can see how much an investor stands to lose when investing money with a hedge fund, in contrast, say, to investing it with an investment manager who charges little or no fees—as the renowned investment manager, Warren Buffett, does. Kay calculates how much less Buffett investors would have today if, instead of investing in the actual Berkshire Hathaway (a collection of investments), they had invested it in a hypothetical Berkshire Hathaway managed by hedge funds with a "2 and 20" annual fee structure. The results are staggering. Instead of creating $62 billion of wealth, those investments would have only created approximately $5.6 billion. In other words, the effect of sacrificing compound interest and lowering the annual profits of the investments by "2 and 20" is to reduce the accumulation by more than 90 percent (Kay 2008). It is not clear whether the average hedge fund investor is fully aware of these implications.

Clearly, however, it is the hope of above-average financial returns that lures investors to deviate from traditional investments that possess more transparency and regulatory safeguards. Does this not imply that hedge funds are duping their investors?

Hedge funds have vigorously opposed legislation that would require them to provide data to the government about their various investments and credit exposure. They protect their secrecy with vigor. Most even hide critical information from their investors. The rationale is strategic: In effect, "If we expose our positions, we expose our strategy. Doing so would sacrifice our competitive advantage." But this strategic absence of transparency, even to their own investors, can create a perverse incentive that separates the interests of fund operators from investors. If a fund is doing poorly, might it not disguise its loss to investors, hoping that things improve later?

The valuation of assets at hedge funds is another important concern in the investor-duping question. It is difficult to value the increasingly complex assets owned by hedge funds, and this has implications for investors. Incorrect valuations can mean that investors pay too much, lose out when they sell, or overpay for performance fees. A key issue is the valuation of derivatives that do not trade on exchanges, such as the collateralized debt obligations (CDOs) that helped spawn the 2008 subprime crisis in the United States. It is easy to imagine a situation where a valuation problem remains undiscovered for years, substantially affecting net asset value. The United Kingdom's Financial Services Authority (FSA) flagged this issue in 2006 when it reprimanded a small UK hedge fund, Regents Park Capital Management, for a discrepancy between the valuations offered to investors and the actual market value of the fund's assets (Kelly 2007). Valuation, Robert Kelly notes, is not an exact science even in the best of circumstances. How much less precise valuation will be, then, in a context where managers may have conflicting interests with investors and in which nontransparency is the norm. Even relatively sophisticated pension fund directors can become prey to such imprecise hedge fund valuation since whatever their financial expertise, they may have little knowledge of the instruments being traded by hedge funds.

Finance professors Dean Foster and Peyton Young recently analyzed hedge fund statistics and concluded that "it is quite easy for a hedge fund manager to 'fake' high performance over an extended period of time without getting caught." Hedge fund managers can undertake calculated gambles by investing money in deals that return substantially above-average returns in contexts where the higher returns derive entirely from a small but extant risk that the entire investment will explode (Foster and Young 2008). This phenomenon has a formal name: It is a called a *Taleb distribution*—that is, a distribution with a high probability of a modest gain and a low probability of huge losses in any period (Wolf 2008). Even if the risk of the rare event is only 10 percent, it can be enough for the manager to collect high returns, to earn his "2 and 20," and to make his investors happy in the process. Of course, if the one-in-ten risk occurs, he will be out of business. But he may well be willing to take that risk since it is not his money, and since it is likely that he will profit handsomely for many years. The manager appears to his clients to be enormously talented. The catch is that his investors don't have any way of knowing that he is gambling with their money, and in turn, no way of knowing that their supposedly talented manager has no talent at all (Foster and Young 2008).

ALLEGED SOCIAL HARM

Finally, hedge funds are alleged to aggravate financial crises and create significant social harm. Bank lending in recent years to hedge funds has been huge. Hedge funds, meanwhile, have been loading up on high-risk debt. With hedge funds, then, we must ask what happens when the good times become bad times, as now appears to be the case. In response to the problems of the Long Term Capital Management hedge fund in 1999, the U.S. Federal Reserve was forced to cobble together a multibillion-dollar bailout because it worried that the hedge fund's meltdown would spark a tsunami in the financial system.

Again, the absence of transparency underlies the purported problem. The economist Paul Krugman observed that when two hedge funds run by Ralph Cioffi of Bear Stearns imploded in the summer of 2006, it shocked investors and helped trigger a financial panic. But subsequent investigation showed that the funds were a disaster waiting to happen. "The funds borrowed huge amounts, and invested the proceeds in questionable mortgage-backed securities . . . and more than 60 percent of their net worth was tied up in exotic securities whose reported value was estimated by Cioffi's own team" (Krugman 2007). Later, in April 2007, the U.S. government spent billions of dollars in a bailout of the Bear Stearns firm. Only a few days earlier, Bear Stearns's CEO spoke confidently about the financial health of his firm.

Before rushing to judgment and condemning hedge funds for the subprime credit crisis of 2008, it is worth remembering that banks, not hedge funds, held the largest share of subprime CDOs in 2008. Moreover, hedge funds were not involved, as the banks were, in creating them and collecting fees for their slicing and dicing. Indeed, the overall situation is so complex that hedge funds often can be credited with playing a role in limiting investors' risks for subprime mortgages. Hedge funds often hold derivatives contracts that pay money to investors when bonds backed by subprime mortgage loans—loans made to less creditworthy borrowers—run into trouble (Scholtes 2007). In this way and in others, hedge funds often serve the vital role of expanding liquidity in the market, and of spreading risk more broadly.

Governments are worried about hedge funds, but how much they worry varies. German Chancellor Angela Merkel attempted in the summer of 2007 to have a strongly worded statement announced at the G8 Summit meeting demanding greater hedge fund transparency But her attempt failed, likely because of resistance from the United States and the United Kingdom.

While less concerned than their European counterparts, American regulators have expressed worry for years about the systemic risks inherent in hedge funds. In the spring of 2006, and long before the advent of the recession of 2008, Federal Reserve Chairman Ben Bernanke granted that market forces offered strong corrective powers for dealing with hedge fund excesses, but added a series of personal concerns about hedge fund risks. He identified the risk that, because hedge funds are now among the most important customers of American banks, and because they have a huge appetite for credit, banks and dealers may be tempted to reduce their margin levels—that is, the level of their holdings that provides a safety net in the event of default. He also worried about whether, in the face of increasingly complex transactions between banks and hedge funds, it is even possible for one side to measure accurately the amount of risk exposure on the other (Bernanke 2006). His concern speaks directly to the issue of transparency. Bernanke cautioned that good management demands that when banks and investors lend to hedge funds, hedge funds must provide transparency appropriate to the lender's determination of risk. Creditors may not "fully internalize the costs of systemic financial problems" and "time and competition may dull memory and undermine risk-management discipline" (Bernanke 2006).

These three allegations, namely tax unfairness, duping, and societal risk, then, are the most salient of the ethical charges made against hedge funds. Of these, it should be noted that only the second and third entail significant problems of transparency and information asymmetry. The first issue, the allegation that the current tax structure unfairly favors hedge fund operators, is significant but not unique to hedge funds. Indeed, it is an historical but arbitrary fact that hedge funds are treated for tax purposes as they are, not unlike the arbitrary tax treatment of thoroughbred horse owners or peanut growers. There may be good public policy reasons for hedge funds' privileged tax status (although I doubt it), but the issue is unconnected to the underlying nature of the hedge fund entity.

HEDGE FUND TRANSPARENCY AND REGULATION

Focusing on the transparency issues in allegations two and three, let us now assess the most popular suggestion for dealing with them, namely government regulation. Why cannot the transparency problems endemic to the hedge fund structure be eliminated though disclosure laws? Data on hedge fund positions could be collected by government authorities and, if necessary, aggregated for public policy purposes. Even more precise data could be disclosed to hedge fund investors. Of course, even without attacking the opacity problem directly, the government can and does establish sanctions for hedge fund conduct through laws that prohibit insider dealing and fraud (Mallaby 2007). But the option to sue for fraud, many argue, cannot substitute for real information that is vital in protecting the public interest.

To be sure, forced-transparency remedies have a successful track record, not only for the financial service industry in particular but for business in general. When information asymmetry in the past meant that pharmaceutical customers were ignorant of the side effects of drugs, governments instituted drug labeling laws. When asymmetry meant that borrowers were ignorant of the true costs of their home and car loans, governments instituted credit disclosure laws. And when asymmetry meant that investors were ignorant of the financial status of the companies whose stock they purchased, governments instituted financial disclosure requirements. Why should not governments require hedge funds to disclose their precise financial positions both to their investors and to the government? This is currently true for registered dealers and brokers under Financial Industry Regulatory Authority (FINRA) rules in the United States, and for broker-dealers in other developed economies.

Such forced disclosure, however, raises special issues of what I call *regulatory recalcitrance*. As is well known, some social problems are more recalcitrant to regulation than others. Two types of recalcitrance are pertinent to the moral problem of transparency, namely:

1. The regulatory process that gathers information and forces disclosure may not only bend entrepreneurial aspirations (as any regulation does) but destroy them. In other words, monitoring and disclosure requirements may constitute a market force of their own, and end up destroying the value of the original aspirations of market participants.
2. The regulatory process that requires monitoring or data collection is either impossible to effect or impossibly costly.

Examples of type 1 recalcitrance are rare but include the self-destructive process of government attempts to regulate the arts. Regulating literature, drama, and cinema has the pernicious effect of destroying the creative process of art. Most modern societies have abandoned attempts to regulate the arts, but Soviet-era governments that attempted to do so paid a high price in the deterioration of artistic quality. In type 1 cases, the regulation that forces disclosure is not exogenous to the creative process; rather, it is internal to it and pernicious. In other words, the regulation directly dampens or eliminates the incentive of hedge fund managers to develop innovative strategies.

Examples of type 2 recalcitrance are more common, and arise often both in private and economic life. The notorious failures of government attempts to regulate private sexual mores show that what government cannot see, it cannot regulate. Some societies manage to regulate private sexual behavior with moderate effectiveness, not from the strength of the regulatory apparatus, but on the basis of the culture's shared religious belief (for example, strict Islamic cultures).

Type 2 regulatory recalcitrance is common in economic life. One of the most obvious instances is bribery. All countries in the world have laws that forbid bribery, yet bribery's prevalence varies widely from country to country. Nor are the differences among countries driven solely by levels of regulatory enforcement. Some differences may be enforcement related, but even much higher expenditures on enforcement would leave bribery difficult to regulate, especially in countries where gift-giving practices are historic and endemic. Bribery with checks or wire transfers is easily monitored. But people can also be bribed with cash payments, physical goods, jobs to family members, free services, or payments to a third party that are channeled into a bribe. In the end, the array of bribing possibilities is almost endless and impossible to monitor and regulate fully. The dramatic differences among nations in levels of bribery owe more to cultural norms than to levels of enforcement.

Other examples of type 2 regulatory recalcitrance include government attempts to prevent employees who move from one firm to another firm from passing trade secrets to their new firm (called *post-employment restraint agreements* or *noncompetes*), and government attempts to prevent digital reproduction (e.g., attempts to forbid software piracy and music downloading).

Important is the fact that bribery, software piracy, and trade secret transfers are inefficient for the market as a whole. They are classic examples of market imperfections. Bribery distorts the market's natural allocation mechanism and promotes economic waste. Software piracy and trade secret transfers corrode the economic incentives that spur creativity and advance social welfare. These points are well established. Hence, to the extent that regulatory control is difficult or impossible, we are brought to consider the cultural and moral attitudes that help explain national differences in behavior.

It is not surprising that market efficiency requires more than market freedom and government regulation. Governments enforce business contracts but would be powerless to enforce them were it not for shared norms of promise keeping and honor. Such moral norms are crucial for facilitating efficient economic activity.

I have argued elsewhere (Donaldson and Dunfee 1999) that rational participants in a market economy will endorse a "hypernorm" or basic moral principle that imposes civic duties on market participants to avoid systematic abuse or sabotage of the overall market system. Such duties of avoidance are important in achieving market participants' shared goal of overall economic welfare. Thomas Dunfee and I have referred to this principle as the "efficiency hypernorm" and linked it to the overall need for moral coordination in a market economy (Gauthier 1986). Such economic duties stemming from the need for coordination are especially relevant to the present problem of transparency, for they include duties on the part of market participants to limit the distortion of information available to market participants—that is, information upon which market efficiency depends. We remember that in a perfectly efficient, ideal market, information availability is perfect.

We all want our society to have a higher level of economic welfare, or what Amartya Sen has called the level of "aggregative resources." By this expression Sen means the sum total of what is available for society (Sen 1992). More bread, more wealth, more health care resources, more educational resources—all of these we presume to be good even prior to considering how the "more" is to be distributed. All other things being equal, more efficiency means greater aggregative resources, and because regulatory regimes are unable to enforce all of the norms necessary for efficiency, market participants possess at least some civic responsibilities to support cooperative practices that enhance efficiency. These include:

- Respecting intellectual property.
- Engaging in fair competition and avoiding monopolies.
- Avoiding nepotism and crony capitalism.
- Not abusing government relationships.
- Providing nondeceptive information to the market (including transparency of relevant information).
- Avoiding bribery.
- Respecting environmental integrity.
- Honoring contracts, promises, and other commitments.

We are now in a position to return to the issue of the possible regulation of hedge funds and determine whether the regulation of hedge funds will encounter either type 1 or type 2 regulatory recalcitrance. The answer is that regulation would encounter both forms of recalcitrance. Type 1 recalcitrance occurs when the regulatory process destroys entrepreneurial aspirations. If we grant the possibility that hedge fund operators may at least sometimes discover novel and creative investment strategies (this appears to be the presumption of investors prepared to pay "2 and 20" to fund operators), then fund operators may be seen as involved in the creation of a form of intellectual property. But unlike other forms of intellectual property such as literature, music, drugs, and novel product design, investment strategies, just as business strategies, are notoriously difficult to protect through patents, copyrights, and trade secret law.

They are also highly perishable: This week's strategy may fail next week and need to be replaced by a new one. The relatively slow reaction of legal regimes to infringements upon intellectual property seems wholly inadequate to protect the creative investment designs of hedge funds. Requiring hedge funds to disclose their positions in detail could well disclose their underlying strategies to competitors. How, then, would proprietary information be protected? "Protection of proprietary information," Ben Bernanke writes, "would require so much aggregation that the value of the information . . . would be substantially reduced" (Bernanke 2006). Regulation that demands disclosure, thus, would inevitably either stifle the incentive of fund executives or violate their right to intellectual property.

Type 2 regulatory recalcitrance also poses problems for the regulation of hedge funds. Collecting sufficiently precise data to avoid social harm seems impossible on a practical level. Ben Bernanke (2006) asks:

> [Should the government create a] database on hedge fund positions? To measure liquidity risks accurately, the authorities would need data from all major financial market participants, not just hedge funds. As a practical matter, could the authorities collect such an enormous quantity of highly sensitive information in sufficient detail and with sufficient frequency (daily, at least) to be effectively informed about liquidity risk in particular market segments? How would the authorities use the information? Would they have the authority to direct hedge funds or other large financial institutions to reduce positions? If several funds had similar positions, how would authorities avoid giving a competitive advantage to one fund over another in using the information from the database?

Because hedge funds are capable of pursuing any strategy that an individual might pursue, such as long positions, short positions, arbitraged currency, mathematical investment models, hedged currency, and so on, it follows that monitoring the economic activity of the existing 9,000 hedge funds in real time, on an ongoing basis, would be as formidable a task as monitoring the real-time economic actions of every single individual in an entire city. This may be bad news for those who have already made up their mind that hedge funds should be regulated regardless. Yet, while frustration with hedge funds is understandable, frustration does not justify concocting irrational regulation as punishment.

Our reasoning here is no different from that used to analyze other difficult contexts where regulatory recalcitrance prevails and where market freedom and law do not by themselves ensure acceptable market outcomes. Again, analogous contexts of regulatory recalcitrance include bribery, corporate/host-country relationships, software piracy, and cronyism. As with other such examples, the implication for hedge funds is not that "anything goes." Rather, the implication is that hedge funds must be pushed to pursue the development of ethical norms and codes that instantiate cooperative action—in other words, industry standards that help resolve the cooperative action dilemma that lies at the bottom of the hedge fund problem. Elsewhere I have called these standards "microsocial norms" (Donaldson and Dunfee 1999).

There is little doubt that microsocial norms work. Stark differences in levels of bribery, nepotism, cronyism, and software piracy must be explained against the backdrop of different cultural, industry, and national norms. During the 1990s and 2000s, substantial progress was made by corporations on issues such as bribery and global supply chain labor standards. For the most part regulation was not involved. Their progress often involved coordination with other key organizations, such as industry associations, nongovernmental organizations (NGOs), and host country governments. Nike and other members of the Global apparel industry coordinated with NGOs on the design and implementation of industry codes of conduct, codes that had measurable impact on labor standards for first-tier suppliers in China and elsewhere. The regulatory apparatus that now constitutes FINRA, and which grew from the National Association of Securities Dealers (NASD), not only began as a securities industry exercise, but even today is governed, especially through its National Adjudicatory Council (NAC), by elected industry participants and appointed independent, but nongovernment, representatives.

Recall that regulation always lags behind novel events, so that sometimes it is only our ethics—or ethics instantiated broadly through industry standards—that can save us from future disasters. The law regulating asbestos in the mid-twentieth century lagged behind the knowledge held by scientists in the industry about the cancerous product's danger, just as laws regulating banking lagged behind bankers' knowledge of the dangers of the leverage they employed in the economic crisis of 2008.

This is not the place or time to speculate about the precise form of industry codes, best practices, and other standards appropriate to hedge funds. But there is little doubt that such norms can reach beyond regulation's grasp. For example, a hedge fund industry standard for desirable transparency between a hedge fund manager and his client would be a standard known to both client and manager and thus available to guide and even arbitrate conflicts between the two. Industry standards, whether formal or informal, provide an agreed-upon benchmark that can guide discussion and arbitrate disputes. Thus, a challenge for the hedge fund industry is to discover, design, and agree upon norms for industry behavior and to contribute to the specifications of best practices in client relations, especially practices affecting transparency.

It does not follow that every single hedge fund activity should escape government regulation. Predatory short-selling is a case in point. If hedge funds gang together and intentionally circulate false information in order to short the shares of a company stock, then their fraudulent activity can be exposed in court. U.S. legislation currently even limits the percentage of stock and the size of the company whose shares may be susceptible to so-called "naked-short" strategies—that is, strategies that promise to deliver shares at a later date without the firm even owning shares.

Nor does our analysis condemn any regulations that might manage to avoid the problems of recalcitrance identified earlier. In April 2009, the European Community (EC) proposed new rules to regulate hedge funds. The new rules exempted managers of funds under €100 million who use leverage—or borrowings. For ones who do not use leverage and have a five-year lock-in period for their investors, a much higher threshold of €500 million applies. Because of the dominance of large firms, the new rules were expected to take in only 30 percent of hedge fund managers but 90 percent of European hedge fund assets (Tait and Masters 2009). Fund managers would have to meet certain reporting, governance, and risk management standards, including some minimum capital requirements (Tait and Masters 2009). The new rules aroused controversy immediately and the obvious ire of a European hedge fund trade association, namely the European Private Equity and Venture Capital Association. Because of such resistance, the implementation of the proposed EC standards remains uncertain at the time of this writing (eventual implementation requires agreement from both the European Parliament and member EU states).

The shape of such regulations avoids many of the regulatory recalcitrance problems identified earlier. By not demanding real-time collection of data for all funds, it limits the impact of type 1 recalcitrance problems in which the regulatory process bends and destroys entrepreneurial aspirations by requiring disclosure of competitively sensitive information. For the same reason, it limits type 2 recalcitrance problems by limiting the kind of data collected and, in turn, the costs of collection. Of course, any collection of data will carry some recalcitrance friction; but some collecting is better than others, and the cost of data collection may be weighed against the benefit of lower systemic risk in the economy.

By limiting more stringent regulatory requirements to large, leveraged firms, regulations like those proposed by the EC target better the problems of systemic risk that lay behind the recession of 2008–2009. With the issue of systemic risk in mind, it is helpful to classify the key stakeholders of hedge fund activity for ethical purposes. These are (1) direct hedge fund investors; (2) indirect hedge fund investors (through, e.g., hedge funds); (3) the national public (citizens of the nation state); and (4) the global public (citizens of all nations). Exhibit 13.1 maps these stakeholders, depicting how as one moves from 1 to 4, the degree to which the respective stakeholder's involvement is voluntary decreases.

The so-called *harm principle* in moral philosophy implies that informed market transactions among adults deserve prima facie protection unless third parties are exposed to significant harm. As Robert Nozick famously quipped, we ought not "prevent capitalistic acts among consenting adults" (Nozick 1975). This implies that as one moves from the bottom to the top of the diagram, the prima facie justification for regulation to gather information increases. To put the matter another way, the trade-offs between the problems of regulatory recalcitrance on the one hand and limiting risk on the other vary depending on the level to which the stakeholder's involvement is *voluntary*. Demands for enhanced provision of sensitive information to regulators to protect a poor farmer in Bangladesh have higher moral priority than demands for enhanced provision of sensitive information to

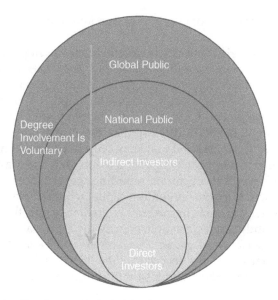

Exhibit 13.1   Hedge Funds: Key Stakeholder Constituencies

protect a wealthy Wall Street speculator making a calculated gamble on a particular hedge fund.

It is difficult to estimate the level of risk to, say, a Bangladeshi farmer from the activities of hedge funds, and such a task lies beyond the scope or competency of this chapter. Yet it is worth noting that hedge funds, including leveraged ones, were not key culprits in the global recession of 2008. Banks and insurance companies with average leverage estimated to be five times that of hedge funds were seen as far more culpable. Nonetheless, as the earlier comment from Bernanke makes clear, leveraged hedge funds often gain leverage through borrowing money from banks. Hence, either closer bank regulation or the collection of selected data from hedge funds relevant to the generation of systemic risk offers the possibility of lessening systemic risk.

These considerations show that certain well-tailored regulations designed to make appropriate trade-offs between the downside of regulatory recalcitrance and the upside of protecting third parties are neither unreasonable nor immoral. Yet, as we have also seen, even such limited regulation will not be fully effective in the absence of industry-level cooperation—in other words, the instantiation of microsocial norms designed to include the inevitably clearer, inside-the-industry perspectives on certain risks.

CONCLUSION

Hedge funds raise important ethical issues, including those of taxation and transparency. I have focused primarily on the latter in order to see whether and what kind of government regulation might aid investors and the general public. We have seen that these conflicts cannot be resolved easily through government regulation because hedge fund activity is subject to two forms of regulatory recalcitrance. In turn, the only practicable resolution lies in the development of sharply tailored regulations designed with an eye to the avoidance of regulatory recalcitrance and the voluntary/involuntary status of key hedge fund stakeholders, along with the development of microsocial norms in the form of industry level codes and the articulation of best practices. Moral coordination, instituted as an industry standard, is essential to help circumvent the inherent limits of regulation. The solution to ethical conflicts in hedge fund opacity, then, is itself partly ethical and not regulatory.

REFERENCES

Anderson, Jenny, and Andrew Ross Sorkin. 2007. Congress weighs end to hedge fund tax. *New York Times*, June 21.

Bernanke, Ben S. 2006. Hedge funds and systemic risk. Speech at Federal Reserve Bank of Atlanta's 2006 Financial Markets Conference. May 16. Sea Island, GA.

Cassidy, John. 2007. Hedge clipping: Is there a way to get above-market returns on the cheap? *New Yorker*, July 2, 1–6.

Donaldson, Thomas, and Thomas Dunfee. 1999. *Ties that bind: A social contracts approach to business ethics*. Boston, MA: Harvard Business School Press.

Foster, Dean P., and H. Peyton Young. 2008. Hedge fund wizards. *Economists' Voice* 5, no. 2.

Gauthier, David P. 1986. *Morals by agreement*. Oxford: Clarendon Press.

Leonhardt, David. 2007. Worth a lot, but are hedge funds worth it? *New York Times*, May 23.

Kay, John. 2008. Just think, the fees you could charge Buffett. *Financial Times*, March 11.

Kelly, Robert. 2007. Hedge fund asset pricing is a crucial issue. *Financial Times*, May 28.

Krugman, Paul. 2007. Gone baby gone. *New York Times*, October 22.

Mallaby, S. 2007. Hands off hedge funds. *Foreign Affairs* 86:91–101.

New York Times. 2007. G8 summit to call for hedge fund vigilance. June 4.

Nozick, R. 1975. *Anarchy, state, and Utopia*. Oxford: Blackwell.

Poirier, John. 2009. U.S. House panel sets May hedge fund hearing-source. *Reuters*, April 30.

Scholtes, Saskia. 2007. Funds attack banks' aid for subprime borrowers. *Financial Times*, May 31.

Schuman, Joseph. 2007. Blackstone agonistes: IPO may amplify taxes. *Wall Street Journal Online*, June 15.

Sen, Amartya Kumar. 1992. *Inequality reexamined*. Cambridge, MA: Harvard University Press.

Tait, N., and B. Masters. 2009. EU unveils hedge fund regulation. *Financial Times*, April 29.

Wolf, Martin. 2008. Why today's hedge fund industry may not survive. *Financial Times*, March 18.

ABOUT THE AUTHOR

Thomas Donaldson is the Mark O. Winkelman Professor at the Wharton School of the University of Pennsylvania. He is the author of four books, including *Ties That Bind: A Social Contract Approach to Business Ethics* (with T. Dunfee) (Harvard

Business School Press, 1999) and *The Ethics of International Business* (Oxford University Press, 1989). He served from 2004 to 2009 as an appointed member of the National Adjudicatory Council of the Financial Industry Regulatory Authority (FINRA, formerly the NASD). In 2002 he testified in the U.S. Senate on the Sarbanes-Oxley corporate reform legislation. He was the winner of the Aspen Institute's 2009 Pioneer Award for lifetime achievement.

CHAPTER 14

Sovereign Wealth Funds

COLLEEN BAKER
Doctoral Student in Ethics and Legal Studies, Wharton School,
University of Pennsylvania

INTRODUCTION

In 2006, Congressional furor and a widespread public outcry greeted the news that Dubai Ports World (DPW), a state-owned company under the control of the United Arab Emirates, would soon manage six ports in the United States by virtue of its acquisition of a British company. In fact, the Committee on Foreign Investments in the United States (CFIUS) had approved this deal. Given the widespread congressional and public opposition, DPW eventually decided to divest itself of the management of these ports. Only a year earlier, a similar response had greeted the news of China National Offshore Oil Corporation's (CNOOC) bid for Unocal, a U.S. oil company. Some opposition parties "portrayed CNOOC as a front for Beijing's strategic energy interests" (Willman 2007). The DPW and CNOOC controversies are perhaps some of the most well-known recent examples of public outcry against foreign government–related investment in the United States. Vehement reactions have likewise characterized other types of foreign government investment in the United States, such as in the case of sovereign wealth funds (SWFs).

Sovereign wealth funds are government-owned investment vehicles and have been called "the new power brokers" (Farrell, Lund, and Sadan 2008). But prior to the current financial crisis, newspaper headlines about SWFs, such as "Who's Afraid of Mideast Money?" or "Russian Wealth Fund Rattles West," also frequently signaled the highly controversial nature of these recently proliferating investment vehicles. Sovereign wealth funds are particularly divisive because, unlike similarly controversial but private investment vehicles such as hedge funds or private equity funds, SWFs as government-owned investment vehicles are ultimately government actors. Their status as government actors has potentially important and unique implications in international financial markets. As economist Lawrence Summers (2007) explained concerning the controversy surrounding SWFs:

> *What has received less attention are the particular risks associated with ownership by government-controlled entities, particularly where the ownership stake is taken through direct investments. The logic of the capitalist system depends on shareholders causing companies to act so as to maximise the value of their shares. It is far from obvious that this will over time be the only motivation of governments as shareholders. They may want to see their national companies compete effectively, or to extract technology or to achieve influence [in a foreign country/market].*

Renowned investor Warren Buffett, however, has offered a slightly different perspective and has cautioned against such concerns, claiming that: "this [SWF investment in the United States] is *our* doing, not some nefarious plot by foreign governments. Our trade equation guarantees massive foreign investment in the U.S." (Buffett 2007). As the Organisation for Economic Co-operation and Development (OECD) and others note, "To date they [SWFs] have been reliable, long-term, commercially driven investors and a force for global financial stability" (OECD 2008).

Although recently the focus of glaring popular controversy, SWFs appear to have faded from public scrutiny in the light of the current worldwide financial crisis. Interestingly enough, the effects of the financial crisis seem likely to precipitate a resurgence of attention to SWFs. The causes of the current financial crisis appear to be many—a prolonged period of overly low interest rates, excessive risk-taking in financial markets, exotic and toxic financial instruments, outdated regulatory structures, and regulatory lapses, to name a few. Although a definitive account of the recent international financial meltdown remains outstanding, it seems likely that in any such account, SWFs will appear in a variety of roles. Some fault the U.S. Federal Reserve (Fed) not only for monetary mismanagement in keeping interest rates too low for too long, and thereby facilitating an asset bubble in the housing market, but in doing so, facilitating an unprecedented influx of foreign investment into the United States, including capital from SWFs. A widespread conviction now exists among many economists and commentators that global trade imbalances played a role in the financial crisis. For example, some suggest that "Without excessive imbalances, the demand for products we now refer to as toxic assets would have been smaller" (Munchau 2009). However, during early rescue attempts in the financial crisis, many SWFs injected large amounts of capital into U.S. financial institutions such as Citigroup, Merrill Lynch, and Morgan Stanley. Most of these SWFs ended up with very heavy losses. But perhaps one of the most interesting roles of the proliferation of SWF investment has been to pave the way for a widespread acceptance of government intervention and investment in financial markets. With the recent, unprecedented interventions of the U.S. government and others around the world in financial markets during the crisis, SWF investment no longer seems as controversial as before.

Before the financial crisis, SWFs ignited controversy due to both micro and macro concerns. The micro concerns focused on issues surrounding individual SWF investments and the benign and malign stories that characterized a SWF's ultimate objectives in undertaking this investment activity. By contrast, the macro concerns related to complex social issues, including questions surrounding the nature of capitalism, the role of government in financial markets, the relationship between the public and private sector, the consequences of significant global trade imbalances, increasingly protectionist policies in many countries, and conflicting international value systems. For example, the growth of SWF investment has precipitated a largely unprecedented occurrence in financial markets: the *uphill* flow of capital—that is, the flow of capital from economically developing markets to economically developed markets. Economists cautioned that the implications of capital flowing uphill from economically developing markets to developed markets are unknown (Summers 2006). What is clear, however, is that the questions surrounding SWF investment are complex. For example, when China invested in

Blackstone, a U.S. private equity firm, did "'bad' Chinese state-owned money [become] transformed into 'good' American private capital" (Schonberg 2008)? And should the large capital infusions by SWFs into U.S. financial institutions during the early stages of the crisis have been refused to keep government actors out of private financial markets?

Economists such as Setser suggest that the answers to such questions might be unnecessary because with the financial crisis, "the sovereign wealth fund moment has passed—at least for the time being" (Setser 2008). Some news stories now claim that "The flows [of SWFs] are neither as big nor as scary as they once seemed" (*Economist* 2009). But this does not diminish the role of SWFs in the international financial markets. Recent reports on SWFs have concluded that "Given the vast pool of assets they represent, SWFs will be important participants in shaping ... [the] future [of global finance]" (Nugee, Rozanov, and Hoguet 2009). While it is impossible to predict the future ambit of SWF activity, their recent ascendance and predictable resurgence as financial market conditions improve suggest a continued need to explore the public policy issues and associated ethical concerns surrounding SWF investment activity.

The discussion of ethical concerns surrounding SWF investment begins with an exploration of both the International Working Group of Sovereign Wealth Funds' (IWG) *Sovereign Wealth Funds Generally Accepted Principles and Practices* ("Santiago Principles") and the Organisation for Economic Co-operation and Development's (OECD) *Guidance on Sovereign Wealth* ("OECD Guidance"). These informal guidelines encapsulate a response to the multiplicity of underlying ethical concerns of both investment recipient countries (IRCs) and SWFs as they relate to the controversy surrounding SWF investment. Ultimately, both the Santiago Principles and OECD Guidance seek to balance concerns about maintaining the free flow of international capital with IRCs' concerns about protecting national security. A tension also implicit in this balancing act is the often differing interests of politicians and businesspersons. I argue that the underlying issues amount to two sides of the same coin: generalized concerns that can be grouped under the label of *corruption*, which for the purposes of this chapter will be understood as the *decay* of something.

One can categorize IRC concerns about SWF investment under the broad label of corruption: corruption of national security, corruption of market processes, corruption of information integrity, corruption of the rule of law, and corruption of domestic industry competitiveness. Conversely, one can also categorize SWF concerns about the response of IRCs to their investments under the broad label of corruption: corruption of open, international financial markets; corruption of the rule of law; and corruption of legitimate concerns about national security. I conclude by suggesting a *balanced-concerns* perspective, which recommends taking a cautious, reasoned approach to SWF investment.

GENERAL BACKGROUND AND DESCRIPTION OF SWFs

In this section, I provide a definition of SWFs, a brief history of their ascent, an exploration of the primary reasons for their recent proliferation, a description of their current size and investing practices, a cursory look at their various roles in the financial crisis, and a summary of the legal regime surrounding SWF investment in the United States.

Basics of SWFs

Sovereign investment can take many forms, including "international reserves, public pension funds, state-owned enterprises, and SWFs" (Kimmit 2008) and can be thought of as creating a "continuum of sovereign investment vehicles" bookended by central banks and state-owned companies (Gilson and Milhaupt 2008, 1354). Although some note that the "distinctions between sovereign wealth funds and other types of government investors are blurring" (Farrell, Lund, and Sadan 2008), this chapter specifically focuses on SWFs for simplicity. Sovereign wealth funds do not have a clearly agreed-upon definition, but I adopt the general definition and description of SWFs in the Santiago Principles since it represents the consensus of 24 countries with SWFs and several permanent observers:[1]

> SWFs are defined as special purpose investment funds or arrangements, owned by the general government. Created by the general government for macroeconomic purposes, SWFs hold, manage, or administer assets to achieve financial objectives, and employ a set of investment strategies which include investing in foreign financial assets. The SWFs are commonly established out of balance of payments surpluses, official foreign currency operations, the proceeds of privatizations, fiscal surpluses, and/or receipts resulting from commodity exports.[2]

Perhaps one reason why there is no generally recognized definition of SWFs is their diversity. For example, SWFs have differing "legal, institutional, and governance structures" and they comprise "fiscal stabilization funds, savings funds, reserve investment corporations, development funds, and pension reserve funds without explicit pension liabilities" (IWG 2008). As the preceding definition suggests, however, SWFs can be generalized into two main categories: commodity-based funds and non-commodity-based funds. The former derive their capital from government commodity revenues or taxes on commodities revenues. Commodity-based SWFs are used for many purposes, including "fiscal revenue stabilization, intergenerational saving, and balance-of-payments sterilization (that is, keeping foreign exchange from stoking inflation)" (Kimmitt 2008). Non-commodity-based SWFs derive their capital largely from official foreign exchange reserves. Global trade imbalances have created massive foreign exchange reserves in some countries. SWF assets, however, can also come from government borrowing or other public or private capital.[3]

The recent intense spotlight on SWF investment activity is relatively new and has already diminished somewhat as a result of the financial crisis. But SWFs have a long history. In 1953, Kuwait created the first SWF, the Kuwait Investment Board, from its oil revenues (Deloitte 2008). The rapid proliferation of SWFs, however, is a more recent development. Since 2005, at least 19 SWFs have been created (SWF Institute 2009). French President Nicolas Sarkozy stated that the purpose of France's recently created SWF is to "give the state the instruments it needs to intervene directly in the economy when it considers that strategic interests of the nation are threatened" (Associated Press 2008). In fact, France has urged other European countries to follow suit in order to protect their own domestic industries. France should not be seen as an anomaly. Countries around the world are increasingly taking such protectionist measures (Samuelson 2009).

Understanding the Recent Proliferation of SWFs

A multitude of economic, political, and social factors are behind the recent proliferation of SWFs. Several macroeconomic factors contribute to the tremendous amounts of financial assets SWFs have available for investment, including general economic growth, high commodity prices, and large global trade imbalances. For example, SWF assets of many countries, particularly those in the Middle East, Norway, and Russia, ballooned with recent high price levels of commodities such as oil and gas. And although the SWF assets of such countries dipped with the global financial crisis and the drop in commodity prices, this trend will likely begin reversing itself as commodity prices are, once again, on the rise. Such countries want to productively deploy their financial assets and they actually stand to lose out on substantial financial returns if they forgo high-yielding investment opportunities. For example, a 2008 McKinsey Global Institute Report calculated that in the case of Asian SWFs, "the opportunity cost of investing excess reserves in relatively low-yielding assets is $123 billion per year, equivalent to 1.3 percent of these countries' GDP" (Farrell, Lund, and Sadan 2008).

Another related macroeconomic factor contributing to SWF investment is that many countries have massive excess foreign exchange reserves resulting from general global trade imbalances. This is particularly true of many Asian SWFs. In October 2009, China had approximately $2.27 trillion in foreign exchange reserves (Batson 2009). For perspective, the increase in China's foreign exchange reserves during six months of early 2009 was $318 billion, which is "a sum nearly equal to the annual gross domestic product of Argentina" (Dyer 2009). Recently, Ben Bernanke, the chairman of the Federal Reserve, expressed concern about such global trade imbalances, suggesting "that it was 'extraordinarily urgent' that the U.S. and Asia adopt policies that prevent a revival of global economic imbalances as the financial crisis ebbs" (Guha 2009). But this is easier said than done. Although global imbalances decreased as a result of the financial crisis, "[a]s the global economy recovers and trade volumes rebound . . . global imbalances may reassert themselves" (Bernanke 2009).

Some sovereigns, such as China, maintain an artificially weak currency in order to boost their country's exports, further contributing to global trade imbalances. This tactic is known as the *competitive devaluation* of a currency, a long-standing strategy that sovereigns sometimes employ to promote export growth. It was a very popular tactic immediately following the Great Depression (Garten 2009). A resurgence of this strategy, however, risks increasing economic nationalism and widespread protectionist measures. Sentiments such as those of Nicolas Sarkozy, quoted earlier, exemplify an increasing trend toward protectionism in response to SWF developments. Reversing export-oriented currency management policies should decrease SWF assets in certain countries, which in turn should help moderate global trade imbalances.

But in addition to a weak Chinese yuan, a sustained period of high levels of U.S. domestic consumption coupled with low domestic savings rates has significantly contributed to the United States' large trade imbalance and its impact on global imbalances. The end result is that the United States needs vast amounts of inflowing capital to finance its large current-account deficit (see Kimmitt 2008). A weak dollar has also made U.S. assets comparatively inexpensive and incentivized SWF investment. But an important underlying question is why "the United States, as the world's greatest power, is the world's greatest borrower" (Summers 2006)? Therefore, in thinking about the pros and cons of SWF investment, it is important to take a holistic perspective. It must be remembered that "[i]f the U.S wants to run a trade deficit of up to 7 percent to 8 percent of GDP, then there will be a lot of consequences. [Foreign entities] can come back and buy us" (Allen 2008). This is also why SWF investment in the United States should come as no surprise.

Social and political factors have also contributed to the recent proliferation of SWFs. Sovereign wealth funds have arguably become symbols of sovereign achievement and prestige, as seen, for example, in rhetoric such as "elite league of SWF nations" and ideas such as "SWFs are increasingly being seen, particularly by the west, as the tools of emerging economies to increase their dominance in global financial system" (Phulgirkar and Gupta 2008). Sovereign wealth funds also excite protectionist rhetoric and tendencies, which has actually encouraged recipients of SWF investment to create their own SWFs in order to safeguard the ownership of national industries.[4] Such SWFs can assist the industrial policy of IRCs by investing in state-favored industries or by providing cheap capital to domestic industries. Another impetus for SWF growth is that SWFs can serve as a protective measure by countries attempting to avoid their past economic fragility, which had exposed their economies to external management and intervention. For example, during the Asian financial crisis of 1997–1998, the International Monetary Fund (IMF) conditioned much of its financial assistance to many Asian countries on programs of domestic "economic austerity." By accumulating vast amounts of foreign reserves, such countries can avoid a repeat of this outside intervention (Allen 2008). Finally, it has been argued that an aging demographic provides an important reason why the United States and Western Europe should welcome the growth of SWF investment. Retirees will need willing buyers when they liquidate their assets to fund their retirement: "[t]hey have lots of stock, but who is going to buy it all?" (Percival 2008).

Current estimates place SWF assets at approximately US$3.6 trillion (SWF Institute 2009). These amounts are thought to be largely unlevered, that is, not debt-based. Therefore, SWFs are generally viewed as stable, long-term investors. Projected estimates of SWF asset growth varies. A State Street report provides estimates of a SWF asset range of $12 to $20 trillion by 2020 (Nugee, Rozanov, and Hoguet 2009); the IMF estimates a range of $6 trillion to $10 trillion by 2013, and Merrill Lynch estimates approximately $8.5 trillion by 2012 (De Ramos 2009). These current and projected amounts make SWFs "systemically significant" international investors (Kimmitt 2008). SWF investment has historically been concentrated in the United States, the United Kingdom, Japan, Australia, India, and Switzerland (Sovereign Wealth Fund Institute 2008), but these investment patterns are likely to change in the future. As of October 2009, the largest SWFs in billions of dollars were UAE-Abu Dhabi ($627), Saudi Arabia ($431), Norway ($396.6), China SAFE ($347.1), China Investment Corp. ($288.8), and Singapore ($247.5). The United States itself has several SWFs: Alaska ($39.8 billion), Alabama ($3.1 billion), New

Mexico ($11.7 billion), and Wyoming ($3.6 billion) (SWF Institute 2009). With these amounts of capital, SWFs are now large enough to "have the potential to distort markets" if they concentrate their resources (Allen 2008).

SWF Relationships with Hedge Funds and Private Equity Funds

For perspective on the total size of this asset pool, SWF assets exceed the combined total amount of assets held by hedge funds, about $1.8 trillion (Lindsay 2010), and private equity funds, about $1.2 trillion (Roxburgh et al. 2009). Furthermore, both hedge funds and private equity funds are themselves often the objects of SWF investment. Sovereign wealth funds have long made capital contributions to hedge funds or been limited partners in private equity funds. Such funds include, among others, Carlyle, Blackstone, Och-Ziff Capital, and Apollo Management, and investments in these funds are estimated to total approximately $450 billion (Farrell, Lund, and Sadan 2008). Korea's SWF is reportedly actively looking to invest in hedge funds in addition to other alternative investments (SWF Institute 2009). Although largely unlevered themselves, SWF investment in hedge funds and private equity funds ultimately contributes to global leverage and, thereby, increased systemic risk (see Johnson 2007). SWFs could also form their own "sovereign hedge funds" in the future. In addition, the creation of a "supra-sovereign-wealth investment fund," a fund of sovereign wealth funds to invest in developing economic markets has been recently suggested (Dyer 2009).

The rise of hedge funds, private equity funds, and SWFs is significant because it signals the "rise of alternative capital pools" in international financial markets. This development "has changed the balance of the global financial system" (World Economic Forum 2008). And some commentators have called for the application of similar regulatory regimes to all three types of investment vehicles (World Economic Forum 2009). Although SWFs are government actors, which fundamentally distinguishes them from both hedge funds and private equity funds, such distinctions could soon blur. Some suggest that in the future, the private equity industry will largely be based upon the financial assets of SWFs and that current private players will likely work for SWFs instead (Thornton, Reed, and Lakshman 2008). The ascent of SWFs suggests that "the mechanisms and structures for accumulating and deploying capital are not pre-existing givens" (Deloitte 2008). With new forms of capital deployment often come new regulatory regimes. The interaction between the two then results in "stable and mature" investment forms (Deloitte 2008). The Santiago Principles and OECD Guidance that I discuss later in this chapter are part of the evolving regulatory response to SWFs.

Sovereign wealth fund investments in the United States have historically been concentrated in debt such as Treasury securities. But SWFs are increasingly migrating to higher-yielding investment opportunities such as equity and, as mentioned earlier, hedge funds and private equity funds. This trend has several implications. First, it could contribute to a weakening of the dollar if demand for U.S. Treasury securities decreases (Barkley 2008). Second, it increases the amount of risk in global financial markets by increasing demand for riskier financial assets that provide higher returns. Third, it contributes to the controversy surrounding these investment vehicles. Although there is a widespread concern that, as government actors, SWFs will invest with both economic and political objectives, it is important to remember that so far SWFs "have consistently behaved as model investors" (Epstein and Rose 2009, 117).

SWF's BENEFITS AND POTENTIAL COSTS

In many ways, SWFs can be viewed as ideal investors. They have low levels of leverage, if any, and generally have long-term investment horizons, which puts them in a better position to withstand short-term market volatility. Their investments also add market liquidity, boost asset prices, and decrease corporate borrowing costs in the economies in which they invest (Kimmitt 2008). Ironically, some suggest that the various regulatory reforms discussed in this chapter, such as additional SWF transparency and disclosure, could create a disproportionate, detrimental focus on short-term results not unlike those faced by public companies in the United States that have high expectations surrounding their quarterly results. At the same time, there is a tricky tension here because SWFs are public actors, and additional disclosure would promote accountability, a definite benefit at a time when the financial crisis has demonstrated the detrimental effects of information deficiencies in global financial markets. Yet, to date, SWFs "represent large, concentrated, and often opaque positions in financial markets" (Kimmitt 2008). Concerns about this opacity are similar to those in the over-the-counter derivative markets, where concentrated, opaque positions resulted in the freezing up of credit markets after Lehman Brothers collapsed.

As noted in the introduction, SWFs arguably contributed to and were representative of several macroeconomic issues that played a part in creating the financial crisis. First, the global trade imbalances that added large amounts of financial assets to SWF's capital also contributed to precarious macroeconomic conditions. Economists argue that one contributing factor to the financial crisis was global trade imbalances, such as those of China, which resulted in large capital inflows, which decreased interest rates, which then increased the attractiveness of riskier securities, such as subprime mortgages, which, in turn, helped create the housing bubble (Samuelson 2009). Second, SWFs invested large amounts of capital in U.S. financial institutions during the early stages of the financial crisis: "From March 2007 through June 2008, Asian SWFs invested $36 billion in Western financial institutions while oil-based SWFs invested $23 billion" (Farrell, Lund, and Sadan 2008). In fact, about 90 percent of SWF investment has "focused on the Western financial sector" (McDermid 2008, citing a report by Global Insight). In general, SWFs suffered substantial losses from these investments. For example, each of Singapore's two SWFs are estimated to have lost many billions of dollars in 2008 (Paris 2009a).

Interestingly, despite the controversy surrounding SWF investment in the United States, their early rescue attempts were largely welcomed. Perhaps Norwegian Finance Minister Kristin Halvorson was correct at the 2008 Davos Economic Summit in his suggestion about the United States and Europe, where SWFs also made significant financial institution investments, that "They don't like us, but they need our money" (O'Grady 2008). In most of these investments in financial institutions, SWFs took passive stakes. Experts suggest that in the future, SWFs are likely to demand increased levels of influence. And because many governments have now invested in their own domestic financial institutions, complex governance issues could arise if multiple government actors have significant stakes in the same company (Moore 2009).

At the same time that the financial crisis has decreased the value of SWF investments, it has also diminished their capital sources, such as commodity prices and export levels. Consequently, the overall capital held by SWFs has decreased. Additionally, the financial crisis could "[provide] an important catalyst for SWFs to re-examine their identity, priorities and objectives in a new financial world order" (Nugee, Rozanov, and Hoguet 2009). For example, some SWFs have increased their focus on their own domestic economies, which have also experienced financial distress. At the same time, economists such as Marko Maslakovic argue that "SWFs have increased their influence on global financial markets since the start of the credit crisis" (quoted in Bradbery 2009). If that ends up being the case, the controversy surrounding SWF investment is likely to revive.

It is important to note that SWF investment in U.S. companies can constitute either a controlling or a noncontrolling position. This is an important distinction. Because SWFs are government-controlled entities, any controlling investment they make in a U.S. company is subject by law to a national security review process by CFIUS. The Committee on Foreign Investment in the United States (CFIUS) is a 12-member, interagency committee headed by the Department of the Treasury and located within the executive branch. The purpose of the CFIUS review process is to strike a balance between encouraging beneficial capital inflows and safeguarding national security concerns while avoiding protectionist measures cloaked as security precautions. In practice, the CFIUS review process has rejected extremely few investments. For example, as noted in the introduction, the CFIUS review process did not block DPW's takeover of the management of six U.S. ports.

The United States is not unique in its regulation of foreign investment. Most countries have some type of regulation in place to address concerns about foreign investment that could potentially harm national security interests. Certain laws in the United States such as the securities laws also subject controlling investments by any investor to additional regulatory requirements. Sovereign wealth funds would likewise be subject to such regulations, but they would still be sovereign actors, meaning that enforcement mechanisms against them would be much more limited than those available against private investors. And whereas a foreign government might assist or at least cooperate with a U.S. enforcement action against a foreign private investor in its jurisdiction, it might not demonstrate the same level of cooperation if the government's SWF itself was the subject of the investigation (Cox 2007). For example, a little over a third of the insider trading cases pursued by the SEC in 2007 involved foreign considerations (Tafara 2008). Sovereign wealth funds are also prohibited from making controlling investments in certain highly sensitive industries such as airlines and nuclear energy (Gilson and Milhaupt 2008).

Although the controlling interest question is an important one, in actual fact SWFs have historically largely avoided taking controlling stakes in U.S. companies. Although noncontrolling investments are not subject to CFIUS review or various other regulations, concern still exists that even noncontrolling positions could allow SWF actors to pursue noneconomic objectives. For example, Gilson and Milhaupt suggest "consider[ing] SWFs' rapid infusion of capital into U.S. commercial and investment banks in the wake of the subprime write-downs. Few domestic financial institutions provided capital. If the investment opportunity was attractive in purely economic terms, why were the SWFs the principal investors" (Gilson and Milhaupt 2008, 1352)? Gilson and Milhaupt provide another example to further suggest the considerable influential role SWFs could provide to government actors: "Could anyone genuinely believe that the investment managers of China Investment Corporation or Singapore's Temasek would hang up the phone if a senior government (or in China's case, Party) official called to offer advice on the fund's handling of a particular investment to advance the country's, rather than the portfolio company's interests" (Gilson and Milhaupt 2008, 1362)?

Their concern is not purely hypothetical. In 2006, Norway's SWF shorted certain debt of Iceland's banking sector, but was "forced to back off after strong protests from Iceland politicians."[5] Finally, even if SWFs have generally taken noncontrolling positions in the past, this does not mean that this strategy will continue. In fact, even now "Middle East families and sovereign wealth funds are slashing their investments and demanding more favourable terms from private equity funds following the financial crisis" (Wigglesworth et al. 2009). And some commentators speculate a likely corporate governance trajectory for SWFs similar to that of large mutual funds, which became highly influential investors in a relatively short period of time (Useem 2008).

GENERAL POLICY ISSUES: BENIGN AND MALIGN EXPLANATIONS

Assuming the influence of SWFs in international financial markets continues to increase, they are likely also to continue arousing passionate controversy. Benign and malign stories—generally designed to influence policies encouraging or discouraging SWF investment—told by the proponents and opponents of SWF investment have arisen in the midst of this firestorm. But it is important to note that the rhetoric surrounding discussions of SWF investment often masks more fundamental and embedded political and social issues related to the government nature of SWFs. As government actors, SWFs are unique. Their public character differentiates them even from foreign private investment.

Proponents of SWF investment argue that such investment should be welcomed by recipient countries because it provides a plethora of benefits. They argue that SWF investment is not only economically beneficial to the United States but also to the global economy as a whole. Such benefits include much needed capital investment, increased financial market stability through long-term investments, additional market liquidity, stronger asset prices (although this also can have negative implications), investment for economically emerging markets, intergenerational savings, and higher investment returns. Furthermore, proponents frequently note, as the OECD states, "To date they [SWFs] have been reliable, long-term, commercially-driven investors and a force for global financial stability" (OECD 2008).

Similarly to other scholars,[6] I have previously argued[7] that increased economic interdependencies through SWF investment could actually increase international cooperation. As commentators suggest, "When SWFs buy a stake in a US company, they also buy a stake in our domestic welfare" (Epstein and Rose 2009, 134). Not only is this due to economic investment, but it also could result arguably from the unique cross-border regulatory coalitions, such as the Santiago Principles, forming in the absence of a global financial regulator to create a governance structure for these markets. Scholars suggest that "an economic enterprise that provides benefits to two different countries embroiled in a dispute contributes to an environment where the leaders of the countries can point to the mutual economic advantages of resolving a conflict as a reason to avoid escalation" (Fort and Schipani 2004, 30). Furthermore, "corporations can build relationships that cross boundaries in a way that might not be accomplished through the traditional political means. Corporations . . . may be able to provide channels for communication that might not otherwise have existed" (Fort and Schipani 2004, 30–31). Sovereign wealth funds likely also have this capacity.

Opponents of SWF investment argue that recipient countries should be highly circumspect about SWF investment since such capital flows could have political motives that endanger national security interests. Some suggest that "governments can be counted upon to act out of more than just economic motivations. It's in their DNA" (Cartwright 2007). For example, Russia has exhibited "a pattern of being very aggressive in using their assets in pursuit of policies unrelated to economics" (White et al. 2008, quoting Evan Bayh). And Michael McConnell, former U.S. Director of National Intelligence, expressed strong concerns about "the financial capabilities of Russia, China and the OPEC countries, and the potential use of their market access to exert financial leverage to achieve political ends" (White et al. 2008). In fact, some economists have termed the U.S. economic situation a "financial balance of terror," creating a geopolitical vulnerability reminiscent of "the effective American use of exchange rate diplomacy to force the hands of the British and French during the Suez crisis" (Summers 2006). Opponents argue that SWF investments could have serious negative effects, including financial market instability resulting from sudden movements of large, concentrated, opaque investment positions; increasing financial market volatility and risk; implementing politically driven rather than economic decisions; harming national security interests; decreasing levels of intellectual property protection; and facilitating anticompetitive effects from SWF access to sensitive government information and preferential financing arrangements which could distort market pricing and competition.

ETHICAL ISSUES SURROUNDING SWFs

As the controversy surrounding SWFs has increased, the IMF and the OECD have spearheaded efforts to develop codes of best practices to govern the behavior of both SWF investors and IRCs to diffuse tensions. The Santiago Principles and the OECD Guidance are the products of these efforts. The Santiago Principles are voluntary best practice guidelines addressing SWF investment practices. The IMF's push to develop these principles, however, was not without opposition. Russia and Kuwait were particularly resistant, the latter pointing to its lengthy and exemplary investment history (O'Grady 2008). Likewise, the OECD has issued tripartite "guidance on recipient country policies towards SWFs" (OECD 2008) focused on recipient country policies, OECD general investment policies, and national security policies. Unfortunately, both the Santiago Principles and OECD

Guidance address mostly micro concerns surrounding SWF investment, and give less attention to consideration of the many underlying macro policy issues that are relevant to SWF investment and arguably at the core of the SWF controversy. This section discusses the ethical concerns surrounding SWF investment by beginning with an exploration of both the Santiago Principles and the OECD Guidance.

Both the Santiago Principles and the OECD Guidance guidelines can be understood as encapsulating general responses to the multiplicity of underlying ethical concerns of both IRCs and SWFs, which are implicitly embedded in the surrounding controversy. As stated previously, I argue that these underlying concerns are really two sides of the same coin: generalized and often related concerns about various issues that can be grouped under the label of *corruption*. Because these concerns are often interrelated, the more extreme positions potentially risk unintended consequences. I suggest, instead, a balanced perspective. For example, many stringent regulations have been proposed to circumscribe SWF investment, including mandating the use of financial intermediaries to invest; only permitting investment in global index funds; removal of voting rights; prohibiting controlling positions; mandating specific disclosure and governance; and creating domestic investment funds to counteract this investment (Epstein and Rose 2009, 119–120). Yet many of these restrictions would have important downsides. For example, stripping SWFs of voting rights could exacerbate agency problems because activist shareholders can positively impact firm performance. To demonstrate the need for a balanced perspective, I will first describe the content of the OECD Guidance and the Santiago Principles, and then explain how a balanced perspective could increase the effectiveness of SWF regulation while also addressing SWF ethical concerns.

The OECD Guidance and Concerns Surrounding IRC Responses

The OECD Guidance surrounding IRC reception of SWF investment, finalized in October 2008, is a three-part approach to balancing the concern for maintaining "an open international investment environment" with the concern of individual IRCs "to safeguard the essential security interests of their people" (OECD 2008). Altogether, it aims to encourage the free flow of international capital and discourage protectionist measures masked as national security precautions in individual IRCs.

The OECD Guidance recognizes both the "constructive contribution" of SWFs and the "legitimate national security concerns [that] could arise" as a result of this investment. The three parts of the OECD Guidance are: (1) the "OECD Declaration on sovereign wealth funds and recipient country policies"; (2) "Guidance that reaffirms the relevance of long-standing OECD investment principles";[8] and (3) "Guidelines for recipient country investment policies relating to national security." Together, these three parts tailor the application of traditional OECD general investment principles of nondiscrimination ("treat SWFs as well as similar domestic investors"), transparency, standstill ("don't introduce new [protectionist] measures"), and progressive and unilateral liberalization to the context of SWF investment. Specifically, the OECD Guidance actively discourages the development of protectionist measures by IRCs, reiterates long-standing OECD policies of nondiscrimination, and, where discrimination is deemed necessary for legitimate national security purposes, calls for transparency, predictability, proportionality, and accountability in such measures. IRCs' adherence to the substance of the OECD Guidance in their development of investment policies relies upon a long-standing OECD process of "peer review" and accompanying potential peer pressures. Additionally, OECD discussions about approaches to investment policy are increasingly involving input from nonmember SWF investor countries such as China, Russia, and Brazil.

The Santiago Principles and Concerns Surrounding SWF Investment

The Santiago Principles, formalized in October 2008, are informal investment guidelines for SWFs that represent the consensus of an extraordinary cross-section of nations. These are voluntary guidelines that are "each . . . subject to home country laws, regulations, requirements, and obligations" (IWG 2008), which "must be ratified by the competent authority in each participating country" (Deloitte 2008). Although informal and nonbinding guidelines, the Santiago Principles should not be dismissed easily since international law scholars have noted a general trend away from international treaties toward more informal agreements (Murphy, 2010) such as those contained in the Santiago Principles. The IWG has also recently produced the "Kuwait Declaration," which established the International Forum of Sovereign Wealth Funds (Forum) for the "continuing exchange of views and study of SWF activities" (IWG 2008).

The Santiago Principles are based upon the following four objectives: "(1) to help maintain a stable global financial system and free flow of capital and investment; (2) to comply with all applicable regulatory and disclosure requirements in the countries in which they invest; (3) to invest on the basis of economic and financial risk and return-related considerations; and (4) to have in place a transparent and sound governance structure that provides for adequate operational controls, risk management, and accountability" (IWG 2008). To implement these objectives, the IWG developed 24 principles applicable to individual SWFs that can be grouped and discussed in three general categories: (1) a SWF's "legal framework, objectives, and coordination with macroeconomic policies"; (2) a SWF's "institutional framework and governance structure"; and (3) a SWF's "investment and risk management" framework (IWG 2008). Taken as a whole, the Santiago Principles are primarily concerned with institutional frameworks, transparency, accountability, and the management of risk. This focus directly addresses the main concerns of opponents to SWF investment. The Santiago Principles were purposely given a broad formulation to facilitate their application in a diversity of "institutional, constitutional, and legal settings" (IWG 2008).

Related and Underlying Concerns about Corruption

As mentioned previously, the fundamental, related purpose of both the Santiago Principles and OECD Guidance is to promote a balancing act between the concerns of IRCs about their national security interests and the concerns of SWFs that their investments be welcomed on a nondiscriminatory basis and receive equal treatment. Embedded in this balancing act is also a tension between government actors and private business interests. Finding an equilibrium between these interests will prevent the corruption of the free flow of capital through large-scale protectionist measures and prevent the corruption of market processes by encouraging more transparent market practices.

The main concern from the perspective of SWF actors is that individual countries will enact excessive investment regulations under the pretense of maintaining national security interests, while really enacting protectionist measures. Hence, what is sometimes left unstated in such discussions, but is at the root of many such concerns, is the particular countries behind SWF investment. For example, there was no public or congressional outcry in the United States when a British company managed the six U.S. ports in the DPW fiasco, but when those ports were to be managed by a member of the United Arab Emirates, a public and congressional outcry arose. In a similar vein, a good deal of Europe's unease with SWF investment likely stems less from SWF investments themselves and more from the countries, such as Russia, behind the investments. Effective regulation must address these national security concerns while also providing avenues for SWF investment.

From the perspective of IRCs, the first set of corruption concerns centers on the corruption of international financial markets and market processes. The integrity of international financial markets can be thought of as an international common good. Maintaining this good, however, is a difficult collective action problem. The potential of SWFs to corrupt market processes could take several forms. The primary concern is that SWF activity be based on political rather than economic motives: "Sovereign wealth funds and their cousins, the state-controlled enterprises, are one example of a class of institutional owners whose behavior can be expected to reflect, in part, non-economic motivations" (Cartwright 2007). Noneconomic motives could include many considerations: to gain access to technology or information, to favor national industries, to secure long-term access to commodities, to serve long-term geopolitical influence, or even to gain the eventual control of a particular industry internationally.

It is particularly challenging to monitor potential misbehavior because, aside from certain limited exceptions such as Norway's SWF, many SWFs have low levels of transparency and disclosure. For markets, or the pricing system, to function properly, additional information disclosure is required. This opacity presents challenges not only for international interests, but also for domestic interests wishing to hold SWFs accountable for their use of public monies. But, as has been noted, transparency is a complex issue because it can relate to a multitude of considerations such as governance structure, investment objectives, and investment strategy (Khanna 2008). While it might be reasonable to demand transparency of governance structure and investment objectives, such demands seem less reasonable in relation to investment strategy (Khanna 2008).

Consequently, an important area of concern related to this lack of domestic accountability is the potential for increased levels of domestic corruption and related agency issues. Lack of transparency and disclosure facilitates this problem. And many of the largest SWFs are located in countries already perceived to be highly corrupt according to Transparency International's Corruption Perceptions Index (Transparency International 2008). It would be naïve to think that the SWFs in such countries would constitute an exception. Such considerations are particularly important when a public matter is involved. Related to these accountability concerns is the fact that many of the largest SWFs are not owned by democratic political regimes. Furthermore, questions about the investment management competency of some SWFs are frequently voiced and represent two primary concerns. First, do SWF managers have the actual skills needed to invest public funds responsibly? Second, what is the benefit of investing such funds through SWFs instead of returning these funds to the private sector and letting individuals themselves decide how to invest this money?

An additional concern is that many SWFs are owned by countries with high levels of domestic poverty. As economists have noted, "It is an irony of our times that the majority of the world's poorest people now live in countries with vast international financial reserves" (Summers 2006). This is a serious and complex international ethical concern. The per capita income of SWF countries varies enormously. Why would a government entity in a poor country make overseas investment when so much infrastructure, education, and health investment is needed on the domestic front? For example, India's proposed SWF has been met with a variety of reactions. India is in a strong position with its foreign exchange reserves. Investing these excesses reserves in U.S. Treasury securities rather than in high-yielding assets is not only very costly, but also arguably forfeits the opportunity to accomplish "strategic objectives" such as energy asset accumulation and contributing to domestic financing demands (Phulgirkar and Gupta 2008). Critics of the idea of an Indian SWF suggest, however, that pressing domestic concerns such as infrastructure, health care, and education should be a higher priority for India's excess reserves (Nair 2008). Similarly, on the one hand it is thought that if Russia used its SWF assets for necessary infrastructure purposes, its SWF's rate of growth would moderate (Sorkin 2008). On the other hand, Russia's finance minister has argued that widespread use of SWF financial assets in the domestic economy could create asset bubbles and stoke inflation (White, Davis, and Walker 2008).

Trends suggest that SWFs will play an increasingly important role in both internal and external development. Robert Zoellick, president of the World Bank, has recently called upon the SWFs of Asia and the Middle East to invest in African development (Weisman 2008). Singapore's Temasek is reportedly planning to invest close to $2 billion in China, India, Mexico, and Brazil in the near future (Paris 2009b); discussions about the creation of a "supra sovereign wealth investment fund" to do just that have already begun. Some think that taking this approach would decrease the opportunities for corruption created when funds are dispersed to "local middlemen" (Dyer 2009). Of course, this route would also allow investors to exert greater local control, which would likely have both positive and negative implications. These combined concerns point to the idea that as public investment vehicles, SWFs should be investing for the benefit of the public, not for the benefit of a variety of possible individuals. Consequently, increased transparency and accountability are necessary to ensure that SWF financial assets are not siphoned off for the benefit of the political and business elite.

A related area of concern can be labeled *rule of law* issues. Maintaining the rule of law can become particularly complex if the regulator and the regulated share the same identity (Cox 2007). Two issues are particularly salient in this area: conflicts of interest and enforcement ability. First, what happens when the regulator is the regulated? A conflict of interest will arise. As mentioned earlier, a foreign entity is less likely to cooperate with the SEC in an investigation of that country's own SWF (Cox 2007). Second, even in a case where enforcement is necessary and provided for by law, enforcement proceedings against sovereigns are extremely difficult and present limited possibilities.

A final area of corruption concern made salient by SWF investment is conflicting international value systems. It has been quipped that one country's ethics is another country's politics. For example, investments by Norway's SWF are reviewed by a Council of Ethics to ensure that they conform to delineated Ethical Guidelines.[9] The Council has decided that several U.S. companies, including Wal-Mart and Freeport-McMoRan Copper & Gold, do not conform to these guidelines, thus requiring divestment by Norway's SWF.

CONCLUSION

Despite all of the surrounding controversy, SWFs have a history of being model investors whose investments offer many benefits. Taking a balanced perspective on SWF investment can help resolve the tensions that exist between the concerns of SWFs and IRCs. These counteracting tensions, properly managed, can work as counterbalancing forces against the corruption tendencies that tempt both constituencies. Sovereign wealth funds already have a long history and should be anticipated to be important financial market participants for the foreseeable future. Therefore, their increasing participation in international financial markets should be cautiously welcomed as their activities could provide many benefits, but could also cause detrimental market disruptions. Therefore, I agree with former SEC Chairman Christopher Cox's recommendation for a "cautious optimism." He writes:

> The optimism would be warranted by the extraordinary progress the world has made in recognizing the importance of markets, and in relying upon them for the allocation of society's resources. The caution comes in recognizing that the rising sun, for all its friendly promise, is still a ball of fire. Whether we ultimately bask in its warmth, or blister under its heat will be determined by wise choices made now, and the continued vigilance of all people dedicated to truly free markets. (Cox 2007)

NOTES

1. Currently, these countries are: Australia: Australian Future Fund; Azerbaijan: State Oil Fund; Bahrain: Reserve Fund for Strategic Projects; Botswana: Pula Fund; Canada: Alberta Heritage Savings Trust Fund; Chile: Economic and Social Stabilization Fund/Pension Reserve Fund; China: China Investment Corporation; Equatorial Guinea: Fund for Future Generations; Islamic Republic of Iran: Oil Stabilization Fund; Ireland: National Pensions Reserve Fund; Korea: Korea Investment Corporation; Kuwait: Kuwait Investment Authority; Libya: Libyan Investment Authority; Mexico: Oil Stabilization Fund; New Zealand: Superannuation Fund; Norway: Government Pension Fund; Qatar: Qatar Investment Authority; Russia: Reserve Fund/National Wealth Fund; Singapore: Temasek Holdings Pte Ltd, Government of Singapore Investment Corporation Pte Ltd; Timor-Leste: Petroleum Fund of Timor-Leste; Trinidad and Tobago: Heritage and Stabilization Fund; United Arab Emirates: Abu Dhabi Investment Authority; and United States: Alaska Permanent Investment Fund. Current permanent observers are: Oman,

State General Reserve Fund; Saudi Arabia: Saudi Arabian Monetary Agency; Vietnam: State Capital Investment Corporation; Organisation for Economic Co-operation and Development; and the World Bank.

2. IWG, 2008. Appendices and References, 27.

3. France planned to access a variety of sources to capitalize its SWF; see Associated Press (2008). And Singapore's Temasek has sold bonds to raise capital; see Lopez (2009).

4. For example, see Associated Press (2008).

5. "Special report: The new competition for global resources" (2008). Available from: The Boston Consulting Group. http://knowledge.wharton.upenn.edu/papers/download/ BCGReport_Competition_for_Global_Resources.pdf.

6. For example, see Epstein and Rose (2009).

7. "The Role of Sovereign Wealth Funds in Promoting Peace Through Commerce," presentation for Peace Through Commerce Conference at George Washington Business School, November 15, 2008.

8. Note that this guidance reaffirms OECD principles originally adopted in 1961.

9. For additional background on Norway's SWF and its Council of Ethics, see Chesterman (2008).

REFERENCES

Allen, Franklin. 2008. Quoted in Huge reserves, emerging market "challengers" and other forces are changing global finance. Knowledge@Wharton, Wharton School of the University of Pennsylvania, September 22.

Associated Press, 2008. France to set up sovereign wealth fund. *Wall Street Journal*, October 24.

Barkley, Tom. 2008. IMF clears way for development of sovereign wealth funds code. *Wall Street Journal*, March 24.

Batson, Andrew. 2009. Chinese reserves hit $2.273 trillion. *Wall Street Journal*, October 15.

Bernanke, Ben. 2009. Asia and the global financial crisis. Speech given at the Federal Reserve Bank of San Francisco's Conference on Asia and the Global Financial Crisis, October 19.

Bradbery, Adam. 2009. Sovereign-wealth funds added assets and influence in 2008. *Wall Street Journal*, March 2.

Buffett, Warren. 2007. Letter to the Shareholders of Berkshire Hathaway Inc., Berkshire Hathaway 2007 Annual Report.

Cartwright, Brian. 2007. The future of securities regulation. Speech given at the University of Pennsylvania Law School, October 24.

Chesterman, Simon. 2008. The turn to ethics: Disinvestment from multinational corporations for human rights violations: The case of Norway's sovereign wealth fund. *American University International Law Review* 23:577–616.

Cox, Christopher. 2007. The rise of sovereign business. Speech given at Gauer Distinguished Lecture in Law and Policy at the American Enterprise Institute Legal Center for the Public Interest, Washington, DC, December 5.

Deloitte Touche Tohmatsu. 2008. Minding the GAPP: Sovereign wealth, transparency, and the "Santiago principles." http://www.deloitte.com/mindingthegaap.

De Ramos, Rita Raagas. 2009. Crisis reshapes role of sovereign wealth funds. *BusinessWeek*, August 21.

Dyer, Geoff. 2009. Immense forex reserves are not a problem but an opportunity. *Financial Times*, October 20.

Economist. 2009. From torrent to trickle. *Economist*, January 22.

Epstein, Richard, and Amanda Rose. 2009. The regulation of sovereign wealth funds: The virtues of going slow. *University of Chicago Law Review* 76:111–134.

Farrell, Diana, Susan Lund, and Koby Sadan. 2008. The new power brokers: Gaining clout in turbulent markets. *McKinsey Global Institute Report*, July.

Fort, Timothy, and Cindy Schipani. 2004. *The role of business in fostering peaceful societies.* Cambridge: Cambridge University Press.

Garten, Jeffrey. 2009. The dangers of turning inward. *Wall Street Journal Online*, March 5.

Gilson, Ronald, and Curtis Milhaupt. 2008. Sovereign wealth funds and corporate governance: A minimalist response to the new mercantilism. *Stanford Law Review* 60:1345–1370.

Guha, Krishna. 2009. Fed chief urges US and Asia to act on imbalance. *Financial Times*, October 20.

International Working Group of Sovereign Wealth Funds (IWG). 2008. Sovereign wealth funds generally accepted principles and practices: "Santiago Principles." http://www.iwg-swf.org/pubs/eng/santiagoprinciples.pdf.

Johnson, Simon. 2007. The rise of sovereign wealth funds. *Finance & Development*, September.

Khanna, Vikram. 2008. Norwegian approach to pension fund management: Martin Skancke, director general of Norway's Ministry of Finance and head of its asset management department, talks to Vikram Khanna about how the Norway government pension fund—one of the world's largest sovereign wealth funds—is managed. *Business Times Singapore*, February 5.

Kimmitt, Robert. 2008. Public footprints in private markets: Sovereign wealth funds and the world economy. *Foreign Affairs* 87, no. 1 (January–February).

Lindsay, Margie. 2010. Global hedge fund AUM hits 1.8 trillion. *Hedge Funds Review*, March 8.

Lopez, Ditas. 2009. Temasek raises $1.5 billion in bond sale. *Wall Street Journal*, October 21.

McDermid, Riley. 2008. Government funds set to grow. *Wall Street Journal*, April 30.

Moore, Heidi. 2009. Wall Street banks: Will sovereign wealth funds speak up? *Wall Street Journal*, January 8.

Munchau, Wolfgang. 2009. At last, a recognition of the deep roots of the crisis. *Financial Times*, September 28.

Murphy, John. 2010. *The evolving dimensions of international law: Hard choices for the world community.* Cambridge, MA: Cambridge University Press.

Nair, Vinay. 2008. Should India set up a sovereign wealth fund? It's a bad idea. Opinion piece, Knowledge@Wharton, March 27.

Nugee, John, Andrew Rozanov, and George Hoguet. 2009. *Sovereign wealth funds: Emerging from the financial crisis.* Boston, MA: State Street Corporation, New Vision Series.

Organisation for Economic Co-operation and Development (OECD). 2008. OECD Guidance on Sovereign Wealth Funds. http://www.oecd.org/document/19/0,3343,en_2649_34887_41807059_1_1_1_1,00.html.

O'Grady, Sean. 2008. Sovereign wealth funds hostile to international code of conduct; World Economic Forum view from Davos 2008. *The Independent* (London), January 25.

Paris, Costas. 2009a. Singapore government fund's loss pegged at $33 billion. *Wall Street Journal*, February 18.

———. 2009b. Temasek to invest more than $1.8 billion in coming months. *Wall Street Journal*, October 22.

Percival, John. Quoted in Huge reserves, emerging market "challengers" and other forces are changing global finance. Knowledge@Wharton, Wharton School of the University of Pennsylvania, September 22.

Phulgirkar, Sharmili, and Sidharth Gupta. 2008. Why India needs a sovereign wealth fund. *BusinessWeek*, October 10.

Roxburgh, Charles, Lund, Susan, Lippert, Matt, White, Olivia, and Yue Zhao. 2009. The new power brokers: How oil, Asia, hedgefunds, and private equity are faring in the financial crisis. *McKinsey Global Institute Report*.

Samuelson, Robert. 2009. China's dollar deception. *Washington Post*, April 6.

Schonberg, Stefan. 2008. Sovereign wealth alarm. *The International Economy*, Winter.

Setser, Brad. 2008. Bonfire of sovereign wealth funds. Blog on the Council of Foreign Relations site, November 25.

Sorkin, Andrew Ross. 2008. Sovereign wealth funds may surpass global foreign reserves. *New York Times Dealbook*, March 12.

Sovereign Wealth Fund (SWF) Institute. 2009. http://www.swfinstitute.org/.

Summers, Lawrence. 2007. Funds that shake capitalist logic. *Financial Times*, July 29.

———. 2006. Reflections on global account imbalances and emerging markets reserve accumulation. L. K. Jha Memorial Lecture at the Reserve Bank of India, Mumbai, March 24.

Tafara, Ethiopis. 2008. Testimony concerning the regulatory framework for sovereign investments, before U.S. Senate Committee on Banking, Housing, and Urban Affairs, April 24.

Thornton, Emily, Stanley Reed, and Nandini Lakshman. 2008. Who's afraid of Mideast money? *BusinessWeek*, January 21.

Transparency International. 2008. Transparency International Corruption Perceptions Index. http://www.transparency.org/.

Useem, Michael. 2008. Quoted in Huge reserves, emerging market "challengers" and other forces are changing global finance. Knowledge@Wharton, Wharton School of the University of Pennsylvania, September 22.

Weisman, Steven. 2008. World Bank calls on sovereign funds to invest in Africa. *New York Times*, April 3.

White, Gregory, Bob Davis, and Marcus Walker. 2008. Russian wealth fund rattles west. *Wall Street Journal*, May 7.

Wigglesworth, Robin, Martin Arnold, and Simeon Kerr. 2009. Mideast investment cuts hit private equity. *Financial Times*, October 19.

Willman, John. 2007. Big spenders: How sovereign funds are stirring up protectionism. *Financial Times*, July 30.

World Economic Forum. 2008. Global Risks 2008. http://www.weforum.org/pdf/globalrisk/report2008.pdf.

World Economic Forum. 2009. The future of the global financial system: A near-term outlook and long-term scenarios. http://www.weforum.org/en/initiatives/Scenarios/GlobalFinancialSystem/index.htm.

ABOUT THE AUTHOR

Colleen Baker is a fifth-year doctoral student in the Ethics and Legal Studies doctoral program at the Wharton School, University of Pennsylvania. She received a BA from the University of Notre Dame, a JD/MBA from the University of Virginia, and has worked in law and information technology, and as an entrepreneur. Her research/teaching interests are in financial regulation, bankruptcy, sovereign wealth funds, sovereign bankruptcy, and legal and ethical issues in economically emerging markets (particularly Latin America). She will be joining the University of Notre Dame Law School as an associate professor in fall 2010.

The author would like to thank the Carol and Lawrence Zicklin Center for Business Ethics for research funding.

PART IV

Financial Services

CHAPTER 15

Marketing of Financial Services

GEORGE G. BRENKERT

Professor of Business Ethics, McDonough School of Business, Georgetown University*

INTRODUCTION

The marketing of financial services and products has become increasingly important as the role of the financial services industry has grown throughout the world and as competition has become more intense (Meidan 1996, 1). Financial services and products provide the means by which people manage their money or gain access to money. Suppliers include banks, credit card companies, stock brokerages, investment funds, and consumer finance companies. The expectation is that attention to the marketing of their services and products improves the effectiveness of the ways in which they are developed, targeted, priced, advertised, and promoted. As such, marketing enhances the competitiveness of the firms involved. To the extent that ethical responsibilities are integrated into these marketing efforts, it may also be expected that there will be fewer occasions for consumer dissatisfaction and greater trust toward those offering financial services.

Unfortunately, the economic and financial crisis of 2008 was an example of how marketing can go astray. There are good reasons to believe that the marketing of financial services and products contributed to this crisis. Mortgage companies marketed home loans to people who could not afford them. Credit card companies raised rates on past purchases, putting increased financial pressure on already overextended consumers. Financial advisers encouraged customers to buy and sell securities in ways that did not contribute to the betterment of their financial situation. And when those at the bottom of the financial scale needed money to get a car or house repaired, payday loans were marketed to them in ways that trapped them in a cycle of debt.

However, this chapter is not simply about ethical issues that appeared during this recent financial crisis. It is more generally about ethical concerns that are always relevant when financial products and services are marketed. The preceding examples simply point to some of the ethical issues that the general topic of the ethical marketing of financial products and services raises.

In this chapter, I can address only a small number of these issues. I limit my discussion here to the marketing of financial services and products to individual

---

*I am indebted to John Boatright for helpful editorial and substantive comments on an earlier version of this chapter.

customers, rather than to other businesses. Within this restricted, though still broad area, I give special attention to ethical issues that arise with regard to the marketing of mortgages, credit cards, and payday loans.[1] These three areas capture a diverse sample of financial services and products that are marketed to a broad range of individuals. Though the ethical issues that arise in these areas are just a few of the topics that the marketing of financial services and products raises, they are important ones.

AN ETHICAL FRAMEWORK

Before looking at these particular issues, we should first briefly consider what ethical marketing framework should be involved in the marketing of financial products and services. To speak of marketing here is not simply to speak of advertising. Advertising is only one part of marketing. Instead, marketing is a set of coordinated activities that are "designed to create, communicate, and convey, through voluntary exchanges, something those targeted will value, and to do so in ways that fulfill the objectives of marketers and/or their organizations" (Brenkert 2008, 13). Understood in this general sense, marketing involves marketing research, product development, segmentation, pricing, distribution, advertising, promotions, and sales. Ideally, all these elements are interconnected by a marketing strategy.

During the latter half of the twentieth century, it was widely held that marketers should guide their actions in accord with the marketing concept. This called on marketers to satisfy the wants or needs of customers in ways that contribute to the profits of the businesses that employ them. "The objective of the marketing process is the profitable sale of services that satisfy customers' financial requirements and needs" (Meidan 1996, 18).

However, this objective is too narrow and simple. Marketers should also follow the law. Still, it is a staple of marketing ethics that just because something is legal it is not necessarily ethical. For example, even if a marketer satisfies the law, there are other marketing activities that could run afoul of ethical concerns, such as when marketers target vulnerable groups with credit cards that they may not be able to handle. Thus, ethical marketing must seek to convey something of value to customers in ways that accord with law and basic ethical values and norms.

An ethical framework for marketing financial services and products would do three things. First, it would identify the basic values and norms (as well as their basis) marketers should follow (*norms identification*). Second, it would indicate how these norms and values would be applied or used in marketing different kinds of financial products and services (*norms application*). Third, it should place this ethical marketing effort within a context in which it could be successful (*norms promotion*). I provide here only a brief sketch of these three parts of an ethical framework.

For norms identification, we can turn to the American Marketing Association (AMA), which has adopted a code of ethics that includes such principles and values as do no harm, honesty, fairness, respect, transparency, trust, and citizenship. In addition, the AMA code calls on marketers to avoid the use of coercion and to reject manipulation (AMA 2009). These are important answers to the first part of an ethical framework. This pluralist set of norms and values should guide the marketing of financial products and services. Though some have viewed these principles as *aspirational* rather than obligatory, to do so would let marketers off the ethical hook much too easily.[2] To *aspire* is to seek to do something or to have an ambition to do it. As such, one may aspire to do or be something even though one does so in half measures and is not required or under an obligation to be successful. However, ethics functions differently (or at least an important part of it does). Ethical principles impose obligations and duties on marketers. Thus, ethics doesn't simply say "Strive not to lie"; it says "Don't lie."[3] One source of the aspirational view of ethics is the assumption that ethical requirements are externally imposed on marketing. But they are not. Ethical requirements emerge from an understanding of *marketing* as an undertaking that presupposes noncoercive exchanges between people who own what they exchange (hence private property) or have authority to exchange those resources.

For example, inasmuch as marketing involves voluntary exchanges, efforts to coerce, manipulate, or influence people to act in ways other than they choose undercut marketing. Thus, there is first a *capacity component* of marketing that is relevant to questions of autonomy and self-direction and hence to norms of openness and respect.

Second, if a person is deceived about an exchange and the person does not really understand what it is he is exchanging or the conditions the exchange involves, the voluntary nature of the exchange is undermined. Thus, there is also a *cognitive component* of marketing. Here norms of honesty, fairness, trust, and truthfulness are relevant.

Third, there is a *relationship component*. The voluntary exchange of items of value creates a relationship between the members of the exchange that may be short-term or long-term, in which the interests of the other member of the exchange may or may not be taken into account. Hence, norms of trust, respect, doing no harm, and openness arise again in a marketing context. However, inasmuch as marketing exchanges frequently take place in a competitive context, one's relationship with other marketers and customers may be different than in a cooperative context.

The second part of an ethical marketing framework, norms application, elaborates on and applies the relevant values and norms in different relationships and situations. This is best done not abstractly but in particular contexts, as I do in the following sections. The ethical determinations made in applying values and norms are not simply subjective responses, but ideally reflective judgments based on appropriate features of the norms and situation. This ethical application component requires that one carefully ascertain the relevant facts of each issue; the pertinent ethical norms and values; possible courses of action; and the extent, degree, and manner in which everyone is affected by alternative actions. Out of such examinations a best, all-things-considered judgment must be rendered that remains subject to review and revision.

Finally, a crucial issue is not simply whether something is ethical, but how we encourage people to do the ethical thing. Crucial to this third part of the ethical framework, norms promotion, are background interrelationships between marketers and their firms, those they target, and society. In short, acting morally or ethically (I understand these to be the same thing here) is always action within a context. The nature of that context plays an important role in whether people act morally. The organization within which people work must be one in which they can make and act on ethical decisions. This will also require laws and regulations that protect organizations from other businesses that are less concerned about ethical marketing.

This chapter focuses primarily on the second part of this ethical framework, applying various ethical principles and values to three important areas of marketing financial services. However, it also, albeit briefly, takes note of steps required to fulfill the third part of an ethical marketing framework, namely norms promotion.

MARKETING MORTGAGES

A house or condominium is one of the iconic possessions in the United States and Canada. It is also the largest single purchase that most individuals will ever make. For this reason, if no other, the marketing that is part of the process by which people acquire a residence deserves close ethical scrutiny. It also deserves examination because the home mortgage industry is widely identified as having played a central role in the credit crisis and financial meltdown of 2008. Of course, it did not accomplish this all by itself. There were many other actors who contributed to this predicament. Further, this was not simply a financial meltdown involving misjudged risk assessments (though it was this). It was also an ethical meltdown arising, in part, from various unethical marketing practices. Unless the ethical dimensions of marketing mortgages are given greater attention than in recent years, we may face similar problems in the future. Three important dimensions of the ethical marketing of mortgages include (1) the relation of the mortgage broker or lender to the borrower; (2) the role of informed decisions in marketing different kinds of loans to customers; and (3) the deception and manipulation of some borrowers that has occurred in getting them to finance their homes.

The Relation of Customers, Mortgage Brokers, and Lenders

The relationship between the providers of a product or service and those whom their marketing targets conditions (or should condition) the nature of that marketing. In the past, a person would find a house through the services of a real estate agent and go to a bank, credit union, or savings and loan company in order to get a loan to buy the house. Though the local bank or credit union that issued a loan often tried to do the best it could for its customers (simply due to the fact the lender and customer were part of the same community and the lender had a concern for its reputation), the lender did not have a fiduciary relationship with its customers—that is, it was not legally or ethically obliged to focus its efforts on serving the best interests of its customer. Still, because the lender, in this case, held on to the loan and received interest and principal payments from the borrower, it was interested in the borrower being able to pay off the loan. The financial futures of the borrower and the lender were joined. Of course, in this system, once the bank had loaned money to others, it had less assets to make additional loans.

Beginning in the 1970s and 1980s, various laws and regulations were changed so that it became possible and desirable to sell those mortgages to other lenders who would package them into mortgage-backed securities that other financial institutions and Wall Street might buy.[4] This opened up more money for those who wanted to buy homes. In addition, in the early twenty-first century, the Federal Reserve cut interest rates to spur lending and spending. This made even more credit available at cheaper rates (see Rozeff 2008). Further, the government encouraged Fannie Mae and Freddie Mac to expand home ownership.[5] Finally, investors on Wall Street were clamoring after investments that offered them the opportunity to increase their profits. Accordingly, there were incentives and opportunities to make many more mortgages available to customers.

These legal and economic changes affected the relation of customers and mortgage lenders and thereby the ways that mortgages were marketed to potential borrowers. One of the crucial tasks responsible marketing faces is to avoid targeting those who are unlikely customers because they would be injured by a marketing exchange due to their vulnerability or lack of resources. However, given the preceding changes, and since many of those who could (on a traditional credit evaluation) own a home already owned one, the companies marketing mortgages targeted groups of people whose creditworthiness was shaky. Some companies disregarded traditional procedures for evaluating creditworthiness and introduced "No Doc" loans—that is, no documents were required in order to obtain a loan. Countrywide had a "SISA" program—stated income, stated assets—in which "[t]he borrower's income and assets were stated but not verified."[6] This approach had initially developed at a time when self-employed people who had good credit ratings sought loans. However, over time, it was applied to almost anyone, regardless of their credit ratings. In addition, because those targeted were at high risk of defaulting on their mortgages, higher rates of interest were charged for their loans. For example, "in 2001, standard mortgage loans carried a 6.5 percent interest rate. The average subprime mortgage rate was over 15 percent" (Legal Helpers 2009).

Further, more and more people went to independent mortgage brokers who marketed these loans and submitted the borrowers' applications to lenders. In fact, by 2007 most "homebuyer's business (70 percent) ... [went] to independent mortgage brokers—some of whom [received] ... bonuses for steering borrowers to higher-interest loans" (Trehan 2007). Inasmuch as those who initially made the loans did not hold them but sold them, they became less worried about whether the borrower could pay off the loan or even what were the financial resources of those who sought loans. Their compensation was based upon the new loans they could generate and the rates of interest that the new loans would pay.

Their compensation was also enhanced by yield-spread premiums (YSP) and prepayment penalties (Ernst, Bocian, and Li 2008, 5). The YSP is a premium that lenders pay brokers to obtain mortgages with higher rates of interest than the borrowers would be qualified to obtain. The prepayment penalty is a charge borrowers have to pay if they seek to change their loan, either by paying it off sooner than required or by changing the terms of their loan. In either case, the aim from the lender's standpoint is, in effect, to lock people into their current loans and into the rates of interest they are paying. Accordingly, because it intended to sell the mortgages it generated to the secondary market, firms such as Countrywide wanted to originate mortgages "with above-market interest rates and other terms [such as prepayment penalties] which would attract premium prices on the secondary market."[7]

The effect of this marketing approach was a large expansion of borrowers who could not afford their loans (subprime loans) by lenders who were indifferent to the borrowers' ability to pay. Borrowers were regarded as responsible for the situations they got themselves into. If they defaulted, that was their problem. The mortgage broker or lending institution had made its fee or commission and then sold the mortgage to some other institution that was stuck with what have come to be called *toxic* mortgages. It was a system built upon a failure to engage in due diligence and a hearty disregard for honesty. Its short-term focus hid significant dangers of defaults.[8] Mortgage brokers and lenders displayed little concern for the injuries that would likely befall their customers or the eventual investors in mortgage-backed securities.[9]

Knowledge of Products: Informed Decisions

Decisions with ethical implications may also be criticized when they are made without an adequate understanding of their nature and consequences. Mortgages are marketed ethically when marketers provide sufficient information to the borrower so that he may understand the nature and implications of the mortgage being offered. When this does not occur, the decision made may be faulty both economically and ethically.

An example of this kind of situation occurred when mortgage brokers promoted adjustable-rate mortgages (ARMs), rather than fixed-rate mortgages, to many borrowers. ARMs start out with (sometimes very) low initial monthly payments, but then after a short period of time, the payments increase (and sometimes dramatically so). There is nothing inherently wrong with such mortgages. If people know what they are and are prepared for their consequences, an adjustable-rate mortgage might be appropriate for the right people at the right time.

However, in many instances the mortgage dealer emphasized "... the very low initial 'teaser' or 'fixed' rates while obfuscating or misrepresenting the later steep monthly payments and interest rate increases or risk of negative amortization."[10] Further, in some cases the interest rate increases could happen once every year or every six months, leading to a continuing adjustment (and increase) in one's monthly mortgage. Finally, in other cases, a person might select a minimum payment option based on the introductory rate of interest. If this was less than the interest accruing on the loan, the unpaid interest was added to the principal of the loan, which resulted in a negative amortization—in other words, the amount the borrower owed grew and grew. In many cases, the amount owed on the loan after five or six years could be tens of thousands of dollars more than the loan for which the borrower originally contracted.[11]

Unfortunately, many people did not understand the complexities and implications of the loans they were taking out. They were encouraged sometimes to make unrealistic assumptions about the increasing value of their houses that would permit them, through refinancing, to avoid paying higher monthly payments. In any case, many soon encountered mortgage payments beyond the amount they were able to pay, and as a result many lost their houses to foreclosures.

Two different marketing sources contributed to this lack of understanding. First, through advertisements and telemarketing calls and solicitations by e-mails and letters, mortgage brokers would tout "low introductory rates and monthly payments that purportedly would save borrowers money over their existing mortgages when the principal amount of the loan would increase, according to court documents" (Gullo and Harris 2008). In addition, television commercials emphasized that the payment rate could be as low as 1 percent, and print advertisements lauded the extra cash available to borrowers because of the low minimum payment on the loan. Television advertisements did not effectively distinguish between the "payment rate" and the interest rate on loans, and any warnings about potential negative amortization in Countrywide's print advertisements were buried in densely written small type.[12] In short, a number of mortgage brokers and lenders failed to adequately and clearly present the terms of the mortgages they were offering. *Caveat emptor* was, in effect, their motto. However, with complicated financial products such as mortgages, especially the ones that involved shifting interest rates, different prepayment penalties, and so on, and with customers having little understanding of such financial instruments, some higher level of responsibility involving due care for the customer is required.

Second, the process whereby the customer agreed to a mortgage was also inadequately informed. For example, when a borrower obtained a "Pay Option ARM" from Countrywide, the only initial monthly payment amount that appeared anywhere in his loan documents was the minimum payment amount. In other words, documents provided to the borrower assumed he would make only the minimum payment. Thus, a borrower would not know the monthly payment necessary to make a payment that would, for example, cover accruing interest, until he received the first statement after the expiration of the teaser rate, well after all loan documents had been signed.[13]

This may be admirable marketing by one who cares only about his bonus or the fees involved, but not one guided by concern for the interests of the borrower or the ethics of marketing. Such marketers display little concern for the cognitive component of the ethical framework noted in the previous section.

Loan Flipping

Suppose you have a mortgage. You are settled into your home. Ethical issues of marketing mortgages haven't ended. A mortgage lender might contact you with the following proposal: If you take out a new loan you will be able to tap into the equity that has accumulated in your home in order to fix up the family room, buy a new car, pay off some other bills, or take a long-desired vacation. Or perhaps the mortgage lender seeks to get a home owner to move from one loan to another loan with the promise that doing so would save him money on his present mortgage payments. In some cases, a good argument might be made for either initiative. Perhaps the interest rates have significantly changed. Maybe a new family room will make the family happy and increase the resale value of the home. In short, in some cases the new or refinanced loan might be in one's best interests. But when this is done in ways that do not benefit the borrower, but simply the loan officer, through charging higher fees, we have a case of what is called *loan flipping*.

This has also occurred in the collapse of the mortgage market in the first part of the twenty-first century. It was alleged that Countrywide was "routinely soliciting borrowers to refinance only a few months after Countrywide or the loan brokers with whom it had 'business partnerships' had sold them loans."[14] One source claims that "80 percent of subprime mortgages involve refinancing existing mortgages" (Legal Helpers 2009). A major problem here is that too often the borrowers did not realize the true costs of the new loan. One of the reasons for this is that these costs are sometimes not accurately and openly portrayed to them. The borrower needed to know that in refinancing a mortgage a person will have "to pay closing costs and fees, and perhaps even additional mortgage loan points."[15] The upshot is that the new loan might cost several thousand dollars in extra charges. Some people have even ended up with a higher-interest loan. In these cases, they have been misled or deceived by the omission or misrepresentation of crucial information. In addition, lenders may also play on people's desires for a special vacation or for extra space in their home. Of course, borrowers should guard against these kinds of appeals. But even if borrowers are to be criticized for their gullibility, this does not license lenders to use marketing techniques that take advantage of these weaknesses and obscure the true costs of the proposed new loans.

Promoting the Ethical Marketing of Mortgages

What can be done to foster more ethical behavior on the part of those marketing mortgages? A number of individual changes could help. For example, lenders might be required to provide worksheets that "allow consumers to compare their final loan terms and closing costs with what was listed on the good-faith estimate" (Singletary 2008).[16] Or mortgage brokers might be required to disclose their fees in advance, and not simply after an application has been submitted to them (see Guttentag 2009). Such steps might help make clearer to borrowers the costs they will be facing. In addition, the penalties imposed on mortgage brokers and originators for deceiving customers need much stronger enforcement. This would require an increase in the number of investigators who go after those engaged in mortgage fraud.[17]

However, more basically, the relation between borrowers and mortgage brokers and lenders needs to be addressed. Instead of a relationship in which brokers and lenders are viewed as focused on their own interests, a more professional relationship is needed in which they should attend to the best interests of their customers. Then when they market loans to potential customers, they would be expected to disclose features of the loans and their fees in a way that would enable customers to make an informed decision in their own best interests and would not encourage them to take out loans inappropriate for their levels of risk and resources. Of course, laws and regulations would also have to be shaped to encourage this relationship on behalf of all those who market mortgages. And for these changes not simply to be an empty gesture, adequate resources would have to be devoted to enforcing such provisions.

CREDIT CARDS

Credit cards have become a fixture of daily life for many people in North America. The average American family has eight credit cards; there are 640 million credit cards in circulation in the United States.[18] In 2008, the average amount of credit debt per household with more than one card [in the United States] was more than $8,000.[19] Since most credit cards do not require that the user pay the full balance at the end of each billing period, they are "a way of borrowing money without security, so [they substitute] . . . for other forms of unsecured lending . . ." (Kahr 2004). For the cost of the monthly interest, credit card holders can extend their payments over a period of time, if they pay a minimum amount specified on the monthly bill.

Credit cards are a $970 billion industry that is the most profitable in the banking sector and has been one of the fastest growing parts of the financial services industry in the past quarter century.[20] In spite of its financial success and the widespread adoption of credit cards by consumers, the credit card industry has also been hit with numerous ethical charges in recent years that relate to the marketing of credit cards. Three of the major marketing ethical issues that credit cards raise are: (1) Who should be targeted for credit card marketing? (2) What should card users know about the cards marketed to them? and (3) How should credit card companies impose charges on users?

Targeting for Credit Cards

Traditionally, credit cards were issued only after the issuer had ascertained that the financial condition of the person seeking the card merited an extension of credit. To make this determination, credit card companies relied on the use of the large databases of credit reporting bureaus to determine an applicant's credit rating or FICO[21] score. This score is used to determine how much one can borrow and the interest rates at which one can borrow. Despite its obvious impact on their borrowing ability, most Americans do not know their FICO score.[22]

In the past, one had to have a relatively high level of creditworthiness to receive a credit card. However, times have changed. Now virtually anyone can obtain a credit card. In fact, there are credit cards that advertise a "100 Percent Guaranteed Approval," that there will be "no credit check," and that applicants will be "approved regardless of credit history." Of course, with such credit cards there are conditions, such as required FDIC-insured bank accounts with a balance of at least several hundred dollars linked to the card, and finance charges being applied without a grace period. However, many other standard credit cards are marketed to those with little or no credit history (e.g., college students, immigrants). In fact, credit card companies increased by 41 percent their direct mail credit card offers to subprime consumers in the first six months of 2006 and 2007; at the same time, they reduced their offers targeting consumers with very high credit by 13 percent.[23]

From the standpoint of credit card companies, the fact that a person has a lower credit rating does not mean that they cannot make money off such a person. Far from it—in fact, a significant portion of their profits come from such customers.[24] Credit card companies have run various risk analyses of potential customers and have made decisions based upon their expectation of being able to make money on people who have a wide range of creditworthiness. The result has been that some people with very shaky creditworthiness have been issued credit cards. And, given the fact that multiple companies may make similar decisions, these less-creditworthy customers may receive multiple cards.

The question is not simply whether targeting people with poor credit ratings is financially rewarding for credit card companies but also whether it is ethically responsible. If a credit card company decides to issue credit cards to those with little credit history or poor credit ratings, then some people will obtain cards who do not have the experiences or resources to use them wisely. They will incur more debt than they can handle, their credit scores will be jeopardized, and their financial circumstances will be negatively impacted for years. In addition, many will experience family conflicts and even suffer bouts of depression. In the case of students, they may have to drop out of college in order to get a job to pay bills. Their parents may have to help out.

There is, of course, a positive side to the extension of such credit, and this is that the mere fact that credit cards are available to a wider range of people is a kind of democratization of credit that would seem desirable. "Low- and moderate-income people now quite often have credit cards, and that wouldn't have been the case, say, 30 years ago" (Yingling 2004). Still, the significance of this benefit assumes that those receiving credit can handle it. What if they cannot?

The argument here is that credit card companies bear some—but not all—of the responsibility for the difficulties that those with poor credit histories will encounter. Credit card companies know in advance that these results will occur, though they do not know with which particular customers they will occur. If ethical marketing seeks to avoid doing harm, then the marketing of credit cards should not use techniques that extend credit cards to members of these groups without warning people of their dangers, seeking to educate them about the dangers, limiting their access to modest amounts until they have proven able to handle larger sums, not raising interest rates that worsen their condition, and offering financial counseling services to those whose debt level exceeds their abilities to handle it.

Information and Deception

Ethical transactions generally require that those taking part have all the relevant information. Accordingly, for credit card applicants and holders to ethically acquire and use credit cards, they must have information regarding their credit cards that is pertinent to their use. Some of that information would include whether the card requires an annual fee and, if so, how much it is. What are the interest charges? When and how may those interest charges change? If they change, what forewarning will one receive? What are the limits to the credit on one's credit cards? What penalties might be incurred if these limits are violated?

In addition, this information must be presented in a manner that is intelligible to the ordinary customer. One should not have to have a degree in finance or accounting in order to understand the conditions that apply to having a credit card. Nor should one have to be a trained investigator in order to learn the relevant facts about a credit card.

These guidelines have not been followed in various cases. For example, some credit cards have advertised low teaser rates that involved charging a very low rate of interest, sometimes even zero percent, at the beginning. However, later the interest rate might rise dramatically (possibly to 30 percent or more) without the customer understanding when or why this was taking place. Capital One was accused of running television ads in Minnesota that advertised credit cards with low "fixed interest rates."[25] Though this feature was offered in the major part of the ad, in the final six seconds of the ad (or in small print in printed ads) Capital One made qualifications that contradicted the fixed-rate offer (Sullivan 2005). As a result, surprised credit card holders found their interest rates rising to three and four times what they had been led to expect.

Most customers also do not understand how long it will take them to pay off their debts if they make only the minimum payment. In fact, "approximately 35 million Americans pay only the required minimum—as low as 2 percent—of their balance each month. Sticking to that rate, it could take years to clear their debt and they'll end up paying far more than the cost of the items or services they bought."[26] The reason is that credit card companies do not tell customers how long it would take to pay off their current debt if they make simply the minimum payment the card requires for that period. They don't want people to know this, since those people might then pay more of the balance due and hence pay less in interest. As Elizabeth Warren says, "They don't tell because they don't want the customer to know, because an informed customer is not as profitable a customer" (Warren 2004).

Companies respond that such information would involve hypothetical numbers. Since a customer can add to his debt going forward, such a number has no real meaning (Warren 2004; Yingling 2004). Yingling argues that a disclosure of how long it would take an individual borrower to pay off his particular loan at the current minimum payment would be wrong 99 percent of the time due to floating rates and added debt (Yingling 2004). Still, this does not mean that hypothetical examples regarding one's current level of indebtedness and the time required to pay it off at minimum payment levels might not help inform credit card holders about the implications of their decisions.

The preceding forms of information regarding ways in which one's interest rate may change, how long it would take to pay off one's debt, the fees that a credit card company may impose, and so on, are all materially relevant to one's use of a credit card. Unfortunately, too often, credit card companies have inadequately shared these kinds of information with cardholders. Though they may assume a rational consumer is capable of protecting himself in a highly competitive environment, their reluctance to openly and directly share information with customers implies a lack of concern with fostering such consumers.

Credit Card Charges and Terms of Agreement

Credit cards are issued based on an agreement with customers that the customer will pay a certain interest rate on outstanding balances that have not been paid following a set period (usually 25 days, at present) after the charges were incurred. However, this agreement has been a unique one inasmuch as once a customer has bought something using the credit card, the credit card company has been able to unilaterally increase (with notice of as little as 15 days) the rate of interest on the card and hence effectively raise the price of the product or service already purchased (Croghan 2009).[27] Thus, if I buy a washing machine for $600 at an interest rate of 9.85 percent but the credit card company subsequently increases my interest rate to 21.75 percent, it has unilaterally increased the price of the washing machine over the period I pay it off.[28] This might occur, for example, if you were late with a payment, even on some other bill. This practice has been termed *universal default*, according to which if one fails to make a payment on any credit card, mortgage, car loan, or the like, or if a credit card company believes that one is taking on too much debt, the interest rate on one's credit card(s) may be raised. The issue here is one of the fairness or the justice of unilaterally changing the terms of the agreement. Of course, if one signs a credit card agreement that permits this, then one has technically agreed to this practice—however, few read these agreements and their only real option is not to have a credit card. In response, to these practices, the Credit Cardholders' Bill of Rights Act became law in 2009 that prohibits such unilateral interest rate increases on existing balances and universal default.[29] Critics point out that there is no other form of contract between a customer and business that is of this nature. If one loses one's job and fails to make a payment on a credit card, one's mortgage rate does not change, nor does the rate one pays for one's car. Credit card companies respond that they raise their rates when the credit rating of the customer has changed—that is, worsened. Defenders of this feature of credit cards argue that the rates they charge for credit loans are linked to the creditworthiness of the customer and that if this has declined (for example, by missing a payment or two on some other credit card or a mortgage), then their creditworthiness has declined; they are more risky and hence should pay higher rates (see Yingling 2004). This argument has only superficial plausibility. One's credit score may change because of a late payment due to any number of reasons unrelated to one's creditworthiness—for example, one was on vacation when the bill came due; the bill was temporarily mixed up with other bills due at a later date; one might even be disputing a charge on another credit card. To have one's interest rates increased not only on future purchases but also on all past purchases strikes most observers as unjust. One made those earlier purchases with a certain interest rate in mind. To have this changed, as well as the total cost of the product, by the unilateral decision of a credit card company is an ethically arbitrary action that should be prohibited.

Some Remedies to Promote Ethics in the Credit Card Industry

The ethical issues raised by the preceding marketing practices may be addressed by emphasizing the ethical values and norms underlying ethical marketing. For example, crucial to ethical marketing is that those who are party to a transaction understand the terms of what they are agreeing to. If customers do not understand the terms of their credit cards and how their rates may be raised or extended over billing periods preceding the most recent one, this should be made clear to them. However, it is not sufficient to enable people to understand practices that may themselves be arbitrary and unfair. Hence, double-cycle billing and increases in interest rates without the opportunity, through prudent handling of one's credit card, to return to lower rates should be ended. Further, if consumers don't understand the implications of making only the minimum payment on their debt, then this should be part of what a person is told. It may also be that certain groups, such as college students or those with weak credit, are more vulnerable to the misuse of credit cards than others.[30] Special precautions should then be taken in marketing to such groups, both proactively as well as after the fact, with regard to ways to mitigate problems that arise. It is possible to extend too much credit to certain individuals.

Similarly, if the fairness of increasing interest on credit charges already made cannot be clearly established, it should be stopped. The practice of raising rates on all one's credit cards because of a problem with one credit card (universal default) without any further justification or clarification for that single problem also raises fairness issues. The reasons a person misses a payment on one card may not imply that his creditworthiness has declined. To stop these practices, the Credit Cardholders' Bill of Rights Act was passed in 2009. It is a case where law and ethics have come together.

Changes such as these might lift much of the ethical, political, and social criticism of credit card companies. Such changes might also begin to foster the kind of relationship between credit card companies and customers that ethical marketers should insist on.

PAYDAY LOANS

Financial services and products are marketed to people from a wide range of economic backgrounds. Mortgages are targeted to those with at least modest means. Credit cards have become increasingly available to a wide range of individuals, though not to the poorest, least creditworthy segment of the population. Payday loans are aimed at those who lack financial resources that many others have. They offer those with poor credit and/or little income small sums of money to pay pressing bills. Accordingly, these products are usually marketed to vulnerable groups such as day laborers, enlisted personnel in the military, some students, and people in inner-city neighborhoods. Payday loans advance the borrower a small amount of money (the average is about $300). The lender does not seek to verify the borrower's ability to repay. Rather, borrowers must have a checking account and demonstrate that they have a job (usually this involves producing a pay stub). They receive their cash usually based on a postdated check they leave with the lender.[31] It might be thought that such loans are unworthy of attention. However, though individual loans are small, this is a $100 billion industry (McGray 2008).[32] "There are more payday outlets than there are McDonald's restaurants" (Miller 2008). "Iowans entered into more than 900,000 payday loans last year, based on state Department of Banking data" (Lynch 2008).These loans come at high rates of interest. A person may take out a loan for $200 for two weeks, but have to repay $230 to settle the loan. Though that may seem simply like an interest rate of 15 percent, those doing this calculation forget that the loan occurs over a two-week period (see Knerl, 2007). "A $15 fee for a $100 two-week loan works out at a 390 percent annual rate."[33] If the fee were $16, that would be an annual percentage rate of 435 percent. Ethical issues of marketing payday loans include (1) what information borrowers have about the terms of the loans; (2) the pricing of the loans; (3) the groups to which they are marketed; and (4) issues of mistrust of traditional financial institutions.

Information

Consider the information that borrowers have regarding these loans. In contrast to credit card charges and some home mortgages, not to mention some car loans, the information at payday loan offices is, seemingly, fairly clear and transparent. At such places there may be "a list of products, services, and prices, a bit like a fast-food menu. Some of the prices are quite high, but the charges are neither confusing nor deceptive" (McGray 2008).

When you go to the Web pages of some of the prominent payday loan companies, you can see very clearly not only what the charges are but also what the annual percentage rates are for those loans. For example, in February 2009, 1 Stop Check Cashing offered a 14-day loan of $200 to customers in Arizona for a finance charge of $35, and a $500 loan for a finance charge of $87.50. In both cases, the page noting these charges also clearly indicates that the annual percentage rate (APR) is 456.2 percent.[34]

It does not appear, at least currently, that customers of payday loans have any difficulty learning what the interest rates are on the loans they take out. This contrasts, as we have seen, with credit cards, as well as with some banking accounts, where higher interest rates and penalties may be imposed in a manner many people consider arbitrary and deceptive. For example, "fees imposed on customers for temporarily overdrawing their [checking] accounts—by accident or on purpose—have been particularly lucrative; banks made $25.3 billion in 2006 on overdraft-related fees, up 48 percent in two years, according to the Center for Responsible Lending" (McGray 2008). One of the reasons some people turn to payday lenders is that they have been hit with unexpected fees from banks and credit cards. They don't trust them. Furthermore, they feel that the implications of bouncing a check are worse than paying a high fee to borrow the money they need. In short, they don't trust credit card companies or mainline banks.

Credit card fees are generally buried in small print that few read and fewer understand. By contrast, at payday loan offices, the fees appear in large, bold print—and they do not change. Though they are much higher, for example, than the interest rates on credit cards, the borrower will not be surprised by sudden changes. At least, they know what they are up against. Or do they?

The other side of this information issue is whether people really understand the implications of taking out a payday loan when they may well not have the funds to pay it back at the end of the loan period (usually 14 days). If the results of some surveys are correct, the large majority of payday borrowers must take out follow-up loans, which trap them into a cycle of taking out loan after loan such that the final cost of borrowing the money they need is much higher than ordinary personal loans. They may be aware of the high interest rates they have to pay, but may not appreciate the difficult situation in which they may be placing themselves by taking out such a loan.

Pricing and Groups Targeted

The pricing of payday loans has been another major topic of ethical concern. Some object that the rates lenders demand are unfair or unjust, even usurious. Payday lenders are said to be loan sharks.

The rates are clearly very high. Given people's circumstances, they may get trapped into taking out successive loans that compound the trouble they face (see Knerl 2007). But are these interest rates unjust or unfair? The people taking out these loans are not physically dragged into the payday loan offices and forced to take out these loans. Sometimes they choose to take their loans at payday offices rather than at ordinary banks.

If the fairness or justness of an interest rate is what people agree to in a market, without deception or fraud, then these interest rates would seem to be fair. But are

there other measures of justice and fairness? One way of considering this issue is
to compare it with other charges that some financial institutions levy. For example
a $100 payday loan for $15 carries an APR of 390 percent. However, if you bounced
a $100 check that carried a $54 nonsufficient funds (NSF)/merchant fee, this would
amount to a 1,409 percent APR. Or if a person had a $100 credit card balance but
a late fee of $37 was assessed, this would amount to a 965 percent APR.[35] Finally,
wire-transfer companies, such as Western Union, may charge fees similar to payday
loans—for example, $15 to send $100—although since some banks have decided to
compete in this area, the fees have dropped by nearly two-thirds (McGray 2008).[36]

In short, the fees people pay for payday loans may not be greater, suitably
viewed, than those charged by credit cards and banks. Still, this doesn't show that
either set of fees is reasonable or just. In some states, such as Ohio, voters have
decided to cap payday loan fees at an APR of 28 percent. Other states are pushing
to limit the amount of fees and interest to 35 percent on an annualized basis. "That's
what the federal government allows payday lenders to charge military personnel
and their families" (Lynch 2008).[37]

There is, obviously, no magic figure here that would be the just price for payday
loans. Other considerations may also enter into our evaluation of the ethical status
of such loans at 24 percent, 35 percent, or higher—for example, the ability of the
borrowers to pay off such loans and their need to take out subsequent loans when
they cannot pay off the initial loan.

Apparently, payday lenders draw approximately "90 percent of their revenue
from borrowers who cannot pay off their loans when due, rather than from one-
time users dealing with short-term financial emergencies" (King, Parrish, and
Tanik 2006, 2). This result is due, it is alleged, to the way in which the repayment
of these loans is set up. "By requiring full repayment within a short period of time
(generally two weeks), with no option to make payments in installments, lenders
compel payday borrowers to return again and again, renewing a loan for another
large fee without being able to pay down the principal" (King, Parrish, and Tanik
2006, 3). In effect, this is a form of loan flipping that was discussed earlier. "Only
one percent of payday loans go [sic] to borrowers who take out one loan per year
and walk away free and clear after paying it off" (King, Parrish, and Tanik 2006,
3). Instead, "ninety-one percent of payday loans go to borrowers with five or more
loan transactions per year" (King, Parrish, and Tanik 2006, 3).[38]

The Community Financial Services Association (CFSA) responds that "in
states that permit rollovers, CFSA members limit rollovers to four or the state
limit—whichever is less. The reality is that a loan cannot be outstanding longer
than eight weeks (two-week loan rolled-over four times)."[39] But the Center for
Responsible Lending contends that "over 60 percent of [payday] loans go to borrowers with 12 or more transactions per year" and that "24 percent of loans go
to borrowers with 21 or more transactions per year" (King and Parrish 2007, 3).
Clearly there is disagreement over the facts here. Only a few states, for example,
report data regarding the number of borrowers who take out a loan, pay it off, and
do not borrow again during that year (see King and Parrish 2007, 7).

Accordingly, one way of addressing the level of interest rates is to tackle the
implications they may have for borrowers who must roll over their loans. Doing this
might involve allowing borrowers to pay back their loans in partial installments,
rather than an all-or-nothing payment, and giving them a longer period to pay

back the loan. Along these lines, at the end of 2008, the state of Virginia passed a law that limits borrowers to one payday loan at a time and extends the time period they have to repay the loan (Fox News 2008). Of course, one effect of this law would be that borrowers can take out fewer loans, though it might increase the amount they borrow at any one time.

Promoting Ethical Payday Lending

Payday loans are a market response to a situation of needy people. "Poor people pay more for just about everything, from fresh groceries to banking; [C. K.] Prahalad, the economist, calls it the 'poverty penalty.' They pay more for all kinds of reasons, but maybe most of all because mainstream firms decline to compete for their business" (McGray 2008). In addition, "some 28 million Americans still go without a bank account ... and more than 50 million have no credit score, which means no access to mainstream credit" (McGray 2008). People go to payday lenders because it is cheaper than having a bank account and paying overdraft fees (McGray 2008).[40]

This situation has arisen, in part, because decades ago, traditional financial institutions left inner cities and ceased to offer short-term, small-denomination loans. Such loans are expensive for banks to originate and maintain. In their place came payday lenders that filled in the financial gap (McGray 2008).

So part of the ethical issue here is the failure of mainline banks to offer loans to those who are among the neediest in the United States. And though banks no longer shy away from low- and medium-income neighborhoods, still their approach is not directed at those borrowers whom payday lenders serve (McGray 2008). "Most banks remain reluctant to fight with check cashers and payday lenders for low-income customers; they don't believe there's enough in it for them" (McGray 2008). By way of contrast, McGray makes the point that payday lenders are successful, at least in part, because they position themselves as part of the community. Borrowers feel more comfortable going to them. Good marketers know the importance of customer relations management.

Accordingly, the ethical marketing issues payday loans raise require action by payday lenders themselves, mainline lending institutions, and the government. According to McGray (2008), one payday loan company is making an interesting effort by providing a rebate on a payday loan into a savings account after six months, if a person pays his loans back and doesn't bounce any checks. "People get payday loans because they have no savings," but this way, heavy payday borrowers will accumulate a small balance (McGray 2008).

The mainline banking industry should consider the needs of those with very modest and minimal incomes. Payday lending could be ended only if the banking industry aggressively sought to serve those who now use payday loans: "They must assist low income families by providing low-cost products that do not involve unexpected fees" (Miller 2008).

State governments have required payday lenders to keep databases regarding their loans, cooling-off periods, repayment plans, or limits to the number of outstanding loans (King, Parrish, and Tanik 2006, 13). The Center for Responsible Lending has found that such reforms "have little impact on the debt trap payday lenders depend on for their revenues" (King, Parrish, and Tanik 2006, 13). Instead, action by policy makers may need to "provide incentives to banks and credit unions to craft responsible small loan products, and [to] ... look at ways to encourage savings among low- and moderate-income families so that they can weather financial emergencies without taking on additional debt" (King and Parrish 2007, 6).

C. K. Prahalad has written about the wealth at the bottom of the pyramid. Those in the mainstream financial realm have not thought long and hard enough about how to develop and market products to those without bank accounts and without credit scores who still need to borrow money, and yet who can be good risks (see McGray 2008).

CONCLUSION

The marketing of financial products and services raises a host of ethical issues. This chapter touches on only a few. However, its intention is to portray these in a manner such that their reality and significance are apparent. I place this discussion within a broader ethical marketing framework that applies not only to the discussion of the topics of this chapter but also to other financial products and services.

As this chapter is being completed, the current administration is considering the creation of a regulatory commission to protect consumers of financial products such as mortgages and credit cards. Whether such a commission will be created, let alone what its powers and reach would be, is unclear at this point. Part of its mandate might be to protect consumers from faulty financial products, just as the Consumer Product Safety Commission protects consumers from poorly designed physical products. However, protection from the faulty marketing of safe financial products is also needed.[41]

The solution to these problems is, in general, not an easy one—if it were, that solution would already be in place. In many cases, large sums of money are involved, something sure to stir the self-interests of individuals as well as the groups and industries of which they are part. Still, if ethics teaches us anything it is that we must look beyond short-term, narrow self-interests to the broader impacts of our actions and practices, as well as to the norms and values that underlie them.

NOTES

1. Some of the other relevant subjects I do not discuss include marketing research and the segmentation of markets as well as more specific issues regarding investments in the stock market, salesforce management, and retirement plans.

2. As recently as 2004, the American Marketing Association suggested that these values and norms were aspirational.

3. It may be granted that this is subject to certain contexts in which other moral norms may override the norm against lying. Still, the obligation not to lie is not simply aspirational.

4. The Depository Institutions Deregulation and Monetary Control Act of 1980 and the Alternative Mortgage Transactions Parity Act of 1982 played important roles in encouraging the development and expansion of adjustable-rate mortgages (ARMs) and interest-only mortgages (see Engel and McCoy 2002, 1275–1277).

5. "The Federal Housing Enterprise Financial Safety and Soundness Act of 1992 directed the Department of Housing and Urban Development (HUD) to significantly increase the volume of low-to-moderate income home loans purchased by Government Sponsored

Enterprises (GSEs)" (Matthews 2009, 247). The reference to GSEs here is a reference to Fannie Mae and Freddie Mac.

6. See *People of the State of California* v. *Countrywide Financial Corporation* in Consumer Law (2008, 20f).

7. Ibid., 5–6.

8. Blame for this situation does not rest simply on mortgage brokers and lenders. Some of the potential borrowers were far less than candid about their resources, creditworthiness.

9. Another way of putting the point here is that a form of moral hazard resulted from the securitization of mortgage loans, since the lenders believed that they were thereby protected from the consequences of borrowers defaulting and consequently lowered their standards for lending and marketing mortgages.

10. Consumer Law (2008, 5).

11. See example in Consumer Law (2008, 12).

12. Ibid., 14.

13. Ibid., 14f.

14. Ibid., 5.

15. Home Loan Basics (2006).

16. HUD has announced a requirement to be implemented in 2010 that lenders add a page to a new standardized HUD-1 settlement sheet. It will "allow consumers to compare their final loan terms and closing costs with what was listed on the good-faith estimate" (Singletary 2008). Singletary argues that this is a small step since "much of the information on the revised statements is something loan originators should have been disclosing and discussing with mortgage applicants anyway."

17. Bart Bartholomew, president of the Colorado Association of Mortgage Brokers, has claimed that "HUD enforces federal statutes, but there are only 30 investigators for the country" (Rozeff 2008).

18. For the number of credit cards per family see http://centerforinvestigativereporting. org/tags/bankingindustry (accessed May 13, 2009). For the number of credit cards in circulation, see Sweet (2009).

19. This figure comes from Sweet (2009), who is reporting a press release from Congressman Luis V. Gutierrez, chairman of the Financial Services Subcommittee on Financial Institutions and Consumer Credit of the U.S. Congress. However, there are differences over this number. Some place the figure as low as $3,000 for 2007 (see Maloney and Schumer 2009); others say it is $5,100 for 2007 (see American Financial Services Association 2009). A higher figure of $10,679 for households is reported by Gordon (2009).

20. The $970 billion figure comes from Trejos and Appelbaum (2008). Regarding the "most profitable" claim, see http://centerforinvestigativereporting.org/tags/ bankingindustry (accessed May 13, 2009). This section has been informed by a valuable program on credit cards, "Secret History of the Credit Card," which appeared on PBS in 2004 (Kahr 2004).

21. "FICO" is an abbreviation for "Fair Isaac Corporation," the name of the corporation that first came up with a score for one's creditworthiness.

22. Most Americans do not know their FICO score: http://www.pbs.org/wgbh/pages/ frontline/shows/credit/more/scores.html (accessed May 13, 2009). If a person has a good credit score, this means that they not only have the resources to meet the debt obligations they may undertake with credit cards but also have the discipline to do so; that their circumstances do not overwhelm their resources and any discipline they

might have; and that they have the knowledge or understanding to handle their debt. Now suppose that a person has a lower credit score. This could be for various reasons. But some factor in the preceding list has affected their handling of their debt.

23. See 24-7 Press Release (2007).

24. In 2007, nearly half of the industry's profits came from so-called "revolvers." See Gary Weiss (2008).

25. ProQuest, 2005.

26. Kahr (2004, 2).

27. When the Credit Cardholders' Bill of Rights takes effect this will be increased to 45 days.

28. "After you have borrowed the $5,000, they can change the interest rate from 9.9 percent to 29.9 percent" (Warren 2004).

29. See Huffman and Bosworth (2009), http://www.consumeraffairs.com/news04/2009/04/obama_credit_cards02.html. It should be noted that there are a number of specific exceptions written into the Credit Cardholders' Bill of Rights that permit the raising of interest rates on existing balances.

30. See Moyer and Shumsky (2008).

31. "Payday lenders do not make loans based on the borrower's ability to repay. Borrowers need only a checking account and a pay stub verifying employment to qualify for a payday loan, which averages about $300" (King, Parrish, and Tanik 2006, 3).

32. Some of the most prominent of these companies are Stop Check Cashing, P.D.Q. Title and Payday Loans, Advance America, QC Holdings, Ace Cash Express, Check 'n Go, and Kinecta.

33. *Economist* (2008).

34. See 1 Stop Check Cashing's web site: www.1stopcheckcashing.com/payday_loan_rates.html (accessed February 26, 2009).

35. These two examples come from Community Financial Services Association (2009), www.cfsa.net/myth_vs_reality.html (accessed February 27, 2009). The calculation of the APR mentioned here assumes a 14-day period.

36. Note that a report of the Pew Charitable Trusts studied households in California and found that "about 58 percent of households in the state are now being charged overdraft fees, credit card late payment fees, out-of-network ATM fees, or check-cashing fees. Across the United States, these fees add up to over $58 billion each year" (Fellowes and Mabanta 2008).

37. Washington, D.C., has capped the interest rates at 24 percent APR (see Hampton Roads 2008).

38. King and Parrish (2007, 8) have a table illustrating the difficulty of paying back a loan after two weeks. They assume that borrowers may require up to four discrete loans a year. When the number of loans a person takes out exceeds this number, they assume that they are rolling over their loans or taking out back-to-back transactions (see King and Parrish 2007, 3).

39. See CFSA (2009). CFSA is an organization that promotes the interests of payday loan companies. Its web site claims that "The Community Financial Services Association of America is the only national organization dedicated solely to promoting responsible regulation of the payday advance industry and consumer protections through CFSA's Best Practices."

40. A supporter of payday lending institutions maintains that "Banks prey on low-income families to a greater degree than payday lenders" (Miller 2008). He goes on to say, "Show

me a financial industry that has a sign that says customers are subject to up to $300 a day in fees and fines." Banks, he says, thrive on bounced-check charges and overdraft fees, and credit card charges can be exorbitant, as well. By contrast, payday lenders let their customers know up front what they'll be paying (Miller 2008).

41. See Goldfarb, Appelbaum, and Cho (2009).

REFERENCES

American Financial Services Association (AFSA). 2009. The right numbers tell a different story. *Opposing Views*. http://www.opposingviews.com/arguments/the-right-numbers-tell-a-different-story (accessed July 29, 2009).

American Marketing Association (AMA). 2009. Statement of ethics. http://www.marketingpower.com/AboutAMA/Pages/Statement percent20of percent20Ethics.aspx (accessed July 28, 2009).

Brenkert, George G. 2008. *Marketing ethics*. Malden, MA: Blackwell Publishers.

Community Financial Services Association. 2009. Myths vs. reality of payday loans. www.cfsa.net/myth_vs_reality.html (accessed February 27, 2009).

Consumer Law. 2008. Complaint for Restitution, Injunctive Relief, Other Equitable Relief, and Civil Penalties. *People of the State of California v. Countrywide Financial Corporation.* http://www.consumerlaw.org/unreported/content/n1588_firstamendedcomplaint.pdf (accessed May 25, 2009).

Croghan, Lore. 2009. Credit card hike fright. *New York Daily News*. http://www.nydailynews.com/money/2009/03/16/2009-03-16_credit_card_hike_fright_banks_raising_ra.html (accessed July 28, 2009).

Economist. 2008. Casting out the money-lenders: Payday lending. *Economist* 389, no. 8607 (November 22). http://www.economist.com/world/unitedstates/displaystory.cfm?story_id=12641615 (accessed December 21, 2008).

Engel, Kathleen C., and Patricia A. McCoy. 2002. A tale of three markets: The law and economics of predatory lending. *Texas Law Review* 80:1255–1370.

Ernst, Keith, Debbie Bocian, and Wei Li. 2008. Steered wrong: Brokers, borrowers, and subprime loans. Center for Responsible Lending, April 8. http://www.responsiblelending.org/mortgage-lending/research-analysis/steered-wrong-brokers-borrowers-and-subprime-l-oans.html (accessed May 25, 2009).

Fellowes, Matt, and Mia Mabanta. 2008. Converting basic financial services fees into prosperity. The Pew Charitable Trusts. http://www.pewtrusts.org/uploadedFiles/wwwpewtrustsorg/Reports/Safe_Banking_Opportunities_Project/SBOPpercent20CApercent20reportpercent20FINAL.pdf (accessed February 27, 2009).

Fox News. 2008. Virginia's new payday loan law may have little effect. http://www.foxnews.com/politics/2008/12/31/lenders-loopholes-virginia-law-limiting-payday-loans/ (accessed May 25, 2009).

Goldfarb, Zachary A., Binjamin Appelbaum, and David Cho. 2009. U.S. may add new financial watchdog. *Washington Post*, May 20. http://www.washingtonpost.com/wp-dyn/content/article/2009/05/19/AR2009051903061.html (accessed May 25, 2009).

Gordon, Marcy. 2009. House passes credit card bill that helps consumers. http://news.yahoo.com/s/ap/20090430/ap_on_go_co/us_congress_credit_cards.html (accessed May 20, 2009).

Gullo, Karen, and Andrew Harris. 2008. Countrywide sued by California, Illinois, over loans (Update 2). Bloomberg, June 25. http://www.bloomberg.com/apps/news?pid=20601103&sid=ayvtiaSnvcBk&refer=us (accessed December 18, 2008).

Guttentag, Jack M. 2009. Mortgage advice and counsel. http://www.mtgprofessor.com/ (accessed May 25, 2009).

Hampton Roads. 2008. Many reasons to pause on ending payday lenders. http://hamptonroads.com/2008/12/many-reasons-pause-ending-payday-lenders (accessed February 27, 2009).

Home Loan Basics. 2006. The dangers of home equity mortgage loan flipping. http://www.homeloanbasics.com/articles/HomeEquityLoans/DangersOfEquityLoanFlipping (accessed July 28, 2009).

Huffman, Mike, and Martin H. Bosworth. 2009. White House, Congress cracking down on credit cards. http://www.consumeraffairs.com/news04/2009/04/obama_credit_cards02.html (accessed May 25, 2009).

Kahr, Andrew. 2004. Secret history of the credit card: *Frontline* interview. www.pbs.org/wgbh/pages/frontline/shows/credit/interviews/kahr.html (accessed November 13, 2008).

King, Uriah, and Leslie Parrish. 2007. Springing the debt trap: Executive summary. http://www.responsiblelending.org/pdfs/springing-the-debt-trap-exec-summary.pdf (accessed February 26, 2009).

King, Uriah, Leslie Parrish, and Ozlem Tanik. 2006. Financial quicksand. Center for Responsible Lending, November 26. http://www.responsiblelending.org/pdfs/rr012-Financial_Quicksand-1106.pdf (accessed February 26, 2009).

Knerl, Linsey. 2007. Confessions of a former payday loan junkie. http://www.wisebread.com/confessions-of-a-former-payday-loan-junkie (accessed May 25, 2009).

Legal Helpers. 2009. Deregulation or take the money and run. http://www.legalhelpers.com/bankruptcy-articles/financial-deregulation-article.html (accessed December 18, 2008).

Lynch, James Q. 2008. Democrats propose limits on payday loans. http://proquest.umi.com/pqdweb?did=1605840891&sid=1&Fmt=3&clientId=5604&RQT=309&VName=PQD (accessed December 21, 2008).

Maloney, Carolyn B., and Charles E. Schumer. 2009. Vicious cycle: How unfair credit card company practices are squeezing consumers and undermining the recovery. http://jec.senate.gov/index.cfm?Fuseaction=Files.View&FileStore_id=42840b23-fed8-447b-a029-e977c0a25544 (accessed May 25, 2009).

Matthews, David J. 2009. Ruined in a conventional way: Responses to credit ratings' role in credit crises. *Northwestern Journal of International Law & Business* 29:245–274.

McGray, Douglas. 2008. Check cashers, redeemed. *New York Times*, November 9. http://www.nytimes.com/2008/11/09/magazine/09nix-t.html?fta=y (accessed February 25, 2009).

Meidan, Arthur. 1996. *Marketing financial services*. London: MacMillan Press Ltd.

Miller, David. 2008. Payday-loan industry thrives in Arizona as banks consider ways to recapture market.

Moyer, Liz, and Tatyana Shumsky. 2008. The worst credit card deals in America. MSNBC. http://www.msnbc.msn.com/id/23257741/ (accessed June 12, 2009).

ProQuest. 2005. Capital One sued for alleged false advertising. http://proquest.umi.com/pqdweb?did=774794151&sid=6&Fmt=3&clientId=5604&RQT=309&VName=PQD (accessed February 24, 2009).

Rozeff, Michael S. 2008. The subprime crisis and government failure. http://www.lewrockwell.com/rozeff/rozeff203.html (accessed July 14, 2008).

Singletary, Michelle. 2008. Mortgage "reform" is just a small step forward. *Washington Post*, November 16. http://www.washingtonpost.com/wp-dyn/content/article/2008/11/15/AR2008111500187.html (accessed November 15, 2008).

Sullivan, Bob. 2005. Capital One sued over marketing practices. www.msnbc.msn.com/id/6781155/ (accessed May 14, 2009).

Sweet, Lynn. 2009. Credit card "bill of rights" passed in House. *Sun Times*. http://blogs.suntimes.com/sweet/2009/04/credit_card_bill_of_rights_adv.html (accessed May 20, 2009).

Trehan, Veena. 2007. The mortgage market: What happened? NPR. http://www.npr.org/templates/story/story.php?storyId=9855669 (accessed December 19, 2008).

Trejos, Nancy, and Binjamin Appelbaum. 2008. New limits imposed on credit card companies. *Washington Post*, December 18. http://www.washingtonpost.com/wp-dyn/content/article/2008/12/17/AR2008121703474.html (accessed May 25, 2009).

24-7 Press Release. 2007. Creditors target subprime borrowers, bankruptcy filers. http://www.24-7pressrelease.com/press-release/creditors-target-subprime-borrowers-bankruptcy-filers-35636.php

Warren, Elizabeth. 2004. *Frontline* interview, September 20. www.pbs.org/wghb/pages/frontline/shows/credit/interviews/warren.html (accessed November 13, 2008).

Weiss, Gary. 2008. Don't get clobbered by credit cards! *Parade*, August 8. http://www.parade.com/hot-topics/0808/dont-get-clobbered-by-credit-cards (accessed June 12, 2009).

Yingling, Edward. 2004. *Frontline* interview, September 16. www.pbs.org/wghb/pages/frontline/shows/credit/interviews/yingling.html (accessed November 13, 2008).

ABOUT THE AUTHOR

George G. Brenkert is a professor of business ethics at the McDonough School of Business of Georgetown University. He is a former president of the Society for Business Ethics, past editor-in-chief of *Business Ethics Quarterly*, and a fellow of the Ethics Resource Center. He has published two books, *Marketing Ethics* (Blackwell) and *Political Freedom* (Routledge). He edited *Corporate Integrity and Accountability* (SAGE), and is co-editor of *The Oxford Handbook of Business Ethics* (Oxford). In addition, he has published numerous articles in such journals as *Business Ethics Quarterly, Journal of Business Ethics, Business & Professional Ethics Journal, Public Affairs Quarterly, Philosophy & Public Affairs, Public Policy & Marketing,* and *Journal of Business Venturing*.

CHAPTER 16

Financial Codes of Ethics

JULIE A. RAGATZ
Fellow at The American College Center for Ethics in Financial Services

RONALD F. DUSKA
Charles Lamont Post Chair of Ethics and the Professions, The American College

INTRODUCTION

Most corporations, professional associations, and educational institutions develop a code of ethics to guide the actions of their members and to formalize a set of standards indicating the sort of behavior expected of their members. This chapter focuses on codes of ethics developed by professional associations governing the practitioners in the financial services industry. Specifically, this chapter examines 11 codes of ethics and explores how these codes of ethics interpret seven common principles. Not all codes contain each of the seven principles, but they overlap enough so that we could call them the seven fundamental principles of ethical behavior in financial services.

Codes of ethics play an important role in guiding the behavior and decisions of financial services professionals. Indeed, in many cases, these ethical obligations become the basis for a moral community among financial services professionals.[1] For example, the Financial Planning Association describes its commitment to ethics as follows: "At FPA, our Core Values represent who we are. They describe our intended state of being. They are so integral to our being that we would not abandon them even if we were penalized for holding them. We want to attract as members those who share our values."

The codes of ethics in financial services are unique insofar as they deal specifically with the obligations that financial services practitioners have in virtue of their status as professionals. Professionals are required to submit their actions to the jurisdiction of four distinct institutions: (1) the laws of the society in which they practice their profession; (2) the regulatory guidelines established by legitimate authorities, such as the Securities and Exchange Commission (SEC), the Financial Industry Regulatory Authority (FINRA), and the various state departments of insurance; (3) the moral norms of the community in which they practice their profession; and (4) the moral principles promulgated by their profession's code of ethics as well as the code of ethics of any specific organization with which they choose to affiliate themselves. These codes of ethics create moral duties that govern professionals' relationships with their clients, their fellow professionals, and society.

It is important to note at the outset that the financial services profession differs in important ways from other professions. There are two visible differences; the first is the depth and breadth of government regulation in the financial services industry relative to the other professions. In most other professions, codes of ethics play a significant role in justifying the autonomy and self-regulative aspects of the profession. "The problem that faces any professional community is one of ethical quality control: how can it regulate itself so as to justify its autonomy while ensuring that the clients of its members and the society as a whole benefit from the profession and the individual professional's actions, rather than becoming their victims" (Brien 1998, 391–392). In the financial services industry, however, ethical quality control is partially monitored and enforced by various branches of the government (an example is the creation of the nonprofit Public Company Accounting Oversight Board [PCOAB] established in accordance with the Sarbanes-Oxley Act). The presence of formal regulatory authorities makes it difficult to assess the profession's role as an autonomous self-regulator.

A second difference is the number of specialized divisions within the financial services industry, such as accounting, investment advisers, and life insurance agents, each of which has its own particular set of obligations and responsibilities. Since the financial services industry encompasses a wider variety of groups relative to other professions, it can be difficult to determine the overall effectiveness of codes of ethics in the financial services industry in a general way. We discuss the question of whether codes of ethics are successful in encouraging higher instances of ethical behavior at the end of this chapter.

WHAT IS A PROFESSION?

It is helpful to begin by taking a closer look at what counts as a profession and what distinguishes professionals from other practitioners.[2]

Solomon Huebner, an educator who worked diligently to establish the financial services industry as a profession, states that a profession emerges when a group of practitioners possesses four characteristics. The first is that professions engage in a vocation that is useful and noble. Professional activities contribute value to society through providing a needed service. For example, doctors provide for the health and comfort of our bodies, and accountants allow for the free market of shares by validating the financial reports and the overall health of corporations. In general, the financial services industry is useful to society because its practitioners help people manage their financial risk and provide for their financial future.

It is instructive to consider Huebner's use of the term *vocation*. According to Lawrence Blum, the concept of a vocation includes a specific place and a designated purpose within society. Vocation carries with it certain values, standards, and ideals. "Vocation implies that the ideals that it embodies are ones that speak specifically to the individual in question. There is a personal identification with the vocation, with its values and ideals and a sense of personal engagement that helps to sustain the individual in her carrying out the activities of the vocation" (Blum 1994, 104). Huebner's use of the term *vocation* points to his belief that an attachment to a vocation results in a personal transformation. For Huebner, it is impossible to become a professional without adopting these professional values. Blum affirms Huebner's insistence on professional values by saying, "An individual with a vocation must believe deeply the values and ideals of the vocation and must in some way choose or at least affirm them for herself" (Blum 1994, 104).

The second characteristic is that the professions require the possession of expert knowledge. To possess expert knowledge is to understand both the universal principle and the concrete particular and, more important, how to apply correctly the universal principle in specific situations. For example, a professional not only understands that he has a moral obligation to act in the best interest of the client but also understands which course of action promotes the best interest of the client in this particular situation. The professional needs to be competent, and so it is a responsibility of the true professional to stay abreast of the latest developments, not only learning latest practices but also understanding why they are beneficial.

The third characteristic of Huebner's definition is that to be a professional means to "abandon the strictly selfish commercial view and ever keep in mind the advantage of the client in the application of that knowledge." The strictly commercial view, according to Huebner, is defined as pursuing one's self-interest to the exclusion of everyone else. The strictly commercial view, then, is extreme in that it promotes unfettered selfishness.

In the English language, the words *self-interest* and *selfishness* have very different meanings. It is important and natural for people to look out for their own interests. In fact, if people are not self-interested, or if they do not have a healthy self-love, they do both their neighbors and themselves a disservice. Andre Comte-Sponville warns us not "to make too much of the distance between them [love of self and love of others]. We can love others, of course, only if we can love ourselves, which is precisely why the Scriptures enjoin us to love thy neighbor 'as thyself'"(Comte-Sponville 1996, 47–48). However, if we pursue our self-interest at the expense of others, we go too far and are selfish.

The fourth characteristic of a professional is a spirit of loyalty to other professionals. Huebner's requirement involves three aspects. First, there are duties of the professional toward his fellow professionals. These duties involve a negative duty to refrain from engaging in malicious gossip about fellow professionals and a positive duty to provide assistance to other professionals in carrying out their responsibilities when it is appropriate. The second aspect requires professionals to work to maintain the positive reputation of the industry in general by not engaging in unethical behavior. This includes monitoring and policing fellow professionals who engage in unethical behavior and calling to task those who fail to uphold professional standards. The obligation of loyalty to the profession is grounded in the fact that the profession is larger than the sum of its members. The important service to society performed by the profession transcends the individual contributions of its members. This obligation goes beyond loyalty to individuals and requires professionals to defend and protect the integrity of the profession itself. Finally, there is the obligation of the professional to the public at large. Professionals have a responsibility to serve the public that depends on their expertise and labor. The American Institute of Certified Public Accountants (AICPA) recognizes this obligation in its Code of Conduct: "A distinguishing mark of a profession is acceptance of its responsibility to the public who rely on the objectivity and integrity of certified public accountants to maintain the orderly functioning of commerce. This reliance imposes a public interest responsibility on certified public accountants."

Professionals take on these additional moral duties for two reasons. The first is that professionals possess expert knowledge, which enables their clients to depend upon them for reliable guidance. The client's dependence upon the professional opens the client up to harm through the professional's intentional or unintentional disregard of the client's interests. It is important to note that many financial transactions require specialist knowledge, which means that the client is, in many cases, entirely dependent upon the expertise of the professional. As financial products have become more complex, it is necessary for people to seek the aid of a professional to ensure their financial future. Hence, the professional has a heightened duty of care on the basis of the vulnerability of the client and the asymmetry of the information. Andrew Brien notes, "It is this dependence and vulnerability of society and its members and the profession's control of vital knowledge that empowers the members of the profession: quite literally the non-professional is at their mercy" (Brien 1998, 301).

A second reason why professionals take on additional moral obligations is that they undertake their role as an expert adviser on a voluntary basis. Professionals offer guidance and advice of their own free will and consequently accept additional moral and legal responsibilities. The AICPA recognizes this point in the Preamble to its Code of Ethics, which states, "Membership in the American Institute of Certified Public Accountants is voluntary. By accepting membership, a certified public accountant assumes an obligation of self-discipline above and beyond the requirements of laws and regulations."

Most codes of ethics governing the various areas of the financial services professions have two elements: principles and rules. The principles are aspirational characteristics that lay out general principles professionals should follow in practicing their profession. For example, most codes use *fairness* as a principle. That means that each professional should treat his clients with a characteristic behavior that is spelled out in the description of that principle. Those principles are then further specified by rules, which promote or prohibit specific activities, such as not commingling clients' funds with one's own funds, reporting the suspicious behavior of fellow professionals to the proper authorities, or specifying how much compensation one can give or receive for work done.

CORE PRINCIPLES IN ETHICS CODES

In this section, we spell out seven basic principles found in the codes of ethics of the following 11 financial services professional associations.[3] These professional organizations represent a broad range of the financial services industry. Most of the codes of ethics governing the financial services industry appeal to several or all of seven aspirational characteristics: integrity, objectivity, competence, fairness, confidentiality, professionalism, and diligence.

The organizations examined are the American Academy of Actuaries; the Institute of Certified Bankers/American Bankers Association; the American Institute of Certified Public Accountants; Chartered Financial Analysts; the Financial Planning Association; the Million Dollar Roundtable; the National Association of Insurance and Financial Advisors; the American College Designees; the National Association of Personal Financial Advisers; Certified Financial Planners; and the Society of Financial Service Professionals.

Appendix A outlines the seven aspirational characteristics that surround the codes (including the actual wording) of these 11 professional associations.

Along with the principles, each of the codes has specific rules, but to spell out the specific rules is beyond the scope of this chapter. One can easily access them by looking at the various codes available on the Internet. We now turn to the enumeration and explication of the principles.

Integrity

Almost every professional code that governs professional associations within the financial services industry requires its members to act with integrity.[4] However, the interpretations of integrity, even within a business context, exhibit a high degree of diversity. Robert Audi and Patrick Murphy cite three prominent definitions of integrity found in the business ethics literature. The first is Lynn Sharp Paine's interpretation of integrity as "moral self-governance." A second is Robert Solomon's definition of integrity as a "super virtue," which "consists not just of individual autonomy and 'togetherness,' but of such company virtues as loyalty and congeniality, cooperation and trustworthiness." The third is taken from John Della Costa, who understands integrity as "equivalent to honesty in a wide sense of that term" (Audi and Murphy 2006, 6–7).

Most interpretations of integrity tie it to honesty. Nevertheless, honesty and integrity are not correlative terms since to have integrity requires more than simply telling the truth. Lying is a symptom of the lack of integrity and does not quite get to the core meaning. For another, more basic meaning we need to get to the word's origin as a mathematical concept. It comes from the word *integer*, which refers to *whole* numbers. Thus, another definition of integrity is the quality or state of being complete or undivided. Therefore, integrity means wholeness, the kind of wholeness referred to when people are praised for "having themselves together."

What does it mean for someone to "have it all together"? The *Merriam-Webster's Collegiate Dictionary* definition of integrity is useful: "firm adherence to a code of especially moral or aesthetic values." This means having a good conscience and adhering to it by doing the right things. Since it is possible to both be honest and lack integrity, honesty is a necessary but not sufficient condition of integrity. To have integrity, therefore, seems to mean to be always *one*.

Daryl Koehn characterizes the person of integrity as someone who is introspective and is able to give an honest reckoning of his own strengths and weaknesses. This self-knowledge allows people of integrity to be comfortable with others. "People of integrity can dwell comfortably anywhere in the world. As long as they can live with themselves, they are satisfied" (Koehn 2008, 131).

These definitions reveal that integrity demands the professional to act according to the same principles in both his personal life and his business life. Integrity, under this interpretation, means integrity as integration. "Integration . . . in moral matters has the advantage of generally making them consistent in their thinking, in their conduct, and what they say connects the two" (Audi and Murphy 2006, 9). The Financial Planning Association (FPA) Code of Ethics captures this in their explanation of integrity: "We strive to have ever more congruence between our words and deeds and to deliver genuine value to those we serve." In other words, a person with integrity speaks with words that do not contradict his actions.

The Certified Financial Planner (CFP) Board of Standards offers another interpretation of integrity: "Integrity demands honesty and candor which must not be subordinated to personal gain and advantage ... integrity cannot coexist with deceit or subordination of one's principles." Therefore, a person with integrity possesses strong moral principles and does not deviate from them out of a desire for personal gain.

Objectivity

A second characteristic common to codes of ethics that govern the financial services industry is objectivity. The ideal of objectivity is grounded in the professional's obligation to subordinate his own interests to the needs and interests of the client. This is particularly important since the professional functions as an advice-giver and is trusted to give sound counsel that is in the interest of the client. Objectivity requires the professional to strive to perceive facts in a way that is not distorted by personal feelings, prejudices, or interests. In short, it requires the practitioner not to be partial to his own perspective or advantage. The CFP Code of Ethics claims that "objectivity requires intellectual honesty and impartiality.... [C]ertificants should protect the integrity of their work, maintain objectivity and avoid subordination of their judgment." The FPA Code of Ethics notes that integrity "is an essential quality for any professional."

Threats to objectivity cluster around two factors: perceptual bias and conflicts of interests. A perceptual bias is a prejudice that distorts perception and leads to faulty beliefs. An expression used in carpentry refers to *cutting on a bias*. To cut on the bias refers to the technique of cutting a piece of fabric or wood against the grain. Since the grain of the wood typically runs in a straight line, to cut on the bias is to cut at an angle. Perceptual bias refers to the same phenomenon insofar as when one is operating under conditions of bias, the world is perceived in a distorted fashion. Overconfidence, anchoring, and sunk costs are just a few examples of the biases, identified by psychologists, that affect the way in which people perceive the world and their place in it.[5]

More attention is paid to the threat that conflicts of interests pose to objectivity, particularly in the financial services industry. Beauchamp defines a conflict of interest as occurring "whenever there is a conflict between a person's private or institutional gain and that same person's official duties in a position of trust" (Jamal and Bowie 1995, 709). The institutional structure of the financial services industry creates compensation structures that some argue cause an unavoidable conflict of interest.[6] The Society of Financial Service Professionals (SFSP) Code of Professional Responsibility recognizes the problems implicit within certain compensation models: "A potential conflict of interest is *inherent* in the relationship between the client and the financial services professional when the professional is compensated by commissions." In any situation in which there is a conflict of interest, most codes of ethics require that members place the interests of the client ahead of their own interests.

Several codes distinguish between actual and apparent conflicts of interest. The AICPA Code of Ethics clearly requires members to be independent not only in mind, or in practice, but also in appearance.[7] The Institute of Certified Bankers (ICB)/American Bankers Association (ABA) Professional Code of Ethics also distinguishes between actual and perceived (apparent) conflicts of interests and urges its members to studiously avoid both situations. Members of the ICB or ABA are required to promise "to conduct my professional affairs in a manner that avoids a conflict of interest or the appearance of a conflict of interest." These organizations' concern with objectivity, in fact as well as in appearance, reflects the importance of maintaining public trust in the integrity and soundness of the financial services industry.

Competence

If a professional is defined as possessing expert knowledge, the professional must be competent in his field. Thus, competence appears as a principle in each of the 11 codes of ethics. The SFSP Code of Financial Responsibility states, "Professionalism starts with technical competence. The knowledge and skills held by a professional are of a high level, difficult to attain, and therefore, not held by the general public." The principle of competence refers to the level of expert knowledge a professional maintains and builds upon through continued education and experience. As the AICPA Code of Ethics states, "competence is derived from a synthesis of education and experience." Every professional organization has educational requirements designed to ensure that its members are able to provide competent service to their clients, as well as serve as an effective advocate or representative of their clients' interests. Most professional organizations require their members to participate in continuing education programs to maintain an acceptable level of technical knowledge throughout the course of their careers. The Code of Ethics that governs the Chartered Financial Analysts (CFA) is one of several codes that specify the importance of continuing education. Chartered financial analysts are required to "maintain and improve their professional competence and strive to maintain and improve the competence of other investment professionals."

The principle of competence also includes the manner in which professionals handle situations where they lack the requisite knowledge to provide acceptable service to their clients. The competent professional is obliged to admit what he does not know. The ICB/ABA Code of Ethics requires its members to promise that "[if] I accept responsibility for handling new and unusual professional activities, but I find that it is beyond my competency, then I agree I am expected to become competent . . . or obtain the assistance of a professional possessing the necessary skills or competency." Several codes explicitly require financial services professionals to recuse themselves from client engagements when they cannot serve the needs of their clients. In short, the competent professional should act only within his area of expertise and defer to outside experts when situations call for such consultation.

The principle of competence shows up in most of the codes of ethics that govern the financial services industry for two reasons. The first is that clients typically lack the information necessary to make decisions in their own best interest. It is this information asymmetry that creates the conflicts of interest discussed in the earlier section on objectivity. "The existence of this kind of information asymmetry can create a conflict of interest situation whereby the professional can serve her interest or the interest of another at the expense of the interest of those who are legitimately depending on the professional for an objective opinion" (Jamal and Bowie 1995, 709). Clients depend on financial services professionals as expert advice givers and trust these professionals to help them make good decisions to secure their financial future. As experts in the field of finance, financial services professionals play an increasingly important role in our society. This is the case since financial products have become incredibly complex, and an increasing number of individuals are responsible for planning for their own retirement and long-term financial security.

The second reason competence shows up in most financial codes arises from a problem that is implicit in agency theory. This is the *adverse selection* problem. Although the client (principal) can observe the actions and behavior of the professional (agent), he is not capable of assessing whether the professional is acting in the client's best interest. Not only does the client usually lack access to the information to which the professional has ready access, such as information about financial products, markets, and terminology, but the client is also uncertain whether the professional is doing a good job in protecting the client's interests. Professional organizations such as the American Medical Association and the American Bar Association were founded, in part, to vouchsafe for the competence of their members and provide assurance to the public that they could put their faith in the expertise of their members. In order for the professions to flourish, the public must have faith in the competence of financial services professional to provide them with the tools necessary to meet their financial goals and objectives.

Fairness

The concept of fairness is either implicitly or explicitly addressed in each of the codes that govern the actions of financial services professionals. As applied in the codes of ethics under consideration, fairness revolves around three concepts. The first is the principle of equality, which requires like things to be treated in like ways. The second is the Golden Rule, which requires professionals to treat their clients in a manner in which they would like to be treated. The final concept is the obligation to give each person or constituency that which is due to them, which often involves balancing the claims of competing parties. These interpretations of fairness overlap considerably but, taken together, they present a comprehensive picture of how the principle of fairness is interpreted by the codes of ethics that govern the behavior of professionals in the financial services industry.

Several codes of ethics explicitly include the principle of fairness. The first canon in the SFSP Code of Professional Responsibility requires its members to apply the principle of fairness. Both the FPA Code of Ethics and the CFP Standards of Professional Conduct include the principle of fairness as one of their seven principles. The American College obliges designees to conduct themselves in accordance with a professional pledge which demands they "make every conscious effort to . . . render that service which, in the same circumstances, I would apply to myself." This promise clearly reflects a commitment to the Golden Rule, which is one of the interpretations of fairness.

The first interpretation of the principle of fairness is a version of the principle of equality, which is the idea that like things should be treated in like ways. Any deviation from this principle requires an explanation to the affected parties in which the decision maker's course of action is justified by showing the relevant differences that justify the disparate treatment. For example, consider a financial services professional who charges one of his clients significantly lower fees for service than he charges another client. Differential pricing, on its face, is not necessarily a violation of the principle of equality. It is possible that the clients concerned differ in *morally relevant ways* and therefore warrant different treatment. Perhaps working with the client who is charged the higher rate demands more of the professional's time and attention because his financial plan is much more complex, while the other client is relatively low maintenance and does not require much in terms of the professional's resources.

However, the differential pricing policy may appear differently if it was discovered that the professional charged his clients varying rates based on their race. This pricing policy raises a troubling moral question since policy is based on characteristics that are irrelevant to the value of the services provided.

What factors are relevant in determining a fair pricing policy? We tend to think that if the professional is providing greater value to the client, it is reasonable to expect the client to compensate the professional accordingly. Many professionals who possess more experience or education demand more in terms of compensation than their colleagues with relatively less experience or education. This strikes most people as appropriate on the assumption that increased education and experience translate into greater value for the client. However, the professional is not required to provide any additional value to the client based on the client's race. In the same way, a professional's race does not contribute to or detract from the value they are able to provide to a client. Quite simply, racial status does not factor into the value proposition at all. The temptation on the part of a professional to base treatment on morally irrelevant differences motivates the FPA to interpret fairness as partially involving, "a subordination of one's own feelings, prejudices, and desires so as to achieve a proper balance of conflicting interests."

A second interpretation of fairness is exemplified in the principle of the Golden Rule: "Do unto others as you would have them do unto you." The SFSP Code of Professional Responsibility endorses the Golden Rule in its first canon: "Fairness requires that a professional treat others as he/she would wish to be treated if in the other's position." The FPA's Code of Ethics states, "Fairness is treating others in the same fashion that you would want to be treated." Applying the Golden Rule often affords an opportunity for professionals to determine exactly which action they should perform in a specific situation. Asking yourself how you would like to be treated can clarify your obligations since, unless there is a relevant difference between you and another person in the very same situation, it seems that you are bound by fairness to treat this person as you would want to be treated. This approach can be quite helpful since people usually understand what is in their best interests in a much clearer manner than they recognize the interests of others. Our perception of our own advantage is not muddled by the prejudice or bias that blocks our objectivity when we consider the interests of others.

The Golden Rule is used in codes of ethics to justify the obligation to disclose material conflicts of interest. When most people make financial decisions that will affect their future security, they want to know whether their adviser has any interest that may conflict with their ability to provide sound advice and suitable recommendations. Therefore, it is incumbent upon the financial services professional to disclose all information that is materially relevant to his recommendations, and this includes conflicts of interest.

The final interpretation of fairness requires that the financial services professional take the legitimate interests of all parties involved into consideration and give each person or constituency what is owed to them. Several codes of ethics explicitly state that professionals are obliged to work toward a proper balancing of interests between all affected parties. Of course, it is often difficult to identify the affected parties and whether the needs and interests of these parties are legitimate and should be taken into consideration. The AICPA, however, provides its members with a broad list of stakeholders to which a CPA should consider herself responsible. "A distinguishing mark of a profession is acceptance of its responsibility to the public. The accounting profession's public consists of clients, credit grantors, governments, employers, investors, the business and financial community, and others who rely on the objectivity and integrity of certified public accountants to maintain the orderly functioning of commerce."

The SFSP's Code of Professional Responsibility requires its members to "perform services in a manner which respects the interests of those he/she serves, including clients, principals, partners, employees and employers." All professionals, because of the different constituencies they serve, as well as their obligation to consider the public interest, are forced to consider what is fairly owed to all the stakeholders affected by their decisions. A common example is the conflict faced by captive agents between their obligations to the company, for whom they act as an agent, and their clients. Ideally, agents and the firms they represent share an interest in working for the good of the client. However, there are circumstances in which the interests of the company diverge from the interests of the client and an agent may be pressured by his employer to profit the firm at the expense of his client.

In brief, professionals have additional obligations besides the ones owed to their clients. The AICPA Code of Professional Conduct recognizes that conflicts are likely to emerge between competing constituencies and recommends that its members "act with integrity, guided by the precept that when members fulfill their responsibility to the public, clients' and employers' interests are best served." Several codes of ethics mention the professional's ethical duties to his employer and to the industry in general. The ICB/ABA requires that its members promise "to conduct my professional affairs in a manner that does not damage the reputation of my employer." Most codes of ethics recognize that professionals are obliged to help their clients within the boundaries of the law and regulation. Maintaining healthy and viable financial services corporations and an efficient and stable regulatory environment ultimately promotes the good of the client.

Confidentiality

Most professions include a duty of confidentiality, and so it is not surprising that all of the codes of ethics in financial services explicitly mention a professional obligation to hold client information in confidence. This is the case since financial services professionals, like physicians and attorneys, possess sensitive information about their clients, and this warrants a duty of confidentiality.

Confidentiality of client information is a requirement based on a promise made to the client not to divulge personal information. Clients not only provide information about the state of their finances and financial goals but also often reveal sensitive information regarding their family dynamics.[8] Moreover, such disclosure is required in order that a financial services provider is able to offer useful guidance and work with them to achieve their financial goals. People often have excellent reasons for not wanting their neighbors, employers, and even certain family members to know about their financial situation and objectives. Consequently, the obligation of confidentiality owed by financial services professionals to their clients is the foundation of a lasting and trusting relationship.

Sissela Bok notes that confidentiality involves "a duty to protect confidences against third parties under certain circumstances. Professionals appeal to such a principle in keeping secrets from all outsiders, and seek to protect even when they would otherwise feel bound to reveal" (Bok 1983, 25). According to Bok, there are four reasons that show the need for confidentiality, three of which support confidentiality and one which argues for professional secrecy. The first is that respect for personal autonomy entails keeping a client's personal information confidential. Part of what is required for respecting a person's autonomy is the acknowledgment of that person's jurisdiction over his own personal information. We believe we have a right to control access to information about ourselves. This is shown in the fact that we view someone surreptitiously gathering information about us as an inappropriate invasion of our privacy. Such an intuitive negative response points to our belief in our right, all things being equal, to control access to information about ourselves.

Ethical questions emerge when the person in question is not a fully autonomous adult—for example, when an individual, not being fully autonomous, lacks the ability to make decisions in his own best interest. Often financial services professions face dilemmas when dealing with the concerns of a client whose ability to act autonomously is called into question.

Consider the decision faced by an estate planner whose client, apparently suffering from dementia, seeks the professional's assistance to implement decisions that are not only out of character but may also have lasting and harmful consequences for the client and his family. In those circumstances, is it permissible for the professional to violate his duty of confidentiality and share his concerns with the client's family? Many factors need to be taken into consideration in such a situation. What is the family dynamic? How severe does the client's impairment appear to be? Are there other options besides speaking with the family? The difficulties raised by this example reinforce the fact that the obligation of confidentiality may not be absolute and is predicated upon the assumption that both parties are both rational and fully autonomous.

The second reason that shows the need for confidentiality is that one must respect the obligations entailed in relationships. Bok correctly notes that one of the ways in which people build trust and intimacy is through the sharing of personal information. According to Bok, confidentiality "presupposes the legitimacy not only of having personal secrets but of sharing them, and assumes respect for relationships among human beings and for intimacy.... Human relationships could not survive without such respect" (Bok 1983, 25).

Financial services professionals may be asked to sell their client list to third parties who are interested in advertising to a particular demographic. Alternatively, a financial services professional might want to use the names and personal information of clients for his own marketing initiatives. Doing this without permission violates the terms upon which information was provided to the financial services professional. Therefore, most codes of ethics emphasize the importance of refraining from using client information for personal gain. While codes might differ on what specific activities are not permitted, their prohibitions are all based on the belief that confidentiality is a mark of respect for the act of trust performed by the client in sharing his information.

This relationship of personal trust is captured in the FPA Code of Ethics. The code states that "a client, by seeking the services of an FPA member, may be interested in creating a relationship of personal trust and confidence with the FPA member. This type of relationship can only be built upon the understanding that information supplied to the FPA member or other information will be confidential."

The third reason showing the need for confidentiality is the client's vulnerability. By sharing personal information, the client places himself in a position of vulnerability. This vulnerability increases the asymmetry already implicit in the relationship with the professional. A client seeks the professional's aid and counsel because he lacks the expertise possessed by the professional. The client, for the most part, is compelled to provide personal information so that the professional can best work toward the client's best interest. While ideally both parties gain from this engagement, the professional is obliged to take pains to protect the information entrusted to him by the client.

The final reason for confidentiality is that it is useful insofar as it serves the common good. Bok argues that even though the professional obligation of confidentiality may hinder the pursuit of the common good or justice, for the most part, the duty of confidentiality creates a situation in which individuals can freely seek advice and counsel of which they might otherwise be deprived.[9] In short, a system that respects confidentiality will work for the public interest better than one that does not.

Professionalism

Each code of ethics featured in Appendix A mentions the importance of professionalism. The principle of professionalism promoted by each of these codes of ethics has three requirements. First, they all require the professional to treat all persons with respect and consideration. Second, they require professionals to act in a way that brings dignity to the profession. Finally, they require professionals to work toward improving the quality of services provided to the public.

The requirement to treat all the persons encountered throughout the course of their business with respect and consideration can be understood on two different levels. First, the professional has an ethical obligation not to treat others as merely a means to his goals. Professionals treat people as mere means when they use other people for their own purposes—for example, treating a client as if he were merely a source of commission income. Treating people as means denies them the right to act autonomously. This obligation, then, would prohibit railroading or other aggressive marketing tactics that undermine a person's ability to pursue an independent course of action. Second, the requirement to treat clients with respect means showing consideration for the client's feelings and circumstances. The American Academy of Actuaries' Code of Ethics requires that its members must "perform actuarial services with courtesy and professional respect and shall cooperate with others in the principal's interests."

The second requirement of the principle of professionalism is to act in a way that maintains and enhances the public image of the profession. For example, among other groups, the ICB/ABA Code of Ethics reminds its members of their "solemn duty to uphold the integrity and honor of my profession and to encourage respect for it." The obligation to protect the reputation of the financial services industry is grounded in the necessity of the public trust that is required for the industry to flourish. At times, this trust has been undermined by the actions of an unscrupulous few, which makes it more difficult for ethical financial services professionals to establish the basic level of confidence necessary to initiate a relationship with prospective clients. All the codes of ethics recognize that the actions of individual members of the profession have consequences that extend beyond their own reputation. Therefore, it is necessary for professionals to consider the effects of their behavior on a larger scale. The FPA Code of Ethics recognizes this obligation in describing one of its core values as stewardship of the profession: "We recognize our responsibility to act with vision, ever mindful of the effects of our actions today and tomorrow on the future."

The final requirement of the principle of professionalism is to improve the quality of services to the public. This requirement reinforces the importance of the public service component of the financial services profession. As is the case in other professions, the concept of a vocation creates a nobler end of professional activities than simply the personal success of the individual practitioner. It is the role of the professional to serve the public by working to ensure the financial security of his clients. This benefits not only the individual client but also society in general. Responsible financial decision making on the part of individuals contributes to a more efficient economy and also to a less strained social safety net. Given the important contribution that financial services professionals make to the greater good, it is evident why several codes of ethics require their members to work together to achieve these benefits.

Diligence

The final principle found in most codes is diligence. The 11 codes of ethics we are considering in this chapter interpret this principle in three different ways. The first interpretation is that diligence requires providing services in a reasonably prompt and thorough manner. One of the ways in which professionals respect their clients is through fulfilling their commitments and obligations within an appropriate time frame. The SFSP Code of Professional Responsibility requires its members "to act with competence and consistency in promptly discharging his/her responsibilities to clients, employers, principals, purchasers and other users of the member's services." An important aspect of diligence is making sure clients have suitable expectations of when work will be completed. Failure of a professional to meet the legitimate expectations of his client creates disappointment and undermines the trust necessary to build a successful client relationship.

A second requirement of the principle of diligence is that professionals provide services with *due care*. Due care requires undertaking one's duties in a painstaking manner. The term *painstaking* implies both a close attention to detail and persistent focus and effort over the course of time. Given the complexity and diversity involved in the activity of financial planning, it is difficult to enumerate specific behaviors that are either diligent or negligent, but it is obvious that diligence demands that the financial services professional act with care and attention at each stage of the planning process.

Several codes of ethics require their members to carefully gather information about a client's background, long-term goals, and sophistication regarding financial markets and products. This is an important example of the principle of diligence since a one-size-fits-all approach is not appropriate, and the professional is compensated on the basis of his ability to apply general principles to a specific individual case. Not only are professionals required to carefully gather information to understand the particular situation and needs of each individual client, but they are also required to exercise due care when giving financial advice and making recommendations to their clients. The ICB/ABA Code of Ethics requires its members to promise "to use reasonable care in expressing opinions involving and related to the performance of my professional duties, and obtain sufficient evidence to warrant an opinion."

A third requirement of the principle of diligence obliges professionals to ensure that their support staff members conduct themselves in a professional manner. Robert H. Colsen, writing on the AICPA Duty of Due Care, explains that diligence for CPAs requires "adequately training, supervising, and evaluating staff members and their work" (Colson 2004, 88). Jamal and Bowie believe that the emphasis on training and supervising staff can be explained by a recognition of the centrality of the moral hazard problem in the professions, and they say that the "monitoring of junior colleagues, who may be naïve about such moral hazard issues, is a professional obligation" (Jamal and Bowie 1995, 709).

EFFECTIVENESS OF CODES

Generally, professional codes of ethics are instituted to raise the level of ethical behavior within the profession. More specifically, a professional code of ethics is usually structured to accomplish three objectives (Higgs-Kleyn and Kapelianis 1999, 364). The first is to assure the public that its members are committed to act in accordance with the highest ethical standards as well as being competent technical practitioners. Frankel argues that codes of ethics can both enhance a profession's reputation in the eyes of the public and establish expectations for professional performance (Frankel 1989, 111). All of the codes of ethics reviewed in this chapter contain an obligation to maintain professional competence and expertise as well as an injunction to work toward the good of society in the practice of professional duties. Several codes of ethics refer to the importance of continuing education in order to maintain professional competence and technical expertise.

The second objective is the fostering of group cohesion around a set of self-legislated values and norms. When individual professionals come together to share their understandings of vocation and their personal values and beliefs with other professionals, increased loyalty to the profession and its ideals can emerge from this conversation. This cohesion is reaffirmed when professionals continue to meet to refine the code of ethics to meet new challenges and developments in the marketplace and professional environment. The process of code development enables experienced professionals to share practical lessons with less-experienced professionals. Frankel notes that codes of ethics also help new members of the profession resolve ethical conflicts: "As a distillation of collective experience and reflection, a code can offer guidance to individual professionals by simplifying the moral universe and by providing a framework for organizing alternative courses of action" (Frankel 1989, 111).

Finally, codes of ethics can serve as the basis for adjudicating disputes that emerge among professionals or between individual professionals and the people they serve. In this way, the code of ethics is established as the benchmark of ethical behavior and functions as the standard against which the actions of individual practitioners should be assessed. By creating and legitimating an ethical standard in the form of a code of ethics, the profession assists individual professionals to challenge the unethical behavior of their colleagues or supervisors. Disagreements can be ideally transformed from individual differences of opinion into conversations as to whether an action is in accord with a shared set of ethical standards. In this way, the code of ethics functions as the basis for continuing conversations about ethics.

Codes of ethics, then, are effective if they work toward meeting these three objectives. The limited literature on professional codes of ethics (as opposed to the more voluminous literature on corporate codes of conduct) does not provide a definitive answer to the question of whether codes of ethics are effective in generally elevating the instances of ethical behavior or in meeting these three objectives. However, it is evident that codes of ethics are insufficient without adequate monitoring and enforcement provisions. Given the problem of adverse selection—namely, that consumers have difficulty evaluating the behavior of experts—much of the monitoring burden falls in an informal way on other professionals. Historically, however, professionals have failed to report their colleagues' ethical violations to the appropriate professional and regulatory authorities.[10]

This negligence belies the professions' commitment to self-regulation and threatens to undermine the public trust upon which their mandate to autonomous self-policing is based. Further, the failure of professionals to defend the code of ethics through sanctioning defectors points to a troubling concern that individual professionals are not truly committed to their stated principles. It also provides ammunition to those who argue that codes of ethics are merely "window dressing" constructs that are "self serving and are more designed to protect the economic interest of the professional than they are for protecting the public from unethical conduct" (Jamal and Bowie 1995, 703). It is perhaps this failure of the self-policing obligation that has motivated recent regulatory encroachments into the financial services industry.

The answer to the question of whether codes of ethics are effective remains vague and indeterminate until further research reveals the extent to which codes of ethics elevate the level of ethical behavior within the financial services industry and achieve the three objectives: public assurance of the ethics and competence of its members, group cohesion around a set of self-legislated norms and values, and the establishment of a standard that can adjudicate conflicts both within and outside the profession. Additional research will reveal both limitations of professional codes of ethics and the opportunities that codes of ethics provide, if properly designed and enforced, to increase instances of ethical behavior among professionals.

APPENDIX A

Exhibit 16.1 provides a synopsis of how the seven aspirational characteristics are presented in the codes of ethics of the 11 organizations considered in this chapter.

Exhibit 16.1 Seven Aspirational Characteristics in Codes of Ethics of Financial Services Professional Organizations

	Integrity	Objectivity	Competence	Fairness	Confidentiality	Professionalism	Diligence
American Academy of Actuaries Code of Professional Conduct	An actuary shall act honesty, with integrity and competence, and in a manner to fulfill the profession's responsibility to the public and to uphold the reputation of the actuarial profession. (Precept 1)	Not specifically noted.	An actuary shall perform Actuarial Services only when the Actuary is qualified to do so on the basis of basic and continuing education and experience, and only when the Actuary satisfies applicable qualification standards. (Precept 2)	Not specifically noted.	An Actuary shall not disclose to another party any confidential information unless authorized to do so by the Principal or required to do so by Law. (Precept 9)	An Actuary shall perform Actuarial Services with courtesy and professional respect and shall cooperate with others in the Principal's interest. (Precept 10). An Actuary shall not engage in any professional conduct involving dishonesty, fraud, deceit, or misrepresentation or commit any act that reflects adversely on the actuarial profession. (Precept 1, Annotation 4)	An Actuary shall perform Actuarial Services with skill and care. (Precept 1, Annotation 1)

| Institute of Certified Bankers (ICB) / American Bankers Association (ABA) | Not specifically noted. | Not specifically noted. | Strive to become and remain proficient in carrying out my professional duties. If I accept responsibility for handling new and unusual professional activities, but I find that it is beyond my competency, then I agree that I am expected to become competent by diligently undertaking the work and study necessary to qualify myself, or to obtain the assistance of a professional possessing the necessary skills or competency. (Number 9) | Not specifically noted. | Safeguard the confidential nature of information concerning the business transactions and condition of my employer and of my employer's present and prospective customers, clients, borrowers or suppliers, except where disclosure of such confidential information is required by state or federal law or regulation. (Number 7) | Owe a solemn duty to uphold the integrity and honor of my profession and to encourage respect for it. I further agree to promote the continual development of the financial services industry as well my respective specialization. (Number 4) | Use reasonable care in expressing opinions involving and related to the performance of my professional duties, and obtain sufficient evidence to warrant an opinion. (Number 10) |

(Continued)

Exhibit 16.1 (*Continued*)

	Integrity	Objectivity	Competence	Fairness	Confidentiality	Professionalism	Diligence
American Institute of Certified Public Accountants (AICPA) Code of Professional Conduct	To maintain and broaden public confidence, members should perform all professional responsibilities with the highest sense of integrity. (Section 54, Article III)	A member should maintain objectivity and be free of conflicts of interest in discharging professional responsibilities. A member in public practice should be independent in fact and appearance when providing auditing and other attestation services. (Section 55, Article IV)	Competence is derived from a synthesis of education and experience. It begins with a mastery of the common body of knowledge required for designation as a Certified Public Accountant. The maintenance of competence requires a commitment to learning and professional improvement that must continue throughout a member's	In discharging their professional responsibilities, members may encounter conflicting pressures from among each of these groups (clients, credit grantors, governments, employers, investors, the business and financial community and others who rely on the objectivity and integrity of Certified Public	A member in public practice shall not disclose any confidential client information without the specific consent of the client. (Rule 301)	A member shall not commit an act discreditable to the profession. (Rule 501)	A member should observe the profession's technical and ethical standards, strive to continually improve competence and the quality of services, and discharge professional responsibility to the best of the member's ability. (Section 56, Article V) Members should be diligent in discharging

responsibilities to clients, employers, and the public. Diligence imposes the responsibility to render services promptly and carefully, to be thorough, and to observe applicable technical and ethical standards. (Section 56, Article V, 04)

Accountants for the orderly functioning of commerce). In resolving these conflicts members should act with integrity guided by the precept that when members fulfill their responsibility to the public, clients' and employers' interests are best served. (Section 53, Article II, 02)

professional life. It is a member's individual responsibility. In all engagements and in all responsibilities, each member should undertake to achieve a level of competence that will assure that the quality of the member's services meets the high level of professionalism required by these Principles. (Section 56, Article 5, 02)

(Continued)

Exhibit 16.1 (*Continued*)

	Integrity	Objectivity	Competence	Fairness	Confidentiality	Professionalism	Diligence
Chartered Financial Analysts (CFA) Code of Ethics / Standards of Professional Conduct	Act with integrity, competence, diligence, respect and in an ethical manner with public, clients, prospective clients, employees, employers, colleagues in the investment profession, and other participants in the global capital markets. (Code of Ethics)	Members and candidates must use reasonable care and judgment to achieve and maintain independence and objectivity in their professional activities. Members and candidates must not offer, solicit, or accept any gift, benefit, compensation, or consideration that reasonably could be expected to compromise their own or another's independence and objectivity. (Standards of Professional Conduct, I.b.)	Maintain and improve their professional competence and strive to maintain and improve the competence of other investment professionals. (Code of Ethics)	Members and candidates must deal fairly and objectively with all clients when providing investment analysis, making investment recommendations, taking investment action or engaging in other professional activities. (Standards of Professional Conduct, III.b)	Members and candidates must keep information about current, former and prospective clients confidential unless (1) the information concerns illegal activities on the part of the client or prospective client; (2) disclosure is required by law; or (3) the client or prospective client permits disclosure of the information. (Standards of Professional Conduct, III.e)	Practice and encourage others to practice in a professional and ethical manner that will reflect credit on ourselves and the profession. (Code of Ethics)	Use reasonable care and exercise independent professional judgment when conducting investment analysis, making investment recommendations, taking investment actions, and engaging in other professional activities. (Code of Ethics)

Financial Planning Association (FPA) Core Values and Code of Ethics	We strive to have ever more congruence between our words and deeds, and to deliver genuine value to whose whom we serve. (Core Values)	An FPA member shall be objective in providing professional services to clients. (Code of Ethics)	Our dedication to competence requires not only lifelong learning, but also that we continually assess our ability to appropriately and effectively address the needs of those we serve. (Core Values)	An FPA member shall perform professional services in a manner that is fair and reasonable to clients, principals, partners, and employers and shall disclose conflict(s) of interest(s) in providing such services. (Code of Ethics	An FPA member shall not disclose any confidential client information without the consent of the client unless in response to proper legal process, to defend against charges of wrongdoing by the FPA member, or in connection with a civil dispute between the FPA member and the client. (Code of Ethics)	An FPA member's conduct in all matters shall reflect credit upon the profession. (Code of Ethics)	An FPA member shall act diligently in providing professional services. (Code of Ethics)

(Continued)

Exhibit 16.1 (*Continued*)

	Integrity	Objectivity	Competence	Fairness	Confidentiality	Professionalism	Diligence
Million Dollar Roundtable Code of Ethics	Not specifically noted.	Always place the best interest of your clients above your own direct or indirect interests.	Maintain the highest standards of professional competence and give the best possible advice to clients by seeking to maintain and improve professional knowledge, skills, and competence.	Not specifically noted.	Hold in strictest confidence, and consider as privileged, all business and personal information pertaining to your clients' affairs.	Maintain personal conduct that will reflect favorably on the life insurance industry and MDRT.	Not specifically noted.
National Association of Insurance and Financial Advisors (NAIFA) Code of Ethics	Not specifically noted.	To present accurately and honestly all facts essential to my client's decisions.	To perfect my skills and increase my knowledge through continuing education.	Not specifically noted.	To maintain my clients' confidences.	To hold my profession in high esteem and strive to enhance its prestige.	To fulfill the needs of my clients to the best of my ability.

| The American College Code of Ethics | Conduct yourself at all times with honor and dignity. | Not specifically mentioned. | Continue your studies throughout your working life so as to maintain a high level of professional competence. | I shall, in light of all conditions surrounding those I serve, which I shall make every conscientious effort to ascertain and understand, render that service which, in the same circumstances, I would apply to myself. (Professional Pledge) | Not specifically mentioned. | Support the established institutions and organizations concerned with the integrity of your profession. | Not specifically mentioned. |

(Continued)

Exhibit 16.1 (*Continued*)

	Integrity	Objectivity	Competence	Fairness	Confidentiality	Professionalism	Diligence
The National Association of Personal Financial Advisers (NAPFA) Code of Ethics	Provide professional services with integrity. Integrity demands honesty and candor which must not be subordinated to personal gain and advantage.	Provide professional services objectively. Objectivity requires intellectual honesty and impartiality.	Maintain the knowledge and skill necessary to provide professional services competently.	Be fair and reasonable in all professional relationships. Disclose conflicts of interest. Fairness requires impartiality, intellectual honesty, and disclosure of material conflicts of interest. It involves a subordination of one's own feelings, prejudices and desires so as to achieve a proper balance of conflicting interests. Fairness is treating others in the same fashion that you would want to be treated.	Protect the confidentiality of all client information.	Act in a manner that demonstrates exemplary professional conduct. Professionalism requires behaving with dignity and courtesy to clients, fellow professionals, and others in business-related activities.	Provide professional services diligently. Diligence is the provision of services in a reasonably prompt and thorough manner, including the proper planning for, and supervision of, the rendering of professional services.

Society of Financial Service Professionals Code of Ethics	A member shall provide professional services with integrity.... integrity involves honesty and trust. A professional's honesty and candor should not be subordinate to personal gain or advantage. (Canon 4)	Not specifically noted.	A member shall continually improve his/her professional knowledge, skill, and competence. (Canon 2)	A member shall perform services in a manner that respects the interests of all of those he/she serves, including clients, principals, partners, employees, and employers.... Fairness requires that a professional treat others as he/she would wish to be treated in the other's position. (Canon 1)	A member shall respect the confidentiality of any information entrusted to, or obtained in the course of, the member's business or professional activities. (Canon 3)	A member shall assist in raising professional standards in the financial services industry. (Canon 6)	A member shall act with patience, timeliness, and consistency in the fulfillment of his/her professional duties. (Canon 5)

NOTES

1. "A profession may, therefore, be viewed as a 'moral community' whose members 'are distinguished as individuals and as a group by widely shared goals, beliefs about the value of those goals...and about the appropriate means for achieving them, and about the kinds of relations which in general should prevail among themselves, and in many cases between themselves and others'" (Camenisch cited in Frankel [1989, 111]).

2. For additional definitions of the term *profession* found in the literature see Higgs-Kleyn and Kapelianis (1999, 363).

3. Mark Frankel distinguishes three forms that professional codes of ethics can take: A code can be *aspirational* if it presents a set of ideals or principles that a professional should use to guide his actions. A code is *educational* when a "conscious effort is made to demonstrate how the code can be helpful in dealing with ethical problems associated with professional practices." Finally, a code is *regulatory* if it promulgates a series of rules to govern professional conduct and establishes policies through which these rules are monitored and enforced. As Frankel notes, these categories are not mutually exclusive, and several of the codes of ethics that we examine in this chapter have elements of all three types (Frankel 1989, 110–111).

4. Audi and Murphy point out that integrity as a moral principle or ideal is primarily applied in the context of business or commercial exchange. "One might be surprised that its [integrity's] main home is in the business world and in the literature of business ethics" (Audi and Murphy 2006, 5).

5. Kahneman and Tversky (1979, 263–291).

6. This is particularly a problem for professionals who are compensated by commission in which they receive a percentage of the value of the product or the service they sell. See Kurland (1991, 759).

7. The AICPA points out seven broad threats to independence: self-review, advocacy threat, adverse interest, familiarity threat, undue interest threat, financial self-interest threat, and management participation threat.

8. Additionally, many financial planning professionals have access to personal information such as a client's social security, credit card, and bank account numbers. A further aspect of confidentiality requires professionals to take adequate precautions to protect against this sensitive information falling into the wrong hands. Many codes of ethics contain explicit instructions regarding the storage and disposal of client information.

9. Bok's point is not uncontroversial. Jamal and Bowie mention that an objection to professional codes of conduct is that they may not represent the moral position of the community. Referring specifically to the professional duty of confidentiality, they write, "attorneys have interpreted these provisions [confidentiality] to mean, that an attorney has no obligation to tell the police where a body of a murder victim may be found even if the attorney knows where it is. Members of the public argue, however, that keeping such information confidential is morally wrong" (Jamal and Bowie 1995, 704).

10. Frankel notes that there may be several reasons for this dereliction, ranging from the desire to protect the profession's reputation and ensure continued public trust to fear of legal retaliation (Frankel 1989, 113). Andrew Brien accounts for this failure by pointing out that it may not be in the best interest of the profession to police itself and its members too vigorously (Brien 1998, 392).

REFERENCES

Audi, Robert, and Patrick E. Murphy. 2006. The many faces of integrity. *Business Ethics Quarterly* 16:3–21.

Blum, Lawrence. 1994. *Moral perception and particularity*. Cambridge, MA: Cambridge University Press.

Bok, Sissela. 1983. The limits of confidentiality. *Hastings Center Report* 13:24–31.

Brien, Andrew. 1998. Professional ethics and the culture of trust. *Journal of Business Ethics* 17:391–409.

Colson, Robert H. 2004. Professional responsibilities: Due care. *CPA Journal* 74:88.

Comte-Sponville, Andre. 1996. *A small treatise on great virtues*. New York: Henry Holt and Company.

Frankel, Mark S. 1989. Professional codes: Why, how and with what impact? *Journal of Business Ethics* 8:109–115.

Higgs-Kleyn, Nicola, and Dimitri Kapelianis. 1999. The role of professional codes in regulating ethical conduct. *Journal of Business Ethics* 19:363–374.

Huebner, Solomon. 1915. How the life insurance salesman should view his profession. Speech, Annual Meeting of Baltimore Life Underwriters Association, Baltimore, MD. February.

Jamal, Karim, and Norman E. Bowie. 1995. Theoretical considerations for a meaningful code of professional ethics. *Journal of Business Ethics* 14:703–714.

Kahneman, Daniel, and Amos Tversky. 1979. Prospect theory: An analysis of decision making under risk. *Econometrica* 47:263–291.

Koehn, Daryl. 2008. Integrity as a business asset. *Journal of Business Ethics* 58:125–136.

Kurland, Nancy. 1991. The ethical implications of the straight-commission compensation system: An agency perspective. *Journal of Business Ethics* 10:757–766.

ABOUT THE AUTHORS

Julie A. Ragatz joined the Center for Ethics in Financial Services at The American College in 2006 as a doctoral fellow. She received an MA degree in social and political philosophy from Marquette University and is pursuing her PhD in philosophy at Temple University. Ms. Ragatz has taught courses in ethical theory and business ethics at universities including Marquette University, Villanova University, and Saint Joseph's University. She has published numerous articles on ethical theory and business ethics. Her second book, *Accounting Ethics*, written with Ronald Duska and Brenda Shay Duska, will be published by Wiley/Blackwell in 2010.

Ronald F. Duska is the Charles Lamont Post Chair of Ethics and the Professions at The American College as well as the director of the American College Center for Ethics in the Financial Services. He is the author, co-author, or editor of numerous books and articles. His most recent books are *Ethics for the Financial Services Professional* (The American College Press, 2008), *Contemporary Reflections on Business Ethics* (Springer Netherlands, 2009), and *Accounting Ethics* (Wiley-Blackwell, 2003). He served as the executive director of the Society for Business Ethics and editor of the society newsletter, and is currently serving on the board of directors of the society.

CHAPTER 17

Banking

CHRISTOPHER J. COWTON
Professor of Accounting and Dean, University of Huddersfield Business School

INTRODUCTION

A *bank* may be broadly defined as a financial institution that is licensed as a taker of deposits and that makes loans and provides other financial services to its customers. The term covers a wide variety of institutions that differ greatly in size and nature—not only historically but also geographically, and within a particular country.

Most countries have a *central bank*, which usually has macroeconomic responsibilities (especially related to monetary policy), acts for the government in other ways (e.g., managing the public debt), regulates banks and other financial institutions, and acts as a lender of last resort to the banking system. Examples include the Federal Reserve Bank in the United States and the Bank of England in the United Kingdom. The operations of central banks are a specialized topic in their own right and are not addressed in this chapter. However, their regulatory role is of some relevance in the following discussion of commercial banking.

There are various ways of categorizing banks other than central banks. One distinction of particular significance in the United States is between *investment* banks and *commercial* banks—a distinction employed by the U.S. Glass-Steagall Act of 1933 (a consequence of the Great Depression), which separated their activities. An investment bank supports and advises on corporations' capital market activities, including mergers and acquisitions and the underwriting of securities issues, and it often engages in proprietary trading. A commercial bank is an institution that accepts deposits of money, makes loans using a proportion of those deposits, and offers related products and services, usually of a financial nature. Although this chapter is about banking in general, its focus is on commercial banking.

Some definitions of commercial banks, particularly in the United States, emphasize the receipt of deposits from, and lending to, businesses, whereas others include institutions that perform similar transactions with individuals or households—so-called *retail* banks. For the purposes of this chapter, the broader definition is used. In any case, in many parts of the world, commercial banks, in the narrow sense, and retail banks do not exist as distinct entities, and the manner in which the discussion in this chapter is framed can be applied to both.

Through their financial intermediation and other activities, commercial banks play a major part in modern economic life. Their problems toward the end of the first decade of the twenty-first century attest to this. Intimately involved in so much economic activity, a reduced ability to function on their part is like reducing the supply of oxygen to the economic body. And if they fail—as history demonstrates they are prone to do, especially if appropriate regulations and safeguards are not in place—the consequences can be severe, not only for their own shareholders and customers but also for businesses and households not connected with the failed bank; even for governments and nation states (Iceland is a recent example).

Although simple in its basic form, commercial banking is a complex professional activity, and like many such activities it entails significant technical and ethical issues. The technical issues that revolve around managing the process of financial intermediation are introduced, quite briefly and in general terms, in the following section. Taking as a springboard the simple model of financial intermediation developed in that section, the principal ethical issues involved are then discussed in three subsequent sections, organized according to three terms—integrity, responsibility, and affinity.

COMMERCIAL BANKS AND FINANCIAL INTERMEDIATION

Commercial banks (hereafter referred to simply as "banks") undertake a variety of activities. Many offer a wide range of financial products and services (for example, financial planning, pensions, mutual funds, and insurance) to their customers. From the customer's point of view, this can make life simpler; from the bank's commercial perspective, it is a means of improving profitability through crossselling. Both the products and services themselves, and the approach to selling them, entail ethical issues. However, at the heart of banks is their *banking* activity, and in order to stay within scope and at an appropriate length, that is the focus of this chapter. Thus this chapter is about banking rather than the complete range of activities undertaken by banks.

The core of banking is financial intermediation. A bank can be described as a middleman or a bridge between those with surplus funds (savers) and those who require credit (borrowers), whether for consumption, working capital, or investment purposes. In attracting funds, commercial banks offer a variety of products, including checking (or current) accounts and savings (or deposit) accounts. Checking accounts rarely offer significant interest, but they have associated benefits and services, and many banks charge for the services attached to such accounts. Savings and similar accounts that offer interest differ from checking accounts in two significant ways. First, they usually do not have services directly associated with them. Second, those that offer higher interest rates tend to require that notice be given before withdrawals can be made; or, at least, some interest already earned is relinquished if a speedier withdrawal is required.

Similarly, banks lend on a variety of bases and terms, including overdraft facilities associated with checking accounts, and term loans. Traditionally, the granting of credit has depended on the exercise of professional judgment by skilled professionals, but increasingly in recent decades the process has been automated by the use of credit scoring. Nevertheless, judgment is still involved, especially for large and nonroutine lending.

Generally speaking, whatever the method by which the interest rate is set, the higher the perceived risk, the higher the interest rate charged—which means that those who are probably least able to pay interest face the greatest interest rate burden. Risk is inherent in lending; the only way to avoid it is not to lend—which is what banks are choosing to do when they turn down a request for credit, at any price. However, risk is not the only issue that impacts whether, and at what rate of interest, a bank is willing to lend. For a given level of risk, the size of the loan also has an impact, with small loans tending to be priced higher (i.e., a higher rate of interest is charged) than larger loans because of the bank's fixed costs of arranging and managing a loan. Very small loans, which may be all that a poor person needs or can afford, tend to be uneconomical for mainstream banks. This can push the poor toward using more expensive or unlicensed lenders—so-called loan sharks—which adds to their financial difficulties.

One response to this has been the development of *microfinance*, the most well-known example of which is Grameen Bank. Although outside the scope of this chapter, microfinance is worth noting as an essentially socially or ethically motivated response to the perceived failure of banks to cater to the needs of the poor. However, some mainstream banks provide assistance for microfinance operations.

In addition to pricing for risk, banks also pursue various means of reducing it, providing safeguards if the borrower defaults on the payment of interest or the repayment of the principal, or is likely to do so. One is the use of third-party guarantors, who stand behind the borrower. Another is for the bank to take security or collateral, often in the form of a fixed charge on a specific asset or assets of the borrower. Mortgage loans are a familiar form of this. Where the borrower is a corporation facing bankruptcy, having security or collateral places the bank ahead of general, unsecured creditors.

The process of financial intermediation can be illustrated by means of a simple diagram (see Exhibit 17.1). Savers make deposits at the bank. Since not all savers are expected to withdraw all their funds at the same time, the bank is able to lend on a proportion of the funds it has received, while keeping a smaller proportion to be able to pay savers who wish to reduce or withdraw their deposits. The bank makes its margin by charging borrowers, on average, a higher rate of interest than it pays, on average, to savers. This margin is intended to cover not only the bank's operating expenses but also losses incurred when borrowers default and fail to pay some or all of the interest and principal they owe.

The process underlying this simple model will be familiar to most readers, but it is worth spelling out its essential nature, since it is drawn on in the remainder of the chapter. As indicated already, the bank can be seen as providing a bridge between saver and borrower. One of the central features of modern capitalism is the

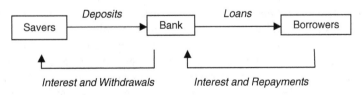

Exhibit 17.1 A Simple Model of Financial Intermediation

way in which much financial capital is freed from ties of family, clan, tribe, and even nation. Banks use money received from savers and lend it, generally subject only to financial considerations, to borrowers with whom the savers have no connection. Exploiting their access to a wide pool of borrowers and using their expertise in assessing and managing lending activities, banks help to ensure that surplus funds are put to financially productive use—subject, of course, to an appropriate level of risk.

However, it is not just a question of acting as a conduit between two parties. A bank can take many small deposits (e.g., from households) and transform them into large loans (e.g., to companies), thus mobilizing savings to contribute to economic growth; this is a major function of banks within an economy. A second transformation is also involved: borrowers usually borrow for much longer periods than depositors are willing to commit their funds for. Again, this is an economically valuable consequence of the bank's financial intermediation, though it also exposes banks to significant financial risk.

For the saver/depositor, the financial intermediation engaged in by the bank provides not only expertise in the use of the funds, but also benefits such as liquidity (they have access to their funds without depending on payments by particular borrowers) and diversification of risk (they effectively have a tiny share in a large portfolio of loans). In this sense, the bank acts not only as a bridge but also as a shield; it breaks the direct relationship between savers and specific borrowers. To change the metaphor again, the bank also acts as a veil, since depositors in general have little or no knowledge of the purposes for which their money has been lent or who has borrowed it.

The preceding paragraph sets out the basic social benefit of banking: the mobilization and transformation of savings to be used in economically productive ways, as reflected in the ability of borrowers to pay interest. However, as the financial crisis of the latter part of the twenty-first century's first decade has shown, there are significant negative consequences when banks, for whatever reason, fail or encounter severe difficulties in honoring their debts to their depositors. Recent events are just one more episode in a long history of banking crises. Regulators attempt to prevent bank failures by such means as specifying capital adequacy ratios so that banks do not overextend themselves by lending too much. Yet even an apparently strong bank can be brought down by a run on it, when a large proportion of savers seek to withdraw their funds simultaneously when they lose confidence in the bank's financial stability—a self-fulfilling prophecy, of course. Regulators seek to prevent such panic occurring by various means, and in many regimes smaller deposits are guaranteed by the state. While beneficial to the stability of the banking system, this is counterproductive if extended to a 100 percent guarantee of all deposits, because big savers then have no incentive to make intelligent decisions about where to deposit their money, instead simply seeking the highest return, perhaps offered by a less reliable, indeed risky, bank. There is a sense in which judging the soundness of a bank, including the control of moral hazard, is a task best performed by a combination of regulators and relatively well-informed depositors.

Thus, the net contribution of banking to society can, in its broadest sense, be viewed as a balancing act between, on the positive side, productive financial transformations brought about through financial intermediation, and, on the opposite side, economic and social disruption if the process goes wrong on a significant scale.

In addition to bringing out the basic nature of banking, Exhibit 17.1 also helps to frame the remainder of the chapter as the principal ethical issues relating to banking are explored. The next section examines ethical issues relating to the left-hand side of the model. In particular, it examines the generation of trust that is necessary for savers to hand over their money to a bank. The section after that considers various possible responsibilities that a bank might have in relation to its lending activities—thus focusing on the right-hand side of the model. The final main section then considers how some depositors might have more highly developed and nuanced interests or concerns regarding borrowers or the purposes for which their money is lent, thus reaching across the bank bridge, or seeing through the veil.

BANKING WITH INTEGRITY

As indicated in the previous section, deposits are needed for the process of financial intermediation to take place. Indeed, historically, banking developed from the custodial role of looking after other people's money. Given the exposure or vulnerability of those who deposit their money at a bank, the most obvious door through which ethics enters banking is *trust*. In entrusting their funds to a bank, depositors are relying upon both the technical competence of the bank (not to lend recklessly, to collect payments, etc.) and the integrity of the bank not to abuse its position—a position not only of holding the money, but also of possessing significant expertise and information not held by depositors. This latter characteristic, *information asymmetry*, is common to situations of moral hazard where a layperson engages with a technical or professional expert.

Depositors, then, can be harmed both by technical incompetence and by a lack of integrity. A good example of the latter within recent memory is the case of the Bank of Credit and Commerce International (BCCI), which engaged in fraudulent activity on a large scale. Typical of the former is when a bank is weakened because a large proportion of its loan book is subject to default—though, as noted earlier, it is depositors' perceptions of likely problems that may be more influential regarding bank failure. However, one of the features of the recent banking crisis is the way in which some of the problems have arisen because of a move away from the traditional model of financial intermediation. First, some lenders, instead of relying upon savers' deposits, attempted to fund their operations by borrowing on the money markets or by relying on brokered deposits, which often entailed high rates of interest. This saved them trouble and expense in terms of retail operations and was effective—until the money markets became tighter and interest rates rose. Second, some lenders securitized bundles of loans and sold them off to other lenders, thus disconnecting information gathering and processing in the lending decision from the creation of assets. A combination of the "market for lemons" (Akerlof 1970) and the "winner's curse" (Thaler 1988) (when bundles of loans were effectively auctioned off) left many institutions with assets that were worth much less than they had thought, especially when the financial crisis hit.

The difference between technical competence and ethical integrity is largely a matter of intentions (Provis 2001). Professional bankers are well aware of the importance of integrity for generating trust. "Since its earliest beginnings banking has been perceived as a business which depends on mutual trust and personal integrity" (Lynch 1991, 3). Although personal integrity is an issue, for the depositor the personal qualities of their contact person (if any) at the bank are not sufficient. When you lend money to a relative or friend, you are trusting a person, whereas when you deposit it at a bank, you are trusting an institution—and the regulators (such as a central bank) that stand behind it. Such a shift in trust from people to institutions is part of the condition of modernity (Giddens 1990). The institution or system needs to be trustworthy, though that does not mean that the personal qualities of individual bankers are irrelevant. In this context, it is instructive to note the everyday use of the phrase *bank on* to mean to rely upon.

One of the ways in which banks have responded to the challenges of engendering trust on the part of savers is in making more explicit the behavior that may be expected of them, for example through codes of ethics (see Cowton and Thompson 2000). Regulators are also important, seeking to prescribe and proscribe certain behaviors of banks and providing a degree of protection for depositors through their monitoring and deposit guarantee activities. Sometimes ethics and regulation are viewed as substitutes for each other, particularly when regulations are extended to remedy a perceived lack of ethics, perhaps in the context of some scandal; witness calls for more regulation when it is felt that banks have not acted with integrity. However, the relationship between banking ethics (at the level of the individual, the bank, or the industry) and external regulation is more complex than this.

Writing detailed rules for complicated businesses, such as banks, where the pace of change is so great and opportunities for moral hazard abound, is very difficult. Indeed, encouraging a rule-based approach can be ultimately self-defeating, since it can lead to a compliance-focused, hollowed-out approach to banking, where what is not forbidden is assumed to be permitted. What is more likely to help generate trust on the part of depositors is to treat ethics (or self-regulation) and external regulation as complementary rather than as substitutes for one another. Thus, initiative for the development and maintenance of trustworthy behavior on the part of banks is best not left solely to regulators but is to be welcomed when it emanates from the banks themselves, either collectively or individually. Indeed, given uncertainty and fear about banks' trustworthiness and reliability, developing a good reputation is probably an astute competitive move on the part of an individual bank.

Howard Davies, former chairman of the UK Financial Services Authority, considered an "ethical, responsible culture" a "win–win" for financial services firms (Davies 2001, 284), and in that context it has been interesting, therefore, to see some commercial banks—those that felt able to do so—emphasizing their trustworthiness in promotional campaigns during and following the recent financial crisis. Of course, there is the question of whether such claims themselves are to be trusted, but—without delving too deeply into an argument familiar in the business ethics literature—it is at least the case that the most sustainable basis for developing a reputation for being trustworthy is to behave with integrity, rather than just talk about it.

To summarize, integrity is important in banking, helping to generate the trust that is vital for a banking system to flourish. It is important that depositors trust banks, otherwise there is no money to lend. The following section moves on to characterize some of the ethical issues that arise in the context of lending that money.

BANKING WITH RESPONSIBILITY

In acting with integrity and competence toward people who deposit money with them, banks should lend responsibly, in the sense of managing the risk and return characteristics of the loan book so as not to put depositors' savings at undue risk. In this regard, depositors' interests are broadly aligned with those of shareholders. However, banks can be argued to have further obligations, including to stakeholders other than depositors and shareholders.

Responsibilities may change in nature or emphasis over time. Many of those faced by banks are faced by other large commercial enterprises too—for example, to be a good employer, a prompt payer of debts, or a fair competitor (Lucas 1998). However, some are specific to banks, or are particularly pertinent for them. Before examining some of them in greater depth, it is worth emphasizing that any conception of a company's social responsibility must start with the nature of its business and the social contribution that that business makes. Thus, for example, while corporate philanthropy might be regarded as one component of corporate social responsibility (CSR), it is just one part. On occasions it even seems to be used as a smokescreen, as an attempt to disguise or at least ameliorate the problematic nature of a company's business or the manner in which it pursues that business. Returning to the point made earlier, banks' fundamental contribution to society is bound up with the beneficial effects of the improved use of surplus funds brought about through competent financial intermediation. If they do not succeed in that, they fail in their contribution to society, whatever the other trappings of CSR they might display.

Nevertheless, between the broad issue of the general contribution of banking and the responsibilities that might be attributed to all or many types of business corporation, there remains a set of particular issues related specifically to banking. These are focused on the right-hand side of Exhibit 17.1 and are concerned with a bank's activities as a lender.

First, particularly given the important role that bank finance plays in many societies, banks can be argued to have a responsibility not to exclude certain groups. This includes a responsibility to lend fairly. The danger is that banks' lending policies, where they are unnecessarily restrictive, will tend adversely to affect certain groups that are denied credit or cannot afford credit on the disadvantageous terms on which it is offered to them. This might prevent those groups from participating in economic life in various desirable ways or drive them to loan sharks and their ilk. Exclusion can happen in various ways, some more deliberate or explicit than others. It might occur, for example, through the so-called redlining of certain geographical areas or the refusal to lend to certain ethnic groups.

Of course, if it is assumed that banks are responsible institutions that seek to maintain their depositors' trust and to earn money for their shareholders, then it might be concluded that any apparent patterns of exclusion exist only because of simple business considerations. However, this can be questioned on several grounds, including that some banks' lending policies—formal or informal—seem to be unjustifiably discriminatory not just in moral (and legal) but also in financial terms. At best, it can be viewed as a kind of laziness not to look more carefully at a particular segment of the market; at worst, it can be viewed as something more perniciously prejudicial.

Second, having lent money, the responsibility of banks can be argued to include not being too hasty to foreclose. Although calling in a loan can be supported in ethical terms as protecting depositors' funds and shareholders' capital, banks should not be overzealous in seeking to safeguard their position. In other words, they should withdraw lending with some consideration for the consequences for other stakeholders—not just for borrowers, but those indirectly affected, too. For example, if a bank calls in a loan from a small firm, it is not only the firm concerned that is affected, but also its network of suppliers and customers, its employees, and other business contacts—with both economic and social consequences. The fear is that some banks seek to withdraw too quickly, at the first possible sign of trouble. Since they do not share in any upside in the firm's performance, there is a temptation for downside possibilities to dominate the decision about whether to continue lending.

Third, as Morison (1995) argues, lending too much is potentially as serious a problem, ethically, as lending too little. There is a connection with the previous point here in that, if too much is lent, then foreclosure is much more likely. Nevertheless, the two are worth distinguishing, for a bank's approach to foreclosure is not necessarily tied to its approach to lending; both may vary according to the degree of profligacy or leniency versus stringency or aggression displayed. Borrowers clearly have a major responsibility in deciding how much to borrow, but so do banks, both in how they encourage borrowing and in how they exercise their expertise in sanctioning loans—bearing in mind that if they are taking security, they might be harmed less than others if things go wrong. In other words, if banks can protect their downside risk reasonably effectively, especially if a relatively high rate of interest is in prospect, they might be more willing to lend to vulnerable borrowers than a proper regard for the interests of those borrowers (and others indirectly affected) would allow.

Finally, beyond issues relating to borrowers, there are questions about the purposes for which loans are made. In particular, in common with other large corporations, banks have been prompted to consider their impact on the natural environment, variously conceived as (for example) sustainability, climate change, or carbon footprint. Like other businesses, banks have a direct impact on the environment (e.g., through their use of stationery and occupation of office buildings). However, they do not—for example—clear rain forests or produce hazardous chemicals; their direct impact is limited compared to many businesses. Their indirect impact, though, is substantial (Thompson and Cowton 2004).

As explained earlier, banks are involved in an incessant search for profitable lending opportunities, and if their industrial borrowers are engaged in activities that significantly and negatively impact upon the environment (especially if the cost is externalized), then the banks are implicated. Given the way in which they transform small, liquid savings into large, long-term loans through financial intermediation, banks make possible industrial activities that would otherwise likely not occur or would occur on a smaller scale. Put another, more positive way, commentators have viewed bank lending as an important lever for limiting or changing business behavior. Thus, for example, the UNEP Statement by Financial Institutions on the Environment & Sustainable Development is a significant element of the work of the United Nations Environment Programme; about 170 financial institutions were signatories as of October 2009. This is one method of encouraging banks not to make loans without considering the environmental consequences of their lending.

This section has focused on the right-hand side of the model, discussing some of the ways in which a bank might be considered to act more or less ethically, or responsibly, in its lending behavior, going beyond what might be considered necessary to protect the legitimate interests of depositors (and shareholders). It has suggested that there are certain responsibilities in the lending process, which might be seen as prima facie duties (Dancy 1991). The section has covered both the treatment of those to whom money is—or is not—lent, and the purpose for which it is lent, focusing on environmental impact. Such concerns might be expressed by any observer of the lending process.

However, the next section turns to the possibility that some depositors, as participants in the process, have a direct, ethically motivated interest in the direction in which their money is loaned or the uses to which it is put. Such depositors have some sense of responsibility for, or affinity with, the use of their deposits. This involves certain deliberate modifications to the conventional financial intermediation process.

BANKING WITH AFFINITY

The model of financial intermediation presented in Exhibit 17.1 separates the saver from the borrower. As explained earlier, the bank sits in the middle of two decoupled processes, with a veil of ignorance—to borrow a well-known philosophical phrase—between depositor and borrower. However, some depositors are uncomfortable with this, and various developments have occurred that offer the potential for concerned savers to deposit their funds with a clear, or clearer, conscience. Such depositors are seeking to make an association, even though there is no direct financial link, between their funds and the loans made by the bank.

These various initiatives may be referred to as *affinity banking*. Lynch (1991) calls similar practices *viewpoint banking*. The term *affinity* is used here for two principal reasons. First, in various fields it stands for relationship by choice, a mutual attraction or resemblance, and hence it seems ideally suited to the coming together of like-minded parties around a values-based or values-influenced financial intermediation process. Second, it is already familiar in a financial context (at least in some countries), referring to credit cards that are associated with a particular organization. The card is branded with the affinity organization's name and logo, and payments are made to it by the card issuer, usually based on initial take-up of the card and usage. Many types of organizations are involved, but among the most prominent beneficiaries of these schemes are charities (Cowton and Gunn 2000; Schlegelmilch and Woodruffe 1995; Worthington and Horne 1993).

Some banks have a lending policy that is avowedly ethical or *responsible*, going beyond the more general ethical codes and environmental policies already referred to. A good example is that of the Co-operative Bank in the United Kingdom. Its Ethical Policy was launched in 1992, capitalizing on the bank's historic roots in the cooperative movement. The policy, which is now incorporated into the bank's Partnership Approach, continues to be refined in response to customer opinion and changing circumstances. It sets out whom the bank will and will not do business with. For example, the bank states that it will not supply financial services to any organization or regime that oppresses the human spirit, takes away the rights of individuals, or manufactures any instrument of torture. Nor will it provide financial services to tobacco product manufacturers. More positively, it will encourage and seek to do business with companies that avoid repeated damage to the environment. The approach is thought to have been a major factor in the bank's success in capturing market share since it was introduced (Cowton and Thompson 1999; Davis and Worthington 1993; Harvey 1995; Kitson 1996; Thompson 1999), including significant growth in the charities sector (Cowton et al. 2000). Savers attracted to the bank because of its stance on various issues are expressing a view not only on its trustworthiness as a custodian of funds, but also on the uses to which those funds are put. The bank's policy provides an opportunity for some savers' ethical values to be more closely aligned with the characteristics of the loan book than is the case with most other banks.

The Co-operative Bank can be depicted as "a conventional bank with an ethical emphasis" (Cowton and Thompson 1999, 10). However, there are other examples of banks or related financial initiatives, many of them of quite recent origin, which seek to go further than the Co-operative Bank in expressing through their product offering a particular set of values or beliefs. The Europe-based Triodos Bank is an instructive example. Triodos has an overarching policy to finance projects that benefit the community, enhance the environment, and respect human freedom. This policy determines the types of projects the bank will and will not finance, but Triodos pushes affinity much further than the Co-operative Bank.

First, because it is relatively small, it is able to provide more detailed information to its depositors about where money has been lent, thus providing an unusually high level of transparency. Second, within the envelope of its standard social and environmental lending criteria, Triodos gives depositors opportunities to specify more precisely the uses to which they wish their funds to be put, through particular accounts, in which the money is then ring-fenced. Examples of areas of application include organic farming and social housing. Thus, Triodos Bank manages to restore a sense of relationship between depositor and borrower which, as explained earlier, tends to be broken in normal banking practice. (For further details see Cowton and Thompson [1999, Chapter 12], and Cowton and Thompson [2001].) Another interesting feature is that, although the Bank's policy is to offer relatively attractive rates of interest, in many cases depositors elect to receive a lower rate of interest than the official rate on the account, in some cases waiving it altogether, thereby helping the borrower by permitting funds to be lent at favorable rates of interest (*interest offset*).

Explicit or implicit interest offset is seen in several other affinity initiatives, which might therefore seem to be as much about personal philanthropy as banking or conventional saving. For example, Shared Interest (Cowton and Thompson 1999, Chapter 9; Moore 1993) seeks to lend to third-world producers while providing a very low return to savers. Such schemes, which emphasize social rather than financial return, pose little threat to mainstream banking because, even though they are growing significantly, they are minuscule in terms of total finance. Nevertheless, they are still of relevance to mainstream banks. First, they provide opportunities for collaboration that might help to deflect some criticisms of mainstream banks; for example, they might support, financially or technically, an organization that has a mission to lend to the poor. Second, the initiatives might be regarded as experiments or sources of ideas for schemes that might subsequently be adopted by mainstream banks in some form.

Finally, although there is not enough space within this chapter to do it justice, mention should be made of the growing phenomenon of Islamic banking. In some cases this is practiced by an independent Islamic bank, in other cases by an Islamic banking unit or subsidiary of a conventional bank, with the Islamic component financially ring-fenced. Islamic banking is widely interpreted to mean a ban on the charging or receipt of interest (*riba*), in accordance with Islamic law (*Sharia*)—though, as in historical debates within Christianity, there is some discussion of whether it is really a matter of not charging *excessive* interest, or usury.

As indicated in Exhibit 17.1, the flow of interest payments is central to the financial intermediation process that lies at the heart of conventional, Western banking. In Islamic banking, this is replaced by alternative mechanisms, including the payment of fees and the sharing of profits and losses or risks, under various financial contract forms (e.g., Mudharabah, Musharakah, Mudaraba)—though some commentators are not convinced that all banking services and products marketed as "Islamic" are really compliant with Sharia. However, it is not only interest that is forbidden (*haram*) in Islamic banking. Attention is also paid to the activities that are being undertaken; for example, all dealings in gambling, pornography, alcohol, and other intoxicants are forbidden, so loans should not be made for those purposes. Overall, Islamic banking involves not only a constrained financial intermediation process, in terms of the direction of lending, but a different type of intermediation process in terms of the nature of the flow of payments between the bank, its depositors, and borrowers. Growing rapidly both in predominantly Muslim nations and among Muslim communities in other countries, Islamic banking poses an interesting challenge to models of banking focused solely on interest and risk.

CONCLUSION

This chapter has sought to provide an overview of ethics in banking by focusing on the core process of financial intermediation that banks engage in through accepting deposits from savers and lending to borrowers who seek credit. Three terms have been used to frame the discussion of some of the salient issues in banking ethics. First, *integrity* (in addition to technical competence) is important to generate the trust necessary for savers to deposit their funds with banks. A minimum level is necessary for any banking system to flourish and so make its fundamental contribution to the economy and society, with banks using information and expertise to channel funds appropriately to economically productive uses. Second, *responsibility* highlights contemporary banks' need to take into account the consequences of their lending policies. I highlighted four prima facie duties: not to exclude certain classes of customers unfairly; not to foreclose too hastily; not to lend profligately; and not to lend without consideration of environmental consequences. Third, and finally, *affinity* refers to a set of relatively novel ways in which depositors and borrowers can be brought into closer association than they are in conventional Western banking, such that the process or outcomes of financial intermediation explicitly align with the depositors' ethical values.

REFERENCES

Akerlof, George A. 1970. The market for "lemons": Quality uncertainty and the market mechanism. *Quarterly Journal of Economics* 84:488–500.

Cowton, Christopher J., Julie E. Drake, and Paul Thompson. 2000. Charities' bankers: An analysis of UK market shares. *International Journal of Bank Marketing* 18:42–46.

Cowton, Christopher J., and Christine J. Gunn. 2000. The affinity credit card as a fundraising tool for charities. *International Journal of Nonprofit and Voluntary Sector Marketing* 5:11–18.

Cowton, Christopher J., and Paul Thompson. 1999. *Ethical banking: Progress and prospects.* London: Financial Times Business.

———. 2000. Do codes make a difference? The case of bank lending and the environment. *Journal of Business Ethics* 24:165–178.

———. 2001. Financing the social economy: A case study of Triodos Bank. *International Journal of Nonprofit and Voluntary Sector Marketing* 6:145–155.

Dancy, Jonathan. 1991. An ethic of prima facie duties. In *A companion to ethics*, ed. Peter Singer. Oxford: Blackwell.

Davies, Howard. 2001. Ethics in regulation. *Business Ethics: A European Review* 10:280–287.

Davis, Peter, and Steve Worthington. 1993. Cooperative values: Change and continuity in capital accumulation—the case of the British Cooperative Bank. *Journal of Business Ethics* 12:849–859.

Giddens, Anthony. 1990. *The consequences of modernity.* Cambridge: Polity.

Harvey, Brian. 1995. Ethical banking: The case of the Co-operative Bank. *Journal of Business Ethics* 14:1005–1013.

Kitson, Alan. 1996. Taking the pulse: Ethics and the British Cooperative Bank. *Journal of Business Ethics* 15:1021–1031.

Lucas, John R. 1998. The responsibilities of a businessman. In *Business ethics: Perspectives on the practice of theory*, ed. Christopher Cowton and Roger Crisp. Oxford: Oxford University Press.

Lynch, James J. 1991. *Ethical banking: Surviving in an age of default.* Basingstoke: Macmillan.

Moore, Geoff. 1993. Banking on concern: Shared Interest Society Ltd and ethical investment in the third world. In *Good business: Case studies in corporate social responsibility.* Bristol: Centre for Social Management, School of Advanced Urban Studies.

Morison, Ian. 1995. Moral conflicts in commercial banking. In *Financial decision-making and moral responsibility*, ed. Stephen F. Frowen and Francis P. McHugh. Basingstoke: Macmillan.

Provis, Chris. 2001. Why is trust important? *Reason in Practice* 1:31–41.

Schlegelmilch, Bodo B., and Helen Woodruffe. 1995. A comparative analysis of the affinity card market in the USA and the UK. *International Journal of Bank Marketing* 13:12–23.

Thaler, Richard H. 1988. The winner's curse. *Journal of Economic Perspectives* 2:191–202.

Thompson, Paul. 1999. The future of commercial banking—the Internet, stakeholders and ethics: A case study of the Co-operative Bank. *Journal of Financial Services Marketing* 3:316–333.

Thompson, Paul, and Christopher J. Cowton. 2004. Bringing the environment into bank lending: Implications for environmental accounting. *British Accounting Review* 36:197–218.

Worthington, Steve, and Suzanne Horne. 1993. Charity affinity credit cards: Marketing synergy for both card issuers and charities. *International Journal of Bank Marketing* 9:301–313.

ABOUT THE AUTHOR

Christopher J. Cowton is a professor of accounting and dean of the University of Huddersfield Business School. He is internationally recognized for his contributions to business ethics, especially his writing on socially responsible/ethical investment and other aspects of accounting and financial ethics. Beyond these areas, his academic publications range from philosophy and biblical studies to operations management and engineering. For several years he has been editor of the quarterly international journal *Business Ethics: A European Review*, and he is a member of the Ethics Standards Committee of the Institute of Chartered Accountants in England and Wales.

CHAPTER 18

Mutual Funds

D. BRUCE JOHNSEN
Professor of Law, George Mason University School of Law

INTRODUCTION

Soft dollars and directed brokerage are two forms of institutional brokerage commission rebate that have persisted for years in the mutual fund industry both in the United States and across the globe, with total yearly volume in the billions of dollars. In the United States, these practices have periodically come under attack from academics, financial market commentators, securities regulators, and politicians as examples of disloyalty and unjust enrichment by fund managers whose duty it is to serve investors. Yet a strong case can be and has been made that they are efficient forms of economic organization that benefit investors. This chapter examines whether they are ethical according to *Integrative Social Contracts Theory* (ISCT) as informed by transaction costs economics.

ISCT is primarily the creation of Donaldson and Dunfee (1999) ("TD2"), who developed it as a practical framework to help businessmen untrained in higher philosophy grapple with the ethical issues they are likely to face. ISCT is intellectually congruent with Western philosophical discourse, as reflected in its reliance on global "hypernorms," and at the same time practical and approachable in its reliance on local "authentic community norms" that allow for substantial "moral free space."

The layered structure of ISCT is akin to the notion of competitive federalism in political and economic theory. It allows for local variation—"laboratories for experimentation"—minimally constrained from above to the extent necessary to mitigate intercommunity spillovers. ISCT emphasizes the moral force of the informed individual's options to exit from and exercise voice in local communities. These options ensure that local norms are subject to evolutionary competitive forces. At the same time, ISCT is sufficiently empirical that it can evolve over time to gradually iterate toward a more useful structure applied to specific business settings. This chapter augments the TD2 conception of ISCT using transaction cost economics. Transaction cost economics suggests that law, ethics, and other evolved institutions serve, at least in part, to constrain socially inefficient behavior (Coase 1937 and 1960).

The following section briefly describes the U.S. mutual fund industry and soft dollars and directed brokerage, two forms of brokerage commission rebate that have been popular in the mutual fund industry but that have also been the target of repeated, and heated, criticism. The third section explains why these practices might be efficient and likely to benefit fund investors once the cost of transacting is considered. The fourth section briefly describes the basics of ISCT and integrates the insights from transaction cost economics to assess the ethical status of these commission rebates. I conclude they are arguably ethical, though admittedly puzzling when viewed from outside the local community of institutional brokers and money managers.

THE MUTUAL FUND INDUSTRY AND INSTITUTIONAL BROKERAGE

The mutual fund industry relies heavily on agents to act on behalf of dispersed shareholders. In such a setting, conflicts of interest are inevitable but by no means crippling. To show how soft dollars and directed brokerage resolve conflicts of interest it is important to have a clear picture of how funds are organized and how soft dollars and directed brokerage actually work.

The Organization and Regulation of Mutual Funds

Mutual funds are investment pools organized as corporations or trusts under state law. To raise capital the fund issues shares to the investing public, with the proceeds placed in a more or less diversified portfolio of risky securities (primarily corporate stocks and bonds, government debt, etc.) and cash to which shareholders have a pro rata claim. A unique feature of mutual funds is that they stand ready to issue and redeem shares at the daily net asset value of the fund next computed based on the reported prices of the underlying portfolio securities. For this reason they are also known as *open-end funds*.[1] Much of Americans' savings is held by mutual funds and managed by advisory firms regulated under the Investment Company Act (ICA) of 1940 and the Investment Advisers Act (IAA) of 1940 (collectively known as "the '40 Act").

The ICA formally mandates that the adviser to a mutual fund be a vertically separate firm. The adviser provides management services through a contract periodically approved by the fund's board of directors or a majority of fund shareholders. In reality, however, the adviser normally creates and promotes the fund, and fund boards almost invariably renew advisory contracts. What is more, even though Section 15(a) of the ICA prohibits direct assignment of the advisory contract, Section 15(f) allows advisory firm owners to profit from a sale of control in the advisory firm that indirectly assigns the advisory contract. The relationship between the adviser and the fund therefore lies somewhere in an economic netherworld between an extended firm and market exchange.[2]

Advisory services include record keeping, custody of shares, and other ministerial functions, but in an actively managed fund they consist most importantly of portfolio management, normally provided by an employee of the advisory firm.[3] As an agent for the fund, an active manager's primary charge is to hold an efficiently diversified portfolio, to use his best efforts to perform or acquire research to identify mispriced securities, and to buy or sell those securities to make a profit for the portfolio before the market fully corrects the pricing error. Once having identified a potentially profitable trade, the manager traditionally hires an institutional securities broker to execute it. In selecting between brokers, the manager has a fiduciary duty to choose the broker that will provide best execution for the fund.

The executing broker is also an agent of the fund. Like the manager, he is subject to a fiduciary duty of best execution of portfolio trades. This requires him to search for willing sellers or buyers and to contract with them for the purchase or sale of the security on the best possible terms for the benefit of the fund. In consideration, the broker typically receives a commission averaging five or six cents per share. Although the manager may be able to trade through a proprietary network or with a discount broker for as little as a penny a share, institutional brokers provide the benefit of specialization, access to a variety of securities exchanges and other exclusive trading networks, and, perhaps most important, anonymity. There is little doubt these specialized agents effectively reduce the total costs of transacting portfolio securities in the vast majority of agency trades.[4]

Because brokerage commissions are treated as a capital expense and included in the price basis of portfolio securities for tax reasons, fund shareholders implicitly pay them in the form of lower net returns.[5] Outsiders to the world of institutional securities brokerage are often shocked to learn brokers routinely provide fund advisory firms or their portfolio managers with benefits as a partial quid pro quo for their promise of premium commission payments on future portfolio trades. Soft dollars and directed brokerage are the primary means by which brokers have provided such benefits.

How Soft Dollars Work

To understand how soft dollars work, Exhibit 18.1 illustrates relations between the parties. P represents the mutual fund's portfolio of securities, whose beneficial owners consist of any number of dispersed shareholders, S. The fund enters into a contract in which it promises to pay the manager, M, a fee consisting of a periodic share of the portfolio's net asset value, say 75 basis points per year.[6] In exchange the manager provides active management by expending effort to identify profitable trading opportunities. Having identified a profitable trade, the manager hires an institutional broker, B, to execute the trade in exchange for commission payments on completion.

In a typical soft dollar arrangement, the broker provides the manager with credits, oftentimes *up front*, to pay a specific dollar amount of his research bill with independent research vendors, V. In exchange, the manager agrees to send the broker future trades at premium commission rates. By way of example, the broker might provide the manager with $60,000 in research credits if the manager agrees to send the broker enough trades over the coming months at seven cents per share to generate $140,000 in brokerage commissions, clearly more than necessary to cover the lowest available commission or the broker's marginal execution cost. In this sense the manager is said to *pay up* for research bundled into the brokerage commission. Once having entered into this agreement the manager orders any of a large number of research products—fundamental analyses, hardware, software, subscriptions, databases, and so on—from independent, or *third-party*, vendors, who in turn receive payment from the broker. If all goes as planned, the manager places the promised trades with the broker at the agreed premium commission

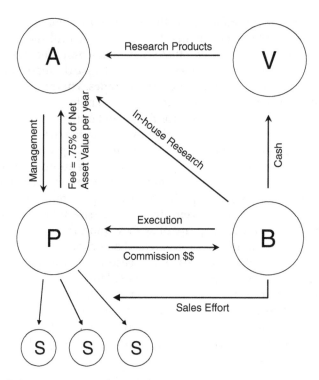

Exhibit 18.1   Relations Between the Parties—Soft Dollars

rate. If not, he can terminate the connection with the broker at any time with no legal obligation to make the promised trades.

Courts and regulators have long regarded brokerage payments as assets of the fund, so-called *client commissions*. Managers' use of client commissions to pay for research with soft dollars has been heavily criticized as an unethical conflict of interest that may lead the manager to favor itself over fund investors. The prospect of unjust enrichment is said to pervert advisers' incentives, leading them to engage in too much trading, to use too much research, and to select brokers to generate research credits rather than to enhance execution quality.[7] The picture that emerges is one in which the entire commission premium is a net drag on fund performance, reducing investor returns dollar for dollar.

It bears emphasizing that none of these criticisms identify a conflict of interest unique to the manager's receipt of *independent* research through soft dollar arrangements. Instead, they identify a conflict inherent in bundling the costs of research and execution together into premium brokerage commissions. Soft dollar brokerage constitutes only one form of bundling. Historically, full-service brokers have provided investment managers with proprietary in-house research and other brokerage services bundled together with execution as part of an informal, long-term relationship. Indeed, this practice predominates to this day, as illustrated by the diagonal arrow in Exhibit 18.1. The main difference between these two forms of institutional brokerage is that proprietary research is generated within the brokerage firm and is accounted for only informally during the long course of a trading relationship, while independent research is transacted in the market for a price—in soft dollars—and provided in arm's-length transactions by independent research vendors. In either case, as part of the Securities Acts Amendments of 1975, Congress provided a safe harbor to fund managers who pay a premium commission for brokerage as long as they determine "in good faith that it was reasonable in relation to the value of the brokerage and research services provided."[8]

How Directed Brokerage Works

Like soft dollars, directed brokerage occurs in the context of premium commission payments by the mutual fund in exchange for institutional brokerage, but rather than providing the manager with research, the broker (or its underwriting affiliate) provides effort selling the fund's shares to the investing public. Exhibit 18.2 illustrates two ways fund shares can be marketed. Historically—but to a lesser extent today—the brokerage firm's retail brokers, RB, provided effort selling the fund's shares to the investing public, S, for an up-front load paid directly by the investor. The investor would write a check for, say, $100 to the RB, who would forward $95 to the fund for the investor's account and retain the $5 load fee as compensation for its selling effort.

In a directed brokerage arrangement, the RB provided effort selling the fund's shares to the investing public in exchange for the adviser's commitment to send the brokerage firm future premium commission business on portfolio trades to

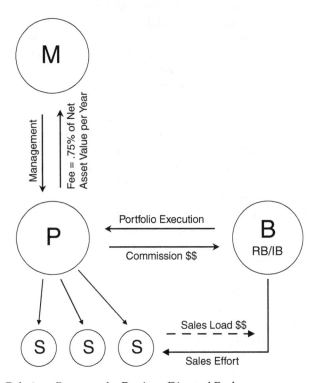

Exhibit 18.2 Relations Between the Parties—Directed Brokerage

be executed by the firm's institutional brokers.[9] Until its prohibition by the SEC in 2004, directed brokerage was one of several *no-load* methods an adviser could use to compensate brokers for their sales effort, often in the context of proprietary *fund supermarkets* that feature funds from a variety of fund families managed by reputable advisory firms. In this context, directed brokerage can be seen as one form of payment for shelf space, similar to what occurs regularly in the retail grocery industry (Klein and Wright 2007; Wright 2007).

Examples of directed brokerage arrangements prior to the SEC's ban involved various *partner programs* between a fund adviser and one or more retail brokers. In exchange for the expectation of having the adviser send trading commission business for its managed funds to the retail broker's institutional affiliate, the retail broker would agree to display the adviser's funds more prominently within its universe of fund listings when making recommendations to its client investors. Fund managers received greater access to the retail broker's sales system, including its branch system, access to individual point-of-sale brokers via training and customer seminars, inclusion in broker events, and invitations to participate in programs broadcast over the retail brokers' internal systems. In some cases the point-of-sale broker and his sales manager received a larger fee for the sale of partner funds than nonpartner funds, with this fee being paid out over time depending on how long the investor remained with the fund.

According to the SEC's release *In re Massachusetts Financial Services Company*,[10] MFS, a prominent fund adviser, negotiated for preferential access to its partners' sales staffs and "heightened visibility" for its fund offerings within their distribution systems. In exchange, MFS paid the retail broker between 15 and 25 basis points for the sale of its fund shares and 3 to 20 basis points per year in trailing fees for fund shares held by its partners' clients more than one year. In some cases MFS paid partners in cash from its own account, but in others it paid with directed brokerage, and there was apparently some evidence to suggest it preferred this method. In any event, MFS made clear to the employees on its trading desk that they could consider partners' sales of fund shares only as "a factor" in allocating portfolio brokerage and that best execution was not to be compromised. MFS cautioned its personnel not to enter into legally binding agreements with partners to promise a specific amount of commission business nor to refer to their arrangements with partners as binding. Nevertheless, some MFS employees casually labeled commission allocations to partners as "obligations," "commitments," or amounts "owed." What is more, from time to time MFS requested that its trading desk increase trading with specific partners to satisfy the commission targets.

MFS informed its fund boards that, subject to best execution, it considered the sale of fund shares as a factor in allocating its funds' portfolio brokerage. It also showed them the exact amount of commission business allocated to every broker-dealer for which consideration of fund sales was a factor. In substance, the SEC found that MFS had entered into bilateral arrangements in which it agreed to allocate specific amounts of fund brokerage commissions, subject to best execution, to broker-dealers for "shelf space" or heightened visibility within their distribution systems. The MFS disclosures to the fund boards were therefore inadequate because they failed to specifically state that the amounts were "used to satisfy bilateral arrangements under the [partner programs]." What is more, the SEC found that MFS avoided using its own assets in consideration for its partner programs by financing the sale of fund shares with directed brokerage. It therefore failed to communicate adequately its reliance on directed brokerage to its funds' boards. Although the SEC release makes no mention of an actual injury to any MFS client, it found MFS had violated various securities laws, assessed it $50 million in disgorgement and penalties, censured it, and imposed various remedial and compliance undertakings.

A TRANSACTION COST ANALYSIS OF INSTITUTIONAL BROKERAGE

Any serious transaction cost analysis of business practice must take seriously the proposition that the parties to a transaction—in this case fund advisers, institutional brokers, and fund investors—share a common interest in increasing the gains from trade. They will adopt new forms of organization that help them do this. Transaction costs stand in their way. Transaction costs are real costs, and so it does not pay the parties to resolve all conflicts of interest or seek the first-best allocation of resources. Nevertheless, cooperation subject to the constraint imposed by transaction costs is a powerful beacon to understand economic organization.

The Role of Prices in Transaction Cost Analysis

Prices as an economic phenomenon are not just about who gets the income from a commercial activity. They are also about providing informative signals to otherwise ignorant market participants—the "man on the spot" (Hayek 1945)—about how best to allocate scarce resources. By relying on prices to allocate resources, both parties to a transaction are encouraged to adjust the goods' attributes to maximize the gains from trade. If, compared to payment on delivery, widget buyers are willing to pay an extra 20 gizmos per widget for credit terms that cost the seller only 15 gizmos, sellers will happily bundle credit terms into the transaction for an increase in price of somewhere between 15 and 20 gizmos. Similarly, if widget buyers are willing to pay an extra 20 gizmos per widget to assure their quality rather than spending the equivalent of 30 gizmos on careful inspection, sellers will happily provide a warranty or some other form of quality assurance as long as the cost of doing so is less than 20 gizmos.

But transfer for a price accomplishes more than efficient bundling. One party's claim that his widget is worth 30 gizmos is more credible when that party is willing to accept 30 gizmos for the widget, and vice-versa for the other party; that is, when the parties "put their money where their mouth is," so-called *smart money*. The transfer has two components: a simple trade of one good for another and reliable information about the value of the respective goods, all bundled attributes considered. However distributed,[11] the parties' gains from trade are a private benefit, but the information itself is a nonrivalrous public good that reliably signals what they consider efficient resource allocation. Only if (and to the extent that) there are substantial spillovers from the transaction—costs or benefits that fall on outsiders—is the informational role of prices undermined (though not entirely eliminated).

The common criticism of this and, indeed, all methods of price allocation is that it gives the rich an advantage over the poor. True, being rich, or well-capitalized, provides one with more opportunities than being poor. In a market system, those of relatively modest means often succeed in outbidding their richer rivals when they are able to generate greater value-added as a result. Value-added, not riches, is what gives market participants pricing power because capital tends to flow to more profitable uses.

One point worth noting about the important role prices play in an economic system is that, as informative as prices may be, they are also costly to use (Coase 1937). Where we see prices emerging for goods, or attributes of goods, that have otherwise been unpriced or bundled with other goods for a single price, it suggests that the informational benefit a new price generates exceeds the transaction cost to the parties involved.

At a very basic level, soft dollars and directed brokerage payments are nothing more or less than garden-variety prices targeted to the agents of fund investors (Coase 1979). These practices unquestionably involve real conflicts of interest, but at the same time they appear superior to the available alternatives once subjected to the scrutiny of transaction cost economics (Johnsen 1994; Horan and Johnsen 2008; Johnsen 2009). Where transacting is costly, perfection is an irrelevant benchmark.

Agency Costs

Agency law tolerates conflicts of interest as long as they are disclosed or, if not disclosed, as long as the agent can demonstrate after the fact that any self-dealing was fair. This is sensible and, I should point out, the empirically evolved common law approach. The phrase *conflict of interest* identifies the set of activities in which agent self-dealing *might* occur. Agency law is, and in this chapter I argue ISCT can be, far more parsimonious than to condemn soft dollars and directed brokerage as unethical per se.

Transaction cost economics introduces the equivalent of friction into the neoclassical model of impersonal exchange of goods whose quality is easily evaluated at the moment trade occurs.[12] In the neoclassical model, the act of exchanging is itself costless, and competition ensures price is equal to marginal production cost. There is no need to rely on specialized agents, and no conflicts of interest arise because all dimensions of the exchange can be fully specified—that is, all goods are what economists characterize as *search* goods. Once transaction costs are introduced, buyers must evaluate quality; sellers must evaluate buyers' ability to pay; and trade is often supported by legally enforceable contracts, reputational capital, long-term relationships, ethical norms, or various other forms of economic organization that rely on specialized agents who are imperfectly motivated. Price cannot equal marginal production cost because transaction costs drive a wedge between the price the buyer pays and the net compensation the seller receives.

This does not mean unjust enrichment occurs on any significant scale, because the parties can profit by avoiding it. In 1976, Jensen and Meckling published the seminal work on principal-agent conflicts.[13] Their positive (descriptive) analysis relies on *agency costs* (a form of transaction costs) to explain how the parties organize their business affairs to maximize the gains from trade. Agency costs consist of *monitoring costs* incurred by the principal, *bonding costs* incurred by the agent, and *residual losses*. The principal can limit divergence from his interest by establishing appropriate organizational incentives for the agent, such as sharing profits or other benefits, and by incurring monitoring costs designed to limit harmful activity by the agent, such as shirking. In some settings it will pay the agent to spend resources bonding himself against actions that would harm the principal. In many agency relationships the parties incur both monitoring and bonding costs. In addition, it is inevitable that some beneficial trade may not occur that would occur absent agency costs. These forgone benefits are the residual losses. As long as residual losses persist, the parties have an interest in innovating new forms of organization to increase the gains from trade (Klein and Murphy 1988). The cost of transacting inhibits this process. Understanding economic organization, including ethical norms, is largely about how the parties adjust the rules to increase the gains from trade.

Institutional Brokerage as an Experience Good

It would be difficult to find an industry that departs more fundamentally from the neoclassical model than institutional securities brokerage. In contrast to search goods, institutional brokerage is what economists recognize as an *experience* good, one that is too costly for the buyer to fully evaluate at the moment trade occurs and whose quality will become apparent only in time or with repeated use. For certain experience goods, the receipt of unexpectedly low quality can impose substantial transaction costs on the buyer in the specific form of search costs. The quality of an institutional broker's execution is costly for a portfolio manager to evaluate owing to the inherent noisiness of securities prices. Excessive price impact on large block trades can easily overwhelm brokerage commissions and create a substantial drag on investor returns.[14] Price impact is an artifact of the high transaction costs managers face achieving best execution.

A conflict of interest arises from the manager's inability to evaluate the broker's execution quality, even after an extended series of trades. If high-quality trades are more costly to perform than low-quality trades, a broker might tout himself as willing to execute high-quality trades and cheat the manager by doing a careless job that leads to excessive price impact. The broker would earn a high commission and save on execution costs. Before the manager could discover the breach, his investors would have suffered diminished portfolio returns.

The market for brokers and fund advisers is competitive in the sense that there are large numbers of each, with active entry and exit and ample organizational innovation. If the cost of legally verifying the quality of broker executions were reasonably low, managers could enter into binding warranties with their brokers and seek money damages on behalf of the portfolio against those whose carelessness or greed led to excessive price impact. Absent egregious conduct by a broker—front-running being a potentially verifiable example[15]—it is impossible for a manager to seek legal recourse against a careless broker because the cost of verifying mere carelessness to an outside party in such a noisy setting is prohibitive. The best the manager can do to protect the portfolio is to terminate brokers whose execution quality proves to be subpar over an extended series of trades.

Execution Quality Assurance

A well-known transaction cost model of how sellers assure the quality of experience goods (Klein and Leffler 1981) shows why, under plausible assumptions, investors would suffer if fund managers paid the lowest available brokerage commission, and why they are better served if managers instead pay up for brokerage in exchange for soft dollar research and other beneficial inputs.

Given the problem of price impact, institutional brokerage is an experience good. What is more, the cost to the broker of avoiding price impact increases the greater care he takes in executing trades. Suppose the manager offers to pay a broker, say, four cents per share for high-quality execution, which is exactly equal to the broker's execution cost. The broker can cheat by secretly providing low-quality execution that costs, say, two cents per share. In noisy securities markets it takes time even for a diligent manager to discover the excessive price impact from low-quality execution and to terminate the broker. In the meantime, the broker earns a short-term profit of two cents per share. Absent brokers' ability to bond themselves against this moral hazard, managers will refuse to pay for high-quality execution, low-quality execution will dominate the market, and investors will suffer excessive price impact that reduces their returns (Akerlof 1970).

Suppose, instead, that the manager offers to pay a broker a premium commission of seven cents per share for high-quality execution. Brokers will welcome this opportunity because it allows them to earn a surplus, or *economic rent*, of three cents per share on each trade, presumably over an indefinite time horizon assuming they refrain from cheating. If the broker were to cheat he could earn a surplus of five cents per share, but only until the manager discovered that his trades create excessive price impact. The Klein-Leffler model shows that there is some commission premium on high-quality trades sufficiently high that the long-term gain to the broker from providing high-quality execution exceeds the short-term gain from cheating. If offered a sufficient commission premium, a wealth-maximizing broker will never cheat.

The harder it is and the longer it takes for the manager to detect excessive price impact—as where the noisiness of securities prices increases—and the higher the broker's discount rate, the higher the commission premium must be to assure high-quality execution. What is more, the manager must presume any broker offering to trade for a low commission is likely to perform poorly and generate excessive price impact. Shopping between brokers for lower commissions is futile where execution quality is unobservable ex ante.[16]

In general, quality assurance requires the buyer to pay a premium price for honoring his commitment. This should come as no surprise. The average consumer routinely buys hundreds of experience goods for which he happily pays a premium price to assure quality—gasoline, golf balls, fine perfume, and even garden-variety aspirin are just a few such goods. Aspirin buyers often pay a premium price for branded tablets, for example, although the generic equivalent is far cheaper and said to be chemically identical. Studies suggest that even those consumers who buy generic aspirin for themselves tend to favor branded aspirin over generic for their children, where quality assurance is considered particularly important.[17] For the producers of high-quality goods, cutting price is simply not an option because it signals to consumers a likely reduction in quality.

If people acting on their own behalf often pay a premium price—they *pay up*—for goods so they can be confident of quality, it is reasonable that agents acting on others' behalf should do the same. Those who condemn fund managers for using investors' money to pay premium commissions for trades claim identical execution can be found for as little as a penny or two per share. The inference is that any excess commission payment above this amount provides no compensating benefit to investors, serving merely to unjustly enrich managers. Unjust enrichment is a normative claim that has little or no foundation in positive economic theory.

Soft Dollars and Directed Brokerage as Performance Bonds

The Klein-Leffler model has one additional feature. Brokers competing for institutional trades stand to earn a surplus equal to the difference between the premium commission they receive on each trade and their cost of executing high-quality trades. In the preceding example this was three cents per share. Standard economic theory tells us that abnormal profits cannot persist in a competitive environment. For normal search goods, competition takes the form of price reductions, but for experience goods a price reduction signals low quality. Consequently, brokers cannot cut their commissions. Instead, they compete by offering to post an up-front performance bond equal to the discounted present value of the quality-assuring premium over the expected time horizon and trading volume.

The use of a quality-assuring performance bond is subject to three competitive conditions. First, the bond must be large enough relative to expected commissions that the broker earns no surplus and merely covers his forgone opportunities. The performance bond capitalizes the broker's expected commission premiums, ensuring he earns only a competitive profit. Second, the bond must be nonsalvageable in the sense that the broker cannot recover it once he has paid or incurred it. Finally, the bond must take the form that provides the greatest possible benefit to the portfolio.

With soft dollars the first condition is met because brokers compete vigorously for managers' business by offering larger soft dollar research payments. The second condition is met because the manager can insist that the broker provide soft dollars up front[18] —whether in the form of third-party or in-house research—and any commitment the manager makes to use a particular broker's services is legally unenforceable as contrary to his fiduciary duty of best execution. A broker who is terminated for poor execution quality will lose its up-front bond. The remaining question is whether soft dollar research provides the greatest possible value to the portfolio. The answer is that investors benefit *more* if the bond takes the form of soft dollar research provided to the manager rather than an equivalent amount of cash paid into the portfolio.

To see this it is important to identify the main conflict of interest the manager faces. The extensive literature on the economics of agency uniformly recognizes that agents whose compensation is based on a fractional share of benefits to the principal have too little incentive to produce gains for the principal if they are required to pay the entire expense out of their own account. Following this logic, if managers were required to pay the entire expense out of their own account, mutual fund investors' concern would not be that they will overuse brokerage and research services but that they will underuse them.

Contrary to prevailing wisdom, the critical conflict of interest for fund managers is that they will tend to spend too little of their own money on raw research, devote too little labor effort to identifying mispriced securities, and do too few profitable trades. If spending a dollar out of his own pocket on research yields a two-dollar increase in portfolio wealth but the manager receives only 15 cents as his fractional share, he may decline to spend the dollar. The limiting case is known as *closet indexing*, in which the manager collects a hefty fee for active management but instead indexes the entire portfolio, saving the cost of researching mispriced securities.

It is unsurprising that the beneficiaries of managed portfolios—whether fund investors, trust beneficiaries, or pension plan sponsors—routinely subsidize their managers' use of brokerage and allow them to bundle the cost of research and other services into the brokerage commission through some form of soft dollar arrangement. Because raw research is a complement to the manager's labor effort in identifying profitable trading opportunities, by subsidizing research the fund increases the manager's effort. With increased effort the manager is likely to identify more profitable trading opportunities and to have good reason to order more trades.

Empirical work suggests soft dollars constitute a self-enforcing bond to assure high-quality brokerage execution and efficiently subsidize manager research (Horan and Johnsen 2008). But what about directed brokerage? Prior to the SEC's complete prohibition on directed brokerage it appears to have met the necessary competitive conditions. First, there is little doubt brokerage firms competed intensely for fund advisers' trading business by offering to sell shares issued by their funds to the investing public. As with soft dollars, the size of the sales effort bond should have approximated the discounted present value of the expected stream of premium brokerage commissions. Second, retail brokers' sale of fund shares to the investing public came in advance, with the manager following up by directing portfolio trades to the firm's institutional brokers based on their *past* success selling fund shares. Owing to the manager's fiduciary duty of best execution, he was free to terminate the broker with the balance of the directed brokerage trading account unpaid. A broker's costly effort selling fund shares was therefore nonsalvageable in the sense that the adviser could terminate the broker with the balance of the trading obligations unfulfilled if the adviser discovered low-quality execution.

The final question is whether a dollar's worth of extra trading commissions used to compensate brokers for their sales effort might have been worth more than a dollar paid to the portfolio in cash. In the absence of concerted sales effort most equity mutual funds would experience net redemptions approaching 18 percent per year.[19] Perhaps more important, uncertainty over near-term redemptions requires a fund to hold higher cash balances than otherwise. Relative to risky securities, cash yields a low expected return. By spending fund resources to sell fund shares to the investing public, a manager can control its net redemptions to reduce cash balances and increase investor returns. Because managers' fees provide them with only a fraction of the investment returns they generate, they would otherwise have too little incentive to spend their own resources selling fund shares. By subsidizing fund share sales, investors reduce the associated conflict of interest.

A widespread but misguided criticism of allowing managers to use fund assets to promote the sale of fund shares is that it gives the adviser a perverse incentive to increase fund assets through share sales, to which its compensation is tied, rather than to increase fund assets through investment performance. These outcomes are not mutually exclusive. By allowing the manager to reduce cash balances, fund sales effort can be an efficient form of performance bond that benefits investors more than dollar for dollar. More important, when the manager sells new shares, his added fees consist of a percentage fee based on the larger asset holdings in the current period *and* additional fees for each subsequent period in which the larger asset holdings persist. The manager's compensation is back-end loaded and contingent on continuing investor satisfaction. Making an unsuitable share sale to a new investor does little to increase the manager's long-run compensation, i.e., wealth (Johnsen 1986), because the investor is likely to become dissatisfied with an unsuitable fund and withdraw sooner rather than later.

A second and more subtle source of efficiency from directed brokerage is the indirect effect it likely had on the brokerage firm's incentive to provide high-quality portfolio trades. Having sold shares of Fund X to its client-investors, a firm that expects future portfolio commission business from Fund X is in position to increase the fund's returns (or prevent them from being eroded) by ensuring that its institutional brokers do a careful job of executing its portfolio trades. By minimizing price impact, it can improve its client-investors' fortunes. Providing the brokerage house with proper incentives to manage various relational spillovers explains why the parties characterized their relationship as a partnership.

Finally, the partner programs targeted by the SEC provided point-of-sale brokers with back-end-loaded compensation. Brokers who sold fund shares retained by investors for more than one year received trailing fees of three or more basis points per year as long as the investor held the shares.[20] In many cases these fees were paid by way of ongoing directed brokerage arrangements. The point-of-sale brokers' compensation therefore increased the longer fund investors held their shares. Holding a broker's sales effort constant, the more suitable the sale to a particular client-investor, the longer the client would have held on to the shares and the higher the discounted present value of the broker's total compensation. The broker's willingness to accept trailing fees bonds the credibility of his promise to provide an appropriate suitability determination.

As long as a dollar's worth of sales effort provided the fund with benefits exceeding a dollar in cash, directed brokerage cost fund investors nothing compared to the alternative and in fact provided it with net benefits. Recall that the size of the performance bond is set by competition, and that the brokerage commission therefore cannot be reduced without suffering a loss of execution quality. As a loyal economic agent, the manager's charge is to spend the competitively determined performance bond on any of a long list of items according to the benefits they provide to the fund. Some forms of soft dollar research surely occupy the top of the list, as recognized and protected by the Section 28(e) safe harbor, but there is no reason to think, a priori, that retail broker sales effort should be precluded from advisers' consideration under the umbrella of "brokerage services" in the soft dollar safe harbor. Presumably, the fund manager's specialized expertise in balancing the associated trade-offs is one of the benefits investors hope to capture from investing in the fund in the first place.

ISCT AND THE ETHICS OF INSTITUTIONAL BROKERAGE REBATES

In this section I make a first pass at combining ISCT and transaction cost economics. I make no claim that this is the last word on the subject. My hope is that my humble efforts here will encourage subsequent scholars to take of the task where I have left it.

The Basics of ISCT

In their book *Ties That Bind*, Donaldson and Dunfee carefully lay out the structure of ISCT and its rationale.[21] They start with the plausible proposition that businesspeople are limited by "bounded moral rationality," which leads them to the following two conclusions. First, those called on to make ethical decisions "are constrained in their ability to discover and process morally relevant facts." Second, even ethical theorists "are constrained in their ability to devise a calculus of morality that coheres well with settled moral opinions" (Donaldson and Dunfee 1999, 29). People therefore face significant ethical uncertainty, a problem compounded in business settings by the huge variety of commercial systems in which people transact.

Owing to this variety, a one-size-fits-all approach would be decidedly inefficient, and no one can doubt that efficiency is at least *one* important concern for business ethics. Just as the substance of commercial (and other) law varies from one community to the next, so too must business ethics be allowed to vary so as to efficiently fill out the behavioral interstices that lie beyond law's effective force. ISCT embraces moral free space sufficient to allow substantial variation in ethical norms across local communities.

Local communities are free within an ISCT framework to specify appropriate ethical norms for commercial conduct as the product of a microsocial contract based on constructive consent. To be authentic, these norms must meet the limited terms of the macrosocial contract derived from social contract theory and fundamental shared principles outside the community—much along the lines of Constitutional values in a federal system—that limit the scope of local community consent. These terms are informed consent, the option for community members to exit and exercise voice, and consistency with what Donaldson and Dunfee characterize as global hypernorms. Some hypernorms are procedural, such as the rights to exit and exercise voice; some are structural, such as those supporting essential political and legal institutions; and some are substantive, such as fundamental conceptions of "the right and the good" (Donaldson and Dunfee 1999, 52). Within the community, authentic norms carry a presumption of moral force as long as they are consistent with these macrosocial contract terms. Local community norms will inevitably come into conflict. This might occur because of globalizing trade that raises issues regarding conflicts of norms. It might also occur *within* an identified community that consists of various vertically related subcommunities, as with corporate stakeholders. When different community norms conflict and both are consistent with the preceding conditions, the conflict is resolved by applying the following six priority rules:

1. Transactions solely within a single community, which do not have significant adverse effects on other humans or communities, should be governed by the host community's norms.
2. Community norms for resolving priority should be applied, so long as they do not have significant adverse effects on other humans or communities.

3. The more extensive the community that is the source of the norm, the greater the priority that should be given to the norm.
4. Norms essential to the maintenance of the economic environment in which the transaction occurs should have priority over norms potentially damaging to that environment.
5. Where multiple conflicting norms are involved, patterns of consistency among the alternative norms provide a basis for prioritization.
6. Well-defined norms should ordinarily have priority over more general, less precise norms.

It is worth noting that Dunfee and Donaldson refrain from overengineering ISCT. They decline to specify the source of hypernorms. They also eschew a detailed listing of hypernorms, apparently leaving that task to ethical theorists applying ISCT as necessary to specific ethical dilemmas.

Transaction Costs and ISCT

Transaction cost economics provides a plausible and potentially empirically testable explanation for soft dollars and directed brokerage according to which they provide clear benefits to investors relative to the alternative forms of organization. With this insight, applying ISCT to these practices to determine whether they are ethical is fairly straightforward. First steps include identifying the macrosocial and microsocial communities within which these practices can be evaluated. There are many candidates for the relevant macrosocial community. A macrosocial community of "all human beings" would ensure that all possible intercommunity spillovers are taken into account, but defining the macrosocial community this broadly would surely be overly inclusive and analytically intractable. Turning the lens of the microscope a few clicks is appropriate.

I propose that the relevant macrosocial community consists of the entrepreneurs and investors who seek to sell and buy the corporate securities held, in part, by mutual funds. Assuming away substantial relevant spillovers on other dimensions, corporate entrepreneurs and investors share a common interest in maximizing the gains from trade through the supply of capital to finance commercial opportunities. There are many alternative ways to do this. Investors can buy and hold corporate securities directly through individual retail brokerage-house accounts or in-person investment advisers or trustees, or they can hold indirectly through pension plans, banks, and insurance companies. They also have the option to hold securities issued and traded in markets outside the United States.

Within the macrosocial community, investors search among the alternatives for the securities likely to provide them with the highest risk-adjusted returns net of the transaction costs of search, monitoring, risk assessment, and so on. On its face, it would appear they have ample opportunities to exit from mutual fund ownership. As it turns out, however, virtually all of these specialized financial intermediaries, both in the United States and elsewhere, engage in some form of institutional brokerage rebate. To err in favor of finding soft dollars and directed brokerage unethical, the only relevant rebate-free alternative is individual retail accounts. The local microsocial community consists of the universe of available mutual fund managers, institutional brokers, and, to some extent, retail brokers selling mutual fund shares. By hypothesis, a corporate investor seeking to exit this community would view the community of retail brokers selling corporate securities directly and managing investor accounts as the relevant alternative, although the practices followed by the various intermediaries listed previously also provide a relevant benchmark to perform the ISCT analysis. Note that exit from mutual fund share ownership to direct corporate share ownership is as simple for an investor to do as calling his retail broker and paying a small transaction fee to make the switch.

Both local communities offer investors some prospect of voice. Although few mutual fund shareholders actually cast their votes, it is far from clear that those shareholders directly holding corporate shares are any more engaged in governance. But even if they were, the effectiveness of voice in mutual fund share ownership must account for the fund's ability to vote the corporate securities it holds in its portfolio. Assuming the fund manager and its board of directors are loyal agents for the common good of fund investors when voting corporate shares, fund investors have added, though indirect, voice in the governance of their investments.

The one sticking point is whether fund shareholders are sufficiently informed about their managers' reliance on soft dollars and directed brokerage to constitute informed consent. Mutual funds are required by SEC regulations to state in their prospectus that the manager receives research from brokers as a quid pro quo for his brokerage allocation decisions. Some have argued that this blanket disclosure is insufficient and have proposed more detailed disclosure identifying which brokers the manager uses, how much trading he does with these brokers, and specifically what research products he receives in exchange. However, this and similar proposals suffer from huge deficiencies. First, keeping track of these details and effectively reporting them to fund shareholders would be costly, and at least part of these costs would be borne by shareholders in the form of higher fees. Second, understanding the details would impose direct costs on shareholders unless, of course, they chose to ignore the disclosure. In all but one of the civil cases following the SEC's action against MFS for failure to adequately disclose its directed brokerage practices, federal courts have granted summary judgment in favor of the defendants because they found the omitted details immaterial in relation to the value of the brokerage commissions at stake, something like a few pennies per \$10,000 of investment (Johnsen 2008b). As the Second Circuit Court of Appeals stated as early as 1996, "If brokerage firms are slightly inflating the cost of their transaction fees, the remedy is competition among the firms in the labeling and pricing of their services, not resort to the securities fraud provisions."[22]

Finally, and most important, the detailed information is very likely proprietary in nature. Which brokers a fund manager uses and how many trades they direct to them is a closely guarded secret. One of the main reasons to trade through a broker is to maintain anonymity to avoid price impact. It is unsurprising that an SEC proposal to mandate detailed disclosure of soft dollar brokerage arrangements was met with a storm of protest from the industry and was quickly abandoned (Johnsen 2008a). Similarly, the innovative forms of organization fund managers used in partnering with brokerage houses over directed brokerage were proprietary. No doubt they were part of the competitive process by which managers and brokers sought to prevail over business rivals. Mandating detailed disclosure of proprietary information can hardly benefit fund shareholders and would very likely hurt them over the long run.

The relevant benchmark for evaluating the partner programs, in which brokers earned back-end-loaded fees, is how investors would fare with individual retail brokerage accounts in which they hold corporate securities directly. In this setting retail brokers have traditionally earned an up-front brokerage commission on each share traded, which can be duplicated as many times as the broker can convince the client to trade. Cases of retail brokers making unsuitable recommendations and churning client accounts are legion. This is probably one reason corporate investors have gradually migrated over the past 50 years away from direct corporate share ownership and toward mutual fund share ownership. And this is true in spite of dramatic reductions in retail brokerage commissions.

The main problem with informed consent is that mutual fund investors are widely dispersed, often hold only a small fraction of a fund's shares, and are largely apathetic monitors owing to the collective action (free-rider) problem they face. No doubt collectively their buy and sell decisions reflect some measure of informed decision making. Mutual fund investments tend to flow toward funds whose managers outperform the market, for example. Simply because individual fund investors know little, in fact, about their manager's brokerage allocation practices does not mean they would object if they did know. The behavior of pension plan sponsors is a relevant example. These sponsors—the firms who manage pension assets for their workforce—directly bear any losses or gains on their portfolio investments, but they face no collective action problem. In this case, the principal is a single entity that is fully capable of monitoring its portfolio managers to gather information about their brokerage allocation practices. Yet pension plan sponsors routinely consent to allowing their managers to receive research rebates from institutional brokers.

The ethical issues at hand with soft dollars and directed brokerage are sufficiently mundane that global hypernorms generally impose no binding constraint in finding them ethical. Once having dealt with the procedural hypernorms of exit, voice, and informed consent, these practices simply do not invoke issues regarding essential political or legal institutions or fundamental conceptions of "the right and the good." It may be that the local norms held by fund shareholders conflict with those held by the fund managers and brokers on which they choose to rely. But given the ease with which investors can exit the community of fund shareholders, the fact that they have chosen not to do so makes a compelling case that soft dollars and directed brokerage are ethical. My transaction cost analysis of these practices is strongly consistent with Donaldson and Dunfee's priority rule 4: Norms essential to the maintenance of the economic environment in which the transaction occurs should have priority over norms potentially damaging to that environment.

CONCLUSION

One of my points in this chapter has been to show that institutional brokerage rebates are likely efficient given the available facts and what we now know about economic organization from transaction cost economics. Because the quality of institutional securities brokerage is difficult to assess, investors can benefit from structuring the temporal flow of costs and benefits in a way that helps to assure high quality. Efficiency increases the size of the pie, but no injustice occurs by serving one party his slice earlier rather than later.

A second point is that ISCT can benefit from further refinements based on transaction cost economics. Among other reasons, this is because innovative but efficient business practices such as soft dollar and directed brokerage often appear puzzling or even evil to outside observers, and their collective outcry of "unethical conduct" can drown out any reasoned analysis. My hope is that transaction cost economics will contribute to the evolution of ISCT and to a deeper understanding of business ethics.

NOTES

1. In contrast, closed-end funds issue shares but do not offer shareholders a redemption option. To cash out, a shareholder must sell his shares to other investors in the market.

2. See Coase (1937); and Klein, Crawford, and Alchian (1978).

3. Mutual funds can be divided into active and passive styles. An index fund attempts to duplicate a specific benchmark such as the Standard & Poor's (S&P) 500 Index and therefore involves little in the way of active management. Most actively managed mutual funds are part of a family of funds that contract for management services with a central advisory firm. Each separate fund has one or more portfolio managers, who are employees of the advisory firm (or possibly independent contractors), each with specific responsibilities and separately negotiated compensation paid by the adviser. In a stand-alone fund the adviser and the manager may be one and the same. For simplicity, I use the terms *adviser* and *manager* interchangeably unless the context requires greater care.

4. Total transaction costs include the brokerage commission, which is an out-of-pocket expense, but it also includes any adverse change in the price (whether bid or ask) at which the broker sells or buys a security between the moment the manager decides to trade and the moment the trade is fully executed—this change is the so-called *price impact*. Price impact is a difficult-to-observe opportunity cost rather than an out-of-pocket expense.

5. Brokerage commissions are added into the price basis of a portfolio security when it is purchased and are netted out when it is sold. Gross investment returns are therefore net of commissions (and other transaction costs).

6. A basis point is one one-hundredth (1/100) of a percentage point.

7. See, for example, Johnsen (1994); see also 2006 Guidance.

8. 15 U.S.C. section 78bb(e) (1988) (as amended).

9. The term *directed brokerage* is sometimes used to refer to the situation in which a pension plan sponsor directs a manager of its pension portfolio to send brokerage commission business to specific brokers in exchange for various benefits they provide to the plan sponsor.

10. Investment Advisors Act Release No. 2224, Investment Company Act Release No. 26,409, 82 SEC Docket 2036 (Mar. 31, 2004).

11. Compared to transacting at a uniform price, for example, price discrimination redistributes the gains from trade between the parties.

12. Johnnie L. Roberts and Richard Gibson, "'Friction' Theorist Wins Economics Nobel," *Wall Street Journal*, October 16, 1991, B1.

13. Jensen and Meckling (1976).

14. The SEC's 2003 *Concept Release* quoted revealing statements by others at note 32: "Virtually all the major institutions have a transaction-cost measuring system in place. They compare their actual execution costs to pre-trade benchmarks from models or peer comparisons from different firms. That puts pressure on the trading desks to control costs. So the guys who aren't doing it are being left behind." (See Alison Sahoo, "SEC Weighs Trading Cost Rule, Seeks Industry Input," Ignites.com, July 22, 2003, quoting Ananth Madhavan.) Additionally, "[M]ore pension funds and investment managers are measuring transaction costs—either by using proprietary systems or third party services. . . . Since the wrenching bear market of 2000–2002, institutions have learned that transaction costs can be a significant drag on performance, and they have begun managing them as intently as they research stocks." (Justin Schack, "Trading Places," *Institutional Investor*, November 2003, 32.) *Request for Comments on Measures to Improve Disclosure of Mutual Fund Transaction Costs*, Investment Company Act Release No. 26,313, 68 Fed. Reg. 74,820, at 74,820–21 (Dec. 24, 2003).

15. Front-running occurs when a broker or his tippee purposely trades a security ahead of the client's trades in anticipation of a price correction. The inevitable result is price impact.

16. For a legal case in which a famous law and economics scholar and now Seventh Circuit judge recognizes that it is not an option for the parties to transact for lower commissions, see *Wsol v. Fiduciary Management Associates, Inc., and East West Institutional Services, Inc.*, 266 F.3d 654 (Seventh Circuit, 2001). (J. Posner: "In either case, FMA, which is to say the fund, would have paid six cents a share per trade; that is the standard fee and there is no proof that FMA could have obtained comparable trading services for less.")

17. See Klein and Leffler (1981, 18) (in 1978 the market share of generic aspirin for children was less than 1 percent compared to a 7 percent share for generic adult aspirin) and http://www.econlib.org/Library/Enc/Brand Names.html.

18. "The traditional soft dollar arrangement works on a simple formula: The soft dollar house provides research or other services to a trader in exchange for a certain amount of trading business *in the future*. The arrangement is normally defined by a ratio: say two dollars' worth of trading commissions for every dollar's worth of research." Jack Willoughby, "Autranet Angers Rivals Again with Soft Dollar Proposal; Suggests SEC Ban Commission Commitments," *Investment Dealers' Digest*, February 20, 1995, 5.

19. See Investment Company Institute, *Investment Company Fact Book* 117 (47th ed. 2007), available at www.icifactbook.org/pdf/2007_factbook.pdf.

20. Morgan Stanley DW, Inc., Securities Act Release No. 8339, Exchange Act Release No. 48,789, 81 SEC Docket 1993, 1993 (Nov. 17, 2003).

21. For related work see Dunfee, Smith, and Ross (1999) and Dunfee (2006).

22. *Feinman v. Dean Witter Reynolds, Inc.*, 84 F.3d 539, 541 (2d Cir. 1996).

REFERENCES

Akerlof, G. A. 1970. The market for "lemons": Quality uncertainty and the market mechanism. *Quarterly Journal of Economics* 84:488–500.

Coase, R. H. 1937. The nature of the firm. *Economica N.S.* 4:386–405.

———. 1960. The problem of social cost. *Journal of Law and Economics* 3:1–44.

———. 1979. Payola in radio and television broadcasting. *Journal of Law and Economics* 22:269–328.

Dunfee, T. W. 2006. A critical perspective of Integrative Social Contract Theory: Recurring criticisms and next generation research topics. *Journal of Business Ethics* 68:303–328.

Donaldson, T. and T. W. Dunfee. 1999. *Ties that bind: A social contracts approach to business ethics*. Boston: Harvard Business School Press.

Dunfee, T. W., N. C. Smith, and W. T. Ross. 1999. Social contracts and marketing ethics. *Journal of Marketing* 63:14–32.

Hayek, F. 1945. The use of knowledge in society. *American Economic Review* 35:519–530.

Horan, S. M., and D. B. Johnsen. 2008. Can soft dollar brokerage benefit the principal? The case of soft dollar brokerage. *International Review of Law & Economics* 28:56–77.

Jensen, Michael C., and William H. Meckling. 1976. Theory of the firm: Managerial behavior, agency costs, and ownership structure. *Journal of Financial Economics* 3:305–360.

Johnsen, D. B. 1986. Wealth is value. *Journal of Legal Studies* 15:263–288.

———. 1994. Property rights to investment research: The agency costs of soft dollar brokerage. *Yale Journal on Regulation* 11:75–113.

———. 2008a. The SEC's mistaken ban on directed brokerage: A transaction cost analysis. *Arizona State Law Journal* 40:1241–1295.

———. 2008b. The SEC's 2006 soft dollar guidance: Law and economics. *Cardozo Law Review* 30:1545–1614.

———. 2009. The SEC's 2006 soft dollar guidance: Law and economics. *Cardozo Law Review*, forthcoming.

Klein, Benjamin, and Keith B. Leffler. 1981. The role of market forces in assuring contractual performance. *Journal of Political Economy* 89:615–641.

Klein, Benjamin, Robert G. Crawford, and Armen A. Alchian. 1978. Vertical integration, appropriable rents, and the competitive contracting process. *Journal of Law and Economics* 21:297.

Klein, B., and K. M. Murphy. 1988. Vertical restraints as contract enforcement mechanisms. *Journal of Law & Economics* 31:265–297.

Klein, B., and Joshua D. Wright. 2007. The economics of slotting contracts. *Journal of Law and Economics* 50:421–454.

Wright, J. D. 2007. Slotting contracts and consumer welfare. *Antitrust Law Journal* 74:439–472.

ABOUT THE AUTHOR

D. Bruce Johnsen is a professor of law at George Mason University School of Law, a leading center for law and economics scholarship. Professor Johnsen holds a BA, an MA, and a PhD, all in economics, from the University of Washington, as well as a JD from Emory University. His scholarship focuses on the economics of property rights, which allows him to address topics as diverse as antitrust, principal-agent relations, Native American institutions, corporate finance and financial institutions, mutual fund organization and management, securities regulation, and business ethics. He has held positions in the Department of Management at Texas A&M University; the Office of Economic Analysis at the U.S. Securities and Exchange Commissions; and, before coming to George Mason University, the Department of Legal Studies at the Wharton School of the University of Pennsylvania. He has published widely in both peer-reviewed social science journals and law reviews and in the popular press.

CHAPTER 19

Pension Funds

DAVID HESS
Assistant Professor of Business Law and Business Ethics, Ross School of Business, University of Michigan

INTRODUCTION

Policy makers and financial planners traditionally refer to financial security for retirement as a "three-legged stool." The three legs are payments from the government (i.e., Social Security), the individual's own personal savings, and pension payments provided by the individual's employer. Controversies and concerns surround all three legs. Some fear that Social Security in the United States is in a crisis and will run a deficit in the near future. Personal savings rates are below levels suggested by experts. Many believe that public pension plans are dangerously underfunded and that private pension plans have shifted significant amounts of risk of sufficient retirement funding onto employees.

This chapter focuses on the concerns related to that third leg of the stool—pension funds—and discusses the ethical issues surrounding the management of pensions to ensure they responsibly meet the retirement needs of employees. As an initial matter, it is important to present some basic background information to guide the discussion that follows. Pension plans are classified based on their sponsor. Public pensions are for any state or local government employee, including public school teachers, police officers, and judges. Private pensions, by contrast, are sponsored by private companies. Typically, private pensions are administered by the company. In some cases, however, if the company has unionized employees, then the union may have significant control over the pension. In the United States, private pensions are regulated by the Employee Retirement Income Security Act of 1974 (ERISA), while the governance of union pensions is regulated by the 1947 Taft-Hartley Act.

Pension plans are also classified based on whether they are a defined benefit (DB) plan or a defined contribution (DC) plan. Under a defined benefit plan, the employer promises to pay an employee a set retirement income based on factors such as the employee's salary and years of service with the employer. To fund that commitment, the employer sets aside sufficient funds to pay those future benefits. In addition to the employer's contribution, employees also typically are required to contribute a percentage of their income to the plan. In a defined contribution plan, the employer and employee contribute funds to an individual retirement account, such as what is commonly known as a 401(k) account in the United States, which

is under the employee's control. Both the employer's and the employee's participation is voluntary, and often the employer's contribution is contingent on the
employee's contribution (e.g., the employer matches funds contributed by the employee up to a specified amount). The employee's retirement income then depends
on the employer's and employee's contributions to the account and any investment
earnings on those funds. In the United States, the vast majority of public pensions
are DB plans while private pensions are more commonly becoming DC plans.

This chapter proceeds by setting out the issues for private pensions and public
pensions separately. Running through both discussions is the idea of fiduciary
duties for those individuals with authority over the pensions. Simply stated, a
fiduciary duty is a legal obligation (through either the common law or statutory
law, such as ERISA) that requires one party to act in the best interests of another.
This is a relationship based on trust, where one party entrusts financial assets, for
example, to another for that party to manage prudently. What fiduciary duties
require of individuals is at the heart of many of the ethical issues for pensions.
The last section of this chapter discusses shareholder activism and social investing
by pension plans. This includes a discussion of both private and public pensions,
though these are primarily issues for public plans.

PRIVATE PENSIONS PLANS

Private pension plans have undergone significant changes in the past few decades.
This section sets out those changes and the ethical issues they have created. The
first subsection discusses the issues created by the shift from DB plans to DC plans.
The next two subsections focus on issues related to the use of DC plans, including
how the use of these plans impacts the ability of employees to build up sufficient
assets for retirement and the duties of the various fiduciaries of a DC plan.

Defined Benefit versus Defined Contribution Plans

Since the early 1980s there has been a dramatic shift in the private sector from
defined benefit plans to defined contribution plans. This includes both the establishment of new plans as DC plans and the decision of employers to change existing
DB plans to DC plans. In 1981 in the United States, of those enrolled in a private
pension plan, 81 percent were in a DB plan. By 2003, that number dropped to
38 percent (James 2008). This shift is due to a variety of factors. DB plans may hurt
a corporation's competitive position due to their growing costs and because they
can impede corporate flexibility (e.g., restructurings, resource allocation) (Clark
and Monk 2008). Deregulation and globalization likely amplified these competitiveness factors. The dramatic nature of the shift to DC plans may be due in part
to the fact that the costs of DB plans were largely unexpected by employers since
pension commitments grew incrementally over time (Clark and Monk 2008). Also
playing a role in the shift away from DB plans is the reduction of government
tax incentives to fund DB plans and changing accounting rules on how to report
pension liabilities (Smith 2007; Walsh 2006).

The shift toward DC plans raises ethical issues related to the choice between
the use of a DB or DC plan and, if the employer elects to shift to a DC plan,
how that shift is implemented. An employer's decision to close a DB plan to

participants and shift employees to a DC plan or to modify its DB plan to a cash balance plan or some other form (see Johnson-Cramer and Phillips 2007) can have a significant impact on employees. Employees have an interest in a sufficient and secure retirement benefit, though there are clearly differences among employees. For example, employees nearing retirement may favor a DB plan, while employees who are early in their careers and expect to change jobs multiple times in the future may favor the portability of a DC plan. Core issues for all employers include fairness of any pension plan changes to existing employees (especially those close to retirement or in retirement), the shifting of investment risks to employees, and any potential reduction of retirement income. For public corporations, shareholders may push against some of these concerns, since they have interests in a company's ability to reduce costs and ensure the corporation has flexibility over the long term to adjust to market conditions, which typically point toward the adoption of a DC plan.

At the heart of this discussion is the core ethical issue of determining the extent of the employer's responsibility for ensuring that employees have an adequate source of income for retirement. For those who believe that DC plans shift too much of that responsibility to employees, critics point out the potential for DB plans to fail due to bankruptcy of the sponsor, payments to retirees that are not offset by new contributions from active employees, and other factors (Gavin and Sloan 2007). Private DB plans are typically insured by the Pension Benefits Guarantee Corporation (PBGC), a federal government corporation that is funded by insurance premiums of participating companies. However, many believe that the PBGC is facing a funding crisis (Gavin and Sloan 2007). In addition, the PBGC may only pay retirees a portion of what they would have received had the company not terminated the plan (Werhane 2007). An additional important factor for determining if an employer is meeting its responsibilities to employees is the employer's motivation for any changes that adversely affect employees, which can range from necessary changes to meet the demands of the business environment to simple attempts of financially healthy companies to opportunistically reduce costs (Windsor 2007).

Ensuring Adequate Retirement Income under a Defined Contribution Plan

Under a DC plan, employees are allowed, but not required, to contribute a certain percentage of their income to a tax-favored retirement account. The employer also may contribute to that account, either by matching employee contributions or making noncontingent contributions. Employees choose how to invest those assets within the options provided by the employer, and therefore they bear the risks of ensuring that they have set aside sufficient assets and invested those assets appropriately to support themselves during retirement.

Many workers are not establishing retirement accounts that will provide them with adequate retirement income. For example, a recent Government Accountability Office (GAO) report found that only one-third of employees were participating in a DC plan with their current employer (and significantly fewer among lower-income employees), and those who were participating had little assets in the plan (GAO 2008b). An additional concern for those participating employees is that many are simply making poor investment choices, such as investing heavily in their employer's stock or avoiding equity investments altogether. This again raises issues of the employer's responsibility to ensure that employees are adequately saving for their retirement.

The Pension Protection Act of 2006 gives employers the ability to attempt to correct some of these problems. First, the Act allows employers to automatically enroll new employees into pension plans and then give them the opportunity to opt out if they so choose. This provision was based on behavioral research showing that individuals are more likely to stay with the default option rather than opt in or opt out (see, e.g., Madrian and Shea 2001). Thus, an employee's right to choose whether to participate is still respected, but the policy makes it more likely that an employee will set aside money for investment.

Second, employers are allowed to provide investment advice to employees through Eligible Investment Advice Arrangements (EIAAs). Prior to the Act, many pensions provided investment education, but not investment advice (Muir 2004). Investment education provides employees with general information on the basics of investing for retirement needs, while investment advice includes personalized recommendations on specific mutual funds, asset allocations, and other matters based on such factors as the individual's financial situation, age, and risk tolerance (Muir 2004). Because this advice is expensive to provide and makes the provider a *fiduciary* (discussed shortly) and potentially liable for inappropriate advice, plan sponsors were unwilling to provide these services. The goal of EIAAs is to make it more likely that employers will make services available to provide sound advice to employees, while also ensuring that the advice provider does not have any conflicts of interest that would influence that advice. For example, under the Act a "fiduciary advisor" cannot receive fees that vary based on the employees' investment options (though, apparently, it is still possible for the adviser to steer the employee toward investments that charge a higher fee). Alternatively, the investment advice can be provided based on a computer model independently certified to be unbiased. By following these requirements, the employer receives liability protection.

Even if an employee is participating in a DC plan, he may harm his chances of having adequate assets for retirement by borrowing against the retirement plan, taking a withdrawal due to a proven financial hardship, or simply cashing out a plan when changing employers. Withdrawals and cash-outs are harmful not only because those assets are now no longer available for retirement, but also because they are taxed at that time as income and may include a penalty for early withdrawal. With respect to loans, employees can typically borrow against their retirement plan for any reason without penalty if they pay back the funds with interest within five years. Employees take advantage of this option to pay medical bills, make housing payments, or pay down credit card debt (Joyner 2008; Weller 2008). Although the loan option sounds valuable to employees, such loans can be extremely costly in the long run. According to one special interest group, a 35-year-old who borrows $30,000 from his retirement fund and repays it over five years can lose $200,000 in retirement savings if the expected rate of return is 6.25 percent, and $600,000 if the rate of return is 10 percent (Joyner 2008).

Some companies have been criticized for making such withdrawals too easy or tempting for employees. For example, some companies provide a service that allows employees to borrow against their private pension by using what is essentially a debit card (Gannon 2008). In other cases, investment adviser encourage employees to take legally permitted penalty-free early withdraws at age 59 1/2, retire early, and invest those funds in other investment vehicles that will supposedly earn a higher rate of return. The Financial Industry Regulatory Authority (FINRA) has sought penalties against firms engaging in such scams that tout unrealistic potential rates of return and provide inadequate counseling on the potential for the employee to lose his entire retirement savings (Gannon 2008).

Fiduciary Duties in Defined Contribution Plans

Under ERISA, a large number of people are potentially considered fiduciaries of the plan and therefore have special obligations of trust to the plan participants. First, the retirement plan must name at least one party (e.g., a specific person, an officeholder, or a committee) as the fiduciary with control over the plan. Second, anyone who exercises discretion in administering the plan or exercising control of its assets is also a fiduciary under ERISA. This includes investment advisers for the plan, but not necessarily accountants or lawyers who are working in their professional capacities to provide advice for the plan. It is important to note that although certain people may be fiduciaries of the plan, such as a member of the board of directors, they only have fiduciary duties with respect to acts on behalf of the plan and not with respect to other company business-related decisions, such as establishing the plan in the first place or determining the employer's contribution for each employee in a DC plan (U.S. Department of Labor 2006; Muir and Schipani 2007; GAO 2008b).

The obligations of these fiduciaries under ERISA developed out of common-law duties of loyalty and care found in trust law. If a fiduciary breaches one of his duties, that individual may be liable for any losses suffered by the plan. First, fiduciaries have a duty of loyalty to act "for the exclusive purpose" of "providing benefits to participants and their beneficiaries." For example, the duty of loyalty is potentially violated if an employer selects a service provider that does not charge a fee to the employer, but passes those fees on to the plan participants (GAO 2008b). Second, fiduciaries have a duty to act with the "care, skill, prudence, and diligence ... that a prudent man acting in a like capacity and familiar with such matters would use."[1] The "prudent man" standard requires fiduciaries to have expertise in investments or hire someone with that expertise to perform the investment functions.

The employer (the sponsor of the plan) that lacks expertise in certain areas of pension administration can fulfill its duty of care by hiring external advisers to make those decisions, such as deciding on the menu of investments available to employees. The employer, however, must still monitor the performance of any such adviser and ensure that the provider does not have any conflicts of interest that could influence its advice. The employer has this duty even if the adviser becomes a fiduciary of the plan, and therefore also has a duty of loyalty to the plan (GAO 2008b). An example of a potential violation of the duty of loyalty by an adviser would be an adviser who plays a role in the selection of the investment options to be included in the plan but also has relationships with potential investment product providers that causes the adviser to select products with higher fees or lower performance than the available alternatives.

PUBLIC PENSION PLANS

Understanding the ethical issues in public pensions requires an understanding of their governance. Public pensions are overseen by a board of trustees that has authority over such matters as investing the plan's assets, administering the plan (e.g., overseeing contributions to the plan, making payments to retirees, and hiring staff), and ruling on complaints filed by beneficiaries. In some cases, one or more of these responsibilities is given to a different government entity. For example, it is not uncommon for one investment board to manage the investments of multiple state and local plans. In some cases, such as in Connecticut, the state treasurer has authority over investment decisions. If the board of trustees has authority over investments, it must determine (with the advice of staff and consultants) the investment policy and strategy and then hire internal and/or external investment managers to carry out the strategy. In administering the plan, the board often has control over such varied matters as making the actuarial assumptions that determine the government's contribution to the plan and determining cost-of-living adjustments for retirees' payments.

The trustees who make these decisions are appointed to the board in one of three ways: (1) those elected by plan members (either retired or active); (2) *ex officio* trustees who serve due to their public office (e.g., state treasurer); or (3) those appointed by a government official or committee. Public pensions can vary significantly in the distribution of board seats among these different categories. For example, on some pension boards, member-elected trustees hold the majority of seats, but on others such trustees are completely absent (Hess 2005). Similar to private pension fiduciaries, the trustees have duties of loyalty and care. The source of these duties is not ERISA—which does not apply to public pensions—but from common-law rules and the state-level statutes that established the plans.

There are three key stakeholders to public pension plans (Hess and Impavido 2004). First, there are the plan participants—which includes both active and retired members—who are interested in the certainty and adequacy of their benefits, as well as the amount of their required contributions to the plan. Second, the government has an interest in a plan that is run efficiently and has strong investment returns, since these factors may reduce the government's required contribution to the plan and free up the funds for other uses. Moreover, a poorly run plan with significant underfunding can have a negative impact on such matters as negotiations with employee unions, property values, and bond and credit ratings (D'Arcy et al. 1999; Hess and Impavido 2004). Third, the taxpayers are the stakeholders ultimately responsible for any underfunding, since taxpayer funds must be used to make up any shortfall. As indicated earlier, there is no uniformity in how these different stakeholder groups are represented on the board, if they are represented at all.

Conflicts of Interest

In governing the pension plan, each category of trustees has significant potential conflicts of interest. These conflicts can be due to a trustee's own personal financial interests or to the trustee's interest in some broader social or political goals. With respect to personal interests, the most basic problem is referred to as *pay to play*, where a money manager, for example, must make some form of donation or gift to the trustee (e.g., a contribution to the trustee's political campaign, a charitable donation in the trustee's name, or meals and entertainment) to receive any consideration for a contract from the fund (Chernoff 2006). Thus, investment managers and others may be selected on the basis of political donations and gifts rather than on merit, which can negatively impact fund performance. In addition, there have been reports of investment management companies hiring trustees after winning a contract with the pension fund or providing trustees with honoraria for attending investment conferences sponsored by that manager (Barrett and Greene 2007). Likewise, trustees rely heavily on consultants, who may have pay-to-play relationships with potential investment managers that would influence the advice those consultants provide (Munnell and Sunden 2005).

Some pensions have attempted to handle these problems by imposing financial limits on donations or gifts, requiring trustees to recuse themselves from decisions where there are potential conflicts, and punishing violators (Chernoff 2006). Some reform proposals also impose limits on investment managers' donations to the governor, since the governor often can appoint trustees or otherwise exert political influence over politically affiliated trustees (Hess 2005).

Trustees also have been criticized for using their position to take actions that further social or political goals not directly related to the beneficiaries' interests. In some cases, the trustees may seek to use the pension's assets to further their own political aspirations. For example, critics claim that some trustees engage their pensions in shareholder activism as a way to improve the trustees' public profile and reputation, rather than in an attempt to improve the pension fund's returns (Romano 1993). The most common criticism is that some politically affiliated trustees use their position to direct government funds away from the pension plan and into other government programs. In some cases, the government simply does not make required contributions to the plan. In other situations, the trustees modify actuarial assumptions in order to reduce the government's required contribution. For example, raising the expected rate of return on investments by 100 basis points (e.g., from 8 percent to 9 percent) can result in a 20 to 25 percent decrease in the government's required contribution (GAO 1996).

Several studies have found that pensions manipulate their expected rate of return and other assumptions to reduce required contributions during periods of fiscal stress (and especially for state funds if the state has a balanced budget amendment) (see Hess [2005] for a review). Politically affiliated trustees have strong incentives to engage in these behaviors because manipulating assumptions not only reduces the required contribution but it can also create the appearance of a more fully funded pension plan. There is some evidence that the presence of member-elected trustees on the board protects against such manipulation (Hsin and Mitchell 1997). Because these trustees' interests are more directly aligned with the beneficiaries, they have an incentive to monitor the behavior of the politically affiliated trustees. Some pensions have instituted reforms to attempt to reduce political influence, such as having the pension hire legal counsel and auditors who are independent of government (Barrett and Greene 2007).

Board Competence and Commitment

A significant challenge facing boards of public pensions is getting trustees with the needed investment expertise and willingness to commit to the board. Many trustees are elected from the plan membership and often do not have the necessary expertise to manage a multimillion-dollar investment fund. In one study, a trustee stated, "Our board members have a three-year term of office, and the learning curve is at least two years" (Hess 2007, 261). Ex officio trustees, who serve due to their political office, may have greater expertise but have priorities elsewhere that cause them to miss important board meetings or fail to prepare adequately (Hess 2005). These factors can lead to the board simply taking actions based on what other pensions are doing (which may not be right for that pension); continuing actions taken by prior boards without careful analysis (e.g., renewing contracts with service providers without reviewing their performance relative to the market of available service providers); or simply acting upon misinformation (Barrett and Greene 2007). One example is pension funds investing in hedge funds when they do not have the expertise to fully understand the investment and its risks and opportunities (GAO 2008a). Reforms used by pensions have included education requirements for trustees, the appointment of investment expert trustees, moving investment decisions to a state board, and prohibitions or limits on particular types of investments (such as hedge funds).

SHAREHOLDER ACTIVISM AND SOCIAL INVESTING

One of the most controversial aspects of DB pensions funds—and especially for public pension funds—is their involvement in shareholder activism and social investing. Shareholder activism refers to pensions placing direct pressure on specific corporations to change their corporate governance practices or their policies on social or environmental issues. Social investing includes refusing to invest in corporations based on some aspect of their social and environmental performance and the incorporation of these nonfinancial factors into the fund's investment policies and practices.

Public pension funds are significantly more active on these issues than private DB pension funds. Private pensions are not active because a corporation does not want its pension to challenge the governance practices of another corporation, since that simply invites retaliation in the future (Useem 1996). In addition, private pension funds are managed mostly externally, and those external money managers provide services for many corporations. Thus, they will not want to vote against management at any particular company, since that may harm their chances of getting business at that company or others in the future (Useem 1996). To a significant degree, this holds, as well, for mutual funds that contract with private pension DC plans. These funds may treat client and nonclient corporations the same, but they use overall voting policies that are management-friendly (Davis and Kim 2005).

There are several reasons for the activism of public pension plans. First, they are independent from management pressures. Second, their political oversight may encourage antimanagement rhetoric against large corporations, which, as discussed later, is also a significant point of criticism. Third, some public pensions have become so large that rather than selling their shares in a company with problems, it makes more sense to engage the corporation and seek improvement (Useem 1996). This is especially true for pensions that have large portions of the portfolio indexed. Fourth, because public pensions seek to provide retirement security for current and past employees, they are concerned more with the long-term performance of their investments than with short-term gains. Fifth, many large pension are what some call *universal owners*, which means that because their investments cover the entire market, they are more concerned with the health of the entire economy than with the financial health of any particular firm (Hawley and Williams 2000). Thus, for example, any short-term gains a corporation receives from externalizing environmental costs is offset by the negative impact those costs have elsewhere in the economy, which affects the performance of the pension's entire portfolio over the long term. It is important to note, however, that although public pensions are closely tied to shareholder activism and social investing, historically only a handful of very large public pensions have been very active (Choi and Fisch 2008; Hess 2007).

Union pension funds are also very active shareholders, and often work directly with public pensions on shareholder campaigns. Starting in the 1990s, union pension funds became very active on corporate governance issues. In some cases, these actions were designed to improve the corporation's overall value for all shareholders, but in other cases their actions were designed to benefit workers at the expense of the nonunion shareholders (Schwab and Thomas 1998; see also Marens 2004, 2008). The use of their power to benefit workers is checked by the fact that union pensions must gain the support of other shareholders to have any chance of forcing changes in corporate behavior (Schwab and Thomas 1998). Although some claim that union activism is troublesome because it is designed to benefit unions at the expense of other shareholders, others argue that passive investment in the equity markets by unions can only serve to harm workers' interests with their own investments (Baker and Fung 2001).

Public pensions became involved in shareholder activism in the 1970s and 1980s when religious investors and others filed shareholder proposals encouraging corporations to adopt the Sullivan Principles, which concerned corporations' operations in apartheid South Africa (Eisenhofer, Barry, and Levin 2007). In some cases state laws were passed requiring divestment, and in other cases the board acted on its own initiative. Other early major campaigns that solidified public pensions as shareholder activists included the Valdez Principles on environmental issues and the MacBride Principles on employment discrimination in Northern Ireland. These were followed by tobacco divestment in the 1990s and divestment from companies doing business in Sudan in the 2000s. These campaigns recognized the unique nature of public pensions, which involves investing state funds directly in corporations. For example, many questioned the logic of the government winning large financial settlements against the tobacco companies and then investing those funds directly in those companies through government pensions.

With respect to corporate governance issues, the California Public Employees' Retirement System (CalPERS) was a pioneer of shareholder activism in the mid-1980s and is still the most well-known shareholder activist. Common corporate governance issues raised by activist pension plans include antitakeover defenses, board structure, and CEO compensation. A common means of pressuring for these changes is the filing of shareholder proposals. In such a proposal, a shareholder requests that a corporation submit some proposed change to a shareholder vote at the corporation's annual meeting. These proposals are only advisory, which means that even if the majority of shareholders vote in favor the proposal, it is not binding on the corporation. However, even proposals that receive well under a majority of shareholder votes when management is recommending a vote against the proposal are viewed as successful and can influence corporate behavior.

In addition to corporate governance matters, shareholder proposals also cover social and environmental issues. Common environmental issues relate to disclosure on how corporations are preparing for any future greenhouse gas regulations and how corporate strategy accounts for the risks of climate change to their business. Social issues include policies on nondiscrimination based on sexual orientation, disclosure of political contributions, and labor standards in developing countries.

In addition to issuing shareholder proposals and developing voting policies on the issues, a few public pension funds have engaged in social investing to encourage greater corporate responsibility. The most common form is negative screening, where the fund divests its holdings in corporations engaging in certain actions, such as divestment from companies doing business in Sudan, as mentioned earlier. A few have moved past just negative social screening and attempt to use positive screens, as well as generally incorporate social and environmental issues into their investment decisions. Some pensions, for example, are attempting to assess how well their external money managers are considering the risks of climate change when making investment decisions (Cooper 2008). Others have taken actions that support the ability of investors to engage in social investing (e.g., pressing for disclosure on greenhouse gases).

Economically targeted investments (ETIs) are a final form of social investing. These are investments designed to improve the local economy where the pension fund beneficiaries live and work, such as by creating jobs or improving low-income housing opportunities (GAO 1995; Hagerman, Clark, and Hebb 2007). Although some initial empirical evidence showed that ETIs reduced such funds' investment performance, more recent studies show no impact (see Hess [2005] for a review). These results can potentially be explained by guidelines issued in the 1990s by the Department of Labor and others that supported the use of ETIs as long as such investments were prudent, even if they did not provide those extra benefits. Current proponents of ETIs claim they are underused, and that in addition to providing significant community benefits, they also can help to diversify the fund's portfolio and achieve a competitive rate of return (Hagerman, Clark, and Hebb 2007).

Do Trustees' Fiduciary Duties Permit Activism and Social Investing?

Since the campaigns to divest from corporations doing business in apartheid South Africa, there have been significant concerns about the restrictions that fiduciary duties place on trustees' ability to engage in social investing and on the appropriateness of making investment decisions on such ethical issues. Some states (e.g., Connecticut) have expressly eliminated the fiduciary duty issue concerns by legislating that the trustee of the state pension fund "may" consider the social and environmental implications of any investment decision (Hess 2007).

Although still unclear in the minds of many trustees, recent reviews support the claim that social investing is not a violation of a trustee's fiduciary duties (Freshfields Bruckhaus Deringer 2005). To understand this, it is important to remember that the trustees' duty is not to maximize the value of individual investments but to improve the value of their entire investment portfolio (Freshfields Bruckhaus Deringer 2005). The duty of loyalty is not violated as long as the trustees are incorporating social and environmental factors into their investment decisions in the expectation of creating long-term value for their portfolio. If, however, the trustees take an action to further their own personal political or social beliefs, then the duty of loyalty may be violated. Likewise, actions designed to directly benefit some third party without regard to the risk/return profile of the investment also would violate the duty of loyalty. However, trustees may consider the social and environmental benefits to society if the investment has a risk/return profile commensurate to other similar investments. With respect to the duty of care, to the extent that social and environmental factors have the potential to impact an investment's return and risk profile, those factors can (and possibly in some cases must) be taken into account. This same analysis also applies to the voting of proxies on social and environmental issues.

This basic analysis applies to both public pensions and private DB pensions operating under ERISA. For example, with respect to proxies, the Department of Labor has stated that voting rights are assets of the plan and that plan managers have a fiduciary duty to vote the shares prudently. The Department of Labor has also stated:

> An investment policy that contemplates activities intended to monitor or influence the management of corporations in which the plan owns stock is consistent with a fiduciary's obligations under ERISA where the responsible fiduciary concludes that there is a reasonable expectation that such monitoring or communication with management, by the plan alone or together with other shareholders, is likely to enhance the value of the plan's investment in the corporation, after taking into account the costs involved.[2]

Criticisms of Shareholder Activism by Pensions

Shareholder activism remains highly controversial. In addition to raising issues related to fiduciary duties, it raises issues of costs and political motivations, both of which can reduce investment returns. This general wariness over government assets being invested in the market has a long history, since even in the 1990s many public pensions had strict limits on the amount of assets that could be invested in equities or had complete bans on such investments (Useem and Hess 2001).

With respect to costs, some suggest that public pension activism does not improve firm performance because the funds are not targeting the right issues or are using a one-size-fits-all approach to governance issues that is not appropriate (Romano 2001; for a review of studies on the effectiveness of shareholder activism, see Gillan and Starks 2007). Thus, they argue, it is a waste of the pension's resources. Others, however, point to the "CalPERS effect"—where corporations that CalPERS has targeted for corporate governance reforms have had significant financial improvements—and argue that targeted activism can be effective (see Eisenhoffer et al. 2007). With respect to social issues, critics maintain that a divestment campaign imposes costs on the pension fund but is unlikely to be effective in creating social change. The critics maintain that boycotting a company's stock will have no effect on that corporation's behavior, since it will not have an impact on the company's stock value (Munnell and Sunden 2005). Thus, the pension fund is devoting attention and resources away from risk/return factors and toward efforts that have no financial or social benefit.

The other major criticism is that activism is driven by political motivations rather than fulfillment of fiduciary obligations (Romano 2001; Bainbridge 2006). The primary example of critics is the attempt of CalPERS to remove the CEO of Safeway Inc. in 2004. CalPERS claimed that it acted based on Safeway's poor performance, but critics claimed that CalPERS (whose board includes union trustees) acted in retaliation for Safeway's hard bargaining with its employees' union (Bainbridge 2006). Likewise, social investment decisions are claimed to be made on the personal political preferences of the trustees, rather than preferences expressed by the fund's beneficiaries and other stakeholders (Munnell and Sunden 2005; Entine 2005).

CONCLUSION

This chapter has reviewed the significant ethical issues raised in designing pension plans to ensure adequate retirement income for private sector and public sector employees. For private sector employees, the increased use of DC plans has shifted responsibility for ensuring adequate assets for retirement from the employer to the employee. This shift has raised significant ethical issues, including conflict-of-interest issues for those advising employees on financial matters and for those that are considered fiduciaries under ERISA. For public pension plans, there are significant governance concerns, including conflicts of interest for members of the board of trustees that impact the investment of pensions' assets. Additional ethical issues are raised by some public pensions' history of social investing and shareholder activism.

NOTES

1. ERISA, 29 United States Code Service, section 1104.
2. Interpretive Bulletin Relating to the Employee Retirement Income Security Act of 1974, 29 C.F.R. § 2509.94-2(3) (1994).

REFERENCES

Bainbridge, Stephen M. 2006. The case for limited shareholder voting rights. *UCLA Law Review* 53:601–636.

Baker, Dean, and Archon Fung. 2001. Collateral damage: Do pension fund investments hurt workers. In *Working capital: The power of labor's pensions*, ed. Archon Fung, Tessa Hebb and Joel Rogers. Ithaca, NY: Cornell University Press.

Barrett, Katherine, and Richard Greene. 2007. The $3 trillion challenge. *Governing*, October: 26–32.

Chernoff, Joel. 2006. Calstrs cracks down on gifts and contributions from vendors. *Pensions and Investments*, November 13:3–4.

Choi, Stephen J., and Jill E. Fisch. 2008. On beyond CalPERS: Developing role of public pension funds in corporate governance. *Vanderbilt Law Review* 61:315–354.

Clark, Gordon L., and Ashby H. B. Monk. 2008. Conceptualizing the defined benefit pension promise: Implications from a survey of expert opinion. *Benefits Quarterly* 24:7–18.

Cooper, Jay. 2008. Climate change takes on new importance. *Pensions and Investments*, March 3:4–5.

D'Arcy, Stephen P., James H. Dulebohn, and Pyungsuk Oh. 1999. Optimal funding of state employee pension system. *Journal of Risk and Insurance* 66:345–380.

Davis, Gerald F., and E. Han Kim. 2005. Business ties and proxy voting by mutual funds. *Journal of Financial Economics* 85:552–570.

Eisenhofer, Jay W., Michael Barry, and Gregg S. Levin. 2007. *Shareholder activism handbook.* New York: Wolters Kluwer Law and Business.

Entine, Jon, ed. 2005. *Pension fund politics: The dangers of social investing.* Washington, D.C.: AEI Press.

Freshfields Bruckhaus Deringer. 2005. *A legal framework for the integration of environmental, social and governance issues into institutional investment.* http://www.unepfi.org/fileadmin/documents/freshfields_legal_resp_20051123.pdf.

Gannon, John. 2008. *Testimony before the U.S. Senate Special Committee on Aging: Saving smartly for retirement: Are Americans being encouraged to break open the piggy bank?* July 16. http://aging.senate.gov/events/hr198jg.pdf.

Gavin, Joanne H., and Ken Sloan. 2007. Pension plan design: An examination of corporate social responsibility. In *Corporate retirement security,* ed. Robert W. Kolb. Malden, MA: Blackwell Publishing.

General Accounting Office (GAO). 1995. *Public pension plans: Evaluation of economically targeted investment programs.* GAO/PEMD 95-13.

———. 1996. *Public pensions: State and local government contributions to underfunded plans.* GAO/HEHS 96-56.

Gillan, Stuart L., and Laura T. Starks. 2007. The evolution of shareholder activism in the United States. *Journal of Applied Corporate Finance* 19:55–73.

Government Accountability Office (GAO). 2008a. *Defined benefit pension plans: Guidance needed to better inform plans of the challenges and risks of investing in hedge funds and private equity.* GAO-08-692 (August).

———. 2008b. *Fulfilling fiduciary obligations can present challenges for 401(k) plan sponsors.* GAO-08-774 (July).

Hagerman, Lisa A., Gordon L. Clark, and Tessa Hebb. 2007. Investment intermediaries in economic development: Linking public pension funds to urban revitalization. *Community Development Investment Review* 3:45–65.

Hawley, James P., and Andrew T. Williams. 2000. *The rise of fiduciary capitalism: How institutional investors can make corporate America more democratic.* Philadelphia: University of Pennsylvania Press.

Hess, David. 2005. Protecting and politicizing public pension fund assets: Empirical evidence on the effects of governance structures and practices. *University of California-Davis Law Review* 39:187–224.

———. 2007. Public pensions and the promise of shareholder activism for the next frontier of corporate governance: Sustainable economic development. *Virginia Law and Business Review* 2:221–263.

Hess, David, and Gregorio Impavido. 2004. Governance of public pension funds: Lessons from corporate governance and international evidence. In *Public pension fund management,* ed. A. R. Musalem and R. Palacios. Washington D.C.: World Bank.

Hsin, Ping-Lung, and Olivia S. Mitchell. 1997. Managing public-sector pensions. In *Public policy towards pensions,* ed. Sylvester J. Schieber and John B. Shoven. Cambridge, MA: MIT Press.

James, Marianne L. 2008. The effect of change in accounting for defined benefit pensions and other postretirement benefit plans on companies' financial statements and stakeholders. *Journal of the International Academy for Case Studies* 14:51–59.

Johnson-Cramer, Michael E., and Robert A. Phillips. 2007. Not how much but how: The ethics of cash balance pension conversions. In *Corporate retirement security,* ed. Robert W. Kolb. Malden, MA: Blackwell Publishing.

Joyner, Tammy. 2008. 401(k) "dippers" robbing future to pay now. *Atlanta Journal Constitution* September 7:1.

Madrian, Brigitte C., and Dennis F. Shea. 2001. The power of suggestion: Inertia in 401(k) participation and savings behavior. *Quarterly Journal of Economics* 116:1149–1187.

Marens, Richard. 2004. "Waiting for the north to rise: Revisiting Barber and Rifkin after a generation of union financial activism in the U.S. *Journal of Business Ethics* 52:10–123.

———. 2008. Going to war with the army you have: Labor's shareholder activism in an era of financial hegemony. *Business and Society* 47:312–342.

Muir, Dana. 2004. Reform of qualified retirement plans: ERISA and investment issues. *Ohio State Law Journal* 65:199–248.

Muir, Dana M., and Cindy A. Schipani. 2007. Fiduciary constraints: Correlating obligation with liability. *Wake Forest Law Review* 42:697–747.

Munnell, Alicia H., and Annika Sunden. 2005. Social investing: Pension plans should just say "No." In *Pension fund politics: The dangers of social investing*, ed. Jon Entine. Washington, DC: AEI Press.

Romano, Roberta. 1993. Public pension fund activism in corporate governance reconsidered. *Columbia Law Review* 93:795–853.

———. 2001. Less is more: Making institutional investor activism a valuable mechanism of corporate governance. *Yale Journal on Regulation* 18:174–251.

Schwab, Stewart J., and Randall S. Thomas. 1998. Realigning corporate governance: Shareholder activism by labor unions. *Michigan Law Review* 96:1018–1090.

Smith, Jeffery. 2007. Reflections on markets, retirement and corporate responsibility. In *Corporate retirement security*, ed. Robert W. Kolb. Malden, MA: Blackwell Publishing.

U.S. Department of Labor (Employee Benefits Security Administration). 2006. *Meeting your fiduciary responsibilities*. http://www.dol.gov/ebsa/publications/fiduciaryresponsibility.html.

Useem, Michael. 1996. *Investor capitalism: How money managers are changing the face of corporate America*. New York: Basic Books.

Useem, Michael, and David Hess. 2001. Governance and investments of public pensions. In *Pensions in the public sector*, ed. Olivia S. Mitchell and Edwin C. Hustead. Philadelphia: University of Pennsylvania Press.

Walsh, Mary Williams. 2006. More U.S. companies ducking out of their pension promises. *New York Times*, January 9: A1 and C4.

Weller, Christian E. 2008. Robbing tomorrow to pay for today. *Testimony before the U.S. Senate Special Committee on Aging: Saving smartly for retirement—Are Americans being encouraged to break open the piggy bank?* July 16. http://aging.senate.gov/events/hr198cw.pdf.

Werhane, Patricia. 2007. Corporate retirement security: A bankrupt oxymoron. In *Corporate retirement security*, ed. Robert W. Kolb. Malden, MA: Blackwell Publishing.

Windsor, Duane. 2007. Ethics of corporate retirement programs. In *Corporate retirement security*, ed. Robert W. Kolb. Malden, MA: Blackwell Publishing.

ABOUT THE AUTHOR

David Hess is an assistant professor of business law and business ethics at the Ross School of Business at the University of Michigan. Professor Hess has a PhD in management from the Wharton School of the University of Pennsylvania and a JD from the University of Iowa College of Law. Professor Hess's research focuses on the role of the law in ensuring corporate accountability and on the governance of public pension funds and their use of sustainable investment strategies.

CHAPTER 20

Insurance

JULIE A. RAGATZ
Fellow at The American College Center for Ethics in Financial Services

RONALD F. DUSKA
Charles Lamont Post Chair of Ethics and the Professions, The American College

INTRODUCTION

In order to appreciate the relationship of ethics to insurance it is necessary to understand the nature of insurance. As a financial instrument for managing risk, insurance is a social institution that plays an essential role in contemporary society in its function of dispersing and distributing risk. Risk management and distribution involve questions of fairness and justice that are intensely debated not only by philosophers and economists but also by industry practitioners, the government, and consumers.

We begin this chapter with a discussion of the nature of insurance. We then turn to a consideration of the history of insurance to understand how insurance arose as a social institution and how the three major types of insurance—life insurance, property and casualty insurance, and health insurance—developed into the forms we recognize today. Each form of insurance shares common ethical issues, such as moral hazard and adverse selection, but each form also poses unique ethical questions. We consider an example of a specific ethical conflict that emerges within each type of insurance: In the field of life insurance we examine the development of life settlements; in property/casualty insurance we examine the controversy over flood damage which emerged after Hurricane Katrina; and concerning health insurance we briefly consider the question of a nationalized health care system. Finally, we conclude with some general comments on the future of the insurance industry at the beginning of the twenty-first century.

THE NATURE OF INSURANCE

The *Encyclopedia Britannica* provides one of the most thorough definitions of insurance available:

> *A contract that, by redistributing risk among a large number of people, reduces losses from accidents incurred by an individual in return for a specified payment (premium). The insurer undertakes to pay the insured or his beneficiary a specified amount of money in*

the event that the insured suffers loss through the occurrence of an event covered by the insurance contract (policy). By pooling both the financial contributions and the risks of a large number of policyholders, the insurer is able to absorb losses much more easily than is the uninsured individual. Insurers may offer insurance to any individual able to pay, or they may contract with members of a group (e.g., employees of a firm) to offer special rates for group insurance.

This definition points to three essential characteristics of insurance. The first is that insurance is a *contract*, which means it is an agreement between parties to provide or receive services under certain conditions. Second, insurance is a form of *risk management* that protects the insured against economic loss. These economic losses can be occasioned through the destruction or loss of property, suffered as a result of medical costs or illness, or financial losses occasioned by a premature death. The third point is that insurance is a *social institution* created through the pooling of risk among a group of insureds. In each form of insurance, individuals voluntarily invest resources, which may not be regained, in order to protect against the possibility of a larger loss they hope does not occur. In order for pooling to be economically successful, it is necessary that the collective shares are sufficient to meet the burden. Successful pooling requires that each member's contribution be fixed according to the rates of payment, which are developed by underwriters, who calculate the probabilities of how many participants are required and the amount they need to contribute to the pool of resources so that there are enough reserves for those who suffer loss.

THE DEVELOPMENT OF MODERN INSURANCE

Insurance, as a method of managing risk and assuring security, has a long history. The oldest insurance contract is believed to have occurred in 1347 in the city of Genoa. Archival research in the city of Florence reveals that insurance contracts were an ordinary event in the principal cities of Italy at this time, although they appeared to be limited to maritime or marine insurance (Holdsworth 1917, 88).

According to Alfred Manes, the history of insurance can be divided into three distinct phases. The first phase, from the middle of the fourteenth century to the end of the seventeenth century, is characterized by the beginnings of the insurance contract and the establishment of maritime insurance. The second period, from the eighteenth century to the first half of the nineteenth century, saw the emergence of the insurance company. The final period, from the mid-1800s until the present time, witnessed the rise of the large international companies and the appearance of social insurance (Manes 1942, 30).

Maritime Insurance

The first period saw the rise of marine insurance, which is generally agreed to be the oldest form of insurance. As Manes states, "The human mind must have thought of indemnity first in relation to sea risks" (Manes 1942, 36). The birth of the insurance contract was "the last term in the evolution of various legal devices invented to provide against the risks of the sea" (Holdsworth 1917, 85). Insurance contracts originated in Italy in the fourteenth century, but they were rarely recognized as such and were often described as sales or even loans in order to avoid falling under the general prohibition on usury.

These contracts were the successor of the maritime loans made in ancient Greece and Rome, which were designed to finance seafaring expeditions. However, the use of so-called sea loans extends beyond ancient Greece and Rome to the civilization of Babylonia in 2000 B.C. and were transmitted to the Greeks and Romans by the Phoenicians (Nelli 1972, 217). Holdsworth distinguishes between maritime loans and maritime insurance, in which the roles of debtor are essentially reversed. "In the maritime loan, the debtor, who has borrowed the money, declares that he has received the sum advanced and promises to restore an equivalent sum on safe arrival of the ship or goods; in insurance the assurer plays the part of the debtor, states that he has received the amount for which the ship or goods are insured, and promises to repay it in the event of the ship or the goods not arriving safely" (Holdsworth 1917, 89).

Fire Insurance and Life Insurance

Eventually, insurances against other dangers to property were developed. The Great Fire of London in 1666 impressed upon Londoners the importance of protecting themselves against the losses to personal property by fire. In 1680, Dr. Nicholas Brabon set up the first fire insurance office in London, and his success encouraged other companies to enter the market (Evans 1987, 89). In 1752, Benjamin Franklin founded the Philadelphia Contributionship for the Insurance of Houses from Loss by Fire in response to a series of devastating house fires in Philadelphia (McChesney 1986, 73). Each home insured by the Contributionship placed a *fire mark*, a plaque affixed to the residence, in order to alert firefighters to stop at their home in case of a fire. A second fire insurance company, the Mutual Assurance Company, opened its doors in Philadelphia in 1740. The Mutual Assurance Company offered protection, at a higher premium rate, to consumers whose properties "were tree-fronted" and were denied protection on these grounds by the Contributionship (McChesney 1986, 73).

At the beginning of the second period, from the eighteenth century to the first half of the nineteenth century, insurance companies began to develop a system of assigning premium payments and assessing risk. It was only in the eighteenth century that the idea of premium income to cover losses and make profits was established (Evans 1987, 89). One of the first examples of this approach was the Scottish Ministers' Widows Fund. Between 1741 and 1744, two Scottish ministers, Alexander Webster and Robert Wallace, established this fund, which collected yearly premiums from all Scottish ministers and then provided annuities to the widows and children of the participants (Hald 2003, 547). In the United States, in 1759, the Presbyterian Ministers' Fund began to provide life insurance for their retired ministers as a way for religious congregations to care for the widows and children of their pastors after their death. These efforts were hindered by the objections of other religious groups who preached to their congregations against life insurance, arguing that it was immoral and a sin to lack faith in providence.[1] This moral argument against life insurance was so powerful that life insurance was illegal in Massachusetts as late as 1809. The aforementioned Presbyterian synods in Philadelphia and New York had a more prudent bent and set up the Corporation for Relief of Poor and Distressed Widows and Children of Presbyterian Ministers in 1759 (Zelizer 1983, 2). The Episcopalians soon followed suit and developed a similar fund to support the dependents of their ministers in 1769. However, these organizations are considered by some scholars of business history not to be life insurance organizations but a hybrid of charity and business (Zelizer 1983, 3).

Although there was some growth between 1787 and 1837, the life insurance industry did not significantly expand in the United States until the 1840s, the beginning of the third period. To appreciate the significance of this growth, consider that the total life insurance in force in the United States grew from $600,000 in 1830 to just under $5 million in 1840. Within five more years, life insurance in force tripled to $14.5 million, and by 1850, the amount of life insurance in force swelled to almost $100 million. This amount was spread among 48 companies, but the three largest companies—Mutual Life Insurance Company of New York (1842), Mutual Benefit Life Insurance Company of New Jersey (1845), and Connecticut Mutual Life Insurance Company (1846)—accounted for half of this amount (Murphy 2002).

Historians and sociologists provide various accounts of the factors that led to the tremendous growth of life insurance in force during this time period, but two factors clearly contributed to it. The first is important changes in the law, both regarding contracts and corporate structures, that occurred in or around 1840. Before 1840 in the State of New York, married women were unable to enter into contracts and therefore could not take out life insurance policies either on themselves or on their husbands. Additionally, any policy that a man undertook with his wife and children as the beneficiaries could be confiscated to pay any debts he had remaining after his death. Since women had the greatest need for life insurance, given their limited access to the labor market and their inability to own property, this placed a serious limitation on the growth of the industry. In 1840, the state legislature of New York passed a law that established the right of a woman to take out a life insurance policy on her husband and protected that policy from creditors of her husband's estate under most circumstances (Murphy 2002). A second factor is that life insurance companies developed a new and more aggressive marketing and selling strategy, which involved personal, door-to-door sales. "In the 1840s, the new companies introduced person-to-person solicitation by thousands of active, high-pressure salesmen who went into the homes and offices of prospective customers" (Zelizer 1978, 596).

The final period in insurance history is the rise of large multinational insurance companies. Significant changes have occurred in both the structure of insurance companies and the types and forms of insurance they offer to consumers. We discuss some of these changes when we look at three different types of insurance: life insurance, property/casualty insurance, and health insurance. However, before we turn to a consideration of these specific forms of insurance, it is helpful to examine two ethical issues that emerge within the social construction of insurance as a pooling mechanism. These are the problems of moral hazard and adverse selection.

MORAL HAZARD AND ADVERSE SELECTION

Before the development of insurance companies, people dealt with catastrophic risk by depending on the goodwill of their communities. Communities and subgroups within communities—for example, the Presbyterian ministers—determined eligibility for participation in the insurance pool or plan, usually on the basis of some form of group membership, such as religion or occupation. The development of the modern insurance company led to questions concerning whether it is ethically permissible to impose limitations on who can participate in an insurance pool. In this section, we discuss adverse selection and moral hazard, which deal specifically with the implications of broadening or narrowing insurance pools.

Adverse selection occurs when a greater proportion of higher-risk individuals purchase life insurance relative to the number of lower-risk individuals. Mark Pauley defines adverse selection as "the tendency for people with higher risk to obtain insurance coverage to a greater extent than persons with lesser risk, when insurers are unable to tell who's high risk and who's low risk" (Pauley 2007, 6). Adverse selection is a result of the information asymmetry between the consumer and the company issuing the health insurance policy. In the case of adverse selection, the issuing company lacks information, which is known to the insureds, regarding their own risk factors.

Adverse selection predicts that since higher-risk individuals are more likely to purchase insurance than lower-risk individuals, these higher-risk individuals will be disproportionately represented in a pool. It suggests that since the pool is composed of a disproportionate number of higher-risk individuals, the amount of monies paid out in claims will be higher than it would be if the pool were better balanced between higher- and lower-risk individuals.

While paying higher premiums in order to purchase adequate risk coverage is acceptable to self-identified higher-risk individuals, if premium rates become too high, lower-risk individuals may be priced out of the market. The ethical problem posed by adverse selection is that these lower-risk individuals may bear the higher costs of participating in a risk pool that contains a disproportionate number of higher-risk individuals relative to the population. The ethical issue at stake is whether it is fair to require that apparently lower-risk individuals (with no known risk factors) participate in a pool composed disproportionately of self-identified, known higher-risk individuals.

The exclusion of known higher-risk individuals from collective pools is a difficult ethical question, which is compounded by the fact that people make decisions without perfect information about themselves or other people. Most people transition from lower-risk to higher-risk states throughout the course of their lives, and may even be unaware that such a shift has taken place. In many cases the precipitating high-risk factor is often due to circumstances outside of the insured's control. It seems that there is an ethical distinction between a higher-risk driver who is classified as such as a result of numerous speeding tickets and a driver who suffers from a degenerative condition. Therefore, another ethical issue emerges, which is whether it is fair to bar participation in the pool to higher-risk individuals when their status as higher-risk participants is beyond their control.[2]

A second ethical issue arising in insurance is the problem of moral hazard. Moral hazard occurs "when the expected loss from an adverse event increases as the insurance coverage increases" (Pauley 2007, 1). A well-known example of moral hazard is the hypothesis that an individual who owns a home that is well insured against fire damage will be less cautious about preventing a house fire than an individual who lacks adequate homeowners insurance. The explanation is that since the former may be more careless since he will not bear the full cost of replacing his home in a case of fire damage. The intuition behind this application of moral hazard is that the more extensive insurance coverage people purchase (in other words, the more risk they are able to transfer to the issuing company), the less incentive they have to take preventive measures against suffering loss. As Baker notes, "the more that a particular risk lies within the control of the insured, the less confidently insurance institutions can insure that risk" (Baker 2003, 259–260). In other words, the more insureds can protect themselves from loss through taking preventive measures (for example, by not leaving lit candles unattended) and the greater the probability that they can inflict harm on themselves by not taking those measures, the more difficult it is for insurers to protect themselves.

Others are concerned about the effect of moral hazard in regards to health insurance. The manifestation of the moral hazard problem in health insurance is slightly different than its application in property insurance.[3] The moral hazard problem emerges, according to this argument, when individuals with more extensive medical coverage consume more medical services than individuals with less extensive medical coverage in similar circumstances. The concern is that if some individuals are using the medical system more than is necessary to maintain health, this is an inefficient distribution of resources that increases the cost of health insurance for everyone.

Concern over moral hazard is partially mitigated by the establishment of a cost-sharing plan. A cost-sharing plan can take one of the following forms (or a combination of forms): deductibles, which are set amounts paid by insureds before the medical benefits provided by the policy take effect; coinsurance, an arrangement whereby the insured and the insurer each pay a fixed percentage of the medical costs after the deductible has been met; and co-pays, a fixed dollar payment an insured pays to access a particular medical good or service. The intuition behind cost sharing is that if individuals are required to bear a portion of the medical costs, they will be more prudent and efficient consumers of medical care.

The practice of cost sharing raises several ethical issues. Opponents argue that if the proportion of medical costs is too high, patients will not seek the medical care they need. This not only harms patients and those who depend on their well-being (children and other dependents as well as employers) but also creates inefficiencies within the medical system as minor health problems grow progressively more serious in the absence of medical care, necessitating more costly treatment in the future. Others take a different view and argue that "cost sharing is virtuous. It causes people to be frugal and wise in their use of medical care, and wise as well in their financial planning" (Pauley 2007, 2). Advocates of cost sharing believe that if there is no cost or a negligible cost to a good or service, the good or service will not be valued as much, and hence it may be more heavily consumed. The resulting inefficiencies of the system raise costs for all participants, and higher costs may place adequate medical coverage beyond the reach of some consumers.

At the heart of this debate is the larger question about the nature of insurance. Proponents of social insurance believe that insurance should function to transfer resources from the healthy to the unlucky individuals who are ill and in need of medical treatment. Social insurance does not discriminate against higher- or lower-risk individuals and simply transfers the funds to each as they are needed. Healthy individuals are willing to pay into a program whose resources they will depend on if they become ill. Another way to organize insurance is to establish an actuarial system. Under this model, premium levels are determined by individual circumstances and history. A health insurance system organized on an actuarial basis looks quite different from a social insurance scheme. Higher-risk insureds and lower-risk insureds would be clustered together into separate pools and consumers could select the level of protection they believe is appropriate to meet their needs. Insurers can then decide to offer protection to those they identify as higher-risk individuals at increased premium levels.

The distinction between these different forms of organizing insurance raises interesting and provocative questions about fairness and the obligations of a community to its more vulnerable and unlucky members, as well as questions about individual rights and the importance of autonomy. Concerns about adverse selection and moral hazard emerge in each of the principal forms of insurance: life, property/casualty, and health insurance. It is to a consideration of these forms of insurance that we now turn.

LIFE INSURANCE

Life insurance is a contract that allows insureds to provide financially for designated beneficiaries in the event of their death. An individual purchases life insurance in order to protect others from the financial losses brought about by his death. Since the traditional beneficiary of a life insurance policy is someone (or some institution) other than the insured, it is generally distinguished from other forms of insurances, such as property and casualty insurance, which are meant to minimize risk to oneself rather than to others.

Both state and religious institutions have good reasons to encourage the purchase of life insurance since it lessens the strain of the social services safety net provided by such institutions. The United States government, in order to encourage the purchase of life insurance, added Section 101 to the Internal Revenue Code. This section exempted the proceeds of a life insurance policy, maturing as a death claim, from taxation as personal income. Favorable tax treatment also makes it possible to purchase life insurance in which portions of the premiums are set aside as savings. This encouraged the development of whole life and universal life insurance policies which could be used for more general financial planning purposes.

An ethical question that sharpened with the development of life insurance was the extent of the responsibility financial providers have to ensure the material security of their loved ones and dependents after their death. A life insurance policy directs resources to a fund that can only be accessed upon the insured's death, and it is reasonable to consider what portion of an individual's resources should be saved for the maintenance of dependents after the insured's death. Individuals need to consider how to balance their obligations to the community and family during their lifetime with their obligations to plan for the long-term care of their dependents and loved ones, while at the same time ensuring they have sufficient resources to meet their own financial needs during the remainder of their life. These questions have grown increasingly important as social norms developed that deemphasized community reliance and stressed individual responsibility and independence.

Life Settlements

A life settlement is a transaction whereby an insured assigns ownership of a life insurance policy to a third party in exchange for a financial remuneration. "In other words, it is the sale of an economic interest in the death of the insured" (Bozanic 2008, 1). The contracting and sale of life settlements creates a secondary market for life insurance. This secondary market has transformed life insurance from a relatively illiquid asset to one that is more liquid. The ultimate result of this new market is a commodification of death that many find ethically repugnant and morally problematic.

The life settlement industry arose in the late 1980s to meet the needs of terminally ill HIV/AIDS patients who were looking to sell their life insurance policies to pay for medical treatment. These contracts, called *viaticals*, provided a way for terminally ill patients to meet their medical expenses through selling their life insurance policies. The terminally ill insured sold his life insurance policy to a third party, who agreed to pay the premiums for the duration of the life of the insured, thus keeping the policy in force. When the terminally ill insured died, the third party collected the death benefit. The third party profited from the difference between the face value of the policy (paid out as a death benefit) and the purchase price of the policy paid to the insured plus the premium payments needed to keep the policy in force. The sooner the insured was expected to die, the higher the settlement offer since the third party would need to outlay less in premium payments before collecting on the investment. Viatical settlements grew increasingly complex and less profitable when advances in medical technology and research made it difficult to accurately predict mortality rates (Bozanic 2008, 7)

The early success of the viatical market led investors to look for other ways to capture the benefits of other securities tied to the death market that did not have the viatical market's uncertainties. The solution was to tie a security to so-called *natural mortality*, which lacked the uncertainty of a security tied to morality occasioned by a terminal illness, or a viatical settlement. This approach had the advantage of leveraging the data the life insurance companies had historically employed to determine the premium structure of life insurance. As Bozanic states, "Applied to the senior market, actuarial science enables investors to achieve more accurate mortality expectations. This increased accuracy makes the rates of return in the senior market more predictable than the market for terminal patients" (Bozanic 2008, 10).

Life settlements emerged as the successor to viatical contracts. A typical life settlement involves a male over the age of 65 or a female over the age of 70. The insured is usually in deteriorating health with a life expectancy of less than 15 years. The life insurance policy generally has a face value of $100,000, is past the two-year contestability period, and has been issued by an insurance company with a rating of A or higher (Flood 2008). The *contestability period* is the time period in which the life insurance company that issued the policy can challenge the validity of the contract.

During this period, insureds make the premium payments on their life insurance policy, even if it has been initiated as a life settlement (in other words, was originally purchased as an investment tool). The premium payments are usually financed through a loan made by the life settlement company. If, after the contestability period has ended, the insured elects to maintain the insurance policy, he is responsible for repaying the loan. If the insured chooses to sell the policy to the life settlement company, the company takes over the premium payments and collects the benefits upon the death of the individual.

As an example of a life settlement, consider Tom, a healthy widower in his late sixties who is approached by his insurance agent about an excellent, risk-free investment opportunity and agrees to participate. An insurance policy is taken out on his life by an irrevocable trust with the beneficiary listed as Tom's family or perhaps a preferred charitable organization. A special purpose lender will loan the trust enough money to pay for the premiums of this new policy for the next two years (the period of contestability). After two years, Tom can choose from three options: (1) pay off the loan and maintain the policy; (2) sell the policy to the investor group, pay off the loan, and keep any profit that remains for himself; or (3) walk away from the loan and allow the lender to collect the insurance policy as collateral.[4]

If Tom selects the second of the three options, the life settlement company will sell Tom's policy to a hedge fund or investment bank, which will warehouse it in order to build a large pool of policies. After the investment bank or hedge fund collects a sufficient number of policies, usually around 200, it converts the pool of policies into an asset-backed security.[5] This process is referred as to *securitization*, defined as "a structured finance process whereby illiquid assets (payment obligations) are transformed into liquid assets (securities)" (Bozanic 2008, 11). These securities, also referred to as *death bonds*, are sold to investors as a low-risk investment that will produce steady returns, around 9 to 13 percent, and lack the volatility often correlated with equities. "Due to the law of large numbers, the bundling of risk across many policies, and the subsequent allocation to many investors, no one investor is unduly exposed to excess risk as he has only a fractional interest in a specific individual's life. All investors enjoy an interest in an asset that generates a smooth stream of income as insureds die off and their life insurance policies pay off" (Bozanic 2008, 12).

One of the ethical issues that emerges from the practice of life settlements is whether it is permissible for the state or the life insurance industry to limit an insured in the use of his property. A troubling consequence of the development of the life settlement industry is that it transforms the concept of *insurable interest* and, some people contend, undermines the traditional purpose of life insurance. There are three traditional understandings of insurable interest, all of which reflect an 1840 law passed by the New York state legislature. This law determined that insurable interest flows from bonds of affection and/or financial interest in the continued life of the insured. Insurable interest means that some form of financial dependency or love is supposed to ensure that the beneficiary (1) has an interest in the continued life of the beneficiary, (2) will experience a loss at the cessation of this life, and (3) will require material compensation to mitigate this loss. The law mandates insurable interest must exist at the time of the issuance of the life policy. If it does not, then the policy is void. It is understood that "insurable interest is lacking when life insurance is underwritten in a scenario where benefits arise or appreciate only from the death, disability or injury of the insured person." The practice of life settlements turns the traditional interpretation of insurable interest on its head. Far from having an emotional or financial interest in the continued life of the insured, the beneficiaries of a life settlement have a financial interest in the hasty death of the insured since they do not receive a return on their investment until the insured's death.

Some argue that if it is permissible for insureds to surrender their policies to the issuing company in exchange for the cash value of the policy, why should they be prevented from selling the same policy to a life settlement company for significantly more money? Defenders of life settlements argue that it is in the interest of life insurance companies to prohibit the sale of any life insurance policy to an outside party. Life insurance companies determine their premium rates on the assumption that certain policies will lapse—that is, some insureds will fail to pay their premiums and their policies will become null and void. If insureds are able to sell policies they no longer need or cannot afford to investors on the secondary market, the lapse rate will decline. This may have a negative effect on insurance companies since they will be required to pay out death benefits on policies that perhaps would have lapsed without the existence of the secondary market. This argument assumes that "life insurance is a form of property, and an owner has fair discretion over what they do with it" (Connolly 2007). If insureds are compelled to sell their policies at a price dictated by the issuing company then it appears that their property rights are being illegitimately limited.

Opponents of life settlements argue that governmental and regulatory bodies frequently circumscribe the use an individual can make of his own property when it is in the best interest of the public. If the development of the life settlement industry undermines the public good, it is morally appropriate to regulate the growth of this product. Life insurance, as we have seen, has historically played an important role in maintaining the safety net in our society. To encourage the purchase of life insurance, the state has given life insurance policies privileged tax status. It is this privileged tax status that the life settlement industry has exploited to develop an attractive product. In this sense, life settlements free-ride on the tax benefit, which was originally intended to incentivize something else entirely.

If the life settlement industry continues to expand, life insurance will begin to be perceived by regulators as an investment product and will be regulated as such. The concern is that if this comes to pass, life insurance may lose its privileged tax status. While a tax on the proceeds of a life insurance policy would certainly hurt the life insurance industry by making its product less competitive, it is possible that it may also have the unintended consequence of making life insurance a less attractive product for some families who need it.

PROPERTY AND CASUALTY INSURANCE

Property and casualty insurance insures one's property against serious loss. From its earliest form as maritime insurance, property and casualty insurance has expanded to cover homeowner policies, personal auto policies, other personal property insurance (renter insurance), commercial property, negligence of legal liability, personal liability insurance, commercial liability insurance, and errors and omissions policies. Like all insurance, property and casualty insurance is a hedge against loss, and as a financial instrument it is generally beneficial for society in helping people overcome catastrophic loss.

Ethical issues arise from abuse of the product, either by companies reluctant to pay legitimate claims, insurance agents misrepresenting the product and its benefits in order to make a sale, or owners of the policies lying to companies about their qualifications or abusing the policy in other fraudulent ways, such as a person buying a policy against fire and setting his property on fire to collect on the insurance.

It is the obligation of any insurance company to meet legitimate claims against policies underwritten by that company. Since the success of property and casualty insurance depends on maintaining the trust of their insureds and, through them, the trust of the public, companies that engage in delaying tactics or consistently underpay on legitimate claims destroy that trust and damage the reputation of the entire industry.

A persistent ethical issue in property and casualty insurance in recent years centers on whether a company should pay certain damage claims. Some of the most well-known incidents arose among the companies handling claims in the aftermath of Hurricane Katrina. Hurricane Katrina was responsible for 1,353 fatalities, and approximately 275,000 homes were destroyed by the storm. As of 2007, insurance companies had paid an estimated $40.6 billion on 1.7 million claims for damages to homes, businesses, and vehicles in six states (Cohen and Rosenberg 2008, 140). One of the most highly publicized cases that emerged from Hurricane Katrina involved a large insurer refusing to pay damages to certain policyholders in Mississippi whose houses were lifted from their moorings and blown upstream to another location.

These insureds filed claims for damages with their insurance companies in the wake of the storm. The insurance companies, in some cases, while conceding that the insured's property suffered serious damage, determined that this damage was the result of flooding. Since flood damage is an uncovered risk in most standard homeowners polices, insurance companies declined to pay the claims for people who did not have flood insurance. After a devastating series of floods in 1927 and 1928, most insurance companies stopped including flood protection in their standard homeowner policies.[6] However, since 1968, the federally funded National Flood Insurance Program (NFIP) has been available, and while there have been several initiatives to encourage more people who live in at-risk zones to participate in NFIP, less than 50 percent of homeowners in these areas have purchased flood insurance (Cohen and Rosenberg 2008, 142).

Damage to property during a hurricane is usually an admixture of water and wind damage, and the proximate cause is not always clear. Since all homeowner policies cover wind-related damage, courts have grappled for decades with the problem of ascertaining an insurer's coverage obligations for hurricane losses resulting from a covered and an uncovered risk. Some of the claimants whose homes were damaged during Hurricane Katrina argued that, as a result of the hurricane winds, their homes were torn from their moorings and deposited in different places, where they suffered additional water damage. These claimants and their attorneys argued that their cases fell under the efficient proximate cause doctrine, which means, "it is sufficient to show that the wind was the proximate or efficient cause of damage, notwithstanding that other factors contributed to the loss" (*Grace v. Lititz Mut. Ins. Co.*, cited in Cohen and Rosenberg 2008, 144). In this case, the insured plaintiffs argued that without the wind damage, their homes would not have been in a position to suffer the far more severe water damage. [7]

For the most part, the courts have rejected the insureds' application of the efficient proximate cause doctrine. In *Leonard v. Nationwide Mutual Insurance*, the court ruled that "to the extent that the property is damaged by wind, and is thereafter also damaged by water, the insured can recover that portion of the loss which he can prove to be caused by wind, but the insured is not responsible for any additional loss it can prove to have been later caused by water" (Cohen and Rosenberg 2008, 142). The situation of insureds who had homeowners policies in which wind was a covered risk but water damage was not, and whose property suffered from both wind and water damage, raises interesting ethical questions.

One question concerns whether the reasonable expectations of the policyholders were violated by the insurer's refusal to pay claims as a result of water damage. Robert E. Keeton argues that judicial decisions involving insureds and the issuing company have traditionally been guided by two broad principles, although he notes that both principles have not been explicitly stated. The first is that "an insurer will be denied any unconscionable advantage in an insurance transaction"; the second is that the "reasonable expectations of applicants and intended beneficiaries will be honored" (Keeton 1970, 961). Keeton argues that as the influence of these two principles becomes more explicit, it is possible to trace the development of a third principle, which also guides judicial decision making. He calls this the "principle of granting redress for detrimental reliance," which Keeton defines as "the objectively reasonable expectations of applicants and intended beneficiaries regarding the terms of insurance contracts will be honored *even though the painstaking study of the policy provisions would have negated those expectations*" (Keeton 1970, 967; emphasis added).

These principles are justified, according to Keeton, on account of the asymmetrical information relation between the insured and the issuing company. The idea is that insurers should not be permitted to benefit from an information asymmetry in unconscionable ways, and redress should be provided to insureds who had reasonable expectations as to the nature and extent of the coverage they were purchasing. Regarding the second principle, Keeton notes that insured are limited to selecting their coverage from the policies offered by the issuing companies or the government. In other words, insureds cannot design a contract that meets their specific need for risk protection. Since they are purchasing a standardized product on the assumption that it will meet their needs, their reasonable expectations regarding this policy should be taken into account in any dispute. Further, Keeton believes that contracts should be clearly written and not contain any provisions or exceptions that would belie the consumer's reasonable expectations. Under Keeton's framework, the question is whether or not the insureds in the case under consideration had a "reasonable expectation" that their homes and property were protected against all forms of hurricane damage.

In the Katrina court case *Leonard v. Nationwide Mutual Insurance Company*, the insured argued that since his agent had informed him that he did not need additional flood insurance, he had a reasonable expectation that his homeowners policy covered all hurricane damage. Although he read his policy and noted the water exclusion, he relied on his agent's advice and did not purchase the additional insurance. However, the courts did not accept his argument. According to Cohen and Rosenberg (2008, 156),

> *Judge Senter rejected this argument, emphasizing that the insurance agent offered no reason for his opinion and never expressly stated that the homeowners policy would provide coverage for water damage. . . . [T]he court concluded that the agent's statement regarding the need for flood insurance was nothing more than an opinion rather than a factual misrepresentation.*

In short, whether the agent misrepresented the extent of coverage to the insured is irrelevant since the agent had no authority to make any statement that contravened the language of the policy. The implication is that if the insured receives an explanation that misrepresents the nature of the coverage and the insured acts on this knowledge, he can receive no redress from the company. It is incumbent upon the insured to understand the policy without relying on the assistance of his agent.

Even if the insured did not have a reasonable expectation in a legal sense, according to Judge Senter, it is possible that he had a reasonable expectation in a moral sense. If insurance practitioners are committed to acting as professionals, rather than as salespersons, the public has a legitimate expectation that their advice is reliable and that to depend upon this advice is reasonable. If insurance practitioners are not professionals, then their advice should be treated with skepticism. However, if this is the case, then the misrepresentation of the industry as a profession is an ethical violation since it creates a false expectation. Since insurance agents represent themselves as professionals, it seems reasonable and prudent for consumers to depend upon their advice and counsel, and agents are morally obliged to give accurate, clear, and sound advice.

However, there certainly may be cases in which the expectation of coverage was not reasonable. Perhaps insureds failed to read their policies and note the covered and uncovered risks. Perhaps they were unwilling, or simply could not afford, to spend the additional money to purchase insurance sufficient to supplement their uncovered risks. Resources used to make these underinsured persons whole would have to be diverted from a legitimate business purpose, or the outlays made up by increasing premium demands on other policyholders. Insurance rests on the pooled resources of the collective, and, all things being equal, each participant should only receive payment for the loss against which he insured himself.

HEALTH INSURANCE

The United States is unique insofar as it is one of the few countries in the world that has opted for a system of voluntary health insurance rather a compulsory program administered by the government (Applebaum 1961, 25). The development of the voluntary health insurance system in the United States can be divided into three stages. The first stage spans the end of the eighteenth century and runs through the beginning of the nineteenth century. This stage is characterized by the establishment of mutual aid societies formed by workers to protect against wage loss in the event of disability or illness, which is primarily what we know as disability insurance (Applebaum 1961, 31). These were collective pools arranged to reduce the risk of ruinous medical costs. Some of the pools were the precursor to unions and engaged in collective bargaining on behalf of their members. However, many pools collapsed as a result of financial difficulties that were brought on by the incorrect application of the principles of actuarial science.

Employers had limited involvement in this first stage, and while a few employers took full responsibility for the medical care of workers, and their dependents, this was rare. For the most part, employer contributions to employee-financed heath collectives were relatively small. The labor movement was particularly suspicious of management involvement in health care insurance, which it viewed as a means to generate employee loyalty without changing the structure of the system under which employees labored (Applebaum 1961, 26).

The second stage, which began with the Great Depression and continued until the beginning of the Second World War, is characterized by the efforts of both consumers and medical providers to develop innovative means of providing affording medical care. A good example of this sort of innovation involved Baylor University Hospital, which in 1929 founded the first Blue Cross Plan. A group of teachers in Dallas wanted to ensure access to affordable hospital care. They negotiated an agreement with Baylor University Hospital whereby if a teacher paid $3.00 per semester, he/she would be eligible to receive three weeks of in-patient care. With over 1,500 participants, the Baylor University Hospital program was successful and inspired similar programs throughout the Southwest (Thomasson 2002, 237).

One reason these plans proved popular with hospital providers is that they supplemented their endowment income, which was rapidly declining as a result of the economic conditions during the Great Depression. A second reason was a fixed benefit plan that limited the amount of benefits insureds could claim from the hospital. In the case of the first Blue Cross Plan at Baylor University Hospital, participants' in-patient treatment was capped at 21 days. The fact that the plan was capped limited the problem of moral hazard since the patients' access to medical resources was fixed. However, this structure may have encouraged some participants to take advantage of the benefit they were paying for and seek out more medical treatment than they would have been willing to pay for otherwise. This example reveals the balance that health insurance providers try to maintain between providing attractive benefit packages and limiting their exposure to loss.

The American Hospital Association (AHA), encouraged by the development of Blue Cross, established a set of standards that all Blue Cross plans were obliged to follow. The AHA mandated that consumers should be free to select both their physician and their hospital. This decision fostered an environment of competition among local hospitals as they competed for business and attempted to keep costs down (Thomasson 2002, 238). Since Blue Cross was believed to be acting in the public's best interest, the government allowed it to operate as a nonprofit corporation. "Under the enabling legislation, plans enjoy the advantages of exemption from the regular insurance laws of the state, are freed from the obligation of maintaining the high reserves required of commercial insurance companies, and are relieved of paying taxes" (Thomasson 2002, 238).

The American Medical Association (AMA) followed in 1930 with the development of Blue Shield. Caught between the Scylla of the possibility of the hospital-provided insurance for physician services and the Charybdis of the possibility of nationalized health insurance embedded in the upcoming Social Security legislation, doctors worked together to organize a framework for prepaid plans that covered physician services (Thomasson 2002, 239). The result was the Blue Shield plan, which allowed physicians to protect the principle of patient choice and also to maintain the right to charge patients the difference between what the insurance plan would reimburse and the actual price of the medical visit.

The third stage of the development of health insurance began at the onset of the Second World War and was characterized by the efforts of the National Labor Relations Board (NLRB) and the unions to expand all employee benefits, including health insurance. Follmann (1965) mentions two factors that contributed to the growth of health insurance. The first was a revision to the Internal Revenue Code which permitted employer contributions to employee welfare funds to be deductible as business expenses. "This development combined with the expansion of the economy ... contributed to the establishment of many new or expanded health and welfare programs" (Follmann 1965, 107). Employer contributions were perceived by corporate managers as a means of building goodwill and loyalty among their current employees, as well as an effective recruitment tool.

The second factor that contributed to the growth of health insurance resulted as a consequence of federal wage policies implemented during the war period in order to control inflation. In 1944–1945, under the "Little Steel Formula," employers were permitted to increase employee benefits in lieu of direct wage increases. The NLRB in 1948–1949, in a case involving W. W. Cross and Company, ruled that corporations were required to submit to collective bargaining regarding the group health benefits of their employees. "The direct consequence of the NLRB decisions, upheld by the federal courts, . . . has been one of the primary reasons for the growth of voluntary health insurance, especially as sold in the group form" (Applebaum 1961, 30).

The Debate over Government-Sponsored Health Care

The issue of whether the United States should mandate some form of compulsory health insurance is, at its heart, a question of economic justice, specifically a question of how to distribute scarce resources. There are many ways to distribute goods: on the basis of merit or need, on the basis of strict equality, or through the forces of the free market.

The original health collectives were distinguished by the freedom of choice of their participants: individuals could choose to join or leave a collective according to their interpretation of their own best interests. Currently, individuals or corporations can shop different health insurance providers and purchase the amount and type of coverage they see as appropriate for their needs. Further, subject to certain limitations imposed by the state, health insurance companies are able to choose who can join the collective they administer. They can determine, also within certain regulatory limitations and the constraints of the market, how much to charge for admission into the collective. The idea is that competition will compel the health insurance companies to make themselves desirable to almost every potential insured by offering generous risk protection at a low price.

Opponents of compulsory health insurance argue that it is ethically inappropriate for a government to compel people to join a collective where they may experience a lower quality of care than they would if they had been permitted to contract for themselves. Additionally, opponents contend that people who are young and healthy may not wish to spend resources on health insurance and should not be forced to participate. The President's 2004 Economic Report argues that a portion of the uninsured are uninsured by choice:

> *Others who lack insurance coverage possess economic or demographic characteristics that suggest many of them remain uninsured as a matter of choice. For example, some have levels of household income that are above the median for the population. Over 32 percent of uninsured individuals report a household income of $50,000 or more. Others have access to employer-provided coverage but opt not to participate. . . . Still others may remain uninsured because they are young and healthy and do not see the need for insurance. (Economic Report of the President 2004, 197)*

This is a particularly tricky question since the presence of young, healthy payers in a collective lowers the price for the aged and infirm. Thus, this arguments runs, not only are people being compelled to act, but they are being compelled to act against what they believe to be in their own best interests.

Proponents of some form of compulsory health insurance object to distributing such an important social good through the market. They point to the fact that many other countries recognize a moral obligation to care for and promote the health of their citizenry. Proponents argue that many Americans find the cost of adequate health insurance and the consequent health care beyond their financial means. Many people, they argue, would certainly purchase health insurance if they could afford to do so. Contrary to opponents of compulsory health insurance, they contend that the decision to forgo health insurance is often made reluctantly and makes them vulnerable to serious financial loss from catastrophic illness. Supporters believe it is particularly necessary for the government to take a more active role in providing health insurance given the decline in employer-sponsored health insurance. While many employers previously provided health insurance for their employees and their dependents, these costs have proved onerous for many companies, and benefits have been eroded as companies have been forced to streamline their expenses in order to compete in the global marketplace—a global marketplace in which many of the dominant economies exist in countries where the government provides health care for their workers.

We have only sketched the outlines of a complex and difficult problem facing all Americans, and the debate over a free-market form of distribution versus some form of compulsory health insurance will likely continue for some time. Solutions to these issues will serve as the beginnings, perhaps, for the fourth stage in the evolution of health insurance.

CONCLUSION

This chapter has presented insurance as a social institution established by a collectivity to mitigate the risk of some form of loss. A necessary condition for insurance to succeed is trust in a promise that the collectivity will make good on its commitment in the participant's time of need. The history of insurance reveals that the institution has been able to evolve to meet both individual and collective needs.

In the future, insurance companies and insurance professionals will be faced with serious ethical challenges. These include determining the legitimacy of life settlements; designing sustainable policies that meet the needs of consumers and promote the long-term growth of the industry in the context of catastrophic losses and natural disasters; and adequately and fairly dealing with the insuring of people against financial loss due to the high costs of health care without strangling the health care system.

We have tried to emphasize the common ethical issues faced by providers, regulators, and consumers of any form of insurance. At a theoretical level, the way we think about the issues of moral hazard and adverse selection has the capacity to profoundly influence how we think about the role of insurance in society. If America continues moving toward a more actuarial model of insurance, insurance contracts will become increasingly specific in order to meet the protection needs of groups at each stage of the risk continuum. This development has the potential to make insurance of all kinds more readily available and attractive to a wide group of Americans. However, the actuarial model may also sharpen the problem of adverse selection and create a class of higher-risk consumers who find themselves priced out of products they desperately need. The social insurance model creates its own set of difficulties, one of which is the problem of moral hazard. The concern is that if participants are able to transfer risk to another party or institution, they will be less attentive to the preventive measures needed to avoid suffering loss and will be more likely to use the benefits they receive in inefficient ways. These inefficiencies may increase the cost of social programs beyond what the collective pool of participants can bear, as well as diverting government resources from other important projects and initiatives.

At its heart, resolution of these ethical conflicts is a question of economic justice. This question affects all Americans who depend upon the social institution of insurance to protect themselves and their loved ones from serious financial loss. How the insurance industry, the government, and consumers respond to these challenges will shape the institution of insurance in the twenty-first century.

NOTES

1. "Putting death on the market offended a system of values that upheld the sanctity of human life and its commensurability. It defied a powerful normative pattern: the division between marketable and the non-marketable, or between the sacred and the profane" (Zelizer 1978, 594).

2. While we have provided an example concerning health insurance, it is possible to apply the problem of adverse selection to other forms of insurance as well. Regarding property insurance, consider the problem posed by flood insurance: "If flood coverage is offered as an option, people living in areas prone to flooding will buy it. Those who live high and dry won't. The pool of covered houses is much more likely to experience damage than the average of all houses. For insurers to break even, they must charge high premiums for flood coverage. More people opt out and eventually the only people covered are those with a high probability of flooding" (Lotterman 2007).

3. Several sources point out the differences between health insurance and other forms of property/casualty insurance such as homeowners insurance or automobile insurance. The first difference is that health insurance policies tend to cover many events that

have little uncertainty, such as dental checkups and physical exams. Second, health insurance policies also tend to cover low-expense items (such as treatment for the flu or an ear infection). Additionally, there are some economists who are doubtful that people consume health care in the same way that they consume other goods. Gladwell quotes Princeton economist Uwe Reinhardt, who argues that "Moral hazard is overblown ... you always hear that the demand for health care is unlimited. This is just not true. People who are very well insured, who are very rich, do you see them check into the hospital because it's free? Do people really like to go to the doctor? Do they check into the hospital instead of playing golf" (Gladwell 2008)?

4. The exact amount that an insured receives in return for surrendering a life policy depends on several different variables besides life expectancy, such as (1) the type of policy being sold; (2) the death benefit attached to the policy; (3) the amount of future premium obligations; (4) the policy's existing cash value; (5) the insurance company; (6) the amount of loans against the policy; and (7) current interest rates, assumptions, and mortality expenses. "The overwhelming factor in the determination of whether there will be a life settlement offer and the amount that will be paid is heath related—i.e. has there been a significant and adverse change in the insured's health since the policy was issued" (Leimberg and Gibbons 2003).

5. The large debt rating agencies, such as Moody's Investors and Fitch Ratings, are expected to start issuing ratings on these death bonds. Hedge funds and other large investors have proved to be a ready market for these bonds in Europe, and it is anticipated that demand for these sorts of asset-backed securities in the United States will be significant. The growth in the life settlement industry has been rapid. It is estimated that sales of life settlements were $2 billion in 2002, and they rose to $10 billion in 2005 and $15 billion in 2006. In spite of the fact that the market for life settlements is constrained by several factors—namely, that the insured need to be senior citizens and that the policies have face value in excess of $100,000—it is predicted that the life settlement industry will be worth upwards of $160 billion in 2030.

6. "Typical language [of a homeowners' policy] will exclude coverage resulting from (1) flood, surface water, waves, tidal water, overflow of a body of water or spray from any of these, whether or not driven by the wind; (2) water which backs up through sewers or drains or which overflows from a sump; or (3) water below the surface of the ground, including water which exerts pressure on or seeps or leaks through a building, sidewalk, driveway, foundation, swimming pool or other structure." *Solomine v. Mass Prop. Ins. Underwriting Ass'n,* 844 N.E. 2d 256, 258 (Mass. App. Ct. 2006) (Cohen and Rosenberg 2008, 142).

7. It is interesting to note that different states have varying standards of coverage in a situation in which damage is the result of two causes, one of which is a covered risk (wind) and one of which is an uncovered risk (water). For example, in Florida, the requirement is that the covered risk (wind) be the proximate cause only applies when the risks are dependent—that is, one event causes the other event (wind damage causing water damage). However, if the events are independent (wind damage did not cause the water damage, but wind damage and water damage happened concurrently), "the concurrent coverage doctrine establishes coverage for the loss if at least one insured risk (covered event) contributed to the loss, *regardless of whether this risk (covered event) was the efficient proximate cause of the loss*" (Cohen and Rosenberg 2008, 145; emphasis added). In response to the state's concurrent coverage doctrine, insurance companies have inserted anticoncurrent causation clauses into their policies. This move/countermove between the State Department of Insurance and the insurance companies raises interesting ethical questions: If the state regulatory organization is attempting to create policies to protect its citizens, is it legitimate for insurance companies to nullify the effects of this regulation

through establishing counterclauses? Conversely, is it appropriate for state regulatory organizations to compel insurance companies to take on greater risk than they would choose to do on their own and which may not be in the best long-term interest of the organization? It is certainly possible for states to develop their own mandatory insurance program for home owners in high-risk areas. Are they, therefore, simply shifting the burden of protecting their citizens to a private company?

REFERENCES

Applebaum, Leon. 1961. The development of voluntary health insurance in the United States. *Journal of Insurance* 28:25–33.

Baker, Tom. 2003. Containing the promise of insurance: Adverse selection and risk classification. In *Risk and morality*, ed. Richard Ericson and Aaron Doyle. Toronto: University of Toronto Press.

Bozanic, Kelly. 2008. An investment to die for: From life insurance to death bonds, the evolution and legality of the life settlement industry. *Penn State Law Review* 113:229–266.

Cohen, Craig A., and Mark A. Rosenberg. 2008. After the storm: Courts grapple with the insurance coverage issues resulting from Hurricane Katrina. *Tort Trial and Insurance Practice Law Journal* 43:139–171.

Connolly, Jim. 2007. Are today's battles déjà vu all over again? *National Underwriter*, April 30:S-5.

Economic report of the president. 2004. Washington D.C.: Government Printing Office.

Evans, Robert. 1987. The early history of fire insurance. *Journal of Legal History* 8:88–91.

Flood, Adam. 2008. Stranger-originated life insurance: How the NAIC tamed an old dog with a new trick. http://works.bepress.com/adam_flood/1.

Follmann, J. F. 1965. The growth of group health insurance. *Journal of Risk and Insurance* 32:105–112.

Gladwell, Malcolm. 2008. The moral-hazard myth. *New Yorker*, August 29.

Hald, Andres. 2003. *A history of probability and statistics and their application before 1750.* Hoboken, NJ: John Wiley & Sons.

Holdsworth, William. 1917. The early history of the contract of insurance. *Columbia Law Review* 17:85–113.

Keeton, Robert E. 1970. Insurance law rights at variance with policy provisions. *Harvard Law Review* 83:961–985.

Leimberg, Stephan R., and Albert E. Gibbons. 2003. Life settlements and the planning opportunities they offer. *Estate Planning* 30:517–521.

Lotterman, Edward. 2007. Flood insurance can be a muddy issue. *Saint Paul Pioneer Press*, September 6.

Manes, Alfred. 1942. Outlines of a general economic history of insurance. *Journal of Business of the University of Chicago* 15:30–48.

McChesney, Fred S. 1986. Government prohibitions on volunteer fire fighting in 19th century America: A property rights perspective. *Journal of Legal Studies* 15:297–335.

Murphy, Sharon. 2002. Life insurance in the United States through World War I. In *EH.Net Encyclopedia*, ed. Robert Whaples. August 14. http://eh.net/encyclopedia/articles/murphy.life.insurance.us.

Nelli, Humbert O. 1972. The earliest insurance contract: A new discovery. *Journal of Risk and Insurance* 39:215–220.

Pauley, Mark. 2007. The truth about moral hazard and adverse selection. Policy Brief Series 36, Center for Policy Research at Maxwell School, Syracuse University.

Thomasson, Melissa. 2002. From sickness to health: The twentieth-century development of U.S. life insurance. *Explorations in Economic History* 39:233–253.

Zelizer, Viviana. 1978. Human values and the market: The case of life insurance and death in 19th century America. *American Journal of Sociology* 84:591–610.

———. 1983. *Morals and markets: The development of life insurance in the United States.* New York: Columbia University Press.

ABOUT THE AUTHORS

Julie A. Ragatz joined the Center for Ethics in Financial Services at The American College in 2006 as a doctoral fellow. She received an MA degree in social and political philosophy from Marquette University and is pursuing her PhD in philosophy at Temple University. Ms. Ragatz has taught courses in ethical theory and business ethics at universities including Marquette University, Villanova University, and Saint Joseph's University. She has published numerous articles on ethical theory and business ethics. Her second book, *Accounting Ethics*, written with Ronald Duska and Brenda Shay Duska, will be published by Wiley-Blackwell Press in 2010.

Ronald F. Duska is the Charles Lamont Post Chair of Ethics and the Professions at The American College as well as the director of the American College Center for Ethics in the Financial Services. He is the author, co-author, or editor of numerous books and articles. His most recent books are *Ethics for the Financial Services Professional* (The American College Press, 2008), *Contemporary Reflections on Business Ethics* (Springer Netherlands, 2009), and *Accounting Ethics* (Wiley-Blackwell, 2003). He served as the executive director of the Society for Business Ethics and editor of the society newsletter, and is currently serving on the board of directors of the society.

We would like to thank Sara Taylor for her insights and helpful comments on this chapter.

CHAPTER 21

Responsible Investing

CÉLINE LOUCHE
Assistant Professor of Corporate Social Responsibility, Vlerick Leuven Gent
Management School

STEVEN LYDENBERG
Chief Investment Officer, Domini Social Investments LLC

INTRODUCTION

Responsible investment is both a product and a practice (Gond and Boxenbaum 2004). Responsible investment (RI) is an investment *product* in the sense that in addition to financial factors, investors acquire, hold, or dispose of companies' shares on the basis of environmental, social, and governance (ESG) factors as well as ethical factors. It is a *practice* in the sense that RI is a way to identify companies with strong sustainability records and to engage with companies to encourage improved ESG performance.

Responsible investment goes by many names—it is variously referred to as socially responsible investing, ethical investing, sustainable investing, triple-bottom-line investing, green investing, best-of-class investing, or most simply as responsible investing. It has evolved over the years from the concerns of religious organizations; environmental, labor, and human rights activists; community groups; and shareholders in the corporations themselves.

Underlying these varied names and approaches is a common theme: *long-term value creation*. Practitioners of RI seek to generate both financial and societal value; to stimulate change toward sustainability within corporations; to steer investments toward the productive and socially beneficial use of capital; and to initiate debate on the proper role of corporations in society. *Value creation* in this context refers not only to economic value, but to the wider impact of companies on society and the natural environment, both today and in the future (World Economic Forum 2005). The RI community implicitly recognizes and acknowledges that investment as an activity impacts society and influences business's behavior and actions. In addition, ESG information helps investors better manage risk and make better informed investment decisions (Lydenberg 2007).

Among the key characteristics of RI are the following:

- Responsible investment encourages a long-term perspective in investing. It does so because (1) environmental, social, governance, and ethical issues cannot always be captured by the market, which tends to be short-term in its perspective; (2) RI seeks to establish trust between stakeholders (employees, communities, customers, suppliers) and corporations, a trust that results from ongoing dialogue and persists over time; and (3) RI encourages corporate managers themselves to adopt a perspective that encompasses corporate social responsibility goals with long-term financial benefits.

- Responsible investment has a broad definition of materiality, which it conceives as relevant to all stakeholders (not just stockowners) and as striking a balance between that relevance (what matters to whom) and significance (how much it matters). This means that RI takes into account in its decision-making issues that have both short-term and long-term implications for investors, other stakeholders, and society in general (AccountAbility 2006).
- Responsible investment adopts a stakeholder perspective. At the core of the conception and practice of RI is the belief that all stakeholders in the corporation matter and that a productive and profitable company will invest in its full range of stakeholders, receive a return from all its stakeholders, and consequently be able to provide a long-term return to its investors (Post et al. 2002).

The objective of this chapter is to provide insights into the activity of responsible investment and to highlight some of its key challenges. The first section presents the history of responsible investment from its roots in the eighteenth century to 2009. The second section maps the different tools and strategies used by responsible investors. The third section focuses on the major players including asset owners, providers of support services, and related organizations. Lastly, the fourth section examines four major challenges the RI field is currently facing.

HISTORY OF RESPONSIBLE INVESTMENT

The concept and practice of responsible investment have evolved over the years in what can be classified as five primary periods. Each phase of this evolution is characterized by its own particular practices and concerns. Each new phase of RI tends to incorporate previous forms that persist and coexist with the new ones.

Although precise figures are difficult to come by, there has been a significant growth of assets under RI management and the number of RI funds over the years, a growth that, it is not an overstatement to say, has been explosive since the late 1990s. In the United States, RI assets under management were at $2.71 trillion in 2007, representing 11 percent of the $25.1 trillion in total assets under management (U.S. SIF 2008). RI assets have increased by 324 percent since 1995, a faster growth than the broader universe of all investment assets under professional management. In Europe between 2002 and 2007, the number of RI funds increased by 150 percent to 447 in 2007 (Lipper FERI 2008). Eurosif has placed the value of the RI market at €2.665 trillion as of December 31, 2007, an increase by 102 percent between 2005 and 2007 (Eurosif 2008). According to Eurosif's figures, RI accounts for 17.6 percent of total European funds under management. Exhibits 21.1 and 21.2 depict the growth in RI funds in the United States between 1995 and 2007. Exhibit 21.3 shows the growth in RI funds in Europe during the period 2002–2007, while Exhibit 21.4

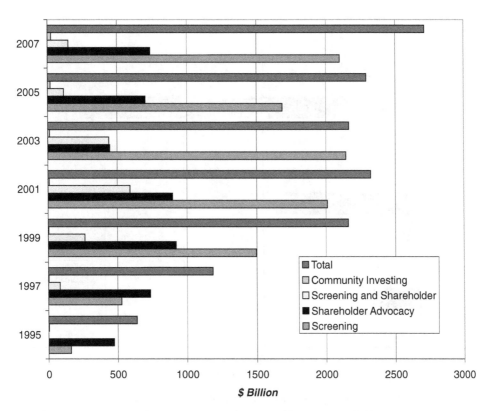

Exhibit 21.1 Responsible Investment in the United States, 1995–2007
Source: U.S. Social Investment Forum, 2008 report.

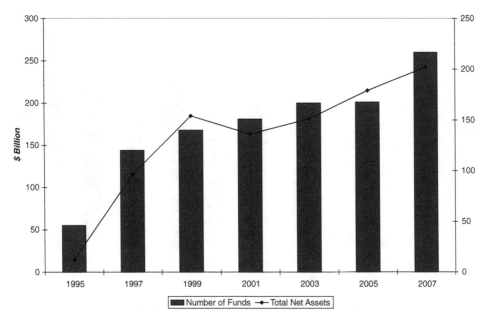

Exhibit 21.2 Responsible Investment Assets and Funds in the United States, 1995–2007
Source: U.S. Social Investment Forum, 2008 report.

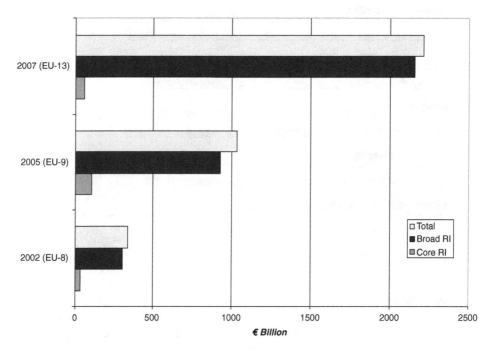

Exhibit 21.3 Broad and Core Responsible Investment in Europe, 2002–2007
Source: SIRI Group, 2007.

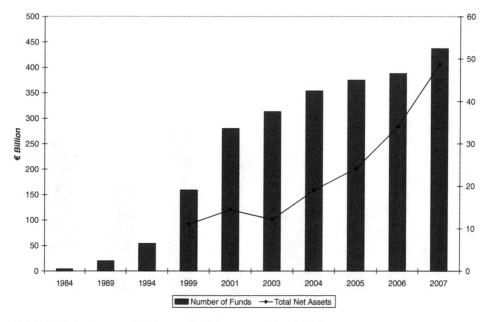

Exhibit 21.4 Responsible Investment Assets and Funds in Europe
Source: SIRI Group, 2007.

outlines the growth in number of European RI funds and their total assets from 1984 to 2007.

Phase 1: Roots

The earliest stage of responsible investment, before it was known as responsible investment, dates back to the eighteenth century (Domini 2001). For several hundred years religious institutions—such as the Society of Friends (Quakers) and the Methodists—were precursors to the modern form of RI in that they believed that investing was not a neutral activity, but implied values. They shunned "sinful" companies whose products conflicted with their basic beliefs. These so-called sin stocks were for the most part those of companies involved in alcohol, tobacco, gambling, and, in certain cases, weapons. One of the emblematic and first RI mutual funds of this first phase was the Pioneer Fund, launched in the United States in 1928.

Phase 2: Development

The second phase dates from approximately 1970 and runs through the late 1980s. It marks the beginnings of RI in the contemporary sense of the term and is typified in the United States by the Pax World Fund, launched in 1971, and in Europe by the Friends Provident Stewardship Unit Trust in 1984.

In the United States, this incarnation of RI originated in part in the political and protest movements of the day. The Vietnam War and apartheid in South Africa were two issues that in particular drove the RI movement of that time. Other citizen movements such as civil rights, women's liberation, and the environment raised issues of crucial concern to the RI movement and became a part of its lobbying of corporations on issues seen as unethical (Louche and Lydenberg 2006). At that time, Ralph Nader and Saul Alinsky, two U.S. consumer and community activists, started to use the shareholder right to appear at corporate annual meetings and to file shareholder resolutions to raise social and environmental issues directly with corporate management. Nader's General Motors campaign leading to the submission of two socially based resolutions on the annual meeting proxy ballot remains an historical moment. These tactics were soon adopted by the RI movement and became an important second tool for the responsible investor.

In the 1980s, RI also took root in Europe. The Friends Provident Stewardship Unit Trust was among the first ethical investment funds in the United Kingdom and a precursor to many similar funds. A number of eco-banks such as Triodos Bank in the Netherlands were also founded during that time.

Simultaneously, a number of RI support organizations were created, such as the Interfaith Center on Corporate Responsibility (ICCR) in 1971, the first two Social Investment Forums in the United States (1980) and the United Kingdom (1983), as well as the first professional RI rating agencies, such as KLD Research & Analytics (United States, 1988) and EIRIS (United Kingdom, 1983).

During this second period, RI developed in a political climate of social protest and was transformed from a faith-based activity (using ethical principles in the construction of investment portfolios) into an activity promoting a public awareness of the social responsibility of corporations and of investing (the self-conscious phenomenon of RI) (Sparkes 2001). This was the period in which RI was first used to lobby corporations to adopt responsible and ethical practices.

Phase 3: Transition

During the early 1990s, RI began a gradual transition to a less confrontational approach with a strong growth in environmental concerns. The Brundtland Report, which highlighted and defined the concept of sustainability, was published in 1987. The Kyoto Protocol on climate change was ratified in 1997. For RI, this meant the emergence of so-called *green* funds, especially in Europe, less concerned with avoidance and stressing identification of specific positive sectors or activities linked to the environment, such as renewable energy and clean technologies.

During this period the number of social rating agencies grew significantly; the first RI index, the Domini 400 Social Index, was launched (1990); and corporate social responsibility (CSR) consultancy organizations such as SustainAbility began to thrive. These developments were typical of the new, more systematic and analytical aspects of this third phase with its emerging emphasis on sustainability and cooperation.

Phase 4: Expansion

The beginning of the twenty-first century heralded a turning point for RI in both its approach and its growth. This fourth period is characterized by the professionalization of the field and a growing worldwide interest in its practice. RI began to find acceptance in the mainstream investment community, leaving behind its more activist image and becoming a more commercially viable endeavor (Déjean, Gond, and Leca 2004; Louche 2004). This evolution was closely linked to the growing importance of corporate social responsibility and the increasing accessibility of CSR reports issued by corporations. The Global Reporting Initiative, launched in 2000, played a crucial role in this growing acceptance of CSR reporting by corporations and the increasing thoroughness and sophistication of these reports.

In the early 2000s, institutional investors started to become broadly involved in RI.[1] This growing interest on the part of institutional investors was partially stimulated by governments in Europe at both the continental and national levels. In several European countries, legislation and regulations required pension funds to publicly state the degree (if any) to which they took into account social, environmental, and governance considerations in their investment decisions. In the United Kingdom, RI pensions disclosure regulation was enacted in 2000, followed shortly thereafter by many other European countries. In addition, in 2001 the Norway Petroleum Fund adopted several RI policies, initiating a movement among major European pension funds toward the incorporation of RI practices. The interest of institutional investors in RI explains the substantial growth of the assets under RI management in Europe during the first decade of the twenty-first century.

With the increasing involvement of institutional investors, a best-in-class approach to stock selection found growing acceptance. This approach stresses broad diversification (no elimination of industries entirely), positive rankings (only the best companies in each industry are included), and quantitative measurements (all companies are scored on sustainability indicators). Companies are evaluated on their performance relative to their peers, rather than in absolute terms. By stressing best practices, the approach promotes societal and financial values and at the same time encourages competition among corporations to achieve social and environmental goals.

Phase 5: Mainstreaming

As the first decade of the twenty-first century drew to a close, RI stood at a crossroads. Its increasing acceptance by institutional investors was marked by such events as the launch of the Principles for Responsible Investment (PRI) in 2006. Subsequently, the PRI grew into a coalition of more than 400 of the largest institutional investors and asset managers worldwide, representing some $15 trillion under management (Hobbs 2008). In many senses RI appeared to be poised to become a mainstream investment practice applied across various asset classes. A number of the members of the PRI, including the French national pension fund (Fonds de Réserve pour les Retraites) and the California Public Employees Retirement System (CalPERS), were extending the concepts of RI to asset classes beyond public equities.

At the same time, however, daily investment practices within the mainstream were apparently increasingly short-term in their time horizon and risky in their approach, as could be seen by the dramatic growth of hedge funds and large private equity firms and the increasing use of exotic financial instruments such as collateralized debt obligations and credit default swaps.

These five phases of the development of RI are summarized in Exhibit 21.5. The challenges faced by RI and its advocates as the financial world entered into a crisis of confidence in 2008, of a scope not seen since the Great Depression of the 1930s, are discussed in more detail in the last section of this chapter.

Responsible Investment and Financial Performance

Throughout the various phases of its development, the question of whether responsible investment imposes costs on financial returns has been the object of ongoing debate and extensive academic study. Advocates of socially responsible investing (SRI) have argued that social and environmental screens can help investors avoid risks unrecognized by traditional stock analysts, help identify high-quality corporate management, and highlight companies that are attuned to emerging issues—all of which should help boost performance (Camejo 2002). Critics have argued that, according to modern theories of portfolio management, any restriction on a universe of potential investments will increase undiversified risks and reduce risk-adjusted returns. Some have asserted that assets managed under such screens are insufficient to move stock prices. Others argue that social and environmental performance affects a company's overall reputation and that companies with stronger reputations can command higher price-to-earnings ratios in the stock markets and borrow at lower rates in the bond markets.[2]

Although this debate is likely to continue, considerable research indicates that, in general, social and environmental screening as recently practiced does not hurt a fund's financial performance. For example, a review of 31 socially screened mutual funds from 1990 to 1998 found that on average they outperformed their

Exhibit 21.5 The Five Phases of Responsible Investment

	Before 1970s Roots	1970s–1980s Development	1990s Transition	2000–2006 Expansion	2006 and Beyond Mainstreaming
Designation	Ethical investment	Socially responsible investment	Green funds: Socially responsible investment	Sustainable investment; best-of-class investing; triple-bottom-line investing	Responsible investment
Dominant logic	Moral and ethical grounds	Political grounds	Sustainability/ environmentalism	Professionalization	Mainstreaming
Dominant actor(s)	Faith-based institutions	Individual shareholder activists	Retail investors	Institutional investors	Mainstream investors
Dominant practice(s)	Avoidance	Shareholder activism	Inclusion	Best in class	Integration
Geographical spread	Essentially the United States	United States; Europe (mainly the United Kingdom)	North America; Europe; Asia; South Africa; Australia and New Zealand; Middle East		

400

unscreened peers, but not by a statistically significant margin (Statman 2000). Similarly, a 2001 academic review of 80 studies on the links between CSR and financial performance found that 58 percent of the studies observed a positive relationship to performance, 24 percent found no relationship, 19 percent found a mixed relationship, and only 5 percent found a negative relationship (Margolis and Walsh 2001).

As responsible investment finds application in asset classes beyond publicly traded stocks—such as fixed income, microlending, real estate, and private equity—this debate as well as an ongoing stream of studies examining RI's financial implications in practice will almost certainly continue (Lydenberg 2005).

TOOLS AND STRATEGIES USED BY RESPONSIBLE INVESTORS

Responsible investors vary in their motives and approaches to the discipline, although their underlying concerns may be the same. Four basic elements determine the final form that RI takes for these investors: (1) the degree of commitment, (2) the strategy adopted, (3) the tools used, and (4) the organizational approach taken. The investors' decisions about each of these elements shape their investment approach, the actions they take, and the types of outcomes they seek.

Degree of Commitment

In their stock selection, responsible investors may apply standards or screens either to the totality or to only part of their portfolio. Most stand-alone RI mutual funds in the United States, such as those run by Calvert, Domini, and Pax World, apply a set of RI screens to all the stocks in their equity funds. By contrast, in the early 2000s, several large European pension funds, such as the Dutch funds ABP and PGGM, allocated a limited portion of their equities to sustainability funds with environmental screens to test the effects of applying RI practices.

A second, alternative approach consists not in screening, but in applying a *responsible engagement overlay* to a part or all of one's assets. For example, this approach was promoted in the early 2000s by F&C Investments in the United Kingdom under the brand name *reo* and involved dialogue and engagement with the managers of the corporations in which investments were made. This approach does not require forgoing investment opportunities due to screening, while still allowing for dialogue and discussion with management on sustainability issues.

Strategies

Four strategies for implementation of RI screening coexist within the RI community. They can be used independently or, as often happens, in combination.

1. *Avoidance.* This approach seeks to avoid investing in companies engaged in businesses or practices regarded as unacceptable or generally harmful to society. It can be based on the exclusion of certain sectors or of certain activities.

2. *Inclusion.* This approach seeks to invest in companies engaged in business areas or practices that are exceptionally beneficial to society, particularly those encouraging a sustainable environment and economic development among the historically underserved.
3. *Relative selection.* This approach aims at selecting sector leaders on environmental, social, and governance (ESG) criteria. It invests across all industries and sectors, selecting the best-performing companies in each.
4. *Engagement.* This approach seeks either to supplement standard setting with contact with companies or to avoid screening altogether and concentrate instead on engaging with companies to voice shareholders' concerns on ESG and ethical issues.

According to surveys conducted in 2008, as much as 70 percent of the American and European RI industry may employ some kind of avoidance strategy, making it the dominant RI strategy (Eurosif 2008; U.S. SIF 2008), while inclusion strategies are employed by less than 10 percent of the European RI industry (Eurosif 2008). The avoidance strategy has been criticized as limited in impact and scope and as conveying a negative message that fails to encourage companies to improve their CSR commitments (Cowton 1999). The first decade of the twenty-first century has seen an increasing emphasis on the inclusion and relative-selection approaches, particularly among institutional investors.

Tools

For each of these four general strategies, a variety of specific tactics have been developed within the RI community since the 1970s.

The *avoidance* strategy has led to the development of a set of negative or exclusionary screening tools. A number of standards or screening tools have been developed that serve to exclude companies or sectors from the investment universe based on criteria relating to their products, services, policies, or actions. These screening tools include the following:

- Screens on products viewed as harmful by faith-based organizations and others concerned with ethical issues. These products include tobacco, alcohol, and gambling. In addition, a substantial Islamic finance practice has grown up in recent years that applies standards based on the teachings of the Koran. Among these is one on usury, which in effect excludes most companies in the financial sector.
- Screens on companies involved in products viewed as more generally harmful to society or the environment, such as land mines, nuclear weapons, nuclear power, ozone-depleting chemicals, pesticides, infant formula, and animal testing.
- Screens on companies doing business in countries generally regarded as contravening international human rights standards, such as Sudan and Burma.
- Screens based on international treaties and standards signed by governments but applicable in general to companies. These screens can relate to weapons of mass destruction or antipersonnel weapons, human rights, labor practices, environmental degradation, and similar issues.

Within this range of screening techniques, the specific exclusions applied are usually tailored to the values of individual and institutional investors and can vary considerably.

The *inclusion* strategy has led to the development of a set of positive screening tools. Tools that have been developed for these positive screens seek out companies or sectors particularly beneficial to society:

- Screens identifying companies promoting environmental sustainability through the development of energy efficiency, renewable and alternative energy technologies, pollution control and prevention, public transportation, and similar initiatives.
- Screens identifying companies promoting economic development and health among the historically underserved, such as mobile telephones, microfinance and microinsurance, vaccines, clean water, and related initiatives.

The *relative-selection* strategy has led to the development of a best-in-class screening tool. Best-in-class generally employs a substantial number of ESG criteria to score and rank companies. It then selects the best-performing (for example, top 10 percent) companies in each industry and excludes the rest. The number of ESG criteria used varies greatly. For example, SAM Group, a longtime proponent of best-of-class screening, uses some 130 criteria, while Asset 4 has developed a methodology that employs approximately 250 key performance indicators that it uses to rate and rank 2,300 companies worldwide.

Exhibit 21.6 provides examples of ESG criteria that are widely used in the RI world and often serve as the basis for best-in-class screening. In constructing scores for ratings, a weighting system is often applied to the different criteria in each sector to reflect the varying degree of importance of ESG issues for different industries. For example, environmental issues may be given a substantial weight in the chemical sector while human resource issues may be overweighted in the computer software industry.

Exhibit 21.6   Examples of Environmental, Social, and Governance Issues

Environmental (E)	Social (S)	Governance (G)
• Emissions	• Stakeholder relations	• Board structure
• Environmental policies	• Working conditions	• Independent directors
• Environmental management systems	• Respect for human rights	• Independent leadership
• Toxic chemicals	• Diversity	• Separation of chairman and CEO
• Genetic engineering	• Workplace health and safety	• Remuneration
• Pollution	• HIV/AIDS	• Shareholder rights
• Water	• Product safety	• Accounting quality
• Energy efficiency	• Treatment of customers	• Audit quality
• Hazardous and solid waste	• Labor relations	• Board skills

The *engagement* strategy has led to the development of a set of engagement tools. Over the past 30 years, shareholder activism and dialogue have become widely used strategies for those seeking to influence corporate behavior on a broad range of issues. Three primary modes of RI engagement have emerged: proxy voting, filing of shareholder resolutions, and dialogue with corporations.

Voting on the shareholder resolutions that appear on corporate proxy statements for annual general meetings is not only the right of all stockholders but the fiduciary obligation of institutional shareholders. Most resolutions appearing on proxy statements relate to corporate governance: election of board members, selection of auditors, approval of compensation packages for corporate executives, and related issues. In addition, resolutions relating to social and environmental matters also appear, particularly at U.S and Canadian companies. Adopting RI voting policies and communicating these policies to corporate management is therefore the most common form of engagement and is essentially applicable to all investors.

Filing shareholder resolutions is a more direct means of engagement with management, used particularly by the RI community in the United States and Canada where filing such resolutions is simpler than elsewhere. Since the early 1970s in the United States, members of the Interfaith Center on Corporate Responsibility have filed well over 100 such resolutions on social and environmental issues each year. Increasingly, unions are also using this tactic to raise corporate governance concerns. Although few proposals on social issues receive majority votes, these resolutions are an important tool in reaching management and initiating dialogue (Forum for the Future 2002).

Dialogue with corporate management is the third widely used form of engagement. RI institutional investors often enter into dialogue with managers on social and environmental issues such as human rights, labor standards, the environment, and diversity, as well as corporate governance matters. Increasingly dialogue is conducted through coalitions of RI investors, such as those participating in the Carbon Disclosure Project (CDP). The CDP is a coalition of institutional investors urging the largest corporations in the world to measure and disclose their carbon emissions.

Between 30 and 40 percent of the U.S. and European RI industries currently engage in some kind of shareholder activism or dialogue (Eurosif 2008; U.S. SIF 2008). While the U.S. RI industry is active in filing shareholder resolutions and public engagement, Europe is notably active in direct private engagement (Louche and Lydenberg 2006).

Organizational Approach

The organizational approaches that asset owners and money managers—be they pension funds or foundations, banks, private money managers, or mutual funds and unit trusts—choose to implement their RI strategies vary depending on whether they choose to conduct these activities internally or outsource them to vendors. Activities that can be outsourced include research, screening, and engagement.

On the research side, responsible investors have the option of either building their own in-house research team to evaluate the social and environmental records of publicly traded companies, or purchasing such services from specialized vendors. The advantage of having an in-house team is that RI investors can focus their research on the specific CSR issues of greatest importance to themselves; or, in the case of the managers of RI funds, they can perform their research on behalf of others and tailor separate portfolios to the concerns of a variety of clients. Examples of asset managers with in-house RI research capabilities—sometimes referred to as *green teams*—include F&C Investments and Morley Asset Management in the United Kingdom; Société Générale in France; Dexia Asset Management in Belgium/France; and Calvert Asset Management, Domini Social Investments, and Pax World Mutual Funds in the United States. These teams typically range in size from 5 to 15 researchers and are charged with developing the RI standards for in-house funds, conducting CSR research on specific companies, and maintaining lists of approved and excluded companies. In most cases, firms with in-house research teams combine their own research with the research provided by one or multiple outside research vendors.

Money managers or asset owners may also decide to rely primarily on outside RI research vendors for their RI research and screening. In this case, the firm typically maintains an internal staff of one to three persons responsible for overseeing research obtained from vendors and creating approved or excluded lists from that research. (See the next section for a listing and description of research providers often used by RI investors.) By using an outside vendor, the manager or asset owner relies on research criteria and screening methodologies developed by what are generally regarded as independent and high-quality parties, thereby avoiding the internal decision making and expense of customized research and screening. This approach is often adopted by money managers wishing to serve an RI clientele along with their other conventional clients, but choosing not to make RI a primary focus.

On the engagement side, similar options for the developing of in-house expertise or the outsourcing of services exist. (See the next section for a description of organizations providing outsourced engagement services.) An additional consideration for RI investors taking up the engagement tactic is whether to act alone or in coalitions with others as they approach corporations on social and environmental issues. As RI becomes an increasingly accepted practice, the trend is toward engagement in broad-based coalitions. One of the largest and most successful of these currently is the Carbon Disclosure Project, which as of 2009 included some 475 institutional investors with combined assets of approximately $55 trillion, seeking disclosure from the largest corporations in the world regarding their carbon emissions. In the United States, since the early 1970s, the Interfaith Center on Corporate Responsibility, a coalition of some 300 institutional investors, mainly religious organizations with combined portfolios worth an estimated $45 billion, has served as a coordinating organization for those engaging with corporations on a wide variety of CSR issues. In the Netherlands, VBDO, the Dutch Association of Investors for Sustainable Development, provides voting services and engages with companies in order to direct corporate policies and behavior toward sustainable performance. It has provided voting advice since 2005 to its clients and engages in dialogue with publicly traded Dutch companies on their behalf.

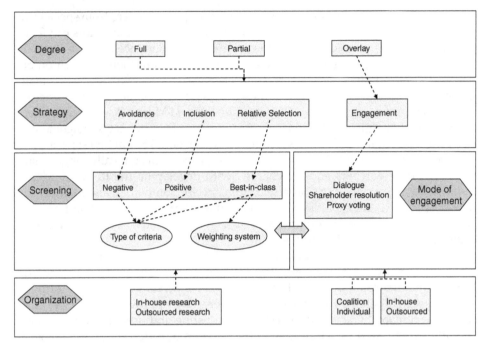

Exhibit 21.7   Map of Approaches to Responsible Investment

Coalitions have the advantages of pooled resources and coordinated action in approaching companies, increasing the chances for a successful engagement. In particular, they raise the level of seriousness of dialogue by assuring corporations of a breadth of concern for specific issues.

The approaches to RI outlined in this section are summarized in Exhibit 21.7.

MAJOR PLAYERS IN THE RESPONSIBLE INVESTING FIELD

As RI has evolved, the number and variety of players in the field has increased. Since the late 1990s RI investors have come to encompass individuals, small institutions, and, increasingly, large government and private pension funds. A growing number of specialized RI research firms and rating agencies, as well as in-house green teams within mainstream money management firms, have also emerged. These in-house teams and outside research firms play a crucial role in supporting the engagement between the financial community and corporate management on social and environmental issues and are important intermediaries between companies and fund managers as they have gained legitimacy in their assessments of companies (Louche, Gond, and Ventresca 2005).

The major players in the RI community today can be divided into three basic categories: asset owners, providers of support services to the RI field, and related organizations.

Asset Owners

The asset owners category refers to retail and institutional investors investing their funds according to RI principles.

Retail Investors

Retail RI investors are individuals wishing to invest in corporations that have positive social and environmental records and to avoid those with more questionable records. They usually invest in RI mutual funds (unit trusts) or, if they are particularly wealthy, through separate accounts managed by private banks or trust offices. They are typically driven by a desire to use their investments as part of a commitment to lives that improve the world.

The retail market for RI products is notably strong in the United States and Japan. In the United States, retail investors, along with religious organizations, were historically one of the driving forces of the RI movement as it evolved during the 1970s and 1980s (Louche and Lydenberg 2006).

According to the U.S. Social Investment Forum, as of 2007 in the United States there were 260 RI mutual funds with $202 billion in assets. These funds primarily serve retail RI investors and retirement savings plans (defined contribution pension plans) for individuals. In Europe, the number of RI retail funds in 2008 was 437, representing €49 billion in assets.

Retail investors may participate in the RI market individually or through retirement savings plans offered by institutional investors. For example, TIAA-CREF, the retirement plan for many college and university professors in the United States, offers its Social Choice Account, which as of year-end 2008 had assets of approximately $6.5 billion.[3]

In Japan, social investing began in the mid-1990s with the launch of a number of retail funds with environmental and sustainability themes (ASrIA 2003; Sakuma and Louche 2008; Solomon, Solomon, and Suto 2004). As of 2007, there were some 34 RI funds in Japan with combined assets of approximately ¥58 billion, or approximately US$3 billion (Sakuma and Louche 2008). Institutional investors currently play a relatively minor role in the Japanese RI market.

Institutional Investors

Since the late 1990s, institutional investors, particularly in Europe, have become a major factor in the responsible investment movement (Albareda and Balaguer 2009). In the 1970s and 1980s in the United States, a substantial number of state and municipal pension funds participated in the South Africa divestment movement to protest the apartheid legal system there. At its peak, many of the major pension funds in the United States, including those of the states of California, New York, New Jersey, Massachusetts, and Wisconsin, with hundreds of billions of dollars in assets, had policies limiting investments in companies doing business in that country (Massie 1997). With the dismantling of apartheid in 1994, these American pension funds pulled back from RI activities.

With the growth of interest in sustainability in Europe starting in the mid-1990s, and the simultaneous privatization of many industries previously in state hands, governments and institutional investors became increasingly interested in responsible investment. Governments, including the European Union, began

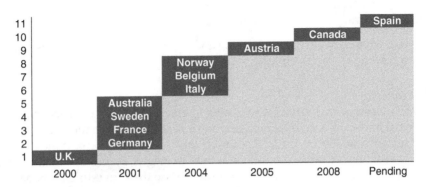

Exhibit 21.8 The Adoption of Disclosure Regulations for Pension Funds

promoting the concept of corporate social responsibility, and various national and local pension funds began adopting aspects of RI. One early move in the promoting of RI among institutional investors came in the late 1990s and early 2000s when the governments of the United Kingdom, Germany, and Sweden, among others, adopted policies requiring pension funds to state whether they took social and environmental considerations into account in their investment practices (see Exhibit 21.8). At the EU level, discussions around increased transparency by institutional investors on their RI practices were underway as of early 2009 (Eurosif 2009).

As a result of these RI disclosure requirements, a number of large European pension plans have increasingly adopted specific RI practices. The Norwegian national pension fund has established specific screens on weapons, human rights, bribery, and the environment.[4] The Swedish national pension plans have varying policies, including several with weapons and human rights screens.[5] The French Fonds de Réserve pour les Retraites (Retirement Reserve Fund) is planning to apply sustainability criteria across all asset classes.[6]

One of the most significant developments in the institutional investor field, however, has been the creation of the Principles for Responsible Investment (PRI),[7] under the aegis of the United Nations Global Compact. Launched in 2006, the PRI had been endorsed by approximately 150 pension funds and other large institutional investors as of early 2009, including major pension funds from throughout the world.

By signing the PRI, they agree to implement six basic practices in their investing:

1. Incorporate ESG issues into their investment analysis and decision making.
2. Incorporate ESG issues into their ownership policies and practices.
3. Seek ESG disclosure.
4. Promote the PRI principles within the financial industry.
5. Work cooperatively to implement the PRI principles.
6. Report on progress in implementing the PRI principles.

The PRI is particularly significant because it provides a forum to institutional investors for consensus building on best practices, collaborative action, engagement, and the promotion of academic work in the field.

Support Services

This second category consists of actors that provide support services to the RI. It consists of money managers, financial consultants, research providers, and those offering engagement services.

Money Managers and Financial Consultants

As the market for RI has grown, the financial community has also responded. Having treated RI with suspicion as it emerged in the 1970s and 1980s, many, if not most, large financial institutions now offer RI services.

A number of mainstream money managers and financial institutions in the United Kingdom have committed to applying responsible investment principles to all of their assets. These include:

- *F&C Investments*. F&C describes its commitment to responsible investment as "fundamental to our global investment philosophy across all our funds." In addition to managing some £3.4 billion in funds with RI screens, it engages with corporate management on behalf of all its own funds, as well as providing an engagement service to others.[8]
- *Hermes Asset Management*. Owned by its largest client, the BT Pension Scheme, Hermes describes itself as "completely committed to responsible investment and the long-term approach that it entails." Hermes manages some £27 billion in funds for a variety of clients, including BT, with an interest in responsible investment.[9]
- *Co-operative Bank*. A part of the Co-operative Group, a large UK consumer cooperative organization, the bank had £18 billion in unit trust assets under management as of September 2008 and analyzes "social, ethical, environmental and other company management issues (e.g., 'fat cat' pay) across all the funds we manage."[10]

RI money managers serve a variety of clients with a variety of social and environmental considerations. One fast-growing segment of the RI market is Islamic investing. Investors in Islamic countries have become increasingly interested in developing and applying approaches based on the teachings of the Koran. As interpreted by most Sharia committees (local committees of clerics charged with applying the Koran's principles to daily life), the Islamic approach resembles traditional Christian RI screening in that, for example, it avoids companies producing alcohol. However, its interpretation of the Koran's condemnation of usury can require the screening out of financial services companies. According to a report by the Oliver Wyman consulting firm, Islamic finance will reach $1.6 trillion in assets by 2012, and as of year-end 2007 had $660 billion under management (Zaywa Finance 2009).

As interest in RI has grown, financial consultants—who serve as gatekeepers for institutional investors, advising them on management practices and helping them implement their financial objectives—are increasingly recognizing responsible investment as a legitimate discipline and advising interested clients on how best to enter the field. Among the major financial consulting firms with RI teams in place as of 2009 were Mercer and Cambridge Associates.

Research Providers
To serve the growing need for data to implement RI strategies and tactics, a number of RI research organizations have sprung up. These organizations provide background data on the social and environmental records of publicly traded companies, rating and ranking their performance. The information they provide is used primarily by institutional investors for investment decisions or shareholder engagement.

In 2007, the French consultancy Observatoire sur la Responsabilité Sociétale des Entreprises (ORSE), in an update of a study originally published in 2001, surveyed the methodologies and services of 30 RI research and rating organizations (ORSE 2007). Among the major firms are EIRIS (United Kingdom), GES Investment Services (Scandinavia), Jantzi-Sustainalytics (Canada and the Netherlands), PIRC (United Kingdom), RiskMetrics Group (including KLD Research & Analytics, United States), SIRIS (Australia), and Vigeo (France).

Engagement Services
Engagement with corporations to encourage positive change has been an important feature of RI since its inception. During the 1970s, engagement was in many senses the primary focus of RI in the United States. Since 2000 it has become increasingly an important part of the sustainable investment movement. Among organizations with a strong focus on engagement as of 2009:

- F&C Investments, which has an engagement protocol called Responsible Engagement Overlay (reo) that it applies to all its assets plus an additional £63 billion of funds managed by other investment institutions.[11]
- Principles for Responsible Investment Engagement Clearinghouse, which provides its institutional investors with a platform for sharing information on engagement activities and encourages collaborative engagement efforts.[12]
- GES Investment Services Engagement Forum, which facilitates collaborative actions among Northern European institutional investors, with a particular focus on encouraging companies to meet international norms on social, environmental, and governance issues.[13]

In addition, proxy voting advisory services, such as RiskMetrics Group and Glass Lewis in North America and PIRC in the United Kingdom, provide recommendations on how to vote on the numerous shareholder resolutions filed each year on corporate governance, social, and environmental issues.

Related Initiatives

The last category of actors covers all other organizations and initiatives that are involved and active in the field of responsible investment. It consists of trade organizations, think tanks, national stock exchanges, and national governments.

RI Associations and Think Tanks

With the growth of RI, a number of associations facilitating networking, meetings, and the promotion of best practices have evolved. These initiatives bring together professional practitioners, researchers, and academics.

The most widespread model for these associations is the *social investment forum*, or SIF. As of 2009, the European Social Investment Forum (Eurosif) served as an umbrella for seven European national SIFs—Belgium, France, Germany, Italy, the Netherlands, Sweden, and the United Kingdom—and was affiliated with four other SIFs in Asia, Australia, Canada, and the United States.[14]

In addition to the Principles for Responsible Investment, other coalitions of investors organized around particular issues, such as the Carbon Disclosure Project and the Investors Network on Climate Risk, are also increasingly emerging and attracting widespread participation. In addition, organizations such as the Enhanced Analytics Initiative have been formed to influence money managers and fund owners to factor into their investment practices those negative and positive externalities relating to ESG that companies have created.

An increasing number of RI academic research initiatives are also underway, including the Moskowitz Research Program at the Center for Responsible Business at the University of California, Berkeley; the Sustainable Investment Research Platform, hosted by the Umeâ School of Business in Sweden and sponsored by the Mistra Research Program on Sustainable Investments; the European Center for Corporate Engagement, a joint initiative of Maastricht University and RSM Erasmus University in the Netherlands; and the Initiative for Responsible Investment at the Harvard University Kennedy School.

National Governments and Stock Exchanges

Also enhancing the growth of SRI around the world have been initiatives by governments and national stock exchanges to promote corporate social responsibility, along with the creation of socially responsible stock indexes by private parties.

To overcome one important barrier to the implementation of SRI in the equities market—the lack of data on the corporate social responsibility records of publicly traded companies—a number of national governments have taken steps, sometimes in conjunction with their national stock exchanges, to encourage and even mandate increased CSR disclosure (Investments 2008). Among countries engaged in these efforts are the following:

- The government of France in 2001 mandated disclosure in financial reports of some 40 key CSR data points by publicly traded companies.
- The government of Malaysia has required publicly traded companies to disclose CSR data in their annual reports since 2007 and imposed CSR requirements for companies listed on its national stock exchange.
- In South Africa, the JSE Limited (formerly the Johannesburg Stock Exchange) has published its SRI Index since 2004, listing companies with the best CSR records.
- The government of Sweden has mandated that companies with state ownership report on their CSR records by 2009, following the guidelines developed by the Global Reporting Initiative.

- The government of Denmark mandated in late 2008 that the 1,100 largest companies in that country begin disclosing CSR data or report on why they do not do so (Cooper 2009).

In addition, a number of RI research firms around the world have created indexes of their own, listing companies they believe fit various criteria for responsible investors. ORSE (2007) lists 12 groups of such indexes, including those maintained by KLD Research & Analytics; SAM Group and Dow Jones; and EIRIS and FTSE. These indexes serve as the basis for a number of financial products.

MAJOR CHALLENGES OF RI TODAY

Despite the growth in interest in RI over the past 30 years, RI remains a niche market within the traditional financial community and a number of important questions confront the field as it continues to evolve. Four of the major challenges are:

1. Can RI become mainstream?
2. Can RI be applied across all asset classes?
3. Can RI develop tools to measure sustainability risks and rewards?
4. Can RI address the issues raised by the financial crises of 2008–2009?

Can RI Become Mainstream?

The increasingly global reach of the RI industry has led some authors to conclude that RI is becoming mainstream (Friedman and Miles 2001; Sparkes and Cowton 2004; World Economic Forum 2005; Zadek, Merme, and Samans 2005). Investment managers, brokers, and fund managers are increasingly interested in RI or specific RI issues such as the environment (Ambachtsheer 2005; PLEON 2005; Taylor Nelson Sofres 2003). A 2007 survey showed that there is a common belief among investors that RI is expected to grow by 25 percent per annum over the next few years and become mainstream by 2015 at the latest (Robeco and Booz & Company 2007).

Money managers such as Generation Investment Management, where former U.S. Vice President Al Gore is a partner, view the practice of sustainable investment as a source of competitive advantage. In addition, regulatory pressures, collaborative initiatives such as the Principles for Responsible Investment, and the trend toward shareholder engagement are bringing RI into the mainstream.

However, a number of hurdles remain before RI will be fully accepted:

- Models quantifying ESG data in stock valuation need to be developed. A 2005 World Business Council for Sustainable Development Young Managers Team and the UN Environmental Program Financial Initiative survey found that young financial analysts felt unequipped to incorporate ESG issues into mainstream company analysis (Jaworski 2007; WBCSD and UNEP Finance Initiative 2005).
- Cross-fertilization between mainstream financial analysts and ESG specialists needs to be encouraged.

- The dominant single-dimensional assessment of companies only on financial dimensions needs to move toward multidimensional models that include ESG issues.
- The communications gap between companies and investors with regard to ESG issues and their relation to materiality needs to be overcome.
- The inherent short-termism of today's financial markets that undercuts the long-term orientation of RI needs to be addressed (Guyatt 2006; Juravle and Lewis 2008).

Can RI Be Applied across All Asset Classes?

Discussions about RI in academic literature and the general press often focus on its theory and practice in relationship to publicly traded corporations. Increasingly RI practices are also applied to other asset classes—most notably cash, fixed income, and real estate, but also private equity and hedge funds.

- The Institute for Responsible Investment (2007) has noted that although the underlying principles of RI remain the same for each asset class, the specific social and environmental issues that they are most naturally suited to address vary from one asset class to another. For example: Cash investments in banks, credit unions, and revolving loan funds are naturally suited for local community economic development, particularly serving the historically underserved. Microfinance is currently a prominent example of RI's integration into the asset class of cash.
- Fixed-income investments in the bonds issued by national and local governments are particularly well suited for the creation of large-scale public goods such as affordable housing, transportation infrastructure, and education. In the United States, Community Capital Management and RBC Global Asset Management's Capital Access Strategies are examples of the use of this asset class to support affordable housing and environmental infrastructure projects.
- Real estate investments are naturally suited to promote environmentally sustainable communities emphasizing proximity to public transportation, walkability, and energy-efficient properties. The UN Environmental Program's Financial Initiative Real Estate Property Working Group, for example, is currently promoting best practices in sustainable real estate development among institutional investors.

A major question for RI is whether it can develop a theory that applies RI to all asset classes.

Can RI Develop Tools to Measure Sustainability Risks and Rewards?

Contemporary investment practice is dominated by the measurement of risk and reward in relation to price-based benchmarks. Risk (usually defined as volatility or *beta*) and rewards (usually defined as excess risk-adjusted returns or *alpha*) do not account for the social and environmental risks and rewards of investments.

Pioneering work has been done by RI research firms such as Trucost in quantifying environmental risk—in Trucost's case, quantifying the carbon footprint of companies and the implied financial risk.[15] The RI research firm Innovest (acquired by RiskMetrics Group in 2009) has produced "intangible value assessments" that capture the social and environmental capital created by firms.[16]

In 2005, Freshfields Bruckhaus Deringer, a prominent international law firm, concluded that investment managers' fiduciary duties should not necessarily preclude or overly hamper RI (Freshfields Bruckhaus Deringer 2005). According to this report ESG information should be taken into account whenever it is relevant to the investment strategy. Where the link between ESG factors and financial performance is recognized, the integration of ESG is not only permissible but even advisable.

How best to report on the full range of social and environmental risks and rewards of investments is a question the RI community needs to address.

Can RI Address Issues Raised by the Financial Crises of 2008–2009?

The worldwide financial crises of 2008–2009 have raised questions about the wisdom of many of the practices of contemporary investing driven by the application of modern portfolio theory (MPT). Whether RI can construct a theoretical framework that justifies its approach as an alternative to certain aspects of MPT remains an unresolved question. Without such a theoretical framework, however, it is unlikely that RI will be able to replace or modify in a meaningful way the investment practices that led to these crises (Lydenberg and Sinclair 2009).

NOTES

1. From the 1970s through 1994 many pension funds and other institutional investors, particularly in the United States, had adopted South African divestment policies, but in general they withdrew from the RI field with the dismantling of apartheid in 1994.
2. For those interested in an extensive annotated bibliography of academic studies on this topic, see the web site maintained by the Center for Responsible Business, sristudies.org.
3. See TIAA-CREF's web site at http://www.tiaa-cref.org/ (accessed April 8, 2009).
4. See Norges Bank Investment Management's web site at http://www.norges-bank.no (accessed April 8, 2009).
5. See http://www.ipe.com/news/Swedish_buffer_funds_exclude_cluster_bomb_investment_29115.php (accessed April 8, 2009).
6. See FRR's web site at http://www.fondsdereserve.fr/ (accessed April 8, 2009).
7. See PRI's web site at http://www.unpri.org/ (accessed April 8, 2009).
8. See F&C's web site at http://www.fandc.com/new/aboutus/Default.aspx?id=82810 (accessed April 8, 2009).
9. See Hermes Investment's web site at http://www.hermes.co.uk/abt_our_philosophy.aspx (accessed April 8, 2009).
10. See Cooperative Bank's web site at http://www.co-operativeinvestments.co.uk/servlet/Satellite/1204616032483,CFSweb/Page/Investments-UnitTrustsAndISAs (accessed April 8, 2009).

11. See F&C web site at http://www.fandc.com/new/institutional/Default.aspx?ID=80961 (accessed April 9, 2009).

12. See the PRI web site at http://www.unpri.org/workstreams/#1 (accessed April 9, 2009).

13. See the GES web site at http://www.ges-invest.com/pages/?ID=70 (accessed April 9, 2009).

14. See the EuroSIF web site at http://www.eurosif.org/about_eurosif/sifs/other_sif_s_around_the_world (accessed April 9, 2009).

15. See Trucost's web site at www.trucost.com (accessed April 9, 2009).

16. See RiskMetrics web site at http://www.riskmetrics.com/sustainability (accessed April 9, 2009).

REFERENCES

AccountAbility. 2006. The materiality report: Aligning strategy, performance and reporting. London: AccountAbility.

Albareda, L., and F. M. R. Balaguer. 2009. The challenges of socially responsible investment among institutional investors: Exploring the links between corporate pension funds and corporate governance. *Business & Society Review* 114:31–57.

Ambachtsheer, J. 2005. SRI: What do investment managers think? Mercer Investment Consulting. www.mercer.com.

ASrIA. 2003. SRI in Asia. www.asria.org.

Camejo, P. 2002. *The SRI advantage: Why socially responsible investing has outperformed financially.* Gabriealla Island, British Columbia: New Society Publishers.

Cooper, B. 2009. Danish reporting rules. *Ethical Corporation*, March: 26–29.

Cowton, C. J. 1999. Playing by the rules: Ethical criteria at an ethical investment fund. *Business Ethics: A European Review* 8:60–69.

Déjean, F., J.-P. Gond, and B. Leca. 2004. Measuring the unmeasured: An institutional entrepreneur's strategy in an emerging industry. *Human Relations* 57:741–764.

Domini, A. L. 2001. *Socially responsible investing: Making a difference in making money.* Chicago: Dearborn Trade.

European Sustainable Investment Forum (Eurosif). 2008. European SRI study. www.eurosif.org/publications/sri_studies.

———. 2009. www.eurosif.org.

Forum for the Future. 2002. Sustainability pays, http://www.cis.co.uk/socacc2002/pdf/SusPays.pdf: Co-operative Insurance Society in association with Forum for the Future.

Freshfields Bruckhaus Deringer. 2005. A legal framework for the integration of environmental, social and governance issues into institutional investment: UNEP FI. http://www.unepfi.org/fileadmin/documents/freshfields_legal_resp_20051123.pdf

Friedman, A. L., and S. Miles. 2001. Socially responsible investment and corporate social and environmental reporting in the UK: An explorative study. *British Accounting Review* 33:523–548.

Gond, J. P., and E. Boxenbaum. 2004. Importing "socially responsible investment" in France and Quebec: Work of contextualization across varieties of capitalism. Paper presented at the EGOS, Ljubljana.

Guyatt, D. J. 2006. *Identifying and overcoming behavioural impediments to long-term responsible investments—a focus on UK institutional investors.* Unpublished PhD dissertation, University of Bath.

Hobbs, M. 2008. UN PRI enlists 400 firms. *Financial Standard* 28 (July). http://www.financialstandard.com.au/news/view/23618/.

Institute for Responsible Investment. 2007. Handbook on responsible investment across asset classes.

Jaworski, W. 2007. Use of extra-financial information by research analysts and investment managers. European Center for Corporate Engagement (ECCE).

Juravle, C., and A. Lewis. 2008. Identifying impediments to SRI in Europe: A review of the practitioner and academic literature. *Business Ethics: A European Review* 17:285–310.

Lipper FERI. 2008. From niche to mainstream. *Hot Topics*. http://www.lipperfmi.com/FERIFMI/Information/Files/Hot%20Topics%20SRI%200807.pdf

Louche, C. 2004. *Ethical investment: Processes and mechanisms of institutionalisation in the Netherlands, 1990–2002*. PhD dissertation, Erasmus University Rotterdam. Rotterdam: Optima Grafische Communicatie. https://ep.eur.nl/retrieve/3259/ESM-dissertation-3003.pdf.

Louche, C., J.-P. Gond, and M. Ventresca. 2005. Legitimating social rating organisations: on the role of objects in the micro-processes of SRI legitimacy-building in Europe. Paper presented at the IABS, Sonoma, California.

Louche, C., and S. Lydenberg. 2006. Socially responsible investment: Difference between Europe and United States. Working Paper. Vlerick Leuven Gent Management School.

Lydenberg, S. 2005. *Corporations and the public interest: Guiding the invisible hand*. San Francisco, CA: Berrett-Koehler Publishers, Inc.

———. 2007. Long term investing. Paper presented at the 2007 summit on the future of the corporation, Paper No. 5.

Lydenberg, S., and G. Sinclair. 2009. Mainstream or daydream? *Journal of Corporate Citizenship*, June.

Margolis, J. D., and J. P. Walsh. 2001. *People and profits? The search for a link between a company's social and financial performance*. Mahwah, NJ: Lawrence Erlbaum and Associates.

Massie, R. 1997. *Loosing the bonds*. New York: Nan A. Talese.

ORSE. 2007. Guide to sustainability analysis organisations. Paris: EDEME, EPE, ORSE.

PLEON. 2005. Accounting for good: The Global Stakeholder Report 2005: Pleon Kohtes Klewes GmbH / Pleon b.v.

Post, J., L. E. Preston, and S. Sachs. 2002. *Redefining the corporation: Stakeholder management and organizational wealth*. Stanford, CA: Stanford University Press.

Robeco and Booz & Company. 2007. Responsible investing: A paradigm shift from niche to mainstream. http://www.booz.com/media/uploads/Responsible-Investing-Paradigm-Shift.pdf

Sakuma, K., and C. Louche. 2008. Socially responsible investment in Japan: Its mechanism and drivers. *Journal of Business Ethics* 82:425–448.

SIRI Group. 2007. Green, social and ethical funds in Europe—2007 review. Milan: SiRi Group/Avanzi.

Solomon, A., J. Solomon, and M. Suto. 2004. Can the UK experience provide lessons for the evolution of SRI in Japan? *Corporate Governance: An International Review* 12:552–566.

Sparkes, R. 2001. Ethical investment: Whose ethics, which investment? *Business Ethics: A European Review* 10:194–205.

Sparkes, R., and C. J. Cowton. 2004. The maturing of socially responsible investment: A review of the developing link with corporate social responsibility. *Journal of Business Ethics*, 52:45–57.

Statman, M. 2000. Socially responsible mutual funds. *Financial Analysts Journal* 56:30–39.

Taylor Nelson Sofres. 2003. Investing in responsible business—the 2003 survey of European fund managers, financial analysts and investor relations officers: CSR Europe, Deloitte, Euronext.

U.S. Social Investment Forum (SIF). 2008. 2007 report on socially responsible investing trends in US—executive summary. Washington, DC: US Social Investment Forum.

WBCSD Young Managers Team, and UNEP Finance Initiative. 2005. Generation lost: young financial analysts and environmental, social and governance issues. http://www.wbcsd.org/web/publications/ymt-perspectives.pdf

World Economic Forum. 2005. Mainstreaming responsible investment. Cologny/Geneva, Switzerland.

Zadek, S., M. Merme, and R. Samans. 2005. Mainstreaming responsible investment. Geneva: Accountability and World Economic Forum.

Zaywa Finance. 2009. Islamic asset to reach $1.6 billion with revenues of $120 billion despite short-term market volatility. April 10. http://www.zawya.com/printstory.cfm?storyid=ZAWYA20090406075859&l=075800090406.

ABOUT THE AUTHORS

Céline Louche is assistant professor at Vlerick Leuven Gent Management School (Belgium). She teaches and researches on corporate social responsibility and sustainability. In her work, she explores the way processes of change take place with a special focus on CSR as a factor of innovation and value creation, socially responsible investment, and stakeholders' processes. Before joining Vlerick, Céline worked five years as a sustainability analyst for SRI at the Dutch Sustainability Research institute. She is member of the Academic Board of EABIS, the scientific committee of the RIODD, and the SRI advisory committee of Dexia Asset Management.

Steven Lydenberg is chief investment officer for Domini Social Investments LLC. He has been active in social investing for 35 years as director of corporate accountability research with the Council on Economic Priorities, investment associate with what is now Trillium Asset Management, and director of research with KLD Research & Analytics. Mr. Lydenberg is the co-author of *Rating America's Corporate Conscience* (Addison-Wesley, 1985) and *Investing for Good* (HarperCollins, 1993), and co-editor of *The Social Investment Almanac* (Henry Holt, 1992). He is the author of *Corporations and the Public Interest: Guiding the Invisible Hand*, published by Berrett-Koehler in early 2005.

CHAPTER 22

Microfinance*

ANTONIO ARGANDOÑA
Professor of Economics, "la Caixa" Chair of Corporate Social Responsibility
and Corporate Governance, IESE Business School, University of Navarra

INTRODUCTION

Although microfinance as a practice is probably very old, the term itself is very recent. It started to be used in the 1960s and 1970s when organizations such as ACCION International, Opportunity International, and Grameen Bank started to grant small loans (less than US$100) to microentrepreneurs, mostly women. These loans were backed by a group guarantee, thus overcoming the lack of collateral which was the main reason why commercial banks neglected the low-income segments of the population.

Since then, microfinance has experienced considerable growth. In 2006, Muhammad Yunus and the Grameen Bank were awarded the Nobel Peace Prize "for their efforts to create economic and social development from below." In awarding the prize, the Nobel committee wrote, "From modest beginnings three decades ago, Yunus has, first and foremost through Grameen Bank, developed microcredit into an ever more important instrument in the struggle against poverty."[1] At present, microfinance is a standard tool in development and poverty reduction policies. It is estimated that in 2007 the volume of outstanding microcredits in the world stood at about US$25 billion, with about 125 to 150 million beneficiaries (*Financial Times* 2008, 1).[2]

The social goal pursued by the microcredit lending agencies gave them an aura of respectability that they have maintained over the decades. However, with the passing of time, critical voices have also emerged: Some of the features that made microfinance attractive have been lost or become blurred, such as the joint liability (see later section on microcredits, discussing group guarantees). Other questionable aspects, such as the high interest rates charged by the microcredits, have been maintained, and microfinancial institutions (MFIs) have placed increasing emphasis on their operations' economic sustainability, which has led some to think that they were not being true to their social function and ethical mission.

---

*This chapter forms part of the activities of the "la Caixa" Chair of Corporate Social Responsibility and Corporate Governance, IESE Business School.

This chapter offers an overview of microfinance and a detailed discussion of the ethical problems associated with it. There is a very extensive literature on microlending,[3] but the literature that is specifically concerned with its ethical dimension is very limited (Hudon 2006, 2007, 2009; Vakulabharanam and Motiram 2007; Vanroose 2007). The following sections discuss the concept and scope of microfinance and the features of the microcredits, after which the chapter turns to issues with a more substantial ethical content: microfinance's social responsibility, the debate over the MFIs' financial sustainability versus their social function, and the ethical issues raised by setting interest rates and the MFIs' right to earn a profit. The chapter closes with some conclusions.

MICROFINANCE

The shortest definition of *microfinance*, and perhaps the most comprehensive, is the provision of financial services to poor, low-income people who, in normal conditions, would not have access to them (the *unbankables*). The reasons for this exclusion may be their location (farmers who live far away from towns); their lack of income (which makes it difficult to repay the loan) or assets (which keeps them from providing any surety); their lack of a financial track record; or other reasons, which altogether mean that the potential client is not profitable for a traditional financial institution. Microfinancial services started with the microcredits, but they also include payment methods (cards, transfers, emigrant remittances), savings instruments (current and savings accounts and other assets), insurance, pension funds, financial leasing, and so on. This extension is based on the realization that microentrepreneurs' needs go much further than credit and may also include training, creation of social networks, education, health, access to land ownership, and information.

Microfinancial services are provided by a broad range of organizations, including commercial banks, nonbank financial companies, public and development banks, and credit unions, both nonprofit and for-profit. The institutional landscape is completed with (1) the providers of funds, which may be the clients themselves (through deposits) or other financial institutions, such as unit trusts, private equity, and public or private donors; (2) partner financial institutions that render services to foundations or NGOs; and (3) supranational organizations that create microlending networks, such as ACCION International, Women's World Banking (WWB), Kreditanstalt für Wiederaufbau (KfW), and the Small Enterprise Education and Promotion (SEEP) Network.

The goal of microfinance is to ameliorate poverty and underdevelopment. It is based on two basic assumptions: (1) The lack of access to financial services is a major (although not the only) cause of poverty, and (2) access to credit is key for the development of entrepreneurial projects that will provide borrowers with a stable income, assets, and the knowledge and skills that will enable them to lift themselves from poverty, thereby extending the impact to the local community (through the creation of jobs and income, the generation of new ideas) and to the country as a whole. This assumption implicitly holds another within it: There is a considerable supply of entrepreneurial ability, even among people without any financial resources or specific training.

MICROCREDITS

Based on the practices of the Grameen Bank, microcredits are usually identified as having the following 12 features (Armendáriz de Aghion and Morduch, 2005):

1. They are for small amounts.
2. The beneficiaries are poor or very poor families and, within them, particularly women.
3. Their goal is to help the beneficiaries put an end to a state of poverty by generating self-employment activities or entrepreneurial projects and, sometimes, enabling construction or purchase of a dwelling; but the microcredits do not cover day-to-day expenses.
4. They are not backed by physical collateral or a contract whose performance can be enforced by law but are founded instead on trust.
5. In order to obtain the credit, the beneficiary must belong to a group (group lending); considerable importance is given to the creation of social capital among the participants.
6. The guarantee is collective, with joint responsibility by the entire group.
7. The microcredit program develops a distinctive credit selection and management methodology and a personalized system for relations between the MFI's staff and its clients; it is the bank that goes to the client and not the client who goes to the bank.
8. Interest and capital are paid in regular installments at frequent periods (every week or fortnight) and in public.
9. The credits are granted in a continuous sequence. The quantity offered in each new credit increases and is conditional upon prior repayment of the previous loans by all of the group's members.
10. The lending program is complemented with compulsory or voluntary savings programs.
11. The interest rates stipulated do not seek to provide an attractive return for investors but to guarantee the program's sustainability. However, the sustainability goal is subordinated to providing a service to the poor.
12. The loans are usually granted through nonprofit organizations or institutions owned by the users themselves (cooperatives), although participation is also open to for-profit institutions.

However, microlending can take many and varied forms, such that, in practice, there is no unanimous—or even majority—agreement on each of these individual features. Let us examine each of these features more closely.

1. *Amount.* A microcredit is the act of lending a small amount, less than what is usually lent in commercial banking. Its amount depends on the borrowers' ability to use it effectively and, above all, on their ability to pay interest and return the capital in various installments.
2. *Beneficiaries.* Microcredits usually target people who are close to the poverty threshold (they live on slightly more than two dollars a day), "poor" people (who live on less than two dollars a day), and "destitute" people (who

live on less than one dollar a day). The ethical problems arising from the microloans' goals and beneficiaries are discussed later in this chapter.

3. *Women*. Preferential lending to women is based on three assumptions: (1) They are better administrators than men; (2) the money they receive will have a greater effect on the family's well-being, particularly on the children; and (3) in many countries, they are discriminated against in the development of their abilities and the roles they can perform, with the consequence that the microcredits may be a useful tool for increasing their empowerment and improving their status and opportunities. In fact, many microcredit programs target primarily women (97 percent, in the case of the Grameen Bank, for example [*Financial Times* 2008]).[4]

4. *Microenterprises*. The microcredit's purpose is not to solve occasional problems caused by lack of income but to start a self-employment program or create or expand a microenterprise. Borrowers may buy a business or farmland, operate a small industrial or craft business, engage in retail sale, street-selling, farming, and so on. The intention is that borrowers be able to generate future income that will enable them to pay interest and return the loan. This purpose of the microcredit is based on two assumptions: (1) that poor people have entrepreneurial abilities that they cannot put to good use due to lack of financial resources, so that providing these resources will enable them to change their lives; and (2) that self-help is much more effective than public or private aid targeting the low-income population.

5. *Other uses*. Rather than restricting the microcredit to an income-generating function, other authors suggest that the borrower be allowed to decide how the funds are used, which may also include covering extraordinary expenses (a wedding, a funeral, or a disease), a temporary fall in income (a bad harvest), the purchase of a trousseau or educational expenses, and so on (Nourse 2001).[5] However, if the microcredit is used for consumption, it may be harder for borrowers to repay it, and its economic impact may be more limited.

6. *Group guarantee*. Microcredits are usually not granted against a physical guarantee but on the basis of trust. Accordingly, credit applicants join groups that perform a variety of functions: share information, negotiate together, monitor other borrowers' compliance, and even share in their members' liability, undertaking to pay their debt if the borrower defaults.

The most distinctive feature of microlending, at least in its early stages, is this group liability. Because the borrowers have no assets, individual guarantees are replaced by that of the group, whose formation is facilitated by the fact that the members already know each other. These members join the group voluntarily and usually live in the same place. The group's meetings with the MFI's representative are held in public, and at these meetings, each member makes her payment in the presence of all the others. The fact that it is a group enables members to monitor each other's compliance and bring pressure to bear on defaulters, appealing to incentives such as reputation loss, shame, or reprisals.

However, many authors criticize joint liability. For example, it raises free-rider problems (Stiglitz and Weiss 1981); the fact that liability is accepted jointly may attract potential borrowers with a higher risk (adverse selection) and encourage higher-risk behaviors (moral hazard). And it may also have a domino effect, when nonpayment by one member of the group induces the others to also default if the liability they would incur is too burdensome (Schreiner 2003). Therefore, if social pressure is to effectively counteract these perverse incentives, it must be very strong, perhaps unjustly so.

7. *Individual guarantee.* In spite of the success achieved with the group credit,[6] many MFIs do not work with groups, and some of those that do are reducing the percentage of their portfolio made up of group loans (including Grameen Bank). This may be for efficiency reasons: Many of the advantages previously discussed (sharing information, peer pressure to abide by the contract, and mutual help) are the result of the group treatment of credit, without any need for joint liability. It may be appropriate in the program's early stages, but when the group and the MFI have obtained the necessary information on each member and the member in question has already acquired some real guarantees and a greater confidence in her project, the individual guarantee may offer more advantages (Drugov and Macchiavello 2008).[7]

8. *Repayment.* When the loan is granted, regular installments are specified for paying interest and returning the capital (the installment amount is constant during the loan period). The first installment is usually a few days (often one week) after the loan is granted, and the installments are also spaced closely together (weekly or fortnightly) during the loan's term (usually 6 to 12 months). Using this procedure, the amount of each installment is low, which facilitates regular payment and reduces monitoring costs.

9. *Bank-client relationship.* The public nature of the transactions and the unique relationship between clients and the MFI also play a major role, which starts with the formation of the group, the discussion of the microcredit's terms, and the provision of the money. It is not the client who goes to the bank but the bank that goes to the client. Meetings are usually held at the borrowers' village or town, often in a public place, such as the market square. The MFI's employee comes weekly or fortnightly, meets with each group of borrowers (attendance is compulsory) to discuss any problems that have arisen, and reviews the credit's status. At this meeting, each member of the group pays her installment in the presence of the other members; if a member cannot pay, she must say so at this time because the meeting is usually not concluded until the employee has received all the payments, either from the borrower or from the other members of the group. Under this system, the defaulter is under very strong pressure from the group, which explains, at least in part, the high repayment rates obtained with these loans.

10. *Credit scaling.* The incentive to repay the loan within the stipulated period is not just based on the social costs (reputation and shame) but also on the fact that honoring the loan's terms by all of the group's members is a necessary condition for entitlement by any one of them to future loans. These loans usually follow a progressive scale: The first loan is small, which makes it easy to return and reduces the group's monitoring costs. When this loan

has been fully repaid, clients may have access to other loans for higher amounts. This is in the interest of each member, because they can now ask for larger sums; in the interest of the group, because their monitoring costs are now lower; and in the interest of the MFI, because its costs are reduced by economies of scale. It is common for the first two or three loans to a client to provide very little return, because the administrative costs are very high compared with the quantity lent (Roodman and Qureshi 2006).

11. *Savings.* The MFIs usually encourage their clients to save voluntarily, or else they impose a compulsory savings amount that is included in the microcredit installments. By this means, the borrower shows her willingness to abide by the terms of the loan; it provides an additional guarantee for the credit and complements the repayment installments; it provides an additional source of income for the family; and it helps develop habits of austerity, good administration, and thinking about the future. Compulsory saving also provides an incentive for punctual performance of one's obligations, because noncompliance of the compulsory saving condition may entail loss of the quantity saved and exclusion from future credits. However, the savings increase the cost of the credit to the borrower and provides a surplus to the MFI, due to the differential between the interest rate paid on the loan and the interest received on the savings.

12. *Interest rates.* The microcredits' interest rates are usually high, often above 100 percent per annum. This raises efficiency and, above all, equity problems, which are discussed later in this chapter.

THE SOCIAL RESPONSIBILITY OF MICROFINANCE

Is microfinance ethical? The most common answer is yes: Microfinancial institutions' moral legitimacy is given by the goal they pursue. But what goal provides moral justification for MFIs? To help determine this, it is helpful to consider (1) how they perform their social responsibility and (2) what are the social results achieved.

The Social Function of Microfinance

In principle, the social function of any organization is justified by its internal and external mission (Pérez López 1993). The former is defined by its contribution to satisfying those needs that drive its members to pool their effort in a common task: how it rewards the labor and capital provided, and how it sustainably and efficiently offers satisfaction, knowledge, and skills to employees, while earning a profit in the case of a business enterprise. The external mission is defined by the needs of clients, suppliers, local community, and other groups that it tries to satisfy, including its actions' impact on outside stakeholders. This external mission is specific to each type of company. In the case of financial institutions, it will be the provision of brokerage services that facilitate the flow of savings toward investment (Argandoña 1995; Merton and Bodie 1995). Each MFI will adapt this generic social function to its nature (commercial bank, hedge fund, insurance company, and so on) and to the environment in which it operates (for example, whether it is a developed or emerging country).

Each MFI defines and implements its mission to a greater or lesser extent and expresses it in a series of voluntary policies: in the case of the MFIs, the provision of financial services (generic social function) to people who until now were excluded from the system (specific function arising from the nature of their activity and the environment they operate in). This is then implemented using different models. Some of them minimally fulfill their social function while trying to maximize profits; others give more weight to social results, although they also try to cover their costs; and, lastly, others emphasize helping the most needy, even if this entails incurring losses, which are covered by donations. We can therefore say that all MFIs fulfill, at least in principle, the generic social function of financial institutions, but the degree to which they assume their specific responsibilities varies in each case, depending on how they have voluntarily defined their external mission.

Social Results

It is not easy to measure the social results of microfinance, because these organizations usually pursue different goals that cannot be measured by applying uniform criteria for society as a whole (economic development, poverty reduction, women's empowerment), for their clients (improve the microentrepreneurs' standard of living), or for the lending institution (its sustainability). Which goal is used, or which goals are combined, is always a more or less arbitrary decision, and the measurement of these variables is also subject to discrepancies.

The empirical studies of the measurement of social results do not show any agreement on the results achieved, not even on one of these variables, and the methods used in most of these studies are subject to serious criticism. Even so, the best empirical studies support the microcredit programs' effectiveness in reducing poverty and empowering women.[8] Dunford (2006) concludes his review of several of these studies by saying that "in sum, the evidence seems sufficient to say that [microfinance]—particularly when provided to relatively poorer women—increases income and savings, improves nutrition and health, and empowers women" (12), and that "many microfinance programs are reaching large numbers of very poor while fully covering their costs" (13). In regard to the effects on the direct beneficiaries (microentrepreneurs and their families), there are many, more or less anecdotal cases of very positive results, although it is not possible to generalize very far from these conclusions.

It would seem, therefore, that an ethical appraisal of microfinance would give a positive finding, at least in regard to its social function and results. But good intentions or positive social results are not sufficient in themselves. Like any human organization, the MFI must also observe ethical criteria in its decisions, which include fairness in granting the microloans, avoiding dependence and overborrowing, and managing with prudence.

SUSTAINABILITY AND THE FIGHT AGAINST POVERTY

The debate on the ethics of microfinance has focused recently on the compatibility between its economic (cost coverage) and social dimensions (outreach). In this section, two issues are discussed: (1) whether the MFIs can and/or should be financially sustainable,[9] and (2) whether they can and/or should try to earn a profit like the commercial banks—that is, whether for-profit organizations should take part in microfinancing.

Microfinance has an economic dimension, and, as such, it is reasonable that it be required to show efficiency in its management, which will manifest in coverage of its costs and production of a surplus. However, microfinance is also an instrument for social policies, and on the one hand, some (the so-called *welfarists*) argue that it should subordinate its strategies and policies to its social function by providing the best possible service at a price that can be afforded by the greatest possible number of people, particularly the poorer people, even if this means that it will always be dependent on donations and subsidies. On the other hand, the *institutionalists*, while acknowledging the social function (outreach), add that financial self-sufficiency is a necessary condition for the MFI's survival and for the expansion of its activity to more potential clients, as its social function requires, without having to resort to a continuous injection of donations. Institutionalists also hold that both goals should be compatible with each other, at least in the medium term.

The debate between these positions has given rise to what Morduch (2000) calls the microfinance *schism*. This debate can be analysed on two levels: historic development and principles.

The Development of Microfinance

From the historic viewpoint, the discussion is a consequence of the organizations' evolution. They started off as subsidized institutions in which the product was new, the clients were not the conventional clients served by commercial banking, and the risk was very high, so that cheap funds provided by subsidies were required to cover start-up expenses. At that time, few people thought that MFIs would ever be self-sufficient.

Over time the MFIs learned to manage their businesses. They improved their procedures, increased their scale, and reduced their costs. Sustainability was no longer a utopia, and, for some of them, it became a necessity because the growth of their businesses forced them to look for broader sources of finance,[10] while the continuity of donations was no longer assured since it was affected by the appearance of other needs requiring the help of agencies and private donors. According to one writer, "The challenge is not to find a willing lender and endow it with sufficient loanable funds but, rather, to find a production function (a technology) that makes it possible to produce quality financial services at reasonable costs for the micro-client and in a profitable manner for the MFO [microfinance organization]" (González Vega 1998, 7). At the same time, commercial banking had also entered the microcredit business, and some nonprofit MFIs have now become for-profit organizations.[11]

In order to be sustainable, microfinance requires a mix of yield and risk that gives it appeal. This may be feasible for some organizations but not for all of them. Hence the danger that some may relinquish their social function for the sake of sustainability—for example, by charging very high interest to increase their profitability, or cutting back on their portfolio of very poor borrowers to reduce their risk (Conning 1999).

Microfinance and Profit

The debate on principles has focused on criticizing those people who seek to earn a profit by doing business with a country's poorest people. However, I feel that this view is mistaken. If someone intends to supply goods and services to those who have nothing (such as severely disabled people or children in a state of complete destitution), it is not reasonable to obtain anything from them because they have no possessions. However, if they can give something, it is reasonable to ask them for a little (such as asking people who go to charity-run community canteens to help clean up afterward), not to obtain a personal profit at their cost but to help them appreciate what they receive, to reduce costs (so that more people can benefit from the service), and to restore their human dignity. Such an argument would be even more justified if beneficiaries are provided with resources that enable them to improve their situation, as is the case with MFIs. Therefore, it seems reasonable for an MFI to require something in exchange from the microcredit's beneficiaries, including return of the capital and payment of interest. To say that these institutions earn profits at the cost of the poor, and not by helping the poor, is to ignore the very nature of business activity, portraying it as predatory.

However, this response does not give a final answer to the question of the compatibility of sustainability and outreach. As Morduch explains, "Much of the enthusiasm [about microfinance] rests on an enticing 'win-win' proposition: microfinance institutions that follow the principles of good banking will also be those that alleviate the most poverty" (2000, 617). Obviously, this is true for some organizations, but it is not necessarily true for all of them. Many MFIs have not achieved a win-win solution nor is it likely that they ever will,[12] either because that is not their chosen strategy or because they are prevented from doing so by such factors as the regulatory framework, government attitudes, competition from other financial institutions, and the impossibility of gaining access to cheap sources of finance.[13]

In any case, a growing number of organizations are trying to make their social function compatible with operational sustainability. This can also mean a rapprochement to the traditional banking model, either as a result of a deliberate decision by the MFIs themselves or because they are forced to do so by the environment in which they operate. It is not known what effects this may have in the long run on the extent, depth, and nature of the microcredits.

THE ETHICAL PROBLEMS ASSOCIATED WITH INTEREST RATES

A large part of the debate between institutionalists and welfarists is concerned with the interest rates charged by the MFIs, which are often very high.[14] This matter raises three economic and ethical issues:

1. Are these high rates justified?
2. What should be the interest rate stipulated for each operation?
3. If, as seems logical, a high interest rate discourages the poorest clients, does this effect give rise to a moral duty for the MFI?

Why Are the Interest Rates So High?

The following arguments are usually given to justify the high interest rates (Goodwin-Groen 2004):

- The alternatives available to microcredit clients also charge very high interest rates. For example, informal lenders and pawnshops may charge up to 20 percent per day (Lewis 2008, 57).
- The profitability of microenterprises in developing countries is probably very high, particularly in the informal economy.[15]
- The real interest rate is high because it includes a risk premium. The lender takes into account the likelihood of a loan not being repaid and increases the interest rate charged on all loans to cover the expected loss. And although the microcredit repayment rate is usually very high (close to 97 percent in many cases), as a group, the borrowers continue to be high risk, particularly because of their vulnerability to external factors, such as poor harvests, epidemics, and recessions.
- The MFIs need capital, which they obtain from private investors, and their cost of capital is high because the MFIs' risk is also high, because it includes their clients' risk premium.
- The interest rates must cover operational and transaction costs, which are usually very high: The clients often live at a considerable distance from towns, they are visited frequently, and the meetings are lengthy. In addition, the administration costs (study and decision making, monitoring, enforcement, and accounting costs) are not less than those of a traditional financial institution, but because the amount of the loans is very small they are unlikely to cover the organization's overhead. (It is just as expensive to process a microcredit for $50 as it is to process a loan for $10,000.)

The conclusion to be drawn from all this is that the high interest rates of MFIs may be justified by the lenders' cost structure and the borrowers' risk. However, the fact still remains that the interest rates are very high—and other costs must be added that are borne by the borrowers, such as the monitoring costs by members of their group (including the time spent in meetings) and compulsory saving.

The Fair Interest Rate

The issue of what interest rate should be charged in a specific operation corresponds to *commutative* justice (Pieper 1966).[16] In a competitive market, in which the prospective borrower has access to several credit providers with similar terms, the resulting interest rate will tend to be equal to the minimum amount needed to cover the provider's costs, and, as a result, there will be no ethical problem at all. However, in the microcredit market, competition is usually limited, so the resulting interest rate will depend on the two parties' relative bargaining power. Because the clients usually have little power, the interest rate imposed will be high (Hudon 2006).

In this case, fair price theory does not recommend what should be the fair interest rate. It cannot be said on the basis of fair price theory that the high rate is unfair, but the MFI should remember that this extraordinary profit is not the outcome of its greater efficiency, but because of the MFI's market power. Then, corporate social responsibility policies should address the best use that could be made of this profit, which might include reducing the interest rate for all or some clients and allocating the extraordinary earnings to social activities.[17]

Exclusion of the Most Needy

If the interest rate is high, it is likely that some potential clients, mainly those with less income, will be excluded from the microcredit system. What are the MFI's moral obligations in this case? This is a problem of *distributive* justice, which addresses the distribution of costs and profits between people in a community (Pieper 1966). There are a number of possible solutions. A lower interest rate could be specified for lower-income borrowers, financed by higher interest rates for those who have more resources (a cross-subsidy), by public or private subsidies from outside organizations,[18] or by waiving part of the institution's profits (provided that this does not endanger its sustainability). As I said earlier, the MFI's external mission should be to establish the needs of the people it seeks to satisfy, and this determination will define its social responsibility on this point.

In any case, the issue of distributive justice goes beyond microfinance's social responsibility in that it also has a political element. The microfinance sector of the economy absorbs indeed a not insignificant volume of subsidies; it generates competition between organizations with very different profiles; it receives different treatments from the authorities; and, in short, it gives rise to vested interests, which often come into conflict, particularly when it must answer the question asked here.

CONCLUSION

Microfinance has undergone considerable growth in recent years and, in general, has enjoyed a very favorable public opinion—which is well deserved, at least in many cases. This chapter has discussed its economic-financial, social, and ethical features—and all of them must be taken into account when judging this reality, which is, at one and the same time, an instrument integrated in development policies, a business opportunity, and a service provided for needy people.

Microfinance rests on certain basic assumptions, such as the role of capital and the importance of access to financial services for economic development; the existence of a large supply of entrepreneurial ability among people without any financial resources or prior training; the importance of social networks as guarantors of the borrowers' conduct; the need for economic efficiency (sustainability) as a condition for the MFIs' survival and growth; and the possibility and effectiveness of a development strategy devised by private institutions, without requiring any direct public involvement (but with the appropriate legal, regulatory, and institutional framework). If any of these assumptions is rejected or challenged, the appraisal made of microfinance might be different.

Microfinance is important for the institutions that offer it, as well as for its clients, the local communities, and society in general. It is based on an ethically correct motivation, and its actions are morally good. Consequently, if it is applied with prudence, honesty, and reasonableness, it deserves a positive ethical appraisal. It also seems to be morally good when judged by its personal, social, and economic effects, although there are reasons for being unsatisfied with the results, either because they have unwanted indirect effects or because they are insufficient in some of their dimensions. In addition, success or failure depends on many factors that are outside an MFI's control, including protection of property rights, adequate incentives, infrastructures and basic services, absence of corruption, adequate regulation of MFIs, and a public policy that fosters it or, at least, does not interfere with microfinance.

Microfinance organizations are not a panacea in the fight against poverty, and microcredit will not render other development policies unnecessary. MFIs have a lot to learn and room to improve—and, in fact, they are learning and changing, both in the technical-financial area (sustainability) and in the ethical area (outreach). As Morduch observes, "There appears to be ample room . . . for a diversity of programs, with competing methods and financial arrangements" (2000, 626), and an extensive variety of MFIs, each one of which will leverage its comparative advantages, as explained by Hudon (2008, 41):

> For-profit institutions have important financial know-how and are able to mobilize important sums. The state-owned institutions understand the local markets and benefit from a strong reputation among the poor. Their social knowledge could become essential to complement the financial knowledge of the for-profit institutions. Cooperatives have the deepest penetration in the market for small deposits. NGOs can play a key role by helping to create experiments with new frameworks to develop the microfinance schemes. They also provide training and management capacity building in order to stabilize and sustain the growth in this field.

This ultimately implies that there is no point in opposing sustainability to outreach, and even less in defending a fundamentalist attitude about what a microfinance program is and should be (Vanroose 2007). In any case, every MFI should be responsible for its decisions on the balance between sustainability and outreach, since it will have to consider its mission and goals, its limiting factors, the intentions of its fund providers (owners, donors, financial markets) and clients, its competitors' strategies, and the constraints of the legal and institutional environments in which it operates.

NOTES

1. See nobelprize.org/nobel_prizes/peace/laureates/2006/press.html.
2. The differences in the figures between the various sources are substantial. Stephens (2008) reports information on almost 900 microfinancial institutions in 2007, with 366,000 employees and more than 40,000 branches throughout the world, more than 64,000 borrowers, and almost $32 billion in credits.
3. See summaries in Armendáriz de Aghion and Morduch (2005), Ghatak and Guinnane (1999), Morduch (1999), and Sengupta and Aubuchon (2008), among many others.
4. Khandker (2005) and Smith (2002) provide empirical evidence to support the efficacy of microcredits targeting women; for evidence against this, see Goetz and Gupta (1996). See also Brau and Woller (2004) for a summary of papers on this subject.

5. In fact, "scattered research suggests that only half or less of loan proceeds are used in business purposes. The remainder supports a wide range of household cash management needs." From "What Is Microfinance" in www.microfinancegateway.org/section/faq percent23Q2, no. 5.

6. Empirical studies on the factors that determine high credit repayment rates include Ahlin and Townsend (2007), Cassar et al. (2007), Hermes et al. (2005), Karlan (2007), Sharma and Zeller (1997), Wenner (1995), Wydick (1999), and Zeller (1998).

7. As a general rule, the commercial banks that engage in microlending prefer individual liability, while the nonprofit institutions prefer group liability. See Cull et al. (2008).

8. For recent reviews of these studies, see Armendáriz de Aghion and Morduch (2005), Goldberg (2005), Morduch et al. (2003), and Watson and Dunford (2006). Khandker (2005) is a particularly careful paper, based on three large-scale programs in Bangladesh; his conclusions are clearly positive.

9. Here, *sustainability* refers to the economic aspect, the coverage of operating expenses and capital costs, not the environmental aspect.

10. In 2007, the 892 MFIs that provided information to Microfinance Information eXchange (MIX) obtained 72 percent of their funds from deposits or commercial debt and only 2.5 percent from subsidies (Stephens 2008, 29). The inability to gain access to sustainable sources of funds accounts for the high percentage of MFIs that do not manage to grow (73 percent of them never get beyond 2,500 clients, according to "Economies of Scale" in www.microfinanceinfo.com/economies-of-scale).

11. This is the case of Banco Compartamos, Mexico's largest MFI, which was created in 1990 as a nonprofit institution. Over the following years, it received $4.3 billion from international development agencies and private donors. In 2000, when it had 60,000 clients, it became a commercial bank; by 2006, it already had 616,000 clients, and it decided to go public in 2007. This operation aroused the interest of investors: 30 percent of its equity was placed for $450 billion, which gave an annual compound rate of return of 100 percent (Rosenberg 2007). Some institutions, such as ACCION International, saw a model in this operation that other MFIs should follow, but there was also strong criticism from those who interpreted it as a betrayal to the spirit of microlending, as Compartamos charged interest to its borrowers at an annual rate of 120 percent, compared with 31 percent charged by similar institutions (Lewis 2008; Yunus 2007).

12. Among the optimists, see González Vega et al. (1997) and Hulme and Mosley (1996). Among those who think that it is not possible to achieve both goals, at least as a general rule, is Morduch (2000).

13. The empirical studies on the effect of a greater sustainability on outreach are not conclusive; for recent summaries, see Goldberg (2005) and Weiss and Montgomery (2004). Hulme and Mosley (1996) and Copestake et al. (2005) show that the poorest people are the least benefited by microcredit, but Khandker (2005) and EDA Rural Systems (2004) come to the opposite conclusion.

14. Cull et al. (2008) calculate that the median interest rate charged by nonprofit, nongovernment MFIs is 25 percent per annum, while the interest rate charged by commercial banks on ordinary loan operations is 13 percent.

15. "For a microentrepreneur, the cost of a microcredit loan represents a small proportion of total business costs. Studies conducted in India, Kenya, and the Philippines found that the average annual return on investments by microbusinesses ranged from 117 percent to 847 percent." (From "International Year of Microcredit," United Nations, 2005; quoted in "What Is Microfinance," www.mcenterprises.org/studycenter/microfinance.) However, Dehejia et al. (2005) and Karlan and Zinman (2006) deny that the demand for microcredits is insensitive to the interest rate, at least for low-income clients.

16. This problem is a variant on the old fair price problem (Messner 1965). Commutative justice is the justice that regulates the relationship between two people: in this case, lender and borrower.

17. Sen (2006) is stricter when he discusses sharing the benefits of globalization. For him, it is not enough that the poor borrower does not come out worse off, in absolute terms. In fact, he argues that profit distribution between the two parties should be biased toward the borrower, and increasingly so the poorer the borrower is and the greater the MFI's market power is (cf. Hudon 2006).

18. Sustainability-driven MFIs are unwilling to accept government aid, which imposes constraints on their characteristic flexibility, innovativeness, and independence.

REFERENCES

Ahlin, C., and R. Townsend. 2007. Using repayment data to test across models of joint liability lending. *Economic Journal* 117:F11–F51.

Argandoña, A. 1995. The treatment of ethical problems in financial institutions and markets. In *The ethical dimension of financial institutions and markets*, ed. A. Argandoña. Berlin: Springer Verlag.

Armendáriz de Aghion, B., and J. Morduch. 2005. *The economics of microfinance*. Cambridge, MA: MIT Press.

Brau, J. C., and G. M. Woller. 2004. Microfinance: A comprehensive review of the existing literature. *Journal of Entrepreneurial Finance and Business Ventures* 9:1–26.

Cassar, A., L. Crowley, and B. Wyndick. 2007. The effect of social capital on loan group repayment: Evidence from field experiments. *Economic Journal* 117:F85–F106.

Conning, J. 1999. Outreach, sustainability and leverage in microlending: A contract design approach. *Journal of Development Economics* 60:51–77.

Copestake, J., P. Dawson, J. P. Fanning, A. McKay, and K. Wright-Revolledo. 2005. Monitoring the diversity of the poverty outreach and impact of microfinance: A comparison of methods using data from Peru. *Development Policy Review* 23:703–723.

Cull, R., A. Demirgüç-Kunt, and J. Morduch. 2008. Microfinance meets the market. Policy Research Working Paper 4630, World Bank.

Dehejia, R., H. Montgomery, and J. Morduch. 2005. Do interest rates matter? Credit demand in the Dhaka slums. Discussion Paper 37, ADB Institute.

Drugov, M., and R. Macchiavello. 2008. Learning and microlending. CEPR Discussion Paper 7011.

Dunford, C. 2006. Evidence from microfinance's contribution to achieving the Millennium Development Goals. Presented at the Global Microcredit Summit, Halifax, November 12–15.

EDA Rural Systems. 2004. *The maturing of Indian microfinance: A longitudinal study*. New Delhi: EDA Rural Systems.

Financial Times. 2008. Conflicts of interests. Life & Arts, December 6–7.

Ghatak, M., and T. Guinnane. 1999. The economics of lending with joint liability: Theory and practice. *Journal of Development Economics* 60:195–228.

Goetz, A. M., and R. S. Gupta. 1996. Who takes the credit? Gender, power, and control over loan use in rural credit programs in Bangladesh. *World Development* 24:45–63.

Goldberg, N. 2005. Measuring the impact of microfinance: Taking stock of what we know. Grameen Foundation USA. www.grameenfoundation.org.

González Vega, C. 1998. Microfinance: Broader achievements and new challenges. Occasional Paper 2518, Ohio State University Rural Finance Program.

González Vega, C., M. Schreiner, R. L. Meyer, S. Navajas, and J. Rodríguez. 1997. A primer on Bolivian experiences in microfinance: An Ohio State perspective. Working Paper, Ohio State University, Rural Finance Program.

Goodwin-Groen, R. P. 2004. Making sense of microcredit interest rates. *Donor Brief* 6 (January).

Hermes, N., R. Lensink, and H. T. Mehrteab. 2005. Peer monitoring, social ties and moral hazard in group lending programmes: Evidence from Eritrea. *World Development* 33:146–169.

Hulme, D., and P. Mosley. 1996. *Finance against poverty*. London: Routledge.

Hudon, M. 2006. Fair interest rates when lending to the poor: Are fair prices derived from basic principles of justice? Working Paper 06/015, Solvay Business School, Université Libre de Bruxelles.

———. 2007. Fair interest rates when lending to the poor. *Éthique et Économique/Ethics and Economics* 5:1–8.

———. 2008. Norms and values of the various MFIs. *International Journal of Social Economics* 35 (1–2):35–48.

———. 2009. Should access to credit be a right? *Journal of Business Ethics* 84:17–28.

Karlan, D. 2007. Social connections and group banking. *Economic Journal* 117:F52–F84.

Karlan, D. S., and J. Zinman. 2006. Credit elasticities in less-developed economies: implications for microfinance. *MIT Research in Action Working Paper*.

Khandker, S. R. 2005. Microfinance and poverty: Evidence using panel data from Bangladesh. *World Bank Economic Review* 19:263–286.

Lewis, J. C. 2008. Microloan sharks. *Stanford Social Innovation Review*, Summer:54–59.

Merton, R., and Z. Bodie. 1995. A conceptual framework for analyzing the financial environment. In *The global financial system: A functional perspective*, ed. D. Crane, K. Froot, F. Mason, A. Perold, R. Merton, Z. Bodie, E. Sirri, and P. Tufano. Boston: Harvard Business School Press.

Messner, J. 1965. *Social ethics: Natural law in the modern world*. Rev. ed. St. Louis, MO: B. Herder Book.

Morduch, J. 1999. The microfinance promise. *Journal of Economic Literature* 37:1569–1614.

———. 2000. The microfinance schism. *World Development* 28:617–629.

Morduch, J., S. Hashemi, and E. Littlefield. 2003. Is microfinance an effective strategy to reach the Millennium Development Goals? *CGAP* Focus Note 24.

Nourse, T. H. 2001. The missing part of microfinance: Services for consumption and insurance. *SAIS Review* 21:61–70.

Pérez López, J. A. 1993. *Fundamentos de la dirección de empresas*. Madrid: Rialp.

Pieper, J. 1966. *The four cardinal virtues: Prudence, justice, fortitude, temperance*. Notre Dame, IN: University of Notre Dame Press.

Roodman, D., and U. Qureshi. 2006. Microfinance as business. Center for Global Development, ABN-AMRO Bank.

Rosenberg, R. 2007. CGAP reflections on the Compartamos initial public offering: A case study in microfinance interest rates and profits. *CGAP* Focus Note 42, June.

Schreiner, M. 2003. A cost-effectiveness analysis of the Grameen Bank of Bangladesh. *Development Policy Review* 21.

Sen, A. 2006. *Identity and violence: The illusion of destiny*. Boston: Norton.

Sengupta, R., and C. P. Aubuchon. 2008. The microfinance revolution: An overview. *Federal Reserve Bank of St. Louis Review*, 90:9–30.

Sharma, M., and M. Zeller. 1997. Repayment performance in group-based credit programs in Bangladesh: An empirical analysis. *World Development* 25:1731–1742.

Smith, S. C. 2002. Village banking and maternal and child health: Evidence from Ecuador and Honduras. *World Development* 30:707–723.

Stephens, B. 2008. MFI benchmark analysis: An industry still expanding, despite challenges. *MicroBanking Bulletin* 17:25–32.

Stiglitz, J. E., and A. Weiss. 1981. Credit rationing in markets with imperfect information. *American Economic Review* 71:393–410.

Vakulabharanam, V., and S. Motiram. 2007. The ethics of microfinance and cooperation. *Éthique et économique/Ethics and Economics* 5.

Vanroose, A. 2007. Is microfinance an ethical way to provide financial services to the poor? Microfinance: Are its promises ethically justified? Working Paper 07/014, Solvay Business School, Université Libre de Bruxelles.

Watson, A. A., and C. Dunford. 2006. From microfinance to macro change: Integrating health, education and microfinance to empower women and reduce poverty. *United Nations Population Fund and Microcredit Summit Campaign.*

Weiss, J., and J. Montgomery. 2004. Great expectations: Microfinance and poverty reduction in Asia and Latin America. Discussion Paper 14, Asian Development Bank Institute.

Wenner, M. 1995. Group credit: A means to improve information transfer and loan repayment performance. *Journal of Development Studies* 32:263–281.

Wydick, B. 1999. Can social cohesion be harnessed to repair market failures? Evidence from group-based lending in Guatemala. *Economic Journal,* 109:463–475.

Yunus, M. 2007. Remarks by Muhammad Yunus, managing director, Grameen Bank. *Microcredit Summit E-News* 5.

Zeller, M. 1998. Determinants of repayment performance in credit groups: The role of program design, intra-group risk pooling and social cohesion. *Economic Development and Cultural Change* 46:599–620.

ABOUT THE AUTHOR

Antonio Argandoña is a member of the Royal Academy of Economics and Finance, chairperson of the Professional Ethics Committee of the Catalan Economics Association, and a member of the Anti-Corruption Committee of the International Chamber of Commerce (Paris). He has been the honorary treasurer and member of the Executive Committee of the European Business Ethics Network (EBEN), and co-founder and secretary general of EBEN-Spain. He is the editor and co-author of *The Ethical Dimension of Financial Institutions and Markets,* and the author of many articles on ethics, economics, and management issues.

PART V

Financial Management

CHAPTER 23

Shareholder Wealth Maximization

DUANE WINDSOR
Lynette S. Autrey Professor of Management, Jesse H. Jones Graduate School of
Business, Rice University

INTRODUCTION

The shareholder wealth maximization (SWM) principle states that the immediate
operating goal and the ultimate purpose of a public corporation is and should
be to maximize return on equity capital. The SWM specification of what is often
termed the *corporate objective* makes operating goal and ultimate purpose the same:
Managers and investors should focus narrowly on SWM.

The question of whether the corporate objective can be a strict emphasis on
SWM or must recognize significant differences between the operating goal for managers and investors and the ultimate social purpose of the public corporation lies
at the intersection of three literatures. In economics and finance literature, SWM is
a standard assumption. This SWM operating goal is expected to yield the most socially efficient allocation of capital. Business ethics, corporate social responsibility,
and stakeholder theory literature emphasizes significant differences between an
operating goal of SWM and the ultimate social purpose of the public corporation.
Corporation law addresses duties, responsibilities, and rights of both financial and
nonfinancial stakeholders. In the United States, the business judgment rule and
in various states corporate constituency statutes permit relaxation in SWM as an
operating goal in favor of stakeholder and social considerations.

This chapter addresses ethical considerations concerning the SWM principle
and its managerial implications. A key factor in understanding SWM is that the
public corporation is simultaneously private property, a web or nexus of contracts,
a governmentally licensed and traded securities registrant, a social benefits entity,
and a locus of stakeholder relationships.

This introduction explains some basic points of general relevance. The second
section discusses the historical background of SWM and some technical considerations including measurement issues. The third section explains justifications for
SWM. The fourth, fifth, and sixth sections explicate three critiques of SWM arising
from (1) business ethics and corporation law, (2) corporate social responsibility
(CSR), and (3) stakeholder theory. The chapter concludes with a summary of the
arguments for and against SWM and their implications for managers.

Shareholder wealth maximization focuses on the motives and behaviors of financial stakeholders. The thesis of separation of ownership and control (Berle and Means 1932) posits that principals (or shareowners) employ agents (or management) who must have some reasonable discretion (e.g., the business judgment rule). At law, officers and directors have a fiduciary duty to safeguard the financial interests of the shareholders (or shareowners). The SWM principle can be stated, however, in two forms.

The stronger form argues that, within any set of legal and ethical constraints, the corporate objective is and should be strictly SWM. The operating goal and ultimate purpose of the public corporation are the same. Fiduciary duty ought therefore to be tightly focused on SWM. From this viewpoint, CSR activity is inappropriate wealth-decreasing altruism unless it yields future positive returns to the firm. This strong form associates with the views that legal and ethical constraints on corporate activity ought to be minimal and that institutions (including common law and social norms) should be market-facilitating. A multinational corporation may be able to select sets of legal and ethical constraints, varying by country, within which it will operate.

There may be a significant difference between management's operating goal and the ultimate social purpose of the public corporation. A weaker form therefore relaxes the strict formulation to a more nuanced argument that the corporate objective is and should be primarily SWM. A relaxation admits, beyond legal and ethical constraints, consideration of CSR and interests of nonfinancial stakeholders. The relaxation understands that managerial responsibility is more complicated than mere fiduciary duty. The relaxation accepts that legal and ethical constraints are and ought to be stronger than minimalist (Windsor 2008).

One must decide which view to accept. One way to combine strong and weak forms is to argue that shareowners can and do make pragmatic choices that best protect their financial interest. A combined approach retains the financial goal and market context of the strong form but expects shareowners to figure out how best to address agents, nonfinancial stakeholders, and gatekeepers (Boatright 2007). The shareowners may decide to act in accord with the weak form in order to advance the SWM goal posited in the strong form.

This chapter explains three key objections to a strong SWM formulation of the corporate objective. These objections are logically admitted by any nuanced statement of SWM as a primary rather than as a singular goal for managers. As previously explained, a goal and a purpose need not be the same. The narrow (but socially penultimate) goal of investors is to maximize financial return. The broader (and ultimate) purpose of a public corporation, a rationale for government licensing, is generation of social benefits. Both corporate social performance (CSP) and financial performance should be positive. The three objections are as follows. First, business ethics functions as a set of supralegal constraints on managerial conduct to avoid wrong acts and social harms. Second, CSR is a justification for corporate contribution of social goods in addition to legal compliance and business ethics. Third, stakeholder theory argues that any business must be a multiple-constituency and a social entity. A continuing debate concerns whether these three objections (business ethics, CSR, and stakeholder theory) justify basic changes in corporate governance principles and/or corporate purpose.

Two competing views about multiple principles can be articulated. A monotonic SWM view is that any two or more principles must be strictly hierarchical (Jensen 2001). Legal and ethical constraints can be antecedent conditions. "Sometimes the aims of the business and rational self-interest will clash with ethics, and when they do, those aims and interests must give way" (*Economist* 2005). Considerations of CSR and stakeholder satisfaction would be subordinate to SWM and function as strategic variables only (Husted and Salazar 2006). A competing view is that two or more corporate goals should be pursued simultaneously. The firm serves a diverse set of social goals. Either there is some win-win combination of goals or else multiple goals must be balanced in some way. An ongoing controversy concerns whether observable varieties of capitalism, addressing these matters differently, will converge or continue to diverge.

HISTORICAL BACKGROUND AND TECHNICAL CONSIDERATIONS

The first important joint stock company was London-based Muscovy Company, which was chartered in the sixteenth century to trade with Russia (Sasse and Trahan 2007, 30). Adam Smith, in *The Wealth of Nations* (1776), commented adversely on Honourable East India Company's (HEIC, 1600–1874) governance problems and the handling of monopoly rule in India. The Dutch East India Company (VOC, 1602–1800) was likely the first to issue public stock (i.e., shares traded on a stock exchange as distinct from a private placement). There was not much attention to corporate governance until the passage of the Joint Stock Companies Act in 1844 in the United Kingdom, and the United Kingdom introduced limited liability only in 1862 (Cadbury 2006, 16). Legal liability of public corporation shareowners today remains limited to capital invested. Bismarck introduced mandatory supervisory boards (i.e., today's two-tier board system) for joint stock companies in Germany in 1870 (Cadbury 2006, 16).

The SWM principle is relatively recent (Englander and Kaufman 2004). The traditional underpinning of public corporations has always been an appreciation of private property rights as the foundation of market capitalism: in theory, capital investors *organize* firms and *hire* agents to manage them. This underpinning aims at prudent conservation. The classical statement occurred in *Harvard College and Massachusetts General Hospital v. Francis Amory* (9 Pick., 26 Mass. 446, 461, 1830, Supreme Court of Massachusetts, for Suffolk and Nantucket, Judge Samuel Putnam): "Do what you will, the capital is at hazard." Trustee Armory, trading in riskier business stocks rather than investing in bonds or real property, lost much of a corpus bequeathed to Harvard College (an annual dividend being paid to the donor's widow) and was sued for recovery. Modifying stricter English common-law standards requiring virtually absolute conservation of capital, the court accepted greater flexibility in the conduct of trustees. The court articulated the guiding principle as follows: "These trustees are not to be made chargeable but for gross neglect and wilful mismanagement."

The capital stock of any for-profit enterprise is divisible into ownership shares for legal definition of duties, responsibilities, and rights, and for purposes of theorizing. The exact form of the enterprise and the related division into shares is a matter of law. Large, publicly traded corporations typically have many owners and diffused ownership, even with large blocks of institutional investors. A shareowner, or shareholder, is an individual or entity owning an equitable interest. The interest (or financial stake), consisting of one or more shares, conveys to the holder limited rights (and liability) to control the entity and to the residual revenues (or profits), if any. A shareowner risks capital in order to obtain return on investment. Rights to control and residual revenues are held jointly by (distributed among) the owners in some proportion to number of (and sometimes type of) shares held. Issues of majority versus minority shareholder rights and types of shares (preferred versus common, voting versus nonvoting) are not the concern of this chapter. The discussion of SWM here proceeds from a basic, idealized conception of the public corporation as a large set of shareholders holding approximately equal rights to control and to profits.

New underpinnings for today's SWM principle developed in the twentieth century. One underpinning is agency theory, positing the separation of legal ownership and effective control. Another underpinning is economic efficiency in real and financial markets: Investors contribute capital to firms in expectation of earning the relatively highest return on investment (Lea 2008). Another underpinning is an understanding of the corporation as a web or nexus of contracts (Lea 2008). This contractual view is the dominant one in economics and finance literature. Managers in a publicly owned corporation with a separation of ownership and control are agents in a position of trust, which is defined as having a fiduciary duty to the principals. This fiduciary duty is to safeguard the assets of the owners. The fiduciary duty is not, however, necessarily to maximize shareholder wealth in the sense of return in addition to safeguarding assets. The fiduciary's first responsibility and concern is always to safeguard corporate assets. Shareholder wealth maximization is a norm for prescribing what the fiduciary should do once asset safety is reasonably assured. Both return and risk are involved in SWM. Higher return implies greater risk.

Shareholder wealth can be defined, at any time, as the market capitalization of the public corporation. This market cap is the number of equity shares outstanding multiplied by the share price at the time of calculation. Market cap is an estimate, by capital markets, of the net worth of the firm. The market cap reflects the firm's tangible assets plus the future expected residual revenues, which may be distributed as dividends or kept as retained earnings. The estimate thus includes the future expected dividend stream. Higher earnings per share (EPS) of common stock (i.e., equity) will tend, ceteris paribus, to increase the market price of each share (and thus the market value of the firm) and to permit in principle either additional investments in profitable projects or higher dividends.

A problem inherent in the market cap definition is that it involves an artificial dimension of subjective valuation by buyers and sellers. There can be artificial bubbles, particularly for real estate and commodities. In a bubble, the price-to-earnings ratio rises, often rapidly. The SWM principle effectively encourages investors to demand, and management to supply, actions that will increase share price over time. There is a significant difference between these management actions and the process of subjective valuation in capital markets. Free cash flow, defined as net operating cash flow minus capital investments, occurs in product markets; and management has direct control of decisions affecting free cash flow, which is then available to exploit opportunities to enhance shareholder value. *Real* free cash flow is more difficult to manipulate than accounting profit. But capital markets independently evaluate the estimated worth of free cash flow or earnings per share or any other relevant measure. This evaluation process might be influenced by management actions and information, but it is not under direct control of management. (Management itself is subject to being disciplined or even replaced by what is termed the market for control of the firm itself.)

How to define the SWM norm as a specific corporate objective and how to measure that objective concretely in order to show an increase or decline in wealth remains a matter of disagreement. There are three different approaches to thinking about measurement: accrual accounting, cash flow, and market value added. The traditional profit-maximization model of the firm embeds the accrual concept of net income (i.e., profit). Accrual profit is a declaration, in accordance with accounting principles, of the difference between revenues and expenses over an accounting time period (such as a quarter or a year). Accounting declaration is subject to manipulation of revenues, expenses, and net income.

The wealth of an investor is more related to cash flows than to accrual profits. The cash-flow model of the firm uses free cash flow computed as net operating cash flow less capital expenditures without respect to specific accounting time periods. One can think of a cash flow return on investment. This real measure avoids accounting distortions or manipulations. Free cash flow can also be computed as net income plus amortization and depreciation less changes in working capital less capital expenditures. Negative cash flow might signal large investments in the firm's future success.

The market value model focuses on the share price of a publicly traded company. For example, Warren Buffett—one of the world's wealthiest billionaires who built Berkshire Hathaway into a major publicly owned investment manager—initially bought some stock in a small company in 1962 at reportedly $7 per share. In October 2006, each share of Berkshire Hathaway was worth about $100,000. Whether that change in wealth was, strictly speaking, maximization (i.e., the most that could have been created over the time period involved) is a different matter.

Stock price, however, may not fully reflect the worth of the shares. There can be unrelated fluctuations in the stock market and other considerations that inflate or deflate a stock's price relative to some true value (which is an estimate by buyers and sellers). Maximization, in this context, requires relatively strong conditions such as efficient capital markets, negligible social costs (i.e., negative externalities), full protection of bondholders from expropriation, and nonappropriation by managers.

Of the three approaches, stock price has the strongest claim to approximating shareholder wealth. Aggregate shareholder wealth, measured as market capitalization or market value, is then the value (i.e., market price) of each share times the number of shares outstanding. The formula for this measurement can be stated as follows:

$$MV = V \times S$$

where MV = market value
         V = value of each share (i.e., of common stock)
         S = number of shares outstanding (i.e., of common stock)

If V (i.e., share price) rises, at a constant S (i.e., number of shares outstanding), then MV rises. The management should focus on getting share price to rise over time. If management issues additional shares, however, then V could fall in response.

One can relate market value to accrual profits or cash flows in the following manner. To grow wealth, managers can increase earnings per share (EPS). MV is the present value of expected future profits or expected future cash flows, which are discounted over time at the equity shareholder's required rate of return r_e. If we let Π stand for either accrual profits or cash flows, depending on the prediction we want to apply, then the formula for this measure can be constructed basically as follows (where successive time periods t are summed from 1 to infinity):

$$MV = \sum_{t=1}^{\infty} \Pi_t / (1 + r_e)^t$$

The market value added (MVA) of a firm is the difference between the value of equity and net debt and the book value of capital invested. If net debt is equal to book value, then the difference between market capitalization and book value of the shareholders' equity is the market value added. The MVA concept is a way of measuring gain over book value.

Stern Stewart & Co. developed in 1989 a concept of economic value added (EVA) to measure wealth generation. EVA measures whether a firm is earning more than its true (i.e., economic) cost of capital. In effect, EVA subtracts a charge for the opportunity cost of capital from net operating profit in order to estimate return on the invested capital. (The opportunity cost of a resource is always the next best return it could earn. The opportunity cost of an equity stock is a risk-free government bond; an equity stock must earn more than the bond in order to show an economic profit.) This EVA is computed as a return on investment less the opening capital (debt and equity) times the weighted average cost of capital (for debt and equity). If debt is D, equity is E, net operating profit after tax is NOPAT (as a notion of return on investment), and weighted average cost of capital is WACC, then the formula is basically as follows:

$$EVA = NOPAT - (D + E) \times WACC$$

Economic profit begins only when capital cost is recovered. A firm could show accrual profit and be losing economic value. An investment project should return more than its cost of capital in order to be profitable (on an economic basis) and increase shareholder wealth.

The SWM principle can be dangerous in three ways. First, as illustrated by Enron and other recent corporate frauds, management may undertake illegal actions to prop up or increase stock prices that have no basis in economic reality. Second, management may trade future economic value for short-term earnings targets. Economic value added, which is effectively net gains after recovering cost of capital invested, may be a superior way of evaluating investment choices. Third, the market for corporate control may not discipline managers but rather exert strong pressure to maximize earnings or short-term share price (Vives 2008,

228–229). A survey of 401 financial executives and in-depth interviews with an additional 20 financial executives found that a majority of the firms involved view earnings, especially earnings per share (EPS), as the key metric for external audiences, even more important than cash flows (Graham et al. 2005). A majority of the executives would avoid initiating a positive net present value (NPV) investment project if the result would fall short of the current quarter consensus earnings. More than 75 percent would exchange economic value for smooth earnings. Their belief is that missing an earnings target or reporting volatile earnings reduces stock price, because investors and analysts have a preference against uncertainty. Managers can decrease this uncertainty to some degree by making voluntary disclosures that reduce information risk. But voluntary disclosure is limited by the need to avoid disclosure precedents that may prove difficult to maintain in the future.

JUSTIFICATIONS FOR SHAREHOLDER WEALTH MAXIMIZATION

The descriptive, instrumental, and normative dimensions of the SWM principle are mutually supporting. The descriptive dimension concerns a particular empirical view of laws, markets, motives, and behaviors. The view posits relatively efficient markets, market-oriented institutions, and self-interested economic rationality. Descriptively, the view posits that management (i.e., officers and directors) has strong fiduciary duties on behalf of shareholders, which are established by law and enforced by the market for corporate control. The instrumental dimension concerns the prescriptively best approach to managing a public corporation on behalf of shareholders and handling the interests of multiple stakeholders in the corporation and its activities. The prescription is that SWM will most efficiently and effectively advance the interests of shareholders and stakeholders and thus social welfare in a market economy.

The normative dimension concerns duties, responsibilities, and rights of the various stakeholders, with particular attention to the fiduciary and stewardship roles of management. Normatively, management should have strong fiduciary duties toward shareholders. There are three normative bases for strong fiduciary duties. One basis is that the agent contracts voluntarily with the principal to act in the principal's best interests and to be trustworthy in this regard. A second basis lies in property rights. The principal is the owner of the tangible assets and residual revenues of the firm. The manager is a trustee for this property. A third basis lies in utilitarianism. This utilitarian interpretation is that free mobility of capital should promote economic development and growth, benefiting everyone in the long run more than other approaches. The empirical evidence over the past two centuries, in this regard, generally (if imperfectly) bears out Adam Smith's prediction in *The Wealth of Nations* (1776) that relatively free markets will outperform alternative approaches for wealth creation (Jensen 2001).

A "primary" goal of shareholder value creation is "a little vague" (Ross et al. 2002, 15). Managers tend to maximize corporate wealth, under their control, rather than shareholder wealth (Ross et al. 2002, 16). "The available evidence and theory are consistent with the ideas of shareholder control and shareholder value maximization. However, there can be no doubt that at times corporations pursue managerial goals at the expense of shareholders. There is also evidence that the diverse claims of customers, vendors, and employees must frequently be considered in the goals of the corporation" (Ross et al. 2002, 17).

There are four key questions concerning the SWM principle. Two intertwined questions are normative. One question concerns the ultimate purpose of a business: In principle, what should a business strive to do? Financial economics theory posits that the ultimate purpose (and immediate operating goal) of any business is to maximize its market value. This corporate objective should, under certain conditions, maximize social welfare. This specification of the corporate objective reflects utilitarianism in the sense that everyone should gain over the longer run from freer markets if the necessary conditions obtain. Nonutilitarian business ethics, corporate social responsibility, and stakeholder theory provide different answers concerning ends and means of business activity. (There are several different theories of business ethics. Utilitarianism, a specific type of teleological or consequentialist ethics, is most closely aligned with market economics. Deontological ethics, best represented by Kant's conception of rational duty, is more closely aligned with CSR and normative stakeholder theory.)

A second normative question concerns property ownership and corporate governance: Who has rights to control or influence the objective function of the corporation? These rights might be moral as well as legal. Linked to SWM as a corporate objective is a particular understanding of the firm, in a capitalist market economy, as attracting and employing capital. (Capital owners need not be the organizers of a firm. Anyone, such as an entrepreneur, might organize a firm and then seek capital.) Allocation of capital is a key dimension of the functioning of the market economy.

A third question is instrumental: What are the practical alternatives for maximizing the firm's value and the shareholders' value—and over what relevant time horizon? And are these alternatives equally satisfactory? Key stakeholders, in addition to shareholders and executives, are customers and employees. A balanced approach to value creation, defined as one empirically treating multiple constituencies as if effectively equal, might perform better in the marketplace than an approach asserting a purely normative theorem.

A fourth, and final, question is descriptive: What are the conditions external to the firm affecting the normative and instrumental answers? Germany, Japan, the United Kingdom, and the United States do not share the same varieties of capitalism. The United States is the prime example of a strongly shareholder-oriented business system. The prevailing assumption is that SWM will tend most efficiently and effectively to resolve stakeholder issues and contribute to social welfare. The public firm is directed by a board of directors elected solely by the shareholders. In Germany, a dual board system and workers' councils reflect a greater degree of attention, in theory at least, to stakeholder management. Depending on conditions prescribed by law, a management board reports to a supervisory board that includes both shareholder and labor representatives. In Japan, although there is a single board like the United States and unlike Germany, banks are important capital sources, and there is an effort to obtain cooperative management-labor relations, as in Germany. The United Kingdom, although more like the United States than Germany or Japan, is arguably an independent development of corporate governance principles and practices. This variation in institutional context significantly affects both normative and instrumental dimensions in each country. Whether globalization will increase convergence or maintain such divergence in descriptive, normative, and instrumental dimensions remains a matter of debate.

Agency is a relationship in which one person or entity (the agent) acts for another (the principal) and typically under conditions of information asymmetries favoring the agent. This principal-agent relationship is ubiquitous in human activities (Mitnick 2008, 44). "At present there is no unified, coherent 'theory of agency'"—which appears in various social and business fields (Mitnick 2008, 45). In public corporations, agency involves potentially conflicting fiduciary and stewardship roles. The fiduciary role involves the relationship between management and shareowners. The stewardship role involves the relationship between management and the organization as an entity and the multiple stakeholders involved with the organization (Preston 1998).

In economics and finance, the key agency concern is contracting and monitoring to align the financial interests of directors, executives, and employees with those of the shareowners. One view of management appropriation of value is that the mechanisms of value diversion do not really matter. The argument is that self-dealing or insider trading, for example, does not reduce shareholder wealth because such mechanisms are simply substitutes for alternative compensation forms that would otherwise be paid to managers by shareholders. In other words, compensation extracted by management is constant at the end of the day, and all that actually varies is the form of transfer. Bebchuk and Jolls (1999) question this view. Their counterargument is that the form of compensation can and does affect the incentives for management effort at enhancing shareholder value. If so, then self-dealing would generate less shareholder wealth than some substitute mechanism yielding the same compensation to management. Ultimately, the question is empirical, if difficult to test. The testable hypothesis is that compensation form does not matter in association with shareholder wealth.

One can argue that transparent, disclosed backdated stock options are simply one form of compensation. Management openly is permitted to select the date for pricing options. Looking backward, management picks the lowest permissible price over some time period in order to obtain the highest feasible compensation. In theory, this self-selection opportunity may be a motivation to improve future shareholder wealth. However, one must then explain why managers engaged in such backdating have frequently kept the activity secret from the shareholders. Basically, to be legal in the United States, backdated options must be fully disclosed (i.e., transparent), approved by the shareholders, and properly treated for accounting and tax purposes. Options that are in-the-money when awarded, for instance, involve taxes due. There are significant financial incentives, therefore, not to disclose backdated options. Backdating may make the company appear to have more money than it really does.

That managers are being sued and prosecuted over backdating secrecy does not accord with the view that backdating is simply one form of compensation. In 2006, William McGuire, chair and CEO of UnitedHealth Group (Minnesota), was forced out in a backdating scandal. In December 2008, a federal judge gave preliminary approval to a settlement in a civil suit by the shareholders. UnitedHealth Group would pay $895 million and Mr. McGuire $30 million to the shareholders

(*Houston Chronicle* 2008). "One financial analyst predicted that an ordinary investor would be thousands of times more likely to contract mad cow disease than to experience the profits bestowed by the backdated insider stock options" (*Houston Chronicle* 2007).

These posited assumptions, or claims, concerning SWM are best regarded as a prescriptive formulation concerning what shareholders' rights ought to be in some idealized conditions. Contracts, incentives, and monitoring ought to assure that the board of directors and top executives are reliable agents who undertake to maximize shareholders' value (Stout 2002, 1195). The costs of assurance may be less than the benefits of assurance. However, the cost-benefit relationship is a purely empirical matter.

CRITIQUE FROM BUSINESS ETHICS AND CORPORATION LAW

The SWM principle is prescriptive in the sense that it is a proposed standard of conduct for officers and directors. This prescription is the dominant, and also a convenient modeling, assumption in the economics and finance literature. The prescription aligns with the neoclassical theory of the firm operating in weakly regulated markets (Coase 1937). The legal duty of officers and directors is to safeguard corporate assets by prudent conduct, not necessarily to increase their own wealth. In practice, officers and directors legally and morally must have some degree of discretionary judgment. In part, such discretion is unavoidable because how to prioritize the competing interests of multiple stakeholders may be conditional and fluid. Management may need to give attention to the preferences of employees, for instance, over the SWM preferences of investors (Jensen 2001). Salience of a specific stakeholder group, including shareholders, may vary over time and by decision situation. An extreme illustration of such conditional and fluid competition of interests has been reported for the Eurotunnel company (Vilanova 2007), which changed its name in 2007.

Whether SWM is or should be a binding legal rule rather than simply a primacy norm is much debated in the U.S. corporation law literature. U.S. legal doctrine affords considerable discretion to officers and directors with respect to conduct of a business. This discretion is known as the *business judgment rule*. Basically, that rule does not defend SWM as the binding requirement for managers. On the contrary, managers must be able to handle the conflicting interests just explained. Corporate constituency statutes in a majority of the American states, adopted mostly as antitakeover deterrence, reinforce that discretion. Basically, SWM is a prescriptive standard of conduct for guiding and evaluating corporate officers and directors. Perhaps even much of the time, SWM is a reasonable standard; but such a standard cannot be made a binding rule of law or conduct for all of the times tough decisions have to be made by managers. Shareholder value is arguably a control principle (who) and not a corporate purpose (why) (Koslowski 2000). At most, shareholder wealth is a goal of shareholders. The merit, or defect, of the prescription depends on the behaviors and outcomes that result.

Stout (2002) argues that, at law, shareholders do not "own" a public corporation and are not the sole residual claimants. "Milton Friedman is a Nobel Prize–winning economist, but he obviously is not a lawyer. A lawyer would know that the shareholders do not, in fact, own the corporation" (Stout 2002, 1191). Shareholders own stock shares (i.e., equity securities), possessing quite limited rights. The board of directors exercises control over corporate assets. The Berle-Means separation thesis (i.e., the separation of widely dispersed ownership and effective management control) means that shareholder influence is both indirect and, on the board of directors, effectively negligible (Stout 2002, 1191). The ownership notion applies at best to a closely held firm with a single controlling shareholder (Stout 2002, 1191).

"Like the ownership argument, the residual claimants argument for shareholder primacy is a naked assertion, and an empirically incorrect one at that" (Stout 2002, 1193). The directors declare a dividend, and that declaration is conditional typically on the firm's financial performance (Stout 2002, 1193). The residual claimant condition obtains only in actual bankruptcy (Stout 2002, 1193), when creditors have priority over shareholders, who receive only what (if anything) is left over after satisfying legal claims of the creditors. For dispersed shareholders to influence the board of directors is a costly action (Stout 2002, 1194). Maximizing the firm's value (or price) is legally binding only at change of corporate control, and then only when the sale is effectively inevitable. This position was emphasized in *Revlon Inc. v. MacAndrews & Forbes Holdings Inc.* (506 A.2d 173, 1986, Delaware Supreme Court). When an external party offers to acquire a publicly traded company, then the directors have a duty to ensure that the offer price is *fair*. Typically, a purchase offer of this type will include some premium over the current market price of shares. A purchase offer is public information, so sometimes there will be a competing bid by another external party.

There are two competing interpretations in the legal literature. One interpretation is SWM is little more than a residual target: If management does not have some reasonable business rationale for doing otherwise, then it should try to create value. *Dodge v. Ford Motor Co.* (204 Mich. 459, 170 N.W. 668, 1919, Michigan Supreme Court) supported the business judgment rule and appreciated trade-offs between immediate profitability and a continuing venture. There is no plain legal duty to SWM, and such a legal rule would be bad public policy and inefficient. The case's specific ruling in favor of a special dividend demanded by the plaintiffs is therefore effectively "a dead letter" (Stout 2008). Management can typically come up with a business rationale for why a special dividend should not be paid, and the courts will likely support management's judgment (Nunan 1988).

The competing interpretation is that the SWM norm remains legally strong. The American Law Institute (ALI) *Principles of Corporate Governance* (1994) provides only three "minor exceptions" to SWM: legal compliance, charitable contributions, and a "reasonable amount of resources" for nonbusiness purposes including public welfare (Macey 2008, 178–179). Practicality is the difficulty: "Maximizing value for shareholders is difficult to do. There is no simple algorithm, formula, or rule that managers can employ to determine what corporate strategy will maximize returns for shareholders" (Macey 2008, 180).

The SWM norm is ineffectual and rhetorical. Management discretion to sacrifice corporate profits in the public interest is necessary, independent of law; and SWM, actually practiced, would override social and moral sanctions on corporate misconduct (Elhauge 2005). An illustration is provided by an answer that Jeff Skilling, later CEO of Enron, reportedly gave in class at the Harvard Business School. He allegedly supported the position that he would keep selling a potentially, but not definitely, harmful (potentially even fatal) product unless government prohibited the product (Fusaro and Miller 2002, 28). The possibility is not hypothetical: Peanut Corp. of America allegedly kept shipping salmonella-tainted peanut products. That company declared bankruptcy in early 2009, and its CEO took the Fifth Amendment before a Congressional hearing.

CRITIQUE FROM CORPORATE SOCIAL RESPONSIBILITY

Firms are expected to practice "corporate citizenship" by engaging in significant community and social philanthropy programs (Sasse and Trahan 2007). The question of whether public corporations should do so is riddled with conflicting opinions concerning strategy and ideology. Friedman (1970) attacked voluntary CSR as agent misconduct. (He noted that a private company can properly operate as a philanthropic enterprise.) Citing the example of Timberland CEO Jeffrey Swartz, Sasse and Trahan (2007) resurrect the unintended results argument of Friedman that corporate philanthropy compromises "distinct roles" that business and government *should* play in market democracies and tends toward socialism. However, Friedman's formulation posits "rules of the game" of law and ethical custom constraining SWM. Adam Smith, in *The Theory of Moral Sentiments* (1759, 339), distinguished between citizenship and good citizenship. The former is simply legal compliance; the latter involves promotion of the general welfare.

An analysis of a sample of 384 U.S. companies, using data pooled from 1998 through 2000, concludes that worse performers in the social domains of environmental issues and product safety are more likely to make larger charitable contributions (Chen et al. 2007). No significant association was found between corporate philanthropy and employee relations. This evidence supports the suggestion that corporate philanthropy involves effort at corporate social legitimization as distinct from corporate social responsibility.

A corporate board cannot exceed its authorized powers (i.e., the legal doctrine termed *ultra vires)* (Hardee 1962, 107). Corporate authority to make charitable contributions was supported under a common-law test of validity, meaning direct benefit to the corporation, in the English case of *Hutton v. West Cork Railway* (23 Ch. Div. 654, 1883) (Hardee 1962, 105). The case concerned distribution of purchase funds following sale of a company at a price determined by arbitration. Upon dissolution, the general meeting determined to pay some of the funds to the company officials for loss of employment and to directors for past services. The officials had no legal claim; the directors had never received any remuneration. Two of the three judges disallowed the payments, on grounds that the company had been dissolved. However, the opinion effectively supported philanthropy for a going concern where there is some direct benefit to the company. By the Insolvency Act of 1986, s.187, and the Companies Act of 2006, s.247, an insolvent UK company can today consider employees' interests.

In the United States, *A. P. Smith Manufacturing Co. v. Barlow* (13 NJ 145, 98 A.2d 581, 1953), a New Jersey state case concerning a $1,500 donation to the annual fund of Princeton University by a New Jersey company, expanded the notion of benefit to be determined by the board of directors. The board of Union Pacific Railroad decided to increase its corporate citizenship activities (Hardee 1962, 105). The company organized test litigation in Utah with formation of a foundation and stimulated passage of a new state law based on a model statute prepared by the American Bar Association. The Supreme Court of Utah, reversing a trial court, sustained the company on common-law grounds while declining to pass, on purely technical grounds, on the new statute. The technical issue (that the statute did not apply to preexisting corporations) was corrected by a new business corporation law in 1961 (Hardee 1962, 105–107).

CRITIQUE FROM STAKEHOLDER THEORY

Since likely there will be a continuing gap between laws and markets, varying by country, a key role of nonfinancial stakeholders is action to expand one or both (Vives 2008, 229). Management and labor are more likely than investors to view a public corporation as a social entity, whose value and growth strategy cannot be summed up entirely by the current equity price (Strine 2007). Stakeholder, team production, and corporate republic views (Blair and Stout 1999; Englander and Kaufman 2004; Strine 2006) favor this interpretation. The basic argument is that the firm is a multiple-constituency organization whose wealth creation is more broadly definable than financial performance (Preston and Donaldson 1999). Critiques are available in Boatright (1996) and Meese (2002).

Jensen (2001, 297) argued that maximization in more than one dimension is logically impossible. If a single-valued objective function must be chosen to guide corporate activities, then in a market economy SWM will maximize social welfare. This prescription has, however, very strong conditions. There must be no externalities and no monopoly; and all goods must be priced. Total market value must include the market values of all financial claims. A key constraint is that SWM is not truly motivational for employees and managers, whose sentiments can affect their productivity effort. Maximizing short-term financial performance (e.g., profits or earnings per share) can destroy long-term value (Jensen 2001, 309). Under these conditions, "no constituency can be given full satisfaction if the firm is to flourish and survive" (Jensen 2001, 309). The government must resolve externality and monopoly issues (Jensen 2001, 308–309).

The business corporation is a wealth-seeking organization (Jensen 2001). It buys and sells, or trades, in a marketplace in order to obtain return on invested capital. There are two minimum conditions for this activity to continue over time. One condition is that the corporation engages in some socially legitimate business. Certain drugs, such as cocaine, heroin, and marijuana, are legally prohibited. Whether such prohibition is sound or effective public policy is not relevant to this chapter. The drug trade is regarded, properly or not, as socially illegitimate. Tobacco products are presently permitted, under certain conditions, but that social legitimacy is being challenged and may ultimately be withdrawn. A second condition is that the corporation creates value in some form. Judge Ben F. Tennille, in *First Union Corporation, Wachovia Corporation, and First Union National Bank v. SunTrust Banks, Inc.*, citing Coase (1937), wrote: "Corporations exist to create value. In purely economic terms, if they do not do that, they cease to exist." As Tennille

(Special Superior Court Judge for complex business cases) points out, in a case concerning the proposed merger of Wachovia and First Union banks, corporations create different types of value: stock price, jobs, community contributions, cheaper and better goods and services, employee or founder personal goal fulfillment, and so forth (Tennille 2001, 4–5).

These two minimum conditions point out a basic problem in assessing SWM. The corporation is both private property and a social institution (Tennille 2001, 5–6, citing Allen 1992). William T. Allen, formerly Chancellor (chief judge) of the Court of Chancery of Delaware (1985–1997), characterizes this duality in terms of a schizophrenic competition between two inconsistent conceptions (Allen 1992, 264–265). One conception views the corporation as the private property of the shareowners. This "property conception of the corporation" or "contract model" bundles wealth-seeking of the principals with the fiduciary duty of the agents. Both terms might be used, because there has been an historical evolution from a private property view dominant in the nineteenth century to a nexus-of-contracts view dominant in the twentieth century (Lea 2008, 1919). The competing conception views the corporation as a social institution, licensed by the government to promote the general welfare. There is thus some duty of loyalty to all concerned with a particular corporation. The legal entity has a public as well as a private purpose. "This view could be labeled in a variety of ways: the managerialist conception, the institutionalist conception, or the social entity conception" (Allen 1992, 265). This view might be characterized as a communitarian theory of the firm (Lea 2008, 1919). A good instance, cited by Lea (2008, 1919), is governmental regulation of social effects such as negative externalities illustrated by pollution. The communitarian theory is closely aligned with stakeholder theory to the extent that the government is treated in the latter as a stakeholder.

Variations in the forms of capitalism were noted earlier. Judge Tennille (2001, 6–7) characterizes three competing systems for corporate value creation: (1) the Japanese *keiretsu* (a business group comprising a set of companies with interlocking business relationships and shareholdings); (2) the European approach involving strong (or close) ownership, strong influence by financial institutions, and state-controlled companies; and (3) the U.S. approach of diverse capital ownership resulting in separation of ownership and control. In Europe, ownership is more concentrated, there are pro-stakeholder institutions, and employment protection is more rigid (Gelter 2009). However, the world is more complicated: There is considerable variation, and the United Kingdom is likely now an independent development. But for present purposes, these three systems will serve. The UK Companies Act facilitates stakeholder interests (Gelter 2009). Each system addresses four tasks differently: (1) defining and ranking corporate values; (2) combining and using financial capital; (3) combining and using human capital; and (4) combining financial capital and human capital.

An open question is whether the U.S. system outperforms the Japanese and European approaches. Judge Tennille (2001, 7) answers favorably for the U.S. system to date. Historically, over the past two centuries, relatively free market systems have performed well at economic development and growth, supporting Adam Smith's prediction in *The Wealth of Nations* (1776). However, the recent global recession, originating in the U.S. subprime mortgage sector and following various corporate scandals there and elsewhere, raises significant questions about a strongly positive answer for the U.S. approach. Yoshimori (2005) suggests that the corporate performance of Toyota and Canon is superior to the corporate performance of GM and Xerox, due partly to the emphasis of the latter on SWM as distinct from sustainable strategy development and corporate governance. Leaving aside the question of whether Yoshimori is in fact correct, it is conceivable that various approaches, rooted in different societal contexts (Tennille 2001, 8), will all perform sufficiently well that the truth of which is strictly better is not a dominating consideration (Henisz and Williamson 1999).

Corporate governance structures in Europe and Japan are more favorable to stakeholder-oriented firms. It may be true that a shareholder board will outperform a stakeholder board and that the purpose of a corporation should be narrowly efficiency rather than broadly social benefits (Williamson and Bercovitz 1996). A rational person should then arguably select the director-primacy model of corporate governance over competing proposals (such as a stakeholder board) as improving social welfare for everyone except the CEO (Dent 2008). However, a recent analysis by three finance professors suggests that stakeholder-oriented firms have advantages and disadvantages, such that the case in favor of shareholder-oriented firms is not automatic or decisive (Allen et al. 2007). The study concludes that stakeholder-oriented firms may have lower output and higher prices—which combination could result in greater value to the firm. (The reason, as the authors note, is effectively an increase in monopoly power, to the potential harm of consumers.) Additionally, consumers (notwithstanding the increase in monopoly power) may prefer to buy goods and services from stakeholder firms; if so, the number of such firms will tend to increase over time. (The study uses a mathematical model of stakeholder governance involving a duopoly of two hypothetical firms selling in competition.)

It is possible that (1) better relations with primary stakeholders (e.g., employees, customers, suppliers, and communities) could increase shareholder wealth, while (2) social initiatives (i.e., CSR activities) not related to primary stakeholders could decrease shareholder wealth (Hillman and Keim 2001). An instrumental stakeholder strategy, by which better stakeholder management results in both greater shareholder wealth and greater benefits for other stakeholders, seems to be a nondebatable win-win thesis.

Several answers may address the social initiative problem. One answer is that the empirical evidence is disputed and arguably contingent on particular circumstances (Margolis and Walsh 2003). The weight of evidence suggests that the average relationship between corporate social and financial performance is basically neutral or mildly positive (Becchetti et al. 2008). If so, limited CSR activities are not likely to endanger corporate earnings materially (Roman et al. 1999, 121). A case does not have to be made that social initiatives are profitable, only that social initiatives are not markedly unprofitable (Bird et al. 2007). Even a thin difference leaves discretion to corporate strategy. A second answer is that social initiatives may serve to enhance or protect corporate reputation as an intangible asset in ways difficult to measure. Market value may depend on intangibles like brand value and reputation (Vives 2008, 205, n. 9). A third answer is that a firm ought to avoid doing wrong and causing social harms; the effort to avoid wrong and social harms may be strengthened by engaging in some social goods (Greenfield 2008).

CONCLUSION

The view that the corporate objective is and should be shareholder wealth maximization (SWM) is a prescriptive, standard assumption in the economics and finance literature. There are normative foundations for the principle in utilitarianism and property rights. The strong form of the principle is arguably not descriptively or instrumentally defensible. There is reason to think that markets in which stock prices are set are seriously imperfect. The principle does not correspond with the actual legal duties of officers and directors. There are objections to strict SWM from business ethics and corporation law, corporate social responsibility, and stakeholder theory (or close variants such as team production and corporate republic conceptions). The corporate objective is better understood as constrained maximization in principle, relaxed to constrained wealth seeking in practice (Jensen 2001). The debate is then over constraints and influences.

The constraints can be understood as a set of antecedent conditions defined by law and ethics. From a deontological perspective, the corporation should commit no wrongs (Greenfield 2008). (An idealized standard may have to be relaxed to a more realistic standard of avoiding or minimizing wrongs.) From a teleological perspective, the corporation should commit no social harms. (Again, an idealized standard may have to be relaxed to a more realistic standard of avoiding or minimizing harms.) This condition is not necessarily one of doing social good, other than as a by-product (i.e., positive externality) of market activities. From a purely financial perspective, wrong conduct may prove very costly to the firm through fines and civil liabilities, loss of reputation and trust, and increased compliance costs occasioned by erosion of integrity. The Foreign Corrupt Practices Act (1977) and the Sarbanes-Oxley Act (2002) are illustrations.

Given compliance with these antecedent conditions, then management should attempt to maximize the sustainable economic value of shareholders' investments over time. Time horizon is a matter of strategic judgment. The shareholders must be concerned to minimize misappropriation of this economic value by management acting as self-interested (i.e., opportunistic) agents. And such agents may undermine efforts at meeting the antecedent conditions.

This corporate objective is further constrained by three strategic considerations bearing on management choices. First, some purpose other than money may be a better strategy and may better enhance employee productivity and stakeholder loyalty (George 2001). Second, sufficient stakeholder satisfaction to ensure loyalty (rather than exit or voice) is strategically valuable. Third, doing some social good (some corporate social responsibility or corporate citizenship) beyond avoidance of wrongs and harms may prove to be a smarter long-run strategy, and may be increasingly demanded or expected by important stakeholders.

REFERENCES

Allen, F., E. Carletti, and R. Marquez. 2007. Stakeholder capitalism, corporate governance and firm value. http://knowledge.wharton.upenn.edu/paper.cfm?paperID=1355.

Allen, W. T. 1992. Our schizophrenic conception of the business corporation. *Cardozo Law Review* 14:261–281.

Bebchuk, L. A., and C. Jolls. 1999. Managerial value diversion and shareholder wealth. *Journal of Law, Economics, & Organization* 15:487–502.

Becchetti, L., S. Di Giacomo, and D. Pinnacchio. 2008. Corporate social responsibility and corporate performance: Evidence from a panel of US listed companies. *Applied Economics* 40:541–567.

Berle, A. A., and G. C. Means. 1932. *The modern corporation and private property.* New York: Commerce Clearing House. Reprinted 1933 by Macmillan.

Bird, R., A. D. Hall, F. Momentè, and F. Reggiani. 2007. What corporate social responsibility activities are valued by the market? *Journal of Business Ethics* 76:189–206.

Blair, M. M., and L. A. Stout. 1999. A team production theory of corporate law. *Virginia Law Review* 85:247–328.

Boatright, J. R. 1996. Business ethics and the theory of the firm. *American Business Law Journal* 34:217–238.

———. 2007. Reluctant guardians: The moral responsibility of gatekeepers. *Business Ethics Quarterly* 17:613–632.

Cadbury, Sir A. 2006. The rise of corporate governance. In *The accountable corporation,* ed. M. J. Epstein and K. O. Hanson. Westport, CT: Praeger Perspectives.

Chen, J. C., D. M. Patten, and R. W. Roberts. 2007. Corporate charitable contributions: A corporate social performance or legitimacy strategy? *Journal of Business Ethics* 82:131–144.

Coase, R. H. 1937. The nature of the firm. *Economics, N.S.* 4:386–405.

Dent, G. W. 2008. Academics in Wonderland: The team production and director primacy models of corporate governance. *Houston Law Review* 44:1213–1274.

Economist. 2005. The ethics of business: A survey of corporate social responsibility. January 22.

Elhauge, E. 2005. Sacrificing corporate profits in the public interest. *New York University Law Review* 80:733–869.

Englander, E., and A. Kaufman. 2004. The end of managerial ideology: From corporate social responsibility to corporate social indifference. *Enterprise & Society* 5:404–450.

Friedman, M. 1970. The social responsibility of business is to increase its profits. *New York Times Magazine,* September 13.

Fusaro, P. C., and R. M. Miller. 2002. *What went wrong at Enron: Everyone's guide to the largest bankruptcy in U.S. history.* Hoboken, NJ: John Wiley & Sons.

Gelter, M. 2009. The dark side of shareholder influence: Managerial autonomy and stakeholder orientation in comparative corporate governance. *Harvard International Law Journal* 50:129–194.

George, W. W. 2001. Medtronic's chairman William George on how mission-driven companies create long-term shareholder value. *Academy of Management Executive* 15:39–47.

Graham, J. R., C. R. Harvey, and S. Rajgopal. 2005. The economic implications of corporate financial reporting. *Journal of Accounting and Economics* 40:3–73.

Greenfield, K. 2008. The disaster at Bhopal: Lessons for corporate law. *New England Law Review* 42:755–760.

Hardee, C. 1962. Philanthropy and the business corporation, existing guidelines—future policy. In *Philanthropy and public policy,* ed. F. G. Dickinson. New York: National Bureau of Economic Research.

Henisz, W. J., and O. E. Williamson. 1999. Comparative economic organization: Within and between countries. *Business and Politics* 1:261–277.

Hillman, A. J., and G. D. Keim. 2001. Shareholder value, stakeholder management, and social issues: What's the bottom line? *Strategic Management Journal* 22:125–139.

Houston Chronicle. 2007. Editorial: Learning failure—Stock option scandal shows many executives and company directors learned little from Enron. *Houston Chronicle* January 4.

———. 2008. Judge approves settlement. *Houston Chronicle* December 19.

Husted, B. W., and J. Salazar. 2006. Taking Friedman seriously: Maximizing profits and social performance. *Journal of Management Studies* 43:75–91.

Jensen, M. C. 2001. Value maximisation, stakeholder theory, and the corporate objective function. *European Financial Management* 7:297–317.

Koslowski, P. 2000. The limits of shareholder value. *Journal of Business Ethics* 27:137–148.

Lea, D. R. 2008. Shareholder wealth maximization. In *Encyclopedia of business ethics and society*, ed. Robert W. Kolb. Thousand Oaks, CA: Sage Publications.

Macey, J. R. 2008. A close read of an excellent commentary on *Dodge v. Ford*. *Virginia Law and Business Review* 3:177–190.

Margolis, J. D., and J. P. Walsh. 2003. Misery loves companies: Rethinking social initiatives by business. *Administrative Science Quarterly* 48:268–305.

Meese, A. J. 2002. The team production theory of corporate law: A critical assessment. *William and Mary Law Review* 43:1629–1702.

Mitnick, B. M. 2008. Agency, theory of. In *Encyclopedia of business ethics and society*, ed. Robert W. Kolb. Thousand Oaks, CA: Sage Publications.

Nunan, R. 1988. The libertarian conception of corporate property: A critique of Milton Friedman's views on the social responsibility of business. *Journal of Business Ethics* 7:891–906.

Preston, L. E. 1998. Agents, stewards, and stakeholders. *Academy of Management Review* 23:9.

Preston, L. E., and T. Donaldson. 1999. Stakeholder management and organizational wealth. *Academy of Management Review* 24:619–620.

Roman, R. M., S. Hayibor, and B. R. Agle. 1999. The relationship between social and financial performance. *Business and Society* 38:109–125.

Ross, S. A., R. W. Westerfield, and J. Jaffe. 2002. *Corporate finance*. 6th ed. New York: McGraw–Hill Irwin.

Sasse, C. M., and R. T. Trahan. 2007. Rethinking the new corporate philanthropy. *Business Horizons* 50:29–38.

Smith, A. 1759. *The theory of moral sentiments*. London: Printed for A. Millar.

Smith, A. 1776. *An inquiry into the nature and causes of the wealth of nations*. London: Printed for W. Strahan and T. Cadell.

Stout, L. A. 2002. Bad and not-so-bad arguments for shareholder primacy. *Southern California Law Review* 75:1189–1209.

———. 2008. Why we should stop teaching *Dodge v. Ford*. *Virginia Law and Business Review* 3:163–176.

Strine, L. E. 2006. Toward a true corporate republic: A traditionalist response to Bebchuk's solution for improving corporate America. *Harvard Law Review* 119:1759–1783.

———. 2007. Toward common sense and common ground? Reflections on the shared interests of managers and labor in a more rational system of corporate governance. *Journal of Corporation Law* 33:1–20.

Tennille, Judge Ben F. 2001. *First Union Corporation, Wachovia Corporation, and First Union National Bank v. SunTrust Banks, Inc.* North Carolina Business Court 9, 01-CVS-10075 (July 20).

Vilanova, L. 2007. Neither shareholder nor stakeholder management: What happens when firms are run for their short-term salient stakeholder? *European Management Journal* 25:146–162.

Vives, A. 2008. Corporate social responsibility: The role of law and markets and the case of developing countries. *Chicago-Kent Law Review* 83:199–229.

Williamson, O. E., and J. Bercovitz. 1996. The modern corporation as an efficiency instrument: The comparative contracting perspective. In *The American corporation today*, ed. C. Kaysen. New York: Oxford University Press.

Windsor, D. 2008. Berle-Dodd debate. In *Encyclopedia of business ethics and society*, ed. Robert W. Kolb, vol. 1, 162–165. Thousand Oaks, CA: Sage Publications.

Yoshimori, M. 2005. Does corporate governance matter? Why the corporate performance of Toyota and Canon is superior to GM and Xerox. *Corporate Governance: An International Review* 13:447–457.

ABOUT THE AUTHOR

Duane Windsor, BA (Rice), PhD (Harvard), is editor of the quarterly journal *Business & Society*, sponsored by the International Association for Business and Society (IABS). He has published a number of books or monographs, as well as scholarly papers appearing in journals, edited books, and proceedings or as conference presentations. His recent work focuses on corporate social responsibility and stakeholder theory. His articles have appeared in *Business & Society, Business Ethics Quarterly, Cornell International Law Journal, Journal of Corporate Citizenship, Journal of International Management, Journal of Management Studies, Journal of Public Affairs,* and *Public Administration Review.*

CHAPTER 24

Earnings Management

LEONARD J. BROOKS JR.
Professor of Business Ethics & Accounting, Executive Director, Clarkson Centre
for Business Ethics & Board Effectiveness, J. L. Rotman School of Management,
University of Toronto

INTRODUCTION

Earnings management occurs when efforts are made successfully to change reported earnings from those that would be normally reported, often with the intent to mislead investors and lenders. It has been practiced in one form or another since the first managers began reporting to owners. In fact, it is probable that earnings management has been pervasive, both over time and throughout the world. A study of 649 *Harvard Business Review* readers, published in 1990, concluded that "a large majority of managers use at least some methods to manage short-term earnings" (Bruns and Merchant 1990). Speaking in September 1998 on "The Numbers Game," Arthur Levitt, then chairman of the U.S. Securities and Exchange Commission, said prophetically:

> *In the zeal to satisfy consensus earnings estimates and project a smooth earnings path, wishful thinking may be winning the day over faithful representation. As a result, I fear that we are witnessing an erosion in the quality of earnings, and therefore, the quality of financial reporting. Managing may be giving way to manipulation; Integrity may be losing out to illusion (Levitt 1998).*

So significant were the risks and consequences of earnings management that Levitt went on to present a nine-point action plan to deal with the problem.

Levitt's view on the seriousness of earnings management practices was confirmed within a few months in two surveys of CFOs. In one by *CFO Magazine*, 78 percent reported being asked to use accounting rules to improve results, 45 percent had been asked to misrepresent results, and 38 percent had done so (Barr 1998). In the second by *BusinessWeek*, 55 percent reported being asked to misrepresent results, and 17 percent reported that they had done so (Barr 1998). Subsequently a study has estimated that for two decades (1980s and 1990s), at least 10 percent of reported operating profits for the S&P's 500 stocks were the result of earnings management techniques ("Economic Focus: Taking the Measure" 2001). Tragically for investors, in specific bankruptcy cases such as Enron, in critical periods, up to 50 percent of reported earnings have been the result of manipulations. Moreover, studies show that earnings management is practiced in countries around the world

(Land and Lang 2002; Bhattacharya, Daouk, and Welker 2003; and Leuz, Nanda, and Wysocki 2003).

Definitive evidence is not available on whether earnings management is practiced more in the United States than elsewhere. It is argued, however, that principles-based accounting, which is the dominant regime outside of the United States, even with its greater reliance on judgment, presents fewer opportunities for earnings management than does U.S. rules-based accounting. An example supporting this assertion would be the 3 percent outside investor rule that facilitated Enron's earnings management disaster. Outside the United States, the substance of external investor control would have been assessed rather than its compliance with a 3 percent threshold. It is worth noting as well that U.S. accounting standards have been influenced by lobbying and political pressure to a greater degree than outside the United States, which may have led to more permissive standards.[1]

Contrary to Levitt's hopes, earnings management has remained a problem in spite of his nine-point plan, although newer, more stringent requirements and penalties have been introduced that make managers think more carefully about providing illusion rather than fact. Even so, the traditional desire of managers and executives to report performance better than or in accord with expectations has induced creative measures of many kinds, some of which are detrimental to investors and others who rely upon those reports. During the 1990s and early 2000s, the advent of more lucrative bonus plans, particularly where stock options were involved, brought creative measures to depress and then overstate reported results in order to maximize cash bonuses and/or stock option gains. Even more recently, in response to the increased scrutiny, transparency, and governance structures introduced by the Sarbanes-Oxley Act of 2002 (SOX), earnings management has moved away from the manipulation of accounting treatments through so-called accruals to the creation of real asset or liability transactions to influence reported results (Cohen, Dey, and Lys 2008). Moreover, the broadened and more stringent application of mark-to-market accounting in 2007[2] effectively curtailed the use of some accrual-oriented techniques and reinforced the need to use real transactions to move or manage in the desired direction. Whatever the intent—to inflate, deflate, or increase the volatility of earnings—earnings management presents an ethical minefield.

Earnings management, as Arthur Levitt noted, represents a degradation of *earnings quality*, which refers to the "ability of reported earnings to reflect the firm's true earnings[3] and to help predict future earnings" (Akers, Giacomino, and Bellovary 2007). Performance reports that are significantly inaccurate or misleading lead to a distortion of the decisions that reliant owners, lenders, and others should take, and to an inability to properly assess the risks that investors face. From an ethical perspective, these negative outcomes raise many problems such as moral hazard,[4] adverse selection,[5] and fairness which may be addressed through analyses focusing on overall consequences, individual rights and duties, fairness, and the virtues expected of executives and the board of directors to which they report.

The aim of this chapter is to explore the motivation for and the practice of earnings management, and to provide insights and an ethical analysis of the topic that are useful to general readers and finance professionals. References are provided to facilitate further study about earnings management and the actions that directors and others may take to guard against it.

MOTIVATIONS TO USE EARNINGS MANAGEMENT

Earnings management occurs when efforts are made successfully to change, in an unwarranted way, reported earnings from those that would be normally reported. For purposes of this definition, normally reported earnings are those in accord with consistently applied, reasonable interpretations of generally accepted accounting principles (GAAP) that would result from transactions designed to maximize the organizational value-added for owners. The desired impact of earnings management is to present an untrue picture of performance that compares favorably or unfavorably with what is expected in order to confer a benefit on one or more stakeholders. Stated succinctly,

> *Earnings management occurs when managers use judgment in financial reporting and in structuring transactions to alter financial reports to either mislead some stakeholders about the underlying economic performance of the company or to influence contractual outcomes that depend on reported accounting numbers (Healy and Wahlen 1999).*

It is worth noting that executives often engage in managing the expectations of current and prospective owners, but that such *expectations management* is not the same as *earnings management*. For example, executives may discuss positive rather than negative aspects of their strategies or performance in the management, discussion, and analysis (MD&A) section of their annual report or in their news releases, but the earnings they report are those that flow normally from such decisions. Therefore, assuming capital markets are reasonably efficient, owners should be able to use the normal performance reports to factor out biased expectations management from their decision making. That said, the desired impact of earnings management can be enhanced by combining it with expectations management.

The purpose of earnings management by executives is to gain some advantage over the current and/or prospective owners of the company or their elected representatives, namely the organization's directors. In so doing, the executives (or perpetrators) generally seek to transfer wealth to themselves at the expense of current or future shareholders.

A positive or overstatement of earnings may lead, in the short term, to:

For the executive(s):
- Higher than warranted bonuses in cash or stock options.
- Higher stock prices leading to additional gains on sale of shares or options.
- Meeting or exceeding analysts' expectations.
- Favorable impact on executive reputation.
- Avoidance of termination.

For the corporation:
- Lower cost of capital.
- Easier borrowing.
- Easier sale of new shares.
- Avoidance of thresholds for regulations and debt covenants.

Of course, the overstatement of earnings may be discovered, which could lead to the opposite effects of those listed and to a permanent loss of credibility for the executives involved and for the corporation in the eyes of its stakeholders. More to the point, regulations spawned by SOX now require CEO and CFO certification of the accuracy of financial reports and of the related internal controls that ensure this accuracy. Knowledgeable false certification can lead to criminal prosecution of the CEO and/or CFO, and if convicted, to fines and jail. In the opinion of some observers, this "criminal prosecution for false certification" provision is the most significant recent reform for reducing earnings manipulation. It has definitely had a chilling effect on earnings management based upon accounting treatments, but has probably encouraged managers to switch to real transactions that are chosen for their short-run impact on profits rather than their long-run economic value-added for shareholders.

Sometimes earnings management is used to *smooth income and earnings* in an attempt to make a favorable impression on investors who have a high regard for earnings predictability and consistent growth. Income smoothing may be achieved by transferring income or expenses from one reporting period to another so that there is an appearance of consistent growth rather than letting income and earnings reflect the volatility of real life. This type of earnings management clouds an investor's ability to identify and properly assess the risk inherent in the stock and to match or manage that risk with a desired risk profile.

Perhaps more important from an ethical perspective, history reveals that many managements start the income smoothing process with the intention of having positive manipulations offset by later negative earnings reports, but find that they must continue to use increasingly large positive manipulations to ensure a constant growth trend. They find themselves on a type of *slippery slope* where an initially small adjustment leads to increasingly larger and much more significant transgressions, leading ultimately to ruin. While it is possible that income smoothing in which positive earnings manipulations are fully offset over time by negative results may lead to higher investor confidence, higher demand for the stock, and lower cost of capital, the risk of such benefits has proven to be too high in memorable cases such as Enron and WorldCom.

Cookie jar accounting is a term that refers to the situation in which earnings are manipulated downward by building up a cushion of costs or revenues (the cookie jar) that can be drawn from (consuming the cookies) in later periods to manipulate earnings upward. The motivation could range from normal income smoothing to the achievement of specific impacts. For example, led by CEO Frank Dunn, the executives of Nortel depressed earnings, creating a cushion that they later released to bolster earnings for two consecutive terms, which was the required trigger condition for substantial bonuses. Dunn and his senior executives were ultimately charged by the SEC (three executives) and the RCMP (two executives) for accounting fraud.[6] Other senior executives returned their bonuses rather than face recovery charges.

Big bath accounting is another commonly used earnings management technique. It refers to situations in which earnings are severely depressed, usually by manipulation, in order to obtain some advantage for the executives or the company. For example, when a company is taken over or new management is installed, there is a tendency to write off against earnings every possible expense, so that subsequent earnings will be artificially high because they are free of such expenses. The underlying purpose is to shift earnings from one period to another. The motivation involved could be to garner executives a higher reputation for gains or higher bonuses, or both, because the performance they are seen to be responsible for will be falsely inflated. Alternatively, this approach to earnings manipulation/management could be used to create tax advantages, such as would be the case in using up tax loss credits as soon as possible or before they expire.

Window dressing and *threshold management* are two additional motivations for earnings management in response to a perceived need to make earnings appear better than they really are. In this context, window dressing refers to the manipulation of earnings so that the organization's performance or its management's performance is seen to be highly desirable in the same way it would be helpful for a retailer who displays his goods for sale in the store window and "dresses up" the window display for maximum impact. Threshold management often takes place to make sure that reported earnings are on the good side of a threshold rather than the bad side. For example, earnings are often managed to appear as just positive rather than just negative, or to be above a threshold expected by senior management or a bonus trigger point.

In one instance from the author's experience as an auditor, a Canadian subsidiary of a U.S. parent continually proposed offsetting adjustments to those desired by the audit firm. Each adjustment was dutifully and thoroughly verified, but well after the audit was finalized it was discovered that the subsidiary's final net earnings multiplied by the year-end exchange rate resulted in a net earnings figure of *exactly* US$1,000,000.00.

The case of Livent's earnings management by Garth Drabinsky and Myron Gottlieb is also revealing. Although Drabinsky was a genius as an impresario of live theater (he thrilled audiences with *Phantom of the Opera*, *Ragtime*, *Kiss of the Spider Woman*, *Sunset Boulevard*, *Showboat*, *Joseph and the Amazing Technicolor Dreamcoat*, *Fosse*, *Candide*, and *Barrymore*), he and Gottlieb continuously ordered the manipulation of earnings so that losses were changed to profits to mislead investors and lenders. How did he do this? He intimidated his accounting staff, one of whom was a former partner of Deloitte who did the audit, into

- Rolling show production costs expenses forward from the correct period to a future period—this raised current earnings, as expenses from one show that had gone into production were moved to another that was still in pre-production.
- Withdrawing expenses already booked and holding them until a later period.
- Misrepresenting loan agreements as revenue by telling the auditors that an agreement with the lender to withdraw funds advanced had been cancelled.

How Earnings Can Be Managed

Depending on the result desired, earnings can be managed up or down by increasing or decreasing the revenues and/or expenses that are the building blocks of earnings. This can be seen algebraically if the relationship between revenues, expenses, and earnings is expressed by the following equation and the impacts of increasing or decreasing revenues and expenses are examined.

$$\text{Revenues} - \text{Expenses} = \text{Net earnings}$$

If the desire is to increase earnings, this can be achieved by raising revenues or decreasing expenses. Alternatively, if the desire is to decrease earnings, revenues could be reduced or expenses could be increased.

Basically, there are two approaches to creating the earnings changes desired:

1. *Accounting choices*—either within the judgment range allowed under GAAP (within GAAP) or outside the range allowed for accounting treatments or policies allowed under GAAP (outside GAAP).
2. *Real transaction choices*—by making real contracts or real economic arrangements that, when recorded using GAAP, move revenues or expenses as desired.

Accounting choices based on judgment are a normal aspect of measuring, correctly recording, and disclosing transactions within a range of GAAP options in order to properly reflect the economic reality of the event or development for current and potential future shareholders. Too frequently, however, CEOs and CFOs are choosing the alternative that best serves their own interests, and not the interests of the shareholders. Sometimes the choices made are biased but within the range allowed by GAAP; whereas, on other occasions, no attempt is made to adhere to the rules provided by GAAP. In the first case, there is a subtle attempt to mislead shareholders or their representatives, namely the board of directors, whereas in the second case the attempt to mislead is much more blatant, although relatively difficult to discover. While it is extremely difficult to attach civil or legal liability in the former case, once discovered the outside GAAP manipulation often leads to both, particularly since the SOX-generated regulations require the CEO and CFO to certify the accuracy of financial disclosure and the internal control systems in place to ensure that accuracy. As a result of this enforceable liability differential, the significant potential for shareholders and other stakeholders to be misled by within-GAAP accounting choices places a high premium on the ethics—the integrity and loyalty—of top management.

Accruals are a common type of accounting choice used to manage earnings, probably because the judgments that have to be made on a continuing basis are not susceptible to accurate point estimates. For example, falsely inflated (deflated) accruals for the following adjustments to assets will decrease (increase) earnings:

- Allowance for doubtful or uncollectable accounts receivable.
- Allowance for obsolete inventory.
- Amortization of intangibles.
- Depreciation of fixed assets.

Conversely, the following accruals that overstate (understate) liabilities will decrease (increase) earnings:

- Contingent liabilities.
- Warranty claims.
- Other one-time charges.

These changes in accruals are often effected by changing the application of an accounting policy or practice, such as changing from accelerated depreciation to straight line depreciation; by adopting a less conservative approach to amortization; or by recording potential bad debts, contingent liabilities, or warranty claims.

It is important to note that changes in accruals do not generally result in corresponding changes in cash flow. As a result, some researchers *erroneously* consider cash flow to be a measure of performance that is relatively immune to manipulation. They should be aware, however, with the recent high-risk changes in the post-SOX regulatory environment, that there has been a trend toward using real transactions to manipulate earnings and that these do produce changes in cash flow.

Real transactions chosen to mislead investors but recorded using acceptable accounting or sometimes questionable policies and entries would include:

- Change in or abnormal discretionary expenses, such as research and development costs or advertising.
- Sale of assets to record gains and leaseback.
- Sales manipulation by product distribution channel stuffing beyond normal demand levels to increase revenue in a period, but with guaranteed take-back of unsold inventory in the next period.
- Increase in production leading to high inventory value that results in a higher than appropriate allocation of overhead cost to inventory rather than to the cost of goods sold, thus increasing net earnings in the short run.
- Sham off-balance-sheet transactions to increase revenue or decrease expenses (as used in the Enron special purpose entities [SPEs] and the Rhythms hedge).

Real transactions are also frequently delayed, advanced, or restructured to defer, advance, or alter the timing of revenue or expense recognition. For instance, a contract to supply six large power generators that are usually invoiced on a completed contract basis when installed and operating could be restructured to include partial invoicing when the units are shipped from the factory, part when installed and operating, and part after three months of operation. Alternatively, the date of completion could be delayed on some technicality to delay the reporting of income.

Both accrual transactions and real transactions have the potential to affect a company's assets and liabilities. Unlike accruals transactions, real transactions generally affect cash flow. Sham transactions such as those used by Enron illustrate how some earnings management transactions can impact earnings and assets but not liabilities since off-balance-sheet financing was used. In these cases Enron used asset sales (which were really disguised loans) to related parties to increase cash and record profits on sales at outrageously high levels. By erroneously considering the related party transactions to be sales rather than loans, no liability was shown.

Whether earnings management is effected through manipulative accounting choices or real transactions, the impact on decision makers is potentially very real and significant. Moreover, since such manipulations may not become known for many years, prevention and early recognition are highly desirable. Consequently, many organizations develop measures within their governance and internal control systems to prevent and control for these problems, not the least of which is the development of an ethical corporate culture in which employees understand the values the organization professes and specifically why earnings management is unethical and therefore not acceptable.

ETHICAL ANALYSIS OF EARNINGS MANAGEMENT

Until recently, many business students, as well as many of the finance community, took the view that business is just a game in which the objective is to win at any cost. Given Enron and other financial scandals, including the subprime lending crisis, the proportion has shrunk but is still significant. These gamesters need to appreciate that the consequences of unethical behavior can be serious for themselves as well as their employers, but first they need to understand what makes an action unethical.

The Association for the Advancement of Collegiate Schools of Business (AACSB) that accredits business schools worldwide has recommended a framework for ethics education of business students in their Ethics Education Task Force (EETF) (AACSB 2004). Applying that framework to earnings management provides a useful starting point for raising the ethical awareness and understanding of finance professionals on these matters. Specifically, the AACSB framework refers to four broad themes that should be present in a business school curriculum:

1. The responsibility of business in society.
2. Ethical decision making.
3. Ethical leadership.
4. Corporate governance.

For ethical decision making, analyses are needed to differentiate an ethical from an unethical act based on the following approaches:

- Consequentialism—study of the consequences of the action.
- Deontology—study of the impact on individual rights, duties, and justice or fairness.
- Virtue ethics—study of the virtues expected.

It is important to note that these analyses are to be performed from the perspective of the consequences to or impacts on stakeholders involved, where stakeholders are those groups that fit within the definition offered by R. Edward Freeman: "...anyone who is affected by or can affect the objectives of the organization" (Freeman 1984). Specifically, for the analysis of earnings management, the following stakeholders should be included:

- Current shareholders.
- Potential future shareholders.
- Board of directors.
- Bankers and other lenders.

- CEO, CFO, and other senior executives.
- Employees.
- Customers or clients.
- Communities.
- Governments.
- Tax and regulatory authorities.

From a *consequentialist* perspective, earnings management is said to benefit current shareholders by smoothing or stabilizing stock price trends, thus reducing volatility and uncertainty for investors and lenders and leading to lower costs of capital. Senior executives and other stock option holders may benefit from falsely stated earnings, but probably only in the short run. However, future shareholders and current shareholders who wish to continue holding their shares may not be able to correctly assess their future risks and returns. The board of directors may also not be able to remunerate senior officers correctly and structure their bonus plans to provide appropriate motivation. Bankers, lenders, governments, tax authorities, and other regulators also have no interest in being misled. In fact, manipulated earnings can give rise to the payment of taxes unnecessarily and/or to underpayment of taxes and tax penalties. Finally, the enforcement of SOX-spawned rules could cause the CEO and CFO, who certify the accuracy of financial disclosures and the adequacy of internal controls, to be prosecuted in criminal court and, if convicted, to be imprisoned. In summary, although earnings management may benefit some parties, these benefits are likely to be in the short term, and when compared to the potential risks for most of the other stakeholders, earnings management should be considered unethical based on an analysis of its consequences.

From a *deontological* perspective, current and potential shareholders have a right to unbiased[7] or unmanipulated information from their agents,[8] and securities regulations should be structured to ensure that is the case. That is a fair expectation from a contracting perspective, although senior management may wish it were otherwise since many of them are motivated to maximize their rewards within the context of their incentive schemes and contracts. In fact, it is quite possible for executives to take advantage of poorly drawn contracts or incentive packages in ways that are legal but not fair or representative of the duty that was expected. Fairness in the distribution of benefits and costs of an action among stakeholders is an important ethical concept, but not one enshrined in law. If the senior executives and others who try to take advantage of earnings management were to put themselves in the position of those they were taking advantage of, this point would be quite evident. As many senior executives and others know, many actions are, in fact, legal but not ethical, although for perpetrators of unethical acts, the consequences are changing for the worse.

It is important to note that the analysis of the ethicality of acts solely by evaluating their consequences will likely lead to a flawed result. Deontological analysis has the capacity to improve the outcome and avoid embarrassment. For example, some may judge the benefits of earnings management to outweigh its costs, perhaps because of their own interests or because losses projected were far in the future. However, an analysis of the fairness involved for all stakeholders and the individual rights subverted (both of which are deontological considerations) would clearly show earnings management to be unethical.

Perhaps the most important lesson for senior executives and others who promote earnings management is that expectations about performance are changing. Unethical actions are increasingly being viewed as unacceptable rather than as part of the game. The discipline of *virtue ethics* suggests that the motivations for actions and the processes those actions involve need to be examined to see whether they match with the virtues expected by the stakeholders involved. Do the motivations, processes involved, and the impact of such actions reflect the character traits expected, including courage, honesty, integrity, fairness, impartiality, and enlightened self-interest? Earnings management involves deception for personal gain. It involves dishonesty, lack of integrity, impartiality, and unenlightened self-interest. By these standards, earnings management is clearly unethical. Even the arguments that it is in the interests of the greater good—lower cost of capital or saving the company—would not change the negative judgment necessitated by virtue ethics.

In some instances, executives and directors will argue that the unfairness to some stakeholders is more than compensated for by the overall benefit of the proposed action. In such situations, the trade-offs involved need to be weighed very carefully. While it may be true that very minor earnings management may be helpful, it should not be forgotten that few decisions affect only the short term, and even those earnings management manipulations that are expected to be short term often need to be repeated, and in larger size, to achieve the stability or growth in earnings that decision makers require. This is a variant of the slippery slope problem, in which a small decision grows incrementally into a big problem. In addition, decision makers should be very wary of the negative medium- and long-term reputational impacts of unethical action on stakeholder support. The trust that many executives and directors seek to engender through earnings management will become mistrust if stakeholders fail to see the demonstration of duties and virtues that they expect. Executives and directors would be wise to consider transparency and ethical management as ways of building and maintaining trust and of managing risks, rather than resort to the manipulation of earnings.

LEADERSHIP AND GOVERNANCE IMPLICATIONS

Recent financial scandals such as Enron, WorldCom, Tyco, and Adelphia, as well as the subprime lending crisis, have underscored the importance of ethical leadership and the development of an ethical corporate culture to guard against unethical acts by executives. Ethical leadership is vital in ensuring that earnings and other performance disclosures are accurate and provide an opportunity to manage risks effectively. Interestingly, the approaches to ethical analysis advocated for business school education that are outlined earlier provide a useful framework for the evaluation of corporate leaders and the ethical aspects of an organization's culture.

It is common now to hear that one of the desirable features in appointing corporate leaders is the *tone at the top*—how top executives think, conduct themselves, and serve as exemplars for the rest of the corporation's employees and agents. In this regard, a criterion for judging an existing or proposed CEO and CFO would be how their reputation and past actions compare with the ethical tests applied to earnings management; for example:

- Do they have a reputation for honesty, fair dealing, openness, transparency, consideration for stakeholders, and leadership in ethical matters?
- Have they been involved in any unethical or questionable actions or activities?
- Have they been forthcoming with past auditors and board audit committees?
- Do they have an understanding of the approaches to ethical analysis developed earlier in this chapter?

While such questions will seem ridiculously idealistic to some, others believe they should be considered a standard part of sound due diligence routines, and many wish they had been part of past assessments of many once well-thought-of corporate leaders. Finance professionals should be wary of executives who exhibit unethical blind spots or tendencies that may get them and/or their corporations into trouble.

The need for an ethical corporate culture has recently been recognized as essential to good corporate governance. Good ethics earns the corporation respect and support from stakeholders and reduces the ethics risks[9] of the corporation (Brooks and Dunn 2020, 16–18). Employees cannot be expected to adhere to corporate policies on ethical performance unless such policies exist, are communicated effectively to them, and are reinforced so that there is no mistake about the company's intention. Top executives must add their encouragement and support or else no one will take the policy seriously. As a result, finance professionals should be looking for the following types of evidence in their evaluation of a corporation's ethical culture:

- Is there a comprehensive, recently revised, code of conduct that captures company policy and is presented with training for sign-off to all employees when they join and annually thereafter?
- Do the senior executives continually support ethical behavior and the code of conduct visibly in both word and deed?
- Is the code integrated into company strategy and operations?
- Is there a credible champion in senior management for the company's code and ethical culture initiatives, supported by a credible, adequately resourced administrative team?
- Is performance in accord with the code monitored, rewards and penalties applied as necessary, and reports thereupon made quarterly to the company's audit or governance committee of the board?
- Is there an effective whistleblowing program in place with quarterly reports to senior management and the audit or governance committee?
- Is there an annual review by the board or one or more of its committees of the company's ethics policies, codes, ethics programs (training, encouragement, monitoring, enforcement, whistleblowing), as well as its leadership and resource framework?

INSTITUTIONAL AND VOLUNTARY MEASURES TO PREVENT EARNINGS MANAGEMENT

Leadership and governance expectations are the aggregate result, in part, of decades of studies, pronouncements, legal requirements, governance guidelines, and leading practices. A list of more important institutional milestones would include the following:

- The Trueblood Committee,[10] which in 1973 affirmed the investor-oriented role of financial reporting and the importance of cash flow information relative to earnings since the latter were subject to management.
- The Treadway Commission,[11] which in 1987 laid out the trust and responsibility framework for companies that raise funds from the public, and for other market participants involved such as directors, lawyers, and accountants, as well as recommendations for improving the integrity of financial reporting. This committee articulated the linkage between governance practices, corporate culture, internal controls, tone at the top, and the accuracy of financial reporting systems and the reports themselves. The continuing influence of this committee is evident in the activities and reports of its successor, the Committee of Sponsoring Organizations of the Treadway Commission, known as COSO,[12] specifically in COSO guidance given on internal controls and on enterprise risk management that have become informal worldwide standards.
- The Financial Accounting Standards Board (FASB), which determines accounting and auditing standards in the United States.
- The International Accounting Standards Board (IASB), which determines accounting auditing and governance standards on an international level.
- The U.S. Securities and Exchange Commission (SEC), which promulgates securities and governance regulation for companies raising funds from the public in the United States, which in 1998, under its then chairman Arthur Levitt, embarked upon a nine-point plan[13] to curb earnings management.
- The Sarbanes-Oxley Act of 2002, which through new SEC rules provided a more stringent governance, reporting, and audit framework in response to the crisis of credibility that followed the Enron and WorldCom bankruptcies, including:
  - Formation of a Public Company Accounting Oversight Board (PCAOB) to oversee accounting, reporting, and audit standard setting and practice, and/or enact standards for disclosure and audit where necessary.
  - Clarification of responsibilities of directors, officers, and auditors, and of audit and governance committee charters.
  - Audit Committee requirements such as:
    - The majority of directors on the audit committee to be independent of management and to exercise independent expert judgment.
    - The establishment of a complaints or *whistleblowing* system to receive and address complaints regarding accounting, auditing, and internal

controls where such a system provides for anonymous submission and for the protection of employees who make the complaints.

- CEO and CFO requirement to sign off on annual and quarterly financial statements, certifying their accuracy and the accuracy of the underlying internal controls in place to ensure this accuracy. In addition, there is specific criminal liability for CEOs and/or CFOs for knowingly making misstatements.
- Independence of auditors—prohibition from offering consulting and other services that might pose a conflict of interest leading to lack of independent audit judgment.
- Greater transparency—reporting requirements for compensation, stock options approved, and insider trading.
- The New York Stock Exchange and similar bodies that issue guidelines for governance expectations.

Each of these institutional developments has been designed to get executives and/or directors to accept greater responsibility for their actions and greater accountability to investors and other stakeholders. Even so, as Levitt pointed out: "This is a financial community problem. It can't be solved by government mandate: it demands a financial community response. . . . I believe we need to embrace nothing less than a cultural change" (Levitt 1998). That change is underway, but it is very slow in developing. New regulations will continue to crystallize stages in the process as they evolve.

While compliance with enacted or promulgated standards is necessary, voluntary adoption of policies and practices that support integrity, transparency, and disclosure in the public interest can be of great assistance in developing an overall corporate culture of integrity that is essential in minimizing corporate risk. For example, the tone at the top of the organization will reinforce desired behavior throughout. Similarly, although SOX-initiated SEC regulations require a whistleblower program for financial matters, instituting such a program for nonfinancial or strategic matters such as those likely to influence consumer or employee support could reduce risks and increase overall support for ethical behavior and, in turn, for integrity in financial reporting. As well, there are many recommended practices, such as the creation of ethics training and reinforcement programs, that are not required but are well advised and valuable voluntary practices.

EARLY RECOGNITION

Even with appropriate scores on the ethicality of leadership and culture, corporations can get into ethical trouble with earnings management, so early recognition of red flags can be quite useful. Finance professionals should be constantly alert for the following potential indicators of earnings management (Mohanram 2003):

- Lack of independent directors noted for their independence, ability, and willingness to challenge proposed transactions.
- Trends in earnings that do not reflect the volatility of the underlying economic realities that the company faces.

- Consistent surpassing of analyst forecasts by a small but relatively constant percentage.
- Changes in depreciation or amortization methods or other accounting policies.
- Real transactions that add proportionately more to earnings than to cash flows.
- Increasing gap between net assets and earnings.
- Increasing gap between cash flow from operations and net earnings.
- Unexpected (large) asset sales, write-offs, or write-downs.
- Large fourth quarter adjustments.
- Qualified audit opinions or (unexplained) change in auditors.
- Large related-party transactions.

CONCLUSION

Earnings management has been widely practiced and will continue to be as the inevitable result of managements' desire to put the best interpretation on their performance. However, it is increasingly important that the significant harm from the manipulations involved is well understood, and that shareholders and other stakeholders are adequately protected. The reporting of earnings is no longer simply part of a buyer-beware culture in which it is accepted that all stakeholders are at the mercy of management. Senior management faces serious legal consequences for financial misstatements, and directors, auditors, and finance professionals are expected to be on guard for deceptions.

It is vital to note, however, that the legally provable standards for fraudulent earnings management are not the only tests of misleading behavior. Greater awareness of the need for ethical behavior and of the possible consequences of ignoring ethical red flags in the character and reputations of executives has focused farsighted executives, auditors, directors, and finance professionals on ethics frameworks by which to challenge, monitor, and judge those who are in a position to manage earnings deceptively. Increasingly in the future, the relevant test will not be whether management can legally get away with earnings management, but rather whether their actions are considered by stakeholders to be evidence of an ethical reputation that they can strongly support.

NOTES

1. See, for example, Granof and Zeff (2002), which documents lobbying and government influence with regard to proposed changes in standards for stock option accounting, derivative accounting, and mergers and acquisitions accounting.

2. The concept of mark-to-market accounting has long been an accepted practice in accounting designed to reduce the value of securities owned when their value was thought to be significantly and permanently eroded. See, for example, the Financial Standards Accounting Board's standard FAS 115 (Accounting for Certain Debt and Equity Securities), which was issued in May 1993. More recently, however, with the advent and popularity of derivative securities, the need for broadened application of the concept gave rise to additional accounting standards internationally, including FAS 157, which was issued in September 2006 with effect for fiscal years beginning after

November 15, 2007. It should be noted that subsequent lobbying pressure caused the FASB to relax the stringency of FAS 157 on April 2, 2009—a measure that immediately increased the reported profits of banks and relieved them of having to meet higher capital requirements during the subprime lending crisis. One quote is indicative of informed reaction: "It may increase reported bank earnings by 20 percent, but it has nothing to do with the reality of bank earnings. It's very important to maintain that distinction," according to William Poole, former Federal Reserve Bank of St. Louis president. See Al Yoon, "U.S. Rulemaker Eases Mark-to-Market's Bite," Reuters, April 2, 2009, http://www.reuters.com/article/newsOne/idUSN0235590020090402, accessed on July 26, 2009.

3. True earnings connotes a type of Hicksian income—"the amount that can be consumed (that is paid out in dividends) during a period, while leaving the firm equally well off at the beginning and the end of the period." Hicks (1939, 176).

4. *Moral hazard* refers to a condition in which an agent who faces different risks and rewards than his principal is inclined, as a result, to take actions that are not appropriate from the principal's point of view.

5. *Adverse selection* refers to making a bad or inappropriate choice of product or action, due to unintended signaling or information asymmetry (agent and principal have different information about an action).

6. "Regulators file charges against Dunn, 3 other former Nortel execs," CBC News, March 12, 2007, http://www cbc.ca/money/story/2007/03/12/secnortel.html (accessed August 8, 2009); Simon Avery, Tara Perkins, and Paul Waldie, "RCMP charge former Nortel executives," BNN Business News Network, June 19, 2008, http:// www.bnn.ca/news/1771.html (accessed August 17, 2009).

7. For a philosophical discussion of justice as impartiality, see Rawls (1971).

8. For a philosophical discussion of rights and duties, see Kant (1964).

9. An ethics risk may exist when the expectations of a stakeholder are not met.

10. *Objectives of Financial Statements*, Report of the Study Group on the Objectives of Financial Statements, Robert M. Trueblood, Chairman, AICPA, NY, October 1973, 71.

11. Report of the National Commission on Fraudulent Financial Reporting, October 1987.

12. Committee of Sponsoring Organizations of the Treadway Commission (COSO), www .coso.org.

13. In Arthur Levitt's speech, "The Numbers Game," referenced earlier, he initiated the following nine-point plan to curb earnings management by technical rule changes by regulators and standard setters to improve transparency, enhance oversight, and initiate a cultural change on the part of management as well as the whole financial community:

    1. SEC to require detailed disclosures about the impact of changes in accounting.

    2. AICPA to require clarified ground rules for the auditing of purchased R&D.

    3. SEC to publish guidance on factors to consider qualitative as well as quantitative factors when determining materiality criteria.

    4. SEC to publish guidance on revenue recognition.

    5. Private sector standards setters (FASB) encouraged to take action where standards are inadequate.

    6. SEC review and enforcement teams will reinforce the regulatory initiatives.

    7. Improved and more professional training and auditing to downplay cost management and increase quality, as well as greater independence of judgment and attention to the public interest on the part of audit committees.

8. A Blue Ribbon Committee sponsored by the New York Stock Exchange and the National Association of Securities Dealers to make recommendations on how to "empower audit committees and function as the ultimate guardians of investor interests and corporate accountability."

9. Challenge "corporate management and Wall Street to reexamine our corporate environment" and "embrace nothing less than a cultural change" to restore integrity in the financial reporting system.

REFERENCES

AACSB. 2004. *Ethics education in business schools.* Report of the Ethics Education Task Force, Association to Advance Collegiate Schools of Business. St. Louis, MO.

Ackers, M. D., D. E. Giacomino, and J. Bellovary. 2007. Earnings management and its implications: Educating the accounting profession. *CPA Journal* 77, 8:62–63.

American Institute of Certified Public Accountants. 1973. *Objectives of Financial Statements.* Report of the Study Group on the Objectives of Financial Statements. Robert M. Trueblood, Chairman.

Barr, S. 1998. Misreporting results. *CFO Magazine.* December 1:36–38.

Bhattacharya, U., H. Daouk, and M. Welker. 2003. The world price of earnings opacity. *Accounting Review* 78:641–678.

Brooks, L. J., and P. Dunn. 2010. *Business & professional ethics for directors, executives & accountants,* 5th ed. Mason, OH: South-Western Cengage Learning.

Bruns Jr., W. J., and K. A. Merchant. 1990. The dangerous morality of managing earnings. *Management Accounting* 72:22–25.

Cohen, D. A., A. Dey, and T. Z. Lys. 2008. Real and accrual-based earnings management in the pre- and post-Sarbanes Oxley periods. *Accounting Review* 83:757–787.

Economic focus: Taking the measure. 2001. *Economist.* November 24.

Freeman, R. E. 1984. *Strategic management: A stakeholder approach.* Boston: Pitman.

Granof, M. H., and S. A. Zeff. 2002. Unaccountable in Washington. *New York Times,* January 23.

Healy, Paul M., and J. M. Wahlen. 1999. A review of the earnings management literature and its implications for standard setting. *Accounting Horizons* 13:365–383.

Hicks, J. 1939. *Value and capital.* Oxford: Oxford University Press.

Kant, I. 1964. *Groundwork of the metaphysics of morals,* trans. H. J. Paton. New York: Harper Torchbooks.

Land, J., and M. Lang. 2002. Empirical evidence on the evolution of international earnings. *Accounting Review* 77:S115–133.

Leuz, C., D. Nanda, and P. D. Wysocki. 2003. Earnings management and investor protection: An international comparison. *Journal of Financial Economics.* 69:505–527.

Levitt, A. 1998. The numbers game. Speech at the NYU Center for Law and Business. September 28.

Mohanram, P. S. 2003. How to manage earnings management. *Accounting World.* October.

National Commission on Fraudulent Financial Reporting. 1987. *Report of the National Commission on Fraudulent Financial Reporting.*

Rawls, J. 1971. *A theory of justice.* Cambridge, MA: Harvard University Press.

ABOUT THE AUTHOR

Leonard J. Brooks Jr. is executive director of the Clarkson Centre for Business Ethics & Board Effectiveness at the J. L. Rotman School of Management, and director of the University of Toronto's Master of Management & Professional Accounting

(MMPA) program and of the Diploma in Investigative & Forensic Accounting (DIFA) program. He has published several books, including *Business & Professional Ethics for Directors, Executives & Accountants*, 5th ed. (South-Western College, 2010); *Ethics & Governance: Developing & Maintaining an Ethical Corporate Culture* (Canadian Centre for Ethics and Corporate Policy, 2008); and *Principles of Stakeholder Management* (Clarkson Centre for Business Ethics, 1999). He served for 14 years on the editorial board of the *Journal of Business Ethics*, and is a Chartered Accountant.

CHAPTER 25

Investor Relations

CYNTHIA CLARK WILLIAMS
Assistant Professor, McCallum Graduate School of Business, and Director of
the Harold S. Geneen Institute of Corporate Governance, Bentley University

LORI VERSTEGEN RYAN
Professor of Management and Director, Corporate Governance Institute, San Diego
State University

INTRODUCTION

The investor relations (IR) function is defined as "a strategic marketing responsibility using the disciplines of finance, communication, and marketing to manage the content and flow of company information to financial and other constituencies to maximize relative valuation" (National Investor Relations Institute [NIRI] 2002).[1] It has undergone a remarkable evolution over the past two decades: It was once a part of the public relations department staffed by communications experts, but has now become, in many companies, a separate department staffed primarily by finance professionals. The number of firms in the Fortune 500 that have an investor relations department has grown from 16 percent in 1984 to 56 percent in 1994 (Rao and Sivakumar 1999) and to 97 percent in 2008.[2] Regardless of the growth and location of the department or the educational background of its managers, the *content and flow of information* still lie at the heart of the role of the investor relations officer (IRO).

Traditional scholarship on investor relations has been dominated by tests of the financial or capital-market-based effects of information disclosure decisions, such as reducing the cost of capital, attracting an analyst following, achieving fair valuation, and managing the agency problems between corporate insiders and outside shareholders (see Healy and Palepu [2001] and Verrecchia [2001] for comprehensive reviews). This approach has placed economic outcomes at the center of most researchers' investigations, and the result has been a rather narrow conception of investor relations as a financial concern, to the exclusion of the ethical implications of the profession. Therefore, in this chapter, we discuss the variety of ethical nuances that arise when IROs make decisions about the content and flow of information that they share with—or withhold from—potential and current investors.

Although analyzing the financial implications of the growth of IR has clearly emerged as the dominant paradigm in research during the 1980s and 1990s, a growing set of scholars has begun to move away from this focus toward a more behavioral and holistic view of the profession. In this alternate view, scholars note that legal mandates and public pressure over the past 15 years have compelled organizations to demonstrate their commitment to shareholder rights by establishing an investor relations department as a boundary-spanning function (Aldrich 1979; Rao and Sivakumar 1999; Useem 1996). Investor relations departments occupy a central position in the organization chart (Rao and Sivakumar 1999), often with the express purpose of "managing the shareholder" (Useem 1996, 168). In this way, the IR function enables managers "to signal their commitment to investors but also to coordinate the disclosure data to investors and analysts and rationalize the management of shareholders" (Rao and Sivakumar 1999, 39).

A key part of managing shareholders is developing disclosure policies and procedures to guide interactions with representatives of the firm's capital and product markets. Because these internal structures are in place, more disclosure activity naturally occurs, creating opportunities to strategically manage disclosures to investors (Gibbins, Richardson, and Waterhouse 1990). Research has also suggested that IR professionals can and should develop close relationships with their firms' shareholders, so that they clearly understand, and thus become more responsive to, their differing needs and preferences (e.g., for information or clarification) (Coyne and Witter 2002).

While managing shareholder relationships can be an ethical endeavor, researchers and practitioners alike have begun to note that some of these IR policies and practices may also be misleading and unethical (Cain, Loewenstein, and Moore 2005; Levitt and Dwyer 2002; Mercer 2005; Useem 1996; Williams and Ryan 2007). At the center of some of the criticism are corporate executives' ethical obligations to shareholders, the fodder of a long-standing debate in business ethics. These obligations encompass fiduciary duty, promise keeping, managing conflicts of interest, and effective corporate governance (e.g., issues of coordination and control). Related to these themes are the recent discussions of transparency, specifically whether withholding information is unethical and whether certain parties have the "right to know." For example, some have noted that the disclosure of more information does not necessarily reduce the likelihood of malfeasance (Karabell 2008).

SHAREHOLDERS, CORPORATE OBLIGATIONS, AND THE PROVISION OF INFORMATION

Although the rights of shareholders and other corporate constituencies are often a hotly debated topic among ethicists, most agree that corporate executives owe their existing investors the duties of loyalty, candor, and care (Boatright 2008). These fiduciary duties stem from the promises made to shareholders at the time of incorporation, placing on executives the moral obligation to both engage in fair dealing and avoid conflicts of interest between their own interests and those of investors (Easterbrook and Fischel 1996). Some authors argue that corporate executives violate these responsibilities when they attempt to withhold or limit information from some shareholder groups—in short, control the content and flow of information—while other researchers note that it is the type of information itself that establishes the moral issue. As such, the mere presence of asymmetric information (Bohren 1998) and negative information (Holder-Webb and Cohen 2007) can impose upon a firm's managers a moral obligation. For example, withholding information about a key executive's health, as in the case of Apple founder and CEO Steve Jobs's five-month medical leave of absence, can create a moral dilemma. On the one hand, executives deserve some privacy, while, on the other, many chose to invest in Apple precisely because of Mr. Jobs and his expertise (Silverglate 2009). Furthermore, the company initially withheld this valuable information and then gave incomplete information. At first, the public was told nothing in response to questions about the CEO's extreme weight loss, and then was told that he was suffering from the common cold. Many have criticized the company for not disclosing accurate information earlier (Hesseldahl 2009; Silverglate 2009).

Indeed, there is a fine line between failing to disclose required information and revealing information that is carefully crafted to hide its true meaning. In response to these troubling trends, some have begun to advocate the idea of *value reporting*, where a manager is obligated to disclose both required information and voluntary information that investors would want to know (DiPiazza and Eccles 2002). Yet such information, too, can be inaccurate, biased, or unclear, as illustrated by the Apple case.

Ethical arguments can be made about the type of information that executives possess and whether they have an obligation to share it, intimately binding information and obligation together in the discussion of ethics and the role of an investor relations officer. Therefore, it is necessary to discuss the nature of the two concepts of information and obligation prior to analyzing the various practices that IROs may be engaging in, whether intentionally or unintentionally.

Information

While executives possess *information* that differs in content and importance, some is legally required to be disclosed to the public while other information can be released voluntarily. The term *voluntary disclosure* means the sharing of information that is not required to be disclosed by law or regulation (Lev 1992). Therefore, it can refer to information that is released in a nonmandatory subject area, or to the provision of information that goes beyond the minimum requirement in a mandatory area (Gray, Javad, Power, and Sinclair 2001), regardless of whether it is good news or bad. In general, in the United States, social and environmental information is voluntary while the majority of a company's financial information is required. However, the lines are beginning to blur as insurance companies in the United States are now required to file an annual climate risk report to disclose the impact of climate change on their business (Ball 2009). Therefore, any type of required information follows the standard of *materiality*, meaning that, if omitted, the information would have a strong likelihood of altering the total mix of information available to a reasonable investor (AICPA 1999).[3] If it is material, then a firm must disclose it.

The Securities and Exchange Commission (SEC) and NIRI note that managers should use their discretion in determining materiality.[4] Some researchers argue that managers misuse their discretion by sharing only voluntary information that is positive (Adams 2002). If correct, this bias would brand the current voluntary social reporting system a failure, because it does not promote transparency but, instead, strategic disclosure (Hess 2007) of the kind that may produce errors of omission. Likewise, others have questioned the very efficacy of disclosure regulation in solving information asymmetry and agency problems in capital markets (Healy and Palepu 2001). Therefore, accountability, transparency, and accuracy are important issues in both required and voluntary information disclosure, a topic that is discussed in detail next.

Obligation

The concept of *obligation* to shareholders has spawned a great deal of discussion, even tension, among business ethicists. Goodpaster (1991) ostensibly set the stage for this disagreement by arguing that the *multifiduciary* view supported by some stakeholder theorists represented a fundamental misunderstanding of the role of a fiduciary: to be partial to one group alone, as in the case of executives toward shareholders, by owing them the duties of loyalty, candor, and care. Boatright (1994) countered that even though fiduciary duties can be owed to multiple constituents simultaneously, shareholders have a unique role, in that they provide certain public policy benefits by helping to keep executives focused on and accountable for shareholder value creation.

Easterbrook and Fischel (1996) offered the field further insight into executives' moral obligations to shareholders in their influential book on corporate law. They note that "entrepreneurs make promises in the articles of incorporation and the securities they issue when they go public," and "also promise, explicitly or otherwise, to abide by the standards of 'fair dealing' embedded in the fiduciary rules of corporate law" (1996, 6). These promises are supported by fiduciary duty because of the difficulties inherent in foreseeing all possible future circumstances, making comprehensive contracting between corporations and their investors prohibitively costly, if not impossible. Other researchers have also noted that managers have an obligation to work in the shareholders' best interest (Davis and Thompson 1994). Philosophical positions support the importance of both promise keeping, in that one party has led another to rely on his or her actions (Oakley and Lynch 2000), and property rights, defined as one's rightful claims in relation to a resource or thing (Heath 2007).

Marcoux (2003) points out that moral obligation is intertwined with the possession and provision of information, thus extending the concept into our present discussion of the IRO's role. He explains that because shareholders are owed certain duties as beneficiaries they embody two main vulnerabilities. Control vulnerability occurs when beneficiaries give control over their assets to another party who is acting in the role of fiduciary in overseeing that asset or project (e.g., a pension or mutual fund). Information vulnerability occurs when the fiduciary has access to beneficiary information that the beneficiary may not even know exists. Information vulnerability also includes the fiduciary's ability to control the flow of information to the beneficiary, such as in the case of withholding information or providing incomplete or erroneous information.

Controlling the flow of information in these ways was a particularly visible issue during the 1990s. Arthur Levitt, SEC chairman from 1993 to 2001, raised concerns about the information advantages that institutional fund managers and analysts enjoyed at the expense of other, primarily small, investors. He argued that companies and their IROs showed favoritism that undermined the integrity of the capital markets. Levitt's speeches often focused on the rights of small investors, whom he considered to be at a disadvantage relative to analysts, brokers, and institutional investors, who commonly were the first to receive information from companies (Levitt and Dwyer 2002). In a 1995 NIRI study, for example, common methods for revealing internal financial forecasts were either via one-on-one conversations or conference calls with selected analysts and investors (according to 65 percent of respondents) or during closed analyst and investor meetings (50 percent of respondents) (NIRI 1995). By 1998, 26 percent of companies surveyed were still using these types of selective disclosure (NIRI 1998), despite NIRI's repeated calls to curtail the practice. While the SEC's Regulation Fair Disclosure (Reg FD) specifically prohibits the practice of selective disclosure, it continues to occur, as we discuss in a subsequent section. A 2005 NIRI study revealed that only 36 percent of respondents were considering discontinuing earnings guidance with analysts (NIRI 2005), a practice that can come dangerously close to disclosing material information about earnings to analysts and not to other investors.

While many investor relations officers do not try to "hype the stock" or intentionally issue misleading information, most realize that they have the power both to broaden the flow and content of information and to restrict it (Useem 1996). Ironically, the IRO must rely on the internal quality and free flow of information from company management in the same manner that investors depend on the IRO's dissemination of sound information. But, ultimately, it is the company disclosure committee and often the IRO who decide how the information is presented (Atkinson 2002), bringing forth some potential ethical quagmires.

Whether researchers argue that managers have a contractual obligation to shareholders (Boatright 1994) or a morally grounded obligation (Goodpaster and Holloran 1994; Hasnas 1998; Marcoux 2003), one fundamental ethical question surfaces: If an IR manager's role is to "manage the content and flow of company information" (NIRI 2002), should she permit the provision of unequal access to that information? For example, should an IRO condone the disclosure of different information content between current shareholders, to whom she owes a fiduciary duty, and potential shareholders whom she wishes to attract? Regardless of one's ethical orientation, the likely answer would be "no," or at least, "it depends." In the remainder of this chapter, we explain why.

MANAGING THE FLOW OF INFORMATION

Over the past several years, a number of management techniques and tools have been used that suggest the existence of questionable efforts to control the flow of company information (Williams and Ryan 2007) or the quality of information (Mercer 2005; Cain et al. 2005). Some of these practices are clearer examples of conflicts of interest and violations of contractual and fiduciary duties than others. Yet all are the province of the investor relations department, which, as noted earlier, has become the office in charge of "managing the shareholder" (Useem 1996, 168).

In research firm Investrend's recent comments to the SEC's Advisory Committee on Smaller Public Companies, certain *ethical* dilemmas were still noted, such as analysts' equity stakes in the companies they cover, inconsistent and selective research, and investor class discrimination favoring institutional owners (*Financial Wire* 2005a; emphasis added). Each of these concerns falls within the IRO's role of managing the content and flow of information. As such, it is useful to break down each of these areas according to the common investor relations practices that present the most pressing ethical concerns. In the area of managing the *flow* unethically, three issues stand out: (1) Some IROs provide information access to those who issue favorable analyst reports; (2) some allow private meetings with certain investors and analysts and not others; and (3) many use tools to track institutional investor activity, potentially violating privacy and restricting the flow to these preferred shareholders only. Regarding the unethical management of *content:* (1) Some IROs unethically edit analyst reports, a practice known as *entanglement*; and (2) some continue to engage in selective disclosure despite its illegality, whereby they provide more detailed (or even different) information to some investors than to others. Issues of transparency, essentially a question of information quality rather than openness, raise the stakes of the ethical implications of both flow and content and are discussed in a later section.

As previously noted, in order to make informed investment decisions, shareholders need the information that management has both access to and control over. Some researchers argue that corporate information should be treated as a public good for all to use (Anonymous 2002). Instead, ample evidence suggests that information is brokered by management so that certain favorable institutional investors and analysts have easier access to management's valuable time and sought-after information, creating a disadvantage among those who are not granted such favorable treatment. Companies use, or allow others to use, a variety of methods to distribute information to their advantage.

Favorable Analyst Treatment

Some securities analysts curry favor with firm management, investment bankers, and equity buyers by recommending the purchase of a particular stock. Historically, sell-side analyst research was an objective, third-party endorsement of a stock sought after by both the firms issuing the stock and investors buying the stock (Mahoney 1991). Sell-side research was considered to be more objective than buy-side research and was similar to having a reporter write a favorable article on the company. Therefore, companies provided sell-side analysts with important information about their stock in hopes of gaining favorable recommendations or preferred pricing on investment banking services. As a result, sell-side analysts began to use unsupported "buy" recommendations to gain access to management and their information network (Solomon 1998; Levitt and Dwyer 2002). They issued very few "sell" recommendations in the 1990s United States bull market, often in order to maintain that access (Sax 2000; Craig 2002). Some company managers were complicit in these practices and shunned analysts who did not offer favorable reports (cf. Levitt and Dwyer 2002). In fact, it was once common for companies to give investment banking firms their business if their analysts issued "buy" recommendations and for analysts to own shares in companies about which they issued opinions.

While recent regulation has discouraged these conflicts, it has not eliminated them entirely. Empirical evidence continues to confirm that such "favor rendering" by executives deters analysts from issuing negative research reports and stock downgrades (Westphal and Clement 2008). Through these actions, executives may clearly violate the fiduciary duties of loyalty, candor, and care owed to their existing shareholders by, in effect, choosing what information to disclose and to whom. The investors who lack this information because they lack access to the senior managers who possess it are then more vulnerable when making investment decisions. Likewise, the information that is disseminated publicly may be made less accurate by this favor rendering.

Private Meetings

Since the enactment of the Sarbanes-Oxley Act in 2002, companies have curtailed the practice of executives speaking directly to sell-side analysts, who sell information to potential clients. These analysts tended to issue glowing recommendations on the initial public offerings managed by their firms, another clear conflict of interest (Levitt and Dwyer 2002). Instead, buy-side analysts, who manage investment portfolios, and large, favored institutional investors now bypass sell-side analysts and meet directly with management, usually in informal gatherings set up by preferred brokerage firms (Zuckerman and Portanger 2004). Not surprisingly, analysts who downgrade a company's stock receive less of this personal access to top management (Westphal and Clement 2008). Further compounding the problem is that more than half of these meetings are paid for by the analyst firms, and the practice is widespread: An estimated 98 percent of investor relations managers use this technique (NIRI 2004).

Private access to management is also garnered via the quarterly conference call. More than 95 percent of respondents to a recent NIRI survey conducted such calls (NIRI 2004) and provided participants with a wealth of valuable information, usually directly from the CEO. Throughout much of the 1990s, such calls were among the benefits of large share ownership, and only rarely were individual investors or the media even allowed to listen in on the calls (Clark 2000). Quite often companies held one call for the media and one for the analysts (Clark 1999). Today, small-stake investors and the media are more often allowed to participate in analyst calls, but in a listen-only manner: 58 percent of NIRI respondents offered access to a toll-free listen-only call, while 31 percent required payment for such access (NIRI 2004). However, 88 percent of companies notify individual investors of the call only by a posting on the company's web site, while they notify 95 percent of institutional investors directly by personal e-mail. In some cases, executives no longer hold conference calls due to the risk of selectively disclosing information to some investors and not to others, which is prohibited under Reg FD (Bushee, Matsumoto, and Miller 2004).

Companies, then, either intentionally or unintentionally limit some investors' access to management, amounting to a form of discrimination, to be sure, but these examples also illustrate the practice of providing valuable investment information to some existing shareholders and not to others, making them vulnerable because of control and information issues (Marcoux 2003). Likewise, it is a violation of management's fiduciary duty to their existing shareholders and of their promise to abide by the standards of fair dealing (Easterbrook and Fischel 1996). It is also a violation of the investor relations code of ethics, which states clearly that members should "provide analysts, institutional and individual investors and the media fair access to corporate information" (NIRI 2006, 1). In sum, holding selective conference calls that include only some shareholders is a clear violation of public policy (i.e., Reg FD), but some managers avoid sanctions by sticking to information that is already in the public domain.

While these private meetings are argued by some to be a new form of governance and shareholder activism (Hess 2007; Reid and Toffel 2008), they may also constitute dissemination of public information to private audiences, which may violate both business ethics and securities law. Announcing conference calls to some investors by e-mail or by web-page posting is a sign of improvement. However, it may constitute a greater hardship for small shareholders, who should receive equal treatment by virtue of both managerial responsibility and public policy. Likewise, analysts who issue reports that they believe are accurate assessments of company performance seem to incur greater difficulty in accessing the valuable flow of information in the future unless they engage in unethical favor rendering (Westphal and Clement 2008). Allowing all shareholders equal access to the same level of information is not only a moral obligation but, as advocates of new governance mechanisms argue, also less expensive, and it makes for more easily comparable evaluations across companies or industries (Hess 2007).

Investor Surveillance and Targeting

A large number of public companies currently use computer *cookies* or stock surveillance vendors that record individual trades to infringe on the anonymity of investors and track their activities (Jones 2007). Large institutional investors, along with some high-net-worth individuals, place a premium on the secrecy of their trades: The vast majority of investors, some 80 percent, intentionally maintain their anonymity by using street names (Borrus 2005), making it difficult for management to determine their exact identities. While certain SEC corporate filings require quarterly data on institutional investing, stock surveillance has become popular because it promises more current, daily trading data. Recently, the integrity of the company's information itself (*Investor Relations Business* 2002), as well as the procedures used by companies selling the data (Pulliam 2004), have come under scrutiny by investors and regulators.

The data typically focus on only the largest shareholders who trade frequently, leaving out a substantial number of owners (*Investor Relations Business* 2002). The convenience of tracking institutional trades biases the information flow in favor of large investors, making them more attractive and apparently more manageable than large numbers of individual holders. As a result, stock surveillance companies help to make institutional investors the dominant and preferred ownership class by enabling firms to piece together information about their behavior. Questions surrounding the quality of some tracking data are cause for more ethical concern, given that firms take action based on these potentially questionable reports.

Companies' recent demands for investor names to facilitate such tracking raise ethical questions concerning shareholder privacy rights. Given the large percentage of investors who prefer anonymity, an ethical justification is needed to support company demands for their identification. Furthermore, investors should be notified, prior to investing, that their names may be made public (DesJardins 2006). Companies claim that their interest in investor information simply mirrors the shareholders' desire for corporate transparency. However, the investors' demands for information rest on a long-standing moral foundation (Goodpaster and Holloran 1994) that includes executive promise keeping and fiduciary duty, while company demands for information rest on less compelling ethical grounds.

Investor relations and corporate director groups have recently called for changes in shareholder communication protocols that they feel have been compromised by proxy rules, in order to allow for more direct and uniform communication to those who directly own the shares. The Shareholder Communications Coalition, a Washington, D.C.-based organization that includes the Business Roundtable, NIRI, and the National Association of Corporate Directors, announced in November 2008 the creation of a new informational web site. This initiative is part of a broader effort to inform the general public and Washington policy makers about significant challenges in the current system used by investors to vote their shares in corporate elections. The current proxy process allows banks, brokers, and other agents to vote the shares of beneficial owners on routine matters if the owners do not do so themselves within 10 days of the annual meeting. This process is clearly oriented more toward promoting the efficiency interests of brokers and banks than toward encouraging effective and efficient communication between companies and their shareholders. The coalition argues that the current system is a complicated and multilayered process routed primarily through intermediaries that are not the economic owners of corporate shares. Instead, the coalition argues that investors should be readily identifiable or, if shareholders want to retain their street names, then they should bear the costs of maintaining their privacy.

While the effort to provide the same content directly to investors of all classes is to be applauded, only weak ethical justification appears to support the publication of private investor identities and trading activity. Investors have a right to privacy, and they should be free to exercise that choice without a financial charge. Furthermore, if investors choose to allow intermediaries to vote their proxies, that, too, is their right, albeit a lax method of fulfilling their monitoring responsibilities.

As this discussion shows, the flow of information from corporations to their shareholders or financial intermediaries entails a variety of ethical dilemmas. The content of that information flow raises a second set of concerns.

MANAGING THE CONTENT OF INFORMATION

Ethical questions surrounding the content of information disseminated by modern firms fall into two related categories: editing analysts' supposedly objective company reports, and disclosing information selectively to different classes of investor.

Editing Analyst Reports

Another questionable practice was prevalent in the 1990s but still continues today: Companies frequently reviewed or outright edited the content of analysts' research reports but did not reveal their role publicly. Further complicating this practice is that these reports were normally considered to be the property of the company producing the report and often copyrighted by the company as sole author. Their authors often received compensation from the company or its investor relations agency (Sax 2000). Editing reports, a practice known as *entanglement*, effectively amounted to the company editing a journalist's article prior to publication. NIRI has attempted to deter this practice for the past several years.

The 2002 global settlement among the top 10 U.S. brokerage firms and the Sarbanes-Oxley Act, both aimed, in part, at preventing analyst conflicts of interest, have begun to encourage independent research. As part of this $1.4 billion global settlement, companies are required to hire three independent research firms in addition to any other securities research firm that they choose to hire. Although a number of companies have begun to offer this type of independent research, many have continued to pen their own, violating both the SEC's Regulation 17(b) and the voluntary industry standards which state that an investor relations firm should disclose both its identity and its compensation information in the event it does issue its own research (*Financial Wire* 2005b). In fact, some reports have been authored by the investor relations firms hired to promote the companies, undermining the definition of *independent*. Other companies have continued to pay for analyst research and justify it by disclosing the nature and extent of the compensation. This disclosure follows both the existing regulatory mandate and the voluntary guidelines for ethical conduct for analyst-corporate relations promoted by the analyst industry's professional organization, the CFA Institute. Yet an obvious question arises: Is it ethical for managers to *pay* for what is assumed to be an objective research report about their company? The NIRI code of ethics suggests that it is not, stating clearly that practitioners have an obligation to represent the interests of shareholders and to treat *all* types of shareholders and the media fairly (NIRI 2006; emphasis added).

From an ethical perspective, the third-party endorsement of sell-side analyst or so-called independent research reports makes company involvement in their writing and/or development suspect. On the one hand, it is troubling if companies pay research analysts—or if these researchers (whether they are employed by a research firm or an IR firm) accept compensation—or if either party *does not* disclose its involvement. However, it can be equally troubling when companies *do* disclose the conflict. Recent empirical evidence reveals that greater disclosure of a conflict can lead to a greater distortion of advice, because it encourages those doing the disclosing to feel "morally licensed" and "strategically encouraged" to exaggerate the company's information or advice (Cain et al. 2005). In fact, the receivers of information often trust those disclosing their involvement even more for divulging the conflicts. Disclosing the conflict, then, is not enough. One must work toward eliminating it in order to preserve credibility.

Furthermore, while companies' fact-checking of analysts' drafts could help to prevent the dissemination of inaccurate information, the ethical nuances of this behavior rest with the manager's intentions, specifically whether this legitimate service is being transformed into a self-serving one. For example, if some managers fashion the reports so that they intentionally appeal to some investors and not to others—versus just checking facts—then it would constitute another case of violating their fiduciary duties and failing to keep their promises to their existing shareholders. Thus, analysts' research reports are another area where the fiduciary manager must exercise a special duty of care for the shareholders' interests in order to avoid entanglement.

Issuing Selective Disclosures

Although discouraged and decreasing in frequency, the practice of selective disclosure still occurs far too often. Specifically, the practice involves issuing forward-looking or material information in oral statements or in handouts to analysts, while excluding the same information in press releases or SEC filings (NIRI 2002).

While Reg FD did cause management to be more cautious concerning such practices (Connelly 2005), with many making significant changes to their analyst and investor communication processes (Rapoport 2005), a handful of prominent companies have consciously violated the regulation. While it has made firms more cautious about selective disclosure, some are still able to engage in the practice due to the difficulties inherent in enforcement or by claiming that *materiality* is open to interpretation. Siebel Systems has twice violated the Reg FD ruling by giving a select group of analysts information that actually contradicted the information it revealed in a conference call to a broader audience (Williams 2004). Recently, Lehman Brothers was accused of disclosing more detailed information to large investors and of misleading the public about its financial condition (Craig 2008; Craig and Smith 2008) in the days leading up to its collapse, in what would appear to be a violation of Reg FD. Several executives from the company now face charges of fraud over misleading statements.

While investors should be able to expect companies to comply with federally mandated rules about the content of information disclosures, management retains a fair amount of discretion over whether and how to offer additional or supplementary information. These voluntary disclosures have been shown to heavily influence investment decisions (Healy and Palepu 2001; Lev 1992). This managerial flexibility also sets the stage for companies to engage in selective disclosures in the wake of damaging news or in the voluntary provision of information (which is not prohibited by law) to those investors whom they wish to court. But by providing more detailed information to one group and not another, even if it is voluntary information, a company can engage in a number of unethical acts, such as re-shaping the firm's shareholder base according to executives' wishes (Williams and Ryan 2007), pursuing more *transient* investors—those with low ownership stability, small stakes, and limited monitoring capabilities (cf. Bushee et al. 2004, 33)—or engaging in outright negligence, as in the case of Lehman Brothers (Craig 2008).

Informing some shareholder groups of corporate performance and projections without simultaneously informing the remaining shareholders has been recognized in legal terms as discriminatory investor treatment through the passage of Reg FD. However, it is also an example of unethical treatment of investors from the perspective of executive promise keeping and fiduciary duty (Williams and Ryan 2007). All shareholders who purchase a company's common stock should have access to identical and timely quantitative and qualitative information from the firm.

Thus, issues arise in investor relations from both the flow and the content of information disseminated by corporations. We now turn to the related, much discussed but little understood concept: corporate transparency.

TRANSPARENCY AND THE "RIGHT TO KNOW"

While it may be clear that companies have an obligation to share the same content with all classes of existing shareholders, the quality of that information is still a murky area. Likewise, some IROs are more forthcoming with certain shareholders than with others, as noted earlier, and are sharing better information, thus controlling the flow of truly transparent information.

Although most companies and investors agree that transparency is good, they typically ascribe different meanings to the term. Indeed, transparency is often ill-defined (Williams 2005) or simply defined by its opposite: opaqueness (Tapscott and Ticoll 2003). While transparency is certainly about the extent to which an organization is open, it is also about the quality of the information disseminated. Companies have been noted to be open, but not credible (Mercer 2005), transparent but not trustworthy (Karabell 2008), open but not accurate (Surowiecki 2002), and even accurate but not timely (Mercer 2005). So transparency is about more than a company's willingness to share information (even if it is in equal measure as required by Reg FD): It is about the precise content of the information as well. Right-to-know advocates who pressure companies for information rarely argue for just any information; they argue for *better* information. Perhaps these advocates know that the quality of the content matters; information that is accurate, complete, and timely is considered to be more forthcoming (Mercer 2005). Disclosure quality may also be conditioned by public pressure and peer comparisons (Cormier, Magnan, and Van Velthoven 2005), often resulting in improved disclosure content. Therefore, we consider *transparency* to mean a firm's disclosure of "relevant, timely and reliable information" (Williams 2008, 121).

Many organizational transparency initiatives are based on this right-to-know requirement. For example, the Toxic Release Inventory (TRI), used widely in empirical research on social and environmental reporting, was part of the 1986 Community Right to Know Act. The TRI, which was enacted following the Union Carbide chemical leak in Bhopal, India, requires companies to report their plants' emissions of certain toxic chemicals. Arming corporate constituencies with this type of information is intended to help them to hold corporations accountable and is part of an expanding governance model that includes social reporting frameworks, such as the Global Reporting Initiative, another right-to-know effort (Hess 2007).

However, many have criticized companies' social disclosures and transparency initiatives as nothing more than selective disclosures made with only positive information and only when firms are hoping to defuse threats to their legitimacy (Deegan 2002; Hess and Dunfee 2007). Companies whose legitimacy depends on high levels of trust and morality (e.g., hospitals, banks, laws firms, schools) are especially susceptible to value challenges by outside constituencies, and companies' responses tend to be more symbolic than substantive (Ashforth and Gibbs 1990). Indeed, many of these social reporting justifications have been criticized for their lack of transparency, noting that their quality is often "woefully poor" (Gray 2001, 13) and that such reports amount to a firm testifying to its own trustworthiness (Swift 2001; Livesey and Kearins 2002). Kolk (2003) found that most Fortune Global 250 firms provided no data about environmental initiatives, but instead simply stated their intentions or policies. Simply put, some firms' struggles to maintain their social legitimacy may drive them to disclose more, but not necessarily complete, information (Hess and Dunfee 2007), representing increases in quantity but not quality. Indeed, accuracy is about *how* the information is presented (e.g., the timeliness, reliability, and relevance), as much as *how much* is presented. As a result, much of the discussion has shifted to imploring companies' investor relations and corporate communications departments to disclose comparable data that is more useful to all corporate constituencies. As Hess notes, accountability is about "getting the right information to the right groups at the right time" (2007, 471).

What, then, is the right information for an IRO to disclose? As previously noted, for the SEC and American Institute of Certified Public Accountants (AICPA), it is information that, if omitted, would have been viewed by the reasonable investor as having significantly altered the total mix of information made available (AICPA 1999). For IROs, this decision often rests on whether or not to share negative news (Mercer 2005; Skinner 1994). The myth about transparency is that it flows from "good" management and substantive action, even "truth," as some have noted (Surowiecki 2002; Karabell 2008). However, more information does not necessarily reduce the likelihood of malfeasance, nor does withholding information necessarily harm a company's growth prospects (Karabell 2008; Surowiecki 2002), simply because it is possible that what is being disclosed is uninformative, irrelevant, harmful, or even deceptive. For example, the problems with both Enron and Parmalat were not the amount of information released, reportedly quite voluminous, but the level of deception contained in the information itself: *how* it was presented.

Others have noted that transparency of irrelevant information can lead to other problems, such as greater public and regulatory scrutiny, less management latitude, and an ineffective focus on short-term results, which is especially problematic for environmental solutions that require long-term investments (Bansal and Kistruck 2006). Similarly, Mercer (2005) found that sharing information about negative news increased the credibility of management but only in the short term, creating a disincentive to disclose it. Skinner (1994) noted that companies share negative news for more self-serving reasons, such as to avoid litigation and a reputation for withholding bad news among analysts, rather than because it is in the best interest of the shareholders and the capital markets to be informed of *all* news. Westphal and Clement (2008) found that senior managers engage in personal and professional favor rendering to neutralize the effect of negative information on analysts, and, in most cases, the analysts capitulate by issuing favorable reports.

As one writer put it following the Wall Street crises in the early 2000s, "transparency is well and good, but accuracy and objectivity are even better" (Surowiecki 2002, 54).[5] So, while managers might reveal negative information, thus being accurate in their information sharing, the information may still be incomplete for analyzing the performance of the company (Mercer 2005), which is a major purpose of corporate reporting and the investor relations function. Likewise, these analyst reports, potentially altered by favor rendering, are no longer objective. In this way, withholding information or altering it can be motivated by self-serving managers who stand to gain personally by the omission (Abraham-son and Park 1994), as was allegedly the case with the CEO of Lehman Brothers (Craig 2008).

In contrast, situations exist where withholding relevant information from shareholders, albeit temporarily, may be in the best interest of shareholders and the company, provided it is done equally among all classes. Some researchers have argued that withholding information rests on whether or not management believes that it will damage their firm's competitive position (cf. Verrecchia 1983, 2001; Dye 2001), such as information on mergers (e.g., prior to setting a price and a post-merger structure [cf. NIRI 2004]), trade secrets (Tapscott and Ticoll 2003), FDA approval letters and clinical trials (Lee 2008), or news about innovations (Karabell 2008). While these types of information are material, an untimely release may harm the profit potential of the information, so they can be legally withheld for a certain period of time (NIRI 2004). Ideally, the information is withheld so that shareholders can earn maximum benefit from the impact of the news. As stewards over share-holder interests, it is also prudent to avoid harm to other corporate constituencies, such as consumers and employees, with an untimely release.

In this way, one could argue that managers who are dealing with such piv-otal sharing and withholding decisions would do best to abide by the basic moral intuition that one has a prima facie duty to avoid doing harm and to make rea-sonable efforts toward that end. While IROs have a prima facie duty to release information that has the potential to be competitively sensitive, they would be acting prudently and reasonably, and within the bounds of current securities law (NIRI 2004), if they were to withhold it temporarily in order to work in the best interest of the shareholders and adhere to their fiduciary duties by exercising care.

EMERGING FUTURE DIRECTIONS

The investor relations function has been in a state of dynamic change over the past two decades. It has shifted focus from a communications-driven function to a marketing-dominated function, and from an emphasis on presenting investors with an accurate portrayal of a company's performance and prospects to one that primarily manages the content and flow of company information to a broad set of constituencies to maximize relative valuation. These changes to the investor rela-tions function—and the concomitant ethical issues of the position—have become challenging in the face of rising shareholder pressure and other social movements described in this chapter. Still, both researchers and practitioners will be confronted with robust issues for future investigation as the business environment continues its ongoing transformation.

For example, the recent debacle in global financial markets has given investor relations officers and executives alike much to think about in terms of content and flow but also in terms of new constituents. First, IROs, as the chief company spokespeople to the investor community, must consider, as we have noted, what and how they will communicate to corporate constituencies. Inherent in that de-cision is the determination of how often they will disseminate information, while also avoiding a potentially damaging short-term focus. Some have noted that such a focus may not only compromise the health of the organization but also cause executives to behave unethically. Thus, the recent global financial debacle requires a rethinking of the very nature of investor communications (Samuelson and Stout

2009). However, the relevance and timeliness of an information event must be weighed against the audience's right to know and the potential harms caused by both short-termism and untimely releases of information.

Next, companies face a fundamentally new investor constituency: the federal government. Major challenges will arise as companies and courts strive to determine how much intervention governmental agents should be allowed in their new role as holders of common or preferred stock. Agents representing taxpayers have, as do all financial intermediaries, a right to information about corporate dealings. However, when backed by the threat of force, made legitimate by government's separate role as market regulator and arbiter, their requests may have unique power among shareholders. A new form of investor discrimination—one that favors the governmental investor, backed by voter fervor—may arise and demand our consideration.

The Obama administration has also granted added weight to the labor union constituency, which could lead to a strengthened union-backed investor base. For example, investor relations officers are likely to be increasingly confronted by heartened representatives of Taft-Hartley and other union pension funds seeking employment reforms and board representation.

More generally, tumultuous markets offer critics of capitalism an opportunity to demand increased regulation and distribution of corporate profits to nonowner constituencies. Researchers should be prepared with robust arguments to inform both the media and the public concerning the economic price that accompanies infringement of investors' property rights. In a global market, firms that are considered to be U.S.-based can easily change allegiances.

Likewise, environmental and socially responsible issues will become more important areas of disclosure (Hockerts and Moir 2004). These so-called ethical reporting initiatives, along with their call to reveal the risks associated with a firm's environmental and social actions (Carbon Disclosure Project [CDP] 2008) and how they address their shortfalls (Reid and Toffel 2008), are likely to drive the content of future disclosure research as well (Hockerts and Moir 2004). Such reports, however, must respond to the criticisms that they lack transparency and use the selective, positive disclosure techniques noted earlier.

Despite the financial focus of much of the existing body of investor relations research, the field embodies a plethora of ethical issues. The management of the flow and content of information between corporations and their shareholders will only become more central in future conversations about the ethical corporation.

NOTES

1. This definition changed slightly from "a corporate, strategic marketing activity combining the disciplines of communication and finance that provides present and potential investors with an *accurate* portrayal of a company's performance and prospects" (NIRI Membership Guide, 1998, emphasis added). The removal of "accurate" from the definition is a notable change.

2. The 2008 statistic was computed by the first author based on a review of web sites of the companies in the Fortune 500, as determined by sales, to mirror the analysis used by Rao and Sivakumar (1999).

3. See also *TSC Industries v. Northway, Inc.*, 426 U.S. 438, 449 (1978), and *Basic v. Levinson*, 485 U.S. 224 (1988).

4. The SEC's Reg FD lists the types of information or events that should be carefully reviewed to determine whether they are material. The SEC cautions that the list is not "exhaustive" but includes the following: (1) earnings information; (2) mergers, acquisitions, tender offers, joint ventures, or changes in assets; (3) new products or discoveries, or developments regarding customers or suppliers (e.g., the acquisition or loss of a contract); (4) changes in control or management; (5) change in auditors or auditor's notification that the issuer may no longer rely on an auditor's audit report; (6) events regarding the issuer's securities—for example, defaults on senior securities, calls of securities for redemption, repurchase plans, stock splits or changes in dividends, changes to the rights of security holders, and public or private sales of additional securities; and (7) bankruptcies or receiverships.

5. Note that Surowiecki is using transparency differently that we are. Following Williams (2008), we use transparency to denote information that is timely, reliable, and relevant.

REFERENCES

Abrahamson, E., and C. Park. 1994. Concealment of negative organizational outcomes: An agency theory perspective. *Academy of Management Journal* 37:1302–1335.

Adams, C. A. 2002. Internal organizational factors influencing corporate social and ethical reporting: Beyond current theorizing. *Accounting, Auditing and Accountability Journal* 15:223–250.

Aldrich, H. E. 1979. *Organizations and environments*. Englewood Cliffs, NJ: Prentice-Hall.

American Institute of Certified Public Accountants (AICPA). 1999. *SEC issues SAB 99 on materiality*. New York: American Institute of Certified Public Accountants.

Anonymous. 2002. Should the SEC expand nonfinancial disclosure requirements? *Harvard Law Review* 115:1433–1455.

Ashforth, B. E., and B. W. Gibbs. 1990. The double-edge of organizational legitimation. *Organization Science* 1:177–194.

Atkinson, A. S. 2002. Ethics in financial reporting and the corporate communication professional. *Corporate Communications* 7:212–218.

Ball, J. 2009. Insurers must disclose climate-change exposure. *Wall Street Journal*, March 18: A6.

Bansal, P., and G. Kistruck. 2006. Seeing is (not) believing: Managing the impressions of the firm's commitment to the natural environment. *Journal of Business Ethics* 67: 165–180.

Boatright, J. R. 1994. Fiduciary duties and the shareholder-management relation: Or, what's so special about shareholders? *Business Ethics Quarterly* 4:393–407.

———. 2008. *Ethics in finance*. 2nd ed. Malden, MA: Blackwell Publishers.

Bohren, O. 1998. The agent's ethics in the principal-agent model. *Journal of Business Ethics* 17:745–755.

Borrus, A. 2005. Investors many not want this hot line. *BusinessWeek*, December 5:82.

Bushee, B. D., D. Matsumoto, and G. S. Miller. 2004. Managerial and investor response to disclosure regulations: The case of Reg FD and conference calls. *Accounting Review*, 79:617–643.

Cain, D. M., G. Loewenstein, and D. A. Moore. 2005. The dirt on coming clean: Perverse effects of disclosing conflicts of interest. *Journal of Legal Studies* 34:1.

CDP. 2008. *Carbon disclosure project report 2008—SandP 500*. London, UK: Carbon Disclosure Project.

Clark, C. E. 1999. Investor influence: Financial conference calls often put press on hold. *Business Media Journal* 7–10.

———. 2000. Making sense of information disclosure: What every public company should know. *Strategist* 6:34–38.

Connelly, J. 2005. The board's eyes and ears on Wall Street. *Corporate Board Member,* January/February.

Cormier, D., M. Magnan, and B. Van Velthoven. 2005. Environmental disclosure quality in large German companies: Economic incentives, public pressures or institutional conditions? *European Accounting Review* 14:3–39.

Coyne, K. P., and J. W. Witter. 2002. Taking the mystery out of investor behavior. *Harvard Business Review* 80:68–77.

Craig, S. 2002. Securities firms do the soft sell on their ratings. *Wall Street Journal,* September 13: C1.

———. 2008. The financial crisis: Lawmakers lay into Lehman CEO; Fuld testifies that he didn't deceive investors ahead of firm's bankruptcy filing. *Wall Street Journal,* October 7: A3.

Craig, S., and R. Smith. 2009. U. S. to ask analysts if Lehman misled. *Wall Street Journal,* October 22: C1.

Davis, G. F., and T. A. Thompson 1994. A social movement perspective on corporate control. *Administrative Science Quarterly* 39:141–173.

Deegan, C. 2002. The legitimising effect of social and environmental disclosures—A theoretical foundation. *Accounting, Auditing and Accountability Journal* 15:282–311.

DesJardins, J. 2006. *An introduction to business ethics.* 2nd ed. New York: McGraw-Hill.

DiPiazza, S. A., and R. G. Eccles. 2002. *Building public trust: The future of corporate reporting.* Hoboken, NJ: John Wiley & Sons.

Dye, R. 2001 Commentary on essays on disclosure. *Journal of Accountancy and Economics* 32:181–235.

Easterbrook, F. H., and D. R. Fischel. 1996. *The economic structure of corporate law.* Cambridge, MA: Harvard University Press.

Financial Wire. 2005a. Investrend research comments about analyst coverage problems to SEC committee. May 25.

———. 2005b. SEC nears paid-for research endorsement, but may leave investors confused about standards. December 12.

Gibbins, M., A. Richardson, and J. Waterhouse. 1990. The management of corporate financial disclosure: Opportunism, ritualism, policies and processes. *Journal of Accounting Research* 28:121–143.

Goodpaster, K. E. 1991. Business ethics and stakeholder analysis. *Business Ethics Quarterly* 1:53–73.

Goodpaster, K. E., and T. E. Holloran. 1994. In defense of a paradox. *Business Ethics Quarterly* 4:423–429.

Gray, R. 2001. Thirty years of social accounting, reporting and auditing: What (if anything) have we learned? *Business Ethics: A European Review* 10:9–15.

Gray, R., M. Javad, D. M. Power, and C. D. Sinclair. 2001. Social and environmental disclosure and corporate characteristics: A research note and extension. *Journal of Business Finance and Accounting* 28:327–356.

Hasnas, J. 1998. The normative theories of business ethics: A guide for the perplexed. *Business Ethics Quarterly* 8:19–42.

Healy, P. M., and K. G. Palepu. 2001. Information asymmetry, corporate disclosure, and the capital markets: A review of the empirical disclosure literature. *Journal of Accounting and Economics* 31:405–440.

Heath, F. E. 2007. Property and property rights. In *Encyclopedia of business ethics and society,* ed. R. W. Kolb. Thousand Oaks, CA: Sage.

Hess, D. 2007. Social reporting and new governance regulation: The prospects of achieving corporate accountability through transparency. *Business Ethics Quarterly* 17:453–476.

Hess, D., and T. W. Dunfee. 2007. The Kasky-Nike threat to corporate social reporting: Implementing a standard of optimal truthful disclosure as a solution. *Business Ethics Quarterly* 17:5–32.

Hesseldahl, A. 2009. Was Apple "adequate but late" on Jobs? Some corporate governance experts question whether the tech giant could have been more forthcoming about its CEO's hormone imbalance. *BusinessWeek*, January 6.

Hockerts, K., and L. Moir. 2004. Communicating corporate responsibility to investors: The changing role of the investor relations function. *Journal of Business Ethics* 52:85–98.

Holder-Webb, L., and J. R. Cohen. 2007. The association between disclosure, distress and failure. *Journal of Business Ethics* 75:301–314.

Investor Relations Business. 2002. Do IROs really need stock surveillance? March 25: 1.

Jones, D. 2007. Where's IR leadership on firms who track investors? *IR Web Report*. http://www.irwebreport.com/daily/2007/10/31/wheres-ir-leadership-on-firms-who-track-investors/ (accessed on November 10, 2008).

Karabell, Z. 2008. The myth of transparency. *Newsweek*, July 7:14.

Kolk, A. 2003. Trends in sustainability reporting by the Fortune Global 250. *Business Strategy and the Environment* 12:279–291.

Lee, J. 2008. News analysis: Pharma giants try to clarify transparency. *PR Week*, June 2.

Lev, B. 1992. Information disclosure strategy. *California Management Review* 34:9–32.

Levitt, A., and P. Dwyer. 2002. *Take on the street: What Wall Street and corporate America don't want you to know*. New York: Pantheon.

Livesey, S., and K. Kearins. 2002. Transparent and caring corporations? *Organization and Environment* 15:233–258.

Mahoney, W. 1991. *Investor relations: The professional's guide to financial marketing and communication*. New York: Simon and Schuster.

Marcoux, A. M. 2003. A fiduciary argument against stakeholder theory. *Business Ethics Quarterly* 13:1–24.

Mercer, M. 2005. The fleeting effects of disclosure forthcomingness on management's reporting credibility. *Accounting Review* 80:723–744.

NIRI. 1995. *Issues in investor communications and corporate disclosure*. Vienna, VA: National Investor Relations Institute.

———. 1998. *Survey of corporate disclosure practices*. Vienna, VA: National Investor Relations Institute.

———. 2002. *Standards of practice*. Vienna, VA: National Investor Relations Institute.

———. 2004. *Standards of practice for investor relations*. Vienna, VA: National Investor Relations Institute.

———. 2005. *The NIRI compensation survey 2005: An assessment of responsibilities, staffing, and salaries of investor relations practitioners*. Vienna, VA: National Investor Relations Institute.

———. 2006. *Regular member code of ethics*. http://www.niri.org/about/CodeOfEthicsRegMember.cfm (accessed April 6, 2006).

Oakley, E. F., and P. Lynch. 2000. Promise-keeping: A low priority in a hierarchy of workplace values. *Journal of Business Ethics* 27:377–392.

Pulliam, S. 2004. Open secrets; tracking stocks: SEC probes firms. *Wall Street Journal*, December 8: A1.

Rao, H., and K. Sivakumar. 1999. Institutional sources of boundary spanning structures. *Organization Science* 10:27–42.

Rapoport, M. 2005. Five years later: Critics felt Regulation FD would choke off the flow of information. Here's why it didn't happen. *Wall Street Journal*, October 17: R8.

Reid, E. M., and M. W. Toffel. 2008. Responding to public and private politics: Corporate disclosure of climate change strategies. Working Paper 09-019, Harvard Business School. http://drfd.hbs.edu/fit/public/facultyInfo.do;jsessionid=HvJlTmLKvslpSmcDQw506v91MQ7glZ2DT3GQr1hQTcnDVpnxbJ4q!-687403865!-1582944782?facInfo=pubandfacEmId=mtoffel percent40hbs.edu#papers.

Samuelson, J. F., and L. A. Stout. 2009. Are executives paid too much? *Wall Street Journal*, February 29: A13.

Sax, I. 2000. Shady side of the street. *Investor Relations*, January: 35–36.

Silverglate, H. 2009. The SEC should leave Steve Jobs alone. *Wall Street Journal*, February 2: A15.

Skinner, D. J. 1994. Why firms voluntarily disclose bad news. *Journal of Accounting Research* 32:38.

Solomon, S. 1998. How to attract analyst coverage. *IR Update*, April: 10.

Surowiecki, J. 2002. The talking cure. *New Yorker*, December 9: 54.

Swift, T. 2001. Trust, reputation and corporate accountability to stakeholders. *Business Ethics: A European Review* 10:16–26.

Tapscott, D., and D. Ticoll. 2003. *The naked corporation: How the age of transparency will revolutionize business*. New York: Free Press.

Useem, M. 1996. *Investor capitalism*. New York: Basic Books.

Verrecchia, R. E. 1983. Discretionary disclosure. *Journal of Accounting and Economics* 5:365–380.

———. 2001. Essays on disclosure. *Journal of Accounting and Economics* 32:97–180.

Westphal, J. D., and M. B. Clement. 2008. Sociopolitical dynamics in relations between top managers and securities analysts: Favor rendering, reciprocity, and analyst stock recommendations. *Academy of Management Journal* 51:873–897.

Williams, C. C. 2004. *Siebel Systems, Inc.: Facing a new regulatory and competitive environment*. Boston: Harvard Business School Publishing.

———. 2005. Trust diffusion: The effect of interpersonal trust on structure, function and organizational transparency. *Business & Society* 44:357–368.

———. 2008. *Trust diffusion: How creating climates of trust can influence organizational effectiveness*. Saarbrücken, Germany: VDM Publishing.

Williams, C. C., and L. V. Ryan. 2007. Courting shareholders: The ethical implications of altering corporate ownership structures. *Business Ethics Quarterly* 17:669–688.

Zuckerman, G., and E. Portanger, 2004. Investor meetings with executives surge, add a risk of data leaks. *Wall Street Journal*, August 31: A1.

ABOUT THE AUTHORS

Cynthia Clark Williams is the director of the Harold S. Geneen Institute of Corporate Governance at Bentley University and an assistant professor in the McCallum Graduate School of Business. She holds a PhD from the honors program at Boston University and an MA from Northwestern University. Her research interests are primarily in the areas of ethics, corporate disclosures, and governance. Her research has been published in *Management Information Systems Quarterly*, *Business Ethics Quarterly*, *Business & Society*, and the *Case Research Journal*, to name a few. She teaches courses in strategy and environmental, social, and governance issues.

Lori Verstegen Ryan is professor of management and director of the Corporate Governance Institute at San Diego State University. Having published in all three journals, she is on the editorial boards of *Academy of Management Review* and *Business Ethics Quarterly*, and is associate editor for corporate governance of *Business & Society*. Ryan is on the Executive Committee of the Social Issues in Management Division of the Academy of Management, past president of the International Association for Business and Society, and active in the Society for Business Ethics. She received her MA in Philosophy and PhD in Management from the University of Washington.

CHAPTER 26

Risk Management

PETER C. YOUNG
E. W. Blanch Sr. Chair in Risk Management, Opus College of Business, University of
St. Thomas

INTRODUCTION

Within the risk management field, the subject of ethics has been long influenced by
insurance theory, and especially by the relationship of moral hazard to insurance. In
this context, *moral hazard* has been defined as "conditions or actions that incentivize
illegal or immoral behavior." In the extreme, moral hazard actually can lead to
a direct increase in loss frequency or magnitude. For example, the presence of
property insurance coverage has been shown, in some circumstances, to increase
the frequency of arson-related losses. Moral hazard offers a reminder that while
risk management actions may have positive intentions and results (reduced losses,
enhanced gains), they may also produce negative effects if not carefully considered.

There are limitations to this particular moral hazard framework. First, reliance
on a definition that is specific to insurance has meant that the term invariably is
linked to loss-producing behavior, whereas a broader definition would emphasize
incentives to take risks while transferring the costs to others. Second, moral hazard
has a strong transactional bias, as one might expect from a concept rooted in economics. Immorality and illegality are seen as responses to the terms and conditions
of transactions—typically economic incentives and disincentives. While useful in
many ways, this context presents very little opportunity to consider the individual's (or an organization's) own values and the cultural context in making choices.
To put it plainly, traditional risk management treatment of ethics has been defined
more by the temptations than by the moral basis for the choices and actions taken.

This chapter attempts to update thinking on the relationship between ethics
and risk management and seeks to broaden the scope of consideration beyond the
moral hazard boundary. Owing to the dramatic degree of change in modern risk
management—what will be called *enterprise risk management*—some initial discussion on current forms and practices is required. As will be seen, enterprise risk
management and some consequent developments have an influence in defining
the relationship between ethics and risk management.

MODERN RISK MANAGEMENT IN OVERVIEW

Despite the great attention risk management has received in recent years, a
comprehensive understanding of current practices has proven elusive. There are

reasons for this situation. The degree and velocity of change in the field are two important factors. For the nonacademic, practitioner sector, most writing has—by necessity—had to be provisional, descriptive, practical, and responsive to fast-changing business conditions. Rarely has this work entered the realm of the conceptual, speculative, or exploratory, and this has meant that many topics simply do not rise to a level of practical interest and, therefore, receive little attention. A good and important illustration of practitioner writing on the subject is the ISO 31000 statement on risk management (ISO 2009).

Speed of change has been a factor influencing academic work as well, but the multidisciplinary nature of modern risk management possibly is more of an impediment. Its broad and varied nature—especially in its current incarnation—has not been well aligned to the existing structure of research parameters within business school disciplines. Is risk management a finance topic, an operations management topic, a business law topic, or something else? In which journals can the research on modern risk management be published? On such small practicalities can intellectual inquiry sometimes founder.

Given these limitations, what can be said about risk management today? Broadly speaking, developments have tended to move risk management from a loosely connected collection of technical specializations—clinical risk management, insurance buying, financial risk management, health and safety, corporate security and intelligence, and so on—to a field where specializations continue, but where the principal focus is on the integration of these specializations under the umbrella of a holistic view of risk management (Ward 2005; Kloman 2002). The governing logic behind this general development might be characterized by the question: *If the individualized management of specific risks is a good idea for organizations, why isn't the systematic management of all risks also a good idea?*

ENTERPRISE RISK MANAGEMENT: THE EMERGING FRAMEWORK

Most areas of management (study and practice) contain specialized or technical knowledge and applications, but they also possess a more nontechnical, integrative face. For example, financial management requires technical knowledge, and consequently most organizations have specialists in financial management. However, it also is true that almost all management positions are seen as having general financial management responsibilities. The same could be said of accounting/audit, marketing, operations, strategy, human resources management, and so on. However, as risk management is a relatively new field, the general face has only just begun to emerge. Put another way, risk management has existed almost exclusively as a technical function (really, as many technical functions), and heretofore has not been understood as an integrated aspect of general management.

To a significant degree, recent advances in risk management may be due to the simple maturation of the field. However, beginning in the mid-1990s, a number of developments occurred that accelerated the emergence of a general face for risk management. These developments, if discussed individually, would make for a very long story, so suffice it to say here that an environment of external expectations began to emerge, first through the establishment of market standards (often in response to a crisis event); then expanded through the release of best practice and guidance statements; followed by influential legislation and even court decisions in key countries; and most recently emanating from new policies in accrediting/rating agencies and governmental responses to the global financial situation (Atkins, Bates, and Drennan 2006).

While all these developments have a degree of independence from one another, a common thread has emerged, which is that key stakeholders expect organizations (both public and private) to practice risk management and that the nature of this risk management is broad, comprehensive, integrative, and strategic (ISO 2009). As a practical matter, this has meant that while the technical specializations within risk management have retained their importance, attention has had to be paid to the general management face of risk management. Put another way, there is an expectation that the CEO is, in effect, the chief risk officer for his organization and that all managers are risk managers within the scope of their responsibilities. Consequently, beyond the specific technical/specialist applications of risk management, there should be ongoing, embedded, general risk management occurring throughout the organization. But what does risk management mean in that context?

The answer to the preceding question is not yet fully understood. It does seem evident that technical specialists will continue to pursue their responsibilities in a manner consistent with the past—though there will be some change inasmuch as their work will now have a different context. Notably, there will be greater explicit expectations for them to interact more frequently with other specialists and generalists.

For top managers (and for generalists at all levels), logic would seem to indicate two types of roles: (1) setting risk policy or interpreting policy, in the case of lower level generalists; and (2) assuring that the intended integration and application of risk practices is taking place in accordance with that policy. The addition of this generalist dimension to the preexisting individual technical functions has earned various labels. For many reasons, the term *enterprise risk management* (ERM) has captured the flag at present, so when discussions of comprehensive, policy-driven, integrated risk management occur, ERM is the shorthand term of reference.

The term *enterprise risk management* does have a number of limitations, especially when applied in settings that are not strictly business related. For example, the phrase seems less relevant in public sector contexts or when multiple organizations or, say, citizen groups are involved. Nevertheless, engagement in the ongoing naming battle is not a good use of space here, so the term *ERM* will be used throughout.

Components of ERM

In reference to the preceding comments, ERM might be said to be divisible into two component areas: risk leadership and risk practice. Risk *leadership* is broadly seen as encompassing risk policy/governance decisions and activities, while risk *practice* focuses on the operational/performance and technical aspects of day-to-day ERM. In Scandinavia, where this categorization first emerged, the assumption is that every person engaged in risk management has some leadership duties but also some practice responsibilities (PRIMO-Denmark 2007, 2008). However, looking at an organization in its totality, the balance of these duties varies greatly at different levels of the organization. At the very top executive and board level, the balance of duties is weighted heavily toward leadership. Unique to this level of leadership, overall risk policy is set and risk management is expressly linked to organizational strategy and governance.

Although ERM presents very interesting new issues in the realm of risk practice (integrating various technical specialties, communication and information-sharing across the organization, creating organizationwide reporting systems), these issues seem to represent extensions of historic activity, and even when ethical matters arise, they tend to replicate long-standing concerns. A focus on risk leadership is more appropriate for this chapter, as within leadership lie most of the newer risk management influences on organizational ethics. For that reason, a short overview of risk leadership is helpful.

Risk Leadership

Risk leadership—as presently understood—might be defined as follows (EIRM 2009):

> *Risk leadership is an attribute of leadership representing a conscious understanding of risk and its impact on decision making. While its visible manifestation is seen in the activities that constitute risk governance, the reference here is on the individual capabilities and methods of a manager or groups of managers to understand the cultural, social and psychological foundations of their approach to decision making as well as their specific role in the implementation of their risk governance responsibilities.*

As the concept of risk leadership is new, there are elements that have yet to be defined. Indeed, the European Institute for Risk Management (EIRM) white paper just cited itemizes a range of as-yet unanswered questions. That list includes:

- How does knowledge of risk relate to and integrate with general knowledge of management?
- How does a manager become usefully conscious of the influence of culture and psychology on his perceptions of risk, as well as on perceptions and the framing of risk generally?
- What analytical methods allow the decision maker to account effectively for risk and uncertainty in analysis?
- To what extent must the leader understand and guide the risk management process?
- How can leaders develop an organized approach to understanding the limits of their knowledge and to knowing how to ask proper questions?
- How does an understanding of risk communication inform their approach to communication?

Undoubtedly, there is much developmental work to do. Recently, however, work on the concept of risk governance has emerged to define some of the instrumentalities of risk leadership. The primary driver of this development is the International Risk Governance Council's (IRGC) white paper, *Risk Governance:*

Towards an Integrative Approach (IRGC 2006). In that document, risk governance is defined as follows:

> Include[s] the totality of actors, rules, conventions, processes, and mechanisms concerned with how relevant risk information is collected, analysed and communicated and management decisions are taken. Encompassing the combined risk-relevant decisions and actions of both governmental and private actors, risk governance is of particular importance in, but not restricted to, situations where there is no single authority to take a binding risk management decision but where instead the nature of the risk requires the collaboration and co-ordination between a range of different stakeholders. Risk governance, however, not only includes a multifaceted, multi-actor risk process but also calls for the consideration of contextual factors such as institutional arrangements (e.g., the regulatory and legal framework that determines the relationship, roles and responsibilities of the actors and co-ordination mechanisms such as markets, incentives, or self-imposed norms) and political culture including different perceptions of risk.

The reason this discussion is relevant to this chapter is the obvious link between risk leadership and general governance and corporate responsibilities. Within the emerging framework of risk leadership is the specific role risk management plays in informing organizational exploration of its values and goals and their influence on forming strategy and on addressing all aspects of governance, corporate social responsibility, and stakeholder relations.

A recent development that seems to underscore the interest in leadership issues is the exploration of reputational risk. While, to date, most of the writing has tended to focus on operational responses to reputational risk exposure, there is evidence that practitioners and scholars are approaching important ethical issues from the vantage point of reputation. A good and recent example is Atkins, Bates, and Drennan's book *Reputational Risk: Responsibility Without Control?* (Atkins, Bates, and Drennan 2006). Additionally, the emerging audit-oriented literature on governance, risk, and compliance has begun to show evidence of an interest in ethics and risk (OCEG 2009). Taken as a whole, this work suggests that risk leadership is the domain where ethics and enterprise risk management most fully meet.

ETHICS AND ENTERPRISE RISK MANAGEMENT

Owing to the range of factors already discussed, it should not be a surprise that there is limited direct reference to the relationship of ethics to enterprise risk management. Therefore, any discussion on the subject will have to be stitched together. The following discussion considers the moral hazard framework, the implications of what is called the contractarian view of risk management, some limited writing on the concept of ethical risks, and some early insights from research on ERM adoptions.

Moral Hazard: The Historical View

The historical basis for looking at ethical impacts of risk management has been the concept of moral hazard (Williams, Smith, and Young 1998). Moral hazard is rooted in economics and thus provides a link to an important and influential theoretical foundation, but it also presents some troubling limitations.

One limitation that should be addressed immediately is that traditional risk management literature has anchored its view of moral hazard in relation to insurance. This means that it has been interpreted as loss-producing behavior influenced by the presence of insurance (or any risk management measure). Such a definition has proven to be somewhat problematic as modern risk management has redirected the focus from the management of downside risks to the management of all risks. Simply put, a more generalized definition (incentivizing risk taking while permitting the costs of risk to be borne by others) seems more flexible in situations where upside risks are also under consideration. Having noted this, the historic definition has had some positive influences.

The theory of risk and uncertainty has long noted the presence and importance of *hazards*. Hazards are defined as conditions that elevate (that is, elevate above ordinary expectation) the probability of loss or the potential severity of loss. The concept of moral hazard emerged from consideration of hazards to reflect the fact that hazards could be the result of human/behavioral—as opposed to environmental—factors, as when the presence of an insurance policy provides motivation for an individual to intentionally create a loss.

The framing of illegal or immoral actions as hazards (or, more precisely, as consequences of morally hazardous conditions) has served a useful purpose inasmuch as it provides a common basis for discussing human behavior–based risks alongside all other risks. Further, moral hazard provides an important caution to risk managers, reminding them that, regardless of good intentions, risk management can produce perverse outcomes if it creates incentives or disincentives that are contrary to intended purposes (Fone and Young 2005).

More broadly, moral hazard illuminates the concept of *reflexivity*, which has emerged in public policy discussions of risk—referring to the idea that societies react to policy measures, and these reactions can alter the fundamental purposes of the policy. Safer roadways can lead to higher-speed driving; certain required safety features on construction equipment can lead to more careless usage. Commonly, the conclusion drawn from both moral hazard and reflexivity is that risk management has to adopt a more strategic (some would say game-theory) approach, and that human reactions to risk management should be anticipated and addressed at the outset. From this line of analysis, it is sometimes observed that, given anticipated reactions and hazards, it occasionally may be more effective to do nothing than to introduce a particular risk management measure. An example of this argument can be found in highway safety literature, where the removal of safety barriers is sometimes suggested as a way to illuminate the "true" risk of, say, a dangerous curve—thus promoting more cautious driving (Adams 2001).

Beyond the historic link to insurance, the key limitation of the moral hazard framework is that it views human behavior primarily in the context of transactional dynamics. Although this may be more a weakness of application than a weakness of the concept itself, writing on moral hazard tends to focus on the incentives and disincentives present in the buying and selling of risk management, and this has left little room for consideration of the moral foundations of the actors and their risk-related decisions and actions. For example, the argument for doing nothing as opposed to doing something presents a different dimension when considered from an ethical perspective than when asked from the perspective of economic efficiency. Yes, perhaps choosing not to install safety barriers on a dangerous curve might reduce overall driving speeds and thereby reduce accidents *in the aggregate*, but what is the ethical duty a state government has to safeguard *any individual driver* from known hazards?

The Contractarian View of Risk Management

A somewhat different approach to ethics and risk management—from *within* the risk management field—came to light in 1998 when Williams, Smith, and Young proposed a theory-linked basis for understanding risk management in modern organizations (Williams, Smith, and Young 1998). Prior to that time, the fragmentation in the field had yielded little in the way of cross-disciplinary connections, and while the authors did not produce a unifying theory, their work was seen as an effort to find risk-related consistencies across a range of theoretical fields.

Their conceptualization is sometimes referred to as the *contractarian* view of risk management, which—in brief summary—poses the argument that organizations are collections of contracts, obligations, commitments, and agreements created or entered into in the service of the overall goals and objectives of the organization. In subsequent commentary, Fone and Young noted that the contractarian view might be seen as risk management from the cellular level, as it presented an organization's risks in the smallest divisible units (Fone and Young 2005). From that construction, it has been argued that risk and uncertainty are facets of each contract, obligation, commitment, and agreement, and that it is in the creation of these arrangements that the first and best opportunity arises to identify, assess, and address risk.

Exploration of the meaning of *obligations, commitments,* and *agreements* gave rise to rather limited discussion of ethics and risk, where it was noted that each such arrangement was not specifically the product of a legal agreement, as was the case with a contract. More broadly, these arrangements rest on a moral foundation. People make commitments to others, for example, based upon values, beliefs, cultural expectations, and a range of other factors outside a legalistic framework.

Although the contractarian idea has not been extended to any great degree since that time, it does have several important implications. Specifically, the contractarian view:

- Assumes that risk management is not a peripheral, narrow technical matter, but an essential and central activity of management.
- Sets forward the idea that risks are strongly entwined with the substance of organizational activity and with the overall goals and purposes of the organization.
- Establishes the view that risks, being a facet of the arrangements that serve as the building blocks of an organization, are interconnected and that the correlation and interrelationship of organizational risks are critical properties of its overall risk profile.
- Has proven to be quite consistent with subsequent modern risk management developments—especially the concept of enterprise risk management.

Recently, a possible formalized pathway into the formation of these arrangements was indirectly presented by Andersen (2006). In his work on strategic risk management, the concept of *real options* was adapted to serve as a strategic planning and execution tool. He argued that strategic choices could be constructed as interlocking sets of options contracts, which served to both commit organizations to certain actions and maintain flexibility to move in different directions if circumstances warrant. Although the author's intentions were not at all geared toward explicit consideration of ethical dimensions of strategic risk management, his work seems promising in better describing how risk management inserts itself into the actual formation of contracts, obligations, commitments, and agreements.

Overall, the contractarian view does present a visible link between ethics and ERM. Importantly, it connects all arrangements to the purposes of the organization—that is, they are entered into in the service of the overall mission of the organization (though for some arrangements, like regulation, the word *imposed* is possibly more apt than *entered into*). In turn, mission and vision are presumed to consciously reflect organizational culture, moral values, and intentions. In this sense, contracts, obligations, commitments, and agreements all reflect the fundamental values of the organization—and this means that values are placed *at risk* but are also safeguarded within each arrangement.

Perhaps the broadest insight to be drawn from the contractarian idea is that all risks are interconnected and that modern risk management expects that addressing risk interconnectedness is a central objective. Although management has always involved complexity, it is nevertheless a new dimension of formal risk management to expressly seek to identify, assess, and address risk complexity in all its manifestations.

Two other insights warrant mention. First, what might be called the *holistic imperative* of modern risk management places a demand on managers that may be—in many senses—impossible to fulfill. The idea that risk management is the management of all organizational risks simply cannot be achieved literally. Organizations face thousands of noncertain situations, and the belief that every one of those situations can be managed is unrealistic. This suggests that ERM must be a high-trust exercise. Top managers are expected to set risk policy, but the actual implementation of risk management is left to the organization as a whole. Systems and processes can anchor many aspects of risk management, but ultimately there is a necessity for all employees to act in a semi-autonomous manner and to use judgment as the risk managers within their area of responsibility. Writing by Weick and Sutcliffe (2001) is an interesting example of emerging, early thinking on trust and reliability.

The other insight is that risk management must be values-based. ISO 31000 (2009), for example, emphasizes that risk management practices should be expected to become embedded in the organization and that they must be consistent with the organization's culture. Significantly, this has been interpreted to mean that an organization's approach to risk management is an expression of moral values and beliefs, not simply an obligation undertaken to comply with external/internal expectations.

Ethical Risks

In 2004, I attempted to provide some substance to the ethics and risk management relationship by considering not the relationship itself, but categories of ethical risks

(Young 2004). This approach was based on the much broader work of the Caux Roundtable (2003). The result was seven generalized ethical risk categories:

1. *The organization and the law I*: What are our responsibilities under civil law?
2. *The organization and the law II*: What are our responsibilities under criminal law?
3. *The organization and stakeholders I*: Have we correctly specified and valued our stakeholders?
4. *The organization and stakeholders II*: What are our nonlegal, value-based obligations to stakeholders?
5. *The organization and stakeholders III*: Do we understand the relationship of fairness to our actions and decisions?
6. *The organization and the world I*: Have we correctly understood societal values and the relationship of those values to ours?
7. *The organization and the world II*: Do we understand the consequences of our behavior on our external environments—particularly with respect to finite or shared resources?

The intention of this paper was speculative and exploratory, and so many of the implications of this structure were left in open-ended form. However, the general thrust seemed to be that stakeholder relationships, relationships to humankind, and relationships with the physical environment might be seen as categories of obligations, commitments, and agreements that exist in a realm outside purely legal requirements.

The implication of the ethical risk framework is that risk management seems better suited to a type of stakeholder relations structure. Or perhaps, to put it more directly, modern risk management is not easily seen from a sole-actor perspective (that is, the organization as a discrete, value-maximizing entity battling the exogenous forces of risk). Rather, as has been suggested elsewhere, modern risk management might best be seen as an aspect of stakeholder relationship management (Andersen and Schroder 2010).

Significantly—perhaps most significantly—this approach undercuts the conventional decision-making assumption in risk management. That is, all risk management measures should maximize firm value, as measured by firm share price (or, in the case of non-publicly traded firms, by some other value-maximization metric). But in a stakeholder frame of reference, the language of value maximization is difficult to integrate. The value of risk management, in its modern manifestation, is possibly more a matter of *optimization* than of *maximization*.

Insights from Current Adoptions

In a recent paper, Andersen argues that all current ERM standards, including ISO 31000, presume a top-down orientation (Andersen 2010). In his judgment, this is problematic as his research shows that decentralization, flexibility, innovation, adaptability, and local control are key ingredients to successful ERM implementations. He identifies a centralization/decentralization tension as present both in the existing standards and in the practices of organizations that have adopted organizationwide risk management.

Andersen's intention is to consider the mechanical process of converting policy to practice, but in doing so he indirectly identifies a framing issue in ethics and risk management. The objective of ERM is to embed processes and methods that become part of the organization's belief and value system. In other words, a successful outcome is an organic approach to risk management as opposed to a distinctly hierarchical, department-oriented management function. The problem is that the transformation process seems to require strong and assertive leadership to provide structure and motivation to get to the intended result.

With a bit of hyperbole, one might refer to this as communism's paradox. In order to achieve the long-term result of the withering away of the state, communist societies chose (found it necessary) to take the view that authoritarian, hierarchical, and bureaucratic means were necessary in order to achieve nonauthoritarian, nonhierarchical, nonbureaucratic ends.

Andersen isolates a much more benign but (seemingly) similar paradox. Enterprise risk management represents such a drastic departure from past risk management practices that it is difficult to imagine an organic or evolutionary transformation. Strong and dynamic change leadership seems necessary, but early evidence suggests that the benefits of ERM lie in its flexible form, variability, and decentralized approach. The ethical question embedded here is this: How can both centralized leadership and decentralized management be accommodated in the same organizational culture? And, more pointedly, what organizational values are put at risk?

SEARCHING FOR THEMES

The connective tissue that exists between the preceding discussions is not necessarily obvious to the naked eye, but it is present. As a basis for discussion, the central connections might be stated as follows:

- A key aspect of the conception of enterprise risk management is that it is a manifestation of organizational culture and values, and that these values are complex and not easily simplified.
- The further complexity of an organization's risk environment means risk policy must be carefully constructed, widely communicated, and reasonably usable in informing day-to-day (and longer-term) decision making.
- The particular emergence of risk leadership and governance places a specific emphasis on the application of risk-based thinking to overall management and governance efforts.
- Practically speaking, the centralization-decentralization dilemma signals possible ethical challenges. When placed in international organizational settings, additional issues arise.
- The emergence of ERM may suggest the beginning of a paradigm shift with respect to the purposes of risk management.

ERM and the Link to Organizational Culture and Values

Perhaps the most universally espoused, and yet unexamined, aspect of ERM today is the belief that it is expected to be a manifestation of an organization's culture and its values—more so, it seems, than even its goals and objectives. General writing on the subject argues that the imposition of a formalized risk management system or process is unlikely to achieve success unless it is expressly consistent with an organization's values and culture. Organizations do not effect such dramatic change if it does not make sense to the organization's culture. Therefore, the more accurate way to understand ERM is as a culturally consistent way of thinking critically about a world with little certainty. Yes, there are processes and methods, but those are the instruments of a specific set of values.

The implication is this: The ERM view of risk management argues that risk management is not just a manifestation of culture and values but is, in fact, a value the organization holds. But, as noted, the literature is very limited in addressing what this means.

The Complexity of the Risk Environment

Extending beyond the previous paragraphs, ERM takes the position that in some real but practical sense all organizational risks are being managed. Stating the purpose this way belies the impossibility of ever identifying, analyzing, and addressing all risks. However, there is a sense in which this is an achievable aspiration through the incorporation of risk-based thinking into the critical-thinking faculties and processes of all managers. In other words, an ERM model that can be guaranteed to unearth and examine all risks is not possible, but equipping managers with sufficient knowledge to react intelligently to risks they encounter (and to imagine risks they have not yet encountered) is possible. In this sense, risk management is a dimension of critical thinking, and indeed—as it is sometimes said—risk management might be reducible to a simple question within any critical thinking exercise: How might we be wrong?

The essence of risk-based thinking, it seems, is a conscious appreciation of human fallibility, the nature of risk and uncertainty, cultural and psychological perceptions of risk and uncertainty, and an understanding of the consequences of risk management decisions and actions. Put together, the fundamental value of risk management thinking is to incorporate a conscious and systematic awareness of our inability to possess certainty, and therefore the necessity to imagine alternative outcomes and alternative approaches.

For specific consideration of ethics and ERM, this means that reflecting on an organization's values, the potential of risk management decisions on ethics, and the identification of ethical risks have to be conscious and explicit aspects of decision making and management.

Risk Leadership/Governance and Ethics

This is perhaps the most evident of insights here. Enterprise risk management, as it is required in most venues, assumes that risk-based thinking is an explicit aspect of organizational governance, and this means that the requirements, values, and relationship considerations that constitute governance give evidence of an explicit recognition of the impact of risk management on the organization's values; and vice versa.

Early anecdotal evidence suggests great difficulty in addressing this fact in practice. For example, organizations laboring under requirements of the London

Stock Exchange have found that it is quite difficult in practice to properly equip directors and executives in order that risk-based thinking can be integrated into the general management decision-making apparatus (Atkins, Bates, and Drennan 2006). The process requires time to help decision makers understand their own views of risk, to help them arrive at a consensus view on which policy can be set, and to have some understanding of the necessary steps to convert policy to practice.

Centralization/Decentralization Dilemma

There is much work to be done with this issue, and so it is raised here for speculative purposes. Simply put, it appears at present that general guidance on the implementation of ERM (and the evidence from early adopters) asks for two seemingly inconsistent things. First, an organization must take a command-and-control approach to initiating ERM, but at some point ERM must transform into a highly flexible, decentralized, organic function.

There simply is no clear evidence yet as to how this happens, but since it is assumed to occur in a manner consistent with organizational values, reason would suggest that there is an ethical impact. Further, anecdotal evidence from global firms indicates that the conversion from policy setting to the implementation stage is fraught with moral challenges when the organization operates on a global basis. ERM assumes a single, clearly articulated risk policy, but the interpretation of that policy is likely to vary widely from culture to culture. So a policy encouraging individual initiative and risk taking will be interpreted differently in, for example, Norway, Brazil, Japan, and South Africa. Can there be a consistent sense of risk management values when cultures look differently at risk?

The Purposes of ERM

Despite its fragmented past, the general philosophical approach to risk management has been scientific-economic, which is to say that risk management's value has tended to be defined by so-called objective assessment of risk frequency and magnitude, of costs and benefits, and of the monetizable (or at least measurable) value of outcomes.

A central purpose for private sector firms is to make money for owners, but ERM represents a departure in that it recognizes that a single overall objective masks a wide range of other goals and purposes. Indeed, as noted earlier, if the stakeholder relationship framework seems more suited to ERM, this means that within each contract, obligation, commitment, and agreement, there may be different goals and objectives present. Optimization is, perhaps, a more relevant way of thinking about risk management than is maximization.

In a way, this manner of thinking overturns much of the historic and even recent thought about risk management, so much so that it might constitute a paradigm shift in our understanding of effective risk management practice. Admittedly, it is too early to state this with much certainty, but while the scientific-economic approach to risk management will continue to make sense in specific cases, ERM is not well-suited to such an approach. Addressing the totality of an organization's risk environment requires due consideration of the immense nonquantitative and nonobjective dimensions of risk—and of the moral value-based nature of ERM.

CONCLUSION

The prevalent dynamic in ERM is the integration of risk management into overall general management decisions and actions. The degree to which this has inverted thinking within the field should not be underestimated. If any views have dominated in the admittedly fragmented world of risk management, they have been geared to the scientific-economic view—which is to say that risk is mainly an objective, measurable phenomenon that, from a management perspective, is best measured and managed in monetizable terms. When joined with economic and financial theories that prevail in business schools, the consideration of subjective and noneconomic factors has been pushed into a secondary role.

As the implications of ERM begin to come into focus, it appears that ERM takes the opposite view. First, risk management is an organizational value, and as such it derives from the organization's moral foundations and culture. If anything, financial goals and the scientific method play a supporting role in fulfilling those values. Second, because risk leadership is so evidently linked with strategy, governance, and stakeholder relationship management, it is likely to be the best forum for discussing the developing relationship between ethics and risk management. Early exploration of the risk leadership concept suggests that risk-based thinking serves to articulate an organization's values with respect to risk, uncertainty, complexity, and ambiguity, and to inform the decisions and actions that are taken.

Third, moral hazard remains an important idea, but understanding the underlying values and ethical foundations also is critical. Risk managers should be clearly mindful that risk management actions can send the wrong signals and can produce unintended effects. But effective risk management probably cannot be viewed as just a matter of creating the right incentives—especially when ERM relies heavily on trust for the day-to-day execution of risk management. Organizational views have to be clearly understood by all managers and be seen to be supported by everyone, in word and deed.

Fourth, the implementation of ERM poses an unusual ethical challenge, as it seems to require two contradictory approaches. This presently is an open-ended matter because there is no clear evidence as to what may resolve the issue. Nevertheless, it does seem likely that the transition from risk leadership to practice is not as clear-cut as early practitioner thinking might suggest. Further, when placed in international or multicultural settings, there seem to be additional challenges as cultures tend to adopt specific views of risk that cannot be assumed to be consistent from one culture to another.

It is, perhaps, unsatisfying to conclude that many unanswered questions remain—but in fact, this is the present situation. This chapter set out to broaden thinking about the relationship of ethics to enterprise risk management, and it is clear the relationship is bidirectional. ERM is intended to be an organizational value or an expression of values, and in that sense it is expressly an ethical undertaking. However, ERM has ethical impacts in that it requires a fuller engagement in the complexity of management, in placing centralizing and decentralizing stresses on organizational culture, and in emphasizing the importance of trust and consistency in the interpretation of values.

Further, it is possible that ERM is transforming the actual nature of risk management and its purposes. When all its facets are considered, it is not terribly illuminating to say that the purpose of ERM is only to maximize organizational value. It may be more proper to say that the purpose of ERM is to ensure consistent treatment of risk and uncertainty across all the stakeholder relationships—and this primarily means a consistency of moral values.

REFERENCES

Adams, J. 2001. *Risk.* London: Routledge.

Andersen, T. J. 2006. *Global derivatives: A strategic risk management perspective.* Upper Saddle River, NJ: Prentice Hall.

———. 2010. Combining central planning and decentralization to enhance effective risk management outcomes. *Risk management: An International Journal* 12:101–115.

Andersen, T. J., and P. W. Schroder. 2010. *Strategic risk management practice.* Cambridge, MA: Cambridge Press.

Atkins, Derek, Ian Bates, and Lynn Drennan. 2006. *Reputational risk: Responsibility without control?* London: Global Professional Publishing.

The Caux Round Table. 2003. *Principles for business.* www.cauxroundtable.org.

European Institute for Risk Management. 2009. *Risk leadership: Searching for core competencies.* Copenhagen: EIRM Press.

Fone, Martin, and Peter C. Young. 2005. *Managing risks in public organisations.* 2nd ed. Leicester: Perpetuity Press.

International Risk Governance Council. 2006. *Risk governance: Towards an integrative approach.* Geneva: IRGC.

International Organization for Standardization (ISO). 2009. *ISO: 31000, risk management—principles and guidelines.* Final Draft. Geneva: ISO.

Kloman, F. 2002. A short history of risk management: 1900–2002. *Risk Management Reports.* February 27.

Open Compliance and Ethics Group (OCEG). 2009. *Governance, risk and compliance capability model: Redbook 2.0.* Phoenix, AZ: OCEG.

PRIMO-Denmark. 2008. *Kommunal risikoledelse-i praksis.* Copenhagen: EIRM Press.

———. 2008. *Risikoledelse-en kommunal opgave.* Copenhagen: EIRM Press.

Ward, S. 2005. *Risk management organisation and context.* London: Witherbys.

Weick, K. E., and K. M. Sutcliffe. 2001. *Managing the unexpected.* San Francisco: Jossey-Bass.

Williams, C. A., M. L. Smith, and P. C. Young. 1998. *Risk management and insurance.* 8th ed. New York: McGraw-Hill Book Company.

Young, P. C. 2004. Ethics and risk management: Building a framework. *International Journal of Risk Management* 6:23–34.

ABOUT THE AUTHOR

Peter C. Young occupies the E. W. Blanch, Senior, Chair in Risk Management in the Opus College of Business, University of St. Thomas. In that capacity, he is responsible for the MBA courses and nondegree programs in risk management. He has been a visiting professor to City University in London and Aoyama Gakuin University in Tokyo, and recently was a distinguished honorary professor at Glasgow Caledonian University in Scotland. He holds a PhD in risk management from the University of Minnesota. He has written four books and has published extensively in academic and practitioner journals.

CHAPTER 27

Bankruptcy

BEN S. BRANCH
Professor of Finance, Isenberg School of Management, University
of Massachusetts, Amherst

JENNIFER S. TAUB
Lecturer and Coordinator of the Business Law Program, Isenberg School
of Management, University of Massachusetts, Amherst

INTRODUCTION

The social stigma once associated with a commercial bankruptcy filing has faded as the American public has come to view it as a common business life-cycle event. Between 20,000 and 80,000 U.S. businesses seek bankruptcy protection each year.[1] Publicly traded corporations represent a small fraction of these filings. In 2001, 263 public companies in the United States made filings. The petition by General Motors in early June of 2009 represented the ninety-ninth such filing that year.[2] Recently, the assets involved in each public company filing have ranged from $20 billion to $691 billion.[3]

Given the number of people and assets affected, large bankruptcy filings gain wide attention. This attention has brought a resurgence of ethically based questions concerning the mode of prioritizing competing financial claims for a limited pool of assets. Also emerging is a desire to grasp the complex process of the U.S. bankruptcy system more effectively.

Accordingly, in this chapter, we explain the basic mechanics of the commercial bankruptcy system. In doing so, we identify attributes that are unique to U.S. law and discuss cross-border insolvency. After that foundation is laid, we provide an historical background and framework for the ethical justification of the bankruptcy system. Then, we identify issues that arise in its administration. Finally, we share some conclusions as to strengths and weaknesses and future direction of the bankruptcy system.

THE COMMERCIAL BANKRUPTCY PROCESS

Most insolvent firms seek protection by voluntarily filing a petition with the federal bankruptcy court. Others are forced into bankruptcy by creditors. Whether voluntary or involuntary, the firm's two main options are liquidation or reorganization, typically managed under Chapter 7 or 11 of the Bankruptcy Code, respectively. Insolvency, however, is not a prerequisite to filing. Some seemingly healthy businesses preemptively initiate a strategic bankruptcy filing in order to avoid or contain contingent liabilities.[4]

Bankruptcy is but one pathway for failing firms. Troubled companies can also be acquired or merged into stronger businesses. They can restructure or work out their debt through private negotiations with creditors. Struggling conglomerates can auction or sell off assets. Large firms may also seek government loans or bailouts. Some may resort to state-law remedies like an assignment for the benefit of creditors and receivership. Very small companies may even cease operations without any official process at all.[5]

Chapter 7

Chapter 7 of the U.S. Bankruptcy Code is designed to govern the process of shutting down an insolvent business and fairly distributing its remaining assets. With a Chapter 7 filing, the U.S. Trustee, an officer of the Department of Justice, appoints a bankruptcy trustee to operate the enterprise and oversee the liquidation, subject to the federal bankruptcy court's oversight. Swiftly taking charge, the trustee may change the office and warehouse locks, commandeer bank accounts, and take possession of the firm's books and records. The trustee then supervises the collection and sale of all business assets and the distribution of the proceeds, if any, to those with valid claims, according to their legally proscribed priority. At the end of a liquidating bankruptcy, the debtor firm is dissolved. Certain assets of the firm may be going enterprises. In such instances, the parent corporation may cease operations, whereas those underlying enterprises that were sold through the liquidation process continue to operate under the control of new owners. Creditors have little influence over the Chapter 7 process, although the trustee has a fiduciary duty to act in their best interests.

Chapter 11

During a Chapter 11 restructuring, the debtor (or more specifically, its senior management) usually continues to operate the business and maintain control of its assets. This *debtor-in-possession* (DIP) initially has up to 120 days to file its reorganization plan. The DIP has 180 days from the filing of the original Chapter 11 petition to solicit and obtain creditor approval. These exclusivity periods can be extended but, under current law, only up to a maximum of 18 and 20 months respectively.[6] Concurrently, upon filing, the automatic stay goes into effect, affording the DIP breathing room from creditors. Under the automatic stay, pending lawsuits are frozen and no one can proceed to collect a judgment or payment related to the debtor's prepetition actions. Additionally, estate property may not be taken to satisfy a prepetition claim without court permission. For example, a supplier who received a check from a debtor prior to filing may not deposit or cash it after the filing.[7]

Creditors play a large role in Chapter 11. Shortly after the petition is filed, the U.S. Trustee appoints a creditors' committee to represent and bargain on behalf of the unsecured creditors. This constituency includes trade creditors, unsecured bondholders, undersecured creditors, and contingent claims holders. Courts may also choose to create additional committees where parties have particular and unique interests. For example, the judge may establish a separate committee for a large class of litigants engaged in a tort lawsuit against the business. Prepackaged bankruptcies ("prepacks") are possible. In the months leading up to a prepack filing, the debtor negotiates with creditors to find a solution. Thus, with a prepack, the debtor simultaneously files a bankruptcy petition and a reorganization plan. While the judge and creditors still need to approve the plan, this process is usually completed in a matter of months instead of years.[8]

The reorganization plan details the proposed distributions to creditors and other claimants. While plans vary, often they cancel the prebankruptcy shares and distribute equity interests (such as stocks and warrants) in the reorganized firm to the former creditors. In addition, claimants may receive cash and bonds.[9] Generally, the market value of what is distributed is considerably below the face amount of the claims but hopefully above what could have been distributed had the firm been liquidated.

When a Chapter 11 plan is confirmed and implemented, the debtor firm is usually discharged of prepetition debts, other than those specifically set out in the confirmed plan. However, whether the enterprise will survive in the long run is a separate question. In fact, the majority of debtors who set out to reorganize through Chapter 11 are eventually liquidated, and according to recent data from the Office of U.S. Courts, only one of eight Chapter 11 bankruptcies results in a successful reorganization (Branch, Ray, and Russell 2007, 7–8).

A Chapter 11 case often depends on obtaining DIP financing. In tough credit markets, firms that might otherwise successfully restructure may be forced into an asset sale under Section 363 of the Code and then liquidation (Glater 2008).

Insolvency across Borders

Given the growth of multinational businesses, insolvency has international implications. Yet the prospect of a single global bankruptcy law to manage multijurisdictional defaults is more of a vision than a reality. Nonetheless, some level of communication and cooperation increasingly occurs (Paulus 2007; Wessels, Markell, and Kilborn 2009). For example, Chapter 15 of the U.S. Bankruptcy Code permits a foreign representative to gain recognition in U.S. courts of a foreign insolvency proceeding. By doing so, the debtor is able to obtain many rights and protections available to debtors based in the United States. Correspondingly, in a number of other countries' bankruptcy courts, U.S. (and other foreign) debtors can gain recognition.

The details of the insolvency laws and processes in various nations differ from those of the United States. A primary distinction between the United States and other nations is the ability for management of the debtor to remain in control of the business through a restructuring. Another difference between the United States and many other jurisdictions relates to the treatment of creditors. In non-U.S. cases, creditors generally have less input in the process and claims are not given the same priorities. Most notably, outside the United States, secured creditors do not have top priority. Under the U.S. rules, secured creditors (who received collateral for their loan or otherwise obtained a valid security interest) by law are to receive the full value of the secured portion of their claims before any other creditors are paid. In many other jurisdictions, the rights of secured creditors are subordinated to many other claimants. For example, amounts owed in administrative claims (e.g., to lawyers, trustees, and appraisers), to employees, and for taxes are paid ahead of the secured creditors (Kilborn 2008). Additionally, in other jurisdictions, liquidation rather than restructuring is the norm (Blashalany).

Note that the relative protection of debtors versus creditors within a bankruptcy system can impact the cost of borrowing generally. In countries with laws that are more protective of defaulting debtors, lenders have an incentive to negotiate for more collateral and/or a higher interest rate up front (Davydenko and Franks 2008).[10]

ETHICAL JUSTIFICATION OF THE BANKRUPTCY SYSTEM

The existing U.S. bankruptcy system, characterized by forgiveness of debts and rehabilitation of the debtor, represents a rejection of old legal practices grounded in ethical theories of retribution and deterrence. Under the laws of ancient Greece and Rome, the punishment for defaulting included enslavement, imprisonment, physical injury, and death (Kilpi 1998, 9–10; see also Newton 2003, 1). Following that tradition, during the Colonial period in America through the mid-nineteenth century, imprisonment for debt was common. Some prominent financiers spent years in debtors' prison, and a few even died there. By 1857, when Massachusetts decided that "imprisonment for debt except in cases of fraud is hereby abolished forever," nearly all of the States had ended this practice (Warren 1972, 52).

While the U.S. Constitution empowered Congress to make uniform bankruptcy laws, the battle to enact legislation was long and fierce. Opponents to one of the early federal bankruptcy bills argued that the proposed *voluntary* filing right favored "dishonest debtors and rogues" and thus was morally offensive. Others, opposed to *involuntary* proceedings, included President Ulysses Grant, who observed that "the mere filing of a petition in bankruptcy by an unfriendly creditor will necessarily embarrass, and oftentimes accomplish the financial ruin of, a responsible business man" (Warren 1972, 115).[11] The current system, a result of the Bankruptcy Code of 1978 (as amended most recently in 2005), attempts to set aside moral judgment and balances the interests of debtors, creditors, and society at large.

The ethical justification for the fresh start is utilitarian. The old approach of injuring, imprisoning, and even executing debtors had significant shortcomings. An imprisoned individual, for example, is particularly unlikely to be able to repay his creditors. In addition, when imprisoned, the individual is unable to meet his family responsibilities, which may well result in additional unpaid debts. This loss of productivity and ability to provide family care will impose a cost upon society. For business debtors, this approach is also impractical given that many different people are engaged in a business enterprise and many creditors need to be paid. To impose individual punishment upon one person for the actions of another decision maker within the firm seems unjust. Also, in theory, the existence of the legal fresh start wherein the creditors may be only partially paid back encourages lenders both to undertake serious due diligence on creditworthiness prior to establishing the terms and conditions of any loans (including sanctions for default) and to diversify risk across sectors and regions.

Finally, some businesses fail for unpredictable and/or unavoidable reasons that may not be due to either incompetence or wrongdoing on the part of the debtor. Too high a penalty for failure is likely to discourage socially desirable risk taking. By allowing insolvent businesses to file, discharge debts, and be rehabilitated where possible, our current regime recognizes that credit must be available so that complex economic and commercial enterprises may thrive. And in order for creditors to have the appropriate incentives to provide financing to viable businesses, an orderly, fair, and predictable set of rules is needed for managing firms when they fail. However, in order to limit the moral hazard of irresponsible borrowing, the system also strives to provide appropriate disciplines for those who fail to meet their obligations.

ETHICAL ISSUES IN THE ADMINISTRATION OF THE BANKRUPTCY SYSTEM

The principal goals of the bankruptcy system are, for a bankrupt enterprise, to preserve as much value as practical and effectuate an orderly, fair, predictable process that resolves conflicts between those with valid claims. To further these goals, the law seeks to establish a fair process that allows the debtor a fresh start where desirable, maximizes the value of the estate, and distributes the assets equitably in furtherance of the greater, common good.

Ethical issues arise when the bankruptcy system is perceived to offend broader societal values. Leading issues include concerns around (1) misuse or abuse of process, (2) debtor empowerment, and (3) estate expansion and distribution.

Misuse or Abuse of Process

In resolving conflicts between those with valid claims, the bankruptcy court needs to employ a fair process. Elements of a fair process include transparency, democracy (an opportunity to be heard and a vote on the outcome), timeliness, and predictability. Perceived abuses of process are often the ones that disturb the public, lead to mistrust of the system, and prompt calls for legal reform.

Issue: Strategic Filing   A commonly cited ethical failing of the bankruptcy system is the so-called strategic or preemptive filing. In particular, some consider abusive the use by large corporations of Chapter 11 proceedings to eliminate or reduce payments associated with (1) collective bargaining agreements, (2) product liability judgments, and (3) pension liabilities and other legacy costs.

Example: Manville   In 1982, Johns Manville pioneered the strategic use of bankruptcy in anticipation of future obligations. When it sought bankruptcy protection, the company had earnings of more than $60 million and a net worth of over $1 billion and was not insolvent on an accounting basis. Manville was, however, the target of litigation from those who claimed to have been injured by its principal product, asbestos (Boatright 2008, 152–153). The company arranged a prepackaged bankruptcy from which it emerged in 1988. It created a trust fund of $2.5 billion in company stock and other assets to pay future claims. Manville thereby sought to contain its legacy liabilities and move forward with its future operations. Since the Manville case, more than 70 firms, including around half of the large U.S. asbestos manufacturers (Bigelow 2007), have sought bankruptcy protection to eliminate massive personal injury liability obligations. In 1994, Congress authorized the use of such trusts to channel all asbestos claims (Brickman and Shapiro 2005). In place of case-by-case litigation, the Code allows the bankruptcy judge to centralize all related mass tort claims into the bankruptcy proceeding (Smith 2008).

Example: A. H. Robins   In 1985, A. H. Robins, manufacturer of the Dalkon Shield, an intrauterine birth control device, filed for bankruptcy protection. In the early 1970s, women in the United States purchased more than 2.7 million shields. Some attributed "birth defects, spontaneous abortions and traumatic infections" to the product. The device was also blamed for 20 deaths. Robins had already paid more than $500 million to settle more than 9,000 lawsuits related to claimed injuries. With more than 5,000 additional suits pending, the firm, which was said to have earned only $10 million on the Dalkon Shield, filed Chapter 11 to stem its losses (Feder 1987). Through the bankruptcy process, more than 200,000 women filed claims. According to a claimant advocate, banks and trade creditors would receive full payment on claims whereas the Dalkon Shield claimants would receive only 35 to 55 cents on the dollar (Lewin 1988).

Example: Northwest Airlines   Over many years, Northwest Airlines allegedly underfunded its employee pension fund, leaving a shortfall of $5.8 billion. Then, according to a Department of Labor investigation, the company filed for bankruptcy just a day before a $65 million payment was due. The pension fund contained assets for more than 60,000 employees (Walsh 2006). Troubled firms commonly fail to build sufficient assets in employee pension funds to cover the actuarial value of the plan's obligations. When the pension plan of a bankrupt enterprise is incapable of meeting its legally mandated obligations, a government agency created in the mid-1970s called the Pension Benefit Guarantee Corporation (PBGC) will step in to take over those obligations, ensuring that current and future retirees continue to receive their monthly payments. However, the amount of the guaranteed payments is limited in such a way that many at the higher pay levels do not receive as much as they would have had under the provisions of the plan. Moreover, other employee benefits, such as health insurance, are not guaranteed by the PBGC and are often canceled without a comparable substitute.[12]

Example: Horizon   In the Horizon Natural Resources reorganization, the judge authorized termination of collective bargaining agreements with the United Mine Workers of America. As a result approximately 3,800 miners and their dependents abruptly lost their company-sponsored health insurance coverage (Dao 2004).

Example: International Steel Group   While some may criticize firms for breaking promises to employees, sometimes the only way to save a business or industry is to reduce these costs. Wilbur Ross, a successful vulture investor,[13] saw an opportunity to make money and create value in an area that many others were afraid to touch. He believed that with the right kind of structure, he could make money in steel. With huge legacy costs and declining demand coupled with strong competition from abroad, steel had epitomized the Rust Belt's decaying industry. Ross, however, believed that if he could put all the pieces together in the right way, he could create a profitable steel company. Accordingly, he set about simultaneously doing the following:

- Purchased the assets of several failing steel companies in bankruptcy for essentially their scrap value.
- Negotiated with the PBGC an arrangement whereby the PBGC assumed billions of dollars in pension obligations of the companies that he was buying.
- Negotiated contracts with the United Steelworkers of America that provided for very substantially reduced wages and benefits and much greater flexibility for how the employer could use labor.

With these various pieces in place, Ross created the International Steel Group in 2002. With a bit of luck, the market price of steel rose from $210 a ton in 2001 to $750 a ton in 2004. Ross was able to sell International Steel for $4.5 billion, making over $2 billion for his investors and pocketing $300 million for himself (Stein 2004).

The Bankruptcy Code places a number of procedural hurdles in front of debtors before a collective bargaining agreement can be rejected. The debtor must make a proposal to the union prior to making a motion to modify the agreement. The debtor must then prove that the modifications are necessary, that all parties are treated fairly and equitably, that the union refused the proposal without good cause, and that the "balance of the equities" favors rejection (Johnson 2006). Recently, courts have grappled with the question of whether the rejection of a collective bargaining agreement gives rise to a damages claim (Updike and Bagby 2008).

Issue: Misuse of Information
Tensions exist in bankruptcy between the need for transparency and the danger of improper sharing and use of information. For example, a member of the creditors' committee has access to nonpublic details about the debtor's business. For the committee member, this information is critical to determining how to restructure the firm and how to pay creditors. However, such information may also be valuable in making investment decisions regarding the debtor's securities. Suppose, as is often the case, a large diverse business such as an investment bank has a representative on the creditors' committee. An information barrier (sometimes called an *ethical wall*) must exist, and often trading restrictions must be placed such that the investment arm of the creditor does not use this "material inside information" in violation of the federal securities laws to trade the debtor's securities (whether equity or debt).

A creditor may choose to exit the process early by trading its claim with an outside investor. This presents a potential legal problem given the material inside information about the debtor that members of the committee obtain. Accordingly, courts have required that an information barrier be put in place between those employees of an investment bank, a member of which also sits on the committee, and those who participate in the trading activity (Sullivan 2008). Trading claims, though, can have important value to investors generally. Research suggests that the post-rehabilitated firm's performance is greater when a vulture investor gains control of the entity (Hotchkiss and Mooradian 1997).

Example: WorldCom   Some unscrupulous investors have exaggerated their debt holdings in order to gain a seat on the creditors' committee. The SEC accused Van Greenfield, the manager of Blue River, of falsely claiming to own $400 million of WorldCom's bonds when he actually held only $6.5 million. Based upon the false claim, the U.S. Trustee named Greenfield to the committee as one of WorldCom's 20 largest creditors (Bilodeau 2005). Greenfield settled the matter without admitting liability.

Issue: Forum Shopping
One of the "most hotly contested corporate reorganization issues" involves forum shopping (Skeel 2001). Increasingly, debtors are highly motivated to use somewhat questionable tactics to select the federal bankruptcy court that will hear their case. Just prior to filing, a firm may incorporate one of its subsidiaries in a state where the bankruptcy court is thought to be more favorable to debtors. Or the debtor with subsidiaries in various states may file that subsidiary for bankruptcy in the state with the most debtor-friendly court; then, the remaining affiliates file for bankruptcy and their cases are consolidated with the initial filing. Firms may wish to avoid the courts in their home states if creditors are likely to have significant influence there (Fitzgerald 2007). A recent study of 182 commercial bankruptcy filings between 1995 and 2003 found that creditors collected 25 percent less from firms filing in New York than in Delaware and recovered more if the firm filed in its home state.[14]

However, others note that the ability to select a filing venue may help the firm survive and thus inure to the benefit of the creditors. Different federal circuits treat certain assets differently. For example, a debtor that depends upon being a licensee of intellectual property might choose to file where judges will allow it to assume licenses without the permission of the licensor. A debtor who is a retailer with many store leases might select the jurisdiction where the court will allow the debtor to file toward the beginning of the month and treat the entire month as an unsecured claim, whereas in other jurisdictions, the postpetition rent would be treated as an administrative claim.

Issue: Role of Professionals
A fair process benefits the key participants and not simply the fee-charging professionals. In other words, a complex, expensive system that rewards the lawyers, accountants, investment bankers, actuaries, appraisers, and others with handsome incomes but provides marginal benefits to the debtors and creditors is unlikely to be seen as fair.[15] Two areas of concern are conflicts of interest and fees.

In the United States, unlike other nations, attorneys serve a central function in the process. In contrast, "[a]ccountants, rather than lawyers, are the leading private bankruptcy professionals in England" (Skeel 2001, 2). Given the reliance on and demand for attorneys, conflicts of interest can arise when a single attorney or law firm (or other professional) represents the interests of many creditors (Rapoport 2002) and when they may have represented or advised both the debtor and/or various creditors in previous matters.

The payment of fees from the debtor to these parties is carefully scrutinized by the court. As one example, attorney fees and other professional fees are paid out of the bankruptcy estate. In a Chapter 11 case, lawyers for one class of creditors might be arguing against lawyers for another class. Meanwhile, the estate is paying the fees of both sides. While only one argument will win, everyone will lose with the run-up in costs. "Spending the estate's funds in an effort to bring additional funds into the estate is one thing. Spending the estate's funds to fight over how to divide up the estate's limited resources is quite another" (Branch, Ray, and Russell 2007, 13).

Debtor Control and Empowerment

A principal feature of the U.S. bankruptcy system is that the debtor retains control. The debtor usually decides whether to file for liquidation or reorganization. If the debtor selects reorganization, other than in extraordinary circumstances, such as when they are suspected of fraud, the managers stay in charge of the operations. Finally, debtors of a reorganized enterprise are allowed a fresh start. Relative to the bankruptcy systems of most other nations, the United States is generally more accommodating and forgiving of its debtors. Until the late twentieth century in most countries in Europe, discharge of debts without the consent of creditors was "unheard of" (Kilpi 1998, 11).

For a commercial bankruptcy managed as a Chapter 11 reorganization, debtor control often means that the same people who operated a business during its decline, who made promises that were not and probably could not be kept, are allowed to stay in control of the enterprise, oversee its rehabilitation, and emerge without the incapacitating debt burdens of the past. Many stakeholders benefit from rehabilitation. Employees may secure ongoing employment and communities, a continuous tax base. Suppliers may suffer a small loss but, in exchange, maintain a long-term customer relationship. Consumers may have more choice in the marketplace, as continued competition among firms may lead to higher quality and lower prices. For the economy at large, a fresh start for bankrupt businesses can mean the more productive utilization of assets rather than dismantling, selling off, and even scrapping valuable equipment and intangibles, and the dispersion of valued employees and other human resources.

Moral Hazard

Some economists express concern that the U.S. bankruptcy system creates a *moral hazard*. That is to say, they worry that debtor-friendly provisions encourage risky behavior that may harm corporate shareholders, creditors, and other stakeholders. Some notice that corporate CEOs manage to capture much of the upside with compensation tied to company stock. Most executives benefit even when the stock rises due to overall market conditions and not the company's performance relative to peers. However, the critics notice that few penalties exist for failure. For these observers, the bankruptcy system further enables the problems with CEO accountability.

Issue: Liquidate or Rehabilitate?

One of the primary debtor control issues is whether the commercial debtor should be allowed a fresh start through Chapter 11 reorganization, or instead should promptly liquidate. Only a relatively small percentage of attempted Chapter 11 reorganizations succeed. Many Chapter 11 filings never result in an acceptable plan and convert to liquidations. Other firms in Chapter 11 do reorganize and come out of bankruptcy only to fail a second and sometimes even a third time. Some believe that too many businesses undergo too many reorganization attempts, straining the system, creating false hopes, and costing stakeholders more in the long-run.

Example: Horizon Horizon Natural Resources (then known as AEI Resources Holdings, Inc.), one of the largest coal mining concerns in the United States, filed Chapter 11 in February 2002 (Jordan 2006). Having negotiated a prepackaged plan with creditors, Horizon quickly emerged from bankruptcy in May 2002 but was unable to pay its creditors and filed for protection again in November 2002.[16]

Studies differ on whether Chapter 11 reorganizations or Chapter 7 liquidations are better for creditors. A study of commercial bankruptcies in New York and Arizona from 1995 to 2001 concluded that creditors recovered relatively more in Chapter 11. While the direct expenses of liquidations are lower and the process is faster, the authors found that Chapter 11's better ability to preserve assets benefited creditors (Bris, Welch, and Zhu 2006). Another study noted that when commercial airlines sold assets in bankruptcy, prices were substantially lower than those received by airlines that made sales outside of bankruptcy. However, the study found no significant difference between prices obtained in Chapter 11 as compared to Chapter 7 (Pulvino 1999).[17] In a study of 459 firms that sought protection between 1991 and 1998, the authors found that the operating performance of firms significantly improved through Chapter 11 (Kalay, Singhal, and Tashjian 2007).

Example: Eastern Airlines Whether Chapter 11 makes sense in each specific case is a separate question. Eastern Airlines filed for bankruptcy protection in March 1989 (Salpukas 1991). Management boasted that creditors would be paid in full, yet the firm failed to survive. Researchers contended that "an overprotective court insulated Eastern from market forces that allowed value-destroying operations to continue long after Eastern should have been shut down." During the course of the bankruptcy, the firm's value declined by more than 50 percent (Weiss and Wruck 1998).

Issue: Fairness to Competitors

Another fresh start ethical issue is whether market intervention for the sake of one firm and its creditors and stakeholders is fair to competitors within the debtor's industry. A debtor firm that comes under federal bankruptcy court protection has advantages over its competitors. With the airlines, for example, some argue that the protection of bankruptcy led to unsound fare wars and other practices that drove down overall profits and thereby weakened the industry. While one of the goals of the bankruptcy system is to maximize wealth for the whole of society, Chapter 11 may also create an implicit subsidy that is not fair to the debtor's competitors.

Issue: Debtor-in-Possession

Another issue stems from the relatively recent practice of allowing senior managers to retain control of the failing business during the bankruptcy rehabilitation process. Prior to the adoption of the 1978 Bankruptcy Code, control of the firm was handed over immediately to outside trustees (Passell 1993).

Many justify the DIP practice as it "allow[s] knowledgeable managers to patch up problems instead of selling a company's assets off piecemeal" and thereby helps to "conserve corporate cash" (Passell 1993). Managers wish to rehabilitate an enterprise in order to retain their jobs and salvage their reputations. However, creditors often prefer to close down the firm and promptly sell its assets when they have certainty of soon getting paid back some portion of what's owed instead of taking a greater risk, waiting longer until payoff, and perhaps receiving even less if the reorganization effort fails.

However, others insist that instead of serving creditors, the managers delay the process and end up serving their own interests. After all, "those closest to the business may be the least able to face reality" (Branch, Ray, and Russell 2007).[18] Moreover, critics of this practice note that some managers actually drive their companies into insolvency due to poor resource allocation, overextension of credit, unwise marketing choices, and the like. By treating blameworthy managers—including those venal leaders who, while acting as DIP, intentionally loot a failing firm—the same as competent managers, the DIP practice may encourage some managers to see little or no disincentive for poor performance, unwise risk taking, and fraud.

Issue: Breathing Room for Debtor

The automatic stay, which takes effect upon the bankruptcy filing, provides debtors with breathing room. While providing the debtor with space to keep the business alive as it works out a plan, the automatic stay can seem unjust at times. Some individuals and businesses that performed under agreements with the debtor now have to wait to see how many if any of the debtor's promises will be honored. To some this seems unfair, particular for those parties who were not privy to the debtor's financial problems. However, the automatic stay is a critical feature of an equitable bankruptcy system. Without this feature, creditors would race to the courthouse to sue and collect from the debtor. With the stay, all similarly situated creditors can be treated equally, with no advantage given to the ones who get to court first. Additionally, creditors are forced to act as a class and reach a compromise instead of each pursuing its own conflicting interests.

Estate Expansion and Distribution

Another foundational principle of the U. S. bankruptcy system is the objective of maximizing the distributable value of the debtor's assets—known as the *estate*. In a commercial bankruptcy, the DIP or, if assigned, the trustee is given the power to pull into the estate as much value as possible. The law provides many tools to accomplish this asset gathering goal. The DIP (or trustee) can, under certain circumstances, "reach back" to reclaim a payment made to a creditor well before the bankruptcy filing. Disadvantageous contracts under which the debtor would have owed future payments, products, or services can be canceled. These powers help the estate's manager create a circumstance in which the dividable pie is enhanced and no particular claimant is able to take an unfair slice or get a portion ahead of time.

Once the assets are gathered, they must be divided. In liquidation they are distributed; in a reorganization they are reinvested into the business or directed or allocated over time to pay back the claimants. Many of the rules and the actual processes involve a balancing of the conflicting interests of the various claimants and stakeholders. The relevant parties' differing time horizons and interests may trigger tensions over how to operate the business after the restructuring. Some of the rules around this balancing are based upon utilitarian considerations of welfare, while others reflect additional normative concerns, such as equity or fairness. For example, some of the so-called blameless bystanders of a bankruptcy can be afforded special treatment. Thus, the small creditors who would not have the time or financial resources to participate in the system are often paid some fraction of their claim (*convenience claims*) early in the process.

The law itself takes care of some of the pie division by establishing rules of priority. First in line for payment are those lenders who received collateral for their loan or otherwise obtained a valid security interest or have a right of set-off against the debtor's property. Collateral can be hard assets like inventory, equipment, and real estate or more intangible items such as future payment streams through accounts receivable and intellectual property licenses. These secured creditors might have their collateral returned or receive cash equal to the value of their collateral up to the amount of their claim. To the extent that the amount still owed by the debtor exceeds the value of the collateral, a lender might have both a secured claim and an unsecured one. The remaining unsecured claims are divided into six classes of descending priority under the Bankruptcy Code. In the highest priority of unsecured claims are items such as administrative expenses of the bankruptcy, employee pension fund accounts, and customer layaway accounts. Often, however, after paying the secured creditors, nothing remains for the other claimants.

Issue: Absolute Priority

Under the "absolute priority of claims" principle, each class of claimants is to be paid the amount of its claim in full before the next class begins to receive a distribution. The class on the margin is to receive a pro rata distribution and those with still lower priority receive nothing. First-lien secured creditors are given priority under the U.S. Bankruptcy Code with regard to the assets securing such claims. This is not often the case in other nations' insolvency regimes. For example, in many countries, employee wage claims and retiree pensions are given higher priority than secured creditors' claims.[19] Recently, problems have arisen when the U.S. government becomes the only lender able to provide DIP financing. As a result of these new and unique circumstances, the government has pressured some classes of creditors to modify the "absolute priority" scheme.

Example: Chrysler In 2009, after receiving billions in federal assistance, privately held Chrysler LLC was forced into bankruptcy by the U.S. government. Using Section 363 of the Code, performing assets of the old Chrysler were transferred to a new Chrysler. Shares in the new Chrysler were then issued to Fiat, a trust for the United Auto Workers' health-care fund, and the U.S. and Canadian governments (Chasan and Halls 2009). The 363 sale process avoided the long process of gaining approval by creditors of a reorganization plan.

As a result of this sale, 55 percent of the equity in the reorganized company plus a $4.5 billion note was used to satisfy part of a $10.5 billion unsecured claim of the UAW. Prior to the sale closing, however, the secured creditors, who were owed $6.9 billion under the plan, were paid only $2 billion (or 29 cents on the dollar). Nearly all of the secured creditors agreed. However, a group of Indiana state pension funds which had purchased Chrysler debt in 2008 for 43 cents on the dollar sued to challenge the plan (Kellogg, Bray, and McLaughlin 2009). Ultimately, the matter was appealed to the United States Supreme Court, which decided not to interfere with the plan's approval.[20] Some heralded this result as being in the best interests of the workers, suppliers, economy, and creditors at large. Others condemn the outcome as unconstitutional and an outright disregard for the law, as creating uncertainty and thus a higher risk premium for distressed credit.

Issue: Claim Rejection

Issues arise both in the process and the substance of claim rejection. Having a claim subordinated or rejected or requiring payments to be returned to the debtor directly harms an individual participant yet furthers the common good of enlarging the pie for future distribution. Thus, all of the tools available to the trustee and DIP, including the use of avoidance powers and treatment of fraudulent transfers, trigger ethical issues. Often a claim is rejected or subordinated on technical grounds. In order to have a secured claim, a creditor must take certain steps, depending upon the type of collateral. Some creditors fail to perform these tasks (such as filing state Uniform Commercial Code statements) upon making the loans or fail to update them when necessary. Yet another tactic is to assert an offsetting claim against the claimant. That step creates a controversy that must be resolved before the original claim is allowed. At that point the debtor may seek to negotiate a reduced amount for the original claim.

The treatment of preferential payments and fraudulent transfers can facilitate the growth of the estate's distributable assets. A preferential payment is a payment made by the debtor to a third party in the window prior to the filing. Generally the window is 90 days for third parties and one year for payments to insiders. Under certain circumstances the payment can be clawed back from the payee and brought into the estate. The theory requiring the return of such payments to the estate is that to prefer certain creditors and diminish the potential pie for the rest is deemed unfair. The recipient of the preference payment, who is required to return it, is subsequently given a claim in the estate for the amount of the clawed-back payment. Thus, 100 percent of the payment amount comes back to the estate, and the creditor receives a claim that is likely to collect only a percentage of its face value when the distributions are made.

Example: Eziba   In 2005, after suspending operations, Eziba, an online retailer, was forced into bankruptcy (Tode 2005). Through its web site, catalogs, and retail outlets, Eziba distributed handcrafted goods made by artisans throughout the world. It boasted to its customers that it paid more than $10 million to people such as basket-weaving war widows from Rwanda. Prior to the bankruptcy, the firm paid off a $500,000 bank loan instead of paying the more than $100,000 it owed to the international artisans. Ultimately, the bankruptcy trustee recovered the $500,000 payment (Tedeschi 2005).[21]

A fraudulent transfer is a payment (or transfer of value) made by the debtor before the filing, at a time when the debtor was considered insolvent, in which the effect is to diminish the net assets of the estate. For example, a sale of an asset made at prices well below the asset's market value might well be found to be a fraudulent transfer. If the court so finds, the transaction is subject to being reversed, thereby restoring value to the estate for the benefit of its creditors.

Example: Revco   In 1988, the drugstore chain Revco D.S. filed for bankruptcy protection. In the process of gathering up the estate's assets, the bankruptcy court looked back in time to the $1.25 billion 1986 management-driven, leveraged buyout (LBO) of the firm (Eichenwald 1991; Labaton 1990). The court-appointed expert questioned whether the shareholders who had tendered their stock in that transaction should have to return their profits to Revco. The theory was that the buyout was financially unsound. That is, the large amount of debt that the firm took on made it insolvent at the time of the closing. Thus, the tendering of shares in exchange for cash was a fraudulent conveyance. In a lengthy report, the expert determined that there were grounds to sue various parties, including the pre-LBO shareholders and the Revco financial advisers, in order to bring those funds back into the estate for the benefit of creditors. However, the use of this tactic has been curtailed. In 1999, the same court that initially advanced the theory, the Third Circuit, in another case limited the trustee's powers, holding that if the tendering shareholder received payment through a broker or other financial intermediary, he could not be the target of a fraudulent conveyance action (Beckerman and Stark 2000).

Issue: Representation on Creditors' Committee
The creditors' committee becomes a location where tensions between claims to the estate materialize. Shortly after the filing, at least one, but sometimes more than one, creditors' committee is formed. For example, the senior and subordinated creditors may each have a committee. The committees are made up of representatives from some portion of those who have a claim in the estate. Not all creditors wish to have a representative on the committee, and some who do are not given a seat. The U.S. Trustee appoints the committee or committees from the ranks of the large creditors.

Example: Enron Controversies among creditors emerged in the Enron bankruptcy. Certain creditors objected to having JPMorgan Chase and Citigroup take lead roles or even serve on the creditors' committee. Opponents argued that these firms helped to structure the off-balance-sheet transactions that facilitated and disguised the demise of Enron. Describing this as the "ultimate conflict of interest," bankruptcy law expert Elizabeth Warren noted that the biggest asset of Enron was the lawsuits against everyone who participated in the fraudulent activity. As members of the creditors' committee, "these firms should be initiating lawsuits against those who injured creditors and shareholders. But the lawsuits they would be initiating would be against themselves" (Wayne 2002).

Other problems arise when, for example, secured creditors who have some collateral can serve on the unsecured creditors' committee. As a legal matter, these undersecured creditors are supposed to look out for the interests of all of the creditors that the committee is charged with representing. As a practical matter, however, they are all too likely to put their own interests ahead of the broader set of creditor interests. To deal with this risk, each class of creditors is given a separate vote. To support the plan, a class must vote two-thirds in dollar value and in majority in number in favor of a plan. Thus, how much any one class of creditors can push its own selfish agenda is limited. That said, if the court deems the plan fair and equitable, and at least the most senior class of impaired creditors supports it, the plan can be "crammed down" against the will of the dissenting class or classes (Weil, Gotshal and Manges 2006).

The power of *equitable subordination* permits an interested party such as the debtor or trustee to seek to make a claim a lower priority for payment than it otherwise would have been if the claimant has a history of misconduct.

Issue: Innocent Bystanders and Small Players

The law does attempt to address the interests of some of the small players who may not have the resources to wait for the process to be completed. Under the relevant provisions, a vendor who ships to a troubled firm that subsequently files for bankruptcy can assert a reclamation claim. This claim technically allows the vendor to repossess the items that have been shipped. These reclamation claims, however, are unsecured and often worth nothing since the lender who has supplied the debtor with a line of credit often has a prior lien on all inventory. As a result, in the 2005 amendments to the Bankruptcy Code, small trade creditors receive better treatment. If a vendor delivers goods to the debtor within 20 days of the bankruptcy petition, the vendor will be given an administrative claim. As noted earlier, this elevates an otherwise lower-priority unsecured claim to the highest class of unsecured claims.

CONCLUSION

Bankruptcy is one of the major events in the business life cycle of many firms. Due to natural causes or management failure or malfeasance, some businesses will, from time to time, need to either wind up or restructure their operations. The modern U.S. bankruptcy system tends to recognize rather than place moral judgments upon this reality. Instead of expecting a debtor to honor all promises (which is the ideal for a solvent entity), our bankruptcy system starts from the place where this is no longer possible. Whether the U.S. system simply furthers (or should further) economic efficiency as the determinant of what is the greatest good or other social policies as well is an important and debatable question. The existence of the bankruptcy option, with the fresh start concept, helps deter lenders from making unwise decisions and shifts some of the risk from the debtor to its lenders, who are in a favorable position to evaluate a business's creditworthiness before extending credit. In addition, the possibility of reorganization as opposed to liquidation tends to limit potential domino effects from failing businesses.

Most of the present debates revolve around (1) whether to shut down or rehabilitate firms and (2) how best to distribute the remaining business assets to their claimants.

While the law shifted in the late twentieth century toward favoring debtors, it has begun to shift back a bit to erode some of those powers and strengthen some creditors' rights. Overall, though, the U.S. regime remains commercial debtor-friendly. In fact, businesses that operate internationally sometimes file in the United States just a day before their foreign filings so as to take advantage of the more favorable treatment of debtors under the U.S. bankruptcy system.[22]

Though moral judgments regarding filing for bankruptcy are minimal, vigorous debate continues over the fairness of the Bankruptcy Code's treatment of different classes of creditors. This can lead to the strategic use of bankruptcy to minimize amounts owed to injured customers and to employees and retirees for past wages, pensions, and health care. Attempts have been made through the legislative process to amend the law to affect these priorities.

Without successful Congressional action, some of the thorny policy issues around whose claims deserve more value have been resolved outside of the legislative process. That is to say, instead of having Congress create amendments to the Bankruptcy Code to elevate certain unsecured claims of employees above those of unsecured creditors, the federal government has been able to achieve the same result through the use of a 363 sale. It is not clear, however, whether the Chrysler example will become more widespread beyond the unique circumstances where the government provides bankruptcy financing.

Some businesses that could enter bankruptcy find ways to bypass the process for other complex reasons. For example, the once-preeminent financial services giant Bear Stearns did not file for bankruptcy in 2008 but instead was purchased by JPMorgan Chase with the multibillion-dollar assistance of the U.S. federal government. Similarly, insurance giant AIG was rescued months later from failure through an initial offer of $85 billion in government assistance. However, venerated investment bank Lehman Brothers was allowed to fail. In the same short window of time, the U.S. government attempted to rescue the credit market and the U.S. financial system through a $700 billion bailout program.

From the preceding discussion, we see that the U.S. bankruptcy system has many critics who point to significant shortcomings. The process can be slow and cumbersome. Bankrupt firms that should be liquidated are sometimes restructured only to fail a second and even a third time. Professional fees can drain away much of the debtor's resources, limiting what is available for the claimants. The system is sometimes abused through forum shopping and strategic filings, which work to the disadvantage of various interested parties. And yet for all its flaws the system works. Unlike a number of other countries, the U.S. process does help weed out unproductive enterprises, and it does allow a second chance for those that have the possibility of making good with a fresh start. In that way, the U.S. bankruptcy system embodies the frontier spirit upon which this nation was founded.

NOTES

1. "U.S. Bankruptcy Filings 1980–2008: Annual Business and Non-Business Filings by Year (1980–2008)," American Bankruptcy Institute, www.abiworld.org. In 2007, there were 28,322 business bankruptcy filings and 822,590 nonbusiness filings. In 2008, there was a sharp increase in filings, with 43,546 business and 1,074,225 nonbusiness. In 2005, the October of which the amendments to the Bankruptcy Code went into effect, there were 39,201 and 2,039,214 respectively. The high-water mark for business filings was in 1986 with over 82,000 filings.

2. "Public Companies Bankruptcies to Make 2009 a Record Year," PTI, June 2, 2009. http://www.dnaindia.com/money/report_public-companies-bankruptcies-to-make-2009-record-year_1261224.

3. "20 Largest Public Bankruptcy Filings 1980–Present," Bankruptcy Data.com, published by New Generation Research, Inc. (with most recent filing the June 1, 2009, filing of General Motors).

4. Insolvency is not a prerequisite for filing. In some cases, solvent firms embroiled in mass tort litigation voluntarily file for bankruptcy to manage and contain current and future claims.

5. It should also be noted that some types of businesses are not permitted to file for bankruptcy. For example, while financial services holding companies can declare bankruptcy, the insolvency of the underlying banks and insurance companies, and securities and commodities brokers, are handled under different regimes.

6. If the DIP's exclusivity period ends without a court-approved reorganization plan, the firm's various claimants can step in and propose their own plan, which would be subject to the same approval process.

7. The Bankruptcy Code provides specific exceptions to the stay. For example, a criminal case may be continued, and certain securities transactions entered into prior to the filing may be settled post-filing. In addition, creditors may petition the court for relief from the stay.

8. Skeel (2001, 228), citing Tashjian et al. (1996, 135).

9. Researchers who studied 139 Chapter 11 cases filed between 1995 and 2001 in Manhattan and Phoenix found that in 80 percent of the bankruptcies of debtors with more than $5 million in assets, the plan involved either (1) canceling the equity holders' stake in the firm and repaying the secured creditors in full, or (2) selling off the firm's assets. McGann (2007).

10. This practice is undertaken in an attempt to help minimize losses upon a potential default. A recent study of bankruptcy codes in France, Germany, and the United Kingdom showed that lenders in France, for example, attempted to shift the cost of bankruptcy to borrowers in this fashion.

11. Notwithstanding the moral tenor of the debates, the practical problems with the proposals were economic. The early federal laws and proposals limited the types of debtors

who could enter the system. Farmers were harmed by this when a tradesman who owed the farmer money defaulted and went bankrupt. While the tradesman would be discharged of all debt, if the farmer, who would now be short of funds, defaulted on his loans, he might land in debtors' prison.

12. "General FAQs About PBGC," www.pbgc.gov.

13. The term *vulture investor* is commonly used to describe those who purchase cheap debt in distressed firms in order to gain bargaining power to renegotiate the terms of repayment through either a workout or bankruptcy process.

14. Fitzgerald (2007), citing an upublished study by Wei Wang, "Bankruptcy Filing and the Expected Recovery of Corporate Debt."

15. Law firms with commercial bankruptcy practices tend to staff up in times of economic downturn. Jones (2008).

16. "Horizon Natural Resources Files Chapter 11," *Business First*, November 14, 2002.

17. Some have argued that the method for valuing assets in bankruptcy, namely allowing the court to determine value, is inefficient and results in lower prices than an auction. However, others claim that whatever errors may be made through judicial valuation are minimal compared to the costs associated with conducting an auction. Easterbrook (1990).

18. A safeguard exists with the board of directors who with a distressed corporation owe duties to the firm's creditors. However, there is a gap between the statement of this duty by the courts and what the courts actually require of directors. Lipson (2007).

19. "Can You Afford to Retire?: Exploring the New Corporate Bankruptcy Strategy," March 16, 2006, http://www.pbs.org/wgbh/pages/frontline/retirement/world/bankruptcy.html. In this segment, Professor Elizabeth Warren notes that Mexico and other countries prioritize obligations to retirees and employees and this is built into the cost of credit: "Banks will adjust their prices accordingly."

20. *Indiana State Police Pension Trust, et al. v. Chrysler LLC et al.,* 556 U.S. __. 2009. Docket No. 08A1096.

21. See also blog of Ethan Zuckerman, "Tedeschi and the New York Times Get It Wrong," April 20, 2007. http://www.ethanzuckerman.com/blog/2005/04/20/tedeschi-and-the-new-york-times-get-it-wrong/.

22. These firms may file under Chapter 15, a model uniform law for foreign proceedings. This allows a non-U.S. company with U.S. assets to benefit from features like the automatic stay.

REFERENCES

Beckerman, Lisa, and Robert J. Stark. 2000. LBOs and fraudulent conveyances: The third circuit does an about-face. *Norton Bankruptcy Law Advisor.* February.

Bigelow, Bruce V. 2007. S.D. diocese follows lead of others in bankruptcy: Companies have used Chapter 11 for years. *San Diego Union-Tribune.* March 18.

Bilodeau, Otis, 2005. U.S. zeroes in on bankruptcy insiders: Efforts to join creditors' panels are called into question. *International Herald Tribune.* November 30.

Blashalany, Matthew. Complex puzzle: Bingham sorts out cross-border insolvencies. http://www.bingham.com/Media.aspx?MediaID=8614.

Boatright, John R. 2008. *Ethics in finance*. 2nd ed. Malden, MA: Blackwell.

Branch, Ben S., Hugh M. Ray, and Robin Russell. 2007. *Last rights: Liquidating a company*. New York: Oxford University Press.

Brickman, Lester, and Harvey D. Shapiro. 2005. Asbestos kills: And more than just people: Jobs, ethics and elementary justice. *National Review*. January 31.

Bris, Arturo, Ivo Welch, and Ning Zhu. 2006. The costs of bankruptcy: Chapter 7 liquidation versus Chapter 11 reorganization. *Journal of Finance* 61:1253–1303.

Chasan, Emily, and Tom Halls. 2009. Judges OK Chrysler sale; appeal to top court likely. *Reuters*. June 5.

Dao, James. 2004. Miners' benefits vanish with bankruptcy ruling. *New York Times*. October 24.

Davydenko, Sergei A., and Julian R. Franks. 2008. Do bankruptcy codes matter? A study of defaults in France, Germany, and the U. K. *Journal of Finance* 63:565–608.

Easterbrook, Frank H. 1990. Is corporate bankruptcy efficient. *Journal of Financial Economics* 27:411–417.

Eichenwald, Kurt. 1991. Talking deals; Bankruptcy court a threat to buyout profits of the 80s. *New York Times*. January 3.

Feder, Barnaby J. 1987. What A.H. Robins has wrought. *New York Times*. December 13.

Fitzgerald, Patrick. 2007. Bankruptcy venue change linked to recovery rates. *Wall Street Journal*. January 24.

Glater, Jonathan D. 2008 Advantage of corporate bankruptcy is dwindling. *New York Times*. November 18.

Hotchkiss Edith S., and Robert M. Mooradian. 1997. Vulture investors and the market for control of distressed firms. *Journal of Financial Economics* 43:401–432.

Johnson, Jeremy R. 2006. The rejection of collective bargaining agreements: New cases and developments. *Current Trends in Insolvency Law*. September.

Jones, Ashby. 2008. Law firms gear up—and wait—for anticipated bankruptcies. *Wall Street Journal*. July 16.

Jordan, Jim. 2006. Mine owned by Kentucky firm with dozens of operations. *Lexington Herald-Leader*. January 4.

Kalay, Avner, Rajeev Singhal, and Elizabeth Tashjian. 2007. Is Chapter 11 costly? *Journal of Financial Economics* 84:772–796.

Kellogg, Alex P., Chad Bray, and David McLaughlin. 2009. Court to hear challenge to Chrysler, Fiat pact. *Wall Street Journal*. June 4.

Kilborn, Jason. 2008. The joy of comparative commercial law. September 10. http://ucclaw.blogspot.com/2008/09/joy-of-comparative-commercial-law.html.

Kilpi, Jukka. 1998. *The ethics of bankruptcy*. New York: Routledge.

Lewin, Tamar. 1988. New threat to A.H. Robins's plan. *New York Times*. May 3.

Labaton, Stephen. 1990. Business and the law; An old weapon against buyouts. *New York Times*. September 17.

Lipson, Jonathan C. 2007. The expressive function of directors' duties to creditors. *Stanford Journal of Law, Business and Finance* 12:224–288.

McGann, Laura K. 2007. Unsecured creditors lose out. *Wall Street Journal*. February 28.

Newton, Grant W. 2003. *Corporate bankruptcy: Tools, strategies, and alternatives*. Hoboken, NJ: John Wiley & Sons, Inc.

Passell, Peter. 1993. Economic watch; critics of bankruptcy law see inefficiency and waste. *New York Times*. April 12.

Paulus, Christoph G. 2007. Global insolvency law and the role of multinational institutions. *Brooklyn Journal of International Law* 32:755–766.

Pulvino, Todd C. 1999. Effects of bankruptcy court protection on asset sales. *Journal of Financial Economics* 52:151–186.

Rapoport, Nancy B. 2002. The intractable problem of bankruptcy ethics: Square peg, round hole. *Hofstra Law Review* 30:977–999.

Salpukas, Agis. 1991. Eastern Airlines is shutting down and plans to liquidate its assets. *New York Times.* January 19.

Skeel, Jr., David A. 2001. *Debt's dominion: A history of bankruptcy law in America.* Princeton, NJ: Princeton University Press.

Smith, Douglas G. 2008. Resolution of mass tort claims in the bankruptcy system. *U.C. Davis Law Review* 41:1613–1664.

Stein, Charles. 2004. Fair or not, Wilbur Ross played the capitalist game. *Boston Globe.* November 14.

Tashjian, Elizabeth, Ronald C. Lease, and John J. McConnell. 1996. Prepacks: An empirical analysis of prepackaged bankruptcies. *Journal of Financial Economics* 40:135–162.

Tedeschi, Bob. 2005. Questioning Eziba's decisions. *New York Times.* April 18.

Tode, Chantal. 2005. Eziba enters bankruptcy, sells assets to overstock.com. *DMNews.* March 17.

Updike, Christopher, and Ingrid Bagby. 2008. Collective bargaining agreements and the bankruptcy code: Are damage claims for rejection of collective bargaining agreements available under Section 1113? *Pratt's Journal of Bankruptcy Law* 4:20–42.

Sullivan, Daniel. 2008. Big boys and Chinese walls. *University of Chicago Law Review* 75:533–568.

Walsh, Mary Williams. 2006. U.S. investigates pension fund at Northwest Air. *New York Times.* March 15.

Warren, Charles. 1972. *Bankruptcy in United States history.* New York: Da Capo Press (originally published by Harvard University Press in 1935).

Wayne, Leslie. 2002. At center of Enron bankruptcy, dispute over big bank creditors. *New York Times.* April 30.

Weil, Gotshal & Manges LLP. 2006. *Reorganizing failing businesses (revised edition): A comprehensive review and analysis of financial restructuring and business reorganization,* ed. Marvin E. Jacob and Sharon Youdelman. Chicago: ABA Section of Business Law.

Weiss, Lawrence A., and Karen H. Wruck. 1998. Information problems, conflicts of interest, and asset stripping: Chapter 11's failure in the case of Eastern Airlines. *Journal of Financial Economics* 48:55–97.

Wessels, Bob, Bruce A. Markell, and Jason Kilborn. 2009. *International cooperation in bankruptcy and insolvency matters.* New York: Oxford University Press.

ABOUT THE AUTHORS

Ben S. Branch is a professor of finance at the University of Massachusetts, Amherst, where he has taught finance, investment, banking, and industrial organization for over 30 years. He previously taught economics at Dartmouth College, the University of Michigan, and the University of Texas, and has served on the boards of several corporations, including the First Republic Bank, BankEast, Bank of New England, and Proactive Technologies. He is currently an associate editor of the *International Review of Financial Analysis.* He has published dozens of journal articles and book reviews. He is the author of *Fundamentals of Investment for Financial Planning* and *If You Are So Smart, Why Aren't You Rich?* He is also a co-author of *Bankruptcy Investing* and *Last Rights: Liquidating a Company.*

Jennifer S. Taub is a lecturer and coordinator of the Business Law Program within the Isenberg School of Management at the University of Massachusetts, Amherst.

Previously, she was an associate general counsel for Fidelity Investments in Boston and assistant vice president for the Fidelity Fixed Income Funds. She graduated cum laude from Harvard Law School in 1993 and earned her undergraduate degree, cum laude, in English from Yale College in 1989. Her areas of research include corporate governance, shareholders' rights, investor protection, mutual fund governance, federal securities laws, and financial regulation.

CHAPTER 28

Acquisitions, Mergers, and Takeovers

ANTHONY F. BUONO
Professor of Management and Sociology, Coordinator, Bentley Alliance for Ethics
and Social Responsibility, Bentley University

ROY A. WIGGINS III
Professor of Finance, Director of the Bentley Microcredit Initiative, Bentley University

INTRODUCTION

Modern-day corporations can choose from a broad range of organizational combinations with differing degrees of *equity ownership* and *contractual control* (Harrigan
1985). One end of this spectrum reflects purely contractual relationships and agreements, including licensing and strategic alliances. In these relationships, no new
equity ownership position or entity is typically created. The middle of the range
includes transactions that are characterized by some degree of partial ownership
and contractual control, like joint ventures. The other end of the spectrum is characterized by full equity ownership and control. Organizations participating in these
strategic alternatives take ownership of the asset and skill base, but they also bear
the full risk of the resulting entity. On a general level, acquisitions, mergers, and
takeovers (AMTs) refer to the combination of two organizations into one larger
entity and are examples of this latter type of transaction.

Virtually every major public corporation—as a merger partner, acquirer or
target—has been involved in an attempted or realized organizational combination
as AMTs have become a basic staple of corporate strategy. The overarching reason
why firms enter into a merger or decide to acquire another company is the belief
that the combination will allow the new entity to attain its strategic goals more
quickly and less expensively than if the firm attempted to do it by internal growth
alone. While proponents argue that well-planned AMTs enhance both the value
of the firm to shareholders and the value of the firm to the larger society (e.g.,
Haspeslagh and Jemison 1991; Wruck 2008), critics (e.g., Moeller, Schlingemann,
and Stulz 2005; Zalewski 2001) respond that far too many of these combinations
are undesirable and ill-conceived. Such AMT deals tend to be dominated by short-
term financial analyses, a focus on historical data rather than future sources of
revenues, and power plays that turn strategy into gamesmanship. Critics suggest
that in these latter instances, AMTs create far more harm than benefit for an array

of internal (e.g., shareholders, managers, employees) and external (e.g., customers, suppliers, unions, local communities) stakeholders, many of which are not directly considered in the decision-making process.

DEFINITIONAL ISSUES

Although the terms *acquisition*, *merger*, and *takeover* are often used interchangeably, there are some subtle and important differences between them. A *merger* is a combination in which two or more previously autonomous companies form a wholly new firm. Merger typically reflects a sense of equality between the two organizations. The equity in the two merging partners is converted into equity in the new, combined organization. Given the nature of the relationship between the merging partners, mergers can be *horizontal* (partners operate in similar product or service spaces in the same industry), *vertical* (partners operate in different stages of the supply chain for similar products or services), or *conglomerate* (partners operate in two or more separate industries). *Acquisition* refers to any transfer of ownership in which one organization is absorbed by another. In this case, the target firm basically disappears and becomes part of the acquiring or bidder firm.

Takeover refers to those situations where a company or an investment group gains enough shares of stock in a publicly traded company that it can control its governance via a plurality of votes for the board of directors. Takeovers can be *hostile* (attempted buyouts of the equity are unsolicited and often unsupported by target management), *friendly* (negotiated or invited offers of solicitation), or *reverse* (a smaller private firm taking over a public firm to gain the target's public listing). Reverse transactions can be either mergers or takeovers and provide a potentially less expensive alternative to going public than doing so through more traditional means like initial public offerings (Gleason, Rosenthal, and Wiggins 2005). Within this context, acquisition and takeover reflect the dominance of the acquiring organization over the target firm.

HISTORICAL CONSIDERATIONS

As a way of understanding the dynamics associated with AMTs and the underlying concerns they raise, it is useful to examine the key characteristics of these organizational combinations and how they have evolved over the past few decades.

AMT Characteristics during the 1980s

Corporate managers were primarily focused on the firm during the 1980s. Although adherence to the shareholder value maximization paradigm was part of the discourse in academic circles, it was not heavily practiced in executive suites. The notion of using equity-based incentives in executive compensation schemes was a relatively new idea with only 20 to 30 percent of total management compensation being tied to stock or market performance. Boardrooms were relatively passive as well, and directors worked closely with the management teams that were influential in selecting them.

When management teams and boards proved ineffective, the "market for corporate control" (Jensen and Ruback 1983) could dispense severe punishment, and a majority of organization combinations during the 1980s had a hostile tenor. Some estimates suggest that almost half of publicly traded firms were party to an outright hostile threat (see, for example, Holmström and Kaplan 2001). Large active investors like Carl Icahn and T. Boone Pickens were characterized as "corporate raiders." In addition to acquiring voting control, they would often take operational control of the firms they pursued, laying off workers and divesting assets as they dismantled the firms they acquired.

Facilitating these organizational changes was an increasing use of debt or leverage to finance the transactions. Replacing equity, cash, or some combination of the two, leverage became the currency of firm buyouts. During this period, Michael Milken and Drexel Burnham introduced the use of non-investment-grade or *junk* bonds, which have been described as *equity disguised as debt*. In a general sense, corporate debt is a hybrid combination of an interest rate instrument and short-selling put options on the firm's equity. In cases of default, equity holders *put* their shares to the debt holders. Junk bonds carry a higher probability of default; thus, the equity put component tends to have a greater impact on the bond's price (see Fridson 1994). Although this form of financing facilitated highly leveraged buyout deals that were largely unhealthy for the larger economy, junk bonds continued to be an important funding vehicle for AMT activity until the credit crunch of the early 1990s (Holmström and Kaplan 2001).

AMT Characteristics during the 1990s

The 1990s saw a tempering of both the hostile and levered characteristics of AMT transactions. The use of hostile takeovers declined for several reasons. During the 1980s, management teams were more focused on firm issues than shareholder concerns, boards tended to be management-friendly, and the notion of an activist shareholder or shareholder group (large block or otherwise) had not become commonplace (see Holmström and Kaplan 2001). Another important constraint for shareholders in the 1980s was access to management. Investors wishing to speak directly to management had to file their intentions with the SEC. It was not until the law was relaxed that friendlier, more informal discussions and communications could take place. During the 1990s, the market for corporate control developed more options than in the 1980s, when a hostile takeover was the predominant means available for correcting underperforming management. Governance mechanisms based on politics and strategic communication began to replace the financially driven, hostile methods (Pound 1992). Examples of these political mechanisms include shareholder committees, director-nominating committees made up of petitions initiated by shareholders, alternative agenda issue campaigns, and friendly monitoring or oversight by larger institutional investors.

At the same time, firms began to implement a battery of takeover prevention measures intended to protect the incumbent management team and existing shareholders. The notion of aligning shareholder and management objectives became a more common focus in corporate offices and boardrooms. Incentive compensation focused more on providing equity opportunities for managers, and stock options and restricted shares of stock became more prevalent means of compensating managers. Boards of directors also took their charge of protecting the interests of shareholders more seriously, which ironically proved to be a double-edged sword in that it also made boards more open to takeovers that benefited shareholders.

The character of large investors began to evolve during this time as well. Single investors became more synonymous with names like Warren Buffett, who sought well-run firms in which to invest and then allowed incumbent management to continue doing what it did best. Buffett's role was more of an enabling one than that of the raiders before him. Institutional investors also became more important players in terms of ownership and control, growing from 25 to 30 percent in the 1980s to as much as 50 percent in the 1990s (Holmström and Kaplan 2001). These investors included a range of firms such as mutual and hedge funds and pension and retirement investment management firms. What makes their involvement both interesting and different is that institutions tend to monitor management teams more intently as they look for higher returns. Concerns for their fund or institutional constituents gave the appearance that they were less loyal to the firm's management than they were to management's most recent performance.

As these ownership and control aspects evolved during the 1990s, so did the means through which AMTs were funded. The credit crunch in the early 1990s, which was compounded by the savings and loan crisis, dealt a blow to the junk bond market, and funding these transactions with equity and cash returned as the prominent means of payment.

AMT Characteristics during the 2000s

In many respects, the 2000s have seen a continuation of many of the trends that began in the 1990s. Less than 5 percent of the completed transactions that reported a transaction attitude on MergerStat (2009), for example, were categorized as "hostile." The preferred method of payment remained cash and equity (60 percent and 19 percent of the completed deals, respectively). Warren Buffett continued to be synonymous with a more business-minded and altruistic single investor. Institutional investors also continued to be important players in terms of ownership and control.

On a related note, media and public emphasis on increasing board independence led to regulatory changes regarding the composition of the board. These changes encouraged, and in some cases mandated, boards to move more fully toward independent directors, with fewer insiders and affiliated friends. Pressure also increased to separate the roles of the CEO and the chair of the board (known as a *dual* structure when one person holds both titles). Research suggests that the percentage of dual CEO-chairs decreased significantly during the late 1990s and early 2000s (Ryan, Wang, and Wiggins 2009). During this same time period, public attitudes toward executive compensation became more critical. Overuse of stock options by firms led to requirements that firms expense these awards at the time of their granting. During the economic crisis that began in 2008, public and government outrage over what appeared to be non-performance-based bonuses reached a peak as all constituents tried to work together to reorient the economy.

AMT Transaction Trends and Valuation

As the preceding discussion illustrates, transaction characteristics have changed dramatically over the past 30 years. An analysis of statistical data in U.S. M&A Reports (MergerStat 2009) confirms that the frequency and value of these transactions changed appreciably over the same time period. For example, U.S. firms engaged in almost 25,000 AMT transactions during the 1980s, the value of which was reported to be roughly $1.4 trillion. Looking at that decade, the smallest number of events occurred in 1980 (1,889 events), with a value of approximately $44.3 billion; the largest number of AMT transactions took place in 1989 (2,366), while the largest value was in the preceding year ($246.9 billion). During the 1990s, over 47,000 events worth an estimated $4.8 trillion were reported. This activity represents nearly a doubling of both the number and value of AMT transactions from one decade to the next. The 2000s continue this trend with almost 88,500 AMTs totaling $8.8 trillion.

An interesting observation is that both the 1990s and 2000s were characterized by high first-year activity (1990 and 2000, respectively) and subsequent drops due to credit or economic issues. In both cases AMT activity did not return to that first-year level until the fifth year of the decade (1994 and 2004, respectively). There is also a noticeable drop from 2007 to 2008, reflecting the severe economic issues revealed during the banking crisis of that year. Finally, the value of AMTs in 2000 reached almost $1.3 trillion on over 11,000 events, which is close to the total value for the 1980s on nearly half of the total number of events. In fact, this annual level was reached or exceeded six times during the past two decades, in 1998–2000 and 2005–2007.

ETHICAL CONSIDERATIONS IN AMTs: PROCESS AND OUTCOMES

There are two fundamental sets of concerns raised about corporate AMTs: The first focuses on whether the combination will create economic value for shareholders; the second emphasizes the effect the combination will have on the companies' implicit contracts with other stakeholders and the larger society. These issues, which reflect both process and outcome considerations, have strong ethical undertones. From a process perspective, questions are typically raised about the appropriateness and fairness of the actions by the parties involved during combination planning, transaction, and implementation. In terms of outcomes, emphasis is placed on the combination's relative benefit or harm (direct and indirect) for all relevant stakeholders (including shareholders) and about the social desirability of these outcomes. Debate about these issues often comes down to questions about fairness, transparency, distributive justice, fulfilling commitments, and the social role of the corporation and its responsibilities to a broader range of constituencies that go beyond shareholders per se (see, for example, Buono and Bowditch 1989; Chase, Burns, and Claypool 1997; Lajoux 1998; Woodstock Theological Center 1990).

The ethical issues in hostile takeovers are clearly more pronounced given the sharp disagreements and pressures between the stakeholders involved, including managers, employees, shareholders, the raiders or takeover firms, suppliers, local communities, and a host of other critical constituencies (Boatright 2008; Hoffman, Frederick, and Petry 1989). However, even with the apparent consensus and mutual agreement between parties in friendly acquisitions, mergers, and solicited takeovers, a number of ethical concerns exist.

HOSTILE TAKEOVERS

A basic tenet of the free market is that organizational combinations intended to maximize the value of the firms for shareholders also have long-term benefits for the larger society. The underlying market for corporate control—that is, the tendency of outside parties (often referred to as *raiders*) to try to buy publicly traded companies—exerts a necessary discipline on managers, whose self-interests often diverge from those of the owners. Thus even hostile takeovers, which imply change and restructuring that can have significant repercussions for the existing management, workforce, local community, and a host of other stakeholders, can have beneficial effects in terms of improving economic performance and generating greater returns to shareholders. The mere fact that a raider is willing to pay a premium (i.e., an amount in excess of the stock's current trading price) for a certain stock reflects the belief that the firm is not achieving its full potential with its present management team. Moreover, many takeovers involve the acquisition of underperforming or undervalued businesses that are unrelated to the strategic core of the parent company. The underlying argument is that managers, as agents of the owners, have a fiduciary responsibility to shareholders to sell off such assets and refocus the company on those areas that promise higher efficiency and return.

Critics argue that many of these takeovers are initiated for the sole purpose of liquidating the target company, especially when there is a gap between the market value of the firm and the breakup value of its assets. A basic proposition of free market capitalism is that market value represents the best estimate of *net present value* (a way of calculating the value of a net cash flow adjusted for the time value of money) of future cash flows. However, detractors contend that beyond a short-term financial return for select parties (typically the shareholders of the acquired firm, investment bankers, and lawyers), a liquidating takeover does not have any long-term benefit to other stakeholders or the larger society. These objections are especially directed at buyouts of successful and profitable companies, where the takeover may lead to layoffs and changes in management and can have a variety of negative effects on the firm's local community and related companies in its supply chain. An underlying question, given the fiduciary duty and responsibilities of corporate officers and directors, concerns what these officers and directors should do when a hostile bid may be attractive to shareholders but is deemed not to be in the best interests of the corporation itself or its other stakeholders.

Another criticism is that the threat of corporate takeover compels managers to show evidence of continuous profitability, forcing them to focus on short-term performance and the attainment of immediate results. This type of myopic decision making is suggested to precipitate a neglect of longer-term investments (e.g., in research and development) as well as a scaling back of commitments to a broader group of stakeholders (e.g., charitable contributions, investments in the surrounding community).

While ethical and social concerns typically focus on the acquirer's motives and actions, target firm management has also come under criticism for a series of questionable tactics intended to discourage unwanted takeovers. Based on an analogy of takeover specialists as sharks, *shark repellent* refers to an exotic array of tactics designed to prevent or stave off unwanted advances, tactics that evolved in response to the growing hostility that characterized takeovers during the 1980s.

These defensive tactics can be classified into several broad categories that include golden parachutes, poison pills, sandbagging, greenmail, corporate restructurings, and voting control issues.

AMT transactions are characterized by high levels of uncertainty, especially for the management of target firms. Consummation of these changes usually results in members of management being dismissed, demoted, or reassigned. To offset some of the fear associated with this uncertainty, many firms have implemented compensation plan components for their top executives that would be triggered by a change-of-control event. Known as *golden parachutes,* these plans promise lucrative benefits and severance payments to current management if they lose their jobs due to a takeover by another company. The benefits from these plans range from paying what an executive would have made in the absence of the change-of-control event to *sweetheart contracts* that would pay multiples of their existing contracts if they were to leave. *Tin parachutes* are a related tactic that focuses on compensating a broader range of employees who might be adversely affected by the AMT event. Affected employees usually receive more compensation than they would under traditional severance packages. These plans may also be a better takeover defense than their golden counterparts due to the fact that the greater numbers of employees can create a larger total payout, even if individual payments are less.

Poison pill tactics are attempts to dilute the value of the target firm shares held by the bidder. Often referred to as *shareholder rights plans,* these tactics give existing shareholders other than the bidding company the right to buy a large amount of stock (either common or preferred) at a low price. The right to buy the additional shares is triggered when someone acquires a certain percentage of the outstanding stock (e.g., 20 to 30 percent). There are several variations on this *right to buy* option. For example, the right to purchase additional shares in the target company is referred to as *flip-in provisions,* while the right to acquire shares in the surviving company is called *flip-over rights plans* or *provisions.* In both cases, shareholders are offered a significant discount for the stock, sometimes as low as 50 percent. The rights can be tied to other securities and assets as well, like offering shareholders the right to trade their shares for or acquire the bonds (*poison pill* or *back-end pill*) or other assets (*asset purchase rights*) of the target firm. In other circumstances, claimholders of other securities in the target firm can be granted additional rights to take some action. For example, *poison-preferred pills* could trigger an increase in preferred dividends and *poison-debt pills* could result in a particular bond issue being called early.

Sandbagging is when a target firm attempts to stall the process, often with the hope that a friendlier, more favorable third-party acquirer or *white knight* will emerge. Lesser known is the *white squire* defense, where an allied group or firm acquires a minority interest in a firm in an attempt to better protect it from becoming a target in the future.

Greenmail, a spin-off of the term *blackmail,* occurs when a target company attempts to pay off a potential raider. In essence, the firm's management pays the raider to cease the takeover attempt. This practice is also known as a *targeted repurchase,* since the firm buys back a large block of its stock from an unfriendly company or raider at a substantial premium to stop the takeover attempt. The funds often come from the firm's cash reserves or proceeds from a debt issue.

Although this tactic is frequently successful in staving off a particular raider, the costs to the firm can be substantial, undermining longer-term investment needs and, quite possibility, the stability of the company.

Management can also employ different types of *corporate restructurings* as an effective takeover defense. With appropriate reserves, the target firm could engage in a *defensive acquisition* of another firm, making itself a less attractive target for someone else. They could also sell or divest attractive assets or subsidiary business units. A *Pac-Man defense* is when a takeover target launches a tender offer for the company that was trying to acquire it. If successful, the target company ends up taking over the company that tried to buy it. A *scorched earth defense*, which is sometimes referred to as a *suicide pill*, is a variation on the defensive acquisition/divestiture strategies. This tactic involves selling off desirable assets or depleting the cash reserves of the target company by making extensive (and not necessarily profitable) acquisitions, possibly incurring large debt in the process. A *crown jewel defense* is employed when the company sells attractive or desirable assets to a friendly third party or spins the assets off into a separate new entity. *Defensive repurchases* or *recapitalizations* also raise the portion of debt in the target's capital structure. In these repurchases, the target buys back shares through either the open market or privately negotiated deals. The recapitalization reduces the cash position and any excess debt capacity as proceeds are paid out to shareholders, often along with new shares.

The term *voting control issues* refers to a class of tactics that enable management to affect or control how the shares outstanding are voted. In an indirect manner, employee or company programs that facilitate employee acquisition of stock may work in management's favor. Pension, profit-sharing, and employee stock ownership plans place voting control for significant amounts of stock into the hands of employees, who are typically on friendly terms with their management. A second mechanism is dual- or multiple-class common stock. In its simplest terms, management issues a high-vote, low-cash-flow stock and another with one vote and high cash flow. Other things being equal, management would prefer to own or control the former class of stock and issue the latter to the broader group of external shareholders, which would make wrestling control away from them a very difficult task.

Related to voting control issues, several state legislatures have drafted, passed, and implemented what have come to be known as *state law defenses*. These laws fall into three broad categories (Case, Shah, and de Pass 1995). First, *control share laws* eliminate the voting rights of shares held by a large blockholder if certain threshold levels are exceeded. Voting rights can only be reinstated after a vote of approval from disinterested shareholders. *Merger moratorium statutes* impose a mandatory waiting period on the consummation of a transaction if the transaction is being led by a large blockholder who exceeds certain prescribed ownership levels. Finally, *cash-out laws* allow nonblockholder shareholders to sell their shares to the bidder at a specified, often prohibitive price once prescribed thresholds have been exceeded.

A final set of control tactics often requires changes or modifications to the corporate charter or bylaws. For example, a *supramajority provision* requires that a large percentage of the shareholders (e.g., up to 80 percent) have to approve a business acquisition or takeover offer. *Fair price provisions* require that all shareholders of a particular class be paid the same price for their shares. This tactic prevents the acquirer from using a two-tier offer, but it also eliminates targeted repurchases or greenmail from management's bag of defense tactics. Finally, firms can move to a staggered board of director structure, where only a small percent of the sitting directors are up for election each year. A board composed of nine members, for example, might hold elections for three directors each year for three years.

While these various tactics may protect the target against an unwanted takeover, they render the company vulnerable to the vagaries of the business cycle and can significantly contribute to company debt. They also raise significant concerns about the duties of the target firm's management as agents of the firm's principals or shareholders. From an agency theory perspective, the underlying question concerns the extent to which these tactics are being utilized to protect shareholder interests or to preserve the entrenched position of the target firm's executives.

ACQUISITIONS AND MERGERS

Although criticism is typically placed on hostile takeovers, even friendly mergers, acquisitions, and solicited takeovers can raise an array of ethical and social concerns. While mergers and acquisitions are often portrayed as carefully calculated strategic acts, in practice they are human transactions that can be very costly with disappointing results. It is important to remember that true value creation in an acquisition or merger is only achieved well *after* the deal is made, when the two firms come together during postcombination integration (Haspeslagh and Jemison 1991; Marks 2003). Yet mergers and acquisitions typically disrupt organizations, often for years, diverting the time and energy of senior management and making organizational members feel stressed, angry, frustrated, disoriented, and frightened. Workplace ethics is especially vulnerable during such strategic transitions. According to a study by the Ethics Resource Center (2003), employees in organizations undergoing mergers or acquisitions observe misconduct and feel pressure to engage in questionable business practices at rates that are nearly double those in more stable organizations.

Although many of the human problems associated with mergers and acquisitions—the fears and uncertainties, stresses, and tensions experienced by employees—and the potentially negative repercussions for a range of external stakeholders cannot be totally eliminated, managers can exert favorable influence on both the integration process and consolidation outcomes (see, for example, Buono 1997 and 2005; Stahl and Mendenhall 2005). There are several concerns, each with a strong social and ethical component, that capture much of this tension.

Competing Claims and Conflicts of Interest

Mergers and acquisitions involve multiple parties, each with distinct interests and needs. Historically, this conflict has largely been framed in terms of the merger partners' or acquiring and acquired firms' shareholders. So framed, legitimate competing claims have been viewed in terms of the interests of the two groups of shareholders. Accordingly, corporate officials were duty-bound to define and pursue the best interests of these individuals. The stakeholder view, in contrast, emphasizes that firms have responsibilities to a broader array of groups that go beyond the immediate interests of shareholders—although the latter continue to occupy a place of prominence among stakeholders.

Although the stakeholder model suggests that a utilitarian orientation (i.e., the greatest good for the greatest number of stakeholders) should help to resolve the difficulties posed by such competing claims, the *greatest* good in a merger or acquisition is difficult to determine and is often a matter of perspective. While shareholders have one set of concerns, other internal stakeholders such as senior managers and employees and external stakeholders such as suppliers, customers, and local communities typically have others. Simply put, what might be in the best interests of one particular stakeholder group might very well conflict with the interests of others. To complicate matters, in most instances, these competing claims involve conflicting rights across different stakeholders, each of which has a legitimate basis.

Executive Compensation and Conflicts of Interest

A reality of acquisitions, mergers, and takeovers is that nonexecutive employees and other stakeholders bear disproportionate risk for poor corporate results, as senior-level executives often receive multimillion-dollar payouts when an acquisition or merger is finalized. In most instances, senior-level executives are able to renegotiate their contracts, not only limiting their financial risk but creating significant remuneration in the process (e.g., golden parachutes). Such change-in-control provisions, which are often part of an executive's employment contract, may not be fully disclosed or understood by the company's compensation committee and, at times, are added only weeks or even days before the finalization of the merger or acquisition. Due to the way in which such corporate reward structures are oriented, individual executives can be biased toward doing a deal rather than giving sound advice to the board, pursuing an offer that would not be in the best interests of all existing shareholders.

Culture Conflict as a Competing Claim

While the tensions between different interests can readily exacerbate combination-related decisions, the subtle nature of many competing claims further clouds the consolidation process. Cultural differences between organizations, for example, often create barriers to integration and consolidation, especially in mergers of equals. Organizational members, an important internal stakeholder group, tend to feel that the culture of the merged organization should be closer to their own culture (i.e., organizational philosophy, values and beliefs, ways of carrying out tasks) than to that of their merger partner. In essence, such competing perceived rights and the resulting collision between different styles, orientations, and values can readily create postcombination difficulties and distract managers and employees from attending to critical business-related activities. This type of conflict is especially prevalent in acquisitions and mergers that involve significant operational integration, where two distinct company populations are expected to work closely together on a day-to-day basis.

Secrecy versus Deception

Tensions typically arise in communication between the managed release of information in an open, honest, and timely manner, and the controlled release of information intended to distort the truth and manipulate people. When faced with a merger or acquisition, managers must make difficult decisions concerning the nature and timing of communication to employees and other relevant publics, which are complicated by a number of legal and operational dilemmas. First, Security and Exchange Commission (SEC) rules limit what can be told about acquisition or merger plans—even to employees—and when such information can be released (in order to prevent insider trading, for example). Second, since the actual details of the combination need to be worked out over several months or even years following the deal, managers often do not have detailed answers to stakeholder questions. Finally, the high level of stress and anxiety associated with the AMT process typically translates into employee feelings of suspicion and a sense of not being fully informed. Critics, however, argue that executives often use such constraints as a convenient shield to deceive and manipulate employees.

These communication-related issues raise concerns about information and property rights. Questions often focus on the extent to which the proposed transaction and its implementation have been carried out in a transparent and honest manner and whether parties with a legitimate right to information relating to the transaction have been given equal access to relevant and appropriate information in a timely manner. Open communication channels are an important factor in minimizing people's fears and creating an informed understanding of the organizational combination. It is important to remember that information needs during an acquisition or merger are quantitatively and qualitatively different from those during normal, everyday interactions.

Employee Participation and the Management of Grief, Loss, and Termination

Mergers and acquisitions often differ in the extent to which organizational members are forced into accepting certain situations or provided with a true opportunity to take part in discussions and decisions. In many instances, precombination planning and execution are tightly controlled by senior-level management, and the resulting change is typically done *to* organizational members rather than *by* or in conjunction *with* them. The ways in which subsequent employee grief, loss, and termination are handled exert a significant impact on employee attitudes and behaviors.

During the initial stages of a merger or acquisition, employees typically experience conflicting emotions ranging from shock, anger, disbelief, and helplessness to hope, excitement, and raised expectations. Following a merger or acquisition, there is typically a mourning period, similar to when a member of an extended family dies, as the erosion of familiar work surroundings and the exit of colleagues and friends signals the end of what was. From a managerial perspective, it is important to assist employees during this transition, helping them to deal with such feelings and the new realities of the combined organization. The handling of employee terminations and staff reductions also sends signals about management's values to the employees. Yet research suggests that most people involved in a merger or acquisition feel that termination decisions are handled arbitrarily and ineffectively.

Insider Trading

From the perspective of the SEC, a *corporate insider* is any officer or director of the firm as well as any beneficial owner with more than a 10 percent ownership stake in the firm's common equity. The origins of the insider trading prohibitions come from common-law restrictions on fraud. In its simplest terms, any party in possession of nonpublic information about a firm should either disclose that knowledge or not use it in trading for his personal benefit. SEC Rule 10b5-1 defines *trading on the basis of inside information* as any instance when a party trades on material nonpublic information. In light of these definitions, there are two distinct notions of insider trading: The first is represented by any trading activity by an insider, and the second is any trading that takes advantage of nonpublic information. The former type of activity is regulated so that disclosures are required; the latter is illegal market manipulation. Corporate insiders have a right to buy and sell on any basis other than possession of material nonpublic information. Providing other parties with such nonpublic information may expose the person providing the information to potential legal action or sanction for breach of confidentiality in violation of his or her fiduciary duty. The legal prohibition is placed on any party, insider or otherwise, in possession of such inside information disclosed to that person by an insider in violation of that insider's fiduciary duty.

AMTs provide opportunity for insider trading during the early conversational or negotiation stages when they are not public knowledge. Nonpublic information on an impending acquisition or merger gives insiders an unfair advantage relative to other investors who do not have similar access to such knowledge. While the occasion or opportunity is there, the majority of the violators in these cases are outsiders who have been tipped off, rather than insiders themselves. Trading by insiders in these instances would be too easily detected and prosecuted.

In order for the SEC to prosecute an insider for illegally trading, it must prove that the defendant had a fiduciary duty to the company and/or intended to personally gain from buying or selling shares based upon this information. Noninsider parties who receive nonpublic information can be held liable if they know or have reason to know that the source of that information breached a fiduciary responsibility (e.g., they received it from an insider) or if they themselves are in breach of a duty to the source (e.g., a lawyer or banker who receives nonpublic information while working for a firm that provides services for the source firm). Current statutes provide for up to treble penalties (gains made or losses avoided), although many cases are settled out of court.

THE ROLE OF THE BOARD OF DIRECTORS

From a broad legal perspective, the board of directors has several principal duties that govern their behavior and choices in all circumstances (Monks and Minow 1995). First, they must have a focused, unbending loyalty to the shareholders of the firm (*duty of loyalty*). Second, each director agrees to exercise due diligence in all their board activities, including reading, processing, and collecting information in a timely and appropriate manner and using that information in their decision making (*duty of care*). Third, directors are required to disclose any and all material information they have about a corporate transaction when they are seeking shareholder approval (*duty of candor*). In contested situations where director behavior and choices are questioned, the courts look first to whether these three duties were adequately and appropriately exercised by the director(s) in question.

Within this legal framework, how directors operate tactically and strategically is as varied and different as the companies they serve. Regardless of these differences, all boards have two broad charges: *monitoring* and *advising*. Directors observe the management of the firm since they are charged with (1) hiring, monitoring, and, if necessary, firing the CEO and his or her C-suite colleagues; and (2) reviewing and approving the strategic plans and processes put forward by these executives, as well as (3) overseeing the financing and the capital expenditures that are required to implement those plans (NACD 2005). All of these monitoring activities are to ensure that the best interests of the shareholders are being adequately served and protected.

Unlike the relatively passive nature of monitoring, the advising function of directors requires a more active relationship with management. The responsibilities in this relationship include advising management about their strategic and operational goals and objectives, matching performance outcomes to these goals and objectives, and participating in conversations about material transactions that do not fall into the normal course of business, like AMTs.

The very nature of these two roles puts directors in a potentially difficult situation when their firm faces AMT transactions. On the one hand, directors should be involved to make sure that interests of the shareholders are considered (possibly through a shareholder vote), protected (ensuring the best possible price per share or outcome), and managed in an orderly and timely fashion. Alternatively, they often find that their own wealth (through equity ownership), position (seat on the board), and reputation (if they fail to protect shareholder interests) are on the line. Management typically shares the wealth, position, and reputation concerns in AMTs.

While director efforts should be aligned with the interests of shareholders by charge, they are often also aligned with managers based on these wealth, positional, and reputational issues. Recent conversations by academics and practitioners that consider how to best realign the shareholder-director relationship have focused on mechanisms that include more independent directors, equity compensation for directors to better align their ownership interests with shareholders, a separation of the CEO and board chair roles, and staggered board memberships. However, the *duty of loyalty* requires that directors put the interests of their shareholders before their own or those of management, especially during the AMT process.

Further complicating the balancing of these competing interests is the ongoing dialogue regarding *corporate constituency statutes* (see Orts 1991; Oswald 1998). These statutes derive from corporate social responsibility debates and stakeholder theories, which encourage directors to consider the interests of other constituent groups like employees, suppliers, customers, and the community. In a general sense, the primary purpose of these statutes is to broaden the range of stakeholder concerns that directors may consider in making and overseeing business decisions.

Although over one-half of the states have adopted these statutes, there is some variation in how they have been crafted. Pennsylvania's statute, which was the first one enacted, has served as a model for many other states. It was modified to stress (1) the "continued independence of the corporation," with attention to both short- and long-term business horizons, and (2) the intent and purpose of any person or firm seeking to gain control of a firm. A second variation, as seen in Georgia and Tennessee, allows the firm to "opt in" or include charter amendments based on the perceived best interest of the firm. In these statutes, even if a firm chooses not to opt in, the constituency statutes would not necessarily pertain to them in the future should a need or desire to benefit from them arise. In essence, these variations underscore that stakeholders do not have any enforcement power and any such decisions are at the discretion of the directors (see Oswald 1998). A third common variation limits the reach of these statutes to "corporate control" events, like AMTs, and any potential change of control transaction would bring these statutes into play. Orts (1991) has criticized such variations, arguing that if these statutes only come into play during an AMT, they have the effect of entrenching management rather than protecting the other constituents as claimed. As such, he contends that this third variation does not provide any protection to a firm's stakeholders in ordinary business situations.

CONCLUSION

The level of respect for organizational members and other key stakeholders as individuals is an important dimension of the AMT process. Historically, the rela- tionship between employer and employee has been governed by the employment- at-will doctrine: The employment contract can be terminated at will by either party at any time for any reason. Although this perspective has been challenged by pub- lic policy questions based on the greater good, it has led to the rather narrow view that employees have only those rights that they are able to negotiate with their employers. Employees and other key stakeholders, however, are not mere abstrac- tions and, as individuals, have a moral right to be treated fairly and with respect and dignity.

To a large extent, the ethical and social impacts of AMTs are dependent on the extent to which these considerations are appropriately dealt with. Hostile takeovers, especially those characterized as liquidation strategies, are criticized for creating significant disruption and often failing to lead to the proposed level of efficiency and effectiveness. Even friendly, collaborative combinations can precip- itate disruption, dislocation, and upheaval. It is generally agreed that corporations are responsible for their actions and have an implicit obligation to their relevant in- ternal and external stakeholders. Yet many AMTs are still driven by cost-reduction tactics rather than strategic planning, with overly ambitious short-term financial goals—often beyond realistic achievement—dominating the process. Thus, in or- der to minimize organizational trauma and adverse effects on relevant stakeholders (e.g., shareholders, employees, customers, suppliers, and local communities), orga- nizations and their management should ensure fairness and due care throughout the AMT process, from precombination planning, through the transaction itself, to postcombination integration.

In addition to the typical financial and legal analyses that accompany AMT planning, such due care should also include social impact analyses that present a coherent rationale for the combination, a three- to five-year business plan on how the combined business will be operated, and an assessment of the effects of the combination on key stakeholders. These analyses should explicitly address the underlying wealth creation strategies and their ramifications for primary stakeholders (e.g., shareholders, employees, customers, and suppliers), and their broader social impacts (e.g., the effect on the local community). Challenges include balancing costs and benefits across different social levels (e.g., local community vs. regional economic concerns) and time periods (e.g., near-term vs. long-term, current generation vs. future generations). Depending on the nature of the acquisition or merger in question (e.g., strategic, financial, operational), early planning and due diligence (i.e., the careful assessment a reasonable person should take before entering into an agreement or transaction with another party) should go beyond financial and legal analyses and include assessments of strategic compatibility, differences in corporate culture, operating style, organizational standards, and business practices. If companies do not address whether and how they will manage these inevitable differences from the outset, they will have to deal with conflict without agreed-upon processes, tools, standards, or principles by which to guide smooth resolution.

Clearly, mergers and acquisitions can be risky strategies, but internal development can be just as risky and even more time consuming. From an ethical and social perspective, AMTs can favorably contribute to the firms involved, their stakeholders, and the larger society if all relevant stakeholders are considered and treated fairly and justly, ensuring that their rights are upheld. Focus should be placed on the extent to which the proposed combination will favorably affect the value of the firms—in essence, creating value and more benefit than harm for the organizations' shareholders, other internal and external stakeholders, and the larger society.

REFERENCES

Boatright, J. R. 2008. *Ethics in finance*. 2nd ed. Malden, MA: Blackwell.

Buono, A. F. 1997. Technology transfer through acquisition. *Management Decision* 35:194–204.

———. 2005. Consulting to integrate mergers and acquisitions. In *The contemporary consultant: Insights from world experts*, ed. L. Greiner and F. Poulfelt. Mason, OH: Thomson/ South-Western.

Buono, A. F., and J. L. Bowditch. 1989. *The human side of mergers and acquisitions: Managing collisions between people, cultures and organizations*. San Francisco: Jossey-Bass.

Case, R., D. Shah, and A. de Pass. 1995. Mergers and acquisitions. In *The WG&L handbook of financial strategy & policy*, ed. D. Logue. Cincinnati, OH: South-Western College Publishing.

Chase, D. G., D. J. Burns, and G. A. Claypool. 1997. A suggested ethical framework for evaluating corporate mergers and acquisitions. *Journal of Business Ethics* 16:1753–1763.

Ethics Resource Center. 2003. *2003 National business ethics survey*. Washington, DC: Ethics Resource Center.

Fridson, M. 1994. Do high-yield bonds have an equity component? *Financial Management* 23:82–84.

Gleason, K., L. Rosenthal, and R. A. Wiggins III. 2005. Backing into being public: An exploratory analysis of reverse takeovers. *Journal of Corporate Finance* 12:54–79.

Harrigan, K. 1985. *Strategies for joint ventures*. Lexington, MA: Lexington Books.

Haspeslagh, P., and D. B. Jemison. 1991. *Managing acquisitions: Creating value through corporate renewal*. New York: Free Press.

Hoffman, W. M., R. Frederick, and E. S. Petry. 1989. *The ethics of organizational transformation: Mergers, takeovers and corporate restructuring*. New York: Quorum Books.

Holmström, B., and S. Kaplan. 2001. Corporate governance and merger activity in the U.S.: Making sense of the 1980s and 1990s. *Journal of Economic Perspectives* 15:121–144.

Jensen, M. C., and R. S. Ruback. 1983. The market for corporate control. *Journal of Financial Economics* 11:5–50.

Lajoux, A. R. 1998. *The art of M&A integration*. New York: McGraw-Hill.

Marks, M. L. 2003. Making mergers and acquisitions work. In *Enhancing inter-firm networks and interorganizational strategies*, ed. A. F. Buono. Greenwich, CT: Information Age Publishing.

MergerStat. 2009. *U.S. M&A Reports*. www.mergerstat.com (accessed January 2009).

Moeller, S. B., F. Schlingemann, and R. Stulz. 2005. Wealth destruction on a massive scale: A study of acquiring firm returns in the recent merger wave. *Journal of Finance* 57:757–782.

Monks, R. A. G., and N. Minow. 1995. *Corporate governance*. Cambridge, MA: Blackwell Publishers.

National Association of Corporate Directors (NACD). 2005. *Report of the NACD Blue Ribbon Commission on director professionalism*.

Orts, E. 1991. Beyond shareholders: Interpreting corporate constituency statutes. *George Washington Law Review* 61:14–135.

Oswald, L. J. 1998. Shareholders v. stakeholders: Evaluating corporate constituency statutes under the Takings Clause. *Journal of Corporation Law* 24:1–28.

Pound, J. 1992. Beyond takeovers: Politics comes to corporate control. *Harvard Business Review* 70:83–93.

Ryan, H., L. Wang, and R. Wiggins. 2009. Board of director monitoring and CEO tenure. Working paper, Georgia State University.

Stahl, G. K., and M. E. Mendenhall, eds. 2005. *Mergers and acquisitions: Managing culture and human resources*. Stanford, CA: Stanford University Press.

Woodstock Theological Center. 1990. *Ethical considerations in corporate takeovers*. Washington, DC: Georgetown University Press.

Wruck, K. H. 2008. Private equity, corporate governance, and the reinvention of the market for corporate control. *Journal of Applied Corporate Finance* 20:8–21.

Zalewski, D. A. 2001. Corporate takeovers, fairness and public policy. *Journal of Economic Issues* 35:431–437.

ABOUT THE AUTHORS

Anthony F. Buono is a professor of management and sociology and founding coordinator of the Alliance for Ethics and Social Responsibility at Bentley University. His primary research, teaching, and consulting interests include organizational change, interorganizational strategies, management consulting, and ethics and corporate social responsibility. He has written or edited 13 books including *The Human Side of Mergers and Acquisitions* (Jossey Bass, 1989) and, most recently, *Client-Consultant Collaboration* (Information Age, 2009) as part of his *Research in Management Consulting* series. He holds a BS in business administration from the University of Maryland, and an MA and PhD with a concentration in industrial and organizational sociology from Boston College.

Roy A. Wiggins III is a professor of finance and the director of the Bentley Microcredit Initiative at Bentley University. His teaching and research focuses on corporate governance, ownership, and control. His research interests include board of director effectiveness and compensation, executive compensation, and corporate expansions such as mergers and acquisitions, joint ventures, and reverse takeovers. He holds a PhD and an MS in finance from Georgia State University. He has a BA in English with a concentration in creative writing from Florida State University.

CHAPTER 29

Executive Compensation

JOHN J. McCALL
Professor of Philosophy and Management, Saint Joseph's University

INTRODUCTION

Outrage. That may be the most commonly reported reaction to executive compensation practices as the first decade of the twenty-first century draws to a close. Business columnists, congresspersons, and the general public on both sides of the Atlantic have used this word in sometimes furious denunciation of executive pay. The current public focus on the compensation of top executives is mostly explained by the fact that large bonuses and severance packages have been awarded to executives of failed companies. Meanwhile, those very companies have received billions of dollars in public funds in order to forestall socially calamitous collapses of vital industries and enterprises.

Examples abound. Merrill Lynch CEO John Thain, excoriated for a lavish $1.2 million refurbishing of his office and for arranging an irregular bonus plan for top executives in the last days before Merrill was acquired by Bank of America, received $17.3 million in compensation while Merrill received a $10 billion government bailout as part of the Bank of America acquisition (Creswell and Story 2009; Dymski 2009; Slack 2009).

Alan Fishman, hired as chief executive officer by Washington Mutual three weeks before the failed bank was seized by federal regulators and its operations taken over by JPMorgan Chase, was entitled by contract to a payout of $18 million in salary, bonus, and severance for his three weeks on the job at WaMu. Though JPMorgan Chase may fight the severance payout, Fishman had already received a signing bonus and salary worth more than $8 million (Protess 2008; Smith 2008).

In Britain, the public outrage forced a revision in Royal Bank of Scotland's plan to pay large bonuses to top bankers. However, the bank, now 70 percent owned by the British government, has agreed to pay its new chief executive a signing bonus of £2.3 million as well as granting performance bonuses potentially worth £2.4 million to the head of its American operations (BBC 2009; Lindsay 2009; Treanor 2009).

Of course, complaints about executive pay have been part of the public discourse since at least the early 1990s. In 2006, some were outraged at the $65 million in pay and potential $83 million pension collected by Hank McKinnell of Pfizer for his five years as CEO and chairman, at a time when Pfizer's share value lagged its industry and dropped by over 40 percent (Morgenson 2006). In 2003, the public was outraged over the $140 million received by Richard Grasso as head of the

New York Stock Exchange, a compensation package some board members say they were unaware of (Thomas and Anderson 2005). As early as 1992, complaints about high executive pay rose from both sides during the U.S. presidential campaign as the top five American CEOs earned a combined total of $322 million in the previous year (McCarrol 1992).

Typically, the issue of executive compensation emerges in the context of economic downturns when layoffs and unemployment are rising while executives are pocketing multimillion-dollar compensation packages. However, the emotional intensity of the public debate in 2009 seems to far exceed that of earlier periods. The intensity is no doubt because the world economy is suffering through its deepest decline since the Great Depression, because unemployment in many places has reached double digits, and because the risky decisions of executives, who continue to garner enormous compensation, are seen by many to have been the cause of the economic collapse.

Public outrage, of course, is not by itself a sufficient basis for judging that the compensation is morally unjustified. In fact, there are any number of recent and serious defenses of executive pay practices (Boatright 2009; Edmans and Gabaix 2009; Evans and Hefner 2009; Gabaix and Landier 2008; Kaplan 2008). Moreover, it is often unclear just what, specifically, is the target of the frequently expressed outrage. Some complaints seem to be about the absolute amount of the compensation; others seem to focus on the pay of American executives relative either to their international peers or to ordinary workers. Still other complaints seem to be about the apparent insensitivity of pay to firm performance. Some target specifically the severance and retirement packages of failed executives who have been forced out by their boards. Finally, some complaints seem to focus on supposedly perverse incentives created by generous use of stock options. Often, these logically distinct complaints are blurred together by politicians, reporters, and citizens in the critiques they offer of executive pay.

It will be important to keep these different complaints separate in the analysis that follows. In particular, since the stock or equity portion of compensation has been a large driver of the increased pay of executives, it will be important to distinguish between complaints about the size of compensation and complaints about its composition. It is perfectly possible to believe that compensation practices encouraged unacceptably risky behavior while not simultaneously holding that the amount of compensation was inappropriate. As we will see, for example, much of the academic debate turns not on the size of the pay but on whether the form of executive compensation, with its heavy reliance on equity, was a wise practice for either shareholders or society at large.

The plan for the remainder of the chapter is to assess the moral acceptability of executive compensation in a more analytic fashion than is often present in the emotional responses reported in the press. The first section describes in some detail the different elements that typically constitute an executive's compensation. Subsequent sections sketch the historical change in compensation and the regulatory responses to those changes; discuss two competing views in the main academic debate over executive pay (both of which use shareholder interests as the touchstone of their analyses); and, finally, approach the issue from a broader horizon by introducing ethical considerations critical for a more complete moral assessment.

THE ELEMENTS OF EXECUTIVE PAY

Executive compensation is typically a complex combination of different elements. Compensation can be in cash, equity, or in-kind perquisites. It can be current or deferred. It can be in the form of salary or bonus. It can include contractually guaranteed elements as well as elements awarded at the discretion of the board of directors. It can be pay that will be received with near certainty or pay that is at risk because it is contingent on performance targets. All of these distinctions between potential components of an executive's pay package can overlap in intersecting ways.

For instance, the salary component is typically contractually guaranteed, but it can also be deferred for later payout. Obviously, pension and severance payments can be both guaranteed and deferred. They can also be pay exposed to risk if the severance or pension includes a stock component (Conway 2008; Walker 2009).

Equity pay is often in the form of restricted shares or stock options. Restricted shares are shares granted with limits requiring that the executive hold the stock for a period of time before it can be sold. Stock options are awards that entitle the recipient to purchase a specified number of shares at a given price (the strike price), usually the price of the stock on the day of the option award. The right to purchase stock at the strike price can be exercised only after a specified date, typically one to three years after the option award. Restricted shares and stock options are by their nature both a form of deferred compensation and a form of compensation that is subject to risk.

Bonuses can be in the form of cash or equity. They can be awarded when the individual executive or the firm meets performance targets. Performance targets can be tied to stock price, to earnings per share, to the completion of mergers or acquisitions, to reductions in workforce costs, to the achieving of other efficiencies, and to almost any other target that the board of directors sets for the executive team. Bonuses, however, are not always tied to performance. Some bonuses are awarded as signing bonuses, often to compensate an executive hired from the outside for the loss of benefits incurred in leaving a previous employer. Bonuses can also be awarded as an incentive to retain or bind key executives and to discourage them from considering offers from other potential corporate employers. Finally, bonuses can be completely discretionary, awarded by a board without any performance target having been met and without any prior agreement that the bonus would be available (Brush 2009a).

Perquisites are often less publicized elements of executive compensation packages, but they can nonetheless be valuable. One study found the median value of perks for executives in a set that approximated the Fortune 1000 as $81,000. Perks include the use of corporate jets, club memberships, automobile use, housing, and the like (Mercer 2008). Executives have also received generous insurance, loans at below-market rates (which were often used to exercise option grants, a practice now prohibited in the United States by the Sarbanes-Oxley Act of 2002), above-market rates of return for deferred pay, and even "gross up" payments to compensate for taxes owed on pay (Bebchuk and Fried 2004).

Obviously, executive pay is a highly complex business. Determining the value of any specific pay package is often difficult. Proxy reports describing compensation can be over 20 pages long and can include elements, such as long-term stock incentives, that may be difficult to value. Packages also vary widely between firms (Trejos 2009; Walker 2009). We will see that this very complexity of executive compensation figures integrally in one powerful academic critique that current patterns of compensation are not in the best interests of shareholders.

HISTORICAL TRENDS IN EXECUTIVE COMPENSATION

While reports on levels of executive compensation exhibit significant variation due to the use of different data sets and different methodologies for measuring total compensation (particularly with respect to valuing equity and pension components of pay), there is one, universally acknowledged fact: The amount executives are compensated has risen dramatically since the early 1990s. In the following paragraphs, we will see just how much U.S. executives are paid, how their pay has changed over time, and how it has changed relative to both ordinary workers and the executives' international peers.

It is important to note that the following paragraphs look not only at CEO pay but also at executive compensation more broadly. For, while most public attention has focused on CEO pay, the fact is that the compensation of many other high-level executives has also seen a dramatic rise. It is important, too, to broaden the focus beyond merely the compensation levels of executives at the economy's largest companies and to consider both the absolute amount and the historical trends in executive pay at smaller public companies. Accordingly, the following paragraphs include information about executives other than CEOs and about firms outside the large-cap Standard & Poor's 500. Including this information will provide some balance against a sensationalist tendency to focus on the most extreme cases and will give a more complete picture of current executive compensation practices.

In 2008, chief executive officers at Standard & Poor's (S&P) 500 firms averaged $10.4 million in pay. Median pay in 2008 was less, at $7.7 million, indicating that some executives took home far more than the average of their peers (AFL-CIO 2009). However, executives at smaller firms earned substantially less. We also see substantial compensation for executives at mid-cap and small-cap firms. In 2003, CEOs at the S&P 400 mid-cap firms earned average compensation of $4 million compared to $9.1 million for CEOs of S&P 500 firms. In that same year, S&P 600 small-cap CEOs had mean earnings of $2 million (Bebchuk and Grinstein 2005). These figures generally exclude the value of CEO pension plans and other deferred compensation, which can be a quite sizable figure. One estimate is that S&P 500 CEOs retire with an average of $10.1 million in their Supplemental Executive Retirement Plans (SERPs), which are special pension plans arranged for high-salary executives (Anderson et al. 2007).

Total compensation awarded to the top four executives below the CEO is also substantial. In 2003, the average compensation for these other four executives, in sum, was $12.3 million in S&P 500 firms, $5.4 million in S&P 400 firms, and $2.7 million in S&P 600 firms (Bebchuk and Grinstein 2005). These figures represent a dramatic increase in executive compensation over the past 20 years. Between 1989 and 2007, average CEO compensation in a set of large publicly traded firms in a *Wall Street Journal* survey increased from $4.6 million to $12.3 million, a growth of 167 percent. Median CEO compensation for these same firms increased from $4.2 million to $8.6 million, a growth of 107 percent (Mishel, Bernstein, and Shierholz 2009).

Relative to their international peers, U.S. executives fare quite well. In 2005, average CEO compensation in the United States was well over two times that of CEOs in 13 other advanced economies. It was nearly twice what was paid to British, German, and French CEOs and nearly four times Japanese CEO pay. This international disparity remains despite the fact that in the past few decades CEO pay in some of those nations increased at rates equal to or greater than that in the U.S. (Kaplan 2008; Mishel, Bernstein, and Shierholz 2009).

U.S. CEO pay is also quite generous relative to the pay of average workers. In 2008, the average S&P 500 CEO, at $10.4 million, earned 280 times the approximately $37,000 annual pay of a typical full-time American worker (as reported by the Bureau of Labor Statistics). The median CEO compensation was still over 200 times the median worker's pay. The average for the large set of over 2,700 CEOs reveals that their pay was only 68 times greater than that of the average worker. These figures, especially for the CEOs of larger firms, reveal another dramatic increase. In 1980, the ratio of CEO to worker pay was approximately 40:1 (Mishel, Bernstein, and Shierholz 2009). These disparities between U.S. executives and their workers dwarf those in most other industrialized nations. In Europe, the ratios are typically closer to 25:1; in Japan, the ratio is closer to 10:1 (Grossman 2009; Mishel, Bernstein, and Shierholz 2009).

The primary explanation for both the rapid increase in executive pay and the widening gap between executives and their workers is that the use of equity-based compensation, in particular the use of stock options, increased markedly in the 1990s. In 1993, equity-based compensation (including both restricted stock and options) was 41 percent of total compensation for S&P 500 CEOs. That percentage increased to 78 percent in 2000 and dropped to 59 percent in 2003 (Bebchuk and Grinstein 2005). And, since compensation for U.S. executives depends more on equity than does the compensation of either ordinary U.S. workers or the CEOs' international peers, the spread between U.S. executives and those two comparison groups was bound to widen.

This increasing spread between ordinary workers and executives is probably most responsible for the waves of public complaint over the past few decades. And the public outcry, in turn, has been responsible for statutory and regulatory responses targeting perceived excesses in executive pay. In response to earlier public criticism in 1992, the Securities and Exchange Commission (SEC) in the United States enacted rules requiring publicly traded companies to include shareholder resolutions on CEO pay and also required greater disclosure of executive pay in the annual proxy statements mailed to shareholders. The Clinton administration pushed for and won legislation capping the tax deductibility of non-performance-based executive pay at $1 million (Jensen, Murphy, and Wruck 2004).

SEC regulations taking effect in 2007 required even more explicit disclosure of executive compensation, including the basis for severance and bonus arrangements. After the stock market crash in late 2008, proposed federal legislation would require greater independence for board of directors compensation committees and would allow shareholders a nonbinding vote on executive compensation packages, a "say on pay" similar to what has been in place in Britain since 2003 (Armstrong 2009; Cho et al. 2009).

Some caution might be in order for these governmental responses to public outrage, however. In the aftermath of the statutory and regulatory actions of the early 1990s, executive pay exploded. Some hold that the greater disclosure requirements imposed at that time by the SEC made it easier to compare CEO pay packages and provided some impetus to a ratcheting-up effect as executives who were paid less than their peers argued for more. And the $1 million cap on the deductibility of non-performance pay simultaneously made $1 million the minimum and greatly increased the use of stock options in compensation packages. Thus, some claim the result of these federal actions had the unintended consequence of inflating executive pay (Jensen, Murphy, and Wruck 2004; Walker 2009).

THE ACADEMIC CONTEST OVER EXECUTIVE PAY

The academic debate over the propriety of recent executive pay practices has been dominated by two competing hypotheses. One view, the *managerial power* perspective, holds that current executive pay results from the ability of management to effectively influence its own compensation. This view generally suggests that current pay is excessive in amount and is dysfunctional in its composition. The alternative view, the *efficient contracting* perspective, holds that executive compensation can be explained as the result of optimal or efficient arm's-length bargaining between high-level executives and the boards that set their pay.

Interestingly, these contesting views share much in common despite the sometimes heated exchanges between their proponents. That is because both take shareholder value as the ultimate criterion by which to assess the propriety of executive compensation. The managerial power hypothesis suggests that shareholders have lost value by the pay-setting practices that have dominated the recent past. The efficient contracting hypothesis argues both that the evidence for efficiency-distorting managerial power is inconsistent with broader corporate trends and that there are good shareholder-value reasons for current practice.

Managerial Power/Rent Extraction

The core idea of the managerial power hypothesis is that upper-level management, because of its position, can influence corporate policy and decisions by the board of directors. This influence allows management to increase its pay at the expense of shareholders. The hypothesis does not suggest that management's power is plenary; rather, it argues that management is inherently limited in what economic rents it can extract. A primary limit is imposed by what the defenders of the view describe as *outrage costs*. While management has influence over its pay, it must avoid actions that engender public and/or shareholder outrage and that might imperil its privileged position. Central to the managerial power explanation, then, is an account of the specific strategies management uses to avoid creating that outrage by disguising pay, by arranging for *stealth pay*. As such, this perspective holds that executives are overpaid and that the complex composition of their pay packages contributes to this overpayment. The managerial power hypothesis, then, is that the more granular features of recent executive pay practices are not reasonably explained as the result of arm's-length bargaining between executives and their firms (Bebchuk, Fried, and Walker 2002; Bebchuk and Fried 2004; Bebchuk and Grinstein 2005).

The features of executive pay that receive the most attention in managerial power accounts include stock options, restricted stock grants, pensions, severance, and bonuses. It will be helpful to address how the managerial power account addresses each of these elements of executive pay in turn. Stock options are, in theory, a reasonable way of overcoming the agency problem that lies at the heart of discussions in modern finance. The problem is how to align the interests of management (agents) with those of the shareholders (principals) they are supposed to represent. Once ownership and control of the modern corporation were separated, it became necessary to design strategies that minimized the potential for management to exercise its control over corporate decisions in ways that enriched them at the expense of investors. It would seem that encouraging executives to see their interests as coincident with shareholders by compensating them with stock options might help to overcome the agency problem.

But proponents of the managerial power hypothesis believe the devil is in the details of recent option grants. Actual option awards were not indexed to general stock market advances, and they had their exercise prices set at the price of the stock on the day of the award. Management power theorists suggest that if companies wanted to use options, they could have indexed them and/or set their exercise prices higher. That, they contend, would provide at least as much incentive and would cost the firm less (Bebchuk and Fried 2004; Walker 2005). Since firms almost never did this, there ought to be suspicion that option design was overly influenced by management (or compensation consultants hired by management). And firms failed to calibrate option awards with incentives because each year they continued to award roughly the same numbers of options to their executives despite the fact that stock prices increased dramatically (Bratton 2005).

Moreover, many firms engaged in practices that removed both risk and incentive from their option grants through repricing. Repricing occurs when a firm lowers the exercise price of existing options whose original strike price is above the current market price. Instead of using risk to link the interests of management to the interests of investors, repricing effectively allows management to hedge against the losses that shareholders suffer (Bebchuk and Fried 2004; Posner 2009). Further evidence for the management power hypothesis is provided by research that establishes a systematic connection between options and the timing of corporate announcements that might influence share price. Often option awards precede news that increases stock price while stock sales by insiders follow the release of good news (Bebchuk and Fried 2004; Henderson et al. 2008).

Finally, some hold that options by their very nature are not the most effective mechanism for binding the interests of executives and investors. Since rising stock prices will offer rewards to option holders while falling prices impose no actual loss, executives may be encouraged by options to pursue overly risky strategies (Bogle 2008; Posner 2009). While this concern focuses on the composition of pay, it would be reasonable to assume that the potentially perverse incentives created by option pay would be magnified when the amount of pay at stake is large. Some suggest, for instance, that this was a primary cause of the widespread use of overleveraged and risky corporate strategies that helped to precipitate the recession of 2007–2009 (Phillips 2008; Posner 2009).

The use of restricted stock grants also comes under criticism by proponents of the managerial power hypothesis. Restricted stock compensation is an outright grant of stock as opposed to an option grant that entitles one to buy stock at a particular price. As such, restricted stock grants continue to have real value even when stock prices fall. While this more effectively makes executives into shareholders than does the use of options, the critics point out that the use of restricted stock grants increased at precisely the time when the stock market was falling in 2001. Falling markets, of course, make options less valuable for executives (Bebchuk and Fried 2004).

Since options and restricted stock constitute such a large portion of executive earnings and are a main reason for the explosion of executive compensation over the past two decades, it is worth noting that the impact of these compensation packages within firms can be substantial. One estimate is that the aggregate compensation of the top five executives in a large database of firms was equal to 12.8 percent of earnings in the period 2000–2002. After the recession of 2001–2002, compensation fell to 9.8 percent of firm earnings (Bebchuk and Grinstein 2005). While this does not establish that shareholders have suffered economically compared to what might have been the case had the share of earnings taken by top management been lower (since the highly compensated management might have been incentivized to produce higher stock prices), there is some reason to question whether the equity awarding practices of the recent past were truly in shareholders' interests.

Additional questions arise about the design of equity pay. The use of equity-based compensation expanded at a rapid pace in the late 1990s but this expansion was not accompanied by any diminution in cash compensation. If the move toward equity compensation was supposed to address the agency problem by realigning management's interests with the interests of shareholders, one might have expected some substitution of equity for cash compensation. However, cash compensation continued to rise through this period, though not at the pace of equity-based pay (Bebchuk and Grinstein 2005; Jensen, Murphy, and Wruck 2004; Walker 2005).

Pensions and severance agreements are two other areas of executive compensation that have come under criticism for being both overly generous and largely hidden from public view, that is until very recently. Until new SEC rules took effect in 2007, the exact value of pension commitments to current and past executives was difficult to determine. Yet those benefits often totaled millions of dollars. Since public discussion of executive pay usually focuses on dollar figures disclosed in proxy statements, the real level of pension compensation is often hidden from public and shareholder view (Bebchuk and Jackson 2005).

Disclosure of severance pay that a firm has committed to has also until recently been largely absent in proxy statements. The SEC rules of 2007 require detailed explanation of termination payments in cases of change in control and termination without cause. Often the commitments firms made were quite large. Moreover, there is no provision in most plans for a reduction of the severance award if the executive found new work (Bebchuk and Fried 2004). It is important to note that since the value of pension and severance pay is usually guaranteed by contract, these forms of compensation are performance insensitive, which raises a question about why boards of directors would commit to such (previously) hidden and large elements of compensation.

Bonuses are a final element of executive compensation that is subject to critique as overgenerous, insufficiently performance sensitive, and open to management manipulation. Performance targets such as earnings per share, cash flow, total revenues, new product development, acquisitions, and the like are ripe for gaming activities by top management. Executives can manage earnings quarterly or yearly by controlling the timing of sales or purchases and by discretionary use of accruals. They can manipulate analysts by managing expectations in guidance given about future performance. In fact, there is an emerging volume of academic literature correlating the incidence of outright fraud, earnings management, and the management of analyst expectations with the strength of incentive plans (Bergstresser and Phillipon 2006; Bollinger and Kast 2003; Cornett et al. 2008; Harris 2008; Harris and Bromiley 2006; Henderson et al. 2008; Marquardt et al. 2009; Ordonez et al. 2009). There is also evidence that performance targets are set in ways that make them easy to achieve, effectively decoupling incentive pay from firm performance (Brush 2009a; Kim and Yang 2009).

Manipulating information or corporate activity in order to meet timed targets can damage long-term firm value, for instance by reducing long-term and growth-enhancing investment in order to temporarily inflate earnings, thus enriching management at the expense of shareholders. Enron is merely the poster child case in point of a much more common earnings management phenomenon (Bebchuk and Fried 2004; Jensen, Murphy, and Wruck 2004). Since the potential for abuse is so significant and well known, critics of executive compensation practices question why boards are willing to base substantial bonus pay on easily gamed performance targets.

The managerial power approach, then, regards the details of executive compensation as confirmation that compensation practices are often not designed in ways that best protect the interests of shareholders and are, rather, designed with a complexity and obscurity that conceals management appropriation of corporate resources. Of course, not everyone accepts the accuracy of this analysis of executive compensation. Critics of the managerial power hypothesis have pointed to a number of facts that would pose challenges to the view: How can it explain that the hiring of new, outside CEOs has increased and that newly hired outside CEOs are paid more than internally promoted CEOs? How is it that increased executive compensation is tied to managerial power at a time when the role of institutional shareholders has increased, as has the incidence of independent directors and pay transparency (Bratton 2005; Yablon 2007)?

Answers to these puzzles are possible, though the nature of the answers does not always neatly accord with a description of the pay-setting process as an exercise of power. As was noted earlier, transparency in pay will not, by itself, be sufficient to rein in compensation unless it is also accompanied by effective influence. There is reason to believe that shareholders are gradually gaining greater influence, but that, too, is a slow process. As an instance in point, shareholder resolutions on pay have been gaining larger shares of proxy votes but are often still short of majorities (Brush 2009b). Moreover, corporations regularly recommend against such proxy measures and have even been able to effectively lobby institutional investors to vote against such measures (Morgensen 2006). And as John Bogle notes, the time horizon for institutional investors is rather limited, with the average stock now held for less than a year (Bogle 2008). Further, the increases in reporting requirements have been implemented only gradually, and they continue to permit extremely complex packages that are difficult for an ordinary investor to fully understand. It is worth noting that it is only with the most recent SEC rules that pay packages have become clearer; the run-up in pay, of course, occurred before those new rules were in force.

And even with more independent directors and increased hiring of new CEOs from outside, there are, nonetheless, factors that explain high pay as something other than shareholder maximizing choices. When hiring a new CEO from the outside, boards are often under pressure to appoint quickly in order to reassure the markets (Yablon 2007). The executive pay decisions by directors, who are limited in time and access to information, are often guided by compensation consultants. Use of consultants will naturally ratchet pay upward since few boards will want to send signals either to the new executive or to the markets with a compensation package below the top quartile of peer corporations. Finally, it is natural that even outside hires will eventually come to have influence over the continued service of current board members, who are often themselves CEOs and who are richly rewarded for their board service (Bratton 2005; Posner 2009; Yablon 2007). These social and psychological factors, of course, do not easily reduce to a simple management power account. Instead, they suggest that the complex social psychology of the institutional pay-setting process makes optimal contracting outcomes difficult to achieve.

Efficient Contracting

The alternative to the management power hypothesis posits that executive compensation is the result of efficient contracting between executives and the boards that represent shareholders. The efficient contract hypothesis attempts to defend as ethically appropriate both the large amount of executive pay and the composition of that pay.

One primary approach is to argue that recent executive pay practices, contrary to the claims of the management power hypothesis, are ex ante rational and voluntary agreements forged by boards of directors in pursuit of shareholders' interests. This approach provides an account of the size of compensation packages as well as of the use of option repricing and generous pensions and severance payments as a potentially reasonable way to structure management incentives so that they might lead to maximal shareholder value.

Efficient contract adherents note that management is often personally risk averse and fears losing income if dismissed for failures in corporate performance. Diversified investors, by contrast, might wish management to be more aggressive in pursuing potentially profitable business strategies (Bratton 2005). The use of equity grants is, as previously noted, one way to align the interests of managers and shareholders. However, since shareholders have diversified risk while management has income risk concentrated in their firm, the use of option grants in compensation might make sense because they provide risk-averse managers with upside potential while mitigating somewhat against loss (Edmans and Gabaix 2009). However, because options are not a guarantee of income, their value to an executive will be less than the value of cash compensation. Hence, in order to compensate an executive for the risk inherent in options, the dollar amount of options will have to be greater. Hence, the use of options is a potentially rational practice that motivates personally risk-averse executives to take reasonable strategic risks for the firm, but it is also a practice that, in a rising market, is likely to inflate executives' earnings.

Large executive earnings are also a potentially rational way to deal with motivating managers to compete for a decreasing number of available positions as they climb the corporate ladder. The tournament analogy explains that since the probability of success decreases with the number of remaining prizes as one advances in competition, participants will be less likely to invest in the competition for top prizes unless the prizes are substantial enough to make up for the possibility of wasted effort. Hence, top corporate jobs must carry substantial compensation if firms are to motivate employees inside and outside the firm to compete for them. Moreover, since monitoring performance is harder for top executives, it makes sense to use share value as a proxy and to link pay to share value through the use of stock and options (Stabile 2002; Thomas 2003). Ex ante, then, it appears a potentially reasonable strategy to pay large sums and to deliver that pay in the form of stock and options.

The practice of repricing can also be made to appear more rational than its description in the management power hypothesis. If a firm wishes to retain an executive because it believes that he has the potential to increase its stock price (either because the firm has confidence in his abilities or because it does not want to send damaging signals to the market), it may have reason to reprice currently underwater options as a way of retaining both incentives and the executive (Colvin 2001; Yablon 2007).

Finally, it may make sense ex ante to agree to significant severance and pension packages. Again, executives are at risk of income loss if they are dismissed and are less diversified than the firm's investors. In order to mitigate the effects of personal risk aversion, it might make sense to offer the executive a partial hedge against income loss in the attempt to increase the incentive to pursue reasonable corporate risks. Without this hedge, it may be difficult to attract and retain the executive talent that a firm seeks (Edmans and Gabaix 2009). Thus, the efficient contract hypothesis argues that it is possible to account for seemingly costly compensation practices as, in reality, reasonable and ethically defensible ex ante arrangements for corporate boards that are attempting to protect shareholder wealth.

Another approach used in defense of recent executive compensation practices has been to argue that they have generally been ex post beneficial to investors while also reflecting more broadly accepted economic norms. Some note that the run-up in executive pay occurred at a time when shareholders were experiencing dramatic increases in the value of their holdings (Gabaix and Landier 2008; Jensen and Murphy 1990; Kaplan 2008). While a straightforward causal account linking pay to corporate performance is difficult to make, it does appear that executive compensation rose in close proportion to the increase in the stock market, lending some credence to the idea that executives were paid appropriately for performance.

Moreover, the rise in executive pay was more than matched by increases in the compensation of other groups. Star athletes and entertainers have seen their pay jump. More dramatically, the compensation of managers of private hedge funds has skyrocketed well beyond the increases seen by executives in publicly traded firms (Kaplan 2008). If current compensation norms across the country are an indication of generally accepted market outcomes, then the pay of corporate executives appears within socially tolerated limits. The efficient contract hypothesis thus attempts to provide accounts that justify recent executive compensation practices. However, as with the explanatory account offered by the management power hypothesis, these attempted justifications are also not without critics.

The attempt to argue that executive compensation is justified as an ex ante rational contract must confront a number of difficulties. First, there are serious questions about whether boards have represented the interests of shareholders effectively. There is certainly evidence of shareholder complaints about perceived excesses in executive compensation over recent years (Biggs 2005; Brush 2009b; Pitman 2009). Many find that boards, even with the increased incidence of independent directors, are still too generous to their executives and fail to adequately discharge their fiduciary duty to shareholders (Bogle 2005, 2008; Posner 2009; Yablon 2007). The fact that even some of the most vocal opponents of the management power hypothesis now admit that recent compensation practices were problematic, both in their structure and their amounts, suggests that something has been amiss in contemporary executive pay. Steven Kaplan, for instance, in commenting on recent practices, says "as in the case with pensions, it seems likely that Boards will respond to adverse shareholder reaction and improved disclosure to make less use of severance when it is not appropriate" (Kaplan 2008). Michael Jensen, widely regarded as one of the fathers of the movement toward equity pay, also has argued that recent practices may have been dysfunctional and may have caused increased management pay at the expense of longer-term share value (Fuller and Jensen 2002; Jensen 2001; Jensen, Murphy, and Wruck 2004). Jensen was even quoted as far back as 2001 saying, "I've generally worried these guys weren't getting paid enough. But now, even I'm troubled" (Colvin 2001). So, even if the past practice has not been due to illicit exercise of management power and has instead been due to a miscalculation by boards, that analysis, while not condemning boards for a past moral failing, must still conclude that pay has been inappropriately set. That concession would seem to entail a fiduciary obligation to reform executive pay going forward, regardless of what moral assessment is made of past practice.

The use of the tournament analogy in the ex ante analysis also raises questions. First, there is a difficult and as yet unanswered question about the net corporate effects of the consequent dramatic gaps in pay between executives and ordinary workers. In theory, the high pay for executives is a necessary motivational tool. There are some, however, who suggest that allowing such wide gaps in corporate pay will have corrosive effects on corporate morale, on the ability to encourage teamwork, and on the retention and/or motivation of critically important managers who do not win the executive suite (Blair and Stout 1999). There are also empirical questions to be answered about just how much remuneration is necessary in order to motivate competition for executive positions and effort by those who occupy them. It might be reasonable to think that the status and authority of executive positions would provide some incremental psychic reward that would reduce the need for monetary compensation. As one very highly compensated executive said, "If I had been paid 50 percent more, I would not have done it better. If I had been paid 50 percent less, I would not have done it worse" (Pitman 2009). As it stands now, the ex ante argument amounts merely to the claim that it is *possible* to provide a narrative that makes recent executive pay compatible with shareholder value.

The attempt to defend the amount and composition of executive compensation by reference to positive results for shareholders and by the comparable pay of others also has been challenged. While it is true that share values increased through the 1990s and early 2000s and that executive pay tracked those increases fairly closely, it may be that the period in question was historically aberrant. A number of commentators suggest precisely that, arguing that the rise in stock prices was an historical bubble, fed by unusually low interest rates. This bubble allowed executives to reap large rewards not from their modest contributions to long-term corporate performance, merely a gain of 1.2 percent by one measure, but from the speculative return created by an overvalued equity market (Biggs 2005; Bogle 2005, 2008).

And while it is undoubtedly true that others, including athletes, entertainers, and hedge fund managers, have seen their compensation grow into the millions, sometimes even far surpassing corporate executives' pay, that fact, by itself, may be insufficient justification. For this to constitute a compelling justification for the distributional outcomes of the market, we would have to believe that the social norms that define the space within which the market operates were adequate ones. That is, merely because a practice is accepted does not mean that it is acceptable. We have examples where socially accepted norms influenced market behavior, yet those norms themselves were morally questionable. The social acceptance of widespread racial and gender discrimination, which was heavily reflected in labor markets, is a case in point.

We should also note that a shift in social attitudes has not been universal. Certainly there have been complaints about the salaries of athletes, entertainers, and hedge fund managers as vigorous as there have been about executives. There is even evidence that the size and composition of executive pay is sensitive to regional variations in attitudes about wealth and inequality (Kuhnen and Niessen 2009). We should not overstate the degree to which recently increasing disparities in wealth and income distributions are in fact socially accepted. Any more complete defense of executive pay, then, must move beyond merely describing it as accepted by the market and must show that it is compatible with more basic ethical considerations.

A BROADER ETHICAL EVALUATION OF EXECUTIVE PAY

How might one assess whether the actual operation of markets is compatible with deeper ethical concerns? What might those deeper ethical concerns be? Interestingly, the public outrage mentioned at the outset of this chapter provides some clues. Expressions of that outrage often rely implicitly on two such more fundamental ethical considerations: the common good and basic fairness.

It has been common in the finance literature over the past decades to argue that pursuit of shareholder value by management is the best way to assure that the society in aggregate reaps economic benefit (Jensen, Murphy, and Wruck 2004). Whether that claim is true (and there are equally numerous challenges to it over the past decades), it has become clear that even sympathetic voices have begun to question whether recent executive pay practices have been good for either share-holders or society at large. Even the usually management-friendly Conference Board recently issued a taskforce report on executive compensation. In it, the task-force called for serious reform in pay practices, including reform of multiyear employment contracts with generous severance, golden parachutes in case of change of control, pay gross-ups for taxes executives owe on their compensation, option repricing, and the like. The taskforce report said, "these . . . 'controversial pay practices'. . . may undermine employee morale, raise 'red flags' for investors, erode the company's credibility, and weaken the trust of key constituencies—employees, shareholders, and the public." Of course, these have been common elements of executive pay in recent years. And, while the concerns raised by the Conference Board address the composition of executive pay, the report must also be seen as critiquing the absolute amount of pay executives have received, since it is these very elements that have been the source of much of their increased pay (Conference Board 2009). That even those who have been sympathetic are now calling for reform of pay practices suggests that those practices have been less than optimal for either shareholders in particular or for society generally.

Another utilitarian concern, not unique to executive compensation, can be raised about the degree of income and wealth inequality that can be tolerated if a society wishes to avoid dysfunction and remain truly democratic. Some social critics question the effect of widening gaps in income on the bonds essential for social cohesiveness. While this is not a concern about executive pay uniquely, it challenges an economic trend of which exploding executive pay is a part (Frank 2007). Of course, these utilitarian arguments depend crucially on contestable empirical claims about the causal effects of executive pay and of inequality more generally. A careful assessment of the truth of those claims is certainly beyond the scope of this chapter. Nonetheless, these *common good* arguments pose questions that need to be taken seriously.

Fairness is the other fundamental moral concern underlying much complaint about executive pay. Of course, as the parent of any teen can attest, an appeal to fairness is often a mask merely for an expression of dislike. Nonetheless, it remains a crucial concept in the moral discourse of our culture. Mere perceptions of unfairness are often sufficient to generate dysfunction within an organization, as the Conference Board report recognizes (Conference Board, 2009). And, despite the woolliness of the concept, it is still possible to give a reasonable operational account of fairness that can be applied to distributional issues.

The fairness of a distribution, when the benefits distributed are the product of a common enterprise, can be determined by the relative contribution made and risk assumed by the respective parties. If we apply these ideas of risk and contribution to the compensation of executives, we might have reason for accepting increased compensation over the past decades. The tasks, and the associated skill sets, required of executives have certainly increased in complexity during that time. Moreover, the risk of termination for executives has also increased. So we might conclude that increased compensation for executives would be fair.

However, distributional fairness is necessarily a relative matter, and it will be crucial to compare the relative risk and contribution of executives with those of others. Certainly, the complexity of tasks for ordinary workers has also increased over the past decades, and their risk of termination has also increased dramatically as job security has declined with the increased incidence of permanent layoffs. Thus, it would seem unlikely that we could justify the dramatically widening gap in pay between U.S. executives and their workers on grounds of relative contribution and risk.

Further, when compared to their international peers, it is also not clear that the widening pay gap can be justified. Corporate leadership everywhere has become more challenging as commerce and finance have become globalized. There is even some reason to think that European executives suffer termination at least at rates comparable to that suffered by American executives (Posner 2009). Thus, a reasonable operational understanding of fairness, based on the relative contribution and risk of the respective parties in a common enterprise, seems to support the public perception that the dramatic increases in U.S. executive compensation over the past 20 years violate norms of basic fairness. It leads to suspicion that the size of executive pay packages is a function of a market that increasingly reflects a winner-take-all approach, despite the fact that this approach conflicts with a deeply and widely held moral understanding about fairness.

CONCLUSION

Obviously, a full moral assessment of executive compensation practices would require a much more detailed analysis than that sketched in these final comments about fairness and the common good. Nonetheless, when even the most sympathetic voices begin to identify serious problems in recent executive pay practices, the contours of such an assessment seem to be emerging. At the very least, executive pay needs reform. Whether the need for reform is due to understandable mistakes made by compensation committees of boards of directors or is, instead, due to managerial rent extraction, almost all experts now seem to agree that the composition of executive pay has been less than optimal, both for corporations and for society. And since the elements of that pay that are most in question are precisely those elements that had the greatest impact on the increased absolute amount of pay, we can conclude that both the size and composition of recent executive compensation call for changes to be made.

As an ethical judgment, an absence of substantial change to both the composition and the amount of executive pay in the future would seem in danger of running afoul of directors' fiduciary duties as well as more fundamental moral principles about fairness and the common good. However, since outsized pay packages have become an expected part of the executive suite, it remains to be seen whether those expectations, and the market that accommodates them, can be reset by more vigilant boards.

REFERENCES

AFL-CIO. 2009. 2008 trends in CEO pay. http://www.aflcio.org/corporatewatch/paywatch/pay/index.cfm.

Anderson, Sarah, John Cavanagh, Chuck Collins, Sam Pizzigati, and Mike Lapham. 2007. *Executive excess: The staggering social cost of U.S. business leadership.* Institute for Policy Studies and United for a Fair Economy. http://www.ips-dc.org/reports/070829/executiveexcess.pdf.

Armstrong, Mike. 2009. Opening up top exec's pay. *Philadelphia Inquirer*, July 17, 2009.

BBC News. 2009. Bonus plan for royal bank manager. *BBC News Channel*. May 24. http://news.bbc.co.uk/2/hi/uk_news/scotland/8065851.stm.

Bebchuk, Lucien, and Jesse Fried. 2004. *Pay without performance*. Cambridge, MA: Harvard University Press.

Bebchuk, Lucien, Jesse Fried, and David Walker. 2002. Managerial power and rent extraction in the design of executive compensation. *University of Chicago Law Review* 69:751–846.

Bebchuk, Lucien, and Yaniv Grinstein. 2005. The growth of executive pay. *Oxford Review of Economic Policy* 21:283–303.

Bebchuk, Lucien, and Robert Jackson. 2005. Executive pensions. *Journal of Corporate Law* 30:823–855.

Bergstresser, Daniel, and Thomas Phillipon. 2006. CEO incentives and earnings management. *Journal of Financial Economics* 80:511–529.

Biggs, John. 2005. Executive compensation: Perspectives from a former CEO. Columbia University Symposium Paper.

Blair, Margaret, and Lynn Stout. 1999. A team production theory of corporate law. *Virginia Law Review* 85:248–328.

Boatright, John. 2009. Executive compensation: Unjust or just right? In *Oxford handbook of business ethics*, ed. George G. Brenkert and Tom L. Beauchamp. Oxford: Oxford University Press.

Bogle, John. 2005. The executive compensation system is broken. Columbia University Symposium Paper.

———. 2008. Reflections on CEO compensation. *Academy of Management Perspectives*, May:21–25.

Bolliger, Guido, and Manuel Kast. 2003. Executive compensation and analyst guidance: The link between CEO pay and expectations management. EFA Annual Conference Paper 861.

Bratton, William. 2005. The academic tournament over executive compensation. *California Law Review* 93:5.

Brush, Michael. 2009a. CEOs earn big bonuses for bad year. *MSN Money*. http://articles.moneycentral.msn.com/Investing/Company Focus/ceos-earn-big-bonuses-for-bad-year.aspx.

———. 2009b. How shareholders are fighting greed. *MSN Money*. http://articles.moneycentral.msn.com/learn-how-to-invest/how-shareholders-are-fighting-greed.aspx.

Cho, David, Zachary Goldfarb, and Tomoeh Murakami Tse. 2009. U.S. targets excessive pay for top executives. *Washington Post*, June 11.

Colvin, Geoffrey. 2001. The great CEO pay heist. *Fortune*, June 25.

Conference Board. 2009. *The Conference Board taskforce on executive compensation*. http://conference-board.org/pdf_free/ExecCompensation2009.pdf.

Conway, Merideth. 2008. Money for nothing and the stocks for free: Taxing executive compensation. Legal Studies Research Paper 08-11, Suffolk University Law School.

Cornett, Marcia Millon, Alan Marcus, and Hassan Tehranian. 2008. Corporate governance and pay for performance: The impact of earnings management. *Journal of Financial Economics* 87:357–373.

Creswell, Julie, and Louise Story. 2009. Thain resigns amid losses at Bank of America. *New York Times*, January 23.

Dymski, Gary. 2009. Performance pay? *Newsday*, February 5.

Edmans, Alex, and Xavier Gabaix. 2009. Is CEO pay really inefficient? A survey of new optimal contracting theories. *European Financial Management* 15:486–496.

Evans, Jocelyn, and Frank Hefner. 2009. Business ethics and the decision to adopt golden parachute contracts: Empirical evidence of a concern for all stakeholders. *Journal of Business Ethics* 86:65–79.

Frank, Robert. 2007. *Falling behind: How rising inequality harms the middle class*. Berkeley, CA: University of California Press.

Fuller, Joseph, and Michael Jensen. 2002. Just say no to Wall Street: Putting a stop to the earnings game. *Journal of Applied Corporate Finance* 14:41–46.

Gabaix, Xavier, and Augustin Landier. 2008. Why has CEO pay increased so much? *Quarterly Journal of Economics* 123:49–100.

Grossman, Robert. 2009. Executive pay: Perception and reality. *HR Magazine* 54:4.

Harris, Jared. 2008. What's wrong with executive compensation?" *Journal of Business Ethics* 85:147–156.

Harris, Jared, and Philip Bromiley. 2006. Incentives to cheat: The influence of executive compensation and firm performance on financial misrepresentation. *Organizational Science* 18:350–367.

Henderson, B. Charlene, Adi Masli, Vernon Richardson, and Juan Manuel Sanchez. 2008. Executive compensation and firm performance around layoffs: Maximizing shareholder value or rent extraction? University of Arkansas Working Paper Series.

Jensen, Michael. 2001. Paying people to lie. Harvard NOM Research Paper 01-03.

Jensen, Michael, and Kevin Murphy. 1990. CEO incentives—it's not how much you pay but how. *Harvard Business Review* 3:138–153.

Jensen, Michael, Kevin Murphy, and Eric Wruck. 2004. Remuneration: Where we've been, how we got here, what are the problems, and how to fix them. Harvard Business School NOM Research Paper 04-28.

Kaplan, Steven. 2008. Are U.S. CEOs overpaid? *Academy of Management Perspectives* May 2008: 5–20.

Kim, Daniel Sungyeon, and Jun Yang. 2009. Beating the target: A closer look at annual incentive plans. American Finance Association 2010 Meetings Paper.

Kuhnen, Camelia, and Alexandra Niessen. 2009. Is executive compensation shaped by public attitudes? American Finance Association 2010 Meetings Paper.

Lindsay, Robert. 2009. RBS hands £2.3M bonus to new executive. *Times Online*, August 19. http://business.timesonline.co.uk/tol/business/industry_sectors/banking_and_finance/.

Marquardt, Carol, Christine Tan, and Susan Young. 2009. Accelerated share repurchases, bonus compensation, and CEO horizons. Working Paper, CUNY.

McCarrol, Thomas. 1992. Executive pay. *Time*, May 4.

Mercer. 2008. Mercer issues study of US CEO compensation trends. *Mercer*. http://uk.mercer.com.

Mishel, Lawrence, Jared Bernstein, and Heidi Shierholz. 2009. *The state of working America 2008–2009*. Ithaca, NY: ILR Press.

Morgenson, Gretchen. 2006. Investors vs. Pfizer: Guess who wins? *New York Times*, April 23.

Ordonez, Lisa, Maurice Schweitzer, Adam Galinsky, and Maz Bazerman. 2009. Goals gone wild: The systematic side effects of over-prescribing goal setting. Working Paper 09-083, Harvard Business School.

Phillips, Kevin. 2008. *Bad money: Reckless finance, failed politics, and the global crisis of American capitalism*. New York: Viking.

Pitman, Joanna. 2009. Bonfire of the bonuses. *Management Today*, July: 47–51.

Posner, Richard. 2009. Are American CEOs overpaid, and, if so, what should be done about it? *Duke Law Journal* 58:1013–1048.

Protess, Ben. 2008. No severance (but a bonus!) for WaMu's 3-week CEO. *ProPublica*. October 3. http://www.probublica.org/no-severance-for-wamus-3-week-ceo/.

Slack, Megan. 2009. Merrill Lynch bonuses were 22 times the size of AIG's. *Huffington Post*, March 31.

Smith, Aaron. 2008. WaMu CEO: 3 weeks work, $18M. *CNNMoney.com*, September 26. http://money.cnn.com/2008/09/26/news/companies/fishman_wamu/index.htm.

Stabile, Susan. 2002. One for A, two for B, and four hundred for C: The widening gap between executives and rank and file employees. *University of Michigan Journal of Law Reform* 36:115.

Thomas, Landon, and Jenny Anderson. 2005. Report details huge pay deal Grasso set up. *New York Times*, February 3.

Thomas, Randall. 2003. Should directors reduce executive pay? *Hastings Law Journal* 54:437.

Treanor, Jill. 2009. RBS bows to government demand to slash bonuses. *Guardian*, February 17. http://www.guardian.co.uk/business/2009/feb/17/rbs-bonus-payments/.

Trejos, Nancy. 2009. How much does your CEO really make? Go figure. *Washington Post*, February 8.

Walker, David. 2005. The manager's share. *William and Mary Law Review* 587:47–62.

———. 2009. The challenge of improving the long-term focus of executive pay. Working Paper 09-22, Boston University School of Law.

Yablon, Charles. 2007. Is the market for CEOs rational? *New York University Journal of Law and Business* 4:89–141.

ABOUT THE AUTHOR

John J. McCall is a professor of philosophy and management at Saint Joseph's University. He is also director of the Pedro Arrupe Center for Business Ethics at the Haub School of Business at Saint Joseph's. He has previously taught at the McDonough School of Business at Georgetown University and the Wharton School at the University of Pennsylvania. His published research in business ethics has covered employment issues, product liability, advertising, and theories of corporate responsibility. He is author/editor, with Joseph R. DesJardins, of *Contemporary Issues in Business Ethics*, 5th ed. (Wadsworth, 2004).

CHAPTER 30

Boards of Directors

DAN R. DALTON
Harold A. Poling Chair of Strategic Management, Kelley School, Indiana University

CATHERINE M. DALTON
David H. Jacobs Chair of Strategic Management, Kelley School, Indiana University

INTRODUCTION

The pillar on which the intersection of finance and ethics rests, always delicate, is leaning precariously. That general foundation is agency theory (for compendia see, e.g., Bratton 2001; Coffee 2001; Dalton, Hitt, Certo, and Dalton 2008; Eisenhardt 1989; Mizruchi 2004; Walsh and Seward 1990), but more specifically the notion that the independence of key corporate parties mitigates the fundamental agency problem (Dalton et al. 2008; Eisenberg 1976; Gilson 1996; Jensen 1993).

The formal development of agency theory arose from the constitutive change in the ownership of publicly traded companies in the United States (e.g., Berle and Means 1932; see also Berle 1959; Bratton 1989, 2001; Mizruchi 2004; Stigler and Friedland 1983). Through the late nineteenth century, the owner of a large-scale enterprise was almost certainly also serving as its presiding officer. Through the first few decades of the 1900s, however, such owners were increasingly less likely to manage their own enterprises. In their place were professional managers who would henceforth direct these enterprises. Even so, the principal owners retained the clear preponderance of the equity in these firms. By contrast, however, the new class of professional managers owned little equity in the firm. From this pervasive separation of ownership of the enterprise from its management came the fundamental agency problem.

The owners would likely require a series of interventions to assure that their interests as owners of the enterprise did not diverge substantially from the interests of its managers (Fama 1980; Fama and Jensen 1983a, b; Jensen and Meckling 1976; Mizruchi 1983; see also Chandler 1977). Shleifer and Vishny (1997; see also Roe 1994, 2005; Ross 1973; Mizruchi 2004) underscored the gravity of the agency problem and noted that evidence for concomitant excesses is robust. Among the suggested means to mitigate such excesses was the assurance that the management of these firms was independent from the stewards of the enterprise—principally its board of directors.

Some 200 years before the formal explication of agency theory, Adam Smith, in *An Inquiry into the Nature and Causes of the Wealth of Nations* (1776; from Hutchins' edition 1952, 324), provided a prescient observation regarding this notion of independence and joint stock companies (the historical equivalent of contemporary publicly traded companies). He noted that managers of other people's money cannot be expected to "watch over it with the same anxious vigilance" as one would expect from owners and that "negligence and profusion, therefore, must always prevail, more or less, in the management of the affairs of such a company." Some years later, Davis (2005, 145; see also Shleifer and Vishny 1977) provided a commendatory summary of the role of agency theory: "This solution to managerialism became perhaps the dominant theory of the public corporation."

From the earliest discussions of the fundamental agency problem, theorists were aware that boards of directors, as the stewards of the shareholders, would not be effective monitors of management if this relationship were tainted by self-interest (Fama 1980; Fama and Jensen 1983a, b; Jensen and Meckling 1976; Mizruchi 1983). Jacobsen (1996, 985), in what he refers to as the "classic articulation" on this point, cites Chief Justice Layton in *Guth v. Loft, Inc.* (5 A.2d 503, 510 [Del. 1939]):

> *Corporate officers and directors are not permitted to use their position of trust and confidence to further their private interests. . . . A public policy, existing through the years, and derived from a profound knowledge of human characteristics and motives, has established a rule that demands of a corporate officer or director, peremptorily and inexorably, the most scrupulous observance of this duty, not only affirmatively to protect the interests of the corporation committed to his charge. . . . The rule that requires an undivided and unselfish loyalty to the corporation demands that there shall be no conflict between duty and self-interest.*

This attention to the independence elements of agency theory and potential conflicts of interests by firms' senior managers and boards of directors abets our discussion of the intersection of ethics and finance. In addition, we should note the passage of United States legislation variously referred to as the top "legal milestone of the last ten years" (Myers 2005, 1), the "most comprehensive public company legislation since the 1930s" (Green 2004, 19), and "the most significant piece of legislation in the history of federal securities regulations" (Bradley and Wallenstein 2006, 67). In the wake of a series of high-profile corporate scandals, the Public Company Accounting Reform and Investor Protection Act of 2002 (aka Sarbanes-Oxley Act, Sarbox, or SOX) was passed by the U.S. Congress with an imposing (423 to 3 vote in the House of Representatives; 99 to 0 vote in the Senate) bipartisan and bicameral mandate (e.g., Bradley and Wallenstein 2006; Gourevitch and Shinn 2005).

SOX sets forth a series of specific requirements regarding the internal governance structures and functions of public corporations (Bradley and Wallenstein 2006; Monks and Minow 2008; Romano 2005; see also Bebchuk, Cohen, and Ferrell 2009; Bhagat, Bolton, and Romano 2008). Specifically relevant to the issue of independence, SOX guidelines set forth that boards of directors' audit committees must be comprised of a minimum of three persons, all of whom must be independent. Since all members of the audit committee must be independent, the chairpersons of audit committees will be independent as well.

Shortly after the passage of SOX, the listing exchanges (e.g., NYSE, NASDAQ) set forth a series of corporate governance guidelines (see New York Stock Exchange Guidelines [2009] and NASDAQ Stock Exchange Guidelines [2009] for a summary; see also Cain [2003] for a broad history and discussion concerning listing exchange standards). Among a host of guidelines were several that are relevant to the discussion of independence. Consider, for example, that the board of directors must be composed of a majority of independent members. Beyond that, the compensation and nominating/corporate governance committees must comprise a minimum of three members, all of whom must be independent. In this case, too, since all members of these committees must be independent, the chairpersons of these committees will also be independent.

In subsequent sections, we focus on two elements of boards' structure and the relationship of each, singly or in concert, to the intersection of ethics and finance. One of these is the composition of the board, specifically issues related to the independence of the board. A second aspect is the leadership structure of the board (*duality*). For this, the issue is the extent to which CEOs simultaneously serve as board chairpersons.

In each of these sections, we also examine what we have referred to as a collision of theories and a collapsing of application. The first issue is the extent to which the reliance on agency theory has compromised other enterprise theories. In the second, we provide a discussion of the extent to which finance, and corporate governance studies more generally, contribute to contemporary applications and practice. Also, we consider the extent to which any of the prior elements currently inform the intersection of ethics and finance.

LEADERSHIP STRUCTURE OF THE BOARD

There is a fundamental element with regard to the board of directors that informs the notion of independence in corporate governance. Often referred to as board leadership structure (Brickley, Coles, and Jarrell 1997; Dalton, Daily, Ellstrand, and Johnson 1998), at issue is the manner by which the board arranges the leadership role of the firm's CEO and the chairperson of the board. The question is in what other capacity, if any, does the CEO of the firm simultaneously serve?

From a structural standpoint, this relatively simple, but nontrivial choice—for which there are actually only two options—has generated an enduring debate. The more common structure is when the same person serves as the CEO and chairperson of the board (e.g., Dalton et al. 1998; Davidson, Jiraporn, Kim, and Nemec 2004; Davidson, Ning, Radowski, and Elsaid 2008; DeRue, Petersen, Mannor, and Morgeson 2009; Finkelstein and D'Aveni 1994; Finkelstein, Hambrick, and Cannella 2009). Alternatively, the role of CEO and chairperson of the board can be held separately by two different persons.

Even near the outset of agency theory, Fama and Jensen (1983a, b; see also Mizruchi 1983) were uncomfortable with the combined structure and argued that it would compromise the ability of the board to reasonably monitor the CEO. Jensen (1993, 866), for example, observed that "Without the direction of an independent leader, it is much more difficult for the board to perform its critical function." Accordingly, advocates for separating these leadership roles are adamant that directors are unable, or unwilling, to dispassionately evaluate the performance, policies, and practices of a firm's CEO when that CEO serves simultaneously as chairperson of the board (Chi 2009; Coombes and Wong 2004; Jensen 1993; MacAvoy and Millstein 2003; Monks and Minow 2008). This has been noted as the functional equivalent of the "CEO grading his own homework" (Brickley et al. 1997, 190).

Others, however, remain unconvinced (Baliga, Moyer, and Rao 1996; Daily and Dalton 1997; Dalton and Dalton 2009; Finkelstein and D'Aveni 1994; Finkelstein, Hambrick, and Cannella 2009; Lorsch and Zelleke 2005). Brickley et al. (1997) suggested, for example, that a board's optimal choice to adopt a dual or unitary board leadership structure is not theoretically obvious. Indeed, agency theory, the foundation on which much of the duality debate has been driven, is not the only viable conceptual lens through which duality might have been viewed.

A COLLISION OF THEORIES

Let us establish from the outset that there is an evident, and assuredly unresolved, fundamental collision of theories that is relevant for the effectiveness of CEO duality. We refer here to the notion of *unity of command* (for an extended discussion, see e.g., Dalton and Dalton 2009; Finkelstein and D'Aveni 1994; Finkelstein, Hambrick, and Cannella 2009), an enduring concept that suggests that any person in an organization should be accountable to one, and only one, individual. A failure to observe this basic guideline may result in inconsistent communications to a subordinate as the two—or more—individuals to whom a subordinate reports may not be of one mind. Not only is this disconnect possible within the organization, it may be observed outside the organization as well. Imagine, for example, a host of external constituencies receiving direction, signals, or disparate information from a single organization but from different corporate spokespersons. It would be a bit awkward, for example, for the CEO of the firm and a separate chairperson of the firm to be inconsistent with their perspectives or directives shared internally or externally. Not surprisingly, then, there is an impressive provenance in support of the unity of command doctrine.

In fact, unity of command has been embraced from the very outset of the formal study of administrative and organizational theory (e.g., Fayol 1949; McCallum 1856; Weber 1947; see also Wren 2005). An early example would be McCallum's pre–Civil War observation that "All subordinates should be accountable to, and be directed by, their immediate supervisor only" (1856, 104). More recently, the United States Marine Corps Officer Training Manual echoes that theme: "Unity of command means that all the forces are under one responsible commander. It requires having a single commander with the requisite authority to direct all forces employed in pursuit of a unified purpose" (Quoted in Dalton 2005, 24).

Obviously, when the positions of CEO and chairperson of the board are separately held, the notion of unity of command is compromised. With that separate leadership structure, there is not a single presiding officer; there are two. Who, then, is the voice of the enterprise? Who, then, is the person from whom both the enterprise's internal and external critical constituencies shall take their direction and with whom they shall directly communicate? More critically, who is in charge? Who is accountable? Contrast this phenomenon to one in which the CEO is the chairperson of the board. In such cases, everyone knows who is in charge and, critically, who is accountable (e.g., Brickley et al. 1997; Lorsch and Zelleke 2005; Lublin 2003).

There is, for us, a compelling contemporary example of a grave lapse of the unity of command guideline. Consider the leadership, or lack thereof, of a firm's executive committee when the CEO does not serve simultaneously as the chairperson of the board.

THE EXECUTIVE COMMITTEE ABSENT A RUDDER?

As noted earlier, the composition of the compensation, nominating, and corporate governance committees is dictated by a specific set of regulations (e.g., SOX and the listing exchanges, such as NYSE and NASDAQ). The executive committee does *not* have this character. In fact, it has been suggested that a fundamental omission of SOX was its silence on a requirement to separate the CEO and chairperson roles (Green 2004). In any case, there are no formal guidelines for the composition or leadership of executive committees. Given that, it need not have any independent members, and could be—and most often is—chaired by the CEO and/or chairperson of the board. Also, it can be composed of as few as two members of the board. The average Fortune 500 board has 11 directors; the average executive committee has just over four members (see, e.g., Dalton and Dalton 2006 for an overview of the executive committee of publicly traded Fortune 500 companies). Accordingly, executive committees have been subject to extreme criticism, accused of being an elite board structure that focuses only on a subset of the board's membership (e.g., Dalton and Dalton 2006; Kenny 2004). Even so, 46 percent of *Fortune* 500 boards maintain an executive committee.

The power of executive committees can be expansive. Consider, for example, the authority of Bank of America under its executive committee's charter: "This Committee shall have the power to direct and transact all business of the Corporation which properly might come before the Board of Directors, except as the Board only, by law, is authorized to perform" (Bank of America Executive Committee Charter 2009).

When a firm has elected to separate the roles of the CEO and the chairperson of the board, who, then, shall be the chairperson of the executive committee? In such circumstances, one can easily imagine the awkwardness at times of various voices waxing from their respective places on high. Notably, such concerns about the risks attendant to a poor execution of unity of command come into particularly sharp focus in a crisis situation.

UNITY OF COMMAND IN A CRISIS ENVIRONMENT

In late 2007 through the first quarter of 2009, we have witnessed more firms that have elected to separate the roles of the CEO and chairperson of the board (e.g., *Agenda* 2006; 2007a, b; 2008a, b; Gribben 2009; Smith 2009). Notably, it has been suggested that "More companies are separating the chairman and CEO positions as boards take a more active role due to a tumultuous economic environment" (Gribben 2009, 1). This is a fascinating development because this decision is exactly the opposite of what one might expect under these challenging circumstances.

Any primer on organizations in crisis would underscore the centrality of a basic tenet, the notion of one voice (Burnett 2002; Fink 1986; Roemer 2007).

As earlier noted, this "one voice" is the face of the corporation, the person in charge, the only person authorized to discuss the organization's challenges, particularly to external constituencies. It would appear, then, that to change the leadership structure by separating the CEO from the board chairperson position under current circumstances would be among the last options, not the first. That point has been emphatically noted (Dalton and Dalton 2009):

> When things are at their most trying, we advocate reliance on a single voice. Consider the leadership demands on, for example, a cardiac surgeon in the operating theater with the patient in extreme distress, a pilot with an aircraft floundering, a military officer challenged with a strategic position imperiled by opposing forces, a quarterback with fourth down and one yard to go and 38 seconds left on the clock. In such circumstances, there is no need for two presiding doctors, two head pilots, two senior military officers, or two quarterbacks. Observers may press their own metaphors, but someone has to make the call and be accountable. Ultimately, there must be one voice, hopefully forged and honed in the crucible of experience. Several voices under such circumstances do not constitute a choir; they are a cacophony.

There is a recent piece that nicely summarizes the issue of whether to change the leadership structure of an enterprise. Dahya, Garcia, and van Bommel (2009) concluded that the abandonment of the combined CEO/chairperson of the board position "appears to be wide of the mark." Faleye (2007, 230), too, suggests that insistence to "separate CEO and chairman duties may be counterproductive" and "may not produce the desired results" (256).

It is, however, an eminently fair question to ask what, if any, differences in the performance of the enterprise have been associated with the choice of leadership structure. We hasten to add that we are unaware of any empirical attention to this question under crisis circumstances. There is, however, an extensive literature dedicated to this basic question of leadership structure and firm performance.

LEADERSHIP STRUCTURE OF THE BOARD AND FIRM PERFORMANCE

There is an expansive body of research, discussion, narrative reviews, and meta-analyses dedicated to the issue of CEO duality. In a level of consistency that is unusual in any literature, this body of work can be easily and uniformly summarized. There is no evidence of substantive, systematic relationships between corporate financial performance and board leadership structure (Baliga et al. 1996; Boyd 1995; Brickley et al. 1997; Coles et al. 2001; Dahya et al., 2009; Dalton et al. 1998; Rhoades, Rechner, and Sundaramurthy 2001). It would seem that such a result would attenuate the apparent interest in board leadership structure. Perhaps it is appropriate to direct our research attention to more promising variables. That is a position that we would embrace, except that there is an alarming misspecification in this body of research.

SEPARATE LEADERSHIP IS *NOT* INDEPENDENT

We should reiterate that the foundation of the efficacy of choosing a leadership structure with a separate CEO and chairperson of the board is anchored in the notion of independence. This choice is made to facilitate a *more independent* board leadership structure. For us, however, this argument fails utterly, because the notion of independence in this context is grossly misspecified. In fact, for the vast majority of cases, when the positions of CEO and board chairperson person are separated, the "independence" problem is actually exacerbated (*Agenda* 2006; Barrett 2008; Dalton and Dalton 2009; Welch and Welch 2006).

The basis of this argument is that a leadership structure with a separate CEO and board chairperson is *not* necessarily indicative of independence. In fact, it rarely results in more independence. In the cases where there is a separate CEO and chairperson of the board, only 16 percent of the chairpersons are independent (Spencer Stuart 2008; see also *Agenda* 2006; Barrett 2008). This is because the "separate" board chairperson in such cases is the former CEO of the company. In fairness, the number of board chairpersons who are actually independent has actually increased in recent years. In 2006, Spencer Stuart's *Annual Board Index* (2006, 9) reported that "only 9 percent of the boards . . . have a truly independent chair." Nonetheless, we see that the great majority of so-called independent chairpersons are not independent. Given this, we are not surprised with Monks and Minow's (2008; see also Gilman 2008) position that the former CEO of the company should not serve on its board at all. Their perspective would clearly disqualify a former CEO from serving as chairperson of the board.

If we consider our prior discussion of the unity of command concept in concert with this rather untidy misspecification issue, we find ourselves in an awkward situation. It is now possible to simultaneously compromise the unity of command guidelines and those of board leadership structure.

PERILOUSLY CLOSE TO THE WORST-CASE SCENARIO

Consider what is apparently a distressingly common scenario. The positions of CEO and board chairperson are separated, but the *separate* chairperson is not independent. So the board chairperson, most likely the immediate past CEO of the firm, is *not* independent.

This outcome, however, constitutes only half of the structural problem. In such situations, not only do we have a separate chairperson who is not independent, we also have a unity of command failure. In addition to confusion about the authority vested in the chairperson as compared to the CEO, there will also be uncertainty about the influence of the former CEO—now chairperson—on the new CEO. In summary, the board does *not* have an independent chairperson but it *does* have a unity of command lapse. This, as we noted, is perilously close to the worst-case scenario.

INDEPENDENCE OF THE BOARD

The independence of board leadership structure is one aspect of the independence concerns set forth in agency theory. Another element relating to the board of directors also suggested as a potential mitigating factor for the fundamental agency problem is the composition of the board of directors (Dalton and Dalton 2009; Dalton, Daily, Johnson, and Ellstrand 1999; Fogel and Geier 2007).

A basic responsibility of the board is to monitor the management of the firm (for compendia, see Cosenza 2007; Dalton et al. 1999; Deutsch 2005; Finkelstein, Hambrick, and Cannella 2009; Gervurtz 2004; Hermalin and Weisbach 2003; Johnson, Daily, and Ellstrand 1996; Lorsch and MacIver 1989; Zahra and Pearce 1989; Zald 1969). It has been repeatedly argued that boards' willingness and ability to responsibly monitor is related to members' independence. An early example, "Directors Who Do Not Direct," by Supreme Court Justice William O. Douglas (1934; see also Karmel 2005) underscores that point. Another classic treatment advocating independent directors is Eisenberg's (1976) book, *The Structure of the Corporation: A Legal Analysis*, published in the same time frame as the early academic work addressing agency theory (e.g., Fama 1980; Fama and Jensen 1983a, b; Jensen and Meckling 1976).

Consider a board, for example, on which the firm's CEO, the chief financial officer (CFO), a senior vice president (SVP), and the general counsel (GC) serves. In this case, we would have four members of management on the board of directors. The agency argument would question the efficacy of this arrangement because the CFO, SVP, and CG of the enterprise almost certainly directly report to the CEO. Critics of such a structure would argue that it is unlikely that such board members would be comfortable criticizing the CEO's performance, practices, and policies. Perhaps the reticence of these officers serving on the board is related to an appreciation that their positions, salary, and perquisites are attributable to the CEO (Baysinger and Hoskisson 1990; Wade, O'Reilly, and Chandratat 1990; Weisbach 1988; Westphal and Zajac 1995).

There is yet another subset of directors who are not independent. Referred to as *affiliated* directors, they have a close personal or professional relationship with the CEO or the firm. Consider, for example, a large vendor of the firm. Presumably, directors with such relationships would be reticent to criticize the CEO because those relationships with the CEO may be compromised along with future business opportunities with the firm. A person with a consultation relationship with the firm may have similar concerns. Obviously, persons with a familial relationship with the CEO may be less likely to dispassionately evaluate the CEO. In these cases, then, the issue is independence, or the lack thereof, of board members.

Persons with such affiliations are not barred from board service. However, as noted in a previous section—based on SOX guidelines and those of the listing exchanges (NYSE, NASDAQ)—board members who are not independent may not serve on the board's audit committee, compensation committee, or its nominating/governance committee. Derivatively, such directors may not serve as chairperson of these committees. For us, such an independence expectation is not unreasonable. As noted in a prior section, however, it is not definitive as there are a host of other conceptual foundations that would actually embrace the participation of *dependent* board members.

ANOTHER COLLISION OF THEORIES

Tenets of resource dependence and the resource-based perspective are in many aspects contradictory to the agency theory independence guidelines (e.g., Daily, Dalton, and Cannella 2003). A foundation of resource dependence theory is that firms must manage the uncertainty in their environments (Pfeffer and Salancik

1978; Selznick 1949; Thompson and McEwen 1958; Zald 1969). Notably, there is an impressive body of research and commentary suggesting that this may often be accomplished through firms' boards of directors (e.g., Booth and Deli 1996; Burt 1980; Goodstein, Gautam, and Boeker 1994; Mizruchi and Stearns 1988; Provan 1980; Stearns and Mizruchi 1993). There may be members of the board with networking and coalition capabilities to enable formal and informal agreements, and other means to secure resources that would otherwise be unavailable to the firm, or available only at higher transaction costs.

Nobel laureate Gary S. Becker (1964), in what has become known as *human capital theory*, may have provided a precursor for the resource-based view (RBV) of the firm when he explained that human competence and the efficacious investment of that competence was a critical aspect of the performance of an enterprise. In his view, it was the accumulation of an individual's education, skills, experience, and expertise that enhanced the cognitive and productive capabilities in the enterprise.

In that spirit, the resource-based view of the firm (e.g., Acedo, Barroso, and Galan 2006; Barney 1991; Barney, Wright, and Ketchen 2001; Thompson and McEwen 1958; Wernerfelt 1984) may inform issues of board composition, its independence—or lack thereof—and its resultant performance. The resource-based view suggests that the acquisition and creation of bundles of rare, valuable, inimitable, and nonsubstitutable resources provide organizations with a sustainable competitive advantage (Barney 1991). Members of boards of directors often possess such a portfolio of experience, expertise, and reputation that can and ought to be brought to bear for the benefit of the firm (Daily et al. 1999).

More recently, the work of Hillman, Cannella, and Paetzold (2000) and Hillman and Dalziel (2003) probe the intersection of resource dependence theory and the resource-based perspective. In that work, they refer to the "capital" of boards or their respective members (e.g., Hillman and Dalziel 2003, 386–387; see also Lester, Hillman, Zardkoohi, and Cannella 2008; Adler and Kwon 2002). The board capital to which they refer is essentially a combination of human capital (e.g., board members' expertise, experience, reputation) and relational capital (e.g., board members' network of linkages with other firms and external constituencies). For us, an interesting aspect of the accumulated work on resource dependence and the resource-based view is that it is silent on the notion of board independence. Consider, for example, that a board member—an important vendor of the firm—could have impressive credentials and a portfolio replete with expertise, experience, and reputation and yet not be independent.

Many observers would aver that these changes toward board independence through the reduction in inside and affiliated directors are utterly consistent with an expectation for improved board monitoring. Paradoxically, however, it has been argued that, *with these changes in independence*, boards have never been more dependent (Dalton 2005; Lorsch 2005). Inside and affiliated directors do—or at least, certainly can—have firm-specific and/or industry-specific knowledge/information. Granted, these members of the board may have been officers of the firm, consultants, former officers, suppliers, customers, bankers, and attorneys, but they were all well acquainted with the firm and with the industry. That directors of these types are currently and decidedly out of favor will be troublesome to those who embrace the resource-based view. As noted by Barney (1991, 101), one means of establishing a competitive advantage is through "the training, experience, judgment, intelligence, relationships, and insight" of individuals within the organization, presumably including senior officers and board members.

There is another aspect of directors who may, in fact, be independent but without the benefit of firm- or industry-based information. On whom will such directors depend for the information necessary to dispatch their stewardship responsibilities? We would expect the primary provider of that information to be the CEO of the firm. This source is not without risk. Surowiecki (2004), for example, reminds us that an effective approach to bias people's judgment is to render them dependent for information. With board members who are armed largely with independence, but without firm/industry backgrounds, is there a threat that some CEOs may be able to leverage this opportunity by providing purposefully selective information?

Obviously, then, there may be some potential for a disconnect between the posited necessity of an independent board and the nature of the board's repository of human capital. Accordingly, it is a fair question, as in the prior section on board leadership structure, to ask whether there is any evidence to suggest that the composition of the board is related to the performance of the enterprise.

COMPOSITION OF THE BOARD AND FIRM PERFORMANCE

As with CEO duality, there is a distinguished and extensive tradition of research, discussion, narrative reviews, and meta-analyses addressing the composition of boards of directors. Fortunately, this body of work is easily summarized. There is no evidence of practical, systematic relationships between board composition and corporate financial performance (Bhagat and Black 1999, 2002; Bhagat et al. 2008; Coles, McWilliams, and Sen 2001; Dalton et al. 1998; DeRue et al. 2009; Fogel and Geier 2007; Gordon 2007; Hermalin and Weisbach 2003; Kaufman and Englander 2005; Rhoades, Rechner, and Sundaramurthy 2000; Wagner, Steimpert, and Fubara 1998; Walsh and Seward 1990).

Fogel and Geier (2007, 35) provide a succinct summary of this work: "[T]here is no predicate, either in logic or in experience, to suggest that a majority of independent directors on a board will guarantee good corporate governance or better financial returns for shareholders." They also argue that the pursuit of board independence is not, even in principle, the appropriate strategy. Bhagat et al.'s (2008, 1814; see also Bebchuk et al. 2009) summary is as direct: They suggest that there is "no relation between director independence and performance." We would also note that, in addition to this dearth of empirical support for the posited board composition/enterprise performance relationship, there are misspecification issues as well. This may be more apparent if we examine the independence of boards in a somewhat broader context.

ARE BOARDS EVER INDEPENDENT?

There are those who argue, irrespective of any categorization of board or member independence, that boards are never independent, dispassionate stewards of the CEO of the firm and other senior officers of the firm. Galbraith (2004, 28), for example, refers to the notion that boards can be independent as an "accepted fraud," and writes that "alleged directors in any sizable enterprise are fully subordinate to the management." This is by no means a novel perspective (e.g., Davis and Thompson 1994; Frederickson, Hambrick, and Baumrin 1988; Gilson and Kraakman 1991; Hermalin and Weisbach 1998; Shivdasani and Yermack 1999). Instead, it has been suggested that board members, irrespective of any notion of independence, are selected—and retained—because they *are* and *remain* sympathetic with the CEO (e.g., Solomon 1978; Wade, O'Reilly, and Chandratat 1990; Westphal and Zajac 1995). Also, it has been rather directly observed that "independent directors often turn out to be lapdogs rather than watchdogs" (Bhagat and Black 1999, 4; see also Bhagat et al. 2008) and that "most independent directors get neutralized in one fashion or another" (Hermalin and Weisbach 1998, 88; see also Smale, Patricof, Henderson, Marcus, and Johnson 1995). Arguing similarly, Sutton (2004) believes that *no* director is independent after he has served five years or more on any given board.

There is another misspecification issue. The notion of *board composition* is apparently something less than universal. It has been demonstrated, for example, that there were 19 distinct operationalizations of board composition reflected in research literature (Daily, Johnson, and Dalton 1999). There were multiple operationalizations of inside director proportion, outside director proportion, and affiliated director proportion. Also, it is interesting that a structural equation confirmatory factor analysis indicated that four psychometrically sound factors could be extracted, but that six of the director *proportion* operationalizations had to be eliminated from the solution. Obviously, some imprecision may have been introduced into the prior research literature. Frankly, the four psychometrically sound constructs are a moot finding. In no case did a study reflect a reliance on these constructs. Instead, the relevant literature relied on a single item, usually some proportion of directors (i.e., independent directors on a company's board) or some subset thereof (a proportion of inside, outside, or affiliated directors).

There is another example, noted in the section on board leadership structure, that warrants revisiting here and that is the executive committee of the board. Under SOX guidelines and those of the listing exchanges (e.g., NYSE, NASDAQ), the audit, compensation, and nominating/corporate governance committees must be totally composed of (and derivatively chaired by) independent directors. These guidelines do not apply to a firm's executive committee. An executive committee could comprise three people, none of whom need be independent. Such a structure would obviously render any notion of board independence moot. With the exception of a single, largely descriptive treatment (Dalton and Dalton 2006) we are aware of no empirical examination of the executive committees of publicly traded companies.

DISCUSSION

There are a host of issues that animate our discussion. As noted in the introductory section, the notion of independence is fundamental to the potential mischief that may result from the basic tenets of agency theory. When the interests of owners and managers diverge, and for a variety of reasons, managers may be able to exact higher rents than are reasonable or would otherwise be accorded them by owners of the firm (Dalton et al. 2008; Eisenhardt 1989; Walsh and Seward 1990). From the beginning of agency theory it has been suggested that such a tendency may be mitigated by adopting measures that enhance the independence of those who manage the enterprise from those who are its stewards (Fama and Jensen 1983a, b; Jensen 1993; Mizruchi 1983). Without such attention, the conflicts of interest that might otherwise arise will exacerbate the fundamental agency problem. Moreover, this focus on the independence/conflict of interest issues is the pivotal element at the intersection of finance and ethics.

This chapter will provide no comfort to those who presumed that attention to board independence factors would be consequential. Instead, we know that there is no evidence supporting a relationship between board leadership structure and enterprise performance (Baliga et al. 1996; Dahya et al. 2009; Dalton et al. 1998). Similarly, there is no relationship between the independence of the board of directors and enterprise performance (Bhagat et al. 2008; Dalton et al. 1998; DeRue et al. 2009; Fogel and Geier 2007; Gordon 2007; Walsh and Seward 1990). Moreover, the comprehensive misspecification and nonspecification of key variables has thoroughly compromised our understanding of these posited empirical relationships (e.g., Dey 2008; Daily et al. 1999).

We must also acknowledge that perhaps scholars have relied too much on agency theory. Hambrick, Werder, and Zajac (2008, 385; see also Fogel and Geier 2007), for example, noted that:

> The extant literature has typically viewed governance as a principal-agent problem between shareholders and management. But useful insights about governance must inevitably have a broader scope, encompassing such quite complex matters as multiple stakeholders, boardroom dynamics, managerial processes, managerial values and motives, and national systems.

Many of the prior sections also suggest a disconnect between theory and practice. Over the broad expanse of organizational studies, there is an enduring concern—more often than not a debate—about the lack of balance between the elegance of research and its concomitant relevance to application and practice (e.g., Bennis and O'Toole 2005; Colquitt and Zapata-Phelan 2007; Hambrick 1994, 2005, 2007; Ireland and Ketchen 2008; Pearce 2004; Pfeffer 1993, 2005, 2007; Pfeffer and Fong 2002, 2004; Rousseau 2006; Walsh, Tushman, Kimberly, Starbuck, and Ashford 2007; Van de Ven and Johnson 2006). Reflected in this body of work is a remarkable breadth of opinion regarding the apparently contentious elegance versus relevance issue.

TO WHAT EXTENT IS THERE ANY RELEVANCE?

Consider, for example, that Birkinshaw and Mol (2009) recently published a book that describes 50 of the most important management innovations in the past 150 years. Pfeffer (2007, 1336) observed that "in none of the 50 instances did the ideas or innovations originate with an academic or in academic research."

In fairness, it is also possible that the body of organizational studies is less than distinguished in its contribution to the relevance end of the continuum. Notably, it is also possible that such results rarely approach the classic standard of "That's interesting!" set by Davis (1971, 399). We would offer that this is apparently the case for much of the work at the intersection of agency theory, the fundamental agency problem, and its often proposed means of mitigation—the independence of a firm's stewards.

Frankly, we join others (e.g., Hambrick 2007; Miller 2007; Rousseau 2006) in thinking that the Academy writ large would benefit from a synthesis period, less dominated by a focus on theory that at times may compromise practice and application. Again, for us this lapse in practice and application is apparent in these issues of board independence.

Fifteen years ago, Hambrick (1994, 13), in comments that were controversial at the time, suggested that

> . . . *if we believe highly in what we do, if we believe in the significance of advanced thinking and research on management, then it is time we showed it. We must recognize that our responsibility is not to ourselves, but rather to the institutions around the world that are in dire need of improved management, as well as to those individuals who seek to be the most effective managers they possibly can be. It is time for us to break out of our closed loop. It is time for us to matter* [emphasis added].

Later, in his concluding remarks he repeated (16), as shall we, "That is our challenge. We should matter. We must matter."

In these times of economic travail, we do have these concerns about the vitality of corporate governance research and the application of that research to practice. We are sensitive, too, about the broader aspects of the elegance/relevance continuum and where a sober tribunal might place it. We are disappointed that these notions of independence, the very essence of the intersection of ethics and finance, are compromised and thus provide little guidance on that dimension, if any. We are as concerned, however, about the contribution to practice and application in these trying times. In many ways our collective contributions are not bounty, but bagatelle. We realize that researchers will have, for a variety of reasons, a predisposition toward different points on the elegance/relevance continuum. Having said that, on these matters of corporate governance and the intersection of ethics, finance, and organizational studies more generally, research in this space does not currently enjoy a compelling voice.

REFERENCES

Acedo, F. J., C. Barroso, and J. L. Galan. 2006. The resource-based theory: Dissemination and main trends. *Strategic Management Journal* 27:621–636.

Adler, P. S., and S.-W. Kwon. 2002. Social capital: Prospects for a new concept. *Academy of Management Review* 27:17–40.

Agenda. 2006. CEO-chairman split not giving boost to independence. December 11:8.

———. 2007a. Boards turning to independent chairs in leadership transitions. July 30:1, 10.

———. 2007b. Call to split CEO, chair roles heat up. October 29:1, 5.

———. 2008a. Credit crisis reviving independent chair debate. April 21:1, 9.

———. 2008b. Companies make indirect concessions to governance. May 19:1, 5.

Baliga, B. R., R. C. Moyer, and R. S. Rao. 1996. CEO duality and firm performance: What's the fuss? *Strategic Management Journal* 17:41–53.

Bank of America Executive Committee Charter. 2009. http://www.media.corporate-ir.net/media_files/irol/71/71595/corpgov/Executive_Committee_Charter_1_07_.pdf (accessed March 25, 2009).

Barney, J. 1991. Firm resources and sustained competitive advantage. *Journal of Management* 17:99–120.

Barney, J., M. Wright, and D. J. Ketchen. 2001. The resource-based view of the firm: Ten years after 1991. *Journal of Management* 27:625–642.

Barrett. A. 2008. Parsing the latest board leadership developments and trends. *Corporate Governance Advisor* 16:19–24.

Baysinger, B. D., and R. E. Hoskisson. 1990. The composition of boards of directors and strategic control. *Academy of Management Review* 15:72–87.

Bebchuk, L., A. Cohen, and A. Ferrell. 2009. What matters in corporate governance? *Review of Financial Economics* 22:783–827.

Becker, G. 1964. *Human capital.* Chicago, IL: University of Chicago Press.

Bennis, W. G., and J. O'Toole. 2005. How business schools lost their way. *Harvard Business Review*, May/June:96–104

Berle, A. A. 1959. *Power without property: A new development in American political economy.* New York: Harcourt Brace.

Berle, A. A., and G. C. Means. 1932. *The modern corporation and private property.* New York: McMillan.

Bhagat, S., and B. S. Black. 1999. The uncertain relationship between board composition and firm performance. *Business Lawyer* 54:921–963.

———. 2002. The non-correlation between board independence and long-term firm performance. *Journal of Corporation Law* 27:231–273.

Bhagat, S., B. Bolton, and R. Romano. 2008. The promise and peril of corporate governance indices. *Columbia Law Review* 108:1803–1882.

Birkinshaw, J., and M. Mol. 2009. *Giant steps in management: Innovations that change the way you work.* London: FT Press.

Booth, J. R., and D. N. Deli. 1996. Factors affecting the number of outside directorships held by CEOs. *Journal of Financial Economics* 40:81–104.

Boyd, B. K. 1995. CEO duality and firm performance: A contingency model. *Strategic Management Journal* 16:301–312.

Bradley, M., and S. M. Wallenstein. 2006. The history of corporate governance in the United States. In *The accountable corporation*, ed. M. J. Epstein and K. O. Hanson. Westport, CT: Praeger.

Bratton, W. W. 1989. The new economic theory of the firm: Critical perspectives from history. *Stanford Law Review* 41:1471–1527.

———. 2001. Berle and Means reconsidered at the century's turn. *Journal of Corporation Law* 26:737–770.

Brickley, J. A., J. L. Coles, and G. Jarrell. 1997. Leadership structure: Separating the CEO and chairman of the board. *Journal of Corporate Finance* 3:189–220.

Burnett, J. 2002. *Managing business crises: From anticipation to implementation.* Westport, CT: Quorum Books.

Burt, R. S. 1980. Cooptive corporate actor networks: A reconsideration of interlocking directorates involving American manufacturing. *Administrative Science Quarterly* 25:557–581.

Cain, K. 2003. New efforts to strengthen corporate governance: Why use SRO listing standards? *Columbia Business Law Review* 1:619–659.

Chandler, A. D. 1977. *The visible hand: The managerial revolution in American business.* Cambridge, MA: Harvard University Press.

Chi, T. 2009. Corporate governance: CII (Council of Institutional Investors) urges Congress to adopt corporate governance reforms. *Corporate Governance Report* 12:4–5.

Coffee, J. C. 2001. The rise of dispersed ownership: The roles of law and the state of the separation of ownership and control. *Yale Law Journal* 111:3–82.

Coles, J. W., V. B. McWilliams, and N. Sen. 2001. An examination of the relationship of governance mechanisms to performance. *Journal of Management* 27:23–50.

Colquitt, J. A., and C. P. Zapata-Phelan. 2007. Trends in theory building and theory testing: A five-decade study of the *Academy of Management Journal* 50:1281–1303.

Coombes, P., and S. C.-Y. Wong. 2004. Chairman and CEO: One job or two? *McKinsey Quarterly*:43–44.

Cosenza, E. 2007. The Holy Grail of corporate reform: Independence or democracy? *Brigham Young University Law Review* 1:1–54.

Dahya, J., L. G. Garcia, and J. van Bommel. 2009. One man two hats—What's all the commotion. *Financial Review* 44:179–212.

Daily, C. M., and D. R. Dalton. 1997. CEO and board chairperson roles held jointly or separately: Much ado about nothing. *Academy of Management Executive* 11:11–20.

Daily, C. M., D. R. Dalton, and A. A. Cannella Jr. 2003. Corporate governance: Decades of dialogue and data. *Academy of Management Review* 28:371–382.

Daily, C. M., J. L. Johnson, and D. R. Dalton. 1999. On the measurement of board composition: Poor consistency and a serious mismatch of theory and operationalization. *Decision Sciences* 30:83–106.

Dalton, D. R. 2005. "Going private" and "going dark": Board compensation, and the downside of independence. *Directors and Boards* 2:4–6.

Dalton, D. R., C. M. Daily, A. E. Ellstrand, and J. L. Johnson. 1998. Board composition, leadership structure, and financial performance: Meta-analytic reviews and research agenda. *Strategic Management Journal* 19:269–290.

Dalton, D. R., C. M. Daily, J. L. Johnson, and A. E. Ellstrand. 1999. Number of directors and financial performance: A meta-analysis. *Academy of Management Journal* 42:674–686.

Dalton, D. R., and C. M. Dalton. 2006. Executive committees: The stealth board body. *Directors and Boards* 30:44–47.

———. 2009. The joint CEO/board chairperson leadership issue in sharp relief. In *Boardroom realities: Building leaders across your board*, ed. J. A. Conger. San Francisco, CA: Jossey-Bass Publishers.

Dalton, D. R., M. A. Hitt, S. T. Certo, and C. M. Dalton. 2008. The fundamental agency problem and its mitigation: Independence, equity, and the market for corporate control. In *Academy of management annals*, ed. A. Brief and J. Walsh. Mahwah, NJ: Lawrence Erlbaum Associates.

Davidson, W. N., P. Jiraporn, Y. S. Kim, and C. Nemec. 2004. Earnings management following duality-creating successions: Ethnostatistics, impression management, and agency theory. *Academy of Management Journal* 47:267–275.

Davidson, W. N., Y. Ning, D. Rakowski, and E. Elsaid. 2008. The antecedents of simultaneous appointments to CEO and chair. *Journal of Management and Governance* 12:381–401.

Davis, G. F. 2005. New directions in corporation governance. In *Annual review of sociology*, ed. K. S. Cook and D. S. Massey, Vol. 31. Palo Alto, CA: Annual Reviews.

Davis, G. F., and T. A. Thompson. 1994. A social movement perspective on corporate control. *Administrative Science Quarterly* 39:141–173.

Davis, M. S. 1971. That's interesting! *Philosophy of the Social Sciences* 1:309–344.

DeRue, D. S., E. Petersen, M. J. Mannor, and F. P. Morgeson. (2009). A two-horse race? The impact of CEO characteristics and governance structures on firm performance. Unpublished manuscript.

Deutsch, Y. 2005. The impact of board composition on firms' critical decisions: A meta-analytic review. *Journal of Management* 31:424–444.

Dey, A. 2008. Corporate governance and agency conflicts. *Journal of Accounting Research* 46:1143–1181.

Douglas, W. O. 1934. Directors who do not direct. *Harvard Law Review* 47:1305–1334.

Eisenberg, M. A. 1976. *The structure of the corporation: A legal analysis*. New York: Little Brown and Company.

Eisenhardt, K. M. 1989. Agency theory: An assessment and review. *Academy of Management Review* 14:57–74.

Faleye, O. 2007. Does one hat fit all? The case for corporate leadership structure. *Journal of Management and Governance* 11:239–259.

Fama, E. F. 1980. Agency problems and the theory of the firm. *Journal of Political Economy* 88:288–307.

Fama, E. F., and M. C. Jensen. 1983a. Separation of ownership and control. *Journal of Law and Economics* 26:301–325.

———. 1983b. Agency problems and residual claims. *Journal of Law and Economics* 26:327–349.

Fayol, H. 1949. *General and industrial management.* London: Pitman.

Fink, S. 1986. *Planning for the inevitable.* New York: AMA.

Finkelstein, S., and R. A. D'Aveni. 1994. CEO duality as a double-edged sword: How boards of directors balance entrenchment avoidance and unity of command. *Academy of Management Journal* 37:1079–1108.

Finkelstein, S., D. Hambrick, and A. A. Cannella. 2009. *Strategic leadership: Theory and research on executives, top management teams, and boards.* New York: Oxford University Press.

Fogel, E. M., and A. M. Geier. 2007. Strangers in the house: Rethinking Sarbanes-Oxley and the independent board of director. *Delaware Journal of Corporate Law* 32:33–72.

Frederickson, J. W., D. C. Hambrick, and S. Baumrin. 1988. A model of CEO dismissal. *Academy of Management Review* 13:255–270.

Galbraith, J. K. 2004. *The economics of innocent fraud.* Boston: Houghton Mifflin.

Gervurtz, F. A. 2004. The historical and political origins of the corporate board of directors. *Hofstra Law Review* 33:89–173.

Gilman, L. 2008. Should a retiring chief executive officer stay on as chairman? *Corporate Board Member*, May/June:12–14.

Gilson, R. 1996. Corporate governance and economic efficiency: When do institutions matter? *Washington University Law Quarterly* 4:327–345.

Gilson, R., and R. Kraakman. 1991. Reinvesting the outside director: An agenda for institutional investors. *Stanford Law Review* 43:863–906.

Goodstein, J., K. Gautam, and W. Boeker. 1994. The effects of board size and diversity on strategic change. *Strategic Management Journal* 15:241–250.

Gordon, J. N. 2007. The rise of independent directors in the United States 1950–2005: Of shareholder value and stock market prices. *Standard Law Review* 59:1465–1568.

Gourevitch, P. A., and J. Shinn. 2005. *Political power and corporate control.* Princeton, NJ: Princeton University Press.

Green, S. 2004. Unfinished business: Abolish the imperial CEO. *Journal of Corporate Accounting and Finance* 15:19–22.

Gribben, K. 2009. More boards strip CEOs of chairman title. *Agenda*, January 20:1–3.

Hambrick, D. C. 1994. What if the academy actually mattered? *Academy of Management Review* 19:11–16.

———. 2005. Just how bad are our theories? A response to Ghoshal. *Academy of Management Learning and Education* 4:104–107.

———. 2007. The field of management's devotion to theory: Too much of a good thing? *Academy of Management Journal* 50:1346–1352.

Hambrick, D. C., A. Werder, and E. Zajac. 2008. New directions in corporate governance research. *Organization Science* 19:381–385.

Hermalin, B. E., and M. S. Weisbach. 1998. Endogenously chosen boards of directors and their monitoring of the CEO. *American Economic Review* 88:96–118.

———. 2003. Boards of directors as an endogenously determined institution: A survey of the economic literature. *Economic Policy Review* 9:7–26.

Hillman, A. J., A. A. Cannella, and R. L. Paetzold. 2000. The resource dependence role of corporate directors: Strategic adaptation of board composition in response to environmental change. *Journal of Management Studies* 37:235–255.

Hillman, A. J., and T. Dalziel. 2003. Boards of directors and firm performance: Integrating agency and resource dependence theories. *Academy of Management Review* 28:383–396.

Ireland, R. D., and D. J. Ketchen. 2008. Interesting problems and interesting research: A path to effective exchanges and between managers and scholars. *Business Horizons* 51:65–71.

Jacobsen, M. A. 1996. Interested director transactions and the (equivocal) effects of shareholder ratification. *Delaware Journal of Corporate Law* 21:91–1025.

———. 1993. The modern industrial revolution, exit, and the failure of internal control systems. *Journal of Finance* 48:831–888.

Jensen, M. C., and W. F. Meckling. 1976. Theory of the firm: Managerial behavior, agency costs, and ownership structure. *Journal of Financial Economics* 3:305–360.

Johnson, J. L., C. M. Daily, and A. E. Ellstrand. 1996. Board of directors: A review and research agenda. *Journal of Management* 22:409–438.

Karmel, R. S. 2005. Realizing the dream of William O. Douglas—The Securities and Exchange Commission takes charge of corporate governance. *Delaware Journal of Corporate Law* 30:79–144.

Kaufman, A., and E. Englander. 2005. A team production model of corporate governance. *Academy of Management Executive* 19:9–22.

Kenny, R. M. 2004. Executive committee: A vestigial appendage. *Directors and Boards* 25:43–46.

Lester, R. H., A. Hillman, A. Zardkoohi, and A. A. Cannella. 2008. Former government officials as outside directors: The role of human and social capital. *Academy of Management Journal* 51:999–1013.

Lorsch, J. W. 2005. Directors challenge value of independence standards. *Agenda*, October: 4.

Lorsch, J. W., and E. MacIver. 1989. *Pawns and potentates: The reality of America's corporate boards*. Cambridge, MA: Harvard University Press.

Lorsch, J. W., and A. Zelleke. 2005. Should the CEO be the chairman. *Sloan Management Review* 46:71–74.

Lublin, J. S. 2003. Separating top posts will hurt CEO's authority some believe. *Wall Street Journal*, January 10:c11.

MacAvoy, P. W., and I. M. Millstein. 2003. *The recurrent crisis in corporate governance*. New York: Palgrave Macmillan.

McCallum, D. C. 1856. Superintendents' report. *American Railroad Journal* 29:225–226.

Miller, D. 2007. Paradigm prison, or in praise of a theoretic research. *Strategic Organization* 5:177–184.

Mizruchi, M. S. 1983. Who controls whom? An examination of the relation between management and board of directors in large American corporations. *Academy of Management Review* 8:426–435.

———. 2004. Berle and Means revisited: The governance and power of large U.S. corporations. *Theory and Society* 33:579–617.

Mizruchi, M. S., and L. B. Stearns. 1988. A longitudinal study of the formation of interlocking directorates. *Administrative Science Quarterly* 33:194–210.

Monks, R. A. G., and N. Minow. 2008. *Corporate governance*. 4th ed. West Sussex, England: John Wiley & Sons.

Myers, R. 2005. The top 10 legal milestones of the last 10 years. *Corporate Board Member* 8:48–62.

NASDAQ Stock Exchange Guidelines. 2009. For a summary see, Comparison of Corporate Governance Guidelines and Codes of Best Practice, http:// www.weil.com/news/ pubdetail.aspx?pub=933 (accessed March 25, 2009).

New York Stock Exchange (NYSE) Guidelines. 2009. For a summary see, Comparison of Corporate Governance Guidelines and Codes of Best Practice http://www.weil.com/news/pubdetail.aspx?pub=933 (accessed March 25 2009).

Pearce, J. L. 2004. What do we know and how do we really know it? *Academy of Management Review* 29:175–179.

Pfeffer, J. 1993. Barriers to the advance of organizational science: Paradigm development as a dependent variable. *Academy of Management Review* 18:599–620.

———. 2005. Why do bad management theories persist? A comment to Ghosal. *Academy of Learning and Education* 4:96–100.

———. 2007. A modest proposal: How we might change the process and product of managerial research. *Academy of Management Journal* 50:1334–1345.

Pfeffer, J., and C. T. Fong. 2002. The end of business schools? Less success than meets the eye. *Academy of Management Learning and Education* 1:78–95.

———. 2004. The business school "business": Some lessons from the US experience. *Journal of Management Studies* 42:1501–1520.

Pfeffer, J., and G. R. Salancik. 1978. *The external control of organizations: A resource dependence perspective.* New York: Harper & Row.

Provan, K. G. 1980. Board power and organizational effectiveness among human service agencies. *Academy of Management Journal* 23:221–236.

Rhoades, D. L., P. L. Rechner, and C. Sundaramurthy. 2000. Board composition and financial performance: A meta-analysis of the influence of outside directors. *Journal of Managerial Issues* 12:76–91.

———. 2001. A meta-analysis of board leadership structure and financial performance: Are "two heads better than one?" *Corporate Governance: An International Review* 9:311–319.

Roe, M. J. 1994. *Strong managers, weak owners: The political roots of American corporate finance.* Princeton, NJ: Princeton University Press.

———. 2005. The inevitable instability of American corporate governance. In *Restoring trust in American business*, ed. J. W. Lorsch, L. Berlowitz, and A. Zelleke. Cambridge, MA: MIT Press.

Roemer, B. 2007. *When the balloon goes up: The communicator's guide to crisis response.* Victoria, BC: Trafford Publishers.

Romano, R. 2005. The Sarbanes-Oxley Act and the making of corporate governance. *Yale Law Journal* 114:1521–1604.

Ross, S. A. 1973. The economic theory of agency: The principal's problem. *American Economic Review* 63:134–139.

Rousseau, D. M. 2006. Is there such a thing as "evidence-based management"? *Academy of Management Review* 31:256–269.

Selznick, P. 1949. *TVA and the grass roots.* Berkeley, CA: University of California Press.

Shivdasani, A., and D. Yermack, D. 1999. CEO involvement in the selection of new board members: An empirical analysis. *Journal of Finance* 54:1829–1853.

Shleifer, A., and R. W. Vishny. 1997. A survey of corporate governance. *Journal of Finance* 52:737–783.

Smale, J. G., A. J. Patricof, D. Henderson, B. Marcus, and D. W. Johnson. 1995. Redraw the line between the board and the CEO. *Harvard Business Review* 73:5–12

Smith, A. 1776. An inquiry into the nature and causes of the wealth of nations. In *Great books of the western world*, ed. R. M. Hutchins. Chicago, IL: Encyclopedia Britannica, 1952.

Smith, D. J. 2009. More firms name separate chairs. *Risk and Governance Weekly*, January 30:1–2.

Solomon, L. D. 1978. Restructuring the corporate board of directors: Fond hope, faint promise. *Michigan Law Review* 76:581–610.

Spencer Stuart. 2006. *Spencer Stuart 2006 Board Index.* Chicago, IL: Spencer Stuart.

———. 2008. *Spencer Stuart Board Index*. Chicago, IL: Spencer Stuart.

Stearns, L. B., and M. S. Mizruchi. 1993. Board composition and corporate financing: The impact of financial institution representation on borrowing. *Academy of Management Journal* 36:603–618.

Stigler, G. J., and C. Friedland. 1983. The literature of economics: The case of Berle and Means. *Journal of Law and Economics* 26:237–268.

Surowiecki, J. 2004. *The wisdom of crowds*. New York: Doubleday.

Sutton, G. 2004. Rules for rock-solid governance. *Directors and Boards* 25:19.

Thompson, J. D., and W. J. McEwen. 1958. Organizational goals and environment: Goal-setting as an interaction process. *American Sociological Review* 23:23–31.

Van de Ven, A., and P. E. Johnson. 2006. Knowledge for theory and practice. *Academy of Management Review* 31:802–821.

Wade, J., C. A. O'Reilly, and I. Chandratat. 1990. Golden parachutes, CEOs, and the exercise of social influence. *Administrative Science Quarterly* 35:587–603.

Wagner, J. A., J. L. Stimpert, and E. I. Fubara. 1998. Board composition and organizational performance: Two studies of insider/outsider effects. *Journal of Management Studies* 35:655–677.

Walsh, J. P., and J. K. Seward. 1990. On the efficiency of internal and external corporate control mechanisms. *Academy of Management Review* 15:421–458.

Walsh, J. P., M. L. Tushman, J. R. Kimberly, B. Starbuck, and S. Ashford. 2007. On the relationship between research and practice: Debate and reflections. *Journal of Management Inquiry* 16:128–154.

Weber, M. 1947. *The theory of social and economic organization*. New York: Oxford University Press.

Weisbach, M. C. 1988. Outside directors and CEO turnover. *Journal of Financial Economics* 20:432–460.

Wernerfelt, B. 1984. A resource-based view of the firm. *Strategic Management Journal* 5:171–180.

Westphal, J. D., and E. J. Zajac. 1995. Who shall govern? CEO/board power, demographic similarity, and new director selection. *Administrative Science Quarterly* 40:60–83.

Wren, D. A. 2005. *The history of management thought*. 5th ed. Hoboken, NJ: John Wiley & Sons.

Zahra, S. A., and J. A. Pearce. 1989. Boards of directors and corporate financial performance: A review and integrative model. *Journal of Management* 15:291–344.

Zald, M. N. 1969. The power and function of boards of directors: A theoretical synthesis. *American Journal of Sociology* 75:97–111.

ABOUT THE AUTHORS

Dan R. Dalton (PhD, University of California, Irvine) is the founding director of the Institute for Corporate Governance, dean emeritus, and the Harold A. Poling Chair of Strategic Management in the Kelley School of Business, Indiana University. A fellow of the Academy of Management, Professor Dalton is widely published with over 300 articles on corporate governance, business strategy, law, and ethics. Additionally, his work has been frequently featured in the business and financial press including the *Wall Street Journal*, *BusinessWeek*, *Fortune*, the *Economist*, *Financial Times*, *Boston Globe*, *Chicago Tribune*, *Los Angeles Times*, *Washington Post*, and the *New York Times*.

Catherine M. Dalton (PhD, Indiana University) holds the David H. Jacobs Chair of Strategic Management at the Kelley School of Business, Indiana University. She also serves as editor of *Business Horizons*, the research director of the Institute for Corporate Governance, and a fellow in the Randall L. Tobias Center for Leadership Excellence. She is widely published in the area of corporate governance, with articles appearing in, among others, *Academy of Management Journal*, *Academy of Management Review*, *Academy of Management Annals*, *Strategic Management Journal*, *Entrepreneurship Theory and Practice*, *Journal of Business Venturing*, *Journal of Management*, *Harvard Business Review*, and *California Management Review*.

Index